COMPARATIVE NEGLIGENCE

SECOND EDITION

THE AUTHOR

VICTOR E. SCHWARTZ is co-author, with the late William E. Prosser and John W. Wade, of the seventh edition of *Cases and Materials on Torts*—the most widely used torts case book in the United States. He has also written a leading treatise on the Multistate Bar Examination. Most recently he has co-authored the first book to deal with the problems of multijurisdictional lawsuits involving a single product.

As head of the Federal Interagency Task Force on Product Liability, Mr. Schwartz was the principal drafter of the Uniform Product Liability Act; he also supervised the Task Force's coordination of all insurance policy issues within the federal government. For his leadership in these projects he was awarded the Special Medal of the Secretary of Commerce.

Mr. Schwartz's efforts were instrumental in the passage of the Risk Retention Act, which facilitates self-insurance by sellers of products. He is counsel to the Product Liability Alliance, which is seeking the enactment of federal product liability law. As a partner in the Washington, D.C. firm of Crowell and Moring, he represents clients, including national corporations, before Congress and in tort litigation.

Mr. Schwartz has chaired the Products, General Liability and Consumer Law Committee of the ABA and the Torts section of the Association of American Law Schools. He is a member of the American Law Institute and has received university and bar association awards for his scholarship.

The author received his law degree magna cum laude from Columbia University, where he was also an editor of the law review. After serving as law clerk to a federal judge, he began practice in Ohio. A former Acting Dean of the University of Cincinnati College of Law, he continues his association with the College as an Adjunct Professor.

COMPARATIVE NEGLIGENCE

SECOND EDITION

By

Victor E. Schwartz

Member, Crowell & Moring
Washington, D.C.
Adjunct Professor of Law
College of Law, University of Cincinnati

THE ALLEN SMITH COMPANY

Publishers

ISBN 0-87473-194-1

DEDICATION

To Deborah Ann Underhill and to her family, who have been a family to me: her parents, George and Ann Underhill, her grandmother, Dorothy Underhill Maxwell, and her brothers, sister and their spouses, Todd and Colleen Underhill, Valerie and Axel Fuchs, Jeffrey and Lisa Underhill.

TABLE OF CONTENTS

CHAPTER 1

THE HISTORY OF COMPARATIVE NEGLIGENCE

CHAPTER 2

THE IMPACT OF COMPARATIVE NEGLIGENCE

CHAPTER 3

THE SYSTEMS OF COMPARATIVE NEGLIGENCE IN THE UNITED STATES

TABLE OF CONTENTS

CHAPTER 8

RETROACTIVE CHANGE TO COMPARATIVE NEGLIGENCE

CHAPTER 9

ASSUMPTION OF RISK

CHAPTER 10

THE GUEST STATUTES

CHAPTER 11

ACTIONS BASED ON NUISANCE

TABLE OF CONTENTS

CHAPTER 12

PRODUCT LIABILITY/STRICT LIABILITY AND COMPARATIVE NEGLIGENCE

CHAPTER 13

WRONGFUL DEATH AND SURVIVAL STATUTES

CHAPTER 14

STANDARD OF CONDUCT MODIFIED FOR PARTY'S CAPACITY

CHAPTER 15

CHOICE OF LAW AND COMPARATIVE NEGLIGENCE

TABLE OF CONTENTS

CHAPTER 16

MULTIPLE PARTIES

CHAPTER 17

FACT FINDING UNDER COMPARATIVE NEGLIGENCE

CHAPTER 18

JUDICIAL CONTROL OF THE FINDERS OF FACT

CHAPTER 19

COUNTERCLAIMS

CHAPTER 20

STRATEGIC CONSIDERATIONS FOR THE ADVOCATE

CHAPTER 21

THE BEST MEANS OF DEALING WITH PLAINTIFF'S NEGLIGENCE

APPENDICES

TABLE OF CONTENTS

ACKNOWLEDGMENTS

This book is a response to numerous requests for an updating of my original treatise in light of the widespread adoption of comparative negligence, by both courts and legislatures, since its publication in 1974.

I would like to acknowledge the efforts of Robert C. Lewis, President of The Allen Smith Company, Publishers, in furthering the success of the first edition and in helping to inspire the second. It has been a pleasure to work with Bob these many years.

I also wish to thank Evelyn F. Rowe, Esquire, a practicing lawyer and Georgetown University Law Center graduate, for her very special assistance. Her scholarship, insights and diligence were indispensable in the creation of the final product.

Finally, I offer my deepest appreciation to Crowell & Moring, the law firm of which I am a partner, for providing the facilities and assistance which helped make this book a reality. Indispensable to the process, too, was the help of my secretary, Alice B. Konicki.

Victor E. Schwartz
Washington, D.C.
November, 1985

CHAPTER 1

THE HISTORY OF COMPARATIVE NEGLIGENCE

Section

1.1 Comparative negligence on the march

Comparative negligence is now truly on the march! In 1950, when Professor Turk's article under that title[1] was published, only five American jurisdictions applied comparative negligence in one form or another to negligence actions generally.[2] These were Georgia,[3] Mississippi,[4] Nebraska,[5] South Dakota,[6] and Wisconsin.[7] Arkansas adopted the principle in 1955,[8] Puerto Rico in 1956[9] and Maine in 1965.[10]

The late 1960's saw the beginning of an all-out attack on the fault system of liability as applied to motor vehicle negligence cases, initiated in academic circles and fostered by some consumer groups and by certain segments of the insurance industry. Other professional groups, meanwhile, were examining various aspects of the fault system—notably the contributory negligence doctrine—with a view to preserving the

---

[1]Turk, *Comparative Negligence on the March*, 28 Chi.-Kent L. Rev. 189, 304 (1950).

[2]For a detailed history of the adoption of comparative negligence, see sections 1.4 and 1.5.

[3]Ga. Code Ann., §§ 46-8-291, 51-11-7.

[4]Miss. Code Ann., § 11-7-15.

[5]Neb. Rev. Stat., § 25-1151.

[6]S.D. Codified Laws, § 20-9-2.

[7]Wis. Stat. Ann., § 895.045.

[8]Ark. Stat. Ann., §§ 27-1763 to 27-1765.

[9]P.R. Laws Ann., tit. 31, § 5141.

[10]Me. Rev. Stat. Ann., tit. 14, § 156.

basic principles while making the system more responsive, not only in motor vehicle cases but in others as well. As a result, the American Bar Association,[11] the American Trial Lawyers Association[12] and the Defense Research Institute[13] all took positions favoring comparative negligence in some form as a substitute for the traditional contributory negligence doctrine. The march of comparative negligence turned into a parade in 1969 when four states—Hawaii,[14] Massachusetts,[15] Minnesota[16] and New Hampshire[17]—all enacted comparative negligence statutes in that one year, followed by Vermont[18] in 1970 and four more states—Colorado,[19] Idaho,[20] Oregon[21] and Rhode Island[22]—in 1971. In 1973 ten jurisdictions—Connecticut,[23] Nevada,[24] New Jersey,[25] North Dakota,[26] Oklahoma,[27] Texas,[28] Utah,[29] Washington,[30] Wyoming[31] and the Virgin Islands[32]—adopted comparative negligence by statute.

Kansas[33] adopted a comparative negligence statute in 1974. In the ten succeeding years statutes were enacted by Montana[34] and New York[35] (both in 1975), Pennsylvania[36] (1976), Louisiana[37] (1979; effective in 1980), Ohio[38] (1980), Indiana[39] (1983; effective in 1985), Arizona[40] and Delaware[41] (both in 1984).

---

[11]Marryott, *The Automobile Accident Reparations System and the American Bar Association*, 6 Forum 79, 82-83 (1971).

[12]American Trial Lawyers Association, *Comparative Negligence* Foreword (ATL Monograph Series, W. Schwartz ed. 1970).

[13]Defense Research Institute, *Pamphlet No. 8, Responsible Reform: A Program to Improve the Liability Reparation System* 23 (1969).

[14]Hawaii Rev. Stat., § 663-31.

[15]Mass. Gen. Laws Ann., ch. 231, § 85.

[16]Minn. Stat. Ann., §§ 604.01, 604.02.

[17]N.H. Rev. Stat. Ann., § 507:7-a.

[18]Vt. Stat. Ann., tit. 12, § 1036.

[19]Colo. Rev. Stat., § 13-21-111.

[20]Idaho Code, §§ 6-801 to 6-806.

[21]Ore. Rev. Stat., §§ 18.470 to 18.510.

[22]R.I. Gen. Laws, §§ 9-20-4, 9-20-4.1.

[23]Conn. Gen. Stat. Ann., § 52-572h.

[24]Nev. Rev. Stat., § 41.141.

[25]N.J. Stat. Ann., §§ 2A:15-5.1 to 2A:15-5.3.

[26]N.D. Cent. Code, § 9-10-07.

[27]Okla. Stat. Ann., tit. 23, §§ 12 to 14.

[28]Tex. Rev. Civ. Stat. Ann. (Vernon), art. 2212a.

[29]Utah Code Ann., §§ 78-27-37 to 78-27-43.

[30]Wash. Rev. Code Ann., §§ 4.22.005 to 4.22.020.

[31]Wyo. Stat., §§ 1-1-109 to 1-1-113.

[32]V.I. Code Ann., tit. 5, § 1451.

[33]Kan. Stat. Ann., §§ 60-258a, 60-258b.

[34]Mont. Code Ann., §§ 27-1-702, 27-1-703.

[35]N.Y. Civ. Prac. Law, §§ 1411 to 1413.

[36]Pa. Stat. Ann., tit. 42, § 7102.

[37]La. Civ. Code Ann., art. 2323.

[38]Ohio Rev. Code Ann., § 2315.19.

[39]Ind. Code, §§ 34-4-33-1 to 34-4-33-13.

[40]Ariz. Rev. Stat. Ann., §§ 12-2501 to 12-2509.

[41]Del. Code Ann., tit. 10, § 8132.

On July 10, 1973, the Supreme Court of Florida[42] adopted the pure form of comparative negligence. This decision was the first in this century, by an American court of last resort, to embrace any form of the doctrine without reliance on legislation.

The Supreme Courts of California[43] and Alaska[44] adopted comparative negligence in 1975; those of Michigan[45] and West Virginia[46] adopted it in 1979. Pure comparative negligence was adopted by the New Mexico[47] and Illinois[48] Supreme Courts in 1981. The Iowa[49] Supreme Court adopted comparative negligence in 1982, followed by the Missouri[50] Supreme Court in 1983 and the Kentucky[51] Supreme Court in 1984.

By early 1985 comparative negligence had replaced contributory negligence as a complete defense in at least forty-four states, Puerto Rico and the Virgin Islands. It has become the prevailing doctrine in the United States. The march of comparative negligence is now a stampede.

1.2 The contributory negligence background

Comparative negligence has been regarded by both courts[52] and writers[53] as a reaction against the contributory negligence defense of the common law. From a purely historical perspective, this characterization may be inaccurate. There is ample evidence that comparative negligence preceded contributory negligence in point of time.[54]

Butterfield v. Forrester

The doctrine of contributory negligence had its origin in the English case of *Butterfield v. Forrester*,[55] decided in 1809. In that case, plaintiff was injured by a fall from his horse when, riding at a fast

---

[42]Hoffman v. Jones, 280 So. 2d 431, 78 A.L.R.3d 321 (Fla. 1973).

[43]Nga Li v. Yellow Cab. Co., 13 Cal. 3d 804, 119 Cal. Rptr. 858, 532 P.2d 1226, 78 A.L.R.3d 393 (1975).

[44]Kaatz v. State, 540 P.2d 1037 (Alaska 1975).

[45]Placek v. Sterling Heights, 405 Mich. 638, 275 N.W.2d 511 (1979).

[46]Bradley v. Appalachian Power Co., 163 W. Va. 332, 256 S.E.2d 879 (1979).

[47]Scott v. Rizzo, 96 N.M. 682, 634 P.2d 1234 (1981).

[48]Alvis v. Ribar, 85 Ill. 2d 1, 52 Ill. Dec. 23, 421 N.E.2d 886 (1981).

[49]Goetzman v. Wichern, 327 N.W.2d 742 (Iowa 1982). The Iowa legislature subsequently codified the *Goetzman* holding in a comprehensive comparative fault and contribution statute. Iowa Code Ann., §§ 668.1 to 668.10.

[50]Gustafson v. Benda, 661 S.W.2d 11 (Mo. 1983).

[51]Hilen v. Hays, 673 S.W.2d 713 (Ky. 1984).

[52]See Maki v. Frelk, 85 Ill. App. 2d 439, 229 N.E.2d 284 (1967), revd. on other grounds, 40 Ill. 2d 193, 239 N.E.2d 445, 32 A.L.R.3d 452 (1968).

[53]See, e.g., Averbach, *Comparative Negligence Legislation: A Cure for Our Congested Courts*, 19 Alb. L. Rev. 4 (1955); Grubb, *Observations on Comparative Negligence*, 23 Ohio Bar 237 (1950); Haugh, *Comparative Negligence: A Reform Long Overdue*, 49 Ore. L. Rev. 38 (1969).

[54]Mole & Wilson, *A Study of Comparative Negligence*, 17 Cornell L.Q. 333, 604 (1932). But see Turk, *Comparative Negligence on the March*, 28 Chi.-Kent L. Rev. 189, 208, 218 (1950). These articles are the best available sources on the history of comparative negligence.

[55]Butterfield v. Forrester, 11 East 60, 103 Eng. Rep. 926 (1809).

pace, he ran into an obstruction left in the road by defendant. The court held that, under these circumstances, plaintiff could not recover. *Butterfield* became the principal authority for the contributory negligence rule—that when a plaintiff's negligence contributes to the happening of an accident, he cannot recover damages from a defendant who negligently injures him.

The *Butterfield* court was not bound to select this rule. There was precedent in the law of admiralty for comparative negligence as a method of handling the case in which a plaintiff was at fault.[56]

Later courts may have given greater scope to the *Butterfield* decision than its various authors intended. There is evidence in Lord Ellenborough's opinion that he intended nothing more than to bar plaintiffs who assumed the risk. The judge stated that, "A party is not to cast himself upon an obstruction."[57] Judge Bayley, in a separate opinion, appears to have regarded the case merely as one in which the plaintiff was the entire cause of the accident as he stated that it "appeared to happen entirely from [plaintiff's] own fault."[58] Certainly *Butterfield* could be read to disallow plaintiff's claim because he had the last opportunity to avoid the accident.

As judges and lawyers know, however, *Butterfield* was not read in any limited sense. Rather, it was given full and broad application in the nineteenth and occasionally in the twentieth century. In fact, in 1854 a Pennsylvania judge called the contributory negligence defense a "rule from time immemorial"[59] and ventured to guess that it was "not likely to be changed in all time to come."[60] The judge was a poor historian,[61] and developments in the law have shown that he was not much better as a prognosticator.

Other major countries of the world,[62] including England,[63] preceded the United States in shifting from the contributory negligence doctrine to comparative negligence. It is only recently that jurisdictions in this country have in substantial numbers joined the trend.[64] However, the contributory negligence rule has been on the decline in most states for much of the twentieth century; the courts have chewed away at it by the use of several doctrines. These decisions, which often cause trouble

---

[56]See R. Marsden, *A Treatise on the Law of Collisions At Sea* 135 (McGuffie 11th ed. 1961); Prosser, *Comparative Negligence*, 51 Mich. L. Rev. 465, 475-476 (1953).

[57]Butterfield v. Forrester, note 55 above, 103 Eng. Rep. at 927.

[58]Id.

[59]Pennsylvania R. Co. v. Aspell, 23 Pa. 147, 149, 62 Am. Dec. 323 (1854).

[60]Id.

[61]See section 1.3.

[62]See Henry, "Why Not Comparative Negligence in Washington?" *in* American Trial Lawyers Association, *Comparative Negligence* 9-10 (ATL Monograph, W. Schwartz ed. 1970).

[63]Law Reform (Contributory Negligence) Act of 1945, 8 & 9 Geo. VI, c. 28.

[64]Prior to 1969 across-the-board comparative negligence was the law in only Arkansas, Georgia, Maine, Mississippi, Nebraska, South Dakota, Wisconsin and Puerto Rico. Since that time 37 states and the Virgin Islands have adopted comparative negligence.

in the law after a state has adopted comparative negligence, are considered in subsections (A) and (B) following.

(A) STANDARD LIMITATIONS ON CONTRIBUTORY NEGLIGENCE

Every state in this country has modified the contributory negligence defense in some manner.[65] It is important to note that the legal effect of all the modifications described in this subsection and in subsection (B) following has been to allow a plaintiff to recover his entire damages. These modifications have not invoked the concept of apportioning damages as does comparative negligence.

Defendant's Reckless Conduct or Violation of Statute

If a negligent plaintiff satisfies a court that defendant's conduct was "intentional" or "reckless," then plaintiff's claim will not be barred by the contributory negligence defense.[66] Or if defendant has violated a statute that was intended to protect plaintiff and others similarly situated from the very risk that befell him (for example, a child injured by a weapon that defendant sold him in violation of law),[67] plaintiff's contributory negligence will be ignored by the law.[68]

Last Clear Chance

In contributory negligence states if defendant had the "last clear chance" to avoid the accident, plaintiff's contributory negligence will not bar his claim.[69] States differ widely as to how broadly they apply this doctrine. Some apply it only if defendant actually discovered plaintiff in a position of inextricable peril and had a reasonable time and ability to avoid the accident but failed to do so.[70] Other states apply the last clear chance doctrine if defendant should have discovered plaintiff, but did not actually discover him.[71] Some states apply last clear chance

---

[65]See James, *Contributory Negligence*, 62 Yale L.J. 691 (1953); Lambert, *The Common Law is Never Finished (Comparative Negligence on the March)*, 32 A.T.L. L. J. 741 (1968); Leflar, *The Declining Defense of Contributory Negligence*, 1 Ark. L. Rev. 1 (1946); Lowndes, *Contributory Negligence*, 22 Geo. L.J. 674 (1934).

[66]See Chapter 5. See generally W. P. Keeton, D. Dobbs, R. Keeton & D. Owen, *Prosser and Keeton on the Law of Torts* § 65, at 462 (5th ed. 1984) [hereinafter cited as W. P. Keeton et al., *Prosser and Keeton on the Law of Torts*] 2 F. Harper & F. James, *The Law of Torts* § 22.6 (1956); *Restatement (Second) of Torts* §§ 481, 482, 500 (1965). See also Sun Oil Co. v. Seamon, 349 Mich. 387, 84 N.W.2d 840 (1957); Cook v. Kinzua Pine Mills Co., 203 Ore. 34, 293 P.2d 717 (1956).

[67]See Chapter 6. See also Tamiami Gun Shop v. Klein, 116 So. 2d 421 (Fla. 1959).

[68]See *Restatement (Second) of Torts* § 283 (1965); Prosser, *Contributory Negligence as Defense to Violation of Statute*, 32 Minn. L. Rev. 105 (1948). See also subsection 1.2(A).

[69]See Chapter 7. See also 2 F. Harper & F. James, note 66 above, at 1241-1263; W. P. Keeton et al., note 66 above, at § 66, suggesting that while some jurisdictions reject the doctrine by name, all apply it in fact.

[70]See Hanson v. N. H. Pre-Mix Concrete, Inc., 110 N.H. 377, 268 A.2d 841 (1970); W. P. Keeton et al., note 66 above, § 66, at 465.

[71]Letcher v. Derricott, 191 Kan. 596, 383 P.2d 533 (1963); W. P. Keeton et al., note 66 above, § 66, at 466. The doctrine of "unconscious" last clear chance.

even though at the time of actual discovery, defendant did not have the then existing ability to avoid the accident.[72] It has been wisely suggested that the more a court dislikes the contributory negligence defense, the more likely it is to broaden the last clear chance exception.[73]

(B) SUBTLE LIMITATIONS ON CONTRIBUTORY NEGLIGENCE

There is a growing body of evidence to support an observation first made by Professor James: judges treat contributory negligence differently from the way they treat negligence.[74] In *Rossman v. La Grega*[75] the New York Court of Appeals was quite explicit on the point:

[W]hen it comes to imposing liability on such a theory as tort, between one whose negligent act does harm to others and one whose negligent act does harm to himself ... the same mechanistic standard ought not be applied undifferentially as to both.[76]

Different substantive rules have evolved as to what facts are material with respect to contributory negligence as compared to defendant's negligence. For example, courts are unlikely to take into account an individual's mental instability where he is a defendant in a negligence suit.[77] Many decisions, however, allow consideration of plaintiff's mental instability when the focus is on whether he was contributorily negligent.[78]

Jury Question

Courts are more likely to send cases to the jury when the issue is whether a plaintiff acted as a reasonable person than when the issue is whether a defendant so conducted himself. Arizona, even before it adopted comparative negligence, provided in its constitution that the

---

[72]Fairport, P. & E. R. Co. v. Meredith, 46 Ohio App. 457, 189 N.E. 10 (1933), affd. 292 U.S. 589, 78 L. Ed. 1446, 54 S. Ct. 826 (1934). The great majority of American decisions requires that defendant have the then existing ability to avoid the accident. See, e.g., Menke v. Peterschmidt, 246 Iowa 722, 69 N.W.2d 65 (1955).

[73]See James, *Last Clear Chance: A Transitional Doctrine*, 47 Yale L.J. 704 (1938).

[74]See James, *Contributory Negligence*, 62 Yale L.J. 691 (1953).

[75]Rossman v. La Grega, 28 N.Y.2d 300, 321 N.Y.S.2d 588, 270 N.E.2d 313 (1971).

[76]Id., 270 N.E.2d at 317.

[77]*Restatement (Second) of Torts* § 283B (1965); Johnson v. Lambotte, 147 Colo. 203, 363 P.2d 165 (1961). But see Breunig v. American Family Ins. Co., 45 Wis. 2d 536, 173 N.W.2d 619, 49 A.L.R.3d 179 (1970). See also section 14.3.

[78]See De Martini v. Alexander Sanitarium, Inc., 192 Cal. App. 2d 442, 13 Cal. Rptr. 564, 91 A.L.R.2d 383 (1961); Emory University v. Lee, 97 Ga. App. 680, 104 S.E.2d 234 (1958); Johnson v. Texas & P. R. Co., 16 La. App. 464, 133 So. 517 (1931), reh. den. 16 La. App. 470, 135 So. 114 (1931); Lynch v. Rosenthal, 396 S.W.2d 272 (Mo. App. 1965) (mentally deficient plaintiff). See also section 14.3.

issue of plaintiff's contributory negligence must be sent to the jury.[79] Courts and legal writers have recognized that often the jury does not follow the instruction on contributory negligence but *sub silentio* applies its own rule of comparative negligence.[80] Of course, when a judge is acting as a trier of fact, he may feel it necessary to apply the letter of the law and the result may be a judgment for the defendant based on a contributory negligence finding.[81]

The contributory negligence defense has also been subtly softened over the years by modification of instructions to the jury. Today a trial judge who instructs that "even the slightest negligence on the part of the plaintiff will bar his claim" is likely to be reversed; this was not true years ago.[82] Moreover, most courts appear to agree that for plaintiff's contributory negligence to bar his claim, it must contribute to the happening of the accident and not merely aggravate his injuries.[83]

Proximate Cause

A very subtle distinction between the assessment of contributory negligence and the assessment of defendant's negligence has arisen

---

[79]Ariz. Const. art. 18, § 5: "The defense of contributory negligence or assumption of risk shall, in all cases whatsoever be a question of fact and shall, at all times, be left to the jury." See Zadro v. Snyder, 11 Ariz. App. 363, 464 P.2d 809 (1970), overruled in Creamer v. Troiano, 108 Ariz. 573, 503 P.2d 794, 797, 798 (1972). However, if there is no evidence from which a reasonable man could find the plaintiff contributorily negligent, the issues need not be submitted to the jury. See W. R. Skousen Contractor, Inc. v. Gray, 26 Ariz. App. 100, 546 P.2d 369 (1976). It has been suggested that the provision creates a de facto comparative negligence system. See M. Franklin, *Injuries and Remedies: Cases and Materials on Tort Law and Alternatives* 308 (1971). See also Anderson v. Muniz, 21 Ariz. App. 25, 515 P.2d 52 (1973), where a verdict for plaintiff was held within the jury's power despite a finding that both parties were negligent. Accord, State v. Cress, 22 Ariz. App. 490, 528 P.2d 876 (1974); Steed v. Cuevas, 24 Ariz. App. 547, 540 P.2d 166 (1975); but see Purchase v. Mardian Constr. Co., 21 Ariz. App. 435, 520 P.2d 529 (1974) (judge may instruct jury that it may find for the plaintiff despite his contributory negligence, but failure to do so is not error); contra, Rhind v. Kearney, 21 Ariz. App. 570, 521 P.2d 1148 (1974) (giving such instruction is reversible error). The Supreme Court of Arizona ruled on the point in Manhattan-Dickman Constr. Co. v. Shawler, 113 Ariz. 549, 558 P.2d 894 (1976): An instruction that the verdict "should" or "may," but need not be in favor of the defendant when the plaintiff is found contributorily negligent was held proper. Arizona's new comparative negligence statute explicitly requires that the plaintiff's negligence or assumption of risk be sent to the jury. Ariz. Rev. Stat. Ann., § 12-2505.

[80]Ulman, *A Judge Takes the Stand* 30-34 (1933). Alibrandi v. Helmsley, 63 Misc. 2d 997, 314 N.Y.S.2d 95 (1970) ("... as every trial lawyer knows, the jury would likely have ignored its instructions on contributory negligence and applied a standard of comparative negligence").

[81]Alibrandi v. Helmsley, 63 Misc. 2d 997, 314 N.Y.S.2d 95 (1970).

[82]See Huey v. Milligan, 242 Ind. 93, 175 N.E.2d 698 (1961); Reep v. Greyhound Corp., 171 Ohio St. 199, 12 Ohio Op. 2d 327, 168 N.E.2d 494 (1960); Mack v. Precast Industries, Inc., 369 Mich. 439, 120 N.W.2d 225 (1963); Lambert, note 65 above, at 756-757.

[83]This trend has been brought into sharp relief in the seat belt cases. See Britton v. Doehring, 286 Ala. 498, 242 So. 2d 666, 672-673 (1970) (collects cases); Berger, *The Seat Belt Defense—Rejection by the Majority of Courts*, A.B.A. Law Notes (July 1969). Prosser thinks the "better view" is contrary and he cites cases; W. P. Keeton et al., note 66 above, § 65, at n.76. Accord, Melesko v. Riley, 32 Conn. Supp. 89, 339 A.2d 479 (1975). See section 4.5.

with respect to the determination of proximate cause.[84] It is hornbook law that for either kind of negligence to be legally significant, the injury incurred must have been among the risks that made a party's conduct negligent in the first place.[85] One can discern in the case, however, that the scope of "risks" is more broadly defined when a court is determining whether a defendant has been negligent than when it is determining whether a plaintiff was contributorily negligent.[86]

Strict Liability

✓ Judicial dissatisfaction with the contributory negligence rule is probably one of the reasons that courts have hesitated to apply the defense in strict liability cases.[87] A few states have gone even further and have held that their comparative negligence statutes are inapplicable in strict liability cases.[88]

1.3   Early development of comparative negligence

Despite the recency of the surge of interest described above in section 1.1, comparative negligence is not a new idea. Some have traced the rudimentary principle behind it—that damages in a tort action should be apportioned between the parties on the basis of fault—to the law of ancient Rome.[89] A form of comparative negligence has been applied in admiralty since the 1700's.[90] There was widespread interest in comparative negligence in the United States in the 1930's.[91]

---

[84]See Chapter 4.

[85]W. P. Keeton et al., note 66 above, § 43, at 281 and § 65, at 457.

[86]Contrast Furukawa v. Ogawa, 236 F.2d 272 (9th Cir. Cal. 1956) (defining risks of plaintiff's negligence) with Gibson v. Garcia, 96 Cal. App. 2d 681, 261 P.2d 119 (1950) (defining risks of defendant's negligence).

[87]See also Lambert, note 65 above, at 745-746 (collecting cases). Accord, Ellithorpe v. Ford Motor Co., 503 S.W.2d 516 (Tenn. 1973); cf. Devaney v. Sarno, 125 N.J. Super. 414, 311 A.2d 208 (1973), affd. 65 N.J. 235, 323 A.2d 449 (1974) (contributory negligence not a defense to strict liability where special circumstances exist—defective seat belt knowingly unused); D'Arienzo v. Clairol, Inc., 125 N.J. Super. 224, 310 A.2d 106 (1973) (unclear warning on bottle of hair dye—need for continuing patch tests). Both courts declined to direct verdicts for the defendants on the issue of contributory negligence in products liability cases, but allowed the jury to consider the issue.

[88]See Chapter 12. The Washington Supreme Court has held the comparative negligence statute inapplicable to strict product liability cases. Seay v. Chrysler Corp., 93 Wash. 2d 319, 609 P.2d 1382, 9 A.L.R.4th 625 (1980). Accord, Albrecht v. Groat, 91 Wash. 2d 257, 588 P.2d 229 (1978). The Washington legislature subsequently amended the statute to cover strict product liability. Wash. Rev. Code Ann., § 4.22.015. However, contributory negligence did constitute a defense to an action in strict liability in Connecticut. Hoelter v. Mohawk Service, Inc., 170 Conn. 495, 365 A.2d 1064 (1976).

[89]Institutes of Justinian, Digest I, XVII, 203; Digest Book 50, tit. 17, Rule 203; Mole & Wilson, A Study of Comparative Negligence, 17 Cornell L.Q. 333, 337 (1932).

[90]Mole & Wilson, note 89 above, at 342-343.

[91]See C. Gregory, Legislative Loss Distribution in Negligence Actions—A Study in Administrative Aspects of Comparative Negligence and Contribution in Tort Litigation (1936).

(A) CIVIL LAW BACKGROUND

Comparative negligence has developed primarily through legislation.[92] As to whether it can really be traced to Roman law, scholars differ;[93] the debate focuses on the interpretation of a provision of Justinian's Digest.[94] Nevertheless, there is agreement that comparative negligence readily found its way into the codes of civil law countries.[95] The civil law acceptance of comparative negligence may explain why Quebec at a very early date adopted a judge-made comparative negligence system.[96]

Civil law influences and a rather specific code provision were not enough, however, to cause Louisiana courts to adopt the principle of comparative negligence.[97] In spite of the civil law historical background and persuasive arguments to the contrary in law reviews,[98] Louisiana allowed the contributory negligence defense until 1979,[99] when the Louisiana legislature enacted a pure comparative negligence statute.[1]

(B) ENGLISH PRECEDENTS

Apportionment of damages first found its way into English law by way of international maritime rules which were increasingly recognized by the English admiralty courts.[2] By about 1700 English courts were consistently applying the rule of equal division in admiralty collision cases. This doctrine was replaced in 1911 by a statute providing for division of damages in proportion to the degree of fault of each vessel—that is, a pure comparative negligence system. The English Parliament

---

[92]See Prosser, *Comparative Negligence*, 51 Mich. L. Rev. 465, 477-494 (1953).

[93]Compare Hillyer, *Comparative Negligence in Louisiana*, 11 Tul. L. Rev. 112, 121 (1936) (supporting the view that comparative negligence principle can be found in Roman law) with Turk, *Comparative Negligence on the March*, 28 Chi.-Kent L. Rev. 189, 218 (1950) (against the view).

[94]Institutes of Justinian, Digest I, XVII, 203; Digest Book 50, tit. 17, Rule 203.

[95]See Hillyer, note 93 above, at 121; Turk, note 93 above, at 241-244 (collecting code provisions of Austria, France, Germany, the Philippines, Portugal and Spain); Malone, *Comparative Negligence—Louisiana's Forgotten Heritage*, 6 La. L. Rev. 125, 128 (1945).

[96]See The Nichols Chemical Co. of Canada v. Amelia Lefebvre, 42 Can. S. C. Rep. 402 (1909); Can. Pac. Ry. v. Frechette, 239 Que. K.B. 459 (1915). Most Canadian provinces have implemented comparative negligence by statute. See Prosser, note 92 above, at 467 and note 9.

[97]La. Civ. Code Ann. art. 2323 (Dart. 1945); Fleytas v. Pontchartrain R. Co., 18 La. 339 (1841); Belle Alliance Co. v. Texas & P. R. Co., 125 La. 777, 51 So. 846, 19 Ann. Cas. 1143 (1910); Inman v. Silver Fleet of Memphis, 175 So. 436 (La. App. 1937), reh. den. 176 So. 657 (La. App. 1937); Mason v. Price, 32 So. 2d 853 (La. App. 1947).

[98]Malone, note 95 above, at 125.

[99]Kuhn v. Oulliber, 225 So. 2d 317 (La. App. 1969); Laney v. Stubbs, 217 So. 2d 468 (La. App. 1968), affd. 255 La. 84, 229 So. 2d 708 (1969); McLelland v. Harper, 38 So. 2d 425 (La. App. 1948).

[1]La. Acts 1979, No. 431, revising La. Civ. Code Ann., art. 2323.

[2]See Turk, *Comparative Negligence on the March*, 28 Chi.-Kent L. Rev. 189, 226 (1950).

enacted a pure comparative negligence law of general application in 1945.[3]

The English admiralty rule of equal division was adopted by the Supreme Court of the United States,[4] but overruled in 1975;[5] since then damages have been apportioned when both parties in a collision at sea are negligent.

1.4 Legislative adoption of comparative negligence

The first significant body of comparative negligence legislation in the United States arose from labor agitation to reform the common-law fault system and make it work for the protection of injured workmen—especially railroad employees.[6] At about the turn of the century the very harsh treatment of injured workmen by the fault system through its trilogy of defenses—contributory negligence, assumption of risk and the fellow-servant rule—led to demands for abolition or modification of the system. A number of state legislatures, as well as the Congress of the United States, in the first three decades of the century enacted laws providing for apportionment of damages in industrial and railroad injury cases.[7]

The utility of a general comparative negligence law was urged by Professors Mole and Wilson in a detailed and scholarly 1932 law review article[8] and by Professor Charles Gregory in a carefully researched book in 1936.[9] Also in 1936 a future President, then a law student, made this perceptive observation:

> [I]f the shifting of loss is to be based on fault, the comparative negligence statutes at least provide a more rational approach to the problem [of distributing costs of automobile accidents] than the crude doctrines of the common law.[10]

Subsections 1.4(A) and (B) following, present a chronological summary account of the enactment of comparative negligence statutes from 1908 to the present.

---

[3]See Law Reform (Contributory Negligence) Act of 1945, 8 & 9 Geo. VI, c. 28.

[4]The Schooner Catharine v. Dickinson, 58 U.S. (17 How.) 170, 15 L. Ed. 233 (1855). See section 3.3.

[5]United States v. Reliable Transfer Co., 421 U.S. 397, 44 L. Ed. 2d 251, 95 S. Ct. 1708 (1975). See also section 3.3. Accord, Shiver v. Burnside Terminal Co., 392 F. Supp. 1078 (E.D. La. 1975) (case decided before *Reliable Transfer*, above).

[6]See Prosser, *Comparative Negligence*, 51 Mich. L. Rev. 465, 475-479 (1953); W. P. Keeton et al., *Prosser & Keeton on the Law of Torts* § 80, at 572-580 (5th ed. 1984).

[7]See subsections 1.4(A) and (B) following.

[8]Mole & Wilson, *A Study of Comparative Negligence*, 17 Cornell L.Q. 333, 604 (1932).

[9]C. Gregory, *Legislative Loss Distribution in Negligence Actions—A Study in Administrative Aspects of Comparative Negligence and Contribution in Tort Litigation* (1936).

[10]Nixon, *Changing Rules of Liability in Automobile Accident Litigation*, 3 Law & Contemp. Probs. 476, 483 (1936).

(A) FEDERAL LEGISLATION

The second Federal Employers' Liability Act,[11] enacted in 1908 and still the law today, provided that an employee of an interstate railroad carrier would not be totally barred by his own negligence from an action against his employer. Rather, the jury would diminish the employee's damages in proportion to the negligence attributable to him. This method of dealing with a plaintiff's negligence, "pure" comparative negligence, was also utilized in more than thirty state statutes that protected railroad employees in intrastate commerce.[12]

Congress incorporated the principle of pure comparative negligence into the Jones Act in 1920.[13] This law protected seamen who suffered physical injury or death in the course of their employment. Pure comparative negligence was also incorporated into the Death on the High Seas Act of 1920.[14]

(B) STATE LEGISLATION

Georgia

Concern about the extreme harm caused by railroads during the 1800's probably prompted a Georgia code provision for diminution of damages if a plaintiff was negligently injured by railroad operations.[15] The Supreme Court of Georgia in rather enterprising fashion combined the principle of this specialized statute with that of another law which provided that a "defendant is not relieved, although the plaintiff may in some way have contributed to the injury sustained"[16] and evolved a general comparative negligence system for the state.[17]

Mississippi

In 1910, the state of Mississippi enacted a pure comparative negligence statute which applied to all negligence actions, not merely industrial accidents.[18] Nevertheless, there is some indication that this statute

---

[11]Act of April 22, 1908, ch. 149, § 3, 35 Stat. 66, 45 U.S.C. § 53. Accord, Seaboard C. L. R. Co. v. Ward, 214 Va. 543, 202 S.E.2d 877 (1974); Kirkland v. Seaboard C. L. R. Co., 230 Ga. 108, 196 S.E.2d 11 (1973).

[12]See Turk, *Comparative Negligence on the March*, 28 Chi.-Kent L. Rev. 189, 334 (1950); Prosser, note 6 above, at 478-479. Some of these statutes are summarized in Appendix C. See also subsection 1.4(B).

[13]Act of June 5, 1920, ch. 250, § 33, 41 Stat. 1007, 46 U.S.C. § 688; Mroz v. Dravo Corp., 429 F.2d 1156 (3d Cir. Pa. 1970). See subsection 3.3(B). Accord, Caddy v. Texaco, Inc., 363 Mass. 36, 292 N.E.2d 348 (1973).

[14]Act of March 30, 1920, ch. 111, § 6, 41 Stat. 537, 46 U.S.C. § 766. See subsection 3.3(B).

[15]Ga. Code Ann., § 46-8-291.

[16]Ga. Code Ann., § 51-11-7.

[17]See subsections 1.5(A) and 3.5(A).

[18]Miss. Code Ann., § 11-7-15. The act was extended in 1920 to include damage to property. See Shell & Bufkin, *Comparative Negligence in Mississippi*, 27 Miss. L.J. 105 (1956). See also section 3.2.

arose, in part, to forestall the possibility that a no-fault workmen's compensation law would be implemented in the state.[19]

The Wisconsin Statute

Legislation[20] giving general application to the 50% form of comparative negligence became effective in Wisconsin on June 16, 1931.[21] The author of the statute traces its origin to the Federal Employers' Liability Act and to Wisconsin legislation that protected intrastate railroad workers.[22] The feature permitting plaintiff to recover if his negligence was "not as great as that of the defendant" had been incorporated into the latter body of law.[23] The author of the statute believed that the benefits of comparative negligence should be extended to injured persons other than railroad employees because it would be equally just in negligence suits in which "human beings [were] pitted against complex machines driven by steam, electricity, etc."[24]

Nevertheless, the Wisconsin example did not immediately generate similar legislative activity in sister states.

South Dakota and Nebraska

In 1941 South Dakota enacted a comparative negligence law that allowed apportionment of damages when plaintiff's negligence was "slight and defendant's was gross in comparison."[25] A similar system had been accepted in Nebraska in 1913.[26] This particular approach to comparative negligence has never drawn a following in sister states.[27]

A Period of Failure

Legislative comparative negligence systems of general application did not "catch on" in the 1930's, 1940's or 1950's. Until the late 1960's states hesitated to apply comparative negligence except in specialized situations involving injured workmen or defendant railroads. The New York Assembly, for example, killed comparative negligence bills in 1930 and 1947.[28] Legislation was offered in Michigan in 1947 but died in com-

---

[19]See Note, *Torts—Effect of Mississippi's Comparative Negligence Statute on Other Rules of Law*, 39 Miss. L.J. 493, 497 (1968).

[20]Wis. Laws 1931, ch. 242, now Wis. Stat. Ann., § 895.045. See subsections 3.5(A) and (B).

[21]Padway, *Comparative Negligence*, 16 Marq. L. Rev. 3, 5 (1931).

[22]Padway, note 21 above, at 5-6.

[23]Id.

[24]Id., at 4.

[25]S.D. Sess. Laws 1941, ch. 160. This act was modified in 1964 and today allows comparison and partial recovery "when the contributory negligence of the plaintiff was slight in comparison with the negligence of the defendant. . . ." S.D. Codified Laws § 20-9-2. See subsection 3.4(B).

[26]Neb. Rev. Stat., § 25-1151. See subsection 3.4(B).

[27]A few comparative negligence statutes of limited application have followed this approach. See Prosser, note 6 above, at 486. See subsection 3.4(B).

[28]Note, *Proposed Statutory Revision: Torts—Doctrine of Comparative Negligence*, 22 N.Y.U. L.Q. Rev. 458 (1947).

mittee.[29] Comparative negligence also failed in Pennsylvania,[30] Oregon,[31] and Washington.[32] In the state of Washington general comparative bills were defeated in every session for over twenty-five years; one finally passed in 1973.[33] In 1950, sixteen states considered but failed to pass comparative negligence legislation.[34]

The reasons for these many failures have not always been made clear. State legislative history is rather thin. Commentators have suggested that major corporate defendants and insurance companies helped to defeat comparative negligence legislation because of their concern that comparative negligence in any form would be too costly.[35]

Arkansas and Maine

In the 1950's one state, Arkansas, did adopt comparative negligence. It first selected pure comparative negligence,[36] but later repealed that act and substituted the then existing Wisconsin modified form under which a negligent plaintiff could recover only if his negligence was "of less degree" than that of the defendant.[37]

The early 1960's saw little development except in 1965, when Maine also adopted the Wisconsin modified comparative negligence system. The Maine statute permitted apportionment of damages unless plaintiff was found by the jury "to be equally at fault" with the defendant.[38]

Attack on the Fault System

In the latter part of the 1960's a new and concerted attack was made on the fault system as a method of distributing the costs of automobile accidents.[39] Proposals for salvaging the system included abolition, or at least modification, of the defense of contributory negligence.[40] The desire to save the fault system appears to have been a decisive spur to the enactment of general comparative negligence legis-

---

[29]See Neef, *Comparative Negligence*, 27 Mich. St. B.J. 34 (1948).

[30]See Note, *Comparative Negligence in Pennsylvania?*, 17 Temp. L.Q. 276, 286 (1943).

[31]Haugh, *Comparative Negligence: A Reform Long Overdue*, 49 Ore. L. Rev. 38 (1969). The Oregon legislature did enact a comparative negligence statute subsequent to the publication of this article. See Ore. Rev. Stat., § 18.470.

[32]Henry, "Why Not Comparative Negligence in Washington?" *in* American Trial Lawyers Association, *Comparative Negligence* 1 (ATL Monograph, W. Schwartz ed. 1970).

[33]Wash. Laws 1973 (1st Ex. Sess.), ch. 138, § 1, now Wash. Rev. Code Ann., §§ 4.22.005 to 4.22.020.

[34]See Lipscomb, *Comparative Negligence*, 1951 Ins. L.J. 667, 674.

[35]See Haugh, note 31 above, at 38.

[36]Ark. Acts 1955, No. 191, § 1. See section 3.2 at note 16.

[37]Ark. Acts 1957, No. 296, § 2. The law has been repealed and replaced by later enactments. See subsection 3.5(B).

[38]Me. Laws 1965, ch. 424, codified at Me. Rev. Stat. Ann., tit. 14, § 156. See subsection 3.5(B).

[39]See R. Keeton & V. O'Connell, *Basic Protection for the Traffic Victim—A Blueprint for Reforming Automobile Insurance* (1965); W. E. Meyer Research Inst. of Law, *Dollars, Delay and the Automobile Victim* (1968); Conard, *The Economic Treatment of Automobile Injuries*, 63 Mich. L. Rev. 279 (1964).

[40]See Turk, note 12 above, at 343-344.

lation. In 1969 and 1970 Minnesota,[41] New Hampshire,[42] Hawaii,[43] Vermont[44] and Massachusetts[45] adopted modified comparative negligence. In 1971 Colorado,[46] Idaho[47] and Oregon[48] enacted similar legislation and the Rhode Island[49] legislature adopted pure comparative negligence. Except for the Arkansas experiment, Rhode Island was the first state to have done this since Mississippi took that step in 1910.[50]

The year 1973 was by far the most active to date in legislative adoption of comparative negligence. Eight states—Connecticut,[51] Nevada,[52] New Jersey,[53] North Dakota,[54] Oklahoma,[55] Texas,[56] Utah,[57] and Wyoming[58]—adopted generally applicable modified forms of comparative negligence, and Washington[59] adopted the pure form. Thus by the end of 1973, counting Florida's judicial adoption,[60] at least twenty-five states were applying comparative negligence in one form or another to all tort actions, and Washington was ready to follow on April 1, 1974.

Legislative Adoption Since 1974

Since the original publication of this book in 1974, comparative negligence has been adopted by the legislatures in: Kansas (1974, modified form),[61] Montana (1975, modified form),[62] New York (1975, pure form),[63] Pennsylvania (1976, modified form),[64] Ohio (1980, modified form),[65] Lou-

---

[41]Minn. Stat. Ann., § 604.01 (effective in any trial commenced after July 1, 1969).

[42]N.H. Rev. Stat. Ann., § 507:7-a (governing all actions and damages sustained on and after August 12, 1969).

[43]Hawaii Rev. Stat., § 663-31 (effective as to claims arising after July 14, 1969).

[44]Vt. Stat. Ann., tit. 12, § 1036 (effective July 1, 1970).

[45]Mass. Gen. Laws Ann., ch. 231, § 85 (effective January 1, 1971).

[46]Colo. Rev. Stat., § 13-21-111.

[47]Idaho Code, §§ 6-801 to 6-806.

[48]Ore. Rev. Stat., § 18-470.

[49]R.I. Gen. Laws, § 9-20-4.

[50]The Canal Zone had adopted pure comparative negligence in 1934 and Puerto Rico in 1956. C.Z. Code, tit. 4, § 1357; P.R. Laws Ann., tit. 31, § 5141.

[51]Conn. Pub. Act No. 73-622, codified at Conn. Gen. Stat. Ann., § 52-572h, replacing Pub. Act No. 72-273, § 6, which had applied comparative negligence to cases involving private passenger motor vehicles.

[52]Nev. Laws 1973, ch. 787, codified at Nev. Rev. Stat., § 41.141.

[53]N.J. Stat. Ann., §§ 2A:15-5.1 to 2A:15-5.3.

[54]N.D. Cent. Code, § 9-10-07.

[55]Okla. Stat. Ann., tit. 23, §§ 12 to 14.

[56]Tex. Rev. Civ. Stat. Ann. (Vernon), art. 2212a.

[57]Utah Code Ann., §§ 78-27-37 to 78-27-43.

[58]Wyo. Stat., §§ 1-1-109 to 1-1-113.

[59]Wash. Laws 1973 (1st Ex. Sess.), ch. 138, § 1 codified at Wash. Rev. Code Ann., § 4.22.005.

[60]Hoffman v. Jones, 280 So. 2d 431, 78 A.L.R.3d 321 (Fla. 1973). See subsection 1.5(D).

[61]Kan. Stat. Ann., § 60-258a.

[62]Mont. Code Ann., § 27-1-702.

[63]N.Y. Civ. Prac. Law, § 1411. See Starr v. Albin Constr. Co., 87 Misc. 2d 858, 386 N.Y.S.2d 623 (1976).

[64]Pa. Stat. Ann., tit. 42, § 7102.

[65]Ohio Rev. Code Ann., § 2315.19.

isiana (1979, pure form),[66] Iowa (1984, modified form),[67] Indiana (1983, modified form),[68] Arizona (1984, pure form),[69] and Delaware (1984, modified form).[70]

1.5 Judicial adoption of comparative negligence

One of the more controversial issues connected with comparative negligence has been whether it can or should be adopted by the judiciary.[71] As indicated in section 1.4 above, until recently the overwhelming majority of states that have adopted comparative negligence have done so by purely legislative action. Nevertheless, a number of serious attempts have been made to implement comparative negligence through judge-made law,[72] and in ten states these attempts have succeeded.[73] In another, Georgia, a comparative negligence doctrine evolved out of a joint enterprise between the legislature and the judiciary.[74] In Hawaii strong judicial language prompted legislative adoption of a comparative negligence system.[75] During the early 1980's the majority of states adopting comparative negligence did so by judicial decision.

This section considers in detail how comparative negligence has been implemented through judicial action. The arguments for and against a court's taking such a step are considered in Chapter 21, sections 21.5 to 21.7.

(A) EARLY ATTEMPTS BY THE JUDICIARY
Nineteenth Century Experiments

As far back as 1858, in the case of *The Galena & Chicago Union Railroad Company v. Jacobs,*[76] the Supreme Court of Illinois attempted

---

[66]La. Civ. Code Ann., art. 2323.

[67]Iowa Code Ann., §§ 668.1 to 668.10. A pure form of comparative negligence was earlier adopted in Goetzman v. Wichern, 327 N.W.2d 742 (Iowa 1982).

[68]Ind. Code, §§ 34-4-33-1 to 34-4-33-13.

[69]Ariz. Rev. Stat. Ann., §§ 12-2501 to 12-2509.

[70]Del. Code Ann., tit. 10, § 8312.

[71]See Juenger, *Brief for Negligence Law Section of the State Bar of Michigan in Support of Comparative Negligence as Amicus Curiae,* 18 Wayne L. Rev. 3 (1972).

[72]See Krise v. Gillund, 184 N.W.2d 405 (N.D. 1971); Peterson v. Culp, 255 Ore. 269, 465 P.2d 876 (1970); Maki v. Frelk, 40 Ill. 2d 193, 239 N.E.2d 445, 32 A.L.R.3d 452 (1968); Haeg v. Sprague, Warner & Co., 202 Minn. 425, 281 N.W. 261 (1938).

[73]Hoffman v. Jones, 280 So. 2d 431, 78 A.L.R.3d 321 (Fla. 1973); Nga Li v. Yellow Cab Co., 13 Cal. 3d 804, 119 Cal. Rptr. 858, 532 P.2d 1226, 78 A.L.R.3d 393 (1975); Kaatz v. State, 540 P.2d 1037 (Alaska 1975); Placek v. Sterling Heights, 405 Mich. 638, 275 N.W.2d 511 (1979); Bradley v. Appalachian Power Co., 163 W. Va. 332, 256 S.E.2d 879 (1979); Scott v. Rizzo, 96 N.M. 682, 634 P.2d 1234 (1981); Alvis v. Ribar, 85 Ill. 2d 1, 52 Ill. Dec. 23, 421 N.E.2d 886 (1981); Goetzman v. Wichern, 327 N.W.2d 742 (Iowa 1982); Gustafson v. Benda, 661 S.W.2d 11 (Mo. 1983); Hilen v. Hays, 673 S.W.2d 713 (Ky. 1984).

[74]See subsections 1.5(A) and 3.5(A).

[75]See Loui v. Oakley, 50 Hawaii 260, 265 n.5, 50 Hawaii 272, 438 P.2d 393, 397 n.5 (1968).

[76]Galena & C. U. R. Co. v. Jacobs, 20 Ill. 478 (1858). See also Phillips, *Maki v. Frelk: The Rise and Fall of Comparative Negligence in Illinois,* 57 Ill. B.J. 10 (1968).

on its own to implement a comparative negligence system. Through that decision and a series of cases which followed, a plaintiff could recover all of his damages "whenever it . . . appear[ed] that the plaintiff's negligence [was] comparatively slight, and that of defendant gross."[77] Similar approaches to comparing negligence were apparently attempted at the end of the nineteenth century in Oregon, Wisconsin and Tennessee, but all of them were abandoned.[78]

It is important to note that these nineteenth century attempts were not pure comparative negligence systems as that phrase is used today. Damages were not apportioned, and the end result in every case was to leave the entire loss on one party or the other although both were at fault.[79] Perhaps such decisions failed as precedents partly because later courts, reassessing the ability of business defendants to bear a loss under the economic conditions then existing, determined that it was advisable not to burden them when contributory negligence was available as a complete defense.[80]

The Georgia System

As indicated in subsection 1.4(B), Georgia has developed a true comparative negligence rule (damages apportioned when plaintiff is negligent) out of a unique blend of judge-made law and statutes. Courts in that state have construed a statute providing for diminution of damages if plaintiff is negligent and is injured in railroad operations together with another statute providing that defendant not be relieved from liability in negligence cases if plaintiff's negligence may in some way have contributed to the injury,[81] to produce a rule that plaintiff in all cases may recover an apportioned part of his damages if defendant's negligence is greater than plaintiff's.[82]

The principles on which these statutes were based had been recognized by Georgia courts as early as 1855, several years prior to their codification.[83]

The developing Georgia comparative negligence law was modified

---

[77]Id., at 497.

[78]See Prosser, *Comparative Negligence*, 51 Mich. L. Rev. 465, 485 (1953).

[79]Id., at 484.

[80]Id., at 485.

[81]Ga. Code Ann., §§ 46-8-291, 51-11-7.

[82]Elk Cotton Mills v. Grant, 140 Ga. 727, 79 S.E. 836, 48 L.R.A. (N.S.) 656 (1913); Berry v. Jowers, 59 Ga. App. 24, 200 S.E. 195 (1939); Wynne v. Southern Bell Tel. & Tel. Co., 159 Ga. 623, 126 S.E. 388 (1925); Moore v. Sears, Roebuck & Co., 48 Ga. App. 185, 172 S.E. 680 (1934); Lamon v. Perry, 33 Ga. App. 248, 125 S.E. 907 (1924); Ocilla v. Luke, 28 Ga. App. 234, 110 S.E. 757 (1922); Smith v. American Oil Co., 77 Ga. App. 463, 49 S.E.2d 90 (1948); Walton v. United States, 484 F. Supp. 568 (S.D. Ga. 1980); Allen v. State, 150 Ga. App. 109, 257 S.E.2d 5 (1979). See Turk, *Comparative Negligence on the March*, 28 Chi.-Kent L. Rev. 189, 304, 330-331 (1950); Goodrich, *Origin of the Georgia Rule of Comparative Negligence and Apportionment of Damages*, 1940 Proc. Ga. B. A. 174; Hilkey, *Comparative Negligence in Georgia*, 8 Ga. B. A. J. 51 (1945).

[83]Macon & W. R. Co. v. Davis, 18 Ga. 679 (1855); Macon & W. R. Co. v. Winn, 19 Ga. 440 (1856); Macon & W. R. Co. v. Winn, 26 Ga. 250 (1858); Flanders v. Meath, 27 Ga. 358 (1859); Macon & W. R. Co. v. Davis, 27 Ga. 113 (1859); Yonge v. Kinney, 28 Ga. 111 (1859).

by the State Supreme Court in 1904 in *Christian v. Macon Railway & Light Company*[84] in a remarkable example of lawmaking without explanation. The Court stated that if plaintiff's "negligence was equal to or greater than the negligence of the defendant," he may not recover any damages at all.[85] This rule was inserted in a headnote and was characterized in the first sentence of the opinion as being "sufficient without elaboration."[86] The Court thus inadvertently laid the groundwork for the majority of comparative negligence statutes of general application in the United States today.

Dean Prosser called the series of Georgia decisions that created this system a "remarkable tour de force of construction by which a statute applicable only to damage inflicted by a railroad was expanded into a general act."[87] Nevertheless, the system itself has remained in force in that state and has not created serious problems for either the courts or the legislature.[88]

Remote Negligence in Tennessee

It has sometimes been said that Tennessee has judicially adopted a form of comparative negligence.[89] It is true that Tennessee courts apportion damages when plaintiff's negligence is "remote."[90] Apparently this means causally remote;[91] therefore, this unique comparative negligence doctrine focuses more on causal connection than on degree of fault of the parties in deciding whether damages should be apportioned. Professor John W. Wade, an adviser and reporter for the *Restatement (Second) of Torts*, after carefully studying the doctrine, called it "elusive."[92]

It is possible that damages are apportioned in Tennessee *only* when defendant had what most states would call "the last clear chance" to

---

[84]Christian v. Macon R. & L. Co., 120 Ga. 314, 47 S.E. 923 (1904).

[85]Id.

[86]Id., 47 S.E. at 923.

[87]W. P. Keeton et al., *Prosser and Keeton on the Law of Torts* § 67, at 471 (5th ed. 1984).

[88]See Seagraves v. Abco Mfg. Co., 118 Ga. App. 414, 164 S.E.2d 242 (1968).

[89]See article by Professor Wade in Symposium, *Comments on Maki v. Frelk—Comparative v. Contributory Negligence: Should the Court or Legislature Decide?*, 21 Vand. L. Rev. 889, 938 (1968). The Supreme Court of Tennessee had denied that the state has comparative negligence. See East Tennessee, V. & G. R. Co. v. Hull, 88 Tenn. 33, 12 S.W. 419 (1889).

[90]See DeRossett v. Malone, 34 Tenn. App. 451, 475, 239 S.W.2d 366, 377 (1950); Elmore v. Thompson, 14 Tenn. App. 78, 100 (1931); Annot., "The doctrine of comparative negligence and its relation to the doctrine of contributory negligence," 32 A.L.R.3d 463, 479-480 (1970). The principle that damages are to be assessed upon a scale of degree of the parties' negligence was held not to be the Tennessee rule for the assessment of damages in Walters v. Glidwell, 572 S.W.2d 657 (Tenn. App. 1978).

[91]See Wade, note 89 above, at 938. See Frady v. Smith, 519 S.W.2d 584 (Tenn. 1974). Contributory negligence, to be proximate, must be the direct and efficient cause of the accident. If plaintiff's negligence is remote, the defendant's negligence is the sole proximate cause.

[92]Wade, note 89 above, at 939 n.4.

avoid the accident.[93] If this is the effect of the Tennessee doctrine, it is far from a general comparative negligence approach. Rather than modifying the defense of contributory negligence, it serves to mitigate the harshness of last clear chance. Instead of giving the plaintiff total recovery when his negligence is "remote," it apportions damages between the parties. The question of whether the plaintiff's negligence was proximate or remote will be removed from the jury only when reasonable minds would not differ on the point.[94]

(B) RESISTANCE TO JUDICIAL ADOPTION

Courts in the United States historically have been reluctant to adopt a general comparative negligence system—one which apportions damages in all kinds of negligence cases. The highest courts in Delaware,[95] Hawaii,[96] Minnesota,[97] New York,[98] North Dakota,[99] Oregon,[1] and Ohio[2] have all specifically declined to take this step. An appellate court in Louisiana declined to apply the doctrine.[3] The Supreme Court of Tennessee declined to address the question but recognized the doctrine as the better rule.[4] An Indiana appellate court case contains dictum rejecting comparative negligence.[5] The highest courts in Illinois,[6] New Mexico,[7] Michigan,[8] and Missouri[9] declined to adopt comparative negligence one or more times before accepting it.

In a 1983 opinion, the Court of Appeals of Maryland[9a] declined to abrogate contributory negligence, stating that abandonment of the

---

[93]See Prosser, note 78 above, at 497. Indeed, it may be that the state of Tennessee has a separate doctrine of last clear chance in which plaintiff's damages are not diminished. See Wade, note 89 above, at 939 n.4.

[94]Frady v. Smith, 519 S.W.2d 584 (Tenn. 1974); Howard v. J. N. Zellner & Sons Transfer Co., 529 F.2d 245 (6th Cir. Tenn. 1976).

[95]McGraw v. Corrin, 303 A.2d 641 (Del. 1973).

[96]See Loui v. Oakley, 50 Hawaii 260, 50 Hawaii 272, 438 P.2d 393 (1968).

[97]Haeg v. Sprague, Warner & Co., 202 Minn. 425, 281 N.W. 261 (1938).

[98]Rossman v. La Grega, 28 N.Y.2d 300, 321 N.Y.S.2d 588, 270 N.E.2d 313 (1971).

[99]Krise v. Gillund, 184 N.W.2d 405 (N.D. 1971).

[1]Peterson v. Culp, 255 Ore. 269, 465 P.2d 876 (1970).

[2]Baab v. Shockling, 61 Ohio St. 2d 55, 15 Ohio Op. 3d 82, 399 N.E.2d 87 (1980). The Ohio legislature enacted a comparative negligence statute in March 1980.

[3]The Court of Appeals of Louisiana declined to apply the doctrine of comparative negligence and thus barred plaintiff's recovery. Bourque v. Olin Corp., 346 So. 2d 1373 (La. App. 1977). The Louisiana comparative negligence statute became effective in 1980.

[4]Street v. Calvert, 541 S.W.2d 576 (Tenn. 1976).

[5]Birdsong v. ITT Continental Baking Co., 160 Ind. App. 411, 312 N.E.2d 104 (1974). The Indiana legislature adopted comparative negligence in 1983, effective in 1985.

[6]Maki v. Frelk, 40 Ill. 2d 193, 239 N.E.2d 445, 32 A.L.R.3d 452 (1968).

[7]Syroid v. Albuquerque Gravel Products Co., 86 N.M. 235, 522 P.2d 570 (1974).

[8]Parsonson v. Construction Equipment Co., 386 Mich. 61, 191 N.W.2d 465 (1971); Kirby v. Larson, 400 Mich. 585, 256 N.W.2d 400 (1977) (split decision).

[9]Steinman v. Strobel, 589 S.W.2d 293 (Mo. 1979). See also Epple v. Western Auto Supply Co., 557 S.W.2d 253 (Mo. 1977); Jensen v. English, 592 S.W.2d 541 (Mo. App. 1979); Chandler v. Mattox, 544 S.W.2d 85 (Mo. App. 1976).

[9a]Harrison v. Montgomery County Bd. of Education, 295 Md. 442, 456 A.2d 894 (1983).

doctrine "involves fundamental and basic public policy considerations properly to be addressed by the legislature."[9b]

A 1984 decision of the South Carolina Court of Appeals[9c] adopting the doctrine of comparative negligence was quashed on appeal to the Supreme Court on the ground that the intermediate appellate court was not empowered to decide the issue.[9d]

Courts that have considered whether to adopt comparative negligence appear to concede that it is superior to the common-law contributory negligence doctrine which bars recovery by the negligent plaintiff. The Supreme Court of Minnesota, in a case in which the plaintiff drove into an intersection on the mistaken assumption that a negligent speeding defendant would slow down, stated, "It would be hard to imagine a case more illustrative of the truth that, in operation, the rule of comparative negligence would serve justice more faithfully than that of contributory negligence."[10]Nevertheless, the courts have held that a legal change of this magnitude should be left to the legislature.

Although the New York Court of Appeals declined in 1971 to embrace comparative negligence, it characterized contributory negligence as follows:

[A] legal concept that created an artificial dichotomy that persisted all through the nineteenth century and is slowly yielding now to the persistent arguments of its critics that it is at once unfair and not well founded in legal principle.[11]

In that case the court did modify the harshness of the common-law doctrine by holding that decedent's contributory negligence was a question for the jury. As has been indicated in section 1.2, one method by which appellate courts attenuate the contributory negligence defense without abandoning it is to allow juries to decide cases containing some evidence of contributory negligence.[12]

(C) AN APPARENT BREAKTHROUGH: MAKI v. FRELK

In 1967 the Illinois Appellate Court, responding to a request from the Illinois Supreme Court, recommended adoption of modified comparative negligence.[13] The Appellate Court rejected the argument that the change should be left to the legislature on the ground that contributory negligence was a judge-made rule that could be abolished if it no long-

---

[9b]Id., 456 A.2d at 905.

[9c]Langley v. Boyter, 325 S.E.2d 550 (S.C. App. 1984).

[9d]Langley v. Boyter, 332 S.E.2d 100 (S.C. 1985).

[10]Haeg v. Sprague, Warner & Co., 202 Minn. 425 at 429, 430, 281 N.W. 261 at 263 (1938).

[11]Rossman v. La Grega, note 98 above, 270 N.E.2d at 317 (1971).

[12]Nevertheless, courts may still be very reluctant to let even a suggestion of comparative negligence enter into their instruction. See Wren v. Steiger, 23 Ohio App. 2d 135, 52 Ohio Op. 2d 161, 261 N.E.2d 191 (1970) (use of the phrase "no matter how negligent defendant may have been" invited comparison of negligence and was error).

[13]Maki v. Frelk, 85 Ill. App. 2d 439, 229 N.E.2d 284 (1967).

er met present-day needs.[14] The court said that contributory negligence might have been "essential" to the growth of industry in the nineteenth century but today resulted in a poor distribution of loss from accidents.[15] The court noted that Illinois courts had disposed of other obsolete doctrines. [16]

In spite of favorable critical comment on *Maki v. Frelk*,[17] the Illinois Supreme Court reversed, deferring to the legislature.[18] The majority accepted the premise that the courts could change a common-law rule that did not contravene statutes or constitutional principles, but it was persuaded that such a change should be made only if the rule were seriously detrimental to public interests.[19] Obviously the majority was not convinced that the contributory negligence rule was harsh enough to deserve judicial correction.

The Illinois Supreme Court noted also that the contributory negligence rule had been incorporated into numerous statutes governing liability in particular cases, such as those concerning injuries caused by negligent firemen or county superintendents of highways.[20] This point of fact was available as a basis for distinguishing the decision in jurisdictions that did not have such specialized statutes.[21] Nevertheless, the general thrust of the Illinois opinion, that the change should be left to the legislature, was followed by the Supreme Courts of Oregon[22] and North Dakota.[23]

Thirteen years after *Maki v. Frelk*, the Illinois Supreme Court adopted pure comparative negligence in *Alvis v. Ribar*,[24] largely on the grounds that in addition to being unfair and outmoded,[25] the contributory negligence rule had been abolished in 36 states.[26] The court dealt with the legislative change argument by noting that six bills had been introduced and had failed to pass between 1976 and 1981 and conclud-

---

[14]Id., 229 N.E.2d at 291.

[15]Id., at 290.

[16]Id., at 285.

[17]See Symposium, note 89 above, at 889; Comment, *Judicial Adoption of a Comparative Negligence Rule in Illinois*, 1967 U. Ill. L.F. 351; Note, *Torts—Comparative Negligence—A Court Moves to Strike the Arbitrary Doctrine of Contributory Negligence*, 17 Buffalo L. Rev. 573 (1968); Phillips, note 76 above, at 10; Note, 43 Notre Dame Law. 422 (1968); Note, *Torts—Contributory Negligence*, 20 S.C. L. Rev. 146 (1968); Annot., "The doctrine of comparative negligence and its relation to the doctrine of contributory negligence," 32 A.L.R.3d 463, 482-488 (1970). In the Vanderbilt Symposium, cited at note 89 above, five out of the six commentators favored the decision. Those in favor were Messrs. Fleming James, Jr., Robert E. Keeton, Robert A. Leflar, Wex S. Malone and John W. Wade. Against, Professor Harry Kalven, Jr.

[18]Maki v. Frelk, 40 Ill. 2d 193, 239 N.E.2d 445, 32 A.L.R.3d 452 (1968).

[19]Id.

[20]Id.

[21]See Juenger, note 71 above, at 43.

[22]Peterson v. Culp, 255 Ore. 269, 465 P.2d 876 (1970).

[23]Krise v. Gillund, 184 N.W.2d 405 (N.D. 1971).

[24]Alvis v. Ribar, 85 Ill. 2d 1, 52 Ill. Dec. 23, 421 N.E.2d 886 (1981).

[25]Id., at 892-893.

[26]Id., at 891-892.

ing that the legislature was waiting for the courts to act.[27] Existing liability statutes were a reflection of then-existing law rather than a ratification of contributory negligence.[28]

Joint Action in Hawaii

Until the year 1973, the strongest language in a majority opinion by any state's high court suggesting full judicial conversion from contributory to comparative negligence appeared in a footnote to an opinion of the Supreme Court of Hawaii.[29] There the court gave notice to the legislature that it might replace contributory with comparative negligence if the legislature failed to act. There was never an opportunity for the court's prediction to be tested; the Hawaii legislature soon passed a statute providing for modified comparative negligence of the Wisconsin type.[30]

(D) JUDICIAL ADOPTION ACCOMPLISHED: HOFFMAN v. JONES

On July 10, 1973, a significant event in the history of judicial lawmaking occurred. In *Hoffman v. Jones*,[31] the Supreme Court of Florida replaced the contributory negligence doctrine with pure comparative negligence. The court directly answered the often stated argument that such a change should be left to the legislature:

Legislative action could, of course, be taken, but we abdicate our own function, in a field peculiarly nonstatutory, when we refuse to reconsider an old and unsatisfactory court-made rule.[32]

The court found the contributory negligence rule unsatisfactory:

Whatever may have been the historical justification for it, today it is almost universally regarded as unjust and inequitable to vest an entire accidental loss on one of the parties whose negligent conduct combined with the negligence of the other party to produce the loss.[33]

Saving the Fault System

The court hinted at its awareness that the entire fault system is under attack and must be reformed in order to have a reasonable chance of surviving:

If fault is to remain the test of liability, then the doctrine of comparative negligence which involves apportionment of the loss among

---

[27]Id., at 895.

[28]Id., at 896.

[29]Loui v. Oakley, 50 Hawaii 260, 265 n.5, 50 Hawaii 272, 438 P.2d 393, 397 n.5 (1968).

[30]See Hawaii Rev. Stat., § 663-31. After the reversal of Maki v. Frelk, note 18 above, the Hawaii Supreme Court appeared to retreat from the suggestion that it would, on its own, establish comparative negligence. See Bissen v. Fujii, 51 Hawaii 636, 466 P.2d 429 (1970).

[31]Hoffman v. Jones, 280 So. 2d 431, 78 A.L.R.3d 321 (Fla. 1973).

[32]Id., at 436.

[33]Id.

those whose fault contributed to the occurrence is more consistent with liability based on a fault premise.[34]

The same theme was stressed later in the opinion:

In the field of tort law, the most equitable result that can ever be reached by a court is the equation of liability with fault. Comparative negligence does this more completely than contributory negligence, and we would be shirking our duty if we did not adopt the better doctrine.[35]

Which Form?

One of the basic factors that has caused courts to shy away from adopting comparative negligence is "the multiplicity of systems" in existence; they have felt that a choice involving so many alternatives should be left to the legislature. This consideration did not trouble the Florida court; it simply adopted the pure form, finding it "the most equitable method of allocating damages in negligence actions."[36] Almost all other states that have judicially adopted comparative negligence have agreed.

New Questions Raised

Another reason courts have hesitated to adopt comparative negligence is that the change raises many new legal questions that could better be (but usually have not been) resolved by the legislature. This did not trouble the Florida court, which answered some of these questions in its opinion:

(1) Last clear chance would no longer be operative in the state (probably because it was no longer needed to ameliorate contributory negligence);[37]

(2) A special verdict procedure could be used to determine the allocation of fault between the parties and the total amount of damages suffered (the court left unclear whether the judge or jury was to make the final calculation);[38]

(3) The opinion established the degree of retroactivity of the decision. A good deal of confusion had arisen about this because an intermediate court in the *Hoffman* case had also applied comparative negligence. In general, the Supreme Court of Florida made the decision applicable to all cases that had not yet come to trial and to any other cases in which the applicability of comparative negligence had been properly raised and preserved.[39]

Obviously, in going beyond the basic issues before it in *Hoffman v. Jones*, the court did engage in legislating of a kind, but it could be rationally contended that the nature and extent of the issue it resolved

---

[34]Id.
[35]Id., at 438.
[36]Id.
[37]Id.
[38]Id., at 439.
[39]Id., at 440. See also section 8.2.

required those additional steps. The opinion could also be criticized for totally ignoring the many cases which held that a court should not adopt comparative negligence on its own. In that regard, the court might have argued that the legal situation in Florida was sufficiently different (perhaps because of the adoption of a no-fault automobile compensation system) from that in other jurisdictions to justify the *Hoffman* result.

Finally, the court was a bit too curt in explaining its method of selecting a comparative negligence system. While this author agrees with the court's choice of the pure form, the minority status of that form among all states adopting comparative negligence, as well as the long-standing controversies about which system is preferable, suggest that the selection process should have been explained more completely.

While it is always easy to criticize a court for what it did not do, it is also proper to praise it for what it did accomplish. The Supreme Court of Florida combined courage and common sense in taking the step it did. To appreciate this fact fully, the arguments for and against the adoption of comparative negligence by the judiciary should be considered. In Chapter 21, sections 21.5 to 21.7, these arguments are considered in more detail.

Unanswered Questions

The court declined to resolve other issues that comparative negligence might raise. In that regard, the court stated that Florida

> [A]lready [had] a body of case law ... dealing with comparative negligence, under our earlier railroad statute. Much of this case law will be applicable under the comparative negligence rule we are now adopting generally.[40]

Further, the court indicated that it was not its proper function

> [T]o decide unripe issues, without the benefit of adequate briefing, not involving an actual controversy, and unrelated to a specific factual situation.[41]

These reasons could have excused the court from deciding any other issues than the adoption of comparative negligence and selection of a form. Probably the court felt compelled to discuss the special verdict question and the retroactivity issue because of the very widespread uncertainty that would result if these matters were left unresolved. Its reasons for deciding to hurdle the last clear chance question are unclear to this author.

---

[40]Id., at 439.

[41]Id. See Blackburn v. Dorta, 348 So. 2d 287 (Fla. 1977) (merging the defense of voluntary implied assumption of risk with contributory negligence under Florida's comparative negligence system).

(E) JUDICIAL ADOPTIONS SINCE HOFFMAN

1975: California and Alaska

Two years after *Hoffman* the Supreme Court of California adopted comparative negligence in *Nga Li v. Yellow Cab Company of California*.[42] The court discussed the unfairness of the contributory negligence rule[43] and said that, because juries tended to ignore it, it detracted from public confidence in the law.[44]

The California Supreme Court had a higher legislative hurdle to jump than other courts that had considered the issue because the California legislature had enshrined a contributory negligence rule of general application in section 1714 of the 1872 Civil Code.[45] After examining the history of the 1872 code, however, the court concluded that the code was meant to "formulate existing common law principles and definitions for purposes of orderly and concise presentation and with a distinct view toward continuing judicial evolution."[46] Code sections were to be construed as inalterable legislative pronouncements only if they represented significant departures from the common law.[47] Section 1714 was intended to codify the then-existing rule of contributory negligence modified by last clear chance, and to serve as a point of departure for the courts in "further development of these concepts according to evolving standards of duty, causation, and liability."[48]

Like the Florida court, the California Supreme Court abolished last clear chance on the ground that it was unjustified in a comparative negligence system.[49] The court also merged certain types of assumption of risk with contributory negligence and suggested that these former defenses, as well as that of plaintiff's willful misconduct, should come within the rule of assessing liability in proportion to fault.[50] The court discussed the choice between pure and modified systems of comparative negligence at some length and concluded that it should adopt the pure form:

> In our view the "50 percent" system simply shifts the lottery aspect of the contributory negligence rule to a different ground.[51]

The California Supreme Court might well be criticized for going to some extremes to explain away specific legislation on the contributory negligence rule. As Justice Clark pointed out in his dissent, the majority conceded that the legislative intent was to adopt contributory negli-

---

[42]Nga Li v. Yellow Cab Co., 13 Cal. 3d 804, 119 Cal. Rptr. 858, 532 P.2d 1226, 78 A.L.R.3d 393 (1975).

[43]Id., 119 Cal. Rptr. at 862-863.

[44]Id., at 863.

[45]Id., at 865.

[46]Id.

[47]Id., at 866.

[48]Id., at 870.

[49]Id., at 872 (citing this treatise).

[50]Id., at 872-873 (citing this treatise).

[51]Id., at 874-875.

gence and last clear chance.[52] Nevertheless, *Nga Li v. Yellow Cab Company* was a landmark case and has become the "textbook" case on judicial adoption of comparative negligence.[53]

The Alaska Supreme Court adopted pure comparative negligence in 1975 in *Kaatz v. State.*[54]

1979: Michigan

In 1977 the Michigan Supreme Court split three to three over the adoption of comparative negligence.[55] Only two years later the court adopted pure comparative negligence in *Placek v. Sterling Heights.*[56] The court noted that almost every common-law jurisdiction outside the United States as well as 32 states in this country had adopted comparative negligence, a "precedent ... so compelling that the question before remaining courts and legislatures is not whether but when, how, and in what form to follow this lead."[57] The Michigan court was able to cite favorable scholarly commentary on the earlier decisions as well as points made by other courts.[58]

The Turn Toward Judicial Decision

Since 1979 six more states have adopted comparative negligence by judicial decision: West Virginia,[59] New Mexico,[60] Illinois,[61] Iowa,[62] Missouri[63] and Kentucky.[64] After 1980 the number of states adopting the rule by judicial decision outnumbered those proceeding by legislation five to three. Language in some of these decisions suggests that state supreme courts are growing impatient with legislative footdragging in the face of an overwhelmingly unfair and obsolete rule.[65]

Future Adoptions

At the end of 1984 only six states—Maryland, Virginia, Tennessee, North Carolina, South Carolina, and Alabama—and the District of Columbia preserved the contributory negligence rule. Most of these states are in the "New South," where tradition dies hard; it has also

---

[52]Id. (Clark, J., dissenting), at 878.

[53]See, e.g., W. Prosser, J. Wade & V. Schwartz, *Cases and Materials on Torts* 603-609 (7th ed. 1982).

[54]Kaatz v. State, 540 P.2d 1037 (Alaska 1975).

[55]Kirby v. Larson, 400 Mich. 585, 256 N.W.2d 400 (1977).

[56]Placek v. Sterling Heights, 405 Mich. 638, 275 N.W.2d 511 (1979).

[57]Id., 275 N.W.2d at 515.

[58]Id., at 517-518, citing Fleming, *Foreword: Comparative Negligence at Last—By Judicial Choice*, 64 Calif. L. Rev. 239 (1976).

[59]Bradley v. Appalachian Power Co., 163 W. Va. 332, 256 S.E.2d 879 (1979).

[60]Scott v. Rizzo, 96 N.M. 682, 634 P.2d 1234 (1981).

[61]Alvis v. Ribar, 85 Ill. 2d 1, 52 Ill. Dec. 23, 421 N.E.2d 886 (1981).

[62]Goetzman v. Wichern, 327 N.W.2d 742 (Iowa 1982).

[63]Gustafson v. Benda, 661 S.W.2d 11 (Mo. 1983).

[64]Hilen v. Hays, 673 S.W.2d 713 (Ky. 1984).

[65]See, e.g., Alvis v. Ribar, note 61 above, 421 N.W.2d at 895-896 (failure of six bills in five years indicates that legislature is waiting for judicial action); Hilen v. Hays, note 64 above, 673 S.W.2d at 713 (bills have been introduced in almost every session since 1968); Gustafson v. Benda, note 63 above, 661 S.W.2d at 14-15 ("We have remained quiescent more than five years while waiting for the legislature to act.").

been suggested that their legislatures are anxious to preserve a favorable climate for industry. Nevertheless, efforts have recently been made in some of these states to enact comparative negligence laws;[66] moreover, the courts may yet decide to join the stampede.[66a]

1.6   No-fault systems and comparative negligence

The present attack on the entire "common law" or "fault" system is grounded on the contention that it is a poor method of distributing the costs of automobile accidents,[67] that it "overpays some claimants while underpaying others."[68] This occurs in part because the system is particularly harsh to plaintiffs in denying recovery because of contributory negligence.

The more conscientious defenders of the fault system reply that if the fault system is given a chance to work, it will not be necessary to engage in highly experimental no-fault accident reparation systems.[69] They argue that the fault system might work well with the abolition of such anachronistic common-law doctrines as contributory negligence and the rule that prohibits contribution among joint tortfeasors. These changes, together with provisions assuring fiscal responsibility of defendants and highly improved pretrial settlement procedures, might result in a risk distribution system that is both fairer and more efficient than the no-fault plans.

These arguments are likely to have great appeal to many state legislators. Reform of the fault system appears to be a compromise between pressures for "no-fault" systems on one side and for the status quo on the other. Because comparative negligence is an important part of this compromise, it is likely to become the law in all states in the near future.

Even in states that adopt a "no-fault system," comparative negligence can be an important part of the law for at least two reasons. First, the well-known no-fault plans apply only to motor vehicle cases.[70] Cases involving slip and fall, product liability, or plane, boat, or train

---

[66]In 1976 the South Carolina legislature enacted a comparative negligence statute applying only to motor vehicle accidents, but the state supreme court found it unconstitutional on equal protection grounds. Marley v. Kirby, 271 S.C. 122, 245 S.E.2d 604 (1978). The court indicated that a general comparative negligence statute would have been valid. 245 S.E.2d at 606. Bills were introduced in the 1984-1985 legislative sessions of Maryland, North Carolina and Virginia. In 1985 the Maryland bill was defeated in the Senate; the North Carolina bill was tabled in the Senate; and the Virginia bill died in committee.

[66a]In 1984, the South Carolina Court of Appeals adopted comparative negligence in a case which was later quashed by the Supreme Court of the state. See notes 9c and 9d, above.

[67]A compilation of detailed criticisms is contained in W. P. Keeton & R. Keeton, *Cases and Materials on the Law of Torts* 457 n.1 (1971).

[68]Id., at 458.

[69]Marryott, *The Automobile Accident Reparations System and the American Bar Association*, 6 Forum 79, 86 (1971); Heft & Heft, *Comparative Negligence: Wisconsin's Answer*, 55 A.B.A. J. 127 (1969).

[70]See W. Prosser & J. Wade, *Cases and Materials on Torts* 631-642 (5th ed. 1971).

accidents will not be affected. Second, most no-fault plans that have proved of interest to legislators retain the fault system for damages exceeding specified limits.[71]

---

[71]The District of Columbia no-fault statute lists six exemptions to the general prohibition against civil actions including survival of wrongful death, substantial disfigurement or disability, and pain and suffering ("noneconomic losses") in connection with medical expenses over an administratively set limit. D.C. Code Ann., § 35-2105. The District is a contributory negligence jurisdiction; thus a slightly injured, mostly responsible participant in an accident is better off than a badly injured, slightly responsible one. In part because of the arbitrariness of the limit, a federal district court judge recently declared the limit unconstitutional. *Court Invalidates Key Part of District's No-Fault Law*, Washington Post, Dec. 8, 1984, at 1. Connecticut, as a part of its no-fault plan, applied comparative negligence to claims exceeding the required first-party insurance coverage for "private passenger motor vehicles." Conn. Pub. Acts 1972, ch. 273, § 6. The latter provision has since been replaced by Connecticut's general comparative negligence statute. The Michigan Supreme Court concluded that the existence of a no-fault act does not preclude the necessity of substituting comparative negligence for contributory negligence. Placek v. Sterling Heights, 405 Mich. 638, 257 N.W.2d 511 at 516, n.7 (1979).

CHAPTER 2

THE IMPACT OF COMPARATIVE NEGLIGENCE

Section

2.1 The definition of comparative negligence

The term "comparative negligence" might be used to describe any system of law that by some method and in some situations apportions costs of an accident, at least in part, on the basis of the relative fault of the responsible parties. As Dean Prosser indicated:

> "Comparative negligence" properly refers only to a comparison of the fault of the plaintiff with that of the defendant. It does not necessarily result in any division of the damages, but may permit full recovery by the plaintiff notwithstanding his contributory negligence.[1]

Nevertheless, the comparative negligence systems that are in operation in the United States today do not operate in that precise manner; rather, they all involve some method of dividing damages when the plaintiff has been contributorily negligent.[2]

An early analysis of comparative negligence suggested that it should be called "damage apportionment" or "comparative damages."[3] The suggestion has merit, but it has not been followed in common parlance. Present statutes that include strict liability use the term "comparative fault," but not all states have been willing to go that far.[4] Therefore, this book uses the term "comparative negligence" to describe the variety of systems of damage apportionment that have been grouped under that label.

There are, indeed, a number of markedly different comparative negligence systems in operation in the United States.

---

[1] Prosser, *Comparative Negligence*, 51 Mich. L. Rev. 465 n.2 (1953).

[2] Id., at 465.

[3] Note, *Torts: Damages: The Rule of Comparative Negligence*, 12 Cornell L.Q. 113 (1926).

[4] See Chapter 12.

Pure Comparative Negligence

The states of Alaska,[5] Arizona,[6] California,[7] Florida,[8] Illinois,[9] Kentucky,[10] Louisiana,[11] Michigan,[12] Mississippi,[13] Missouri,[14] New Mexico,[15] New York,[16] Rhode Island[17] and Washington,[18] the Commonwealth of Puerto Rico,[19] the Federal Employers' Liability Act,[20] admiralty cases,[21] and a number of state statutes of limited scope[22] apply "pure" comparative negligence as that term is used in the present work and by other authorities. Under this system a contributorily negligent plaintiff may recover even though his negligence was greater than defendant's, but his damage award will be reduced in proportion to the amount of negligence attributable to him. This system and problems peculiar to it are described in detail in section 3.2.

Modified Comparative Negligence

There are three major forms of "modified" comparative negligence in operation in the United States today. The feature they have in common is that the percentage of a plaintiff's negligence in relation to the case as a whole does not necessarily serve as a basis for apportioning damages.

1. *Equal Division.*—First of the three kinds of modified comparative negligence is the equal division or former admiralty rule. In that system, damages were almost always equally divided regardless of the contribution the negligent parties made to the accident.[23] Admiralty cases are now governed by pure comparative negligence,[24] and the equal division rule is limited to contribution among joint tortfeasors in states that have not adopted comparative apportionment.[25]

2. *Slight-Gross System.*—The second major form of modified comparative negligence is the "slight-gross" system which is applied in all neg-

---

[5]Kaatz v. State, 540 P.2d 1037 (Alaska 1975).
[6]Ariz. Rev. Stat. Ann., § 12-2505.
[7]Nga Li v. Yellow Cab Co., 13 Cal. 2d 804, 119 Cal. Rptr. 858, 532 P.2d 1226, 78 A.L.R.3d 393 (1975).
[8]Hoffman v. Jones, 280 So. 2d 431, 78 A.L.R.3d 321 (Fla. 1973).
[9]Alvis v. Ribar, 85 Ill. 2d 1, 52 Ill. Dec. 23, 421 N.E.2d 886 (1981).
[10]Hilen v. Hays, 673 S.W.2d 713 (Ky. 1984).
[11]La. Civ. Code Ann., art. 2323.
[12]Placek v. Sterling Heights, 405 Mich. 638, 275 N.W.2d 511 (1979).
[13]Miss. Code Ann., § 1454.
[14]Gustafson v. Benda, 661 S.W.2d 11 (Mo. 1983).
[15]Scott v. Rizzo, 96 N.M. 682, 634 P.2d 1234 (1981).
[16]N.Y. Civ. Prac. Law, § 1411.
[17]R.I. Gen. Laws, § 9-20-4.
[18]Wash. Rev. Code Ann., § 4.22.005.
[19]P.R. Laws Ann., tit. 13, § 5141.
[20]Act of April 22, 1908, ch. 149, § 3, 35 Stat. 66, 45 U.S.C. § 53.
[21]Act of June 5, 1920, ch. 250, § 33, 41 Stat. 1007, 46 U.S.C. § 688 (Jones Act).
[22]See Appendix C.
[23]The Schooner Catharine v. Dickinson, 58 U.S. (17 How.) 170, 15 L. Ed. 233 (1855).
[24]United States v. Reliable Transfer Co., 421 U.S. 397, 44 L. Ed. 2d 251, 95 S. Ct. 1708 (1975).
[25]See section 16.7.

ligence actions in Nebraska[26] and South Dakota[27] and in a limited number of actions in other states.[28] Under this system, if a plaintiff's negligence is slight and defendant's is gross in comparison, the plaintiff can recover, but his damages will be diminished by the percentage of fault attributable to him. This approach and the peculiar problems that arise under it are described in detail in section 3.4.

3. *50% System.*—The third and most popular form of modified comparative negligence is the 50% or Wisconsin system[29] and its derivatives. Under this system as originally adopted in Wisconsin, plaintiff's contributory negligence does not bar his claim if it is less than that of a particular defendant but his damage award is reduced by the percentage that his fault contributed to the happening of the accident as a whole. If plaintiff's contributory negligence is equal to or greater than that of defendant, the common-law contributory negligence rule applies and plaintiff receives nothing. This system, now called the "49% rule," is the law in Arkansas,[30] Colorado,[31] Georgia,[32] Idaho,[33] Kansas,[34] Maine,[35] North Dakota,[36] Utah,[37] West Virginia,[38] and Wyoming.[39]

In 1969 New Hampshire adopted a variant of this approach which allows plaintiff to recover 50% of his damages when his negligence is equal to that of a defendant.[40] The New Hampshire variant has become increasingly popular in recent years. It has been adopted by Connecticut,[41] Delaware,[42] Hawaii,[43] Indiana,[44] Iowa,[45] Massachusetts,[46] Minnesota,[47] Montana,[48] Nevada,[49] New Jersey,[50] Ohio,[51] Oklahoma,[52] Ore-

---

[26]Neb. Rev. Stat., § 25-1151.

[27]S.D. Codified Laws, § 20-9-2.

[28]See Appendix C.

[29]Wis. Stat. Ann., § 895.045 before 1971 amendment.

[30]Ark. Stat. Ann., § 27-1765.

[31]Colo. Rev. Stat., § 13-21-111.

[32]Christian v. Macon R. & L. Co., 120 Ga. 314, 47 S.E. 923 (1904).

[33]Idaho Code, § 6-801.

[34]Kan. Stat. Ann., § 60-258a(a).

[35]Me. Rev. Stat. Ann., tit. 14, § 156.

[36]N.D. Cent. Code, § 9-10-07.

[37]Utah Code Ann., § 78-27-37.

[38]Bradley v. Appalachian Power Co., 163 W. Va. 332, 256 S.E.2d 879 (1979).

[39]Wyo. Stat., § 1-1-109.

[40]N.H. Rev. Stat. Ann., § 507:7-a. See Orcutt & Ross, *Comparative Negligence in New Hampshire*, 12 N.H.B.J. 6 (1969).

[41]Conn. Gen. Stat. Ann., § 52-572h.

[42]Del. Code Ann., § 10-8132.

[43]Hawaii Rev. Stat., § 663-31.

[44]Ind. Code, § 34-4-33-4.

[45]Iowa Code Ann., § 668.3.

[46]Mass. Gen. Laws Ann., ch. 231, § 85.

[47]Minn. Stat. Ann., § 604.01, subd. 1.

[48]Mont. Code Ann., § 27-1-702.

[49]Nev. Rev. Stat., § 41.141.

[50]N.J. Stat. Ann., § 2A:15-5.1.

[51]Ohio Rev. Code Ann., § 2315.19.

[52]Okla. Stat. Ann., tit. 23, § 13.

gon,[53] Pennsylvania,[54] Texas,[55] and Vermont,[56] and in 1971 Wisconsin[57] itself changed to the New Hampshire variant, perhaps in response to judicial criticism of its original rule.[58] The difference between the "49%" and the New Hampshire rules is not without significance: attorneys who have practiced with some frequency under comparative negligence suggest that juries are inclined to return "50/50" verdicts which would, of course, bar recovery under the "49% rule."

The states that utilize the Wisconsin system and its derivatives differ from each other on a number of points. For example, some use mandatory special verdicts and some do not.[59] Problems peculiar to the 50% system and its derivatives are detailed in section 3.5.

2.2 Causes of action governed by comparative negligence

Tort law can be divided into three bases of liability. As set forth by the late Dean Prosser[60] they are:

1. Intent of the defendant to interfere with the plaintiff's interests.
2. Negligence.
3. Strict liability, or liability "without fault," where the defendant is held liable in absence of any intent which the law finds wrongful, or any negligence.

The question arises as to whether a particular comparative negligence statute or doctrine should govern claims brought on liability theories other than common-law negligence: for example, an intentional tort[61] or strict liability action.[62] It also may arise where a tort claim is not denominated as negligence at all, as in an action for nuisance.[63] The same question may arise if plaintiff's claim is based on a wrongful death or survival statute.[64] Each of these problems of applicability is explored in detail in subsequent chapters, but an overview at this point might be helpful.

Statutory Guidelines to Applicability: Examples

In many instances comparative negligence statutes themselves provide no clear guide to their application other than to common-law neg-

---

[53]Ore. Rev. Stat., § 18.470.

[54]Pa. Stat. Ann., tit. 42, § 7102.

[55]Tex. Rev. Civ. Stat. Ann. (Vernon), art. 2212a.

[56]Vt. Stat. Ann., tit. 12, § 1036.

[57]Wis. Laws 1971, ch. 47, amending Wis. Stat. Ann., § 895.045.

[58]See Vincent v. Pabst Brewing Co., 47 Wis. 2d 120, 177 N.W.2d 513 (1970); Holzem v. Mueller, 54 Wis. 2d 388, 195 N.W.2d 635, 640-641 (1972).

[59]See sections 2.2 and 17.4.

[60]See W. P. Keeton et al., *Prosser and Keeton on the Law of Torts* § 7, at 31-32 (5th ed. 1984). The fundamental organization of the *Restatement of Torts* reflects this division.

[61]See section 5.2.

[62]See, e.g., Austin v. Raybestos-Manhattan, Inc., 471 A.2d 280 (Me. 1984). See also Chapter 12.

[63]See Chapter 11.

[64]See Chapter 13.

ligence actions. In Delaware,[65] Hawaii,[66] Kansas,[67] Massachusetts,[68] New Hampshire,[69] New Jersey,[70] North Dakota,[71] Oklahoma,[72] Pennsylvania,[73] Texas,[74] Vermont,[75] Wisconsin,[76] and Wyoming,[77] the statutes specifically indicate that they are to be operative in cases in which the plaintiff seeks "to recover damages for negligence." In Connecticut,[78] Ohio,[79] and South Dakota,[80] the statutes explicitly deal with harms when they are "caused by negligence" or "based on negligence." The Idaho[81] and Utah[82] statutes add "gross negligence." These statements, instead of providing guidance, merely raise the question of how strictly the word "negligence" is to be interpreted.

The statutes of Mississippi and Rhode Island proclaim that they are to be operative in all actions brought for personal injuries.[83] Does this imply that the contributory negligence defense is to vest where it did not prior to the enactment of the statute?

The "Fault" Statutes

Maine's statute suggests that the legislature gave some thought to the problems adverted to in this section. It is operative when "any person suffers death or damage as a result partly of his own fault and partly of the fault of any other...."[84] Two paragraphs later the statute defines "fault" as follows:

> Fault means negligence, breach of statutory duty or other act or omission which gives rise to a liability in tort *or* would, apart from this section, give rise to the defense of contributory negligence.[85]

Although the italicized "or" creates some ambiguity in the statute, the legislative intention probably was to apportion contributory negligence whenever that defense would have been operative under prior law and

---

[65]Del. Code Ann., tit. 10, § 8132. The Delaware Supreme Court has held that the Uniform Commercial Code warranty provisions entirely occupy the product liability field and has therefore refused to adopt strict product liability in tort. Cline v. Prowler Industries of Maryland, Inc., 418 A.2d 968, 15 A.L.R.4th 765 (Del. 1980).

[66]Hawaii Rev. Stat., § 663-31(a).

[67]Kan. Stat. Ann., § 60-258a(a).

[68]Mass. Gen. Laws Ann., ch. 231, § 84.

[69]N.H. Rev. Stat. Ann., § 507:7-a.

[70]N.J. Stat. Ann., § 2A:15-5.1.

[71]N.D. Cent. Code, § 9-10-07.

[72]Okla. Stat. Ann., tit. 23, § 13.

[73]Pa. Stat. Ann., tit. 42, § 7102.

[74]Tex. Rev. Civ. Stat. Ann. (Vernon), art. 2212a.

[75]Vt. Stat. Ann., tit. 12, § 1036.

[76]Wis. Stat. Ann., § 895.045.

[77]Wyo. Stat., § 1-1-109(a).

[78]Conn. Gen. Stat. Ann., § 52-572h(a).

[79]Ohio Rev. Code Ann., § 2315.19(A)(1).

[80]S.D. Codified Laws, § 20-9-2.

[81]Idaho Code, § 6-801.

[82]Utah Code Ann., § 78-27-37.

[83]See Miss. Code Ann., § 11-7-15; R.I. Gen. Laws, § 9-20-4.

[84]See Me. Rev. Stat. Ann., tit. 14, § 156.

[85]Id. Emphasis added.

not to apply the defense in any form in other cases. The statute is a bit confusing in that the word "fault" includes nonfault, as for example in strict liability. When the Maine Supreme Court considered the question it held that in a strict product liability case, plaintiff's failure to discover a defect was not a fault, but that his assumption of risk, if any, would be a fault.[86]

The Arkansas legislature apparently saw the same problem when, in 1973,[87] it replaced its previous comparative negligence statute with one using "fault" instead of "negligence" and "fault chargeable to a claiming party" instead of "contributory negligence." The word "fault" was defined as including "negligence, willful and wanton conduct, supplying of a defective product in an unreasonably dangerous condition, or any other act or omission or conduct actionable in tort."[88] In 1975 Arkansas enacted a further modification which expanded the meaning of "fault" to include "any act, omission, risk assumed, breach of warranty, or breach of legal duty which is a proximate cause of damages sustained by any party."[89]

Indiana,[90] Iowa,[91] and Minnesota[92] have also enacted comparative fault statutes, although the Indiana statute expressly excludes strict product liability.[93] The New York statute uses the term "culpable conduct."[94] Nebraska[95] and Washington[96] have amended their statutes to include strict liability. Colorado,[97] Connecticut,[98] Idaho,[99] and Michigan[1] have enacted separate product liability statutes including a comparative fault provision.

Court Rulings on Applicability: Examples

The courts of Hawaii,[2] Kansas,[3] Montana,[4] Oregon,[5] Rhode Island,[6]

---

[86] Austin v. Raybestos-Manhattan, Inc., 471 A.2d 280 (Me. 1984).

[87] Ark. Acts 1973, No. 303.

[88] Ark. Stat. Ann., § 27-1763.

[89] Ark. Acts 1975, No. 367 (modifying Ark. Stat. Ann., § 27-1763).

[90] Ind. Code, §§ 34-4-33-1 to 34-4-33-13.

[91] Iowa Code Ann., ch. 668.

[92] Minn. Stat. Ann., § 604.01.

[93] Ind. Code, § 34-4-33-13.

[94] N.Y. Civ. Prac. Law, § 1411.

[95] Neb. Rev. Stat., § 25-1151, amended by Laws 1978, L.B. 655.

[96] Wash. Rev. Code Ann., §§ 4.22.005 and 4.22.015, replacing § 4.22.010 ("damages caused by negligence" statute).

[97] Colo. Rev. Stat., § 13-21-406.

[98] Conn. Gen. Stat. Ann., § 52-572o.

[99] Idaho Code, § 6-1404.

[1] Mich. Comp. Laws, § 600.2949, amplifying judicially created comparative negligence. See Placek v. Sterling Heights, 405 Mich. 638, 275 N.W.2d 511 (1979).

[2] Kaneko v. Hilo Coast Processing, 65 Hawaii 447, 654 P.2d 343 (1982).

[3] Kennedy v. Sawyer, 228 Kan. 439, 618 P.2d 788 (1980).

[4] Zahrte v. Sturm, Ruger & Co., 661 P.2d 17 (Mont. 1983).

[5] Sandford v. Chevrolet Div. of General Motors, 292 Ore. 590, 642 P.2d 624 (1982).

[6] Fiske v. MacGregor Div. of Brunswick, 464 A.2d 719 (R.I. 1983).

Utah,[7] and Wisconsin[8] have applied a general comparative negligence statute to strict liability. The New Jersey statute has been held to apply only when the plaintiff's conduct constitutes a voluntary and unreasonable assumption of risk.[9] Courts in New Hampshire,[10] North Dakota,[11] and Texas[12] have found the general comparative negligence statute inapplicable but have fashioned a comparative fault rule for strict liability cases.

The comparative negligence doctrine has been held to apply to bailments[13] and to negligent examination of real estate titles.[14] However, application of the doctrine was held inappropriate in actions based on negligent misrepresentation[15] and legal malpractice[16] as well as actions brought under a Dram Shop Act.[17]

The concept of comparative negligence was held applicable in several derivative causes of action[18] as well as in a rescue case.[19]

In *Portee v. Jaffee*,[20] the New Jersey Supreme Court held that a parent's recovery for the emotional harm received from watching the death of her child must be reduced by the decedent's percentage of negligence as well as any contributory negligence on the parent's part.

The Louisiana courts have held that the comparative negligence statute does not apply to collisions between automobiles and pedestrians[21]; the driver must bear the entire loss unless he was not negligent at all.[22] By contrast, the Massachusetts Supreme Court has held that the Massachusetts comparative negligence statute supersedes a statute

---

[7]Mulherin v. Ingersoll-Rand Co., 628 P.2d 1301 (Utah 1981).

[8]Dippel v. Sciano, 37 Wis. 2d 443, 155 N.W.2d 55 (1967); accord, Collins v. Eli Lilly Co., 116 Wis. 2d 166, 342 N.W.2d 37 (1984).

[9]Cartel Capital Corp. v. Fireco of New Jersey, 81 N.J. 548, 410 A.2d 674, 19 A.L.R.4th 310 (1980).

[10]Thibault v. Sears, Roebuck & Co., 118 N.H. 802, 395 A.2d 843 (1978).

[11]Day v. General Motors Corp., 345 N.W.2d 349 (N.D. 1984).

[12]Duncan v. Cessna Aircraft Co., 665 S.W.2d 414 (Tex. 1984).

[13]Mannis v. Pine Hills Taxi Co., 87 Misc. 2d 680, 386 N.Y.S.2d 301 (1976). Cf. Insurance Co. of Pennsylvania v. Estate of Guzman, 421 So. 2d 597 (Fla. App. 1982) (plaintiff was entitled to comparative fault instruction in case of stolen aircraft only because case went to the jury on both negligence and bailment theories).

[14]Russell v. Hixon, 117 N.H. 35, 369 A.2d 192 (1977).

[15]Carroll v. Gava, 98 Cal. App. 3d 892, 159 Cal. Rptr. 778 (1979) (comparative fault principles, designed to mitigate the often harsh consequences of personal injury, not appropriate in context of ordinary business transaction).

[16]Corceller v. Brooks, 347 So. 2d 274 (La. App. 1977).

[17]Feuerherm v. Ertelt, 286 N.W.2d 509 (N.D. 1979). See section 6.2.

[18]Lieberman v. Maltz, 99 Misc. 2d 112, 415 N.Y.S.2d 382 (1979); Eggert v. Working, 599 P.2d 1389 (Alaska 1979) (loss of consortium); Meyer v. State, 92 Misc. 2d 996, 403 N.Y.S.2d 420 (1978); Hasson v. Ford Motor Co., 19 Cal. 3d 530, 138 Cal. Rptr. 705, 564 P.2d 857 (1977); Hamm v. Milton, 358 So. 2d 121 (Fla. App. 1978).

[19]Ryder Truck Rental, Inc. v. Korte, 357 So. 2d 228 (Fla. App. 1978).

[20]Portee v. Jaffee, 84 N.J. 88, 417 A.2d 521 (1980).

[21]Drum v. United States Fidelity & Guaranty Co., 454 So. 2d 267 (La. App. 1984); Turner v. New Orleans Public Service, Inc., 449 So. 2d 139 (La. App. 1984).

[22]Baumgartner v. State Farm Mut. Automobile Ins. Co., 356 So. 2d 400 (La. 1978).

making the contributory negligence of a nonpassenger a complete defense in a street railway accident.[23]

Interests Protected

On occasion, cases arise involving property damage to intangibles in which a plaintiff has been contributorily negligent. In *Darnell Photographs, Incorporated v. Great American Insurance Company*,[24] the plaintiff suffered damage due to the negligent failure of the defendant insurance company to increase his coverage. The district court determined that this was not an "injury to property" to which the comparative negligence statute would apply and barred the claim.[25] The Court of Appeals reversed, interpreting the phrase to cover any damage resulting from negligent invasion of property rights, tangible or intangible.[26]

In *Lippes v. Atlantic Bank of New York*,[27] the court allowed the phrase "injury to property" to encompass injuries arising from commercial transactions, thus permitting recovery of damages under the comparative negligence statute. By broadening the meaning of "injury to property" to include any manner of commercial torts, the court concluded that the defendant's culpable conduct justified apportionment of damages between the parties. But a Texas court refused to apply comparative fault in a banking case where the plaintiff's negligence and fraud were raised as a defense to breach of contract of deposit and conversion.[28] The court held that Uniform Commercial Code section 3-406, which makes negligence that "substantially contributes" to an unauthorized signature a complete defense, controlled.

One federal court has held that Florida comparative fault rules apply to securities violation claims based on negligence.[29] Another federal court applied the Michigan rule to an employment discrimination claim based on negligent evaluation and discharge, finding the employee 83% negligent for having a bad attitude, performing badly, and failing to see the handwriting on the wall in time to improve.[30]

---

[23]Mirageas v. Massachusetts Bay Transp. Authority, 391 Mass. 815, 465 N.E.2d 232 (1984).

[24]Darnell Photographs, Inc. v. Great American Ins. Co., 33 Colo. App. 256, 519 P.2d 1225 (1974).

[25]Id.

[26]Id. Contra, Miller v. Pine Bluff Hotel Co., 286 F.2d 34 (8th Cir. Ark. 1961) (Arkansas comparative negligence statute applied only to physical damage to tangible property).

[27]Lippes v. Atlantic Bank of New York, 69 A.D.2d 127, 419 N.Y.S.2d 505 (1979) (citing this treatise).

[28]Behring International, Inc. v. Greater Houston Bank, 662 S.W.2d 642 (Tex. App. 1983).

[29]Starkenstein v. Merrill Lynch Pierce Fenner and Smith, Inc., 572 F. Supp. 189 (D. Fla. 1983). See Note, *A Comparative Fault Approach to the Due Diligence Requirement of Rule 10b-5*, 49 Fordham L. Rev. 561 (1981).

[30]Chamberlain v. Bissell, Inc., 547 F. Supp. 1067 (W.D. Mich. 1982).

Skiing Accidents

In at least five states,[31] statutes have been adopted to bar recovery from ski area operators for injuries resulting from any risk inherent in the sport of skiing notwithstanding the comparative negligence laws of the states.

2.3 Adjustments in tort law and procedure when comparative negligence is adopted

A state which converts from contributory to comparative negligence may be confronted with a number of problems left unresolved by the statute[32] or decision under which the new doctrine is adopted. These problems must be dealt with by the courts on a case-by-case basis or addressed through additional legislation.

Judicial Problem-Solving

At first glance the adoption of comparative negligence may seem only a simple reform, perhaps long overdue. Commentators[33] and courts[34] have said that its adoption makes no change in substantive law except to modify the contributory negligence defense. Yet constitutional issues have been raised concerning the doctrine; South Carolina's statute was held to be defective on equal protection grounds because it applied only to motor vehicle accident actions.[35] If no substantive difference is involved, why have courts that clearly prefer comparative negligence over contributory negligence hesitated to effect the change by judicial decision?[36] And why did Arkansas, having adopted one system of comparative negligence, find it necessary to switch to another system two years later?[37]

The reasons for such difficulties are threefold. First, there is disagreement as to which is the preferable comparative negligence sys-

---

[31]Pa. Stat. Ann., tit. 42, § 7102(c); Mass. Gen. Laws Ann., ch. 143, § 71P; Mont. Code Ann., § 23-2-737; Utah Code Ann., § 78-27-53; Vt. Stat. Ann., tit. 12, § 1037.

[32]See, e.g., Idaho Code, §§ 6-803 to 6-806 (effect of comparative negligence on contribution among joint tortfeasors); N.H. Rev. Stat. Ann., § 507:7-a (burden of proof); Ore. Rev. Stat., § 18.470 (assumption of risk); R.I. Gen. Laws, § 9-20-4.1 (no set-off of damages).

[33]See Leflar, *Comparative Negligence—A Survey for Arkansas Lawyers*, 10 Ark. L. Rev. 54, 61 (1955).

[34]Natchez & S. R. Co. v. Crawford, 99 Miss. 697, 717, 55 So. 596, 599 (1911).

[35]Marley v. Kirby, 271 S.C. 122, 245 S.E.2d 604 (1978), revd. on other grounds 273 S.C. 16, 253 S.E.2d 370 (1979); accord, Ramey v. Ramey, 263 S.C. 680, 258 S.E.2d 883 (1979), cert. den. 444 U.S. 1078, 62 L. Ed. 2d 761, 100 S. Ct. 1028 (1980) (court also concluded that guest statute was unconstitutional). In Stockman v. Marlowe, 271 S.C. 334, 247 S.E.2d 340 (1978), decided under the former statute, contributory "recklessness," "willfulness" and "wantonness" were held not to be a complete bar to recovery. For discussion of constitutional issues see Chapter 16.

[36]See, e.g., Peterson v. Culp, 255 Ore. 269, 465 P.2d 876 (1970); Maki v. Frelk, 40 Ill. 2d 193, 239 N.E.2d 445, 32 A.L.R.3d 452 (1968); Haeg v. Sprague, Warner & Co., 202 Minn. 425, 281 N.W. 261 (1938).

[37]See Rosenberg, *Comparative Negligence in Arkansas: A "Before and After" Survey*, 13 Ark. L. Rev. 89 (1959); see also section 2.2.

tem.[38] Second, an enormous number of "adjustments," substantive or otherwise, must be made in the tort law once a form of comparative negligence has been adopted. These adjustments may consist of or result in changes above and beyond the mere modification of one defense theory. Finally, some difficulties arise simply because an old, familiar doctrine has been replaced by something new.

Prior to adoption of comparative negligence in a particular jurisdiction, courts may have made a number of modifications mitigating the harshness of the contributory negligence defense. For example, they may have held that a negligent plaintiff should receive a full recovery if defendant had the last clear chance to avoid the accident.[39] If the legislature, in its subsequent framing of a comparative negligence statute, does not address the question of whether this or other modifications should be preserved in the law, courts may have the burden of reexamining them.

In addition to contributory negligence and its modifications, many other tort law doctrines may have to be viewed in a new light by courts with the advent of comparative negligence. The defense of assumption of risk as a total bar to recovery may suddenly seem unduly harsh, particularly where contributory negligence no longer has that effect.[40] Courts may also be required to reconcile guest statutes with the comparative negligence doctrine.[41]

The introduction of comparative negligence may result in new judicial perspectives on doctrines and procedures apart from tort law. For example, using modern conflicts theory a court may consider, as one criterion for making a choice of law, "which jurisdiction has the better legal principle;"[42] the fact that one of the jurisdictions has comparative negligence could affect the court's choice.[43]

Legislative Problem-Solving

In framing comparative negligence statutes, legislatures have the opportunity to select a basic system with great care[44] and to resolve various collateral legal questions. When the first edition of this book was published in 1974, legislatures were making surprisingly little use

---

[38]American Trial Lawyers Association, *Comparative Negligence* 75-83 (ATL Monograph Series, W. Schwartz ed. 1970); Ghiardi, *Comparative Negligence, The Case Against a Mississippi Type Statute*, 10 For the Def. 61 (1969). The greatest difference of opinion is directed at whether Mississippi's pure comparative negligence system, which in theory permits plaintiff to recover unless he is 100% negligent, is preferable to Wisconsin's modified comparative negligence system, which bars plaintiff's claim when his negligence is greater than defendant's.

[39]See Chapter 7.

[40]See Springrose v. Willmore, 292 Minn. 23, 192 N.W.2d 826 (1971); Blackburn v. Dorta, 348 So. 2d 287 (Fla. 1977). See also Chapter 9, "Assumption of Risk."

[41]See Chapter 10.

[42]See Clark v. Clark, 107 N.H. 351, 222 A.2d 205 (1966).

[43]See Decker v. Fox River Tractor Co., 324 F. Supp. 1089, 1090 (E.D. Wis. 1971); Chapter 15.

[44]See Chapter 3, describing the alternative systems in detail.

of this opportunity; generally they were enacting broadly phrased statutes and leaving it to the judiciary to solve collateral problems on a case-by-case basis.[45]

Statutory approaches to such collateral problems may be illustrated by the ways in which various legislatures have dealt with the relation of the assumption of risk defense to comparative negligence law.[46] As of 1985 thirteen states had statutes which addressed this problem. Connecticut and Massachusetts abolished assumption of risk as a defense,[47] thus making it necessary for defendant to plead the same facts as a special case of contributory negligence. Oregon and Utah defined contributory negligence as including assumption of risk;[48] Oregon later followed Connecticut in abolishing assumption of risk.[49] Arizona,[50] Arkansas[51] and New York[52] included assumption of risk in their comparative fault statutes; in these states it is necessary to look to case law to determine what "assumption of risk" means.[53] Indiana,[54] Iowa[55] and Minnesota[56] have adopted the Uniform Comparative Fault Act definition of "fault," which includes "unreasonable assumption of risk not constituting an enforceable express consent."[57] Washington appropriated the term "unreasonable assumption of risk" but not the "express consent" language.[58] Oklahoma, in one section of its act, provided that the defenses of contributory negligence and assumption of risk should always be jury questions, thus implying that the two defenses were to remain separate,[59] but at the same time omitted assumption of risk from the section providing for comparison,[60] thus implying that it was still to be considered a complete defense.

---

[45]In part this may have been because the two basic "founding father" statutes were drawn in very simple terms. See Miss. Code Ann., § 11-7-15 and Wis. Stat. Ann., § 895.045. See also C. Gregory, *Legislative Loss Distribution in Negligence Actions—A Study in Administrative Aspects of Comparative Negligence and Contribution in Tort Litigation* 154-172 (1936). By way of contrast, Canadian comparative negligence statutes historically have been more detailed. See, e.g., R.S. Ont. 1960, Ch. 261.

[46]See Chapter 9 for a detailed discussion of this subject.

[47]Conn. Gen. Stat. Ann., § 52-572h(c); Mass. Gen. Laws Ann., ch. 231, § 85.

[48]Ore. Rev. Stat., § 18.470; Utah Code Ann., § 78-27-37.

[49]Ore. Rev. Stat., § 18.475. See also Thompson v. Weaver, 277 Ore. 299, 560 P.2d 620 (1977).

[50]Ariz. Rev. Stat. Ann., § 12-2505.

[51]Ark. Stat. Ann., § 27-1763 ("risk assumed").

[52]N.Y. Civ. Prac. Law, § 1411.

[53]See Chapter 9.

[54]Ind. Code, § 34-4-33-2.

[55]Iowa Code Ann., § 668.1.

[56]Minn. Stat. Ann., § 604.01(1a).

[57]Unif. Comp. Fault Act § 1(b) (1979), 12 U.L.A. 39 (Supp. 1985). See section 21.4.

[58]Wash. Rev. Code Ann., § 4.22.015.

[59]Okla. Stat. Ann., tit. 23, § 12.

[60]Id., tit. 23, § 11.

Special Verdict Provisions

Some legislatures specifically provided for procedures to accompany comparative negligence verdicts.[61]

The statutes of Colorado,[62] Hawaii,[63] Indiana,[64] Iowa,[65] Kansas[66] and New Jersey[67] require the jury to return special verdicts setting forth (1) the plaintiff's total damages and (2) the percentage of plaintiff's fault.

The Ohio statute[68] requires the jury to return a general verdict accompanied by answers to interrogatories on the same two issues. The court then uses the jury findings to determine plaintiff's award. In Idaho,[69] Minnesota,[70] North Dakota,[71] Oregon,[72] Utah,[73] and Wyoming[74] the statutes make special verdicts mandatory only if requested by counsel. In Maine, the statute requires only that the jury record the total damages, but it may on its own reduce that award "by dollars and cents, and not by percentage, to the extent deemed just and equitable, having regard to the claimant's share in the responsibility for the damages. . . ."[75] New Hampshire[76] and Vermont[77] specify general verdicts in their statutes.

A 1949 amendment to the Wisconsin law deleted the previous requirement that diminution of damages be made "by the jury." This led the courts of that state to find a legislative intent to establish a mandatory special verdict procedure similar to that now embodied in the Colorado, Hawaii, and New Jersey statutes.[78]

By way of contrast, the Arkansas legislature repealed a comparative negligence statute that had a special verdict procedure and enacted a new statute[79] that did not contain such a scheme. This was

---

[61]See section 17.4 for a detailed treatment of special verdicts.

[62]Colo. Rev. Stat., § 13-21-111(2).

[63]Hawaii Rev. Stat., § 663-31(b).

[64]Ind. Code, § 34-4-33-6.

[65]Iowa Code Ann., § 668.3(2).

[66]Kan. Stat. Ann., § 60-258a(b).

[67]N.J. Stat. Ann., § 2A:15-5.2.

[68]Ohio Rev. Code Ann., § 2315.19.

[69]Idaho Code, § 6-802.

[70]Minn. Stat. Ann., § 604.01, subd. 1.

[71]N.D. Cent. Code, § 9-10-07.

[72]Ore. Rev. Stat., § 18.480.

[73]Utah Code Ann., § 78-27-38.

[74]Wyo. Stat. Ann., § 1-7.2(b).

[75]See Me. Rev. Stat. Ann., tit. 14, § 156.

[76]N.H. Rev. Stat. Ann., § 507:7-a.

[77]Vt. Stat. Ann., tit. 12, § 1036.

[78]See Baierl v. Hinshaw, 32 Wis. 2d 593, 146 N.W.2d 433 (1966) (indicating amount of discretion with respect to form); Heft & Heft, *Comparative Negligence: Wisconsin's Answer*, 55 A.B.A. J. 127, 128 (1969); Ghiardi & Hogan, *Comparative Negligence—The Wisconsin Rule and Procedure*, 18 Def. L.J. 537, 545-555 (1969).

[79]Ark. Acts 1961 (1st Ex. Sess.) No. 61, § 4. The 1961 act has since been repealed, but the 1973 act replacing it also omits reference to special verdicts. Ark. Stat. Ann., §§ 27-1763 to 27-1765.

interpreted by the Supreme Court of Arkansas as intending to leave the matter of special verdicts in comparative negligence cases to the trial court's discretion.[80]

Liability of Joint Tortfeasors

Increasingly, comparative negligence statutes address themselves specifically to the question of whether there should be contribution among joint tortfeasors and how shares should be determined.[81] These questions are especially important if the state has adopted one of the early versions of the Uniform Contribution Among Tortfeasors Act which provided for *pro rata* shares.[82] The Idaho law states that contribution should be apportioned among joint tortfeasors "when there is such a disproportion of fault . . . as to render inequitable an equal distribution among them of the common liability. . . ."[83] Utah's law is similar to Idaho's.[84] The Minnesota statute and most others adopted since the mid-1970's direct that in all cases contribution is to be apportioned among joint tortfeasors according to the percentage of fault attributable to each.[85] The Indiana statute, on the other hand, preserves the bar to contribution among tortfeasors.[86]

In *Kohr v. Allegheny Airlines, Incorporated*[87] the Seventh Circuit announced a new rule governing contribution among joint tortfeasors in cases of mid-air collisions occurring in national air space. The state rule of contribution will not apply; rather, contribution will be apportioned according to the fault of each defendant. In effect, the court imposed a rule of "federal common law." The court predicated its holding on the basis of the interstate nature of the accident as well as the general federal interest in the area of air transportation. The Nevada, New Hampshire, North Dakota, Texas, and Vermont statutes also apply pure comparative negligence as the basis for apportionment among tortfeasors.[88]

To be contrasted with defendants' obligations toward one another by way of contribution is the very separate issue of a joint tortfeasor's obligation to plaintiff.[89] Only a few statutes address this question. The Idaho, Maine, Minnesota, New Jersey, North Dakota, Utah and Wyo-

---

[80]See Cobb v. Atkins, 239 Ark. 151, 388 S.W.2d 8, 12 (1965).

[81]See Chapter 16 for a detailed treatment of this subject.

[82]Unif. Contribution Among Tortfeasors Act, § 2 (1955), 12 U.L.A. 87.

[83]See Idaho Code, § 6-803(3).

[84]Utah Code Ann., § 78-27-40(2).

[85]See Minn. Stat. Ann., § 604.01, subd. 1. See also Ariz. Rev. Stat. Ann., §§ 12-2501 to 12-2503; Iowa Code Ann., § 668.5; Mont. Code Ann., § 27-1-703; Pa. Stat. Ann., tit. 42, § 7102(b); Wash. Rev. Code Ann., § 4.22.040.

[86]Ind. Code, § 34-4-33-7.

[87]Kohr v. Allegheny Airlines, Inc., 504 F.2d 400 (7th Cir. Ind. 1974). See section 16.7.

[88]1973 Nev. Stat., ch. 787, § 1, subd. 3(b); N.H. Rev. Stat. Ann., § 507:7-a; N.D. Cent. Code, § 9-10-07; Tex. Rev. Civ. Stat. Ann. (Vernon), art. 2212a, § a(b); Vt. Stat. Ann., tit. 14, § 1036.

[89]See W. P. Keeton et al., *Prosser and Keeton on the Law of Torts* § 47, at 328-330 and § 50, at 336 (5th ed. 1984).

ming statutes make it clear that each joint defendant is jointly and severally liable for the entire amount of defendants' obligation to the plaintiff.[90] Arizona and Minnesota have adopted the provision of the Uniform Comparative Fault Act which allows percentage shares to be reallocated if a judgment is found to be uncollectible after one year;[91] this system can also result in imposing complete liability on one of several tortfeasors.

On the other hand, the New Hampshire and Vermont statutes limit each defendant's obligation to "that proportion of the total dollar amount awarded as damages in the ratio of the amount of his causal negligence to the amount of causal negligence attributed to all defendants against whom recovery is allowed."[92] Kansas enacted a nearly identical statute in 1974.[93] Iowa,[94] Nevada,[95] and Texas[96] provide for joint and several liability except that a defendant whose negligence was less than plaintiff's is liable only for his proportionate share.

Retroactivity

With respect to the issue of whether or not the statute is to have retroactive application,[97] the statutes in Arizona,[98] Colorado,[99] Delaware,[1] Hawaii,[2] Indiana,[3] Iowa,[4] Kansas,[5] Louisiana,[6] Massachusetts,[7] Minnesota,[8] New Hampshire,[9] New Jersey,[10] New York,[11] Ohio,[12] Oklahoma,[13] Pennsylvania,[14] and Vermont[15] specifically state that they

---

[90]See Idaho Code, § 6-803(3); Me. Rev. Stat. Ann., tit. 14, § 156; Minn. Stat. Ann., § 604-01, subd. 1; N.J. Stat. Ann., § 2A:15-5.3; N.D. Cent. Code, § 9-10-07; Utah Code Ann., § 78-27-40(2); Wyo. Stat., § 1-7.3(c). Accord, Markey v. Skog, 129 N.J. Super. 192, 322 A.2d 513 (1974) (common liability of each joint tortfeasor to the plaintiff creates the right of contribution, which accrues when one defendant pays more than his pro rata share).

[91]Ariz. Rev. Stat. Ann., § 12-2508; Minn. Stat. Ann., § 604.02(2); Unif. Comp. Fault Act § 2(d) (1979), 12 U.L.A. 39 (Supp. 1985).

[92]See N.H. Rev. Stat. Ann., § 507:7-a; Vt. Stat. Ann., tit. 12, § 1036.

[93]Kan. Stat. Ann., § 60-258a.

[94]Iowa Code Ann., § 668.4.

[95]Nev. Rev. Stat., § 41.141(3)(a).

[96]Tex. Rev. Civ. Stat. Ann. (Vernon), art. 2212a, § 2(c).

[97]See Chapter 8 for a full discussion of retroactivity.

[98]Ariz. Sess. Laws 1984, ch. 237, § 1; Ariz. Rev. Stat. Ann., § 12-2505.

[99]Colo. Rev. Stat., § 41-2-14.

[1]64 Del. Laws, ch. 384 (1984); Del. Code Ann., tit. 10, § 8132.

[2]Hawaii Sess. Laws 1969, ch. 227, § 2.

[3]Ind. Code, § 34-4-33-9.

[4]Iowa Acts 1984, H.B. 2487.

[5]Kan. Stat. Ann., § 60-258b.

[6]La. Civ. Code Ann., art. 2323.

[7]Mass. Acts 1969, ch. 761, § 2.

[8]Minn. Laws 1969, ch. 624.

[9]N.H. Rev. Stat. Ann., § 507:7-a.

[10]N.J. Laws 1973, ch. 146, § 4.

[11]N.Y. Civ. Prac. Law, § 1413.

[12]Ohio Rev. Code Ann., § 2315.19.

[13]Okla. Sess. Laws 1979, ch. 38.

[14]Pa. Stat. Ann., tit. 42, § 7102.

[15]Vt. Acts 1969, No. 234 (Adj. sess.), subsection (b).

are to be effective only from a certain day forward. In the absence of language similar to that in the Uniform Comparative Fault Act ("This Act applies to all [claims for relief] [causes of action] accruing after its effective date"), it has occasionally been necessary to litigate the meaning of "effective."[16] The Montana[17] and Washington[18] legislatures amended their statutes at a later date to resolve this question. In absence of guidance from the legislature, the courts have had some difficulty in deciding whether the new comparative negligence acts are in any degree retroactive.[19]

2.4 Liability insurance

Insurance Costs

In 1981 a committee of the North Carolina Legislative Research Commission prepared a comprehensive report[20] on the subject of comparative negligence for the General Assembly of the state. This most interesting study includes a section on the findings of the committee concerning the effects of comparative negligence laws on liability insurance costs. Questionnaires were sent to insurance commissioners in thirty-five states that had adopted the doctrine and twenty-four states responded. Also, the committee wrote to several major national insurance associations for figures or published studies on the subject.

The report discussed the responses to the survey and in its conclusion, the committee said:

A thorough search revealed no recent comprehensive, in-depth study on the actual experience of any state. The Committee did receive articles and memoranda from major insurance associations suggesting an increase in insurance premiums as a result of adoption of a comparative negligence system. However, the contention that rates would increase appears to be based primarily on [a] California study. The study was based on predicted settlement figures, rather than on actual rate changes.

The majority of the Insurance Commissioners responding to the Committee's questionnaire indicated that in their opinion comparative negligence had no effect on insurance premiums in their states.

---

[16]See, e.g., Wilfong v. Batdorf, 6 Ohio St. 3d 100, 6 Ohio B.R. 162, 451 N.E.2d 1185 (1983), overruling Viers v. Dunlap, 1 Ohio St. 3d 173, 1 Ohio B.R. 203, 438 N.E.2d 881 (1982), discussed in Chapter 8.

[17]Mont. Laws 1981, S.B. 162, amending Mont. Code Ann., § 27-1-703.

[18]Wash. Laws 1982, ch. 100, § 3, defining the 1981 transition from one comparative negligence statute to another.

[19]See Chapter 8; Annot., "Retrospective application of state statute substituting rule of comparative negligence for that of contributory negligence," 37 A.L.R.3d 1438 (1971). See also Grabs v. Missoula Cartage Co., 169 Mont. 216, 545 P.2d 1079 (1976) (Supreme Court of Montana applied comparative negligence to a case tried prior to ((but decided after)) effective date of state's statute, without discussing the issue of retroactivity. The statute does not deal with the issue of retroactivity).

[20]North Carolina Legislative Research Commission, *Laws of Evidence and Comparative Negligence* (Report to the General Assembly, 1981). See additional remarks on insurance costs in sections 21.1, 21.3 and 21.9.

Commissioners in several other states indicated that they did not have any data upon which to base an estimate or opinion.

Thus, the Committee was unable to find any strong evidence to support the contention that insurance rates would increase substantially as the result of adoption of a comparative negligence system in North Carolina.

Thus, there is still no hard evidence to support a widely held belief that the introduction and application of comparative negligence produces an increase in liability insurance costs.

Uninsured Motorist Coverage

Experts on the topic of uninsured motorist coverage have speculated on whether or how, in comparative negligence jurisdictions, plaintiff's own negligence should reduce his compensation under the uninsured motorist clause in his policy.[21] In one of the few cases on the subject, a jury found plaintiff's total damages to be $25,000, but also found her to be 15% responsible for the accident. The defendant was plaintiff's own insurance carrier. Her policy's maximum uninsured motorist coverage was $10,000, which, the company contended, should be reduced in proportion to her negligence. The court held with the plaintiff that comparative negligence should operate only to reduce her total damages to $21,500, and that she should receive the maximum amount under her policy plus the statutory penalty and a reasonable attorney's fee. The court thus awarded plaintiff the same amount she would have been entitled to claim in an action against the insurer, had there been one, of the motorist who was the main cause of the accident.[22]

---

[21]1 A. Widiss, *Uninsured and Underinsured Motorist Insurance* § 7.5, at 199 (2d ed. 1985).

[22]Alexander v. Pilot Fire & Casualty Ins. Co., 331 F. Supp. 561 (E.D. Ark. 1971).

CHAPTER 3

THE SYSTEMS OF COMPARATIVE
NEGLIGENCE IN THE UNITED STATES

3.1 Introduction

In section 2.1, above, it was indicated that all comparative negligence systems in operation in the United States today involve some method of dividing damages between plaintiff and defendant when plaintiff has been contributorily negligent. It was also suggested, however, that states have chosen a number of markedly different methods for making this important apportionment. This chapter discusses in detail precisely how these methods differ from one another. The benefits and liabilities of each are discussed in Chapter 21, especially in section 21.3.

Under pure comparative negligence, plaintiff's contributory negligence is taken into account by reducing his award in proportion to his fault.[1]

---

[1]See, e.g., Erie R. Co. v. Schleenbaker, 257 Fed. 667 (6th Cir. Ohio 1919), cert. den. 250 U.S. 666, 63 L. Ed. 1197, 40 S. Ct. 13 (1919); Auslender v. Boettcher, 78 Colo. 427, 242 P. 672 (1925); Grand Trunk W. R. Co. v. Lindsay, 233 U.S. 42, 58 L. Ed. 838, 34 S. Ct. 581 (1914); Cumberland Tel. & Tel. Co. v. Cosnahan, 105 Miss. 615, 62 So. 824 (1913); Louisville & N. R. Co. v. Wickton, 55 F.2d 642 (5th Cir. Miss. 1932); Cobb v. Williams, 228 Miss. 807, 90 So. 2d 17 (1956); Wells v. Bennett, 229 Miss. 135, 90 So. 2d 199 (1956); Shows v. Hattiesburg, 231 Miss. 648, 97 So. 2d 366 (1957); Buford v. Horne, 300 So. 2d 913 (Miss. 1974); Placek v. Sterling Heights, 405 Mich. 638, 275 N.W.2d 511 (1979); La. Civ. Code Ann., arts. 2323, 2324; Walker v. Louisville & N. R. Co., 571 F.2d 866 (5th Cir. Miss. 1978); Transit Casualty Co. v. Spink Corp., 78 Cal. App. 3d 509, 144 Cal. Rptr. 488 (1978), vacated 94 Cal. App. 3d 124, 156 Cal. Rptr. 360 (1979). See also Mole & Wilson, *A Study of Comparative Negligence*, 17 Cornell L.Q. 333, 604 (1932); Prosser, *Comparative Negligence*, 51 Mich. L. Rev. 465 (1953); Shell & Bufkin, *Comparative Negligence in Mississippi*, 27 Miss. L.J. 105 (1956); Turk, *Comparative Negligence on the March*, 28 Chi.-Kent L. Rev. 189, 304 (1950); Comment, *Comparative Negligence: Some New Problems for the Maine Courts*, 18 Me. L. Rev. 65 (1966); Note, *Torts—Effect of Mississippi's Comparative Negligence Statute on Other Rules of Law*, 39 Miss. L.J. 493 (1968).

Modified comparative negligence systems depart from "pure" systems in one of two basic ways. First, damages may not be apportioned at all in some situations where both plaintiff and defendant are negligent; in effect, in a limited number of cases the contributory negligence defense returns. This occurs in Nebraska and South Dakota where plaintiff's negligence is more than slight;[2] in such a situation, he recovers nothing. It occurs in Arkansas, Colorado, Georgia, Hawaii, Idaho, Kansas, Maine, Minnesota, North Dakota, Oklahoma, Oregon, Utah, West Virginia and Wyoming where plaintiff's negligence is equal to or greater than that of the defendant.[3] The plaintiff is barred in Connecticut, Massachusetts, Montana, Nevada, New Hampshire, New Jersey, Ohio, Pennsylvania, Texas, Vermont, the Virgin Islands and Wisconsin when his negligence is greater than defendant's.[4]

Second, damages may be divided equally rather than in proportion to the fault of the parties. Equal division is the method by which many states handle contribution among joint tortfeasors.[5] This system was formerly used in the United States in admiralty cases involving ship

[2]See section 3.4.

[3]Ark. Stat. Ann., §§ 27-1764, 27-1765; Colo. Rev. Stat., § 41-2-14; Ga. Code Ann., §§ 94-703, 105-603; Idaho Code, § 6-801; Hawaii Rev. Stat., § 663-31; Kan. Stat. Ann., § 60-258a; Scales v. St. Louis-S.F.R. Co., 2 Kan. App. 2d 491, 582 P.2d 300 (1978); Me. Rev. Stat. Ann., tit. 14, § 156 (action won't be defeated by reason of *fault* of the person suffering damage, but damages will be reduced to the extent that the "jury thinks just and equitable"; the claimant cannot recover if he is equally at fault; in practice, plaintiff's damages are reduced in proportion to his percentage of causal negligence); Minn. Stat. Ann., § 604.01; N.D. Cent. Code, § 9-10-07; Okla. Stat. Ann., tit. 23, § 11; Ore. Rev. Stat., § 18.470; Utah Code Ann., § 78-27-32; Bradley v. Appalachian Power Co., 163 W. Va. 332, 256 S.E.2d 879 (1979); Wyo. Stat., § 1-7.2. See, e.g., Peterson v. Haule, 304 Minn. 160, 230 N.W.2d 51 (1975); Wagner v. International Harvester Co., 611 F.2d 224 (8th Cir. Minn. 1979); Bauer v. Graner, 266 N.W.2d 88 (N.D. 1978); Anderson v. Gailey, 97 Idaho 813, 555 P.2d 144 (1976), revd. on other grounds, 100 Idaho 796, 606 P.2d 90 (1980).

[4]Conn. Gen. Stat. Ann., § 52-572; Mass. Gen. Laws Ann., ch. 231, § 85; Mont. Code Ann., § 27-1-702; Nev. Rev. Stat., § 41.141; N.H. Rev. Stat. Ann., § 507:7-a; N.J. Stat. Ann., §§ 2A:15-5.1 to 2A:15-5.3; Ohio Rev. Code Ann., § 2315.19; Pa. Stat. Ann., tit. 17, § 2101; Tex. Rev. Civ. Stat. Ann. (Vernon), art. 2212a, §§ 1, 2; Vt. Stat. Ann., tit. 12, § 1036; V.I. Code Ann., tit. 5, § 1451; accord, Keegan v. Anchor Inns, Inc., 606 F.2d 35 (3d Cir. V.I. 1979); Wis. Stat. Ann., § 895.045. See, e.g., Nimmer v. Purtell, 69 Wis. 2d 21, 230 N.W.2d 258 (1975); Reiter v. Dyken, 95 Wis. 2d 461, 290 N.W.2d 510 (1980); Reyes v. Missouri P. R. Co., 589 F.2d 791 (5th Cir. Tex. 1979); Willingham v. Hagerty, 553 S.W.2d 137 (Tex. Civ. App. 1977); Gonzales v. Reyes, 564 S.W.2d 100 (Tex. Civ. App. 1977).

[5]See generally W. P. Keeton et al., *Prosser and Keeton on the Law of Torts* § 50, at 340 (5th ed. 1984); Note, *Adjusting Losses Among Joint Tortfeasors in Vehicular Collision Cases*, 68 Yale L.J. 964, 981-984 (1959).

collisions;[6] damages in these cases are now apportioned on the basis of pure comparative negligence.[7]

Modified systems of comparative negligence are usually more complicated and difficult to administer than "pure" comparative negligence. It is reasonable to ask why so many states have preferred the modified form. The late Dean Prosser stated that it was "impossible to justify the [modified] rule[s] on any basis except one of pure political compromise."[8] In effect, modified systems were a political halfway house between retaining the contributory negligence defense and abandoning it.

Perhaps the adoption by so many states of the modified form can also be explained by legislative concern that pure comparative negligence vests too much power in the hands of the jury,[9] and that some brake is needed to prevent the rewarding of highly negligent plaintiffs with more than ample damages. Some legislators may sincerely believe that it is morally wrong to award any damages to a party who is more at fault than the defendant.[10] The soundness of these and other arguments in favor of modified systems will be considered in Chapter 21.[11]

The present chapter first considers "pure" comparative negligence and then the basic forms of modified comparative negligence along with their special attributes. It should be remembered that other "modified" forms of comparative negligence could be imagined.[12] Classification here is based on what is present law and what are likely to be future approaches to modified comparative negligence in the United States.

3.2 Pure comparative negligence

The simplest comparative negligence rule is commonly called "pure"

---

[6]The Schooner Catharine v. Dickinson, 58 U.S. (17 How.) 170, 15 L. Ed. 233 (1855). See also United States v. Atlantic Mut. Ins. Co., 343 U.S. 236, 238, 96 L. Ed. 907, 72 S. Ct. 666 (1952); The Eugene F. Moran, 212 U.S. 466, 53 L. Ed. 600, 29 S. Ct. 339 (1909) (four offending vessels, equal division of damages). See generally, G. Gilmore & C. Black, *The Law of Admiralty* ch. VII (1957); G. Robinson, *Handbook of Admiralty Law in the United States* § 115 (1939); Albritton, *Division of Damages in Admiralty—A Rising Tide of Confusion*, 2 J. Mar. L. & Commerce 323 (1971).

[7]United States v. Reliable Transfer Co., 421 U.S. 397, 44 L. Ed. 2d 251, 95 S. Ct. 1708 (1975); Walsh v. Zuisei Kaiun K. K., 606 F.2d 259 (9th Cir. Wash. 1979); Bangor & A. R. Co. v. The Ship Fernview, 455 F. Supp. 1043 (D. Me. 1978).

[8]Prosser, note 1 above, at 494.

[9]See, e.g., Cotton, *Comparative Negligence is NOT in the Public Interest*, 17 La. B.J. 205 (1969); Ghiardi, *Comparative Negligence, The Case Against A Mississippi Type Statute*, 10 For the Def. 61 (1969); Powell, *Contributory Negligence: A Necessary Check on the American Jury*, 43 A.B.A.J. 1005 (1957).

[10]See, e.g., Ghiardi, note 9 above, at 61.

[11]See section 21.3.

[12]Turk, note 1 above, at 345 (suggests possibility of adopting Canadian system).

comparative negligence.[13] Under this system, the contributorily negligent plaintiff's damages are reduced by the jury in proportion to the amount of negligence attributable to him. The jury is instructed to take this step unless plaintiff's negligence was the sole proximate cause of the harm that befell him.[14] Thus, if a jury determines that a motor-cyclist-plaintiff going sixty miles an hour in a fifty m.p.h. zone was 90% at fault, while a defendant-truckdriver who negligently failed to apply his brakes to avoid an accident was 10% at fault, the plaintiff will recover $10,000 of his $100,000 damages. The first general state comparative negligence statute of the pure type was Mississippi's, enacted in 1910.[15] Arkansas enacted a pure comparative negligence statute in 1955,[16] but this was superseded two years later by a statute which authorized recovery only when plaintiff's negligence was "of less degree" than defendant's.[17] In 1971 the state of Rhode Island enacted a pure comparative negligence statute covering damage to persons and property.[18] In 1973 Florida adopted pure comparative negligence judicially[19] and Washington adopted it by statute.[20]

In 1975 California[21] and Alaska[22] adopted pure comparative negligence judicially and New York adopted it by statute.[23]

Following a case in which the court split over the question,[24] Michi-

---

[13]See, e.g., Mole & Wilson, *A Study of Comparative Negligence*, 17 Cornell L.Q. 333, 604 (1932); Prosser, *Comparative Negligence*, 51 Mich. L. Rev. 465 (1953); Shell & Bufkin, *Comparative Negligence in Mississippi*, 27 Miss. L. J. 105 (1956); Turk, *Comparative Negligence on the March*, 28 Chi.-Kent L. Rev. 189, 304 (1950); Comment, *Comparative Negligence: Some New Problems for the Maine Courts*, 18 Me. L. Rev. 65 (1966); Note, *Torts—Effect of Mississippi's Comparative Negligence Statute on Other Rules of Law*, 39 Miss. L. J. 493 (1968); Annots., "Comment Note—The doctrine of comparative negligence and its relation to the doctrine of contributory negligence," 32 A.L.R.3d 463 (1970); "Modern development of comparative negligence doctrine having applicability to negligence actions generally," 78 A.L.R.3d 339 (1977).

[14]See, e.g., Camurati v. Sutton, 48 Tenn. App. 54, 342 S.W.2d 732 (1960); Stewart v. Kroger Grocery, 198 Miss. 371, 21 So. 2d 912 (1945); Mississippi Ex. R. Co. v. Summers, 194 Miss. 179, 11 So. 2d 429 (1943).

[15]Miss. Laws 1910, ch. 135. This act applied only to personal injury and death cases, but was amended in 1920 to include actions for property damage (Miss. Laws 1920, ch. 312). The present statute is reprinted in Appendix B. (Miss. Code Ann., § 11-7-15). See Walker v. Louisville & N. R. Co., 571 F.2d 866 (5th Cir. Miss. 1978).

[16]Ark. Acts 1955, No. 191, § 1, which read in part: "In all actions hereafter accruing for negligence ... the contributory negligence of the person injured ... shall not bar a recovery, but the damages awarded shall be diminished in proportion to the amount of negligence attributable to the injured person...."

[17]Ark. Acts 1957, No. 296, § 2. The law has been repealed and replaced by later exactments. See subsection 3.5(B).

[18]R.I. Gen. Laws Ann., § 9-20-4.

[19]Hoffman v. Jones, 280 So. 2d 431, 78 A.L.R.3d 321 (Fla. 1973).

[20]Wash. Rev. Code Ann., § 4.22.010, since repealed and replaced by § 4.22.005. See Prybysz v. Spokane, 24 Wash. App. 452, 601 P.2d 1297 (1979).

[21]Nga Li v. Yellow Cab Co., 13 Cal. 3d 804, 119 Cal. Rptr. 858, 532 P.2d 1226, 78 A.L.R.3d 393 (1975). Accord, Transit Casualty Co. v. Spink Corp., 78 Cal. App. 3d 509, 144 Cal. Rptr. 488 (1978), vacated 94 Cal. App. 3d 124, 156 Cal. Rptr. 360 (1979).

[22]Kaatz v. State, 540 P.2d 1037 (Alaska 1975).

[23]N.Y. Civ. Prac. Law, § 1411.

[24]Kirby v. Lársen, 400 Mich. 585, 256 N.W.2d 400 (1977).

gan adopted pure comparative negligence in 1979;[25] the same year, Louisiana adopted it by a statute which became effective in 1980.[26]

In 1981 the Supreme Court of New Mexico, in *Scott v. Rizzo*,[27] and the Illinois Supreme Court, in *Alvis v. Ribar*, adopted the pure form of comparative negligence.[28] In 1982 the Iowa Supreme Court adopted pure comparative negligence,[29] but the legislature enacted a modified comparative fault statute in 1984.[30] The Missouri Supreme Court adopted pure comparative negligence in 1983[31] and the Kentucky Supreme Court did the same in 1984.[32]

Pure comparative negligence also exists in a number of limited state statutes applicable to damage caused by intrastate railroads[33] or to injuries suffered by persons in their employment.[34] The United States Supreme Court has adopted pure comparative negligence as the rule for collisions at sea.[35]

Federal Statutes

Pure comparative negligence is also embodied in a number of important federal statutes. The most frequently litigated is the Federal Employers' Liability Act, which covers all employees of railroad common carriers who are injured in their employment while engaged in any activity which furthers interstate commerce or directly or closely and substantially affects it.[36] The Merchant Marine Act of 1920[37] and the Jones Act[38] also contain sections embodying pure comparative negligence. The Federal Death on the High Seas Act of 1920[39] applies pure comparative negligence to death from wrongs occurring more than one

---

[25]Placek v. Sterling Heights, 405 Mich. 638, 275 N.W.2d 511 (1979).

[26]La. Civ. Code Ann., art. 2323. The statute reads in part: "When contributory negligence is applicable to a claim for damages ... the amount of damages recoverable shall be reduced in proportion to the degree or percentage of negligence attributable to the person suffering the injury, death or loss." The act also provides that a plaintiff who is more at fault than a particular defendant cannot recover damages in an amount greater than defendant's percentage of fault.

[27]Scott v. Rizzo, 96 N.M. 682, 634 P.2d 1234 (1981).

[28]Alvis v. Ribar, 85 Ill. 2d 1, 52 Ill. Dec. 23, 421 N.E.2d 886 (1981).

[29]Goetzman v. Wichern, 327 N.W.2d 742 (Iowa 1982).

[30]Iowa Code Ann., ch. 668.

[31]Gustafson v. Benda, 661 S.W.2d 11 (Mo. 1983).

[32]Hilen v. Hays, 673 S.W.2d 713 (Ky. 1984).

[33]See Appendix C.

[34]See Appendix C.

[35]United States v. Reliable Transfer Co., 421 U.S. 397, 44 L. Ed. 2d 251, 95 S. Ct. 1708 (1975).

[36]Act of April 22, 1908, ch. 149, § 3, 35 Stat. 66, 45 U.S.C. § 53. See Reed v. Pennsylvania R. Co., 351 U.S. 502, 100 L. Ed. 1366, 76 S. Ct. 958 (1956); Caddy v. Texaco, Inc., 363 Mass. 36, 292 N.E.2d 348 (1973).

[37]Act of June 5, 1920, ch. 250, § 33, 41 Stat. 1007, 46 U.S.C. § 688.

[38]Act of March 4, 1915, ch. 153, § 20, 38 Stat. 1185, 46 U.S.C. § 688. Provisions of the Jones Act and Merchant Marine Act, both now embodied in 46 U.S.C. § 688, incorporate by reference the federal statutes applicable to "personal injury to railway employees" or "death in the case of railway employees." See, e.g., Kirkland v. Seaboard C. L. R. Co., 230 Ga. 108, 196 S.E.2d 11 (1973).

[39]Act of March 30, 1920, ch. 111, § 6, 41 Stat. 537, 46 U.S.C. § 766.

marine league from the shore of any state. Further, the Supreme Court of the United States has ruled that there is a cause of action in admiralty for death due to violation of maritime rules within one marine league of a state.[40] The Court adopted pure comparative negligence in that context.[41] The Canal Zone also has pure comparative negligence as a general rule in civil litigation.[42]

Foreign Statutes

A number of foreign countries have adopted pure comparative negligence.[43] England, by the Reform Act of 1945, adopted a pure comparative negligence system.[44] England also applies pure comparative negligence in admiralty under the Brussels Maritime Convention of 1901 and 1910.[45]

Plaintiff's Gross Negligence

Pure comparative negligence gives a jury room to make some award to the plaintiff even when he has been grossly negligent. For example, in *Cobb v. Williams*,[46] the defendant negligently entered an intersection. The plaintiff had proceeded when visibility was poor, was traveling at an excessive rate of speed and did not slow down or give warning when he approached the intersection. Nevertheless, the Supreme Court of Mississippi ruled that plaintiff's contributory negligence did not justify dismissal.

In *Melancon v. I.M.C. Drilling Mud*[47] the captain of a vessel who was injured by shifting cargo was found 70% negligent in failing to secure it, but he recovered 30% of his damages.

In *Zavala v. Regents of University of California*,[48] a visitor to a uni-

---

[40]Moragne v. States Marine Lines, Inc., 398 U.S. 375, 26 L. Ed. 2d 339, 90 S. Ct. 1772 (1970).

[41]Id., 398 U.S. at 405-409.

[42]C.Z. Code, tit. 5, § 1357, applied in Panama R. Co. v. Davies, 82 F.2d 123 (5th Cir. C.Z. 1936). See also P.R. Laws Ann., tit. 31, § 5141: "A person who by an act or omission causes damage to another through fault or negligence shall be obliged to repair the damage so done. Concurrent imprudence of the party aggrieved does not exempt from liability, but entails a reduction of the indemnity."

[43]Switzerland, Spain, Portugal, Austria, Germany, France, Phillipines, China, Japan, Russia, Poland, Thailand, and Turkey all have provisions in their codes for comparative negligence in one form or another. In addition, all Canadian provinces have adopted comparative negligence, as have England, New Zealand, and Western Australia. For citations, see Mole & Wilson, note 13 above, at 339; Turk, note 13 above, at 189.

[44]Law Reform (Contributory Negligence) Act of 1945, 8 & 9 Geo. 5, ch. 28, which reads in part as follows: "Where any person suffers damage as the result partly of his own fault and partly of the fault of any other person or persons, a claim in respect of that damage shall not be defeated by reasons of the fault of the person suffering the damage, but the damages recoverable in respect thereof shall be reduced to such extent as the court thinks just and equitable having regard to the claimant's share in the responsibility for the damage."

[45]Article 4, Brussels Collision Liability Convention, 1910.

[46]Cobb v. Williams, 228 Miss. 807, 90 So. 2d 17 (1956).

[47]Melancon v. I.M.C. Drilling Mud, 282 So. 2d 532 (La. App. 1973).

[48]Zavala v. Regents of University of California, 125 Cal. App. 3d 646, 178 Cal. Rptr. 185 (1981).

versity campus fell off a balcony while under the influence of beer and marijuana. The University was found 20% at fault for serving beer to an intoxicated person, and the plaintiff was allowed to recover that share of his damages. The court cited the California rule allowing comparative fault when defendants act wantonly and willfully and said it should apply to plaintiffs as well.

It is unusual for a court to reduce the amount of plaintiff's award under pure comparative negligence, but there are occasions when a court will take that step.

In *Dendy v. City of Pascagoula*,[49] a teenage plaintiff suffered quadriplegia when he dived off a town dock without checking the depth of the water. The Supreme Court of Mississippi would not bar a recovery, but it reduced the jury award of $550,000 to $100,000 because of the plaintiff's contributory negligence.

Similarly, in *Fournier v. United States*,[50] the Federal District Court in Mississippi would not bar a wrongful death claim because decedent was extremely intoxicated when she fell down defendant's stairs and met her death. Nevertheless the court, acting as jury, reduced her damages by 50%. In *Gulf and Ship Island Railroad Company v. Bond*,[51] a plaintiff's decedent who was extremely careless about looking where he was going was killed by a train exceeding the legal speed limit. The jury awarded $10,000. The court held that the decedent's contributory negligence would not bar recovery as a matter of law but said that the jury "in assessing damages ... did not deduct enough because of the contributory negligence of the deceased. The negligence of the deceased was greater than the negligence of the railroad company; and the statute imposing the duty of diminishing damages should be observed by juries in rendering verdicts."[52] The court ordered a remittitur to $7500.

As these cases show, pure comparative negligence does not mean that "anything goes" or that plaintiff must always recover substantial damages.[53] Obviously, the pure comparative negligence statutes leave much to the appellate court's discretion as to how often and on what terms it should interfere with a jury verdict. The Supreme Court of Mississippi has been more inclined to check that the jury in fact

---

[49]Dendy v. Pascagoula, 193 So. 2d 559 (Miss. 1967).

[50]Fournier v. United States, 220 F. Supp. 752 (S.D. Miss. 1963).

[51]Gulf & S. I. R. Co. v. Bond, 181 Miss. 254, 179 So. 355 (1938), corrected 181 Miss. 277, 181 So. 741 (1938).

[52]Id., 181 Miss. at 276, 179 So. at 361-362.

[53]Ghiardi, *Comparative Negligence, The Case Against A Mississippi Type Statute*, 10 For the Def. 61, 64 (1969).

reduced plaintiff's award when he was contributorily negligent than have the federal courts in administering the F.E.L.A.[54]

On occasion, a plaintiff whose award is substantially reduced due to his own negligence may still recover his costs without apportionment. For example, in *Florida East Coast Railway Company v. Hunt*[55] a plaintiff's award was reduced by 90% due to his contributory negligence. Nevertheless the court granted the plaintiff's motion to tax costs to the defendant. The court held that costs were not governed by that state's pure comparative negligence rule. Likewise, a California court refused to apportion costs in a case where the plaintiff was found 40% negligent, holding that he was still the prevailing party, although the court noted that the result might have been different had the defendant recovered on a cross-claim.[56]

Defense Under Pure Comparative Negligence

The careful defense lawyer can keep pure comparative negligence from giving the negligent plaintiff a blank check. The attorney in that role can explain in summation the simple mechanics of the system as well as its fairness. In that connection, an empirical study of the operation of pure comparative negligence in Arkansas revealed that the system did not in fact lead to runaway verdicts for negligent plaintiffs.[57] It should be remembered that defendant will probably be deemed to have the burden of pleading and proving that plaintiff's negligence contributed to the accident.[58] There are Mississippi cases, moreover, that have allowed a jury to reduce plaintiff's award even though defendant

---

[54]See Powell, *Contributory Negligence: A Necessary Check on the American Jury*, 43 A.B.A. J. 1005 (1957). Compare Dendy v. Pascagoula, 193 So. 2d 559 (Miss. 1967); Gulf & S. I. R. Co. v. Bond, 181 Miss. 254, 179 So. 355 (1938), with Rogers v. Missouri P. R. Co., 352 U.S. 500, 1 L. Ed. 2d 493, 77 S. Ct. 443 (1957); Webb v. Illinois C. R. Co., 352 U.S. 512, 1 L. Ed. 2d 503, 77 S. Ct. 451 (1957); Arnold v. Panhandle & S. F. R. Co., 353 U.S. 360, 1 L. Ed. 2d 889, 77 S. Ct. 840 (1957). See Cullinan v. Burlington Northern, Inc., 522 F.2d 1034 (9th Cir. Mont. 1975). In a FELA case the appellate court will not reverse unless the damages awarded are grossly excessive. Accord, Kelloch v. S. & H. Subwater Salvage, Inc., 473 F.2d 767 (5th Cir. La. 1973).

[55]Florida E. C. R. Co. v. Hunt, 322 So. 2d 68, 82 A.L.R.3d 520 (Fla. App. 1975). Accord, Spicuglia v. Green, 302 So. 2d 772 (Fla. App. 1974); but see United Furniture Co. v. Register, 328 So. 2d 566 (Fla. App. 1976) (defendant discharged from liability; error to deny him costs).

[56]Hyatt v. Sierra Boat Co., 79 Cal. App. 3d 325, 145 Cal. Rptr. 47 (1978).

[57]Rosenberg, *Comparative Negligence in Arkansas: A "Before and After" Survey*, 13 Ark. L. Rev. 89 (1959).

[58]See, e.g., Yazoo & M.V.R. Co. v. Lucken, 137 Miss. 572, 102 So. 393 (1925), citing Mobile & O. R. Co. v. Campbell, 114 Miss. 803, 75 So. 554 (1917); Jefferson v. Pinson, 219 Miss. 427, 69 So. 2d 234 (1954); see also Shell & Bufkin, note 13 above, at 118.

See also Southern Pacific Transp. Co. v. Allen, 525 S.W.2d 300 (Tex. Civ. App. 1975); Chmela v. State, Dept. of Motor Vehicles, 88 Wash. 2d 385, 561 P.2d 1085 (1977) (under pure comparative negligence the requirement of a security deposit by an uninsured motorist involved in a fatal automobile accident was upheld as the facts presented "a reasonable possibility of judgment").

neglected to plead a contributory negligence defense, where the facts demonstrated that plaintiff was indeed negligent.[59]

Comparison with Multiple Defendants

One appealing feature of a pure comparative negligence system is the simplicity with which it is applied where multiple defendants are to some degree negligent. All are liable to the plaintiff even though some were less negligent than the plaintiff. This is not true under the Wisconsin modified system.[60]

Contribution Among Tortfeasors

Wisconsin, which applies a variant of the 50% rule[61] as a general rule in negligence cases, follows pure comparative negligence where multiple defendants seek contribution among themselves.[62] It is important to note in jurisdictions having comparative negligence legislation similar to Wisconsin's, that the Wisconsin Supreme Court, in *Bielski*, a thoroughly reasoned opinion, has ruled against applying its "modified" comparative negligence statute to the doctrine of contribution.[63]

In overturning the common-law rule of no contribution among joint tortfeasors in a slight-gross comparative negligence state, the Supreme Court of Nebraska stated that a joint tortfeasor may seek contribution when he discharges more than his "proportional share" of the common liability.[64] The Seventh Circuit has adopted pure comparative negli-

---

[59]See, e.g., Winstead v. Hall, 251 Miss. 800, 171 So. 2d 354 (1965); Carr v. Cox, 255 So. 2d 317 (Miss. 1971); Gilliam v. Sykes, 216 Miss. 54, 61 So. 2d 672 (1952); Herrington v. Hodges, 249 Miss. 131, 161 So. 2d 194 (1964). But see Altom v. Wood, 298 So. 2d 700 (Miss. 1974). In the absence of any pleading or instruction on contributory negligence the jury awarded $2,500 when the evidence was that the plaintiff's damages exceeded $10,000. On appeal, the court found the negligence of the plaintiff, if any, to be slight and ordered an additur of $10,000.

[60]See sections 16.5 and 16.6. See also Walker v. Kroger Grocery & Baking Co., 214 Wis. 519, 252 N.W. 721, 92 A.L.R. 680 (1934); Quady v. Sickl, 260 Wis. 348, 51 N.W.2d 3 (1952). Plaintiff could recover nothing against one defendant whose fault was no greater than his own; his recovery against the other defendant must be reduced in the proportion that plaintiff's negligence bore to the total of all three, rather than as between two; the remaining defendant must bear the liability for the negligence of the party released; from Prosser, note 13 above, at 507. See also Farr, *Submitting the Comparative Negligence Question in Multiple Party Cases*, 34 Wis. B. Bull. 13 (1961).

[61]Wis. Stat. Ann., § 895.045: "Contributory negligence shall not bar recovery in an action by any person or his legal representative to recover damages for negligence resulting in death or in injury to person or property, if such negligence was not greater than the negligence of the person against whom recovery is sought, but any damages allowed shall be diminished in the proportion to the amount of negligence attributable to the person recovering." See sections 3.5 and 16.8.

[62]See Bielski v. Schulze, 16 Wis. 2d 1, 114 N.W.2d 105 (1962), discussed at length in section 16.7.

[63]See also Liberty Mut. Ins. Co. v. General Motors Corp., 65 Hawaii 428, 653 P.2d 96 (1982); Little v. Miles, 213 Ark. 725, 212 S.W.2d 935 (1948); Missouri P. R. Co. v. Star City Gravel Co., 452 F. Supp. 480 (E.D. Ark. 1978), affd. 592 F.2d 455 (8th Cir. Ark. 1979) (applying Arkansas law); Sitzes v. Anchor Motor Freight, Inc., 289 S.E.2d 679 (W. Va. 1982); Packard v. Whitten, 274 A.2d 169 (Me. 1971); Idaho Code, §§ 6-803, 6-804; Minn. Stat. Ann., § 604.02(3); N.H. Rev. Stat. Ann., § 507:7-a; Vt. Stat. Ann., tit. 12, § 1036.

[64]Royal Indem. Co. v. Aetna Cas. & Surety Co., 193 Neb. 752, 229 N.W.2d 183 (1975).

gence in contribution among joint tortfeasors in regard to aviation collisions.[65]

The Louisiana statute states that a defendant may seek to enforce contribution whether he admits or denies liability on the obligation.[66]

Setoffs

A minor complication can arise in a pure comparative negligence system when a defendant attempts a setoff against a negligent plaintiff. Even a defendant who was more than 50% negligent can cross-claim for a percentage of his damages from a negligent plaintiff. Rhode Island appears to have precluded setoffs in this context.[67] It has been suggested that setoffs should always be barred when damages are paid in fact by a liability insurance company;[68] allowing a setoff in such a context would defeat the comparative negligence goal of providing at least some compensation within the framework of a fault system.

3.3   The equal division system and maritime law

(A) THE EQUAL DIVISION RULE

The simplest form of modified comparative negligence was also the first to be formally recognized—the equal division system.[69] When plaintiff and defendant were both negligent, damages were divided equally. Thus, if plaintiff suffers $10,000 worth of damages as a result of defendant's negligence and his own, he recovers $5000. In 1854 the Supreme Court adopted this rule in *The Schooner Catharine v. Dickinson,* a ship collision case.[70] Until 1975 equal division continued to be the rule for United States admiralty ship collision cases.

The equal division system was severely criticized because of its unfairness where negligence is grossly disproportionate between the

---

[65]Kohr v. Allegheny Airlines, Inc., 504 F.2d 400 (7th Cir. Ind. 1974).

[66]La. Civ. Code Ann., art. 1805.

[67]See R.I. Gen. Laws, § 9-20-4.1.

[68]See section 19.3; see also Flynn, *Comparative Negligence: The Debate,* 8 Trial 49, 52 (1972). For an example of the inequities that can occur when setoff is mandatory, see Willingham v. Hagerty, 553 S.W.2d 137 (Tex. Civ. App. 1977).

[69]Hillyer, *Comparative Negligence in Louisiana,* 11 Tul. L. Rev. 112 (1936) (unclear whether earliest system was equal division of damages); Malone, *Comparative Negligence—Louisiana's Forgotten Heritage,* 6 La. L. Rev. 125 (1945) (no comment that equal division of damages was earliest); Mole & Wilson, *A Study of Comparative Negligence,* 17 Cornell L. Q. 333, 604 (1932) (equal division used where proportion of damages not ascertainable); Turk, *Comparative Negligence on the March,* 28 Chi.-Kent L. Rev. 189, 304 (1950) (never really says this was the earliest system).

[70]The Schooner Catharine v. Dickinson, 58 U.S. (17 How.) 170, 15 L. Ed. 233 (1855).

parties.[71] The federal courts developed a number of doctrines to limit the unfairness of the rule. In some cases they were able to apply state or foreign law under choice of law[72] or jurisdictional[73] principles. Some courts applied a "major/minor cause" rule, ignoring the libelant's fault if it was minor compared to the libelee's,[74] or imposing a burden on the libelee to prove the libelant's fault by clear and convincing evidence.[75] Last clear chance provided an additional escape hatch.[76] Most of these methods had the disadvantage of imposing the entire loss on one party.

In 1975 the Supreme Court overruled *The Schooner Catharine* in *United States v. Reliable Transfer Company.*[77] The case showed the arbitrary results that could arise under the equal division system. The

---

[71]See, e.g., Luckenbach S.S. Co. v. United States, 157 F.2d 250 (2d Cir. N.Y. 1946); Eastern S.S. Co. v. International Harvester Co., 189 F.2d 472 (6th Cir. Ohio 1951); Tank Barge Hygrade, Inc. v. The Tug Gatco New Jersey, 250 F.2d 485 (3d Cir. Pa. 1957); St. Louis-San Francisco R. Co. v. Motor Vessel D. Mark, 243 F. Supp. 689 (S.D. Ala. 1965); Ahlgren v. Red Star Towing & Transp. Co., 214 F.2d 618 (2d Cir. N.Y. 1954); Oriental Trading & Transport Co. v. Gulf Oil Corp., 173 F.2d 108 (2d Cir. N.Y. 1949); see also Staring, *Contribution and Division of Damages in Admiralty and Maritime Cases,* 45 Calif. L. Rev. 304 (1957).

[72]See, e.g., Atlantic Transport Co. v. Imbrovek, 234 U.S. 52, 58 L. Ed. 1208, 34 S. Ct. 733 (1914); Atlantic Transport Co. v. Maryland, 234 U.S. 63, 58 L. Ed. 1213, 34 S. Ct. 736 (1914); Campbell v. H. Hackfeld & Co., 125 Fed. 696 (9th Cir. Hawaii 1903). See also *Restatement (Second) of Conflict of Laws* §§ 6(e), 145 (1971); Tooker v. Lopez, 24 N.Y.2d 569, 301 N.Y.S.2d 519, 249 N.E.2d 394 (1969); Reich v. Purcell, 67 Cal. 2d 551, 63 Cal. Rptr. 31, 432 P.2d 727 (1967).

[73]Executive Jet Aviation, Inc. v. Cleveland, Ohio, 448 F.2d 151 (6th Cir. Ohio 1971), affd. 409 U.S. 249, 34 L. Ed. 2d 454, 93 S. Ct. 493 (1972). See also Houston-New Orleans, Inc. v. Page Engineering Co., 353 F. Supp. 890 (E.D. La. 1972) (occurrence of injury at sea creates admiralty jurisdiction, regardless of place of wrongful act or omission); but see Pfeiffer v. Weiland, 226 N.W.2d 218 (Iowa 1975) (locality only a significant factor in determining if maritime law applies); Pryor v. American President Lines, 520 F.2d 974 (4th Cir. Md. 1975) (injury occurred on land during loading process, admiralty jurisdiction does not commence until goods come to rest on ship); accord, Sacilotto v. National Shipping Corp., 520 F.2d 983 (4th Cir. Md. 1975). Compare Fort v. Lewis, 649 S.W.2d 204 (Ky. App. 1983), decided after *Reliable Transfer* but before Kentucky adopted comparative negligence: in a case involving the collision of two pleasure boats, the court arguably went out of its way to find admiralty jurisdiction so that comparative negligence would apply.

[74]See, e.g., The City of New York, 147 U.S. 72, 37 L. Ed. 84, 13 S. Ct. 211 (1893); Mystic S.S. Corp. v. SS Amalfi, 307 F. Supp. 885 (E.D. Va. 1969); In re Harbor Towing Corp., 310 F. Supp. 775 (D. Md. 1970), affd. 438 F.2d 535 (4th Cir. Md. 1971); P. S. Fish Industries, Inc. v. St. George Packing Co., 307 F. Supp. 458 (S.D. Tex. 1969).

[75]See, e.g., Ore S. S. Corp. v. The Pan Virginia, 123 F. Supp. 346 (D. Md. 1954), affd. Pan American Petroleum & Transp. Co. v. The Steelore, 220 F.2d 688 (4th Cir. Md. 1955); Federal Ins. Co. v. S.S. Royalton, 194 F. Supp. 543 (E.D. Mich. 1961), revd. 312 F.2d 671 (6th Cir. Mich. 1963).

[76]See, e.g., The Cornelius Vanderbilt, 120 F.2d 766 (2d Cir. N.Y. 1941); Petition of Marina Mercante Nicaraguense S.A., 364 F.2d 118 (2d Cir. N.Y. 1966), cert. den. 385 U.S. 1005, 17 L. Ed. 2d 544, 87 S. Ct. 710 (1967); accord, Arundel Corp. v. The City of Calcutta, 172 F. Supp. 593 (E.D. N.Y. 1958). See also Annot., "Last clear chance in admiralty," 3 A.L.R. Fed. 203 (1970).

[77]United States v. Reliable Transfer Co., 421 U.S. 397, 44 L. Ed. 2d 251, 95 S. Ct. 1708 (1975); accord, Pan-Alaska Fisheries, Inc. v. Marine Constr. & Design Co., 402 F. Supp. 1187 (W.D. Wash. 1975) (citing this treatise), vacated on other grounds, 565 F.2d 1129 (9th Cir. Wash. 1977). See also Walsh v. Zuisei Kaiun K. K., 606 F.2d 259 (9th Cir. Wash. 1979); Bangor & A. R. Co. v. The Ship Fernview, 455 F. Supp. 1043 (D. Me. 1978).

plaintiff's vessel was 75% responsible for the accident (due to its own navigational error); the fault of the United States Coast Guard was only 25% (due to failure to maintain a breakwater light). Nevertheless the plaintiff was awarded 50% of his damages.[78] The Supreme Court concluded that the equal division rule had prevailed by "sheer inertia" and its sole virtue—ease of application—was far outweighed by the unjust results which obtained under it.[79] Of course, if the fault of both parties is equal, damages will still be divided equally.[80]

Continued Vitality of *The Pennsylvania* Doctrine

The rule of *The Pennsylvania*,[81] decided when equal division was the law, provided that if a party violates a safety statute, he bears the burden of proving that his negligence did not contribute to the collision. Subsequent cases have held that the burden of proof will still shift, but the result will be apportionment of damages, not equal division.[82]

Last Clear Chance

The application of the doctrine of last clear chance to admiralty cases may be limited now that the equal division system has been abandoned. In *S. C. Loveland, Incorporated v. East West Towing, Incorporated*[83] a negligently moored barge broke loose and damaged a bridge tended by the Florida Department of Transportation. Department employees saw the barge approaching but failed to act effectively to prevent the accident. The court refused to apply the doctrine of last clear chance to shift total liability onto the Department. The court apportioned damages, declaring that the last clear chance rule had been applied selectively in admiralty to modify the now discarded equal division rule and there was no further need of it under pure comparative negligence.

(B) PURE COMPARATIVE NEGLIGENCE IN MARITIME LAW

Since 1890 it has been perfectly clear that pure comparative negli-

---

[78]Reliable Transfer Co. v. United States, 497 F.2d 1036 (2d Cir. N.Y. 1974).

[79]United States v. Reliable Transfer Co., 421 U.S. at 410.

[80]Id., at 411; see, e.g., Bunge Corp. v. M. V. Furness Bridge, 396 F. Supp. 852 (E.D. La. 1975). However, the Fifth Circuit Court of Appeals later reversed, finding the vessel owner solely liable as the wharf owner had no duty to warn vessels about a hidden defect. Bunge Corp. v. M/V Furness Bridge, 558 F.2d 790 (5th Cir. La. 1977).

[81]The Pennsylvania, 86 U.S. (19 Wall.) 125, 22 L. Ed. 148 (1874); accord, Board of Cmrs. v. M/V Agelos Michael, 390 F. Supp. 1012 (E.D. La. 1974).

[82]See, e.g., Crown Zellerbach Corp. v. Willamette-Western Corp., 519 F.2d 1327 (9th Cir. Ore. 1975); Tug Ocean Prince, Inc. v. United States, 584 F.2d 1151 (2d Cir. N.Y. 1980); Alamo Chemical Transp. Co. v. M/V Overseas Valdes, 398 F. Supp. 1094 (E.D. La. 1975).

[83]S. C. Loveland, Inc. v. East West Towing, Inc., 415 F. Supp. 596 (S.D. Fla. 1976). The Fifth Circuit Court of Appeals affirmed, holding the last clear chance doctrine inapplicable in the action. S. C. Loveland, Inc. v. East West Towing, Inc., 608 F.2d 160 (5th Cir. Fla. 1979), reh. den. 611 F.2d 882 (5th Cir. Fla. 1980).

gence, not the equal division system, applies in personal injury cases arising under maritime law.[84] From that time, admiralty courts have followed the practice of diminishing damages recovered to the extent of libelant's contributory negligence. Numerous federal statutes have also incorporated the pure comparative negligence doctrine for personal injury cases arising under maritime law. The Jones Act and the Merchant Marine Act of 1920[85] both incorporated the comparative negligence provision of the Federal Employers' Liability Act.[86] Remedies under these two acts are exclusively for maritime employees in claims against their employers, but other claims brought in admiralty are also governed by pure comparative negligence. The Death on the High Seas Act of 1920[87] is an example.

Wrongful Death

For a long period of time courts have struggled to find a legal basis for actions for wrongful death. The Death on the High Seas Act of 1920[88] allowed a cause of action when a fatal injury occurred more than one marine league from shore. However, within one league of shore the survivor's claim was subject to state law, under which decedent's contributory negligence might bar the claim.[89] This should no longer occur; in *Moragne v. States Marine Lines, Incorporated* the United States Supreme Court ruled that, apart from the statute, the maritime law would supply a cause of action for a wrongful death, and that this would apply even within one marine league of shore when the accident was caused by a violation of maritime duties.[90] It is now clear that pure

---

[84]The Max Morris, 137 U.S. 1, 34 L. Ed. 586, 11 S. Ct. 29 (1890), first applied in The Lackawanna, 151 Fed. 499 (S.D. N.Y. 1907). See also Webster v. Davis, 109 F. Supp. 149 (S.D. Cal. 1952); Nygren v. American Boat Cartage, Inc., 290 F.2d 547 (2d Cir. N.Y.1961); Socony-Vacuum Oil Co. v. Smith, 305 U.S. 424, 83 L. Ed. 265, 59 S. Ct. 262 (1939); King v. Testerman, 214 F. Supp. 335 (E.D. Tenn. 1963).

[85]Act of March 4, 1915, ch. 153, § 20, 38 Stat. 1185; Act of June 5, 1920, ch. 256, § 33, 41 Stat. 1007. The applicable provisions of both are now embodied in 46 U.S.C. § 688. See, e.g., Garrett v. Moore-McCormack Co., 317 U.S. 239, 87 L. Ed. 239, 63 S. Ct. 246 (1942). See also G. Gilmore & C. Black, *The Law of Admiralty* § 1-10 at 21, 22, n.77 (1957). See also Noack v. American S.S. Co., 491 F.2d 937 (6th Cir. Ohio 1974) (casual worker along waterfront held to be a seaman within scope of Jones Act); accord, Brown v. ITT Rayonier, Inc., 497 F.2d 234 (5th Cir. Ga. 1974).

[86]See text at notes 36 to 38, section 3.2.

[87]Act of March 30, 1920, ch. 111, § 6, 41 Stat. 537, 46 U.S.C. § 766: "In suits under this chapter the fact that the decedent has been guilty of contributory negligence shall not bar recovery, but the court shall take into consideration the degree of negligence attributable to the decedent and reduce the recovery accordingly."

[88]Act of March 30, 1920, ch. 111, §§ 1 to 8, 41 Stat. 537, 46 U.S.C. §§ 761 to 768.

[89]See, e.g., Hess v. United States, 361 U.S. 314, 4 L. Ed. 2d 305, 80 S. Ct. 341 (1960); Feige v. Hurley, 89 F.2d 575 (6th Cir. Ky. 1937); Truelson v. Whitney & Bodden Shipping Co., 10 F.2d 412 (5th Cir. Tex. 1925), cert. den. 271 U.S. 661, 70 L. Ed. 1139, 46 S. Ct. 474 (1926); The A. W. Thompson, 39 Fed. 115 (S.D. N.Y. 1889). See also Annot., "Action for death caused by maritime tort within a state's territorial waters," 71 A.L.R.2d 1296, 1319 (1960).

[90]Moragne v. States Marine Lines, Inc., 398 U.S. 375, 26 L. Ed. 2d 339, 90 S. Ct. 1772 (1970), overruling The Harrisburg, 119 U.S. 199, 30 L. Ed. 358, 7 S. Ct. 140 (1886). Accord, Hebert v. Otto Candies, Inc., 402 F. Supp. 503 (E.D. La. 1975).

comparative negligence applies and that contributory negligence is no longer a total bar to such a claim.[91]

Unseaworthiness Doctrine

In recent years the doctrine of unseaworthiness has been used more often than the Jones Act as the method of recovery by injured seamen,[92] because under this doctrine recovery can be had even though the defendant used due care.[93] The doctrine at one time applied also to longshoremen and other harbor workers, who were thus permitted to utilize it as a vehicle for recovery.[94] The 1972 amendments to the Longshoremen's and Harbor Workers' Compensation Act replaced the unseaworthiness doctrine with negligence as the basis of liability of shipowners to harbor workers.[95]

A federal district court in Washington has interpreted the legislative intent of the 1972 amendments as prohibiting the defense of assumption of risk in actions by longshoremen.[96] Although the unseaworthiness doctrine is a no-fault theory, the courts apply pure comparative negligence to diminish recovery.[97] It has been held that where the unseaworthiness was not the proximate cause, but the seaman was 100% contributorily negligent, he could not recover at all.[98]

---

[91]Moragne v. States Marine Lines, Inc., note 90 above, 398 U.S. at 405-408. See also Hornsby v. Fish Meal Co., 431 F.2d 865 (5th Cir. La. 1970); Guilbeau v. Calzada, 240 So. 2d 104 (La. App. 1970); Green v. Ross, 338 F. Supp. 365 (S.D. Fla. 1972), affd. 481 F.2d 102 (5th Cir. Fla. 1973).

[92]G. Gilmore & C. Black, note 85 above, at §§ 6-38, 6-44.

[93]See, e.g., Mahnich v. Southern S. S. Co., 321 U.S. 96, 88 L. Ed. 561, 64 S. Ct. 455 (1944); Mitchell v. Trawler Racer, Inc., 362 U.S. 539, 4 L. Ed. 2d 941, 80 S. Ct. 926 (1960).

[94]Seas Shipping Co. v. Sieracki, 328 U.S. 85, 90 L. Ed. 1099, 66 S. Ct. 872 (1946).

[95]Act of Oct. 27, 1972, Pub. L. 92-576, § 18(a), 86 Stat. 1263, 33 U.S.C. § 905(b). See, e.g., Bess v. Agromar Line, 518 F.2d 738 (4th Cir. S.C. 1975); Ramirez v. Toko Kaiun K.K., 385 F. Supp. 644 (N.D. Cal. 1974); Birrer v. Flota Mercante Grancolombiana, 386 F. Supp. 1105 (D. Ore. 1974); but see Scalafani v. Moore McCormack Lines, Inc., 388 F. Supp. 897 (E.D. N.Y. 1975), affd. without published opinion 535 F.2d 1242, 1243 (2d Cir. N.Y. 1975) (1972 amendments to the Longshoremen's and Harbor Worker's Compensation Act do not apply to injuries received before the amendments' effective dates); Lopez v. Delta S.S. Lines, Inc., 387 F. Supp. 955 (D. P.R. 1974) (declaring stevedoring an abnormally dangerous activity subject to strict liability); Streatch v. Associated Container Transp., Ltd., 388 F. Supp. 935, 29 A.L.R.Fed. 771 (C.D. Cal. 1975) (strict product liability is a part of the federal maritime common law, thus the 1972 amendments to the LHWCA did not affect a longshoreman's right to recover on the theory of strict products liability).

[96]Davis v. Inca Compania Naviera S.A., 440 F. Supp. 448 (W.D. Wash. 1977) (assumption of risk doctrine inconsistent with comparative negligence standards of the 1972 amendments to the Longshoremen's and Harbor Worker's Compensation Act).

[97]See, e.g., Pope & Talbot, Inc. v. Hawn, 346 U.S. 406, 98 L. Ed. 143, 74 S. Ct. 202 (1953); Sams v. Haines, 299 F. Supp. 746 (S.D. Ga. 1969); Muller v. Lykes Bros. S.S. Co., 337 F. Supp. 700 (E.D. La. 1972). Accord, Lambert v. United States, 479 F.2d 50 (5th Cir. Fla. 1973); Scott v. Fluor Ocean Services, Inc., 501 F.2d 983 (5th Cir. La. 1974); Marchese v. Moore-McCormack Lines, Inc., 525 F.2d 831 (2d Cir. N.Y. 1975). Further, if a contributorily negligent plaintiff employed by a party other than the shipowner breaches his warranty of workmanlike performance, the shipowner may be entitled not only to reduction in the plaintiff's award, but full indemnity from his employer. See Sousa v. M/V Caribia, 360 F. Supp. 971 (D. Mass. 1973); Nye v. A/S D/S Svendborg, 358 F. Supp. 145 (S.D. N.Y. 1973), affd. in part and revd. in part 501 F.2d 376 (2d Cir. N.Y. 1974).

[98]See, e.g., Cumberland v. Isthmian Lines, Inc., 282 F. Supp. 217 (E.D. La. 1967).

Property Damage Claims

Pure comparative negligence may also apply to claims for property damage that occurs at sea from causes other than collision. It is substantially less clear than in the area of personal injury that pure comparative negligence applies in this context; but it is equally certain that the equal division rule is not firmly embedded there.[99]

Strict Product Liability

In 1983 the Fifth Circuit adopted a rule of pure comparative fault in maritime strict product liability personal injury cases in *Lewis v. Timco, Incorporated*.[1] The plaintiff had been seriously injured while operating hydraulic tongs on a drilling barge in the territorial waters of Louisiana.[2] The trial court apportioned 20% of the fault each to the manufacturer of the tongs and an equipment rental company, 10% to a second rental company, and 50% to the plaintiff.[3] The plaintiff argued that under strict liability he should be allowed to recover all of his damages.[4] The appellate court reviewed the application of pure comparative fault to cases brought under the unseaworthiness doctrine, the Jones Act, the Death on the High Seas Act and the Longshoremen's and Harbor Workers' Compensation Act and concluded that, in the interests of uniformity in maritime law, the doctrine should apply to strict product liability as well.[5] The court noted that comparative fault applied to product liability in wrongful death cases under the Death on the High Seas Act and said it would be inconsistent to apply a different rule when the plaintiff was injured, not killed.[6]

The Fifth Circuit has also ruled that knowing and voluntary assumption of risk will be subsumed into comparative fault in maritime product liability cases.[7]

3.4   The slight-gross system and its derivatives

(A) THE NINETEENTH CENTURY SYSTEMS

As far back as 1858, Illinois developed a general rule that a negligently injured plaintiff could recover fully "wherever it ... appears

---

[99]Turk, *Comparative Negligence on the March*, 28 Chi.-Kent L. Rev. 189, 231-232 (1950).

[1]Lewis v. Timco, Inc., 716 F.2d 1425 (5th Cir. La. 1983), revd. and rendered in part 736 F.2d 163 (5th Cir. La. 1984), noted, 15 Tex. Tech. L. Rev. 983 (1984). See also Pan-Alaska Fisheries, Inc. v. Marine Constr. & Design Co., 565 F.2d 1129 (9th Cir. Wash. 1977) (applying strict product liability in an admiralty property damage action, with damages apportioned on comparative fault principles).

[2]Lewis v. Timco, Inc., note 1 above, 716 F.2d at 1426.

[3]Id., at 1427; in the later proceeding the Court of Appeals held that plaintiff was not contributorily negligent; 736 F.2d, at 167.

[4]Id.

[5]Id., at 1427-1428. See also notes 85, 87, 88 and 95 above.

[6]Id., at 1428.

[7]National Marine Service, Inc. v. Petroleum Service Corp., 736 F.2d 272 (5th Cir. La. 1984).

that the plaintiff's negligence is comparatively slight, and that of the defendant gross."[8] The rule did not operate as a modern comparative negligence rule, in that there was no attempt to apportion the loss between the parties. Plaintiff recovered all or nothing.

The late Dean Prosser found case law evidence that this system was applied for a period of time in Oregon, Wisconsin, and Tennessee.[9] Nevertheless, it eventually was abandoned in all of the states. The reason the system fell into disuse was threefold. First, courts had a great deal of difficulty with defining "slight" negligence: while it was sometimes defined as "a degree of negligence less than a failure to exercise ordinary care,"[10] this definition was difficult to apply and the definitional conundrum created burdensome appeals. A second difficulty with the system was that it did not really comport with the fault principle because the entire loss was always placed on one party. Finally, courts developed what they believed were better methods of modifying the contributory negligence defense—such as last clear chance. These developments reduced the need to rely on the early "slight-gross" comparative negligence system.

The only vestige of this early system that remains in the law today is in Tennessee. There, plaintiff's contributory negligence will reduce, but not bar, his claim if his negligence was "remote" in comparison with that of the defendant.[11] The Tennessee courts have had their share of difficulty applying this doctrine.[12] It can be argued that it places the plaintiff in a worse position than the normal contributory negligence defense does; there is some evidence in the Tennessee cases that plaintiff's contributory negligence will bar his claim unless defendant had what other states would call the last clear chance to avoid the accident.[13]

---

[8]Galena & C. U. R. Co. v. Jacobs, 20 Ill. 478, 497 (1858).

[9]Prosser, *Comparative Negligence*, 51 Mich. L. Rev. 465, 485 (1953).

[10]Annot., "The doctrine of comparative negligence and its relation to the doctrine of contributory negligence," 32 A.L.R.3d 463, 476 (1970).

[11]See, e.g., McCullough v. Johnson Freight Lines, Inc., 202 Tenn. 596, 308 S.W.2d 387 (1957); McClard v. Reid, 190 Tenn. 337, 229 S.W.2d 505 (1950); Anderson v. Carter, 22 Tenn. App. 118, 118 S.W.2d 891 (1937); Bejach v. Colby, 141 Tenn. 686, 214 S.W. 869 (1919); Louisville, N. & G. S. R. Co. v. Fleming, 82 Tenn. 128 (1884). See also McDermott, *Remote Contributory Negligence*, 2 Tenn. L. Rev. 109 (1924); Comment, *Remote Contributory Negligence: A Tennessee Concept*, 22 Tenn. L. Rev. 1030 (1953); article by Professor Wade in Symposium, *Comments on Maki v. Frelk—Comparative v. Contributory Negligence: Should the Court or Legislature Decide?*, 21 Vand. L. Rev. 889, 938, 939 (1968).

[12]See Comment, *Remote Contributory Negligence: A Tennessee Concept*, note 11 above, at 1030. See also Symposium, note 11 above, at 939, n.4 (on confusion as to the precise meaning of remote contributory negligence: "A series of court of appeals cases has defined the 'remote cause' as 'that which may have happened and yet no injury have occurred, notwithstanding that no injury could have occurred if it had not happened.' DeRossett v. Malone, 34 Tenn. App. 451, 475, 239 S.W.2d 366, 377 (1950); Elmore v. Thompson, 14 Tenn. App. 78, 100 (1931)").

[13]Prosser, note 9 above, at 497.

(B) MODERN SLIGHT-GROSS STATUTES

In 1913, Nebraska adopted a comparative negligence statute, still in effect today, providing:

> In all actions brought to recover damages for injuries to a person or to his property caused by the negligence of another, the fact that the plaintiff may have been guilty of contributory negligence shall not bar a recovery when the contributory negligence of the plaintiff was slight and the negligence of the defendant was gross in comparison, but the contributory negligence of the plaintiff shall be considered by the jury in the mitigation of damages in proportion to the amount of contributory negligence attributable to the plaintiff; and all questions of negligence and contributory negligence shall be for the jury.[14]

In 1941 the state of South Dakota adopted identical legislation[15] which has since been slightly modified.[16] Similar legislation exists in numerous limited applications in many states.[17]

These comparative negligence systems differ from those of the nineteenth century in two important ways. First, they allow for the apportionment of damages. When the plaintiff's negligence is slight and defendant's gross in comparison, plaintiff does not recover his entire claim; rather, the amount of his award is reduced by the percentage of negligence attributable to him. In that regard, the modern slight-gross system is similar to pure comparative negligence and the 50% system.

As is shown below, the history of Nebraska and South Dakota cases applying these statutes shows a trend away from trying to define "slight negligence" in the abstract and toward making a comparison of negligence between plaintiff and defendant. The result is very close to a de facto 50% system.

Computation of Award

For a period of time, in Nebraska, it seemed possible that the negligent plaintiff's damages would be computed by the ratio of his negligence to that of defendant.[18] Nevertheless, it is clear today in both South Dakota and Nebraska that a negligent plaintiff's damages will

---

[14]Neb. Rev. Stat., § 25-1151. See generally Baylor, *Comparative Negligence in Nebraska*, 10 S.D. B. J. 146 (1941); Grubb, *Comparative Negligence*, 32 Neb. L. Rev. 234 (1953); Johnson, *Comparative Negligence—The Nebraska View*, 36 Neb. L. Rev. 240 (1957).

[15]S.D. Sess. Laws 1941, ch. 160; S.D. Code Supp. 1960, § 47.0304-1.

[16]S.D. Codified Laws, § 20-9-2. See generally Hanson, *Comparative Negligence*, 31 S.D. B.J. 11 (1962); Nelson, *The Status of Comparative Negligence in South Dakota*, 7 S.D. L. Rev. 114 (1962); Note, *Comparative Negligence: A Look at the South Dakota Approach*, 14 S.D. L. Rev. 92 (1969).

[17]See Prosser, *Comparative Negligence*, 51 Mich. L. Rev. 465, 477-482 (1951).

[18]See Baylor, note 14 above, at 152-153, citing Patterson v. Kerr, 127 Neb. 73, 254 N.W. 704 (1934) and Morrison v. Scotts Bluff County, 104 Neb. 254, 177 N.W. 158 (1920).

be reduced by the percentage of total negligence attributable to him.[19] For example, a plaintiff who is found to have been 10% at fault in the accident will recover 90% of his damages from a defendant who was 90% at fault.

Comparing Fault

A second important way in which modern slight-gross systems differ from their nineteenth century forebears is that "slight" negligence is not determined in the abstract, but only in comparison with the negligence of the defendant.[20] This makes the system easier to operate.

A number of South Dakota rulings prior to 1964 did require plaintiff to show that his negligence was "slight" in the absolute sense.[21] In response to a law review article by Judge Hanson[22] of the Supreme Court of South Dakota, the state legislature amended its statute to make it clear that the "slightness" of plaintiff's negligence should not be determined in the abstract but only in comparison with the negligence of the defendant.[23] It should be noted that the 1964 amendment also eliminated the word "gross" from the comparative negligence statute.[24] Thus, in South Dakota, plaintiff now has to show only that his negligence was slight "in comparison with the negligence of the defendant," not that the defendant's negligence was gross in comparison.[25]

Directed Verdict

Both South Dakota and Nebraska Supreme Courts have struggled to formulate a standard whereby a trial court could determine whether a defendant should be granted a directed verdict on the ground that

---

[19]See, e.g., Hanisch v. Body, 77 S.D. 265, 90 N.W.2d 924 (1958); Foland v. Dugan, 74 S.D. 586, 57 N.W.2d 166 (1953); Morrison v. Scotts Bluff County, 104 Neb. 254, 177 N.W. 158 (1920); Hiner v. Nelson, 174 Neb. 725, 119 N.W.2d 288, 291 (1963); Darnell v. Panhandle Cooperative Assn., 175 Neb. 40, 120 N.W.2d 278, 287 (1963) ("deduct . . . such amount as her contributory negligence . . . bears to the whole"). See also Robinson v. Mudlin, 273 N.W.2d 753 (S.D. 1979); Hartman v. Brady, 201 Neb. 558, 270 N.W.2d 909 (1978).

[20]See, e.g., Bezdek v. Patrick, 167 Neb. 754, 94 N.W.2d 482 (1959); Nugent v. Quam, 82 S.D. 583, 152 N.W.2d 371, 376 (1967); Johnson v. Roueche, 188 Neb. 716, 199 N.W.2d 1 (1972); C. C. Natvig's Sons, Inc. v. Summers, 198 Neb. 741, 255 N.W.2d 272 (1977); Sandberg v. Hoogensen, 201 Neb. 190, 266 N.W.2d 745, 5 A.L.R.4th 1185 (1978).

[21]See, e.g., Associated Engineers, Inc. v. Job, 370 F.2d 633, 640 (8th Cir. S.D. 1966), which concerned a 1962 verdict on appeal and applied the South Dakota statute in its pre-1964 form.

[22]Hanson, note 16 above, at 11.

[23]". . . the fact that the plaintiff may have been guilty of contributory negligence shall not bar a recovery when the contributory negligence of the plaintiff was slight in *comparison* with the negligence of the defendant . . ." (emphasis added). S.D. Codified Laws, § 20-9-2, incorporating amendment by S.D. Sess. Laws 1964, ch. 149.

[24]Before the 1964 amendment the section read in part: ". . . the fact that the plaintiff may have been guilty of contributory negligence shall not bar a recovery when the contributory negligence of the plaintiff was slight and the negligence of the defendant was gross in comparison. . . ." S.D. Code § 47.0304-1 (Supp. 1960).

[25]See Nugent v. Quam, 82 S.D. 583, 152 N.W.2d 371 (1967); Urban v. Wait's Supermarket, Inc., 294 N.W.2d 793 (S.D. 1980).

plaintiff's contributory negligence was more than slight.[26] There have been admissions by both courts that this task may be impossible and cases must be finally determined "on their facts."[27]

Sandberg v. Peter Kiewit Sons Company, a 1966 Eighth Circuit case,[28] contains facts which, in both South Dakota and Nebraska, might support a directed verdict for defendant. Plaintiff drove his automobile onto an uncompleted portion of an interstate highway. Defendant construction company, in having negligently removed the barricades block-

---

[26]See, e.g., Ford v. Robinson, 76 S.D. 457, 80 N.W.2d 471 (1957) (employee could have pushed pickup truck without exposing his wrist to the injury received; the danger of his position was much more obvious to him than to his fellow employee. "In determining whether negligence on the part of an injured plaintiff is more than slight, thus removing his case from the application of the comparative negligence statute, it is proper to consider the comparative knowledge of the parties as to the existence of facts or circumstances resulting in peril." 80 N.W.2d at 473). Audiss v. Peter Kiewit Sons Co., 190 F.2d 238 (8th Cir. S.D. 1951), applying South Dakota law (where the deceased, while driving a truck, ran into a slow-moving heavy road roller which, because of its neutral color, tended to blend at night with the road on which it was parked, whether deceased was guilty of more than slight negligence in failing to reduce his speed in time was a question of fact which the lower court should not have withdrawn from the jury). Pleinis v. Wilson Storage & Transfer Co., 75 S.D. 397, 66 N.W.2d 68 (1954) (decedent's driving into back of truck without trying to stop amounted to more than slight negligence as a matter of law; failure to have flares out was not gross negligence in comparison even though truck was stopped on road, since lights were on and driver had been flagging down cars). Winburn v. Vander Vorst, 75 S.D. 111, 59 N.W.2d 819 (1953) (no more than slight negligence existed where plaintiff did not realize defendant's truck was stopped unlawfully on public highway without lights or warning flares and plaintiff tried to stop behind truck rather than go around it because a car was coming in the opposite direction). Allen v. Kavanaugh, 160 Neb. 645, 71 N.W.2d 119 (1955) (motorist who saw parked automobile on highway at night from over 300 feet but made no attempt to use the clear passage in his own lane of travel but instead drove into the parked automobile was guilty of more than slight contributory negligence as a matter of law; judgment for defendant notwithstanding the verdict). Rogers v. Shepherd, 159 Neb. 292, 66 N.W.2d 815 (1954) (road was covered with ice and snow and two motorists were approaching from opposite directions, both traveling down the middle of the road; defendant went over the hill at about 35 m.p.h., saw decedent about 100 feet away and attempted to apply his brakes lightly while turning right out of the traveled way; defendant was going downhill with no chains; plaintiff's deceased was going uphill with chains, and there was no evidence as to his speed, attempts to stop, or whether he saw defendant; but decedent's view was unobstructed and he could have observed the situation as soon as defendant could; "A failure to look and to see that which if seen would avoid an accident is as a matter of law more than slight negligence." 66 N.W.2d at 819, citing Evans v. Messick, 158 Neb. 485, 63 N.W.2d 491 (1954); judgment for plaintiff reversed, action dismissed). Snodgrass v. Nelson, 369 F. Supp. 1206 (D. S.D. 1974), affd. 503 F.2d 94, 19 Fed. R. Serv. 2d 378 (8th Cir. S.D. 1974) (although plaintiff drove on left side of roadway with view obstructed to avoid disabled vehicle, her negligence was no more than slight compared to that of defendant). Karna v. Byron Reed Syndicate, #4, 374 F. Supp. 687 (D. Neb. 1974) (negligence of plaintiff in walking into negligently placed glass door in lobby with which he was familiar was more than slight as a matter of law); Hrabik v. Gottsch, 198 Neb. 86, 251 N.W.2d 672 (1977) (plaintiff, in not keeping constant lookout while crossing four-lane highway between intersections, was guilty of more than slight contributory negligence as a matter of law). Accord, Central Constr. Co. v. Republican City School Dist., 206 Neb. 615, 294 N.W.2d 347 (1980); Circo v. Transit Authority of Omaha, 217 Neb. 497, 348 N.W.2d 908 (1984).

[27]"The uncertainty in [the] legislative concept is intrinsic." Audiss v. Peter Kiewit Sons Co., 190 F.2d 238, 242 (8th Cir. S.D. 1951), quoting Friese v. Gulbrandson, 69 S.D. 179, 8 N.W.2d 438, 442 (1943).

[28]Sandberg v. Peter Kiewit Sons Co., 364 F.2d 206 (8th Cir. Neb. 1966).

ing off the area, was in part responsible for plaintiff's error. Nevertheless, the evidence was clear that the plaintiff proceeded on the highway when he knew or should have known that it was closed, and that he drove sixty miles per hour. Therefore, when his car slammed into a muddy drop-off which caused the automobile to be projected across a ten-yard mud area into an eighteen-inch abutment, his negligence was deemed more than slight in comparison with that of defendant.[29] As the court indicated, "ordinarily where there is room for difference of opinion,"[30] it is for the jury to decide whether plaintiff's negligence was more than slight. But when reasonable minds could draw but one conclusion—that plaintiff abandoned any caution whatsoever—the verdict would be directed for defendant.[31]

It is very important to note that, although the Nebraska and South Dakota statutes expressly state that questions arising under them are to be left to the jury, courts in both states will direct verdicts when the factual pattern is such that "reasonable minds could draw but one conclusion."[32] Perhaps if the defendant convinces the court that it would be impossible to imagine a clearer example of "more than slight" contributory negligence than in the case before it, the court may direct a verdict for the defendant.[33]

The Blackmun Guidelines

Some helpful guidelines were set forth by Justice (then Judge) Blackmun in an Eighth Circuit opinion applying South Dakota law as it existed before the 1964 amendment of its comparative negligence statute.[34] First he noted that the "cases in which the quality of the plaintiff's contributory negligence has been found to raise an issue for the fact finder, rather than to be more than slight as a matter of law, for the most part are those in which one of several forms of mitigating circumstances presents itself."[35] He gave as examples cases involving collisions where a plaintiff made a left hand turn after looking and signaling or slowing down. On the other hand, "where a plaintiff failed to

---

[29]Id., at 210.

[30]Id., at 208, quoting Day v. Metropolitan Utilities Dist., 115 Neb. 711, 214 N.W. 647, 650 (1927), quoting Disher v. Chicago, R. I. & P. R. Co., 93 Neb. 224, 140 N.W. 135 (1913). Accord, In re Estate of Tichota, 190 Neb. 775, 212 N.W.2d 557 (1973).

[31]Sandberg v. Peter Kiewit Sons Co., note 28 above, 364 F.2d at 210. See also Thomas v. Owens, 169 Neb. 369, 99 N.W.2d 605 (1959); Corbitt v. Omaha Transit Co., 162 Neb. 598, 77 N.W.2d 144 (1956).

[32]Sandberg v. Peter Kiewit Sons Co., note 28 above, 364 F.2d at 210. See also Buick v. Stoehr, 172 Neb. 629, 111 N.W.2d 391, 398 (1961), citing Thomas v. Owens, 169 Neb. 369, 99 N.W.2d 605 (1959); Corbitt v. Omaha Transit Co., 162 Neb. 598, 77 N.W.2d 144 (1956); Hickman v. Parks Constr. Co., 162 Neb. 461, 76 N.W.2d 403, 62 A.L.R.2d 1040 (1956); Ries v. Daffin Corp., 81 S.D. 134, 131 N.W.2d 577, 579 (1964); Flanagan v. Slattery, 74 S.D. 92, 49 N.W.2d 27, 29 (1951). Accord, Meyer v. Bankers Dispatch Corp., 471 F.2d 1290 (8th Cir. Neb. 1973); Hrabik v. Gottsch, 198 Neb. 86, 251 N.W.2d 672 (1977).

[33]Sandberg v. Peter Kiewit Sons Co., note 28 above, 364 F.2d at 210.

[34]Associated Engineers, Inc. v. Job, 370 F.2d 633, 641 (8th Cir. S.D. 1966). See notes 23 and 24 above.

[35]Id., at 641.

look or signal before turning, recovery was barred as a matter of law."[36]

In situations in which plaintiff was as much aware of a situation of danger as the defendant[37] it is likely that both Nebraska and South Dakota might deem his negligence more than slight in comparison with that of defendant. Justice Blackmun thought it was important to focus on:

> [T]he quality of a plaintiff's negligence: the precautions he took for his own safety; the extent to which he should have comprehended the risk as the result of warnings, experience, or other factors; and the foreseeability of injury as a consequence of his conduct.[38]

Slight Comparison

Because Justice Blackmun's opinion dealt with South Dakota law as it existed before the 1964 amendment of the comparative negligence statute,[39] it does not focus on the comparison aspect which characterizes present South Dakota and Nebraska law. Today in both states "slight" is a term of relation and will vary depending on the conduct of both parties.[40] Thus, when an individual was killed by a heavily intoxicated hit-and-run driver, his heirs recovered in a wrongful death action even though decedent had been violating a safety statute by walking on the wrong side of a highway.[41] If the defendant had been less culpable in this case, he might have had a directed verdict in his favor.[42] Thus, plaintiff's negligence will not be deemed "more than slight" simply because he violated a safety statute; one must look at the facts, including defendant's negligence, in order to make such a determination.[43]

Some perspective can be put on the South Dakota-Nebraska systems by contrasting them with the comparative negligence system that bars plaintiff's recovery if he is more than 50% negligent. The rule in Wisconsin is that plaintiff's negligence can be more than slight but not

---

[36]Id. Compare Roberts v. Brown, 72 S.D. 479, 36 N.W.2d 665, 668 (1949) and Barnhart v. Ahlers, 79 S.D. 186, 110 N.W.2d 125, 127-128 (1961) with Flanagan v. Slattery, 74 S.D. 92, 49 N.W.2d 27, 30-32 (1951). Accord, Meyer v. Bankers Dispatch Corp., 471 F.2d 1290 (8th Cir. Neb. 1973).

[37]Associated Engineers, Inc. v. Job, 370 F.2d 633, 641 (8th Cir. S.D. 1966).

[38]Id.

[39]Id., at 640. See notes 23 and 24 above in this section.

[40]See, e.g., Nugent v. Quam, 82 S.D. 583, 152 N.W.2d 371 (1967); Crabb v. Wade, 84 S.D. 93, 167 N.W.2d 546 (1969); Smith v. Gunderson, 86 S.D. 38, 190 N.W.2d 841 (1971); Darnell v. Panhandle Cooperative Assn., 175 Neb. 40, 120 N.W.2d 278 (1963); Brackman v. Brackman, 169 Neb. 650, 100 N.W.2d 774 (1960); Sayers v. Witte, 171 Neb. 750, 107 N.W.2d 676 (1961); Johnson v. Roueche, 188 Neb. 716, 199 N.W.2d 1 (1972); Kloewer v. Burlington Northern, Inc., 512 F.2d 300 (8th Cir. Neb. 1975); Snodgrass v. Nelson, 369 F. Supp. 1206 (D. S.D. 1974), affd. 503 F.2d 94 (8th Cir. S.D. 1974).

[41]See Crabb v. Wade, 84 S.D. 93, 167 N.W.2d 546 (1969).

[42]Id., 84 S.D. at 98-99, 167 N.W.2d at 549.

[43]See Smith v. Gunderson, 86 S.D. 38, 190 N.W.2d 841 (1971); C. C. Natvig's Sons, Inc. v. Summers, 198 Neb. 741, 255 N.W.2d 272 (1977) (plaintiff negligent as a matter of law yet defendant's negligence greater).

"greater than that of the defendant."[44] The Supreme Court of Nebraska, on the other hand, in 1970 in *Burney v. Ehlers*,[45] indicated that Nebraska rule is not one in which "a certain percent [of contributory negligence] will bar recovery as a matter of law."[46] Further, recent South Dakota decisions tend to indicate that as long as the defendant's negligence is greater than plaintiff's, plaintiff's negligence will not bar recovery.[47]

New Trial on Damages

Although the South Dakota and Nebraska courts have become more in harmony with each other by their reluctance to direct verdicts except where plaintiff's negligence was clearly greater than that of the defendant's, they differ on an important procedural point. Nebraska will grant defendant a new trial on the issue of damages alone when the court believes that the trier of fact did not make a correct apportionment of damages.[48] It seems clear that the Supreme Court of South Dakota will not do this; when it believes that the apportionment of damages has not been properly made, it remands for a new trial on both liability and damages.[49]

Mandatory Instruction

The two states may differ on another important point as well. Nebraska requires a trial court to give an instruction on comparative negligence, even if defendant fails to request it, as long as there is evidence to support a finding that plaintiff's negligence was more than slight in comparison with that of the defendant.[50] In South Dakota a defendant may waive his right to the instruction by failure to request it.

Contribution Among Joint Tortfeasors in Nebraska

In *Royal Indemnity Company v. Aetna Casualty and Surety Company*,[51] Nebraska abolished the common-law rule of no contribution among joint tortfeasors. Each tortfeasor will remain liable to the plaintiff for the full amount of the judgment, but may seek contribution if anyone discharges more than his "proportionate" share of the common liability. The court did not specify whether contribution would be based on equal division among the joint tortfeasors or on the percentage of negligence attributable to each.

---

[44]See Hammer v. Minneapolis, S. P. & S. S. M. R. Co., 216 Wis. 7, 255 N.W. 124, 126 (1934) (contrasting Wisconsin's general law with one of its limited comparative negligence laws).

[45]Burney v. Ehlers, 185 Neb. 51, 173 N.W.2d 398 (1970).

[46]Id., 173 N.W.2d at 400.

[47]See Crabb v. Wade, 84 S.D. 93, 167 N.W.2d 546 (1969); Smith v. Gunderson, 86 S.D. 38, 190 N.W.2d 841 (1971).

[48]See Scofield v. Haskell, 180 Neb. 324, 142 N.W.2d 597, 602 (1966).

[49]See Hanisch v. Body, 77 S.D. 265, 90 N.W.2d 924 (1958).

[50]See Sober v. Smith, 179 Neb. 74, 136 N.W.2d 372 (1965).

[51]Royal Indem. Co. v. Aetna Cas. & Surety Co., 193 Neb. 752, 229 N.W.2d 183 (1975).

3.5   The 50% system and its derivatives

The 50% systems of comparative negligence have a vital principle in common: contributory negligence will not bar a recovery by a plaintiff at fault as long as the amount of that fault remains below a fixed level in comparison with the negligent defendant.[52] This general approach has been by far the most popular general comparative negligence system among the states: of the forty-four states that had adopted comparative negligence by 1985, twenty-eight selected a 50% system.[53] The Virgin Islands' comparative negligence statute is also a 50% system.[54]

(A) THE ORIGINS OF THE 50% SYSTEM

Georgia Origins

The 50% comparative negligence systems and their derivatives can be traced to a series of Georgia cases of over a century ago where it was suggested that the plaintiff's contributory negligence should not bar his claim when it was less than the defendant's.[55] As set forth in subsections 1.4(B) and 1.5(A), Georgia's comparative negligence law developed from the Supreme Court's broad construction of two early negligence statutes.[56] The principle that contributory negligence returns as an absolute defense when plaintiff's negligence equals that of the defendant was fixed indelibly in Georgia law in a 1904 decision.[57]

Wisconsin Origins

Wisconsin placed a similar limitation on plaintiffs' claims in a statute dealing with the rights of railroad employees injured in the course

---

[52]Knoeller, *Review of the Wisconsin Comparative Negligence Act—Suggested Amendment*, 41 Marq. L. Rev. 397 (1958); Ghiardi and Hogan, *Comparative Negligence—The Wisconsin Rule and Procedure*, 18 Def. L. J. 537 (1969); Heft & Heft, *Comparative Negligence: Wisconsin's Answer*, 55 A.B.A. J. 127 (1969); Prosser, *Comparative Negligence*, 51 Mich. L. Rev. 465 (1953); Padway, *Comparative Negligence*, 16 Marq. L. Rev. 3 (1931); Campbell, *Wisconsin's Comparative Negligence Law*, 7 Wis. L. Rev. 222 (1932); Whelan, *Comparative Negligence Statute*, 20 Marq. L. Rev. 189 (1936); Whelan, *Comparative Negligence*, 1938 Wis. L. Rev. 289; Annot., "The doctrine of comparative negligence and its relation to the doctrine of contributory negligence," 32 A.L.R.3d 463 (1970).

[53]Ark. Stat. Ann., § 27-1764; Colo. Rev. Stat., § 13-21-111; Conn. Gen. Stat. Ann., § 52-572h; Del. Code Ann., tit. 10, § 8132; Ga. Code Ann., §§ 46-8-291, 51-11-1; Hawaii Rev. Stat., § 663-31(a); Idaho Code, § 6-801; Ind. Code, § 34-4-33-4; Iowa Code Ann., ch. 668; Kan. Stat. Ann., § 60-258a; Me. Rev. Stat. Ann., tit. 14, § 156; Mass. Gen. Laws Ann., ch. 231, § 85; Minn. Stat. Ann., § 604.01, subd. 1; Mont. Code Ann., § 27-1-702; Nev. Rev. Stat., § 41.141; N.H. Rev. Stat. Ann., § 507:7-a; N.J. Stat. Ann., § 2A:15-5.1; N.D. Cent. Code, § 9-10-07; Ohio Rev. Code Ann., § 2315.19; Okla. Stat. Ann., tit. 23, § 11; Ore. Rev. Stat., § 18.470; Pa. Stat. Ann., tit. 42, § 7102; Tex. Rev. Civ. Stat. Ann. (Vernon), art. 2212a, § 1; Utah Code Ann., § 78-27-37; Vt. Stat. Ann., tit. 12, § 1036; Bradley v. Appalachian Power Co., 163 W. Va. 332, 256 S.E.2d 879 (1979); Wis. Stat. Ann., § 895.045; Wyo. Stat., § 1-1-109.

[54]V.I. Code Ann., tit. 5, § 1451.

[55]See subsection 1.5(A), and cases cited at note 82.

[56]Ga. Code Ann., §§ 46-8-291, 51-11-7.

[57]Christian v. Macon R. & L. Co., 120 Ga. 314, 47 S.E. 923 (1904). See subsection 1.5(A).

of their employment.[58] The 50% principle of this statute became the heart of a comparative negligence statute of general application passed by the Wisconsin legislature in 1931.[59]

The draftsman of the statute, who was at various times a practicing attorney and a judge, perhaps inserted the rule that a plaintiff could not recover if his negligence was equal to or greater than that of the defendants in order to assure passage of the bill.[60] However, his discussion of the merits of his own act does not reflect this.[61] The Wisconsin bill later became the starting point for the development of general comparative negligence laws in many other states.

The current status of such laws is discussed in subsections (B) and (C) below.

(B) THE 50% NEGLIGENT PLAINTIFF

The 50% systems of the various states differ from each other in a number of ways, and they have developed a number of special problems; but one key variation must be mentioned before any of the others is discussed. In ten of the states that have adopted a form of this system, contributory negligence will bar a plaintiff if it is either equal to or greater than the negligence of the defendant.[62] In a majority of states having such a system, however, plaintiff's negligence will bar his claim only if it is greater than that of the defendant.[63]

The original 50% statute, the 1931 Wisconsin act, provided that the plaintiff's negligence would reduce his recovery in proportion to his own fault, but would not bar recovery as long as his negligence was

---

[58]See dissenting opinion of Chief Justice Hallows in Vincent v. Pabst Brewing Co., 47 Wis. 2d 120, 177 N.W.2d 513 (1970). Hallows traces the development of the railroad legislation, which originated as a reaction to the fellow-servant rule (Wis. Laws 1875, ch. 173) and imputed liability for negligence of a fellow-servant to the railroad, maintaining contributory negligence as a defense. There were several intervening steps, and the 1913 Act (Wis. Laws 1913, ch. 644) provided for a comparison of negligence to reduce the recovery.

[59]Wis. Laws 1931, ch. 242, § 1, which read: "Contributory negligence shall not bar a recovery in an action by any person or his legal representative to recover damages for negligence resulting in death or in injury to person or property, if such negligence was not as great as the negligence of the person against whom recovery is sought, but any damages allowed shall be diminished by the jury in the proportion to the amount of negligence attributable to the person recovering."

See Padway, *Comparative Negligence*, 16 Marq. L. Rev. 3, 5 (1931).

In 1971 Wisconsin amended its law to substitute "not greater than" for "not as great as." See the following subsection.

[60]See Prosser, *Comparative Negligence*, 51 Mich. L. Rev. 465, 494 (1953): "It appears impossible to justify the rule on any basis except one of pure political compromise."

[61]See Padway, note 59 above, at 4.

[62]Arkansas, Colorado, Georgia, Kansas, Idaho, Maine, North Dakota, Utah, West Virginia and Wyoming.

[63]Conn. Gen. Stat. Ann., § 52-572h; Del. Code Ann., tit. 12, § 8132; Hawaii Rev. Stat., § 633-31; Ind. Code, § 34-4-33-4; Iowa Code Ann., ch. 668; Mass. Gen. Laws Ann., ch. 231, § 85; Minn. Stat. Ann., § 604.01; Mont. Code Ann., § 27-1-702; Nev. Rev. Stat., § 41.141; N.H. Rev. Stat. Ann., § 507:7-a; N.J. Stat. Ann., § 2A: 15-5.1; Ohio Rev. Code Ann., § 2315.19; Okla. Stat Ann., tit. 23, § 12; Ore. Rev. Stat., § 18.470; Pa. Stat. Ann., tit. 42, § 7102; Tex. Rev. Civ. Stat. Ann. (Vernon), art. 2212a; Vt. Stat. Ann., tit. 12, § 1036.

less than that of defendant; beyond that, contributory negligence would continue as a bar. This principle has been incorporated in a number of statutes of limited application.[64]

"Not as Great as" States

Arkansas adopted a pure comparative negligence system by statute in 1955, but in 1957 repealed and replaced it with a law providing that plaintiff could recover only if his negligence was "of less degree" than that of defendant.[65] A 1961 act[66] reenacted the provisions to place railroads on an equal basis with respect to comparative negligence without changing the "less degree" language. Later amendments in 1973 and 1975 revised the law to refer to the "fault" rather than the "contributory negligence" of the parties.[67] Currently, the Arkansas law contains the following provision: "If the fault chargeable to a party claiming damages is of less degree than the fault chargeable to the party or parties from whom the claiming party seeks to recover, then the claiming party is entitled to recover the amount of his damages after they have been diminished in proportion to the degree of his own fault."[68]

In 1965, Maine applied the same basic principle, but used different language in stating it, in the enactment of its general comparative negligence statute: "If . . . claimant is found by the jury to be equally at fault, the claimant shall not recover."[69] Maine's statute is a bit unusual, moreover, in that the jury is not instructed to reduce the negligent plaintiff's award strictly on the basis of the percent of negligence attributable to him, but rather "to the extent deemed just and equitable, having regard to the claimant's share in the responsibility for the damages. . . ."[70]

In 1969, Hawaii[71] and Minnesota[72] adopted statutes allowing contributory negligence to return as a total bar to recovery when plain-

---

[64]See, e.g., Ark. Stat. Ann., § 73-916 (applied in Missouri P. R. Co. v. Brown, 195 Ark. 1060, 115 S.W.2d 1083 (1938); Mich. Comp. Laws, § 419.52 (applied in Bruce v. Michigan C. R. Co., 172 Mich. 441, 138 N.W. 362 (1912); Wis. Stat. Ann., § 192.50(3) (applied in Zeratsky v. Chicago, M. & S. P. R. Co., 141 Wis. 423, 123 N.W. 904 (1909). See generally Prosser, *Comparative Negligence*, 51 Mich. L. Rev. 465, 478-480 (1953).

[65]Ark. Acts 1955, No. 191, § 1; Acts 1957, No. 296, § 2. See Rosenberg, *Comparative Negligence in Arkansas: A "Before and After" Survey*, 13 Ark. L. Rev. 89 (1959).

[66]Ark. Acts 1961 (1st Ex. Sess.), No. 56, §§ 1, 2, codified at Ark. Stat. Ann., §§ 27-1730.1 and 27-1730.2. See Martin v. United States, 448 F. Supp. 855 (E.D. Ark. 1977) (contributory negligence will be considered in mitigating damages), mod. 586 F.2d 1206 (8th Cir. Ark. 1978).

[67]Ark. Acts 1973, No. 303, §§ 1-3; Acts 1975, No. 367, §§ 1-3, codified at Ark. Stat. Ann., §§ 27-1763 to 27-1765.

[68]Ark. Stat. Ann., §§ 27-1765.

[69]Me. Laws 1965, ch. 424, codified at Me. Rev. Stat. Ann., tit. 14, § 156.

[70]Id.

[71]Hawaii Rev. Stat., § 663-31(a).

[72]Minn. Stat. Ann., § 604.01, subd. 1. See also Wagner v. International Harvester Co., 611 F.2d 224 (8th Cir. Minn. 1979) (when one party is entirely responsible, comparative negligence does not apply).

tiff's negligence is equal to that of defendant. Colorado,[73] Idaho,[74] North Dakota,[75] Oklahoma,[76] Oregon,[77] Utah,[78] Wyoming,[79] and Kansas,[80] followed suit, although some of these states later adopted the New Hampshire variant.[81]

In 1979 the West Virginia Supreme Court, in *Bradley v. Appalachian Power Company*,[82] became the first court to adopt a modified form of comparative negligence. The court barred recovery whenever a party's negligence or fault equals or exceeds the combined negligence or fault of any other party or parties involved.

The New Hampshire Variant

In 1969 New Hampshire became the first state to permit partial recovery by a plaintiff who is found exactly 50% (equally) at fault.[83] Vermont adopted an identical provision the next year.[84] Under this modification, the 50% negligent plaintiff will be able to recover half his damages.

In 1971 Wisconsin, the original 50% state, following the report of a legislative interim study commission, amended its statute so as to permit reduced recovery by the 50% negligent plaintiff.[85] It is to be anticipated that other states which borrowed the original Wisconsin statute may modify their statutes and that new states will avail themselves of the Wisconsin legislative study. As a matter of fact, of the eight states that adopted modified comparative negligence statutes in 1973, four—Connecticut,[86] Nevada,[87] New Jersey,[88] and Texas[89]—chose the "not greater than" language of the New Hampshire statute and the Wisconsin amendment in preference to the "not as great as" language of the original Wisconsin statute.

In 1976 Pennsylvania adopted the New Hampshire variant of the 50% system;[90] by 1985, Delaware, Hawaii, Indiana, Iowa, Massachu-

---

[73]Colo. Rev. Stat., § 41-2-14(1).

[74]Idaho Code, § 6-801. See Anderson v. Gailey, 97 Idaho 813, 555 P.2d 144 (1976), revd. on other grounds, 100 Idaho 796, 606 P.2d 90 (1980).

[75]N.D. Cent. Code, § 9-10-07. See Bauer v. Graner, 266 N.W.2d 88 (N.D. 1978).

[76]Okla. Stat. Ann., tit. 23, § 11.

[77]Ore. Rev. Stat., § 18.470.

[78]Utah Code Ann., § 78-27-37.

[79]Wyo. Stat., § 1-7.2(a).

[80]Kan. Stat. Ann., § 60-258a. See also Scales v. St. Louis S. F. R. Co., 2 Kan. App. 2d 491, 582 P.2d 300 (1978).

[81]See the following subsection.

[82]Bradley v. Appalachian Power Co., 163 W. Va. 332, 256 S.E.2d 879 (1979).

[83]N.H. Rev. Stat. Ann., § 507:7-a.

[84]Vt. Stat. Ann., tit. 12, § 1036.

[85]Wis. Laws 1971, ch. 47, amending Wis. Stat. Ann., § 895.045.

[86]Conn. Gen. Stat. Ann., § 52-572h(a).

[87]Nev. Rev. Stat., § 41.141(1).

[88]N.J. Stat. Ann., § 2A:15-5.1.

[89]Tex. Rev. Civ. Stat. Ann. (Vernon), art. 2212a, § 1. See also Reyes v. Missouri P. R. Co., 589 F.2d 791 (5th Cir. Tex. 1979).

[90]Pa. Stat. Ann., tit. 17, § 2101.

setts, Minnesota, Montana, Ohio, Oklahoma, Oregon, and the Virgin Islands had adopted this variant.[91]

Theoretically only a very small percentage of plaintiffs would be found exactly 50% negligent, so that the difference between "not as great as" and "not greater than" language would be relatively insignificant. However, as a matter of practice, juries vexed with the problem of apportioning fault between two negligent parties often return verdicts that they were equally at fault.[92] The result could be particularly devastating in states such as Colorado, Hawaii, and Massachusetts, which followed the Wisconsin practice of requiring special verdicts apportioning negligence while keeping from the jury information as to the legal effect of its apportionment. In these states, the jury might mistakenly believe that a verdict apportioning fault equally would result in an award to the plaintiff of half his damages.[93] Many states requiring special verdicts now allow the court to instruct the jury on the effect of its findings on the ultimate outcome.[94]

The Vital Point

In all of the 50% systems and their derivatives, a negligent plaintiff will have his damages reduced by the percentage he was at fault in the accident up to the "vital point" at which the contributory negligence defense, in fact, returns in its full common-law application. Thus, in Wisconsin today a plaintiff who suffered $10,000 damages in an accident, but was 50% at fault, recovers $5,000. If the accident had occurred prior to amendment of Wisconsin's statute on June 22, 1971, plaintiff would have recovered nothing, since his fault was equal to that of the defendant.[95]

The rather dramatic difference in outcome that occurs in 50% systems once the plaintiff's negligence has reached the vital point at which contributory negligence becomes a bar is rationalized by a certain fundamental view of the fault system. It is thought by many that it is

---

[91]Del. Code Ann., tit. 10, § 8132; Hawaii Rev. Stat., § 663.1; Ind. Code, § 34-4-33-4; Iowa Code Ann., ch. 668; Mass. Gen. Stat. Ann., ch. 231, § 85; Minn. Stat. Ann., § 604.01; Mont. Code Ann., § 27-1-702; Ohio Rev. Code Ann., § 2315.19; Okla. Stat. Ann., tit. 23, § 13; Ore. Rev. Stat., § 18.470; V.I. Code Ann., tit. 5, § 1451.

[92]See dissent in Vincent v. Pabst Brewing Co., 47 Wis. 2d 120, 177 N.W.2d 513, 517, 520 (1970). See also Moses v. Scott Paper Co., 280 F. Supp. 37 (D. Me. 1968) and Towle v. Aube, 310 A.2d 259 (Me. 1973).

[93]See dissent in Vincent v. Pabst Brewing Co., 47 Wis. 2d 120, 177 N.W.2d 513, 520; Wisconsin Legislative Council; minutes of Judiciary Committee on Automobile Accident Liability 6-7 (July 16, 1970).

[94]Colo. Rev. Stat., § 13-21-111(4); Conn. Gen. Stat. Ann., § 52-572h(b); Seppi v. Betty, 99 Idaho 186, 579 P.2d 683 (1978); Ind. Code, § 34-4-33-5; Iowa Code Ann., § 668.3(5); Nev. Rev. Stat., § 41.141(2)(1); Roman v. Mitchell, 82 N.J. 336, 413 A.2d 322 (1980); N.D. Cent. Code, § 9-10-07; Adkins v. Whitten, 297 S.E.2d 881 (W. Va. 1982). See also Danforth v. Danforth, 156 Ga. App. 236, 274 S.E.2d 628 (1980) (it was error to give comparative negligence instruction implying that plaintiff could recover even if he were more than 50% at fault).

[95]See Lupie v. Hartzheim, 54 Wis. 2d 415, 195 N.W.2d 461 (1972). Accord, Schuh v. Fox River Tractor Co., 63 Wis. 2d 728, 218 N.W.2d 279 (1974).

indefensible to allow a party who is more at fault to recover from one who is less at fault.[96] As indicated in section 21.3, this rationale has been severely criticized, but it obviously has had great appeal to state legislators.

(C) MULTIPLE PARTIES IN A 50% SYSTEM

Chapter 16 covers most of the problems in regard to multiple parties under a comparative negligence system. Nevertheless, there are special concerns relating to apportionment between multiple plaintiffs and defendants under a 50% system which should be discussed at this point.

Combine Defendants' Negligence?

One significant problem when there are multiple defendants is whether plaintiff's negligence is to be compared with all defendants jointly (as a "unit") or with each defendant separately. Obviously if plaintiff's negligence surpasses the vital point when compared with the negligence of all defendants combined, he recovers nothing.

There is a difference among the states, however, as to whether a plaintiff may recover from a particular defendant when plaintiff's negligence is greater than the particular defendant's, but less than that of all the defendants combined. Under Arkansas decisions applying the state's comparative negligence statute, plaintiff is entitled to recover if his negligence is less than the negligence of all defendants combined (the unit rule).[97] In Wisconsin, however, plaintiff recovers from a particular defendant only when his negligence was equal to or less than that of the particular defendant.

An example might clarify the difference in approaches. Suppose a jury finds in a single accident that:

1. Plaintiff was 30% at fault,

2. Defendant A was 20% at fault, and

3. Defendant B was 50% at fault.

In Wisconsin, plaintiff could recover 70% of his damages but only against defendant B. In Arkansas, he could recover that portion of his damages against either defendant.

Wisconsin courts appeared to be in the process of revoking the old rule so as to allow the percentage of negligence of all the defendants to be combined when comparing them with plaintiff's negligence.[98] How-

---

[96]Ghiardi, *Comparative Negligence, The Case Against a Mississippi Type Statute*, 10 For the Def. 61, 64 (1969).

[97]Walton v. Tull, 234 Ark. 882, 356 S.W.2d 20, 8 A.L.R.3d 708 (1962); Riddel v. Little, 253 Ark. 686, 488 S.W.2d 34 (1972) (where plaintiff's negligence was less than 50% of all the codefendants', he was entitled to recover from each or all of them as joint tortfeasors even though his negligence equaled that of a particular defendant).

[98]See Soeldner v. White Metal Rolling & Stamping Corp., 473 F. Supp. 753 (E.D. Wis. 1979); May v. Skelley Oil Co., 83 Wis. 2d 30, 264 N.W.2d 574 (1978). See section 16.6.

ever, in 1980 the Wisconsin Supreme Court, in *Reiter v. Dyken*,[99] refused to combine the defendants' negligence for purposes of determining whether plaintiff would be allowed to recover. The court reasoned that the legislature would provide a more appropriate forum for the resolution of this particular problem.

The overwhelming majority of modified comparative negligence states that have considered the question follow the Arkansas unit rule approach,[1] including at least two states that had based their statutes on the Wisconsin statute.[2] In recent years states enacting comparative negligence legislation have chosen to include the unit rule in the statute.[3] Hawaii amended its statute to clarify the rule.[4] Outside Wisconsin

---

[99]Reiter v. Dyken, 95 Wis. 2d 461, 290 N.W.2d 510 (1980).

[1]See note 97 above. Mountain Mobile Mix, Inc. v. Gifford, 660 P.2d 883 (Colo. 1983); Conn. Gen. Stat. Ann., § 52-572h; Del. Code Ann., tit. 10, § 8132; Hawaii Rev. Stat., § 663-31(a); Ind. Code, § 34-4-33-4; Iowa Code Ann., § 668.3(1); Kan. Stat. Ann., § 60-258a(a); Mass. Gen. Laws Ann., ch. 231, § 85; Nev. Rev. Stat., § 41.141(1); Hurley v. Public Service Co. of New Hampshire, 123 N.H. 750, 465 A.2d 1217 (1983); N.J. Stat. Ann., § 2A:15-5.1; Ohio Rev. Code Ann., § 2315.19(A)(1); Okla. Stat. Ann., tit. 23, § 13; Ore. Rev. Stat., § 18.470; Pa. Stat. Ann., tit. 42, § 7102; Tex. Rev. Civ. Stat. Ann. (Vernon), art. 2212a, § 1; Jensen v. Intermountain Health Care, Inc., 679 P.2d 903 (Utah 1984); Vt. Stat. Ann., tit. 12, § 1036; Bradley v. Appalachian Power Co., 163 W. Va. 332, 256 S.E.2d 879 (1979).

The 1976 Pennsylvania statute, Pa. Stat. Ann., tit. 42, § 7102, has posed some interesting ambiguities. The first part of the statute states that the plaintiff's contributory negligence "shall not bar a recovery by the plaintiff... where such negligence was not greater than the causal negligence of the defendant or defendants against whom recovery is sought...." The second part, under the caption "Recovery against joint defendant; contribution," states, "The plaintiff may recover the full amount of the allowed recovery from any defendant against whom the plaintiff is not barred from recovery." This commentator and at least one other have construed this statute to follow the Wisconsin rule. V. Schwartz, *Comparative Negligence* § 3.5(C) (1981 Supp.); Timby, *Comparative Negligence*, 48 Pa. B. A. Q. 219, 231 (1976); but other commentators have assumed or argued that the unit rule was intended. See, e.g., Sherman, *An Analysis of Pennsylvania's Comparative Negligence Statute*, 38 U. Pitt. L. Rev. 51, 65-66 (1976); Griffith, Helmsley & Burr, *Contribution, Indemnity, Settlements, and Releases: What the Pennsylvania Comparative Negligence Statute Did Not Say*, 24 Vill. L. Rev. 494, 501 (1978-1979); Beasley & Tunstall, *Jury Instructions Concerning Multiple Defendants and Strict Liability After the Pennsylvania Comparative Negligence Act*, 24 Vill. L. Rev. 518, 530-531 (1978-1979). Beasley and Tunstall suggest that the second part of the statute means that the statute is intended to have no effect on existing immunities such as that between spouses. Id. at 530. The Pennsylvania courts have followed the Beasley and Tunstall approach in construing the statute to exclude employers from comparative fault determinations under worker's compensation immunity. William Harter and Cleaver Brooks, A Div. of Aqua-Chem., Inc. v. Yeagley, 310 Pa. Super. 449, 456 A.2d 1021 (1983); Kelly v. Carborundum Co., 307 Pa. Super. 361, 453 A.2d 624 (1982). In *Kelly v. Carborundum* a dissenting judge points out that joinder of an employer for determination of comparative negligence shares is necessary if the unit rule is to work properly. *Kelly* at 635-636 (Cirillo, J., dissenting). In late 1984 an intermediate appellate court ruled that the unit rule was intended: the legislative history did not indicate an intent to adopt Wisconsin comparative negligence law in its entirety, and every other state using "or defendants" language had adopted the unit rule. Elder v. Orluck, 483 A.2d 474 (Pa. Super. 1984).

[2]Colorado and Utah. See note 1 above.

[3]Del. Code Ann., tit. 10, § 8132; Iowa Code Ann., § 668.3(1); Ind. Code, § 34-4-33-4.

[4]Hawaii Rev. Stat., § 663-31.

only Georgia,[5] Idaho,[6] Minnesota,[7] and Wyoming[8] still use the Wisconsin rule.

The merits of the Wisconsin rule are rather on the surface; the approach preserves the principle that a defendant who is less at fault than plaintiff should not be held liable. Nevertheless, the Wisconsin rule can result in an unfair burden on a defendant in the position of defendant B in the example above. He will be unable to recover any contribution from defendant A because such a right is predicated on initial liability to the plaintiff.

Further unfairness can arise if a court permits a rather questionable strategy, developed by defendants in Wisconsin, of broadening the number of "defendants" among whom apportionment of fault will be distributed, thereby reducing plaintiff's chances of success against any of them. Thus, in 1963 the Supreme Court of Wisconsin indicated that even a tortfeasor who had settled and who was not a party to the lawsuit could be deemed a party for the purpose of apportionment of negligence.[9] In 1972, the court reaffirmed this principle when plaintiff had released three defendants and subsequently dismissed his claim against them; they still were to be considered as defendants for the purpose of apportionment.[10] The result of these rulings is to increase the possibility that the percentage of fault of each defendant who actually is in the case will be less than that of the plaintiff. If this does indeed occur, plaintiff will recover nothing against that defendant.

Joint and Several Liability

A very important question on which there is some difference among the states with a 50% system is whether the common-law principle of joint and several liability[11] is preserved under comparative negligence. The statutes of at least seven states make it clear that each joint defendant is severally liable for the entire amount of all defendants' obligations to the plaintiff.[12] Thus, in the example given above, the 30% negligent plaintiff could recover 70% of his damages from defendant B, even though B's negligence was only 50%; and in states following Arkansas, he could recover 70% from either defendant B or defendant A, whose negligence was only 20%. This would be in accord with the common-law principle of joint and several liability.

---

[5]Mishoe v. Davis, 64 Ga. App. 700, 14 S.E.2d 187 (1941).

[6]Odenwalt v. Zaring, 102 Idaho 1, 624 P.2d 383 (1980).

[7]Horton v. Orbeth, Inc., 342 N.W.2d 112 (Minn. 1984).

[8]See W. P. Keeton et al., *Prosser and Keeton on the Law of Torts* § 50, at 339-340 (5th ed. 1984).

[9]Pierringer v. Hoger, 21 Wis. 2d 182, 124 N.W.2d 106 (1963).

[10]Payne v. Bilco Co., 54 Wis. 2d 424, 195 N.W.2d 641 (1972).

[11]See W. P. Keeton et al., note 8 above, § 47, at 328-330 and § 50.

[12]Idaho Code, § 604.01, subd. 1; N.J. Stat. Ann., § 2A:15-5.3; N.D. Cent. Code, § 9-10-07; Utah Code Ann., § 78-27-41(1); Wyo. Stat., § 1-7.4(1). See, e.g., Markey v. Skog, 129 N.J. Super. 192, 322 A.2d 513 (1974).

Joint Liability Abolished

The New Hampshire, Kansas and Vermont statutes limit each defendant's obligation to "that proportion of the total dollar amount awarded as damages in the ratio of the amount of his causal negligence to the amount of causal negligence attributed to all defendants against whom recovery is allowed."[13]

The New Hampshire and Vermont statutes have not been much litigated; the Kansas courts, however, have interpreted the statute to abrogate joint and several liability.[14] Ohio and Indiana have recently enacted statutes subject to the same interpretation.[15] In these states, in the example given above, plaintiff could recover only 50% of his damages from defendant B. If the state follows the Arkansas rule on recovery from several defendants, plaintiff could in addition recover 20% of his damages from defendant A.

Perhaps it could be successfully argued that the limitation of these statutes was not intended to apply when defendants were joint tortfeasors. Such a construction, although not in accord with the letter of the statute, would be within the spirit of comparative negligence: that is, that plaintiff's recovery should not be reduced below the percentage of his fault.

The Middle Ground

The Texas statute takes a compromise position on joint liability of multiple defendants under comparative negligence. It provides that "Each defendant is jointly and severally liable for the entire amount ... except that a defendant whose negligence is less than that of the claimant is liable ... only for that portion ... which represents the percentage of negligence attributable to him."[16] Iowa and Nevada have adopted the same rule.[17] Thus, in the example given above, plaintiff could recover only 20% against defendant A but could proceed against defendant B for 50% plus any portion of the 20% not recovered from A.

Reallocation

Arizona, Minnesota, and Montana have adopted provisions similar to the one in the Uniform Comparative Fault Act provision with regard to multiple tortfeasors.[18] At the time of trial damages are apportioned according to percentage shares of fault. If a tortfeasor turns out to be judgment-proof, the court may, upon motion made within one year of

---

[13]N.H. Rev. Stat. Ann., § 507:7-a; Kan. Stat. Ann., § 60.258a(d); Vt. Stat. Ann., tit. 12, § 1036.

[14]Brown v. Keill, 244 Kan. 195, 580 P.2d 867 (1978); Lester v. Magic Chef, Inc., 230 Kan. 643, 641 P.2d 353 (1982).

[15]Ohio Rev. Code Ann., § 2315.19(2); Ind. Code, § 34-4-35-5(b)(4). See Stearns v. Johns-Manville Sales Corp., No. C79-2088 (N.D. Ohio Feb. 17, 1984), citing this treatise.

[16]Tex. Rev. Civ. Stat. Ann. (Vernon), art. 2212a, § 2 (c).

[17]Iowa Code Ann., § 668.4; Nev. Rev. Stat., § 41.141(3)(a).

[18]Ariz. Rev. Stat. Ann., § 12-2508; Minn. Stat. Ann., § 604.02(2); Mont. Code Ann., § 27-1-703(3) (omits time limit); Unif. Comp. Fault Act, § 2(d), 12 U.L.A. 39 (Supp. 1985) (see section 21.4).

the original judgment, reallocate damages among the remaining parties, so that the plaintiff still obtains damages that were arguably the responsibility of the judgment-proof party. However, his recovery is reduced by the percentage that he, the plaintiff, was at fault. Thus, if the judgment-proof's share was $100 and the plaintiff was 30% at fault, the remaining joint tortfeasors are responsible for 70%, or $70.

Multiple Plaintiffs

A final point about multiple parties focuses on how apportionment is handled when there are multiple plaintiffs. While there is little case law on the matter, it seems relatively clear that the amount of an individual plaintiff's recovery will not be reduced simply because there is another negligent plaintiff in the case.[19] Thus, if a number of plaintiffs are injured by a single explosion, the negligence of each will be separately considered in regard to the negligence of the defendant. The only time a plaintiff must bear the burden of another plaintiff's negligence under comparative negligence is when preexisting principles or tort or agency law would impute that negligence to him.

---

[19]See, e.g., Polistina v. Polistina, 183 N.J. Super. 291, 443 A.2d 1086 (1982). Vroman v. Kempke, 34 Wis. 2d 680, 150 N.W.2d 423 (1967); Callan v. Wick, 269 Wis. 68, 68 N.W.2d 438 (1955). See also Bouchard, *Apportionment of Damages under Comparative Negligence*, 55 Mass. L.Q. 125, 136 (1970).

CHAPTER 4

CAUSATION

Section

4.1   Cause in fact

One of the great breakthroughs in analysis of proximate cause was accomplished when courts and legal scholars attempted to isolate problems of causation in fact from proximate cause.[1] If one can excise questions of policy and focus upon simple physical causation, then one has isolated causation in fact. As Dean Prosser stated:

> [T]he simplest and most obvious problem connected with "proximate cause" is that of causation in "fact." This question of "fact" ordinarily is one upon which all the learning, literature and lore of the law are largely lost. It is a matter upon which lay opinion is quite as competent as that of the most experienced court. For that reason, in the ordinary case, it is peculiarly a question for the jury.[2]

Defendant's Negligence as Cause in Fact

Under a comparative negligence system, just as under a common-law fault system, defendant's negligence in order to be legally operative must be a "cause in fact" of plaintiff's injuries. For example, in *Altiere v. Bremer*,[3] plaintiff contended that defendant's negligently operated automobile had injured her child. Nevertheless, the court permitted a verdict for defendant to stand, because the evidence indicated that the child dashed in front of the automobile.[4] Even assuming that the defendant was negligent, if she could not have stopped in time while traveling at a normal speed, her act of negligence was not a cause in fact of plaintiff's harm. As the court stated, "the jury could have reasonably concluded that the accident was unavoidable and that

---

[1]See W. P. Keeton et al., *Prosser and Keeton on the Law of Torts* § 41 (5th ed. 1984); H. Hart & M. Honoré, *Causation in the Law* (1959); Malone, *Ruminations on Cause-In-Fact*, 9 Stan. L. Rev. 60 (1956).

[2]W. P. Keeton et al., note 1 above, § 41 at 264-265.

[3]Altiere v. Bremer, 39 Wis. 2d 548, 159 N.W.2d 264 (1968).

[4]Id., 159 N.W.2d at 266.

[defendant's] negligence, if any, was not a substantial factor in causing the accident."[5]

Again, in *Leanna v. Goethe*,[6] it was alleged that plaintiff-motorcyclist was injured when defendant negligently made a left turn without giving any signal. The jury found the defendant negligent, but it also apparently determined that the plaintiff would not have seen the signal if it had been given. Therefore, the defendant's negligence was not a cause in fact of the accident and the Supreme Court of Wisconsin upheld a verdict for the defendant.[7]

Plaintiff's Negligence as Cause in Fact

The cause in fact issue must also be considered when it is alleged that plaintiff was negligent. In order for plaintiff's negligence to be material and thus subject to comparison with that of defendant, plaintiff's negligence must have been a cause in fact or must at least have contributed to his injury.

In *Martinson v. Polk County*[8] plaintiff was injured when he drove into a ditch that defendant had negligently left unguarded. Defendant apparently argued that plaintiff was negligent in maintenance of his brakes and that this should have been considered in making the award. The court held under the facts that it could be found that even if plaintiff's brakes had been in perfect condition, he still would have met with the same accident and injury; therefore, the jury did not have to take plaintiff's negligence into account in making its award.

There are limits to how far a plaintiff can press this argument. An appellate court may review jury findings on the issue and reverse if it determines that a reasonable person must find plaintiff's negligence was causal.[9]

---

[5]Id. See also Farley v. M M Cattle Co., 515 S.W.2d 697 (Tex. Civ. App. 1974) (failure of defendant to give plaintiff a horse that would rein properly not cause in fact of collision as plaintiff did not attempt to rein horse. The Supreme Court of Texas subsequently reversed and remanded for a new trial, as the Court found sufficient evidence to raise a fact issue of negligence. Farley v. M M Cattle Co., 529 S.W.2d 751 (Tex. 1975), later app. 549 S.W.2d 453 (Tex. Civ. App. 1977)). See also Thomas v. Sarrett, 505 S.W.2d 345 (Tex. Civ. App. 1974) (under conditions of near invisibility, defendant's failure to keep proper lookout not cause in fact of collision).

[6]Leanna v. Goethe, 238 Wis. 616, 300 N.W. 490 (1941).

[7]See also Cole v. Tullos, 228 Miss. 815, 90 So. 2d 32 (1956) (jury to decide whether accident would have been avoided if employer had informed employee of danger from cotton picker); Ledford v. Pittsburgh & L. E. R. Co., 236 Pa. Super. 65, 345 A.2d 218 (1975) (unexpected stop of train did not contribute to injury of employee who lost grip on bar on side of railroad car while investigating cause of delay).

[8]Martinson v. Polk County, 227 Wis. 447, 279 N.W. 61 (1938). See also Courville v. Home Transp. Co., 497 S.W.2d 788 (Tex. Civ. App. 1973) (plaintiff's intoxication not cause in fact of collision or second collision involving third party); Stockton v. Longmore, 498 S.W.2d 440 (Tex. Civ. App. 1973) (plaintiff's failure to keep proper lookout not cause in fact of collision since normal driver would not have had time to react after defendant began to make turn).

[9]McCarthy v. Behnke, 273 Wis. 640, 79 N.W.2d 82 (1956).

Summary

The issue of cause in fact appears to be treated very much the same under comparative negligence as it is where contributory negligence is a complete bar to recovery. However, it is not an issue to be ignored; it may serve to prevent any comparison of negligence on the part of either plaintiff or defendant.

4.2 The concept of proximate cause

Proximate cause is one of the most richly discussed topics in the entire law of torts, and it is not the purpose here to reexamine aspects of that topic that have been amply discussed elsewhere.[10] It is important to note, however, that proximate cause differs from the simpler question of cause in fact. Assuming that plaintiff's or defendant's negligence was a physical cause of the accident, was it a proximate, or legal, cause? At this juncture, considerations of policy, either expressed or unexpressed, enter into a court's decision.

Does the introduction of comparative negligence alter a court's treatment of proximate cause, either with respect to defendant's negligence as a proximate cause of plaintiff's injuries, or with respect to plaintiff's negligence as a proximate cause of his own injuries? In 1972, a writer focusing on this problem stated that "[C]onsiderations of proximate cause under comparative negligence should theoretically remain as they existed before the Act."[11] Nevertheless, that writer did not undertake a careful examination of whether this theory is applied in fact. Some writers have perceived that some differences may arise.[12] However, there has been no careful exploration of the impact of comparative negligence on proximate cause. This is done in sections 4.3 to 4.5, following.

4.3 Defendant's negligence as a proximate cause

If one focused solely on the Mississippi cases under comparative negligence, one would have to conclude that comparative negligence has had no noticeable effect on whether a defendant's negligence was a

---

[10]See Green, *Rationale of Proximate Cause* (1927); W. P. Keeton et al., *Prosser and Keeton on the Law of Torts* Ch. 7 at 263 & note 1 (5th ed. 1984) (collecting citations to law review articles).

[11]Laugesen, *Colorado Comparative Negligence*, 48 Den. L.J. 469, 486 (1972).

[12]See Prosser, *Comparative Negligence*, 51 Mich. L. Rev. 465, 494-497 (1953); Note, *Legal Cause, Proximate Cause, and Comparative Negligence in the F.E.L.A.*, 18 Stan. L. Rev. 929 (1966). See, e.g., George v. Guerette, 306 A.2d 138 (Me. 1973) (the Supreme Court of Maine found the giving of an "unavoidable accident" instruction was error and could cause confusion under comparative negligence; nevertheless, defendant could prevail if plaintiff's negligence was the sole proximate cause of the accident). In St. Louis S. R. Co. v. Pennington, 261 Ark. 650, 553 S.W.2d 436 (1977), the Arkansas Supreme Court declared that the negligence of the plaintiff and defendant in cases of comparative negligence are "concurring causes."

proximate cause of plaintiff's injury.[13] A surface reading of the Wisconsin cases produces a similar conclusion. That state has adopted the very general "substantial contribution" test of the *Restatement of Torts*.[14] For the most part the Supreme Court of Wisconsin has struggled with proximate cause issues through the years in a manner not dissimilar to that in states that have not adopted the *Restatement* test.

Blameworthiness Affecting Proximate Cause

In Wisconsin, in apportioning negligence between two or more persons, the jury is permitted to consider both the degree of blameworthiness and the nature of the causal relation.[15] Of course, the court must first determine whether the jury may find defendant's conduct a legal or proximate cause of the accident. The Wisconsin court has said that defendant's negligence must have made a substantial contribution to the accident or injury;[16] underlying the court's determination of this issue "lurks the idea of responsibility."[17]

The fact that comparative negligence applies may have a bearing on the court's determination whether defendant's negligence made a substantial contribution. For example, in *Cirillo v. City of Milwaukee*,[18] plaintiff suffered injuries in a gymnasium class when he was pushed to the floor by fellow students. The plaintiff sought to hold the teacher responsible because he had absented himself from the class of forty-eight high school boys for over twenty-five minutes. In other states, it is likely that plaintiff would not have a claim; a court would determine that the proximate cause of the injury was either plaintiff's own conduct or the act of the boys who pushed him down.[19] Nevertheless, the Supreme Court of Wisconsin held that the defendant's absence could be considered a substantial factor in plaintiff's injuries.

Careful reading of the *Cirillo* case suggests that the court was influenced by the fact that it could apportion responsibility under comparative negligence. The defendant-teacher would not be responsible for the entire damage; some would be apportioned to the plaintiff him-

---

[13]See Miss. Code Ann., § 11-7-17, annotations under "Proximate cause." See also Standard Furniture Co. v. Wallace, 288 So. 2d 461 (Miss. 1974) (plaintiff involved in collision with two vehicles; court found the faulty brakes of one, while negligence per se, not to be a contributing cause of the accident and allowed recovery only against the other). A Florida court ordered a new trial to determine whether defendant's negligence proximately caused injuries to a young go-cart driver, a finding which would permit recovery for the plaintiff under comparative negligence. Balart v. Michel's Kartway, Inc., 364 So. 2d 90 (Fla. App. 1978).

[14]See Schultz v. Brogan, 251 Wis. 390, 29 N.W.2d 719 (1947). See also *Restatement (Second) of Torts* § 465 (1965).

[15]See Kohler v. Dumke, 13 Wis. 2d 211, 108 N.W.2d 581 (1961).

[16]See Schultz v. Brogan, 251 Wis. 390, 29 N.W.2d 719, 721 (1947).

[17]*Restatement of Torts* § 431, Comment a (1934), quoted in Schultz v. Brogan, 251 Wis. 390, 29 N.W.2d 719, 721 (1947).

[18]Cirillo v. City of Milwaukee, 34 Wis. 2d 705, 150 N.W.2d 460 (1967).

[19]See, e.g., District of Columbia v. Cassidy, 465 A.2d 395 (D.C. App. 1983); Ohman v. Board of Education, 300 N.Y. 306, 90 N.E.2d 474 (1949); Guyten v. Rhodes, 65 Ohio App. 163, 18 Ohio Op. 356, 29 N.E.2d 444 (1940).

self and some to the boys who pushed him down. The fact that the court could limit the defendant's responsibility in the primary litigation allowed it to temper a proximate cause limitation extant in other states.

In a similar case, the California Supreme Court, in *Hoyem v. Manhattan Beach City School District*,[20] indicated that if it could be proved that a pupil's off-school premises injury was proximately caused by the school district's negligent supervision, the district may be held liable for the resulting damages. Judge Tobriner reasoned that a jury may well conclude that the defendant school district could have reasonably foreseen the temptation of the student to leave the school premises, and that the conduct of the third-party motorcyclist did not necessarily represent a superseding cause which would cut off the district's liability. Thus, the proximate cause issue should have been submitted to the jury.

In *George v. Guerette*[21] the Supreme Court of Maine noted the recent adoption of comparative negligence might render a proximate cause instruction on "unavoidable accident" confusing. The court held that it should no longer be used in the state. Maine courts, unlike those in other states, determine liability entirely on the basis of causation; culpability is considered at the damages phase of jury deliberations.[22]

In 1978 a federal district court in *Bangor & A. R. Company v. The Ship Fernview*[23] apportioned the liability between the parties, since the negligence of both parties proximately caused the accident, notwithstanding a presumption that a moving vessel that strikes a stationary object is at fault.

In dictum, the Supreme Court of Wisconsin was even more explicit in regard to this point. The court stated:

> The contribution of [substantial factors] under our comparative negligence doctrine are all considered and determined in terms of percentages of total cause.

> Under this concept of causation, the act of knowingly allowing a minor who is intoxicated or who might reasonably become so to drive an automobile might well lie in the chain of causation if such intoxication contributed to an injury and might be considered a substantial factor along with other substantial factors.[24]

The lesson of these opinions is clear. Cases in which, prior to the

---

[20]Hoyem v. Manhattan Beach City School Dist., 22 Cal. 3d 508, 150 Cal. Rptr. 1, 585 P.2d 851 (1978).

[21]George v. Guerette, 306 A.2d 138 (Me. 1973).

[22]Id., 306 A.2d at 144. See also Jackson v. Frederick's Motor Inn, 418 A.2d 168 (Me. 1980), noted, 34 Me. L. Rev. 207 (1982). In *Jackson* the jury found the defendant liable under Maine's modified comparative negligence rule but reduced the plaintiff's damages by more than half; the Maine Supreme Court upheld the verdict on the ground that causation and blameworthiness could be considered separately.

[23]Bangor & A. R. Co. v. The Ship Fernview, 455 F. Supp. 1043 (D. Me. 1978).

[24]Blashaski v. Classified Risk Ins. Corp., 48 Wis. 2d 169, 179 N.W.2d 924, 927 (1970) (dictum). See also Dwyer v. Erie Invest. Co., 138 N.J. Super. 93, 350 A.2d 268 (1975).

adoption of comparative negligence, plaintiff might have lost under proximate cause rules, because the acts of plaintiff or third parties were regarded as a "supervening cause," may now be sent to the jury for decision because it can reach a "fair" decision by apportioning some of the blame to defendant and some to third parties or to the plaintiff himself.

Under comparative negligence *the jury* can still find defendant's negligence as the sole proximate cause and not be required to apportion damages at all.[25]

Causation Under F.E.L.A.

A more dramatic change in proximate cause rules—one that is easier to spot—has occurred in the application of comparative negligence under the Federal Employers' Liability Act. The Supreme Court of the United States indicated in *Rogers v. Missouri Pacific Railroad Company*[26] that the railroad should be liable whenever its negligence "played any part, however small, in the injury or death which is the subject of the suit."[27] While it is not crystal clear how much this test departs from traditional proximate cause, the new phraseology shows that the reach of causation is broader under F.E.L.A. than at common law.[28]

In *Patterson v. Norfolk & Western Railway Company*,[29] for example, a railroad employee who contracted tuberculosis from a co-worker recovered from the employer for negligently failing to provide a safe place to work.

Under the Jones Act, even the slightest negligence of the employer justifies some recovery by the seaman.[30]

A Kansas railroad company was successful in bringing into the suit a third-party defendant, by filing a claim against the company for its negligence in contributing to the decedent's cause of death.[31]

It is unlikely that the F.E.L.A. cases will be applied to general comparative negligence acts adopted in the states. The Supreme Court in *Rogers* was attempting to implement a general congressional purpose to allow recovery to injured railroad employees for injuries suffered in the course of employment whenever there is any rational basis for doing so; such a purpose is peculiar to the F.E.L.A. and therefore

---

[25]Mosca v. Middleton, 342 So. 2d 986 (Fla. App. 1977), cert. den. 354 So. 2d 983 (Fla. 1977).

[26]Rogers v. Missouri P. R. Co., 352 U.S. 500, 1 L. Ed. 2d 493, 77 S. Ct. 443 (1957), reh. den. 353 U.S. 943, 1 L. Ed. 2d 764, 77 S. Ct. 808 (1957).

[27]Id., 352 U.S. at 508, 77 S. Ct. at 449. See also Adams v. Seaboard C. L. R. Co., 296 So. 2d 1 (Fla. 1974).

[28]See Note, *Legal Cause, Proximate Cause, and Comparative Negligence in the F.E.L.A.*, 18 Stan. L. Rev. 929 (1966). But see Ledford v. Pittsburgh & L. E. R. Co., 236 Pa. Super. 65, 345 A.2d 218 (1975) (if there is no causal connection between the defendant's negligence and the injury, recovery is barred even under the F.E.L.A.).

[29]Patterson v. Norfolk & W. R. Co., 489 F.2d 303 (6th Cir. Mich. 1973).

[30]Spinks v. Chevron Oil Co., 507 F.2d 216 (5th Cir. La. 1975), clarified 546 F.2d 675 (5th Cir. La. 1977).

[31]Soper v. Kansas City S. R. Co., 77 F.R.D. 665 (D. Kan. 1978).

would be unlikely to have application elsewhere. In addition, F.E.L.A. applies pure comparative negligence so that *any* causal negligence on the part of the employer would justify *some* recovery by the employee.

4.4   Plaintiff's negligence as the sole proximate cause

Traditionally it has been argued in support of the contributory negligence defense that plaintiff should not recover when his negligence is the "proximate cause" of the accident.[32] As the late Dean Prosser demonstrated, this rationale is unsupportable because it assigns to "proximate cause" a meaning that is broader than that utilized in other situations.[33] Usually there are a number of causes that may be deemed proximate as long as each was a substantial factor in producing the accident.[34]

A plaintiff who, for reasons of policy, cannot be charged with contributory negligence may be barred from recovery because he was the sole proximate cause of the accident. Thus, in *Korbelik v. Johnson*[35] a five-year-old child who darted in front of a car was denied recovery because her conduct was the sole proximate cause of her injuries. This was true in spite of the fact that she was legally incapable of contributory negligence.

The linkage between "proximate cause" and contributory negligence can eviscerate the underlying purpose of a comparative negligence system. Even in cases where there are other contributing causes, a court may hold that plaintiff's claim is barred because his negligence was the "sole proximate cause" of the accident. In effect, the contributory negligence defense returns under a different name.

Violation of Rules Under F.E.L.A.

Prior to 1943, plaintiffs in F.E.L.A. cases could not recover if they had violated a company rule or order and the violation contributed to the injury or accident. The Supreme Court of the United States had said that plaintiff's violation was the "sole proximate cause" of his injury.[36] In 1943, however, the Supreme Court retreated from this position and treated violation of company rules as a form of assumption of risk, which had, in effect, been eliminated as an absolute defense by a 1938 amendment to the Act.[37] Nevertheless, the late Dean Prosser

---

[32]See Annot., "The doctrine of comparative negligence and its relation to the doctrine of contributory negligence," 32 A.L.R.3d 463, 470 (1970). See also Pittman v. Volusia County, 380 So. 2d 1192 (Fla. App. 1980).

[33]See W. P. Keeton et al., *Prosser and Keeton on the Law of Torts* § 65 at 452 (5th ed. 1984).

[34]Id.

[35]Korbelik v. Johnson, 193 Neb. 356, 227 N.W.2d 21 (1975).

[36]Great N. R. Co. v. Wiles, 240 U.S. 444, 60 L. Ed. 732, 36 S. Ct. 406 (1916).

[37]Tiller v. Atlantic C. L. R. Co., 318 U.S. 54, 63-64, 87 L. Ed. 610, 63 S. Ct. 444, 143 A.L.R. 967 (1943).

found cases which still applied the discarded rationale;[38] it is one that might arise in the future.

Sole Proximate Cause in Mississippi

In Mississippi defendant will prevail if he can persuade the jury that the plaintiff's conduct was the "sole proximate cause" of the accident.[39] This is extremely important under pure comparative negligence, for it provides one way a defendant can defeat plaintiff's claim even though both parties were negligent. Thus, in *Bates v. Walker*,[40] plaintiff alleged that the accident was caused by the defendant's failure to observe his automobile at a crossroad but defendant argued that the accident was caused solely by plaintiff's proceeding through a red flashing light. A jury was permitted to decide that plaintiff's negligence was the sole proximate cause of the accident.

The Train Crossing Cases

In *Illinois Central Railroad Company v. Smith*,[41] plaintiff's decedent was killed when his automobile was hit by a moving train. The jury returned a verdict for the plaintiff and the defendant appealed on the ground that decedent's failure to stop, look and listen was the sole proximate cause of the accident. The Supreme Court of Mississippi reexamined the evidence and determined that decedent did not see or hear the train because he was neither looking nor listening; it concluded that "the decedent's failure to look or listen for the train was the sole proximate cause of the collision of the train with his automobile. . . ."[42]

A dissent in the *Smith* case pointed out how close a case of this kind can be. It found evidence that the train could have stopped in time but that the defendant's fireman negligently thought that a brake valve was to be used only when an engineer dropped dead.[43] Less than a year later in a strikingly similar case, the Supreme Court of Mississippi let the jury decide whether a decedent who entered a railroad crossing had been the "sole proximate cause" of his own death.[44]

Arguably, the train crossing cases may be nothing more than decisions on cause in fact; even if the defendant had not been negligent, plaintiff would have been injured.[45] However, not all the crossing cases

---

[38]See Prosser, *Comparative Negligence*, 51 Mich. L. Rev. 465, 495 (1953).

[39]See Bates v. Walker, 232 Miss. 804, 100 So. 2d 611 (1958); Salster v. Singer Sewing Machine Co., 361 F. Supp. 1056 (N.D. Miss. 1973).

[40]Bates v. Walker, 232 Miss. 804, 100 So. 2d 611 (1958).

[41]Illinois C. R. Co. v. Smith, 243 Miss. 766, 140 So. 2d 856 (1962).

[42]Id., 140 So. 2d at 859.

[43]Id.

[44]Green v. Gulf, M. & O. R. Co., 244 Miss. 211, 141 So. 2d 216 (1962). See also Newman v. Missouri P. R. Co., 545 F.2d 439 (5th Cir. Miss. 1977) (determination of whether failing to stop at railroad crossing constitutes negligence is a question for the finder of fact).

[45]See New Orleans & N. R. Co. v. Dixie Highway Express, Inc., 230 Miss. 92, 92 So. 2d 455 (1957).

could be so characterized,[46] and it is arguable that on occasion in Mississippi, the contributory negligence defense comes back into the law under the rubric "sole proximate cause."

Sole Proximate Cause in Minnesota

Recent Minnesota cases have followed Mississippi's interpretation of sole proximate cause. In two automobile collision cases[47] the jury found the defendant negligent, but denied recovery on the ground that the defendant's negligence did not contribute to the happening of the accident. Both were cases in which the court could have found the plaintiff's negligence as great or greater than the defendant's and denied recovery without reaching proximate cause.

Sole Proximate Cause in Wisconsin

In contrast to Mississippi, Wisconsin appears very circumspect about barring a claim on the ground that plaintiff's conduct was the "sole proximate cause" of the accident. For example, in *Menden v. Wisconsin Electric Power Company*[48] a maintenance man was killed when he took hold of live wires which defendant had negligently maintained. Decedent handled the live wires although he knew they were "hot" and that there was no immediate need to do so. In those circumstances, the Supreme Court of Wisconsin deemed decedent's act an intervening cause and barred the claim. Nevertheless, the court in dictum said that had there been any need for immediate intervention or if the wires had not clearly appeared "hot" or "live," the jury would have been permitted to compare decedent's negligence with that of the defendant.[49] Even under the facts before it, the court relied on an alternative holding that the decedent's negligence was "greater" than that of the defendant.

More recently in Wisconsin, a plaintiff claimed injuries from a fall into an open elevator pit.[50] The defense sought to avoid application of the comparative negligence statute by arguing that plaintiff's walking into the pit without assuring himself that the elevator was there was an intervening and supervening proximate cause of the accident, thereby terminating defendant's responsibility. The court declined to accept this proposition but rather treated plaintiff's causal negligence as con-

---

[46]See Green v. Gulf, M. & O. R. Co., 244 Miss. 211, 141 So. 2d 216 (1962); Thompson v. Mississippi C. R. Co., 175 Miss. 547, 564, 166 So. 353, 357 (1936) (dissenting opinion).

[47]Ramirez v. Miska, 304 Minn. 4, 228 N.W.2d 871 (1975) (plaintiff failed to brake his car; defendant may have been speeding); Vanderweyst v. Langford, 303 Minn. 575, 228 N.W.2d 271 (1975) (plaintiff failed to brake, use lights, and maintain a proper lookout; defendant may have braked improperly and may have been speeding).

[48]Menden v. Wisconsin Elec. Power Co., 240 Wis. 87, 2 N.W.2d 856 (1942).

[49]Id., 2 N.W.2d at 858.

[50]See Presser v. Siesel Constr. Co., 19 Wis. 2d 54, 119 N.W.2d 405 (1963).

tributory negligence and therefore subject to comparison with defendant's fault in failing to maintain barricades.[51]

The Wisconsin Supreme Court in *Leckwee v. Gibson*[52] found multiple acts of negligence of both parties to a motorcycle-automobile collision as factors to be considered in apportioning causal negligence. The Court held that the automobile driver's acts were the "dominant causes" of the accident and were thus, as a matter of law, at least as negligent as the acts of the motorcyclist.

Summary

It may be that, under pure comparative negligence, the defense that plaintiff's negligence in the accident was the "sole proximate cause" of the injury should be preserved in order to avoid placing liability upon a defendant whose responsibility for the occurrence was extremely limited. In other situations, defendant can be protected by the apportionment of damages and courts should not thwart legislative intent by bringing back the contributory negligence defense under the label "sole proximate cause."

4.5 Plaintiff's negligence as a contributing proximate cause

As noted in section 1.2, courts developed both explicit and subtle limitations on the contributory negligence defense. One of the most subtle distinctions was based on the concept of proximate cause. Frequently, plaintiff was able to avoid the contributory negligence defense by convincing the court that his negligence was not a "proximate cause"[53] of the injury or that plaintiff was not negligent with respect to the particular hazard that injured him.[54] In effect, a general rule developed that a negligent plaintiff was not barred when his failure to exercise reasonable care for his own safety resulted in injury from a differ-

---

[51]Id., 119 N.W.2d at 409. See also Siblik v. Motor Transport Co., 262 Wis. 242, 55 N.W.2d 8 (1952) (plaintiff caught his hand under a tire); McGuire v. Ford Motor Co., 360 F. Supp. 447 (E.D. Wis. 1973) (plaintiffs pushing stalled car were not sole proximate cause relieving manufacturer of liability). But see Collins v. Ridge Tool Co., 520 F.2d 591 (7th Cir. Wis. 1975) (plaintiff plumber injured by pipe-cutting machine was 100% responsible under Wisconsin law since the machine was an open and obvious hazard). See also Jacobs v. Stack, 63 Wis. 2d 672, 218 N.W.2d 364 (1974).

[52]Leckwee v. Gibson, 90 Wis. 2d 275, 280 N.W.2d 186 (1979). See also Stewart v. Wulf, 85 Wis. 2d 461, 271 N.W.2d 79 (1978) (trial court has a duty to announce when causal negligence of plaintiff is greater than that of defendant).

[53]See Montambault v. Waterbury & Milldale Tramway Co., 98 Conn. 584, 120 A. 145 (1923); Dewire v. Boston & M. R. Co., 148 Mass. 343, 19 N.E. 523, 2 L.R.A. 166 (1889); Guile v. Greenberg, 192 Minn. 548, 257 N.W. 649 (1934).

[54]See Furukawa v. Ogawa, 236 F.2d 272 (9th Cir. Cal. 1956); Smithwick v. Hall & Upson Co., 59 Conn. 261, 21 A. 924, 12 L.R.A. 279, 21 Am. St. Rep. 104 (1890); Gray & Bell v. Scott, 66 Pa. 345, 5 Am. Rep. 371 (1870). See also Note, *Contributory Negligence Towards a Hazard Other Than That Causing Injury; Recommended Changes in Application*, 1958 Wash. U.L.Q. 111; Note, *Negligence—Contributory Negligence—Causal Relation Required*, 22 Minn. L. Rev. 410 (1938); Note, *Plaintiff's Violation of a Statute as Affecting Recovery for Negligence—Proximate Cause*, 41 Ky. L.J. 317 (1953).

ent "risk" or different "hazard" than that which made him negligent in
the first place.[55]

Foreseeability As Part of Contributory Negligence Defense

In the abstract, proximate cause concepts applied to plaintiff's negligence should be the equivalent of those applied to defendant's negligence.[56] Nevertheless, courts operating under the contributory negligence doctrine have often been grudging in defining a foreseeable risk or hazard for the purpose of determining plaintiff's negligence. The legal effect of this attitude has been to limit the contributory negligence defense.

For example, in *Furukawa v. Ogawa*,[57] plaintiff was injured by a fall from a refuse-laden ramp into a garbage pit. He knew that the debris on the ramp created or increased the risk of falling. When plaintiff fell, his leg caught on a projection from defendant's truck parked in the pit below. The court upheld a verdict for the plaintiff on the ground that, while plaintiff may have been negligent with respect to the risk of falling, he was not necessarily negligent with regard to the risk of falling onto a projection from the truck. In effect, he was not negligent with respect to the projection because he did not know of it and did not appreciate the amount of danger in the fall!

In *Smithwick v. Hall & Upson Company*[58] plaintiff disregarded warnings not to work on the part of a slippery platform which lacked a guardrail. He was injured when a nearby wall collapsed and knocked him to the ground. The court held that plaintiff's contributory negligence did not bar his claim because he was damaged by an "entirely different" risk than the one that made him negligent. In another case, a plaintiff injured on a railroad track avoided the contributory negligence defense because the court determined he was negligent only with respect to the risk of being hit by eastbound, not westbound, trains.[59]

In effect, these and other courts have construed foreseeable risks more narrowly when the question was whether plaintiff's contributory negligence was a proximate cause of his injuries than when the question was whether defendant's conduct was a proximate cause of the accident. This is relatively easy to do because there is no fixed way of defining "risks."[60]

A Change Under Comparative Negligence?

It may be questioned whether courts will, under comparative negligence, continue to construe risks narrowly when deciding whether

---

[55]See W. P. Keeton et al., *Prosser and Keeton on the Law of Torts* § 65, at 457-458 (5th ed. 1984); *Restatement (Second) of Torts* § 468 (1965).

[56]See Green, *Contributory Negligence and Proximate Cause*, 6 N.C. L. Rev. 3 (1927).

[57]Furukawa v. Ogawa, 236 F.2d 272 (9th Cir. Cal. 1956).

[58]Smithwick v. Hall & Upson Co., 59 Conn. 261, 21 A. 924, 12 L.R.A. 279, 21 Am. St. Rep. 104 (1890).

[59]Kinderavich v. Palmer, 127 Conn. 85, 15 A.2d 83 (1941).

[60]See R. Keeton, *Legal Cause in the Law of Torts* (1963).

plaintiff's negligent conduct was the proximate cause of his injuries. An examination of the Mississippi and Wisconsin cases suggests that the construction would change.[61] For example, in the case of the plaintiff who knowingly walked on the slippery ramp and fell onto a projection, a court might say the foreseeable hazard was falling. The same might be true of the plaintiff in the *Smithwick* case: the foreseeable risk might be held to be falling from the platform.

Again, the plaintiff who was hit by a westbound rather than an eastbound train might find that his contributory negligence was now being considered and compared. A court might hold that by going upon the track he ran the risk of being hit by a train.

The reason that a more equitable handling of foreseeable risk issues as between plaintiff and defendant is likely to occur under comparative negligence is that the court is no longer constrained to find an escape from the contributory negligence defense.[62] Of course, where the accident that befell a plaintiff is different from the risk he might have anticipated, this can and should be taken into account by the jury in determining plaintiff's relative degree of negligence in any comparative negligence system. In *Thoen v. Lanesboro School District No. 229,*[63] plaintiff's failure to wear a hard hat while working on a power line did not expose him to a foreseeable risk of head injury when struck by a school bus.

The line drawn on foreseeable risks under comparative negligence may be quite fine. For example, if a plaintiff in Georgia knowingly rides in a car with an intoxicated driver, his negligence may be compared with that of the driver, but not with that of a defendant in another car involved in a collision,[64] unless the plaintiff contributes to the happening of the accident.[65]

In a Texas case plaintiff failed to act as an ordinarily prudent person when he deliberately walked into a pool of wax to retrieve a hose; the court determined that this behavior was a contributing cause of the injury and therefore reduced plaintiff's recovery.[66]

In sum, a comparative negligence system allows a court to be more "even-handed" with the application of proximate cause concepts in

---

[61]Cf. Daves v. Reed, 222 So. 2d 411 (Miss. 1969).

[62]Cf. Note, *Contributory Negligence Towards A Hazard Other Than That Causing Injury; Recommended Changes in Application,* 1958 Wash. U.L.Q. 111. See Adams v. Mackleer, 239 Pa. Super. 244, 361 A.2d 439 (1976) (lack of headlight on bicycle precludes recovery only if its absence was a proximate cause of the accident).

[63]Thoen v. Lanesboro School Dist. No. 229, 296 Minn. 252, 209 N.W.2d 924 (1973).

[64]Jones v. Petroleum Carrier Corp., 483 F.2d 1369 (5th Cir. Ga. 1973); Petroleum Carrier Corp. v. Jones, 127 Ga. App. 676, 194 S.E.2d 670 (1972).

[65]Ullman v. Overnite Transp. Co., 508 F.2d 676 (5th Cir. Ga. 1975) (served a driver drinks).

[66]Guffey v. Borden, Inc., 595 F.2d 1111 (5th Cir. Tex. 1979). See also Parker v. Highland Park, Inc., 565 S.W.2d 512 (Tex. 1978) (negligence of both plaintiff and defendant must be compared so long as there is a finding of proximate cause in each case). The Texas Supreme Court abolished the "duty to warn" doctrine regarding open and obvious dangers in the same case.

regard to both plaintiffs and defendants. Because of this, lawyers and courts should be suspicious of old contributory negligence cases where the "risk" or "hazard" incurred by plaintiff's contributory negligence was narrowly confined by courts.

F.E.L.A. Standards

It would seem unlikely that a plaintiff's award would be reduced under a comparative negligence system if his negligence were not a proximate cause of his injury under general principles of common law. Nevertheless, this result was suggested in *Page v. St. Louis Southwestern Railway Company*,[67] in an opinion interpreting the comparative negligence section of the Federal Employers' Liability Act.[68] The *Page* opinion focused on the fact that the Supreme Court of the United States had replaced the common-law "proximate cause" requirement with a rule that allowed recovery whenever defendant's negligence "played any part, however small, in the injury or death which is the subject of the suit."[69] A major tenet of the *Page* opinion was that a system of comparative negligence will not work unless the test for causation is the same for both parties—that is, unless a single standard of legal cause is applied to both.[70] Therefore, if plaintiff's negligence "played any part, however small" in causing the accident, it may be considered by the jury and plaintiff's award reduced. In effect, if plaintiff was negligent in any respect the jury may consider this, even though the hazard that in fact caused plaintiff's injury was totally unforeseeable.[71]

The logic of abandoning common-law concepts of proximate cause with regard to either plaintiff's or defendant's conduct is unsound. One function of a legal cause standard in a comparative negligence system is to signify when a comparison is to be made. The court can make that determination. As one commentator has pointed out, "the legal cause test not only tells the jury when a comparison is to be made but also what is to be compared."[72] It should be utilized for both parties. It has been argued that, because the general legislative purpose behind the F.E.L.A. was to increase the likelihood that performing the hazardous occupation of railroading would be compensated in the event of job-related injuries,[73] a dual standard of proximate causation under F.E.L.A. might be justified. Some courts have taken that position, purportedly influenced by their reading of the legislative history of the

---

[67]See Page v. St. Louis S. R. Co., 349 F.2d 820, 822-824 (5th Cir. Tex. 1965) (dictum).

[68]Act of April 22, 1908, ch. 149, 35 Stat. 66, 45 U.S.C. § 53.

[69]See Rogers v. Missouri P. R. Co., 352 U.S. 500, 508, 1 L. Ed. 2d 493, 77 S. Ct. 443, 449 (1957), reh. den. 353 U.S. 943, 1 L. Ed. 764, 77 S. Ct. 808 (1957).

[70]Page v. St. Louis S. R. Co., 349 F.2d 820, 824 (5th Cir. Tex. 1965).

[71]See Note, *Legal Cause, Proximate Cause, and Comparative Negligence in the F.E.L.A.*, 18 Stan. L. Rev. 929, 935 (1966).

[72]Id., at 935.

[73]See Rogers v. Missouri P. R. Co., 352 U.S. 500, 507-508, 1 L. Ed. 2d 493, 77 S. Ct. 443, 449 (1957).

F.E.L.A.[74] Nevertheless, today there is little or no evidence that the occupation of a railroad worker is more hazardous than, for example, driving a taxicab on the streets of New York.[75]

In the ordinary comparative negligence statute, unless a court can find sound policy reasons for a difference in the context of a particular kind of case, proximate cause tests for defendant and plaintiff should be the same. Comparative negligence itself is flexible enough to provide for a fair disposition of the matter in the context of the fault system; further plaintiff "helping" is unnecessary.

4.6 Plaintiff's negligence increasing injury

A fact pattern that presented a riddle to the common law was plaintiff's negligent conduct prior to an accident that "played no part in bringing about the accident" but rather "aggravated the ensuing damages."[76] A number of courts reasoned that such conduct could not be contributory negligence because it did not contribute to the happening of the accident.[77] Further, plaintiff's damages could not be reduced under the "avoidable consequences rule" because that only "comes into play after a legal wrong has occurred, but while some damages may still be averted. . . ."[78]

In *Brazil v. United States,*[79] subsequent acts of the plaintiff which further aggravated his injuries were held by an Alabama district court to reduce the amount of his recovery.

The Seat Belt Cases

How to handle plaintiff's negligence when it aggravates his injuries but does not cause the accident is a frequent practical problem today. It has arisen where plaintiff automobile passenger failed to fasten an available seat belt,[80] or where an injured motorcyclist failed to wear a protective helmet or use other safety equipment.[81] The overwhelming majority of courts have declined to treat such conduct as contributory

---

[74]See Missouri-Kansas-Texas R. Co. v. Shelton, 383 S.W.2d 842 (Tex. Civ. App. 1964).

[75]See Note, *Legal Cause, Proximate Cause and Comparative Negligence in the F.E.L.A.*, 18 Stan. L. Rev. 929, 933, n. 26 (1966).

[76]See W. P. Keeton et al., *Prosser and Keeton on the Law of Torts* § 65, at 459 (5th ed. 1984).

[77]See Mahoney v. Beatman, 110 Conn. 184, 147 A. 762, 66 A.L.R. 1121 (1929); Hamilton v. Boyd, 218 Iowa 885, 256 N.W. 290 (1934). See also Comment, *Mahoney v. Beatman: A Study in Proximate Cause,* 39 Yale L. J. 532 (1930). Kerby v. Abilene Christian College, 503 S.W.2d 526 (Tex. 1973) (driving with school bus door open not causal negligence).

[78]W. P. Keeton et al., note 76 above, § 65, at 458.

[79]Brazil v. United States, 484 F. Supp. 986 (N.D. Ala. 1979). Alabama is still a contributory negligence state.

[80]Annot., "Automobile occupant's failure to use seat belt as contributory negligence," 92 A.L.R.3d 1025 (1974); Annot., "Nonuse of automobile seatbelts as evidence of comparative negligence," 95 A.L.R.3d 239 (1977).

[81]See Dare v. Sobule, 674 P.2d 960 (Colo. 1984); Annot., "Failure of motorcyclist to wear protective helmet or other safety equipment as contributory negligence, assumption of risk, or failure to avoid consequences of accident," 40 A.L.R.3d 856 (1971).

negligence.[82] These decisions are based, in part, on the proposition that it is too harsh to deny all recovery to a plaintiff whose only failure was to buckle a seat belt or wear a helmet—failures which in no way contributed to the happening of the accident.[83] Of course, in the unusual case where failure to wear a seat belt is a cause in fact of the accident, the jury may consider whether the plaintiff was negligent in not using the belt and may allocate fault accordingly.[84]

Certainly, it is unfair to bar plaintiff's claim when his alleged negligent act contributed to only part of his injuries. Recognizing this, some courts have applied logic and common sense: they have, in effect, applied comparative negligence for apportionment of damages in this very limited situation.[85]

The Seat Belt Under Comparative Negligence

When a state has a general system of comparative negligence, apportioning damages is much easier in seat-belt cases because the courts are accustomed to dealing with damage apportionment between negligent plaintiffs and defendants. This may explain why Wisconsin is one of the few states to give any recognition to the so-called seat-belt defense.[86]

New York and Florida courts allow the plaintiff's nonuse of a seat

---

[82]See Britton v. Doehring, 286 Ala. 498, 242 So. 2d 666 (1970) (collecting seat belt cases); Rogers v. Frush, 257 Md. 233, 262 A.2d 549, 40 A.L.R.3d 847 (1970) (helmet case). Accord, Amend v. Bell, 89 Wash. 2d 124, 570 P.2d 138, 95 A.L.R.3d 225 (1977); Pritts v. Walter Lowery Trucking Co., 400 F. Supp. 867 (W.D. Pa. 1975); Ford Motor Co. v. Bland, 517 S.W.2d 641 (Tex. Civ. App. 1974); Nash v. Kamrath, 21 Ariz. App. 530, 521 P.2d 161 (1974); King Son Wong v. Carnation Co., 509 S.W.2d 385 (Tex. Civ. App. 1974), affd. 516 S.W.2d 116 (Tex. 1974); Birdsong v. ITT Continental Baking Co., 160 Ind. App. 411, 312 N.E.2d 104 (1974); Churning v. Staples, 628 P.2d 180 (Colo. App. 1981); Taplin v. Clark, 6 Kan. App. 2d 66, 626 P.2d 1198 (1981). See also Breault v. Ford Motor Co., 364 Mass. 352, 305 N.E.2d 824 (1973) (nonuse of seat belt not assumption of risk); accord, Melesko v. Riley, 32 Conn. Supp. 89, 339 A.2d 479 (1975). See also Kopischke v. First Continental Corp., 187 Mont. 471, 610 P.2d 668 (1980); Polyard v. Terry, 148 N.J. Super. 202, 372 A.2d 379 (1977), revd. on other grounds 160 N.J. Super. 497, 390 A.2d 653 (1978) (no duty to wear seat belt, therefore no contributory negligence).

[83]See Berger, *The Seat Belt Defense—Rejection by the Majority of Courts*, A.B.A. Law Notes (July 1969); Note, *The Emerging Seat Belt Defense: Two Views*, 5 Akron L. Rev. 129 (1972).

[84]Curry v. Moser, 89 A.D.2d 1, 454 N.Y.S.2d 311 (1982) (plaintiff fell out of the car when door opened on a turn, and was run over by the following car).

[85]See Mays v. Dealers Transit, Inc., 441 F.2d 1344 (7th Cir. Ind. 1971) (anticipating Indiana law); Barry v. Coca Cola Co., 99 N.J. Super. 270, 239 A.2d 273 (1967); Walker and Beck, *Seat Belts and the Second Accident*, 34 Ins. Couns. J. 349, 352 (1967). See also Werber, *A Multidisciplinary Approach to Seat Belt Issues*, 29 Clev. St. L. Rev. 217 (1980) (collecting arguments and factual support for the defense).

[86]See Foley v. West Allis, 113 Wis. 2d 475, 335 N.W.2d 824 (1983). See also Grobe v. Valley Garbage Service, Inc., 87 Wash. 2d 217, 551 P.2d 748 (1976) (declined to permit defendant to prove plaintiff was not wearing seat belt since contention was not part of the record originally certified, and plaintiff's preparation time was inadequate).

belt to be considered in the mitigation of damages, but not in determining liability.[87]

This is not to say that any state with comparative negligence will automatically adopt the seat-belt defense. The court may hold that the defense should not be allowed because it sets too high a standard of care (statutes usually require the installation but not the wearing of seat belts), or that it is impossible to determine precisely how the wearing of a seat belt would have mitigated damages.[88] The point is that if a court thinks that for reasons of policy it should recognize this defense, it can more readily and easily do so if its state has a general system of comparative negligence.[89]

For example, the Wisconsin Supreme Court readily understood that the seat-belt defense can be applied only when the defendant proves how the wearing of a seat belt would have reduced plaintiff's damages.[90] Further, the situation of a plaintiff whose failure to use care for his own safety only aggravates his injuries and in no way contributes to the happening of the accident itself fits within Wisconsin's developed concept of "passive" negligence.[91] Under the Wisconsin system, such negligence is relevant only to the claim brought by the passively negligent plaintiff against the actively negligent defendant; it is of no relevance in any counterclaim by the defendant. This is certainly logical and should be the approach taken in other comparative negligence jurisdictions regardless of the form that they have adopted.

Seat Belts—A Change in Public Policy?

Courts have often deferred to legislatures on the seat-belt issue; they have cited the American's general reluctance to wear belts and the legislatures' refusal to require their use as evidence that the reasonable person does not necessarily wear a seat belt. However, public policy appears to be changing;[92] recent developments in the automotive safety field may provide more forceful incentives to use seat belts. In

---

[87]Spier v. Barker, 35 N.Y.2d 444, 363 N.Y.S.2d 916, 323 N.E.2d 164, 80 A.L.R.3d 1025 (1974); Insurance Co. of North America v. Pasakarnis, 451 So. 2d 447 (Fla. 1984). See also Annot., "Nonuse of seat belt as failure to mitigate damages," 80 A.L.R.3d 1033 (1974).

[88]See Miller v. Miller, 273 N.C. 228, 160 S.E.2d 65 (1968); Fischer v. Moore, 183 Colo. 392, 517 P.2d 458 (1973); Amend v. Bell, 89 Wash. 2d 124, 570 P.2d 138, 95 A.L.R.3d 225 (1977); Berger, *The Seat Belt Defense—Rejection by the Majority of Courts*, A.B.A. Law Notes (July 1969).

[89]See, e.g., Ottem v. United States, 594 F. Supp. 283 (D. Minn. 1984) in which the court rendered damages in a motorcycle/automobile collision case. The court found that plaintiff's only negligence was his failure to wear a helmet; defendant's negligence was the sole proximate cause of the accident. Further, the plaintiff would have been totally and permanently disabled in any case. Accordingly, the court left the medical cost and lost income awards intact but reduced the pain and suffering award by 25%.

[90]See Bentzler v. Braun, 34 Wis. 2d 362, 149 N.W.2d 626 (1967). This is no easy matter. See Defense Research Institute, *The Seat Belt Defense in Practice* (Monograph No. 6, 1970).

[91]See Theisen v. Milwaukee Auto. Mut. Ins. Co., 18 Wis. 2d 91, 118 N.W.2d 140 (1962).

[92]See, e.g., Hampton v. State Highway Comm., 209 Kan. 565, 498 P.2d 236 (1972); Robinson v. Lewis, 254 Ore. 52, 457 P.2d 483 (1969).

July 1984 the National Highway and Traffic Safety Administration promulgated a rule allowing automobile manufacturers not to install air bags or passive belts should two-thirds of the U.S. population be covered by state mandatory use laws by 1989.[93]

So far, only New York has enacted a law that meets NHTSA standards requiring a $25 fine for noncompliance and allowing mitigation of damages in civil litigation.[94] As of May 1985, Illinois, Michigan, Missouri, New Mexico and New Jersey had enacted statutes that prescribe lesser fines or no mitigation of damages or both.[95] It has been suggested that such omissions are deliberate because some state legislatures want the air bag requirement to survive.[96]

The history of child safety seat laws indicates, absent political considerations, that statutes may go in any direction. Over the past few years, many states have enacted laws requiring drivers to secure small children or infant passengers in special safety seats.[97] Legislatures have often considered the effect the statute should have on civil liability. Some statutes simply bar admission of any evidence of noncompliance in a civil personal injury action.[98] Others say that evidence of noncompliance is inadmissible on "negligence," leaving open the question of admissibility on damages.[99] The District of Columbia statute also makes evidence of *compliance* with the statute inadmissible on contributory negligence.[1] Some of the large comparative negligence states have been silent on the question.[2] Wisconsin has taken a middle ground by making evidence of noncompliance admissible but not conclusive.[3] Admittedly there are policy considerations regarding helpless children that might not apply to adults. When New York enacted its mandatory

---

[93]49 Fed. Reg. 28,962 (1984).

[94]N.Y. Laws 1984, ch. 365.

[95]Ill. Laws 1984, 83-1507 (no diminution of recovery; noncompliance not evidence of negligence; fine not to exceed $25); Mich. Pub. Acts 1985, 1, § 1 (mitigation of damages not to exceed 5 percent; no specific fine; law to expire if federal government requires passive restraints); 1985 Mo. Legis. Serv. S. No. 43 (not comparative negligence; expert evidence required to mitigate damages; reduction in damages may not exceed 1% of damages *after* comparative negligence deduction); N.M. Laws 1985, ch. 131 ($25-$50 fine but no comparative negligence or fault; silent on mitigation); N.J. Laws 1984, ch. 179 (fine will not exceed $20 for a third offense).

[96]*Auto Makers and Safety Activists Reverse Usual Positions Regarding Seat Belt Laws*, Wall Street J., Jan. 3, 1985, at 13.

[97]See, e.g., Cal. Veh. Code, § 27360; D.C. Code Ann., § 40-1202; Fla. Stat. Ann., § 316.613; Minn. Stat. Ann., § 169.685.

[98]See, e.g., Minn. Stat. Ann., § 169.685; Md. Transp. Code Ann., § 22-412.2; S.D. Codified Laws, § 32-37-4.

[99]See, e.g., D.C. Code Ann., § 40-1207; Md. Transp. Code Ann., § 22-412.2(i); Fla. Stat. Ann., § 316.613(3).

[1]D.C. Code Ann., § 40-1207.

[2]See, e.g., Cal. Veh. Code, § 27360; N.Y. Veh. & Traf. Law, § 1229-c (before the 1984 amendment).

[3]Wis. Stat. Ann., § 347.48(d).

seat-belt law, it allowed noncompliance to be used to mitigate damages, thus leaving its judicially created seat-belt defense intact.[4]

The wearing of seat belts should be encouraged by tort law. The comparative negligence concept provides a practical way to reach this goal in a way that is also fair to both parties.

---

[4]N.Y. Laws 1984, ch. 365, § 1, applying to the infant seat statute as well.

CHAPTER 5

INTENTIONAL, RECKLESS, AND GROSSLY NEGLIGENT CONDUCT

Section

5.1 Introduction
5.2 Intentional torts
5.3 Willful, reckless, or grossly negligent conduct by defendant
5.4 Punitive damages for willful, reckless, or grossly negligent conduct
5.5 Willful, reckless, or grossly negligent conduct by plaintiff

5.1 Introduction

It has been a fundamental of common law that the contributory negligence defense is unavailable when defendant's conduct was *intended* to inflict harm upon the plaintiff.[1] Out of this basic rule a large number of courts in the United States derived other limitations on the contributory negligence defense: that it is unavailable when defendant's conduct was "willful," "wanton" or "reckless."[2] Some

---

[1]See W. P. Keeton et al., *Prosser and Keeton on the Law of Torts* § 65, at 412 (5th ed. 1984).

[2]See, e.g., Sun Oil Co. v. Seamon, 349 Mich. 387, 84 N.W. 2d 840 (1957); Cook v. Kinzua Pine Mills Co., 203 Ore. 34, 293 P.2d 717 (1956); Vaughn v. Baxter, 488 P.2d 1234 (Okla. 1971); Bennett v. Woodard, 60 Tenn. App. 20, 444 S.W.2d 89 (1969); Phelps v. Magnavox Co. of Tennessee, Inc., 62 Tenn. App. 578, 466 S.W.2d 226 (1970); Scott v. Instant Parking, Inc., 100 Ill. App. 2d 293, 241 N.E.2d 517 (1968); Maddox v. Hunt, 281 Ala. 335, 202 So. 2d 543, 28 A.L.R.3d 1373 (1967); Evans v. Pickett, 102 Ariz. 393, 430 P.2d 413 (1967); Scholz v. United States, 271 F. Supp. 111 (D. Conn. 1967); Green v. Millsboro Fire Co., 385 A.2d 1135 (Del. Super. 1978), modified 403 A.2d 286 (Del. 1979); DeElena v. Southern Pacific Co., 121 Ariz. 563, 592 P.2d 759 (1979); Harrington v. Collins, 298 N.C. 535, 259 S.E.2d 275 (1979); Hawkins v. Ivy, 50 Ohio St. 2d 114, 4 Ohio Op. 3d 243, 363 N.E.2d 367 (1977); Holloway v. Cronk, 76 Mich. App. 577, 257 N.W.2d 175 (1977); Iverson v. Iverson, 56 Ill. App. 3d 297, 13 Ill. Dec. 108, 370 N.E.2d 1135 (1977); Jackson v. Brantley, 378 So. 2d 1109 (Ala. App. 1979), affirmed ex parte 378 So. 2d 1112 (Ala. 1979); Jarvis v. Sanders, 34 N.C. App. 283, 237 S.E.2d 865 (1977); Junk v. East End Fire Dept., 262 Pa. Super. 473, 396 A.2d 1269 (1978); McKeown v. Calusa, 172 Ind. App. 1, 359 N.E.2d 550 (1977); Siders v. Gibbs, 39 N.C. App. 183, 249 S.E.2d 858 (1978); Miller v. United States, 442 F. Supp. 555 (N.D. Ill. 1976), affd. 597 F.2d 614 (7th Cir. Ill. 1979) (recovery warranted even if breach of duty of defendant was merely negligent rather than willful, as risk was hidden); Skinner v. Baker, 67 Ill. App. 3d 773, 24 Ill. Dec. 202, 384 N.E.2d 1360 (1978); Spring v. Toledo, P. & W. R. Co., 44 Ill. App. 3d 3, 2 Ill. Dec. 887, 357 N.E.2d 1330 (1976), affd. 69 Ill. 2d 290, 13 Ill. Dec. 686, 371 N.E.2d 621 (1977); Stephens v. United States, 472 F. Supp. 998 (C.D. Ill. 1979); Lostritto v. Southern Pacific Transp. Co., 73 Cal. App. 3d 737, 140 Cal. Rptr. 905 (1977). But see Southern Pacific Transp. Co. v. Lueck, 111. Ariz. 560, 535 P.2d 599 (1975) (an Arizona jury may balance the plaintiff's wanton contributory negligence against the defendant's wanton conduct so as to bar recovery); Ewing v. Cloverleaf Bowl, 20 Cal. 3d 389, 143 Cal. Rptr. 13, 572 P.2d 1155 (1978); O'Connor v. G & R Packing Co., 74 A.D.2d 37, 426 N.Y.S.2d 557 (1980); Wollaston v. Burlington Northern, Inc., 188 Mont. 192, 612 P.2d 1277 (1980).

See generally 2 F. Harper & F. James, *The Law of Torts* § 22.6 (1956); W. P. Keeton et al., note 1 above, § 65, at 462; *Restatement (Second) of Torts* §§ 481, 482, 500 (1965).

courts even extended the rule to situations in which defendant was "grossly negligent."[3]

Courts adopted these limitations on the contributory negligence defense, even while rejecting both last clear chance and comparative negligence,[4] because in these cases defendant's conduct was so culpable it was *qualitatively* different from the plaintiff's.[5] The basis of the limitation is culpability rather than causation. In effect, where the conduct of the defendant was highly culpable in that it showed a total disregard for plaintiff's safety, it would give too much power to the contributory negligence defense to bar a claim.

Modern Comparative Negligence Distinguished

The courts denying the contributory negligence defense in cases where defendants acted recklessly are not applying comparative negligence as we know it today. Damages are not apportioned; plaintiff obtains a full recovery.[6] On the other hand, the fault of the parties is compared and some courts have held that the contributory negligence defense returns if *both* parties are reckless.[7] At least one court refused to differentiate between negligence and gross negligence because this would invite comparisons by the jury as in a comparative negligence system.[8]

While it is true that, in order to apply the limitation in question, courts must characterize conduct as "willful," "wanton" or "reckless" conduct, most of the complexities of comparative negligence are avoided in applying this simple limitation on contributory negligence. Professors Harper and James perhaps described the limitation best in calling it "a step in the direction of comparative negligence, though a crude one."[9]

What happens to this limitation once a state converts to a comparative negligence system? Is a negligent plaintiff to recover some or all of his damages when the defendant's conduct was intentional, willful, reckless, or grossly negligent? A common-law plaintiff often obtains punitive damages when these legal labels are applied to defendant's

---

[3]See Astin v. Chicago, M. & St. P. R. Co., 143 Wis. 477, 128 N.W. 265 (1910), ovrld. Bielski v. Schulze, 16 Wis. 2d 1, 114 N.W.2d 105 (1962); Cole v. Woods, 548 S.W.2d 640 (Tenn. 1977).

[4]Melby v. Anderson, 64 S.D. 249, 266 N.W. 135 (1936) (equating "gross negligence" in the guest act with willful and wanton misconduct).

[5]See Falls v. Mortensen, 207 Ore. 130, 295 P.2d 182, 187 (1956), ovrld. on other grounds, Lindner v. Ahlgren, 257 Ore. 127, 477 P.2d 219 (1970).

[6]See 2 F. Harper & F. James, note 2 above, § 22.6; W. P. Keeton et al., note 1 above, § 65, at 462.

[7]See Elliott v. Philadelphia Transp. Co., 356 Pa. 643, 53 A.2d 81 (1947); Tabor v. O'Grady, 61 N.J. Super. 446, 161 A.2d 267 (1960); *Restatement (Second) of Torts* § 482(2) (1965).

[8]See Melby v. Anderson, 64 S.D. 249, 266 N.W. 135, 137 (1936). South Dakota later adopted comparative negligence.

[9]See 2 F. Harper & F. James, note 2 above, § 22.6, at 1215.

conduct.[10] Will punitive damages be available under comparative negligence? This chapter explores these questions and concludes with a short section on what happens under comparative negligence when *plaintiff's* conduct is "intentional," "willful," "reckless" or "grossly negligent."

5.2 Intentional torts

At common law, contributory negligence was not a defense to liability when defendant's conduct could be characterized as an intentional wrong.[11] Under comparative negligence, the result is likely to be the same and defendant will be unable to use plaintiff's negligence to diminish the award.[12]

Most of the comparative negligence statutes are clear on this.[13] The Massachusetts statute is typical in stating that "Contributory negligence shall not bar recovery in any action ... to recover damages for *negligence*," then going on to speak of diminution of damages.[14] The legislature was referring to claims predicated on negligent and not intentional wrongs. Plaintiff's negligence remains immaterial when he seeks relief for an intentional wrong.

In a Wisconsin case,[15] plaintiff, a man in his seventies, alleged that a relatively young, 278-pound defendant physically tossed him out of a meeting of the town council. Defendant contended that plaintiff had disturbed the orderly progress of the meeting of the council and, therefore, defendant's actions were privileged. The trial court permitted the jury to consider whether plaintiff's conduct should serve to reduce his award and it applied the comparative negligence statute.

The Supreme Court of Wisconsin recognized that plaintiff's claim was for battery, an intentional tort. Further, the court observed, the proper defense was based on privilege and the question for the jury was whether the privilege was exceeded.[16] The court stated:

> For some reason (perhaps the type of insurance coverage available to defendants, or some similar consideration), the parties treated the use of excessive force as merely negligent conduct, and considered

---

[10]See Sebastian v. Wood, 246 Iowa 94, 66 N.W. 2d 841 (1954); W. P. Keeton et al., note 1 above, § 2, at 9-10.

[11]See W. P. Keeton et al., *Prosser and Keeton on the Law of Torts* § 66, at 462 (5th ed. 1984). But see Sindle v. New York City Transit Authority, 33 N.Y.2d 293, 352 N.Y.S.2d 183, 307 N.E.2d 245 (1973) (teenager falsely imprisoned on school bus chose an unreasonable means of escape by climbing through a broken window and his claim was subject to the contributory negligence defense).

[12]See Schulze v. Kleeber, 10 Wis. 2d 540, 103 N.W.2d 560 (1960) (battery); Alsteen v. Gehl, 21 Wis. 2d 349, 124 N.W.2d 312 (1963) (intentional infliction of emotional harm).

[13]See, e.g., Mass. Gen. Laws Ann., ch. 231, § 85; Minn. Stat. Ann., § 604.01; Vt. Stat. Ann., tit. 12, § 1036.

[14]Mass. Gen. Laws Ann., ch. 231, § 85 (emphasis added).

[15]Schulze v. Kleeber, 10 Wis. 2d 540, 103 N.W.2d 560 (1960).

[16]Id., 103 N.W.2d at 564.

that the comparative negligence statute ... would apply if plaintiff
was negligent and the injury was caused by the conduct of both.

We consider that the questions in the special verdict as to [plain-
tiff's] negligence in resisting removal, and as to comparison of negligence were surplusage. Once the jury determined that [defendant]
used excessive force, the only remaining question pertinent to liability was whether the excessive force caused the injury.[17]

The general point is important with respect to comparative negligence statutes; if the defendant's conduct is intentional wrongdoing,
the statute has no application.[18] Of course, the attorney is left with the
problem of what is an intentional wrong. In most jurisdictions this
would include not only conduct inflicted with a wrongful purpose, but
also that engaged in when defendant knew "that a particular result
was substantially certain to follow."[19]

When evidence in a tort action demonstrated the existence of elements of an intentionally induced breach of contract by the defendant,
the Colorado Appeals Court in *Carman v. Heber*[20] reinstated a full
award of damages to the plaintiff, even though she had been found 40%
negligent. The comparative negligence statute was held inapplicable
upon this finding of the defendant's intentional wrongdoing.

Similarly, a federal court refused to apply Wyoming's comparative
negligence statute to a Section 1983 civil rights claim and pendent
state claims by a candidate for public office whose opponents, by their
allegedly outrageous conduct, blew his cover as a protected witness.[21]
The court held that the Wyoming statute was inapplicable to intentional as well as to willful and wanton conduct.

The Supreme Court of Utah refused to apply comparative negligence to a claim for battery in a barroom brawl.[22] The court held that
the trial court had correctly refused a comparative negligence instruction where it had given proper instructions on self-defense and mutual
combat.

Plaintiff's attorney should be alert to the possibility of characterizing a defendant's conduct as "intentional" as compared with negligent
or even grossly negligent; if a court adopts the attorney's perspective
on the facts, he will avoid the possibility that his client's damage award
will be reduced because he failed to act with reasonable care for his
own safety.

---

[17]Id.

[18]Id.; Alsteen v. Gehl, 21 Wis. 2d 349, 124 N.W.2d 312 (1963) (intentional infliction of
emotional harm); Stephan v. Lynch, 136 Vt. 226, 388 A.2d 376 (1978) (concepts of comparative negligence inapplicable when son's wrongful acts against his mother were deliberate, and not negligent).

[19]See W. P. Keeton et al., note 11 above, § 8, at 35.

[20]Carman v. Heber, 43 Colo. App. 5, 601 P.2d 646 (1979) (citing this treatise).

[21]Bell v. Mickelsen, 710 F.2d 611 (10th Cir. Wyo. 1983).

[22]Cruz v. Montoya, 660 P.2d 723 (Utah 1983).

"Fault" Statutes

The Maine statute[23] is somewhat ambiguous with respect to intentional torts, in that it uses the term "fault" rather than "negligence." "Fault" is defined as "negligence, breach of statutory duty or other act or omission which gives rise to a liability in tort *or* would, apart from this section, give rise to the defense of contributory negligence."[24] This definition is broad enough to cover intentional torts as well as negligence. Can it be that the legislature intended to provide for reduction of awards in cases where at common law plaintiff could have recovered his full damages regardless of his own fault?

The clue to the legislative intent may be found in the positioning of the language calling for diminution of damages. The statute provides that "a claim ... shall not be defeated by reason of the fault of the person suffering the damage, but the damages ... shall be reduced ...."[25] It thus appears that, despite the apparent breadth of the Maine statute, it means to compare fault and apportion damages only in those instances where, but for the statute, contributory negligence would have been a complete bar to recovery.[26] This should not include intentional torts.

The Arkansas statute as amended in 1973 contained a similar ambiguity, defining fault as "negligence, willful and wanton conduct, supplying of a defective product in an unreasonably dangerous condition, or any other act or omission or conduct actionable in tort."[27] Again, the position of the diminution clause was important: the proviso, "where such fault is chargeable to the person injured ... recovery shall be diminished in proportion to such fault," was subsidiary to the language repealing the contributory negligence defense.[28] In 1975 Arkansas enacted a new comparative fault statute that appears to resolve the ambiguity.[29] "Fault" is defined to include "any act, omission, conduct, risk assumed, breach of warranty or breach of any legal duty which is a proximate cause of any damage sustained by any party."[30] The diminution clause was also rewritten and now reads:

> In all actions for damages for personal injuries or wrongful death or injury to property in which recovery is predicated on fault, liability shall be determined by comparing the fault chargeable to a claiming

---

[23]Me. Rev. Stat. Ann. 1964, tit. 14, § 156 (emphasis added).

[24]Me. Rev. Stat. Ann., tit. 14, § 156, third paragraph (emphasis added). If the statute used "and" instead of the italicized "or," the meaning would have been clear.

[25]Me. Rev. Stat. Ann., tit. 14, § 156, first paragraph.

[26]See Note, *Comparative Negligence: Some New Problems for the Maine Courts*, 18 Me. L. Rev. 65, 73-74 (1966). This note, written soon after enactment of the Maine statute, uses the phrase "comparative negligence" throughout, makes no point of the fact that the statute uses "fault" instead of "negligence," and appears to assume that the statute is inapplicable to intentional torts.

[27]Ark. Acts 1973, No. 303, § 1, codified at Ark. Stat. Ann., § 27-1763.

[28]Ark. Acts 1973, No. 303, § 3, codified at Ark. Stat. Ann., § 27-1765.

[29]Ark. Acts 1975, No. 367, §§ 1-3, codified at Ark. Stat. Ann., §§ 27-1763 to 27-1765.

[30]Ark. Stat. Ann., § 27-1763.

party with the fault chargeable to the party or parties from whom the claiming party seeks to recover damages.[31]

The Arkansas Supreme Court recently refused to apply comparative fault to an intentional tort but relied on proximate cause analysis rather than the language of statute. In *Kubik v. Igleheart*[32] the plaintiff allegedly operated his motorboat dangerously close to the defendant's dock in violation of several safety statutes, whereupon the defendant shot him. The defendant claimed that he had intended to fire a warning shot and hit the plaintiff accidentally. The court characterized the defendant's act as intentional but upheld the refusal of a comparative negligence instruction on other grounds: namely, that the plaintiff's fault was not the proximate cause of his injuries. Thus the court left open the questions whether a plaintiff's negligence can be the cause of another's intentional tort and, if so, whether comparative fault would then apply; seemingly it would.

New York's "Culpable Conduct" Statute

The New York comparative negligence law provides that "the *culpable conduct* attributable to the claimant or to the decedent, including contributory negligence or assumption of risk, shall not bar recovery"[33] and that "culpable conduct claimed in diminution of damages ... shall be an affirmative defense to be pleaded and proved by the party asserting the defense."[34] A lower New York court appears to have applied New York's statute to reduce damages in an intentional tort case. In *Comeau v. Lucas*[35] the plaintiff was attending a party and was assaulted by a member of a rock band that had been engaged to play there. He sued the band member for battery and the parents of the sixteen-year-old hostess for negligent supervision of the party. The trial court granted summary judgment for the defendant on the negligence claim but allowed the battery claim to go to the jury. The jury awarded the plaintiff $250,000 in compensatory damages and reduced the award by 10% on account of the plaintiff's drinking and disorderly behavior. The Appellate Division reinstated the negligence claim and upheld the instruction on comparative negligence. The court offered no explanation as to why comparative negligence should apply to a battery.

Consent Defense

If a plaintiff expressly or impliedly permits an intentional act by defendant resulting in injury to the plaintiff, the consent defense, of course, still bars recovery.[36] But this does not mean that plaintiff's inadvertent negligent conduct contributing to his harm will be a defense to his action for intentional injury.

---

[31]Ark. Stat. Ann., § 27-1764.

[32]Kubik v. Igleheart, 280 Ark. 310, 657 S.W.2d 545 (1983).

[33]N.Y. Civ. Prac. Law, § 1411.

[34]N.Y. Civ. Prac. Law, § 1412.

[35]Comeau v. Lucas, 90 A.D.2d 674, 455 N.Y.S.2d 871 (1982).

[36]See Moore v. Atchison, T. & S. F. R. Co., 26 Okla. 682, 695, 110 P. 1059, 1064 (1910); W. P. Keeton et al., note 11 above, § 18.

5.3 Willful, reckless, or grossly negligent conduct by defendant

The term "willful misconduct" is most ambiguous.[37] At times, the courts may consider "willful" synonymous with "knowing" or "intentional"—that is, done for a set purpose, or with substantial certainty of the consequences of the action.[38] If the court interprets "willful" in this very limited sense, it is unlikely, when comparative negligence is adopted, that any "contributory negligence" of plaintiff will be taken into account in a cause of action based on willful conduct.[39]

Willful Short of Intentional

On the other hand, "willful" has been used in guest statutes,[40] and sometimes in other connections, as synonymous with "wanton" or "reckless."[41] Thus, the defendant's conduct may be called willful although he has "no intent to cause harm" when he "intentionally performs an act so unreasonable and dangerous that he knows, or should know, it is highly probable that harm will result."[42] In effect, willfulness is equated with "reckless disregard" as defined by the *Restatement*.[43] To make any sense out of this second characterization of "willful misconduct," it is perhaps best to describe it by the rather equivocal phrase "negligent willful misconduct." When a jurisdiction giving this meaning to "willful misconduct" adopts comparative negligence, contributory negligence in such cases should be handled the same way it is handled when the defendant's acts constitute reckless conduct.

As has been indicated in a number of jurisdictions and under the *Restatement of Torts*, when a defendant's conduct is characterized as "negligent willful misconduct" or "reckless conduct," the contributory negligence defense does not apply.[44] One reason is that the defendant's negligence, gauged in terms of culpability, is so close to intentional wrongdoing that he should not have the benefit of contributory negligence.[45] Another important reason for attaching this legal consequence to willful or reckless conduct was to ameliorate the hardship of com-

---

[37]See Falls v. Mortensen, 207 Ore. 130, 295 P.2d 182, 187-188 (1956).

[38]See Farmers Ins. Exchange v. Hewitt, 274 Minn. 246, 143 N.W.2d 230, 238 (1966) (case demonstrates ambiguity in later defining willful as reckless).

[39]See S.D. Codified Laws, § 20-9-1; Georgia Power Co. v. Deese, 79 Ga. App. 704, 51 S.E.2d 724 (1949).

[40]See specialized treatment in section 10.3. See also Siders v. Gibbs, 39 N.C. App. 183, 249 S.E.2d 858 (1978) (owner-passenger may recover against other motorist whose negligence was willful and wanton).

[41]See 45 *Words and Phrases* 240-243 (Permanent ed. 1940).

[42]Donnelly v. Southern Pacific Co., 18 Cal. 2d 863, 118 P.2d 465, 468 (1941). See Ryan v. Foster & Marshall, Inc., 556 F.2d 460 (9th Cir. Ore. 1977).

[43]*Restatement (Second) of Torts* § 500 (1965).

[44]See section 5.1 above, at note 2. See also DeElena v. Southern Pacific Co., 121 Ariz. 563, 592 P.2d 759 (1979) (plaintiff's claim not defeated by contributory negligence when "wanton" negligence on part of defendant is established); Harrington v. Collins, 298 N.C. 535, 259 S.E.2d 275 (1979); Hawkins v. Ivy, 50 Ohio St. 2d 114, 4 Ohio Op. 3d 243, 363 N.E.2d 367 (1977); International Assn. of Bridge, Structural & Ornamental Ironworkers, Local 387 v. Moore, 149 Ga. App. 431, 254 S.E.2d 438 (1979).

[45]See section 5.1 above, at note 5.

mon-law contributory negligence.[46] Once a state has adopted comparative negligence this latter reason for the rule is removed, but the first remains. Thus the courts are presented with a very difficult issue if the legislature has given no guidance.

Case Law Under Comparative Negligence

There is a growing body of case law.

Mississippi: Even though defendant has engaged in reckless or negligent willful misconduct, Mississippi compares negligence and reduces the award.[47] However, this is not a particularly persuasive precedent because the Mississippi courts had not evolved an exception to contributory negligence as a defense when defendant's conduct was reckless.[48]

Wisconsin: Under Wisconsin law prior to comparative negligence, if defendant was grossly negligent or reckless, plaintiff's contributory negligence was not taken into account.[49] In *Bielski v. Schulze*[50] the Supreme Court of Wisconsin discussed the issue of whether comparative negligence should apply if a defendant was "grossly negligent." In prior decisions that court had interpreted "grossly negligent" to be the same as "reckless" and "wanton."[51] In effect, it had regarded gross negligence not merely as different in degree from ordinary negligence but as different in kind.[52] The court held in *Bielski* that the doctrine developed by the Wisconsin courts that gross negligence would negate the contributory negligence defense "no longer fulfills a purpose in comparative negligence."[53] Therefore, the jury could apportion damages if plaintiff was negligent even though defendant was "reckless" or "grossly negligent." It is only when defendant's conduct fits within the concept of intentional tort that contributory negligence is ignored.[54]

In a more recent case, *Wangen v. Ford Motor Company*, the Wisconsin Supreme Court reconsidered fault categories, saying that *Bielski* had effectively abolished gross negligence as a separate type of conduct for purposes of comparison.[55] However, conduct that might be characterized as "reckless, wanton or willful" was to be distinguished from

---

[46]See W. P. Keeton et al., *Prosser and Keeton on the Law of Torts* § 65, at 462 (5th ed. 1984).

[47]See Anderson v. Eagle Motor Lines, Inc., 423 F.2d 81 (5th Cir. Miss. 1970) (applying Mississippi law); Moore v. Abdalla, 197 Miss. 125, 19 So. 2d 502 (1944).

[48]South Dakota had specifically allowed contributory negligence as a complete defense even though defendant's conduct was reckless or wanton. Wittstruck v. Lee, 62 S.D. 290, 252 N.W. 874, 92 A.L.R. 1361 (1934). Today, when defendant's conduct is reckless, South Dakota applies the statute and makes a comparison. See Crabb v. Wade, 84 S.D. 93, 167 N.W.2d 546 (1969).

[49]See Astin v. Chicago, M. & St. P. R. Co., 143 Wis. 477, 128 N.W. 265 (1910).

[50]Bielski v. Schulze, 16 Wis. 2d 1, 114 N.W.2d 105 (1962).

[51]Id., 114 N.W.2d at 112.

[52]See Barlow v. Foster, 149 Wis. 613, 136 N.W. 822 (1912).

[53]Bielski v. Schulze, 16 Wis. 2d 1, 114 N.W.2d 105, 113 (1962).

[54]See Alsteen v. Gehl, 21 Wis. 2d 349, 124 N.W.2d 312, 316-17 (1963) (the court determined intentional infliction of emotional harm could not be based merely on recklessness). See also Davies v. Butler, 95 Nev. 763, 602 P.2d 605 (1979) (citing this treatise).

[55]Wangen v. Ford Motor Co., 97 Wis. 2d 260, 294 N.W.2d 437, 13 A.L.R.4th 1 (1980).

gross negligence. The issue before the court was whether punitive damages would be available in this context, so the court did not reach the question of whether a plaintiff's negligence would be compared with a defendant's willful or wanton conduct.

Arkansas: In *Billingsley v. Westrac Company*[56] a federal court applying the 1961 Arkansas law[57] reached a result similar to the holding in *Bielski*. Defendant had driven his large tractor-trailer across a highway at night while attempting to make a turn and plaintiff's decedent crashed into its unlit side. The court indicated that even if defendant's conduct was "willful and wanton," the Arkansas comparative negligence statute would be applied and decedent's negligence would diminish or bar recovery if it contributed to the accident. The court reached this result in spite of clear Arkansas precedent that the contributory negligence defense is unavailable if defendant acted in reckless disregard of the rights of others.[58] The court said in its opinion that "the purpose of a comparative negligence statute is thwarted whenever there is a judicial characterization of an act as something other than negligence."[59]

The argument of the court in *Billingsley* is a bit conclusory. State legislatures have left little written history to show the purpose behind comparative negligence statutes.[60] Certainly they were intended to mitigate the defense of contributory negligence and it could be argued that allowing contributory negligence to mitigate damages where it would not have been allowed for any purpose prior to enactment of the comparative negligence statute thwarts this legislative purpose.

Further, some legislatures have been specific and included the term "gross negligence" in the adoption of a comparative negligence statute.[61] If "willfulness" or "recklessness" is different in kind from negligence, arguably the comparative negligence statutes are not applicable to actions based on such a theory.[62]

It should be noted that the Arkansas legislature in effect adopted the result of the *Billingsley* case in its 1973 act which used the term "fault" instead of "negligence" and specifically defined "fault" to include "willful and wanton conduct."[63] This, however, does not neces-

---

[56]Billingsley v. Westrac Co., 365 F.2d 619 (8th Cir. Ark. 1966).

[57]Ark. Acts 1961 (1st Ex. Sess.), No. 61, compiled as Ark. Stat. Ann., §§ 27-1730.1 and 27-1730.2.

[58]See St. Louis, I. M. & S. R. Co. v. Freeman, 36 Ark. 41, 50 (1881).

[59]Billingsley v. Westrac Co., 365 F.2d 619, 623 (8th Cir. Ark. 1966). See also Rone v. Miller, 257 Ark. 791, 520 S.W.2d 268 (1975) (appellate court held that the evidence sustained a jury verdict that the defendant was guilty of reckless or wanton misconduct, but nevertheless reversed to allow a jury to consider apportionment of damages based on the plaintiff's contributory negligence).

[60]Wisconsin Legislative Council, minutes of Judiciary Committee on Automobile Accident Liability (July 16, 1970).

[61]See Idaho Code, § 6-801; Nev. Rev. Stat., § 41.141; Utah Code Ann., § 78-27-37.

[62]See section 5.1 above, at note 5.

[63]Ark. Acts 1973, No. 303, § 1, codified at Ark. Stat. Ann., § 27-1763. For discussion of the 1975 amendment of the Arkansas law, see section 5.2 above, at note 28.

sarily indicate that the 1961 legislature intended the same result when it enacted the statute under which *Billingsley* was decided.

The Supreme Court of Wisconsin may have come close to the mark in its reasoning in *Bielski,* discussed above in this section. The statutes arguably are not wholly plaintiff-oriented, but rather attempt to apportion damages more precisely in terms of fault than does the common law under the contributory negligence defense. If that is the general legislative purpose, then even when defendant's conduct was "willfully negligent" or "reckless" or "grossly negligent," plaintiff's damages should still be subject to apportionment if he was ordinarily negligent. If this approach is taken by courts, they will gain another advantage in avoiding the very difficult problem of drawing the line between negligent and reckless conduct. A study of cases indicates that it is much easier to state in words where to draw the line than to apply those words in concrete fact situations.[64]

Oklahoma: The *Billingsley* rationale was adopted by an Oklahoma District Court in *Amoco Pipeline Company v. Montgomery*[65] when it announced that comparative negligence allows the apportionment of damages in those cases where conduct is classified as gross or ordinary negligence or willful and wanton negligence.

New Jersey: In *Draney v. Bachman*[66] the Superior Court of New Jersey adopted a variant of the Wisconsin rule in *Bielski.* The court found that gross negligence was different from ordinary negligence only in degree and that it fell within New Jersey's comparative negligence system. However, if a defendant engages in willful or wanton conduct, his conduct falls outside the ambit of the comparative negligence statute; he will not be able to assert the plaintiff's contributory negligence as a defense. As in contributory negligence, if both plaintiff and defendant are willfully or wantonly negligent, no recovery will be allowed on either side.

Oregon: In *Ryan v. Foster and Marshall, Incorporated*[67] the Ninth Circuit Court of Appeals applying Oregon law held that plaintiff's comparative ordinary negligence could not be used to offset defendant's gross negligence, characterized as "conscious indifference to or reckless disregard of the rights of others."[68]

Wyoming: The Wyoming Supreme Court, in *Danculovich v. Brown,*[69] found that when the defendant's conduct was wanton or will-

---

[64]See, e.g., Cope v. Davison, 30 Cal. 2d 193, 180 P.2d 873, 879 (1947); Tighe v. Diamond, 149 Ohio St. 520, 37 Ohio Op. 243, 80 N.E.2d 122, 126 (1948). See generally 2 F. Harper & F. James, *The Law of Torts* § 16.15 (1956).

[65]Amoco Pipeline Co. v. Montgomery, 487 F. Supp. 1268 (W.D. Okla. 1980) (citing this treatise).

[66]Draney v. Bachman, 138 N.J. Super. 503, 351 A.2d 409 (1976). Accord, Burd v. Vercruyssen, 142 N.J. Super. 344, 361 A.2d 571 (1976).

[67]Ryan v. Foster & Marshall, Inc., 556 F.2d 460 (9th Cir. Ore. 1977).

[68]Id., at 461.

[69]Danculovich v. Brown, 593 P.2d 187 (Wyo. 1979).

ful, the plaintiff's damages would not be reduced under that state's comparative negligence statute. The Court also declared that consideration as to whether a defendant's conduct was willful or wanton as opposed to grossly negligent was a jury question; if the jury finds the defendant's conduct to be willful and wanton, recovery would be allowed.

Nevada: In a wrongful death action, the Nevada Supreme Court declined to abrogate the long-standing rule that mere negligence on the part of the plaintiff would not constitute a defense to the willful or wanton misconduct of the defendant.[70] The Court interpreted the legislature's inclusion of the phrase "gross negligence" in the comparative negligence statute to mean that gross negligence is not equivalent to willful or wanton misconduct. While the former may be compared to a plaintiff's contributory negligence, the latter may not. This behavior should be left "outside the purview of the comparative negligence statute."[71]

California: Prior to the adoption of pure comparative negligence, California ignored a plaintiff's contributory negligence if a defendant's conduct was "willful or wanton." Under comparative negligence it is likely that damages will be apportioned in cases where the plaintiff is contributorily negligent if the defendant's conduct falls short of intentional wrongdoing. In its decision adopting pure comparative negligence, the California Supreme Court noted Dean Prosser's suggestion that contributory negligence should be no defense at all because reckless conduct is different in kind from ordinary negligence,[72] but it also observed that "a comprehensive system of comparative negligence should allow for apportionment of damages in all cases involving misconduct which falls short of intentional."[73]

In *Sorensen v. Allred*,[74] a California court allowed the comparison of fault between plaintiff's negligent illegal left turn and defendant's willful and wanton drunk driving and speeding. The court based its decision in part on the trend toward comparing fault regardless of the basis for liability, citing several cases involving mixed strict liability and negligence.[75] The court concluded:

> We are not here comparing apples and oranges ... but rather two varieties of oranges ... or at worst oranges and lemons, since the

---

[70]Davies v. Butler, 95 Nev. 763, 602 P.2d 605 (1979) (citing this treatise).

[71]Id., 602 P.2d at 610.

[72]Nga Li v. Yellow Cab Co., 13 Cal. 3d 804, 119 Cal. Rptr. 858, 532 P.2d 1226, 1241, 78 A.L.R.3d 393 (1975).

[73]Id. See Lostritto v. Southern Pacific Transp. Co., 73 Cal. App. 3d 737, 140 Cal. Rptr. 905 (1977) (contributory negligence held no defense to willful misconduct). In a later decision on a pre-*Li* action not reviewed on principles of comparative negligence, the California Supreme Court indicated that if the plaintiff's decedent was contributorily negligent, this would not bar recovery if the defendant's misconduct was willful. Ewing v. Cloverleaf Bowl, 20 Cal. 3d 389, 143 Cal. Rptr. 13, 572 P.2d 1155 (1978).

[74]Sorenson v. Allred, 112 Cal. App. 3d 717, 169 Cal. Rptr. 441, 10 A.L.R.4th 937 (1980).

[75]See Chapter 12.

underlying comparison is being made between two types of negligence which the jury found to be almost equal in causing the accident.[76]

Full Recovery as a Deterrent

If the court is still compelled to distinguish between negligent and reckless conduct with respect to punitive damages,[77] not much litigation time will be saved. Further, there may be some loss of the deterrent effect that might be engendered by a total award for plaintiff where defendant has been reckless.

It is this author's view that the likelihood is slight that wanton or reckless conduct would be effectively deterred by complete loss of the contributory negligence defense. For this reason and because the core of comparative negligence is full apportionment on the basis of fault, courts should adopt the Wisconsin approach and should apportion damages when the plaintiff has been negligent and defendant's conduct falls short of being intentional even though defendant's conduct has been grossly negligent, reckless or "willful negligent misconduct."

5.4 Punitive damages for willful, reckless, or grossly negligent conduct

For a period of time, punitive damages were allowed only when an intentional tort was committed. As the late Dean Prosser indicated, the purposes of such damages were multifold and included punishment of the defendant as well as general and specific deterrence.[78] Some opinions added as a purpose that punitive damages would serve to reimburse the plaintiff for elements of damages that are not legally compensable, "such as wounded feelings or the expenses of suit."[79] Nevertheless, the general thrust of punitive damages is not to compensate the plaintiff, but to reprove defendants and deter wrongful conduct.

A number of decisions have allowed the jury to award punitive damages when the defendant did not intentionally cause harm but did exhibit a "conscious and deliberate disregard of the interests of others."[80] The courts may call such conduct "gross,"[81] or "reckless."[82] The adoption of comparative negligence in a jurisdiction that has allowed punitive damages when defendant's conduct falls short of

---

[76]Sorenson v. Allred, 169 Cal. Rptr. at 445, 10 A.L.R.4th at 944.

[77]See W. P. Keeton et al., note 46 above, § 2 at 9-10.

[78]See W. P. Keeton et al., *Prosser and Keeton on the Law of Torts* § 2, at 9 (5th ed. 1984).

[79]Id.

[80]See Sebastian v. Wood, 246 Iowa 94, 66 N.W.2d 841 (1954) (drunken driving); Dorn v. Wilmarth, 254 Ore. 236, 458 P.2d 942 (1969).

[81]See Hicks v. McCandlish, 221 S.C. 410, 70 S.E.2d 629 (1952).

[82]See cases cited in note 80 above.

intentional wrongdoing is unlikely to change the result—punitive damages will still be awarded.[83]

Case Law

Mississippi appears to have had no problem with respect to the award of punitive damages when defendant's conduct has been reckless.[84] There appears to be no reason why the comparative negligence system should be interpreted to alter the law in this regard.

The court in *Kozar v. Chesapeake and Ohio Railway Company*[85] held that the comparative negligence provisions in the F.E.L.A. do not bar a recovery by an employee of punitive damages, even when he has been contributorily negligent. The court ruled that the employee's negligent conduct is not a defense to a claim for punitive damages unless he acts with reckless disregard for his own safety.[86]

It would seem possible, where both parties reach a high degree of culpability, that a jury might be permitted to apportion punitive damages under a comparative negligence system. However, there appear to be no cases in which apportionment has been allowed.

In *Amoco Pipeline Company v. Montgomery*,[87] an Oklahoma District Court permitted an award of punitive damages to defendant's counterclaimants with no setoff allowed. The court reasoned that punitive damages are intended to punish the wrongdoer and as such bear no relationship to compensatory damages.

The Wisconsin Exception

The general proposition that enactment of a comparative negligence law does not abolish punitive damages for defendant's "aggravated negligence"[88] found an exception for a time in Wisconsin. In *Bielski v. Schulze*[89] the Supreme Court of that state appeared to have abolished the concept of aggravated negligence for all purposes; this included doing away "with the basis for punitive damages in negligence cases."[90] In Wisconsin, therefore, punitive damages were awarded only for an intentional tort. The court's conclusion in *Bielski* was based to some extent on the comparative negligence statute. Since it had already decided that aggravated negligence by a defendant would no

---

[83]Such a question could arise in Oregon. See Falls v. Mortensen, 207 Ore. 130, 295 P.2d 182 (1956) (awarding punitive damages when defendant was reckless); Ore. Rev. Stat., § 18.470. See also Danculovich v. Brown, 593 P.2d 187 (Wyo. 1979) (court indicated that the availability of an award of punitive damages would be beneficial in a proper case of willful and wanton misconduct).

[84]See Teche Lines, Inc. v. Pope, 175 Miss. 393, 166 So. 539 (1936). See also Ryan v. Foster & Marshall, Inc., 556 F.2d 460 (9th Cir. Ore. 1977).

[85]Kozar v. Chesapeake & O. R. Co., 320 F. Supp. 335 (W.D. Mich. 1970).

[86]See generally, Annot., "Recovery of punitive damages in actions under Jones Act or Federal Employers' Liability Act," 10 A.L.R.Fed. 511 (1972).

[87]Amoco Pipeline Co. v. Montgomery, 487 F. Supp. 1268 (W.D. Okla. 1980) (citing this treatise).

[88]This is a shorthand description for reckless or willful conduct.

[89]Bielski v. Schulze, 16 Wis. 2d 1, 114 N.W.2d 105 (1962).

[90]Id., 114 N.W.2d at 113.

longer serve to block a jury's consideration of plaintiff's negligence, there was little need for preserving the concept.

Despite the adequacy of the reasons for abolishing the concept of gross or aggravated negligence, the court in *Bielski* added, as a reason for denying punitive damages, that the criminal law could best punish and deter such conduct. This latter argument is part of the general controversy as to whether punitive damages are ever appropriate for aggravated negligence or other applications in tort law.[91] The Supreme Court of Wisconsin may have merely muddied the waters by introducing this point in a discussion relating to comparative negligence.

In 1980 the Wisconsin Supreme Court reconsidered its position on punitive damages in *Wangen v. Ford Motor Company*,[92] a product liability case involving allegations of reckless conduct in the design of an automobile gasoline tank that exploded in a rear-end collision. The court said that the real effect of *Bielski v. Schulze* was to abolish gross negligence as a concept separate from negligence; punitive damages would continue to be available for "outrageous" conduct that fell short of an intentional tort.

Ford argued that punitive damages were inappropriate in a comparative negligence setting because the plaintiffs would be allowed to introduce evidence of the defendant's wealth that might bias the liability case. The court responded that if punitive damages were not allowed the jury would be likely to increase compensatory damages. While the Wisconsin court's argument seems unresponsive to Ford's concern about the corporate wealth evidence, commentators have suggested dealing with this problem by holding a separate trial on punitive damages after liability has been determined or by allowing the judge to set the amount.[93]

Separation of Punitive Damages Law

In sum, the law of punitive damages and the law of comparative negligence are separate and should be so considered by courts—despite the ruling in *Bielski v. Schulze*. In a situation where both parties commit acts of aggravated negligence, the court might consider whether punitive damages might be apportioned.

---

[91]See Wheeler, *The Constitutional Case for Reforming Punitive Damages Procedures*, 69 Va. L. Rev. 269 (1983); Owen, *Problems in Assessing Punitive Damages Against Manufacturers of Defective Products*, 49 U. Chi. L. Rev. 1 (1982); Defense Research Institute, *The Case Against Punitive Damages* (monograph Aug. 1969); Note, *The Imposition of Punishment by Civil Courts: A Reappraisal of Punitive Damages*, 41 N.Y.U. L. Rev. 1158 (1966) (against); Vratsenes v. N. H. Auto, Inc., 112 N.H. 71, 289 A.2d 66 (1972) (against); Morris, *Punitive Damages in Tort Cases*, 44 Harv. L. Rev. 1173 (1931) (for); Note, *Exemplary Damages in the Law of Torts*, 70 Harv. L. Rev. 517 (1957) (for).

[92]Wangen v. Ford Motor Co., 97 Wis. 2d 260, 294 N.W.2d 437, 13 A.L.R.4th 1 (1980). See the Uniform Product Liability Act, S. 100, 99th Cong., 1st Sess. § 12 (1985).

[93]Wheeler, note 91 above, at 301-302; Owen, note 91 above, at 52-53.

5.5 Willful, reckless, or grossly negligent conduct by plaintiff

Under the contributory negligence defense, there is no special rule applicable to plaintiff's contributory negligence amounting to aggravated negligence. There is no need to formulate a rule; plaintiff's claim is barred as soon as he is negligent. The only time it is necessary to characterize plaintiff's conduct as aggravated negligence is when defendant is proven reckless and the contributory negligence defense is abolished; if plaintiff is also reckless, the contributory negligence defense will probably return.[94]

The various labels of aggravated negligence—"reckless," "wanton," "grossly negligent"—have no practical value when applied to plaintiff's conduct under comparative negligence. Under pure comparative negligence, plaintiff's negligence, however aggravated, must be compared with that of the defendant. Some Mississippi cases have been rather specific about this,[95] as has at least one California case.[96]

50% States

In states that bar plaintiff's claim when his negligence is equal to or greater than that of the defendant, it would seem that a "grossly negligent" or "reckless" plaintiff might have difficulty having his case heard by the jury. Nevertheless, with an occasional exception,[97] courts in those states have not used the characterizations of aggravated negligence as a method for determining that plaintiff's negligence was equal to or greater than defendant's.[98] Rather, their focus has been more directly centered on comparing the magnitude of negligence of the parties.[99]

Slight-Gross States

The Nebraska statute and the original South Dakota statute were identical in limiting plaintiff's recovery to instances where "the contributory negligence of the plaintiff was slight and the negligence of the defendant was gross in comparison ...."[1] Under this language, the South Dakota courts attempted to determine in the abstract whether plaintiff's negligence was more than slight.[2] However, the South Dako-

---

[94]See *Restatement (Second) of Torts* § 482(2) (1965).

[95]See McClellan v. Illinois C. R. Co., 204 Miss. 432, 37 So. 2d 738 (1948); Gulf & S. I. R. Co. v. Bond, 181 Miss. 254, 179 So. 355, 361 (1938).

[96]Zavala v. Regents of Univ. of California, 125 Cal. App. 3d 646, 178 Cal. Rptr. 185 (1981) (comparing plaintiff's intoxication with defendant's negligence in serving beer to an intoxicated person).

[97]See Central R. R. & Banking Co. v. Smith, 78 Ga. 694, 3 S.E. 397 (1887) (grossly negligent plaintiff barred when he walked upon defendant's railroad track).

[98]See Bielski v. Schulze, 16 Wis. 2d 1, 114 N.W.2d 105 (1962) (abolishing these terms with respect to defendant's conduct).

[99]See section 3.5 above.

[1]Neb. Rev. Stat., § 25-1151; S.D. Code Supp. 1960, § 47.0304-1. See Hartman v. Brady, 201 Neb. 558, 270 N.W.2d 909 (1978) (recovery of plaintiff not barred when his negligence was slight and defendant's negligence gross).

[2]See discussion in Crabb v. Wade, 84 S.D. 93, 167 N.W.2d 546 (1969).

ta statute was amended in 1964 to permit recovery when "the contributory negligence of the plaintiff was slight in comparison with the negligence of the defendant ...."[3] Since then, abstract characterizations of plaintiff's conduct have had no significance in South Dakota; rather, direct comparison is made. This has always been the practice under the Nebraska statute.[4]

Consent by Plaintiff

In one situation—when plaintiff's intentional and voluntary conduct causes his injury—his claim is barred in any comparative negligence jurisdiction. Put another way, plaintiff has consented to the negligent infliction of the harm that befell him. For example, if a plaintiff knowingly and voluntarily walks in front of defendant's speeding car, he is deemed to have consented to the injury he receives, no comparison is made and his claim is barred.

In *Lucas v. Long Beach*[5] a policeman who negligently failed to inspect a jail cell was found not liable for the wrongful death of a prisoner who hanged himself, as the prisoner's intentional conduct was the superseding cause of the injury.

The doctrine of volenti non fit injuria is so deeply entrenched in American law that it is unlikely that a court would interpret the comparative negligence statute to abolish the consent defense.[6] Moreover, since consent negatives the wrongful element of a defendant's intentional tort, a fortiori it would also do so with regard to negligent conduct.[7] Nevertheless, courts must be most careful in distinguishing consent from extreme contributory negligence; and it is rare, indeed, that true consent can be found.

---

[3]S.D. Codified Laws, § 20-9-2.
[4]See section 3.4 above.
[5]Lucas v. Long Beach, 60 Cal. App. 3d 341, 131 Cal. Rptr. 470 (1976).
[6]See W. P. Keeton et al., *Prosser and Keeton on the Law of Torts* § 18 (5th ed. 1984).
[7]See Moore v. Atchison, T. & S. F. R. Co., 26 Okla. 682, 695, 110 P. 1059, 1064 (1910).

CHAPTER 6

VIOLATION OF CRIMINAL SAFETY STATUTES

Section
6.1 Negligence per se
6.2 Defendant's violation of statute
6.3 Plaintiff's violation of statute

6.1 Negligence per se

When criminal legislation prescribes a standard of conduct for the purpose of protecting life, limb or property from a certain type of risk, and when failure to meet the statutory standard causes harm to the interest sought to be protected, American courts will readily consider that statutory requirement in determining rights and obligations in civil litigation.[1] There has been surprisingly little serious discussion of reasons for this approach;[2] nevertheless, a majority of jurisdictions have given decisive effect to violation of such statutes in civil cases. The courts hold that a party who violates the statute is negligent per se.[3] If the court deems the statute applicable, an unexcused violation amounts to negligence and there is nothing left for the jury to decide on this issue. Most commonly this doctrine of negligence per se is

---

[1]See W. P. Keeton et al., *Prosser and Keeton on the Law of Torts* § 36 (5th ed. 1984); 2 F. Harper & F. James, *The Law of Torts* § 17.6 (1956); *Restatement (Second) of Torts* §§ 285, 286 (1965). See, e.g., Arthur v. Flota Mercante Gran Centro Americana S.A., 487 F.2d 561 (5th Cir. La. 1973) (failure to move substantial hardware on gangway in violation of regulation negligence per se); Smith v. Kahler Corp., 297 Minn. 272, 211 N.W.2d 146 (1973) (failure to maintain adequate lighting in cocktail lounge as required by statute negligence per se); Rudelson v. United States, 431 F. Supp. 1101 (C.D. Cal. 1977), affd. 602 F.2d 1326 (9th Cir. Cal. 1979) (violation of federal aviation regulation by air traffic controller negligence per se).

[2]See Morris, *The Role of Criminal Statutes in Negligence Actions*, 49 Colum. L. Rev. 21 (1949); James, *Statutory Standards and Negligence in Accident Cases*, 11 La. L. Rev. 95 (1950); Thayer, *Public Wrong and Private Action*, 27 Harv. L. Rev. 317 (1913).

[3]See materials cited in note 1 above. Some courts suggest that violation of a statute or, more commonly, an ordinance, is only "evidence of negligence." However, if the acts which led to the violation of statute were not in themselves negligent, the court may find the violation not to be negligence per se. See Antee v. Sims, 494 S.W.2d 215 (Tex. Civ. App. 1973) (defendant used due care in braking to avoid collision; crossing over center line as a result not negligence per se). Further, some courts apply the doctrine of negligence per se only if the statute is one designed to protect a particular class of persons from their inability to protect themselves, with other statutory violations being only evidence of negligence. See deJesus v. Seaboard C. L. R. Co., 281 So. 2d 198 (Fla. 1973) (dicta). However, other courts have considered such statutes as imposing strict liability and preclude the apportionment of damages. See Zerby v. Warren, 297 Minn. 134, 210 N.W.2d 58 (1973). See also In re Petition of Alva S.S. Co., 616 F.2d 605 (2d Cir. N.Y. 1980) (shipowner's failure to comply with a fire department order constitutes negligence per se); Scott v. Independent School Dist., 256 N.W.2d 485 (Minn. 1977) (school district negligent per se when it did not enforce regulation of wearing of protective safety glasses in industrial arts classes).

applied to defendant's conduct, but it also can serve to brand plaintiff negligent as a matter of law.[4]

Judicial Extension of Legislative Policy

It is important to realize that usually the legislature does not require that the courts apply to civil cases the standard established by a criminal statute; rather the courts do it on their own. Perhaps the best explanation is that courts believe that the legislation reflects a community standard of care which the courts can fully implement by utilizing it in civil cases.[5]

As has been suggested, the usual effect of applying a criminal statute is to characterize the violator's conduct as negligent. Nevertheless, at times, more may be accomplished. A duty may be imposed on defendant where there was none at common law.[6] A defendant's violation *may* make the defense of contributory negligence unavailable.[7] If plaintiff has violated a statute, his conduct may be deemed contributory negligence as a matter of law; under the contributory negligence rule, this bars his claim.[8]

Criminal Violations Under Comparative Negligence

Under comparative negligence, what is the effect when a party violates a criminal safety statute that a court deems applicable? If both parties are negligent but one has violated a statute, will damages be apportioned? These questions are explored in this chapter in light of what has already occurred in comparative negligence jurisdictions and in consideration of the reasons underlying the concept of negligence per se.

6.2   Defendant's violation of statute

When a defendant violates a criminal safety statute a court will regard his conduct as negligent per se under comparative negligence if that was the rule in the jurisdiction before comparative negligence.[9]

---

[4]See W. P. Keeton et al., note 1 above, § 36, at 232.

[5]See Clinkscales v. Carver, 22 Cal. 2d 72, 136 P.2d 777 (1943) (applying civil statute that would be invalid in criminal case for want of complete publication); Thayer, note 2 above, at 322.

[6]See Ney v. Yellow Cab Co., 2 Ill. 2d 74, 117 N.E.2d 74, 51 A.L.R.2d 624 (1954) (ordinance forbidding leaving key in ignition); Rappaport v. Nichols, 31 N.J. 188, 156 A.2d 1, 75 A.L.R.2d 821 (1959) (ordinance forbidding sale of liquor to intoxicated person); Gould v. Allstar Ins. Co., 59 Wis. 2d 355, 208 N.W.2d 388 (1973) (ordinance requiring maintenance of premises in a reasonably safe condition); Feuerherm v. Ertelt, 286 N.W.2d 509 (N.D. 1979) (Dram Shop Act violation creates liability not recognized at common law).

[7]See *Restatement (Second) of Torts* § 483 (1965); Annot., "Contributory negligence as a defense to cause of action based upon violation of statute," 10 A.L.R.2d 853 (1950); Prosser, *Contributory Negligence as Defense to Violation of Statute*, 32 Minn. L. Rev. 105 (1948).

[8]See W. P. Keeton et al., note 1 above, § 36, at 232.

[9]See Johnson v. Chemical Supply Co., 38 Wis. 2d 194, 156 N.W.2d 455 (1968); Gulf & S. I. R. Co. v. Bond, 181 Miss. 254, 179 So. 355 (1938), mod. 181 Miss. 277, 181 So. 741 (1938); Rudelson v. United States, 431 F. Supp. 1101 (C.D. Cal. 1977), affd. 602 F.2d 1326 (9th Cir. Cal. 1979).

However, this means only that defendant must be found negligent; plaintiff's negligence still may be used to diminish his award.[10]

Under modified comparative negligence, the fact that defendant violated a statute does not necessarily establish as a matter of law that his negligence was equal to or greater than the negligence of the plaintiff.[11] This is in accord conceptually with the result under the contributory negligence defense; where the defendant violates a statute that "merely fixed a standard of care," plaintiff's contributory negligence may still be considered by the jury.[12]

Criminal Violation Barring Contributory Negligence

Under the contributory negligence doctrine there are only two situations where defendant's violation of a criminal statute bars the defense of contributory negligence. The first is relatively simple; it is when the legislature specifically provides for such a bar. The second is when "the effect of the statute is to place the entire responsibility for [plaintiff's] harm . . . upon the defendant."[13]

Full Damages Under Comparative Negligence

With regard to the first situation — the existence of legislation specifically barring the contributory negligence defense where a criminal statute is violated — it would seem that such legislation would remain in effect upon adoption of comparative negligence, and that a negligent plaintiff would recover his full damages. Of course, a court's decision in such a matter is easiest when the comparative negligence statute itself spells out which statutory violations will bar the contributory negligence defense completely. This is done in the F.E.L.A. by a proviso that "no such employee who may be injured or killed shall be held to have been guilty of contributory negligence in any case where the violation

---

[10]See Gulf & S. I. R. Co. v. Bond, 181 Miss. 254, 179 So. 355 (1938), mod. 181 Miss. 277, 181 So. 741 (1938) (court found as a matter of law that jury should have apportioned damages although defendant violated safety statute); Scott v. Independent School Dist., 256 N.W.2d 485 (Minn. 1977).

[11]See Frederick v. Hotel Investments, Inc., 48 Wis. 2d 429, 180 N.W.2d 562, 565 (1970).

[12]See Skarpness v. Port of Seattle, 52 Wash. 2d 490, 326 P.2d 747 (1958); Dart v. Pure Oil Co., 223 Minn. 526, 27 N.W.2d 555, 171 A.L.R. 885 (1947).

[13]Restatement (Second) of Torts § 483 (1965)

by such common carrier of any statute enacted for the safety of employees contributed to the injury or death of such employee."[14]

Usually, comparative negligence statutes are not so specific. They often have general language suggesting that apportionment is appropriate in all cases based on negligence.[15] Therefore, a problem can arise when a defendant has violated a safety statute which expressly barred the contributory negligence defense, but which was enacted prior to the comparative negligence law. In states that apply comparative fault to strict liability, courts and legislatures must decide whether statutory liability is intended to be strict or absolute.

The Arkansas Rule

This problem was presented in *Bond v. Missouri Pacific Railroad Company*,[16] where defendant railroad violated a 1911 Arkansas statute requiring it to maintain a lookout and barring the contributory negligence defense where the railroad was in violation.[17] The 1957 general comparative negligence statute then applicable in Arkansas applied by its terms to "all actions hereafter accruing for negligence."[18] The legislature had made no reference in the 1957 statute to the lookout statute. The court said that since the legislature had not specifically repealed or modified the lookout statute, it would not find a repeal by implication and the contributory negligence defense could not be raised even to diminish the award. The decision was made easier by precedent that the 1911 lookout statute had survived a 1919 comparative negligence statute applicable only to railroads.[19]

This holding seems sound and should be applied in similar situations. Comparative negligence statutes appear to be addressed only to situations where the contributory negligence defense acted as a total bar under prior law. A careful legislature, however, can assist the

---

[14]Act of April 22, 1908, ch. 149, § 3, 35 Stat. 66, 45 U.S.C. § 53. See, e.g., Osteen v. Seaboard C. L. R. Co., 305 So. 2d 241 (Fla. App. 1974) (defendant's violation of safety statute precludes consideration of plaintiff's contributory negligence). The only way the defendant can avoid total liability when he violates a safety statute is to determine that the plaintiff's negligence was the sole proximate cause of the accident. In Metcalfe v. Atchison, T. & S. F. R. Co., 491 F.2d 892 (10th Cir. Colo. 1974) the defendant argued that the plaintiff's contributory negligence in standing between two railway cars equipped with uncouplers which did no comply with the regulations was the sole proximate cause of his injury. The court found the failure to provide automatic uncouplers to be the proximate cause of the accident and allowed a complete recovery. But see Bertholf v. Burlington Northern R., 402 F. Supp. 171 (E.D. Wash. 1975) (violation of Occupational Safety and Health Act by employer railroad does not preclude reduction of damages in relation to plaintiff's negligence since O.S.H.A. expressly inapplicable to F.E.L.A. cases).

[15]See Colo. Rev. Stat., § 13-21-111 ("Contributory negligence shall not bar recovery in any action by any person to recover damages for negligence . . ."); Mass. Gen. Laws Ann., ch. 231, § 85 ("Contributory negligence shall not bar recovery in any action by any person . . . to recover damages for negligence. . . .").

[16]Bond v. Missouri P. R. Co., 233 Ark. 32, 342 S.W.2d 473 (1961).

[17]Ark. Stat. Ann., § 73-1002.

[18]Ark. Acts 1957, No. 296, § 2.

[19]Ark. Stat. Ann., § 73-1004.

courts by indicating whether prior statutes that barred or curtailed the contributory negligence defense are still viable.

Entire Responsibility Statutes

As stated above in this section, a second situation in which defendant's violation of a statute may bar the contributory negligence defense is when "the effect of the statute is to place the entire responsibility for [plaintiff's] harm ... upon the defendant."[20] The courts have not provided precise guidelines for determining whether a statute has this effect. Some courts have not adopted this exception at all.[21] As indicated by a Comment thereto, the *Restatement (Second) of Torts* does not attempt to delineate "the various types of statutes which have been enacted for such a purpose, nor the principles of statutory construction by which the purpose of a particular statute is to be determined."[22]

Standard of Conduct Statutes

It has developed from the case law, however, that statutes that merely fix a standard of care do not bar the contributory negligence defense. It is barred only by statutes intended to protect a person such as the plaintiff from his own inability to protect himself.[23]

As an example, in one case a plaintiff sought damages for fishing gear which burned while stored in defendant's building. Although defendant failed to comply with the fire ordinances, plaintiff's negligence in storing goods in such a structure could be considered; defendant merely violated a fixed standard of care.[24]

A defendant's violation of a statute does not necessarily establish that his negligence exceeds that of the plaintiff. In *Gurin v. Harris*[25] a Georgia court upheld a defendant's verdict despite the fact that the defendant violated a safety statute in connection with the accident.

Child Labor Laws

On the other hand, when defendant employs a minor in violation of a child labor law, the minor's negligence is not considered in an action for his injuries during employment. Courts find a legislative determination that the employment is negligence because children are likely to be unappreciative of risks and are prone to be careless.[26]

Prosser made a valiant attempt to list other kinds of statutes that

---

[20]*Restatement (Second) of Torts* § 483 (1965).

[21]See Prosser, *Contributory Negligence as Defense to Violation of Statute*, 32 Minn. L. Rev. 105 (1948); Annot., "Contributory negligence as a defense to a cause of action based upon violation of statute," 10 A.L.R.2d 853 (1950).

[22]*Restatement (Second) of Torts* § 483, Comment c at 539 (1965).

[23]Skarpness v. Port of Seattle, 52 Wash. 2d 490, 326 P.2d 747 (1958).

[24]Id.

[25]Gurin v. Harris, 129 Ga. App. 561, 200 S.E.2d 368 (1973).

[26]See Lenahan v. Pittston Coal Mining Co., 218 Pa. 311, 67 A. 642, 12 L.R.A. (N.S.) 461, 120 Am. St. Rep. 885 (1907); Karpeles v. Heine, 227 N.Y. 74, 124 N.E. 101 (1919); Dusha v. Virginia & Rainy Lake Co., 145 Minn. 171, 176 N.W. 482 (1920).

might bar the contributory negligence defense.[27] However, there is a surprising diversity in the cases. In *Tamiami Gun Shop v. Klein*[28] defendant, a commercial gun dealer, sold a weapon to a minor in violation of a state statute and city ordinance. The gun went off by accident, severely injuring the child. The court held that the child's contributory negligence should not be considered because the statute was meant to protect him against the risk of the very type of accident that did occur.

In contrast to this result, in a remarkably similar case where defendant sold a rifle to a twelve-year-old boy, the Supreme Court of New Mexico declined to hold that a similar ordinance was enacted for the child's benefit and it allowed the jury to consider his contributory negligence.[29]

New York and Wisconsin courts have held that when an absolute statutory duty exists under that state's labor law, plaintiff's damages will not be reduced under the comparative negligence statute.[30] In the Wisconsin case, *D. L. v. Huebner*,[31] a thirteen-year-old boy lost a hand in a piece of farm machinery and sued his employer and the manufacturer. The trial court threw out the claim against the employer and found the plaintiff 40% at fault. The Wisconsin Supreme Court reinstated the claim against the employer, finding him strictly liable under the state's child labor law and refusing to apply comparative fault. The court held not only that the violation of the statute was a proximate cause of the accident but that the statute presumes causation in order to protect children from injury. The court added that there were strong public policy reasons for not changing the law.

Scaffold Laws

Again, the New York Court of Appeals deemed a window cleaner's contributory negligence immaterial when defendant violated a safety statute designed for the worker's protection.[32] The New York courts have continued to impose absolute liability in cases coming under the state's "Scaffold Law," which applies to any construction or maintenance job requiring the use of scaffolds, ladders, or some other kind of support.[33] At the same time, the New York courts have applied compar-

---

[27] See Prosser, note 21 above, at 105 (including violation of factory acts and other statutes for the protection of workmen or laws prohibiting sale of weapons to children).

[28] Tamiami Gun Shop v. Klein, 109 So. 2d 189 (Fla. App. 1959), cert. dismissed 116 So. 2d 421 (Fla. 1959).

[29] Zamora v. J. Korber & Co., 59 N.M. 33, 278 P.2d 569, 570 (1954).

[30] Long v. Murnane Associates, Inc., 68 A.D.2d 166, 416 N.Y.S.2d 413 (1979); D. L. v. Huebner, 110 Wis. 2d 581, 329 N.W.2d 890 (1983).

[31] D. L. v. Huebner, 110 Wis. 2d 581, 329 N.W. 2d 890 (1983).

[32] Koenig v. Patrick Constr. Corp., 298 N.Y. 313, 83 N.E.2d 133, 10 A.L.R.2d 848 (1948).

[33] N.Y. Lab. Law, § 240. See Kalofonos v. State, 115 Misc. 2d 692, 454 N.Y.S.2d 645 (Ct. Cl. 1982) affd. 104 A.D.2d 75, 481 N.Y.S.2d 415 (1984); Reinhart v. Long Island Lighting Co., Inc., 91 A.D.2d 571, 457 N.Y.S.2d 57 (1982); Evans v. Nab Constr. Corp., 80 A.D.2d 841, 436 N.Y.S.2d 774 (1981); Sullivan v. Held, 81 A.D.2d 663, 438 N.Y.S.2d 359 (1981); accord, Carlton v. Verplaetse, 120 Ill. App. 3d 795, 76 Ill. Dec. 184, 458 N.E.2d 584 (1983) (applying absolute liability to the Illinois Structural Work Act).

ative fault to the safe workplace statute,[34] leading to litigation over which of the two laws covers a particular workplace accident.[35]

The Supreme Court of Nebraska permitted a window washer's contributory negligence to be considered although defendant violated a safety code by failing to install safety bolts.[36] The court held that the statute was not intended to protect individuals against their failure "to exercise self-protective care."[37]

Dram Shop Cases

The North Dakota Supreme Court, in *Feuerherm v. Ertelt*,[38] declared that the comparative negligence statute was not applicable to actions brought under the Dram Shop Act. Liability was imposed upon the defendant bar owner purely for violating the statute, without regard to his own negligence or fault. Therefore, any defense based on the plaintiff's alleged negligent conduct would be inapplicable.

Michigan applies comparative negligence in dram shop actions where it would be available to the intoxicated person as a partial defense, i.e., where the other person involved in the accident was partly at fault.[39] In a case where the plaintiff passenger had assisted the driver in getting drunk by paying for the beer, the court found the plaintiff's fault a complete defense.[40] Illinois allows comparative contribution from a dram shop to a defendant driver, although liability to accident victim plaintiffs remains strict.[41]

Reduction of Damages Denied

The rule that violation of a safety statute precludes assertion of the contributory negligence defense is somewhat amorphous. Nevertheless, it does exist and the question arises whether it will continue under comparative negligence. In a 1928 Mississippi case, *Hartwell Handle Company v. Jack*, a child who had been employed in violation of the

---

[34]N.Y. Lab. Law, § 241. See Long v. Forest-Fehlhaber, 55 N.Y.2d 154, 448 N.Y.S.2d 132, 433 N.E.2d 115 (1982); Baehre v. County of Erie, 94 A.D.2d 943, 464 N.Y.S.2d 69 (1983); Halftown v. Triple D Leasing Corp., 89 A.D.2d 794, 453 N.Y.S.2d 514 (1982); Larabee v. Triangle Steel, Inc., 86 A.D.2d 289, 451 N.Y.S.2d 258 (1982); Duva v. Flushing Hospital & Medical Center, 108 Misc. 2d 900, 439 N.Y.S.2d 268 (1981); accord, Hardy v. Monsanto Enviro-Chem Systems, Inc., 414 Mich. 29, 323 N.W.2d 270 (1982); Brons v. Bischoff, 80 Wis. 2d 80, 277 N.W.2d 854 (1979).

[35]See Ryan v. Morse Diesel, Inc., 98 A.D.2d 615, 469 N.Y.S.2d 354 (1983); Phillips v. Flintkote Co., 89 A.D.2d 724, 453 N.Y.S.2d 847 (1982).

[36]Wertz v. Lincoln Liberty Life Ins. Co., 152 Neb. 451, 41 N.W.2d 740, 17 A.L.R.2d 629 (1950).

[37]Id., 41 N.W.2d at 744.

[38]Feuerherm v. Ertelt, 286 N.W.2d 509 (N.D. 1979). Accord, Suskey v. Loyal Order of Moose Lodge No. 86, 472 A.2d 663 (Pa. Super. 1984); Pautz v. Cal-Ros, Inc., 340 N.W.2d 338 (Minn. 1983).

[39]Lyman v. Bavar Co., Inc., 136 Mich. App. 407, 356 N.W.2d 28 (1984).

[40]Dahn v. Sheets, 104 Mich. App. 584, 305 N.W.2d 547 (1981).

[41]Morgan v. Kirk Bros., Inc., 111 Ill. App. 3d 914, 67 Ill. Dec. 268, 444 N.E.2d 504 (1982).

child labor law was seriously crippled by his employer's machine.[42] The court held that the child's contributory negligence could not be used to reduce his award under the comparative negligence statute. The court reasoned that the purpose of the child labor statute was to protect minors from the consequences of their own negligence, lack of care or caution, and that to allow their contributory negligence to be considered would defeat this very purpose.

A Georgia court in *Bennett Drug Stores v. Mosely*[43] held plaintiff's decedent's contributory negligence immaterial when defendant violated a safety statute intended to protect decedent from his own inadvertence. There, defendant-pharmacist sold plaintiff carbolic acid in violation of a statute which required the seller to make inquiry of the purchaser as to whether he was aware the substance was poisonous and whether he was using it for legitimate purposes. Plaintiff's decedent died when he drank the carbolic acid. The court did not enter into a discussion of the state's comparative negligence rule; it simply ignored decedent's contributory negligence on the basis of the purpose of the safety statute.

Reduction of Damages Permitted

There are arguments and some authority that plaintiff's negligence should always be considered even if defendant violated a safety standard designed for plaintiff's protection. For example, in the Mississippi child labor case discussed above, a dissenting judge pointed out that the comparative negligence statute by its terms is to apply in all actions based on negligence and that the majority opinion had, in effect, held that the child labor statute partially repealed the comparative negligence statute.[44] Moreover, the comparative negligence statute could be harmonized with the child labor statute, in that the child would still recover some damages and his recovery would be reduced only if he was negligent in light of his age, experience, and intelligence.

The Mississippi case was somewhat different from the more usual case, in that the applicable child labor law was enacted after rather than before the comparative negligence statute. Implicit in the dissenting judge's opinion is the argument that if the legislature enacting the child labor law had intended to make an exception to the comparative negligence law, it would have said so. In the more usual situation where the comparative negligence statute follows the safety statute in time of enactment, this argument would cut the other way.

Under California's judicial adoption of pure comparative negligence a defendant air traffic controller's violation of a federal aviation regu-

---

[42]Hartwell Handle Co. v. Jack, 149 Miss. 465, 115 So. 586 (1928), affd. per curiam 122 So. 216 (1929).

[43]Bennett Drug Stores, Inc. v. Mosely, 67 Ga. App. 347, 20 S.E.2d 208 (1942).

[44]Hartwell Handle Co. v. Jack, 149 Miss. 465, 115 So. 586, 590 (1928).

lation did not bar reduction of the plaintiffs' damages by their own negligence.[45]

Section 205-a of the New York General Municipal Law provides a cause of action for firemen when they cannot recover in negligence.[46] In *Koehler v. New York*[47] the Queens County Supreme Court held the comparative negligence statute applicable to such actions; liability under Section 205-a is therefore not absolute in nature.

Reading Legislative Intent

There is logic in the dissenting judge's opinion in *Hartwell Handle Company v. Jack*, the Mississippi case discussed above in this section.[48] In enacting the child labor law, the legislature did not explicitly abolish the mitigating effect of contributory negligence. Whenever a court fathoms an "intent" in the absence of any specific legislative language or history, it is really guessing. Clearly the child labor law was intended to protect children against injuries they might incur in factories, but could the court be certain that the legislature intended that the child who was negligent under standards adjusted for his age and experience should obtain a full recovery? A comparative negligence statute should provide some guidelines for application of a statute intended to protect persons against a risk of harm springing from their own negligence.

Wisconsin Policy

The Supreme Court of Wisconsin has given very strong indications that it will not ignore contributory negligence even when defendant has violated a safety statute designed to protect plaintiff against his own negligence. In *Presser v. Siesel Construction Company*,[49] a construction worker at a Nike missile base fell into a pit that was left unguarded in violation of a "safe place to work" statute. Plaintiff argued that his contributory negligence should not be subject to apportionment under the comparative negligence statute and relied on a New York case[50] that had held a worker's contributory negligence immaterial when defendant had violated a similar law. The Supreme Court of Wisconsin distinguished the New York case, in part, on the ground that "In New York contributory negligence is a complete bar to the action whereas in Wisconsin under the comparative negligence

---

[45]Rudelson v. United States, 431 F. Supp. 1101 (C.D. Cal. 1977), affd. 602 F.2d 1326 (9th Cir. Cal. 1979).

[46]N.Y. Gen. Mun. Law, § 205-a.

[47]Koehler v. New York, 102 Misc. 2d 398, 423 N.Y.S.2d 431 (1979).

[48]Hartwell Handle Co. v. Jack, 149 Miss. 465, 115 So. 586, 590 (1928).

[49]Presser v. Siesel Constr. Co., 19 Wis. 2d 54, 119 N.W.2d 405 (1963). Accord, Buerosse v. Dutchland Dairy Restaurants, Inc., 72 Wis. 2d 239, 240 N.W.2d 176 (1976) (plaintiff's ordinary negligence may be compared with negligence based on violation of safe place statute).

[50]Koenig v. Patrick Constr. Corp., 298 N.Y. 313, 83 N.E.2d 133, 10 A.L.R.2d 848 (1948).

statute ... such defense is not."[51] Wisconsin, the court said, "as a matter of public policy has been committed to the doctrine of comparative negligence."[52]

Wisconsin still imposes strict liability under its child labor laws.[53] Nevertheless, the thrust of Wisconsin decisions under the safe place statutes indicates that today the state's Supreme Court would be likely to permit plaintiff's contributory negligence to be considered even though defendant violated a statute intended to protect plaintiff against his own acts of negligence.[54]

Minnesota Policy

In *Peterson v. Haule*[55] the Minnesota Supreme Court ruled that apportionment of damages was proper although defendant had violated a statute requiring glass doors to be marked. In *Simchuck v. Fullerton*[56] apportionment was allowed despite defendant's violation of a right-of-way statute.

The violation of a strict liability statute, however, will probably preclude the apportionment of damages in Minnesota. In *Zerby v. Warren*[57] the Minnesota Supreme Court held that neither contributory negligence nor assumption of risk would be available as defenses when a defendant retailer violated a statute forbidding the sale of glue to minors. The Court construed the statute as imposing strict liability in tort for its violation.

Nebraska Permits Defense

Nebraska permits contributory negligence to be shown, even to the point of barring recovery under its slight-gross rule, unless the applica-

---

[51]Presser v. Siesel Constr. Co., 19 Wis. 2d 54, 119 N.W.2d 405, 411 (1963). See also Fitzgerald v. Badger State Mut. Casualty Co., 67 Wis. 2d 321, 227 N.W.2d 444 (1975) (the court upheld a jury's apportionment of negligence despite defendant construction company's violation of a statute requiring the maintenance of adequate barriers and lighting at a construction site on the highway).

[52]Presser v. Siesel Constr. Co., 19 Wis. 2d 54, 119 N.W.2d 405, 411 (1963).

[53]D. L. v. Huebner, 110 Wis. 2d 581, 329 N.W.2d 890 (1983).

[54]See Frederick v. Hotel Investments, Inc., 48 Wis. 2d 429, 180 N.W.2d 562 (1970); Lovesee v. Allied Development Corp., 45 Wis. 2d 340, 173 N.W.2d 196 (1970); Gould v. Allstar Ins. Co., 59 Wis. 2d 355, 208 N.W.2d 388 (1973) (reduction of damages permitted when plaintiff negligently dived off pier which was not properly marked in violation of Wisconsin safe place statute); Kaiser v. Cook, 67 Wis. 2d 460, 227 N.W.2d 50 (1975) (reduction of damages permitted when defendant violated safe place statute by failure to maintain barriers at a race track and plaintiff negligently sat in the unprotected areas of the grandstand).

[55]Peterson v. Haule, 304 Minn. 160, 230 N.W.2d 51 (1975).

[56]Simchuck v. Fullerton, 299 Minn. 91, 216 N.W.2d 683 (1974).

[57]Zerby v. Warren, 297 Minn. 134, 210 N.W.2d 58 (1973). But see Steinhaus v. Adamson, 304 Minn. 14, 228 N.W.2d 865, 88 A.L.R.3d 613 (1975). See also Scott v. Independent School Dist., 256 N.W.2d 485 (Minn. 1977).

ble safety laws "expressly abrogate the defense of contributory negligence."[58]

In so holding, the Nebraska Supreme Court referred in dictum to the rule of Section 483 of the first *Restatement of Torts*, which barred the contributory negligence defense where defendant had violated a statute designed to protect "a person in a class unable 'to exercise self-protective care' ";[59] but the court said the plaintiff window-washer in the case before it was not such a person, presumably because he was an independent contractor, had solicited the business, knew of the risks and failed to use an available alternative safety device. Other decisions on facts strikingly similar to those in this case have barred the contributory negligence defense on the rationale of Section 483, even without express statutory language abrogating the defense. The New York Court of Appeals, ruling out contributory negligence as a defense in such a case, held it "of no moment" that plaintiff was an independent contractor and pointed out that "Workmen ... who ply their livelihoods on ladders and scaffolds ... usually have no choice but to work with the equipment at hand, though danger looms large."[60]

Kansas Permits Defense

The protective purpose of a Kansas statute which prohibited the sale of explosives to minors was held not to be defeated by comparative negligence principles in *Arredondo v. Duckwall Stores, Incorporated.*[61] The Kansas Supreme Court deemed the statute not to be an "exceptional" one wherein the contributory negligence defense would not lie.

The Better Rule

It is this author's view that under comparative negligence, unless the legislature specifically states to the contrary, plaintiff's fault should be considered even though defendant has violated a safety statute designed to protect plaintiff from his own inadvertence. This result is suggested by the specific language usually found in comparative negligence statutes to the effect that apportionment is to be made in all cases predicated on negligence. There may be some justification in retaining the rule that plaintiff's negligence should not be considered when defendant has violated a statute specifically designed to protect

---

[58]Wertz v. Lincoln Liberty Life Ins. Co., 152 Neb. 451, 41 N.W.2d 740, 17 A.L.R.2d 629 (1950). In Epperson v. Utley, 191 Neb. 413, 215 N.W.2d 864 (1974), the Supreme Court of Nebraska upheld a jury finding for the defendant despite his entry into an intersection at an unlawful speed. As the doctrine of negligence per se is derived entirely from statute and not subsequent decisional law, the court upheld a refusal to instruct on a repealed statute which provided for forfeiture of right-of-way for entry into an intersection at an unlawful speed.

[59]Wertz v. Lincoln Liberty Life Ins. Co., 41 N.W.2d 740, 744 (1950), quoting *Restatement of Torts* § 483 (1934).

[60]See Koenig v. Patrick Constr. Corp., 298 N.Y. 313, 83 N.E.2d 133, 135, 10 A.L.R.2d 848 (1948) (window cleaner fell off ladder not equipped with safety devices required by statute).

[61]Arredondo v. Duckwall Stores, Inc., 227 Kan. 842, 610 P.2d 1107 (1980).

plaintiff against his own negligence and when that specific type of negligence has occurred. Nevertheless, the great difficulty encountered by courts[62] (and apparent in the *Restatement (Second) of Torts*[63]) in setting forth the means of identifying such statutes suggests that the rule should be abolished.

Although this particular rule barring contributory negligence was not directly spawned by courts' dislike of the contributory negligence defense, it arose in an atmosphere where plaintiff was placed in an all or nothing recovery situation. Under comparative negligence it would seem proper, even where defendant violated a statute designed to protect plaintiff against his own inadvertence, to permit the jury to make some apportionment if it finds that plaintiff was at fault with respect to the cause of his own injuries. Of course the jury must give due regard to the gravity of defendant's offense and to the totality of circumstances. If the matter is approached in this way, it can be anticipated that mitigation of damages, if any, will be very slight.

6.3 Plaintiff's violation of statute

When plaintiff violates a criminal safety statute intended to protect him against risk of the very harm that occurred, most American courts following the contributory negligence doctrine have barred his claim; plaintiff was negligent per se.[64]

A few courts have in the past given even more force to violations of criminal statutes by plaintiffs and barred their claims even though the breach did not relate to the harm that actually occurred; this was called by some the "outlaw" effect.[65] For example, a Massachusetts court once held that a driver of an unregistered automobile had no right of action if involved in a collision.[66] Today, under either comparative negligence or contributory negligence, it is unlikely that the "outlaw" approach will be applied; plaintiff will be deemed negligent per se only if the statute violated was intended to protect against the risk of harm that befell him.[67]

The courts that applied the "outlaw" effect to plaintiffs whose conduct violated a statute gave too much weight to such breaches. A few

---

[62]See notes 28 and 29, above, and accompanying text.

[63]*Restatement (Second) of Torts* §483, Comment c at 539.

[64]See *Restatement (Second) of Torts* § 469 (1965); Note, *The Plaintiff's Breach of Statutory Duty as a Bar in an Action of Tort*, 39 Harv. L. Rev. 1088 (1926).

[65]See Note, *Effect of Sunday Law on Negligence Actions Where Duty Based on Sunday Contract*, 13 B.U.L. Rev. 365 (1933).

[66]See W. P. Keeton et al., *Prosser and Keeton on the Law of Torts* § 36, at 223 and note 29 (5th ed. 1984).

[67]Id., § 36, at 232–233. See, e.g., Swaner v. City of Santa Monica, 150 Cal. App. 3d 789, 198 Cal. Rptr. 208 (1984) (violation of statute barring sleeping on the beach would not bar recovery against city for failing to keep drivers from racing on the beach at night); Hansen v. Washington Natural Gas Co., 27 Wash. App. 127, 615 P.2d 1351 (1980), revd. on other grounds, 95 Wash. 2d 773, 632 P.2d 504 (1981) (violation of jaywalking statute will not bar recovery for injury at street excavation site).

courts have gone to the other extreme and held that plaintiff's violation of a safety statute should not constitute contributory negligence since such statutes were enacted for the protection of others, not of the plaintiff himself.[68] These decisions were severely criticized by the late Dean Prosser[69] and are unlikely to be followed under comparative negligence. They were probably based on a desire to limit the contributory negligence defense.[70]

Claim Allowed to Statutory Offender

Jurisdictions with comparative negligence have deemed plaintiff's violation of a criminal safety statute negligence per se.[71] This, however, does not answer the more difficult and material question under comparative negligence: whether plaintiff's claim will be barred when he has violated an applicable criminal safety statute.

Admiralty Jurisdiction

In maritime law the violation of a safety statute is negligence per se.[72] Ordinarily, in admiralty, if a moving vessel strikes a stationary object, the moving vessel is presumed to be at fault. But if the owner of the stationary vessel has violated a safety statute by blocking the waterway, the presumption is overcome and fault will be compared.[73]

Pure Comparative Negligence

Under pure comparative negligence a plaintiff's claim will not be barred by his violation of a safety statute. In *Winfield v. Magee*[74] plaintiff-truck driver sought damages for personal injuries sustained when defendant negligently drove out of a narrow driveway onto a highway and collided with plaintiff's vehicle. Defendant argued that the plaintiff's claim should be dismissed because he was in violation of the law, in that his truck was on the left side of the road. The Supreme Court of Mississippi indicated that under the state's comparative negligence statute, plaintiff's conduct "would be only contributory negli-

---

[68]W. P. Keeton et al., note 66 above, at 203, citing Dohn v. R. N. Cardozo & Bros., 165 Minn. 193, 206 N.W. 377 (1925); Watts v. Montgomery Traction Co., 175 Ala. 102, 106, 57 So. 471 (1912). See also Brownstone Park, Ltd. v. Southern Union Gas Co., 537 S.W.2d 270 (Tex. Civ. App. 1976) (since purpose of state building code is protection of building's inhabitants, and not absolution of service company from liability, plaintiff's violation of building code not negligence per se).

[69]W. P. Keeton et al., note 66 above, at 232–233.

[70]Cf. Cavanaugh v. Boston & M. R. R., 76 N.H. 68, 79 A. 694 (1911) (explicit on this point with regard to the "last clear chance" doctrine).

[71]See Johns v. Secress, 106 Ga. App. 96, 126 S.E.2d 296 (1962); Winfield v. Magee, 232 Miss. 57, 98 So. 2d 130 (1957); Johnson v. Chemical Supply Co., 38 Wis. 2d 194, 156 N.W.2d 455 (1968). Accord, Petrella v. Izzo, 117 R.I. 459, 367 A.2d 1078 (1977).

[72]Board of Comrs. v. M/V Agelos Michael, 390 F. Supp. 1012 (E.D. La. 1974). See also In re Petition of Alva S.S. Co., 616 F.2d 605 (2d Cir. N.Y. 1980) (violation of fire department regulation constituted negligence per se).

[73]Board of Comrs. v. M/V Agelos Michael, 390 F. Supp. 1012 (E.D. La. 1974). See subsection 3.3(C).

[74]Winfield v. Magee, 232 Miss. 57, 98 So. 2d 130 (1957).

gence which would cause the damages to be reduced ...."[75] In effect, plaintiff's statutory negligence was treated the same as ordinary negligence.

Modified Systems

Under modified comparative negligence, the question whether plaintiff's statutory negligence will bar his claim is closer. Nevertheless, decisions to date indicate that violation by plaintiff of a safety statute does not automatically bar his claim and eliminate apportionment of damages.[76]

Slight-Gross System

Under the slight-gross system in Nebraska, the fact that plaintiff violated a safety statute does not automatically mean that his conduct was more than slightly negligent in comparison with defendant's.[77] Similarly, South Dakota decisions indicate that although plaintiff violated a safety statute, the jury may determine that his negligence was "slight" when compared with the defendant's.[78]

50% System

Obviously, under a comparative negligence system that bars plaintiff's claim when plaintiff's negligence is equal to or greater than that of the defendant,[79] there is a great temptation to bar a plaintiff who has violated a criminal safety statute. Nevertheless, an examination of the decisions shows that the courts have not succumbed to the temptation. For example, in *Johns v. Secress*,[80] plaintiff-automobile driver sustained serious injuries in an intersection collision with a defendant who was driving eighty miles per hour. Defendant contended that plaintiff's claims should be barred because he entered the intersection without obeying a stop sign, thus violating a state safety statute. The Georgia court rejected this contention and affirmed a verdict granting plaintiff a reduced award. The court was most explicit:

---

[75]Id., 98 So. 2d at 131–132.

[76]See, e.g., Reed v. Little, 680 P.2d 937 (Mont. 1984) (statutory violations in rear-end collision were evidence of negligence but did not necessarily bar recovery). Cf. Barker v. Kallash, 63 N.Y.2d 19, 479 N.Y.S.2d 201, 468 N.E.2d 39 (1984), in which the fourteen-year-old plaintiff was barred from recovery, the comparative fault statute notwithstanding, because his conduct in making a pipe bomb was an egregious violation of public policy.

[77]See Union P. R. Co. v. Denver-Chicago Trucking Co., 202 F.2d 31 (8th Cir. Neb. 1953) (applying Nebraska law); Continental Can Co. v. Horton, 250 F.2d 637 (8th Cir. Neb. 1957). It should be noted that in Nebraska violation of a statute is only evidence of negligence; see Union P. R. Co., 202 F.2d at 35.

[78]See Weeks v. Prostrollo Sons, Inc., 84 S.D. 243, 169 N.W.2d 725 (1969). Older cases suggested that if plaintiff violated a safety statute, his negligence was more than slight; see Friese v. Gulbrandson, 69 S.D. 179, 8 N.W.2d 438 (1943); Haase v. Willers Truck Service, 72 S.D. 353, 34 N.W.2d 313 (1948). These cases can be explained by a practice followed before the 1964 amendment of the South Dakota statute; that state used to determine in the abstract whether plaintiff's negligence was more than "slight." Since the 1964 amendment, this practice is no longer followed. See section 3.4.

[79]See section 3.5.

[80]Johns v. Secress, 106 Ga. App. 96, 126 S.E.2d 296 (1962).

While an act defined by the law as negligence per se is not issuable, in the sense that no issue may be made as to the act being or not being negligence, yet it is still within the exclusive province of the jury to determine whether one shown to have been guilty of negligence per se, was guilty of greater negligence than another shown to have been guilty of some other kind of negligence per se or merely of negligence as a matter of fact and to compare the two and determine which is greater.[81]

The general hesitancy of Wisconsin courts to rule as a matter of law that a plaintiff's negligence equaled or exceeded that of the defendant suggests that that state would be in accord with the Georgia rationale.[82] Wisconsin and other states with a 50% comparative negligence system should adopt the Georgia approach because it is in accord with general principles of comparative fault, as well as for practical considerations. For example, an act of common-law contributory negligence can create a higher risk to plaintiff than a statutory violation.[83] Therefore, it makes more sense to let the jury weigh the fault of the parties in relation to each other, as the comparative negligence statute dictates, than to bar plaintiff's claim simply because he has violated a safety statute. This is the approach taken in Massachusetts' general comparative negligence statute, which provides that the plaintiff's violation of a safety statute is evidence of negligence but not a bar to recovery.[84]

More importantly, a rule automatically barring plaintiff could in effect bring back the contributory negligence defense. There are so many safety statutes and ordinances today that it is unusual for plaintiff to be negligent without having violated one.

In sum, the thrust of all comparative negligence statutes is toward apportionment of damages when both parties were at fault. This intent would be severely circumscribed if plaintiff's claim were always barred when he violated a criminal safety statute.

---

[81]Id., 126 S.E.2d at 298.

[82]See Johnson v. Chemical Supply Co., 38 Wis. 2d 194, 156 N.W.2d 455, 460 (1968) (plaintiff's claim not barred though he obliterated safety warning on steel barrel containing volatile substance).

[83]Id.

[84]Mass. Gen. Laws Ann., ch. 231, § 85.

CHAPTER 7
LAST CLEAR CHANCE

Section

7.1 The rationale of last clear chance under the contributory negligence defense

The most frequently applied limitation on the contributory negligence defense is the so-called last clear chance doctrine.[1] It was first crystallized in the nineteenth century case of *Davies v. Mann*,[2] where plaintiff left his ass with fettered forefeet helpless on the highway and defendant proceeding at "a smartish pace" ran into the animal. The doctrine has been in search of a lucid rationale ever since. In *Davies v. Mann* itself, the opinion of Baron Parke shows that he thought the doctrine necessary to protect helpless contributorily negligent plaintiffs from being injured by the subsequent acts of highly culpable defendants.[3]

The proposition that a wrongdoer with the last opportunity to avoid an accident is more culpable than a helpless plaintiff is true in the context of *Davies v. Mann*, but not always in other situations. The late Dean Prosser posed the hypothetical case of a plaintiff lying drunk in the street and defendant properly driving an automobile who sees him and excitedly steps on the accelerator instead of the brake.[4] In such a situation, the mere fact that the defendant was the last actor does not make him more culpable than the plaintiff. Nevertheless, the assumption that the last wrongdoer is the more culpable has adhered as a rationale underlying the last clear chance doctrine.[5]

The Proximate Cause Rationale

The most frequently asserted rationale for the last clear chance doctrine is that where defendant has the last chance, his act and not plaintiff's prior negligence is the "proximate cause" of the accident. This rationale is merely verbal and "cannot stand the most superficial analy-

---

[1]See W. P. Keeton et al., *Prosser and Keeton on the Law of Torts* § 66 (5th ed. 1984); 2 F. Harper & F. James, *The Law of Torts* §§ 22.12 to 22.14 (1956); James, *Last Clear Chance: A Transitional Doctrine*, 47 Yale L.J. 704 (1938); MacIntyre, *The Rationale of Last Clear Chance*, 53 Harv. L. Rev. 1225 (1940).

[2]Davies v. Mann, 10 M. & W. 546, 152 Eng. Rep. 588 (1842).

[3]Id., 152 Eng. Rep. at 589: "Were this not so, a man might justify driving over goods left on a public highway, or even over a man lying asleep there, or the purposely running against a carriage going on the wrong side of the road."

[4]See W. Prosser & J. Wade, *Cases and Materials on Torts* 517 (5th ed. 1971).

[5]See James, note 1 above, at 718-719 (demonstrating that the assumption becomes particularly weak as the time between plaintiff's act and defendant's becomes shorter).

sis if it purports to apply to plaintiff the test of legal cause generally used today in the inquiry as to a defendant's liability."[6] If plaintiff's negligent wrongdoing causes injury to a third party, he may be liable to the third party even though the principal defendant had in relation to plaintiff "the last clear chance."[7]

The emptiness in the "proximate cause" explanation of last clear chance has been recognized in a few judicial decisions.[8] Nevertheless, as indicated in a 1972 opinion of the Supreme Court of Iowa, an overwhelming number of courts in this country base their application of last clear chance on proximate cause; the act of the last wrongdoer insulates plaintiff's prior contributory negligence.[9]

Limitation of an Unpopular Doctrine

The overwhelming number of writers on last clear chance[10] and some courts[11] have stated that the purpose of the doctrine is simply to limit the effect of the contributory negligence defense. In point of fact, this "benefit" may have caused last clear chance to survive even though it has always lacked a solid rationale and is awkward to apply.

Conscious Last Clear Chance

With respect to the extent of the confusion in application of the doctrine, one can find different versions of it coexisting in the same jurisdiction.[12] Some general agreement can be found in a majority of jurisdictions. They do apply the doctrine when:

1. plaintiff has placed himself in inextricable peril, that is, can no longer escape by the exercise of reasonable care, and
2. defendant knows of plaintiff's position, and
3. although able to do so, defendant fails to exercise reasonable care to avoid the accident.[13]

This is so-called "conscious" last clear chance.

Unconscious Last Clear Chance

Some jurisdictions apply last clear chance where defendant *should have known* that plaintiff was in a position of inextricable peril even

---

[6]2 F. Harper & F. James, note 1 above, § 22.23 at 1244.

[7]See Cordiner v. Los Angeles Traction Co., 5 Cal. App. 400, 91 P. 436 (1907).

[8]See Petition of Kinsman Transit Co., 338 F.2d 708, 719 (2d Cir. N.Y. 1964) ("a notion as faulty in logic as it is wanting in fairness").

[9]See Ackerman v. James, 200 N.W.2d 818, 829-830 (Iowa 1972) (collecting cases). Accord, Minyard v. Hildebrand, 24 Ariz. App. 465, 539 P.2d 939 (1975).

[10]See materials cited in note 1 above.

[11]See Petition of Kinsman Transit Co., 338 F.2d 708 (2d Cir. N.Y. 1964); Cushman v. Perkins, 245 A.2d 846 (Me. 1968); Case Note, 2 Creighton L. Rev. 376 (1969).

[12]See DeMuth, *Derogation of the Common Law Rule of Contributory Negligence*, 7 Rocky Mtn. L. Rev. 161 (1935).

[13]See *Restatement (Second) of Torts* § 479 (1965). The mere fact that the plaintiff has negligently placed himself in a position of danger does not, in itself, make the position one of inextricable peril. See Burns v. Ottati, 513 P.2d 469 (Colo. App. 1973) (child negligently crossing heavily traveled street not in a position of inextricable peril); Street v. Calvert, 541 S.W.2d 576 (Tenn. 1976), approving *Restatement (Second) of Torts* § 479.

though he did not actually know. This is the so-called "unconscious last clear chance" situation.[14]

Some courts and the *Restatement (Second) of Torts* mitigate the requirements even further by allowing recovery when plaintiff was merely inattentive and could, by the exercise of reasonable care, have extricated himself from the position of peril at the time defendant's negligence became operative.[15] In such a situation, almost all states would require that defendant have actual knowledge of plaintiff's position and of his inattention, and have the ability after such knowledge to avoid the injury by the exercise of reasonable care.[16] As Prosser has noted, if the defendant does not discover the inattentive plaintiff but merely could do so by proper vigilance,

[I]t is obvious that neither party can be said to have a "last clear" chance. The plaintiff is still in a position to escape, and his lack of attention continues up to the point of the accident, without the interval of superior opportunity of the defendant, which has been considered so important.[17]

Remarkably, Missouri and possibly a few other states have applied last clear chance even in that situation.[18] To further confuse the issue, one court has applied the doctrine to a plaintiff who was neither helpless nor inattentive. In *Fish v. Ovalle*[19] the plaintiff stepped in front of the defendant's automobile and refused to move even after the car had moved forward twice. The third time it moved forward, the plaintiff was injured. The court held that the doctrine of last clear chance applies even when the defendant recognizes the peril and could have avoided it by the exercise of reasonable care if the plaintiff recognizes that he will not do so.

Plaintiff's Last Clear Chance

To add to the confusion, a few courts have held that a plaintiff cannot recover if he had the "last clear chance" to avoid the accident.[20] Where contributory negligence is a complete defense, this serves little

---

[14]See W. P. Keeton et al., note 1 above, § 66 at 466.

[15]Id.

[16]See *Restatement (Second) of Torts* § 480 (1965). See also Street v. Calvert, 541 S.W.2d 576 (Tenn. 1976), approving *Restatement (Second) of Torts* § 480.

[17]See W. P. Keeton et al., note 1 above, § 66 at 467. See also Brewer v. Apalachicola N. R. Co., 303 So. 2d 652 (Fla. App. 1974); Perry v. Gulf, M. & O. R. Co., 502 F.2d 1144 (6th Cir. Tenn. 1974) (both cases involved inattentive plaintiffs who failed to observe approaching trains despite unobstructed vision. Both courts declined to apply last clear chance as the negligence of the plaintiff was concurrent with that of the defendant).

[18]See W. P. Keeton et al., note 1 above, § 66 at 467. Missouri abolished last clear chance in Gustafson v. Benda, 661 S.W.2d 11 (Mo. 1983).

[19]Fish v. Ovalle, 512 S.W.2d 718 (Tex. Civ. App. 1974).

[20]See Umberger v. Koop, 194 Va. 123, 72 S.E.2d 370 (1952); Island Express, Inc. v. Frederick, 35 Del. 569, 171 A. 181 (1934); Louisville & N. R. Co. v. Patterson, 77 Ga. App. 406, 49 S.E.2d 218 (1948). Florida's holding to this effect in Miami Beach R. Co. v. Dohme, 131 Fla. 171, 179 So. 166 (1938) appears to have been at least clouded by its 1973 adoption of comparative negligence. See Hoffman v. Jones, 280 So. 2d 431, 438, 78 A.L.R.3d 321 (Fla. 1973).

purpose other than to come "out at exactly the same place as the defense of contributory negligence without the doctrine at all...."[21]

One point about the last clear chance doctrine is clear. When it is applied against a defendant, plaintiff recovers his entire damages and there is no apportionment.[22] Because the last clear chance doctrine has the effect of transferring from the plaintiff to the defendant an entire loss which was in fact attributable to the fault of both, it is important to know whether the doctrine survives the adoption of comparative negligence. Section 7.2 will discuss that problem. Section 7.3, then, is a short exposition on what occurs under comparative negligence when plaintiff had the "last clear chance" to avoid the accident.

7.2   Defendant's last clear chance under comparative negligence

There has been an extraordinary amount of discussion on what would appear to be a rather narrow problem: whether the last clear chance doctrine can be applied under comparative negligence.[23] This abundance of discussion is not surprising in view of the dramatic effect last clear chance can have under comparative negligence; if it is applied, plaintiff avoids any apportionment of his damages and recovers the entire amount.

As might be anticipated, there is sharp division, both under limited[24] and general comparative negligence statutes, as to whether last clear chance applies. The divisions have arisen because there has been surprisingly little guidance from the legislatures; only in the Connecticut statute and in the 1955 Arkansas statute was the problem specifically confronted. Those statutes indicated that last clear chance would no longer be applied.[25] The Arkansas statute, however, was subsequently

---

[21]W. P. Keeton et al., note 1 above, § 66 at 454.

[22]Id., § 66 at 464. Prosser notes a few cases where damages were apportioned because part of them were inflicted before the last clear chance had occurred; see § 66 at 464, n. 13.

[23]See C. Gregory, *Legislative Loss Distribution in Negligence Actions—A Study in Administrative Aspects of Comparative Negligence and Contribution in Tort Litigation* 126–133 (1936); Budd, *The Validity of Retaining the Last Clear Chance Doctrine in a State Having a Comparative Negligence Statute,* 1 Ga. S.B.J. 500 (1965); Garner, *Comparative Negligence and Discovered Peril,* 10 Ark. L. Rev. 72 (1955); Laugesen, *Colorado Comparative Negligence,* 48 Den. L.J. 469, 485–486 (1972); MacIntyre, *Last Clear Chance After Thirty Years Under the Apportionment Statutes,* 33 Can. B. Rev. 257 (1955); Shell and Bufkin, *Comparative Negligence in Mississippi,* 27 Miss. L.J. 105, 109 (1956); Annot., "Application of last clear chance doctrine in comparative negligence case," 59 A.L.R.2d 1258 (1958); Note, *Comparative Negligence and the "Jackass Doctrine" (Last Clear Chance),* 6 S.D. L. Rev. 96 (1961); Note, *Doctrine of Last Clear Chance Retained by Comparative Negligence Statute,* 52 Harv. L. Rev. 1187 (1939); Case Note, *Negligence: Last Clear Chance Doctrine Superseded by Comparative Negligence Statutes,* 8 U. Fla. L. Rev. 339 (1955); Note, *Comparative Negligence: Some New Problems for the Maine Courts,* 18 Me. L. Rev. 65, 90, 92 (1966); Case Note, 2 Creighton L. Rev. 376 (1969).

[24]Barnes v. Red River & G. R. R., 14 La. App. 188, 128 So. 724 (1930) (applied); Soles v. Atlantic C. L. R. Co., 184 N.C. 283, 114 S.E. 305 (1922) (applied); Loftin v. Nolin, 86 So. 2d 161 (Fla. 1956), noted in 8 U. Fla. L. Rev. 339 (1955) (rejecting application of last clear chance).

[25]Ark. Acts 1955, No. 191; Conn. Gen. Stat. Ann., § 52–572h(c).

repealed and a new comparative negligence statute was enacted that did not mention last clear chance.[26] The current Arkansas statute also omits mention of last clear chance.[27] The courts of that state may have taken the statutory change as a sign that last clear chance should apply.[28]

In 1981 the state of Washington adopted a new comparative fault statute modelled in part on the Uniform Comparative Fault Act, which states that comparative fault

> applies whether or not under prior law the claimant's contributory fault constituted a defense or was disregarded under applicable legal doctrines, such as last clear chance.[29]

Retention of Last Clear Chance

States with general comparative negligence laws that have clearly retained last clear chance include Georgia,[30] Nebraska[31] and South Dakota.[32] New Hampshire and Michigan appear also to have retained the doctrine.[33]

Abolition of Last Clear Chance

To date, Alaska, California, Connecticut, Florida, Illinois, Maine, Missouri, Nevada, Oregon, Texas, Washington, Wisconsin, and Wyoming have general comparative negligence doctrines under which it is crystal clear that the last clear chance doctrine does not apply. Connecticut and Oregon specifically abolished the doctrine by statute.[34] Wisconsin courts avoided the whole problem by rejecting last clear

---

[26]See Ark. Stat. Ann., §§ 27–1730.1 and 27–1730.2 (since repealed).

[27]Ark. Stat. Ann., §§ 27–1763 to 27–1765.

[28]See Ed Hopson Produce Co. v. Munoz, 230 Ark. 179, 321 S.W.2d 203 (1959) (court appears to assume the viability of the "discovered peril" doctrine).

[29]Wash. Rev. Code Ann., § 4.22.005; Unif. Comp. Fault Act, § 1(a), 12 U.L.A. 40 (Supp. 1985).

[30]See Grayson v. Yarbrough, 103 Ga. App. 243, 119 S.E.2d 41 (1961). For a while it appeared that Georgia had abandoned the doctrine; see Smith v. American Oil Co., 77 Ga. App. 463, 49 S.E.2d 90 (1948). The Supreme Court of Georgia put this question to rest in Southland Butane Gas Co. v. Blackwell, 211 Ga. 665, 88 S.E.2d 6 (1955), modified Fountain v. Thompson, 252 Ga. 256, 312 S.E.2d 788 (1984). See also Conner v. Mangum, 132 Ga. App. 100, 207 S.E.2d 604 (1974); cf. Shuman v. Mashburn, 137 Ga. App. 231, 223 S.E.2d 268, 85 A.L.R.3d 741 (1976) (plaintiff injured diving into defendant's swimming pool while intoxicated was not entitled to instruction on last clear chance, since he was not in a position of inextricable peril immediately prior to diving and defendant could not appreciate peril in time to avoid injury).

[31]See, e.g., Whitaker v. Burlington Northern, Inc., 218 Neb. 90, 352 N.W.2d 589 (1984); Whitehouse v. Thompson, 150 Neb. 370, 34 N.W.2d 385 (1948); Parsons v. Berry, 130 Neb. 264, 264 N.W. 742 (1936).

[32]See Vlach v. Wyman, 78 S.D. 504, 104 N.W.2d 817 (1960).

[33]See Hanson v. N. H. Pre-Mix Concrete, Inc., 110 N.H. 377, 268 A.2d 841, 844 (1970); Macon v. Seaward Constr. Co., 555 F.2d 1 (1st Cir. N.H. 1977) (jury must take last clear chance components into account but no longer necessarily reach an all-or-nothing result); Bell v. Merritt, 118 Mich. App. 414, 325 N.W.2d 443 (1982); Wilson v. Chesapeake & O. R. Co., 118 Mich. App. 123, 324 N.W.2d 552 (1982).

[34]1973 Conn. Pub. Act No. 73–622, § 1(c); Conn. Gen. Stat. Ann., § 52–572h(c); Ore. Rev. Stat., § 18.475(1).

chance even before the state adopted comparative negligence,[35] and the state has reaffirmed its rejection since its comparative negligence statute became operative.[36] In *Loftin v. Nolin*[37] Florida held the last clear chance doctrine inconsistent with its comparative negligence statute applicable to railroads; later, when it adopted general comparative negligence by judicial action, the Florida Supreme Court said without further discussion that "of course" last clear chance would no longer apply.[38]

Despite the Florida and Wisconsin decisions the highest court of neither state had engaged in a full discussion of the issue. As of 1974 the only state court to undertake that burden was the Supreme Judicial Court of Maine in a 1968 case.[39] Subsequently the California and Alaska supreme court decisions adopting pure comparative negligence engaged in a discussion of the rationale of last clear chance under comparative negligence. Both courts rejected the simultaneous operation of both doctrines: the California court because last clear chance is incompatible with the principle of liability in proportion to fault;[40] the Alaska court because last clear chance was no longer needed to limit the operation of the contributory negligence defense.[41] The Supreme Court of California declared that the last clear chance doctrine would result in a "windfall to the plaintiff in direct contravention of the principle of liability in proportion to fault" under comparative negligence.[42] The Supreme Court of Alaska also declared that last clear chance would no longer be a defense under comparative negligence, as its only value was to ameliorate the harshness of contributory negligence.[43]

In 1979, the Wyoming Supreme Court declared that the doctrine of last clear chance has been rendered unnecessary under that state's comparative negligence statute due to the apportionment of damages.[44] The Nevada Supreme Court deemed the doctrine of last clear chance inappropriate in view of the comparative negligence statute as amended by the 1979 legislature.[45]

The Texas Supreme Court abolished last clear chance in *French v.*

---

[35]See Switzer v. Detroit Inv. Co., 188 Wis. 330, 206 N.W. 407 (1925).

[36]See Butts v. Ward, 227 Wis. 387, 279 N.W. 6, 116 A.L.R. 1441 (1938); Wilmet v. Chicago & N.W. R. Co., 233 Wis. 335, 289 N.W. 815 (1940).

[37]Loftin v. Nolin, 280 So. 2d 161, 59 A.L.R.2d 1257 (Fla. 1956).

[38]Hoffman v. Jones, 280 So. 2d 431, 438, 78 A.L.R.3d 331 (Fla. 1973). Accord, Beltran v. Waste Management, Inc., 414 So. 2d 1145 (Fla. App. 1982).

[39]Cushman v. Perkins, 245 A.2d 846 (Me. 1968) noted in 2 Creighton L. Rev. 376 (1969).

[40]Nga Li v. Yellow Cab Co., 13 Cal. 3d 804, 119 Cal. Rptr. 858, 532 P.2d 1226, 78 A.L.R.3d 393 (1975).

[41]Kaatz v. State, 540 P.2d 1037 (Alaska 1975).

[42]Nga Li v. Yellow Cab Co., 13 Cal. 3d 804, 824, 119 Cal. Rptr. 858, 872, 532 P.2d 1226, 1240, 78 A.L.R.3d 393 (1975).

[43]Kaatz v. State, 540 P.2d 1037 (Alaska 1975).

[44]Danculovich v. Brown, 593 P.2d 187 (Wyo. 1979).

[45]Davies v. Butler, 95 Nev. 763, 602 P.2d 605 (1979). See Nev. Rev. Stat., § 41.141.

Grigsby,[46] declaring that comparative negligence was meant to do away with doctrines that placed the entire loss on one side or the other. English precedent appears to have limited the application of last clear chance to a situation in which defendant recklessly injures a plaintiff in peril.[47]

In 1981 the Illinois Supreme Court abolished last clear chance in the course of adopting comparative negligence;[48] the West Virginia Supreme Court did so in reconsidering its original position in *Bradley v. Appalachian Power Company*.[49] The Missouri Supreme Court's 1983 decision in *Gustafson v. Benda*[50] was unusual in that the case was certified only on the question of last clear chance; the court abolished last clear chance and proceeded to adopt comparative negligence!

States Where Result Uncertain

Surprisingly, even though Mississippi has had comparative negligence since 1910, it is uncertain whether it has totally abolished last clear chance. Writers in that state's major law review believe, or at least hope, that the doctrine has been abandoned.[51] Nevertheless, the Fifth Circuit has assumed that last clear chance survives in Mississippi.[52] In *Underwood v. Illinois Central Railroad Company* that court said, "the last clear chance doctrine . . . is firmly imbedded in the jurisprudence of Mississippi."[53] Moreover, there is some indication in state decisions that the doctrine is still alive.[54] The Supreme Court of Missis-

---

[46]French v. Grigsby, 571 S.W.2d 867 (Tex. 1978); Scott v. Webb, 583 S.W.2d 846 (Tex. Civ. App. 1979) (doctrine of discovered peril no longer proper issue since adoption of comparative negligence). See also Missouri-Kansas-Texas R. Co. v. Alvarez, 670 S.W.2d 338, 347 (Tex. App. 1984), revd. on other grounds, Alvarez v. Missouri-Kansas-Texas R. Co., 683 S.W.2d 375 (Tex. 1984).

[47]See Harvey v. Road Haulage Exec., [1952] 1 K.B. 120; Davies v. Swan Motor Co., 2 K.B. 291, 1 All Eng. 620 (1949).

[48]Alvis v. Ribar, 85 Ill. 2d 1, 52 Ill. Dec. 23, 421 N.E.2d 886 (1981).

[49]Ratlief v. Yokum, 280 S.E.2d 584 (W. Va. 1981).

[50]Gustafson v. Benda, 661 S.W.2d 11 (Mo. 1983).

[51]See Price, *Applicability of the Last Clear Chance Doctrine in Mississippi*, 29 Miss. L.J. 247 (1958); Shell and Bufkin, *Comparative Negligence in Mississippi*, 27 Miss. L.J. 105, 109 (1956); Note, *Effect of Mississippi's Comparative Negligence Statute on Other Rules of Law*, 39 Miss. L.J. 493 (1968).

[52]See Underwood v. Illinois C. R. Co., 205 F.2d 61, 63 (5th Cir. Miss. 1953). In a later decision regarding the same case, the court determined that the plaintiff did not prove defendant had the last clear chance. Illinois C. R. Co. v. Underwood, 235 F.2d 868 (5th Cir. Miss. 1956), cert. den. 352 U.S. 1001, 1 L. Ed. 2d 546, 77 S. Ct. 557 (1957).

[53]Underwood v. Illinois C. R. Co., 205 F.2d 61, 63 (5th Cir. Miss. 1953).

[54]See Mississippi C. R. Co. v. Aultman, 173 Miss. 622, 642, 160 So. 737, 740 (1935), appeal dismissed 296 U.S. 537, 80 L. Ed. 382, 56 S. Ct. 108 (1935) (when an engineer saw and appreciated the danger it was his duty to use every reasonable means to prevent the collision; no discussion of apportionment). See also Johnson v. Columbus & G. R. Co., 192 Miss. 627, 7 So. 2d 517 (1942); Young v. Columbus & G. R. Co., 165 Miss. 287, 147 So. 342 (1933). Accord, Newman v. Missouri P. R. Co., 421 F. Supp. 488 (S.D. Miss. 1976), affd. 545 F.2d 439 (5th Cir. Miss. 1977) (only conscious last clear chance survives in Mississippi; engine crew that did not see automobile on crossing in time to avoid collision did not have the "last clear chance" but rather had a "better chance" to avoid it; damages were apportioned).

sippi has never been precisely clear on the point, but it appears to apply the doctrine when defendant had a conscious last clear chance.[55]

An Ohio intermediate court has declared that the last clear chance doctrine did not survive the enactment of statutory comparative negligence.[56]

In New Hampshire, although last clear chance is no longer used to render an all-or-nothing result, the First Circuit has held that its components are still applicable. In *Macon v. Seaward Construction Company*[57] it was held permissible to instruct the jury that it might consider whether the defendant had time to avoid the accident.

That Colorado probably will abandon last clear chance is indicated by omission from the revised pattern jury instructions of a last clear chance instruction.[58] The only thing clear with respect to F.E.L.A.[59] and admiralty[60] cases is that they are divided over the issue. There has been little indication from other comparative negligence law jurisdictions as to whether they will continue to apply last clear chance.

It is uncertain whether last clear chance will continue to apply to the admiralty jurisdiction. One district court has held that the last clear chance doctrine was applied in admiralty only to mitigate the harshness of the divided damages rule and will no longer be available under pure comparative negligence.[61]

Arguments for Preserving Last Clear Chance

In order to understand the total picture with respect to last clear chance, it is more important to focus on the reasons for and against application of the doctrine in a comparative negligence jurisdiction than it is to consider how courts have "voted" to date. The arguments for retention of last clear chance are rather simple. First, where a legislature did not indicate the doctrine was to be abolished, one can argue

---

[55]See cases cited in note 54 above.

[56]Mitchell v. Ross, 14 Ohio App. 3d 75, 14 Ohio B. R. 87, 470 N.E.2d 245 (1984).

[57]Macon v. Seaward Constr. Co., 555 F.2d 1 (1st Cir. N.H. 1977).

[58]See Colo. Jury Instructions, 9:18, cited in Laugesen, *Colorado Comparative Negligence*, 48 Den. L.J. 469, 493 (1972); see also dictum in Burns v. Ottati, 513 P.2d 469, 472 (Colo. App. 1973).

[59]See Seaboard C. L. R. Co. v. Daugherty, 118 Ga. App. 518, 164 S.E.2d 269 (1968), cert. den. 397 U.S. 939, 25 L. Ed. 2d 120, 90 S. Ct. 950 (1970) (firmly rejecting); Deere v. Southern Pac. Co., 123 F.2d 438 (9th Cir. Ore. 1941) (applying); Annot., "Tests of causation under Federal Employers' Liability Act or Jones Act," 98 A.L.R.2d 653, 682 (1964).

[60]See, e.g., The Steam Dredge No. 1, 134 F. 161, 165–168 (1st Cir. Me. 1904) (rejecting); Annot., "Last clear chance doctrine in admiralty," 3 A.L.R. Fed. 203 (1970) (majority rule is to reject). The Second Circuit has applied last clear chance when the defendant was well aware of the danger and could easily have avoided it. The purpose of application was to avoid the harsh rigidity of the equally divided damages rule in cases in which one party is only slightly at fault. See Petition of Marina Mercante Nicaraguense, S.A., 364 F.2d 118 (2d Cir. N.Y. 1966), cert. den. 385 U.S. 1005, 17 L. Ed. 2d 544, 87 S. Ct. 710 (1967); Arundel Corp. v. The City of Calcutta, 174 F. Supp. 593 (E.D. N.Y. 1958).

[61]S.C. Loveland, Inc. v. East West Towing, Inc., 415 F. Supp. 596 (S.D. Fla. 1976), affd. 608 F.2d 160 (5th Cir. Fla. 1979), cert. den. 446 U.S. 918, 64 L. Ed. 2d 272, 100 S. Ct. 1852 (1980). See section 3.3 above, at note 47.

that there was a legislative intent that it should continue.[62] A second argument is that the underlying rationale of last clear chance is proximate cause, in that defendant had the last opportunity to avoid the accident but did not use it, and, since the comparative negligence statute does not speak to proximate cause, it should not change the last clear chance doctrine.[63] Further, the same linguistic argument can be stated under the heading of "duty": defendant under comparative negligence still has a duty to avoid injuring a party who has negligently placed himself in inextricable peril.[64]

Arguments Against Last Clear Chance

The arguments that call for abolition of last clear chance when comparative negligence has been adopted answer the contentions stated above and add persuasive points that suggest abolition as the correct position. It is true that a strict reading of many comparative negligence statutes could betoken an intent to apportion damages only where contributory negligence would have been a complete defense prior to enactment.[65] Nevertheless, the general purpose underlying comparative negligence statutes suggests that they be construed to allow damage apportionment on the basis of fault.[66] If a broad last clear chance doctrine were to survive, it would be a serious restraint on comparative negligence because it would sharply reduce the number of cases in which this kind of apportionment could be accomplished.[67]

To the argument that last clear chance survives because it is based on proximate cause, the answer is a bit more complex. The proximate cause of an accident is the same regardless of who is injured in the accident. If responsibility is governed by last clear chance and last clear chance is a matter of proximate cause, then the responsibility should be the same regardless of who is injured. Yet it is clear that if a plaintiff places himself in a position of inextricable peril and causes injury to a third party, plaintiff's conduct is the proximate cause and he is responsible for the injury even though another defendant's conduct immediately caused the accident.[68]

---

[62]Only the Connecticut statute (Conn. Gen. Stat. Ann., § 52–572h(c)), the Washington statute (Wash. Rev. Code Ann., § 4.22.005), a repealed Arkansas statute (Ark. Acts 1955, No. 191) and a few Canadian statutes (see Walker v. Forbes, 56 Ont. L.R. 532, 2 D.L.R. 725 (1925), 59 A.L.R.2d 1261, 1263 note 9, 1269 (1958)), have ever directly addressed themselves to the issue.

[63]See Neilsen v. Richman, 68 S.D. 104, 299 N.W. 74 (1941).

[64]See Mississippi C. R. Co. v. Aultman, 173 Miss. 622, 160 So. 737, 740 (1935), appeal dismissed 296 U.S. 537, 80 L. Ed. 382, 56 S. Ct. 108 (1935).

[65]See, e.g., Minn. Stat. Ann., § 604.01; R.I. Gen. Laws, § 9-20-4; Vt. Stat. Ann., tit. 12, § 1036.

[66]See Cushman v. Perkins, 245 A.2d 846, 850 (Me. 1968). See also Nga Li v. Yellow Cab Co., 13 Cal. 3d 804, 119 Cal. Rptr. 858, 532 P.2d 1226, 78 A.L.R.3d 393 (1975).

[67]See Price, *Applicability of the Last Clear Chance Doctrine in Mississippi*, 29 Miss. L.J. 247, 248 (1958).

[68]See Budd, *The Validity of Retaining the Last Clear Chance Doctrine in a State Having a Comparative Negligence Statute*, 1 Ga. S.B.J. 500 (1965). See also Britton v. Hoyt, 63 Wis. 2d 688, 218 N.W.2d 274 (1974) (dicta).

For example, if a party leaves his truck, unlighted and abandoned on the highway and defendant negligently crashes into it with the result that a third party is injured, both the owner of the abandoned truck and the party who immediately brought about the accident are liable to the third party.[69]

Since the argument that last clear chance is a branch of proximate cause fails, that rationale should not serve to sponsor the retention of last clear chance under comparative negligence.

Policy Based on Comparative Culpability

Finally, policy does not support the rule that a defendant who has a last clear chance should always be held liable to one who has placed himself inextricably in peril. It has been argued in support of the rule that as between the two parties, the one with the last opportunity is always more culpable. This is an overgeneralization. Plaintiff can recklessly place himself in a position of peril and be injured by a less culpable defendant. For example, a daredevil who sleeps on a darkened highway may be more negligent than the driver who later injures him.[70] Moreover, as the time between the respective negligent acts decreases, last clear chance almost totally breaks down as a gauge of fault.[71]

As indicated in section 7.1, the true reason for the popularity of last clear chance was that it served to modify the harshness of the contributory negligence rule.[72] Nevertheless, it wrought complexities in the law, and jurisdictions sharply divided (sometimes internally) with respect to the scope of its application.[73]

As the Supreme Court of Maine recognized,[74] "the last clear chance rule is but a modification of the doctrine of contributory negligence." Therefore, when the "absolute bar disappeared . . . the last clear chance rule disappeared with it. . . ."[75] The overwhelming number of writers would agree with the Maine court that the last clear chance doctrine is totally out of harmony with comparative negligence—a system which requires each party to bear the cost of his own fault.[76]

---

[69]See Hill v. Edmonds, 26 A.D.2d 554, 270 N.Y.S.2d 1020 (1966); Petition of Kinsman Transit Co., 338 F.2d 708, 719 (2d Cir. N.Y. 1964) ("As against third persons, one negligent actor cannot defend on the basis that the other had 'the last clear chance.' ").

[70]See text at note 4, section 7.1.

[71]See James, *Last Clear Chance: A Transitional Doctrine*, 47 Yale L.J. 704, 718–719 (1938).

[72]See W. P. Keeton et al., *Prosser and Keeton on the Law of Torts* § 66 (5th ed. 1984); 2 F. Harper & F. James, *The Law of Torts* §§ 22.12 to 22.14 (1956); James, note 71 above at 704; MacIntyre, *The Rationale of Last Clear Chance*, 53 Harv. L. Rev. 1225 (1940); Petition of Kinsman Transit Co., 338 F.2d 708 (2d Cir. N.Y. 1964); Cushman v. Perkins, 245 A.2d 846 (Me. 1968); Case Note, 2 Creighton L. Rev. 376 (1969).

[73]See note 12, section 7.1, and accompanying text.

[74]Cushman v. Perkins, 245 A.2d 846, 850 (Me. 1968).

[75]Id. See also Bruce v. McIntyre, Ont. L. Rep., 2 Dom. L. Rep. 799 (1954), affd. Can. S.C. 251, 1 Dom. L. Rep. 785 (1955).

[76]See note 23 above.

Modified Comparative Negligence Systems

Of course, when a state has modified comparative negligence, [77] a strong argument could be made that last clear chance should still apply when negligence is not compared. This may be why Nebraska and South Dakota[78] have retained last clear chance. Moreover, in *Cushman v. Perkins*, the Supreme Court of Maine recognized that the doctrine might still apply under a diluted comparative negligence system like that of Nebraska and South Dakota where the contributory negligence defense still has some virility.[79]

Finally, it should be noted that the jurisdictions that have retained the last clear chance rule along with comparative negligence have not given very broad scope to the doctrine. Recent cases indicate that in all such jurisdictions, last clear chance is applied only in situations where defendant knew that plaintiff was in peril (conscious last clear chance)[80] and failed to use reasonable care to avoid the accident. Since it is extremely difficult for plaintiffs to show that defendant had a conscious last clear chance,[81] the difference among the cases in this area may be more apparent than real. Nevertheless, it is this author's view that unless there is a special, expressed statutory policy to retain it, the last clear chance doctrine should not survive where negligence is compared.

7.3 Plaintiff's last clear chance under comparative negligence

A few states with contributory negligence apply a doctrine where plaintiff's claim is barred if he had the last clear chance to avoid the accident.[82] There is no apparent reason to do this; it is merely the contributory negligence defense coming back under another name.[83]

Nevertheless, such a doctrine can do serious damage if it survives after a state adopts comparative negligence. This has, in fact, occurred in Georgia,[84] but there a special statute dictates the result.[85] In that state, if the plaintiff by ordinary care could have avoided the consequences to himself caused by defendant's negligence, he is not entitled

---

[77]See sections 3.3 to 3.5.

[78]See notes 29 and 30 above.

[79]See Cushman v. Perkins, 245 A.2d 846, 850 (Me. 1968) ("in cases where the plaintiff's negligence is less than defendant's").

[80]See notes 13 and 14, section 7.1, and accompanying text.

[81]See Hanson v. N. H. Pre-Mix Concrete, Inc., 110 N.H. 377, 268 A.2d 841 (1970).

[82]See W. P. Keeton et al., *Prosser and Keeton on the Law of Torts* § 66, at 464 (5th ed. 1984).

[83]Id.

[84]See Grayson v. Yarbrough, 103 Ga. App. 243, 119 S.E.2d 41 (1961); Stephenson, *Plaintiff's Last Clear Chance and Comparative Negligence in Georgia*, 6 Ga. S.B.J. 47 (1969).

[85]Ga. Code Ann., § 51-11-7.

to recover. In other cases, the defendant is not relieved although the plaintiff may in some way have contributed to the injuries sustained.[86]

Obviously, application of the last clear chance doctrine to bar plaintiff's claim under a comparative negligence system would serve to eviscerate the very purpose of the system itself, to allocate damages on comparative fault. Therefore, unless the legislature specifically directs, once comparative negligence is adopted, courts should not apply last clear chance to bar a plaintiff's claim.

---

[86]Sanders v. Davila, 550 S.W.2d 709 (Tex. Civ. App. 1977), decided before French v. Grigsby, 571 S.W.2d 867 (Tex. 1978); see section 7.2, note 46, and accompanying text.

CHAPTER 8

RETROACTIVE CHANGE TO COMPARATIVE NEGLIGENCE

Section
8.1 Introduction
8.2 Retroactivity of judicial change
8.3 Legislative intent to change prospectively
8.4 Legislative change presumed prospective
8.5 Constitutionality of retroactive legislative change

8.1 Introduction

When comparative negligence is introduced in a state, its general effect is to allow causes of action to survive that would have been barred by the old contributory negligence defense. It must then be determined whether the new doctrine applies to conduct occurring before announcement of the new doctrine.[1]

The new doctrine may have come about through legislation[2] or by judicial action under the common law.[3] In either event a court may be faced with the question of retroactive application. While the statute of limitations has run on causes of action arising before the enactment of statutes cited in the first edition of this book, some states have only recently instituted comparative negligence, and the courts continue to refine the doctrine.[4]

Retroactive Statutes

The retroactivity question that has most often confronted the courts is whether a comparative negligence *statute* is to be given retroactive effect. Will a court construe the statute to "give to preenactment conduct a different legal effect from that which it would have without the passage of the statute"?[5]

If the statute is deemed retroactive, problems of constitutional

---

[1]See Annot., "Retrospective application of state statute substituting rule of comparative negligence for that of contributory negligence," 37 A.L.R.3d 1438 (1971); Note, *Comparative Negligence: Some New Problems for the Maine Courts,* 18 Me. L. Rev. 65, 71–73 (1966). See also on the general problem of retroactive application of law: Hochman, *The Supreme Court and the Constitutionality of Retroactive Legislation,* 73 Harv. L. Rev. 692 (1960); Smead, *The Rule Against Retroactive Legislation: A Basic Principle of Jurisprudence,* 20 Minn. L. Rev. 775 (1936); Smith, *Retroactive Laws and Vested Rights,* 5 Tex. L. Rev. 231 (1927); Stimson, *Retroactive Application of Law—A Problem in Constitutional Law,* 38 Mich. L. Rev. 30 (1939).

[2]See section 1.4.

[3]See section 1.5.

[4]See, e.g., Caterpillar Tractor Co. v. Boyett, 674 S.W.2d 782 (Tex. App. 1984), refusing to apply retrospectively the multiple-defendant rules of Duncan v. Cessna Aircraft Co., 665 S.W.2d 414 (Tex. 1984) retrospectively.

[5]Hochman, note 1 above, at 692.

dimension can arise under both state and federal due process clauses.[6] This complex and policy-laden issue has been reached in only a few cases under comparative negligence laws.[7] As will be demonstrated in section 8.4 below, courts have generally avoided this issue by finding a legislative intent to make the statutes operate prospectively only.

8.2 Retroactivity of judicial change

As of 1985, ten state courts of last resort have adopted comparative negligence by common-law decision.[8] The possibility of others doing so is not remote.[9] If a court takes this step, it must determine the extent to which its ruling will be applied retroactively.

In the past, there have been occasions when a major judge-made change in tort law was applied retroactively only to the particular case before the court and was made prospective as to all other cases.[10] However, that treatment was usually justified by the fact that reliance had been placed on continuation of the prior law. The most common example is the judicial abolition of governmental or charitable immunity in situations where governmental or charitable agencies had, in reliance on the old rule of immunity, failed to secure liability insurance.

Reliance on Contributory Negligence

It is difficult to conceive of a situation in which a defendant might have acted or failed to act to his detriment, either in insurance matters or otherwise, in justifiable reliance on continuation of the contributory negligence rule. In the absence of such reliance, it seems appropriate to apply the general rule that a judge-made change in tort law can be fully retroactive.[11] In that regard, a number of judge-made changes have been applied retroactively without any discussion of the issue.[12] Further, the Wisconsin Supreme Court adopted comparative negligence as a rule for contribution cases by judicial action and apparently made it fully retroactive.[13]

---

[6]Id.

[7]See section 8.5.

[8]Alaska, California, Florida, Illinois, Iowa, Kentucky, Michigan, Missouri, New Mexico, and West Virginia.

[9]See section 1.5.

[10]See Battalla v. State, 10 N.Y.2d 237, 219 N.Y.S.2d 34, 176 N.E.2d 729 (1961) (allowing recovery for negligent infliction of emotional harm although plaintiff suffered no physical impact); Sinkler v. Kneale, 401 Pa. 267, 164 A.2d 93 (1960) (cause of action allowed for infant injured in the womb); Rowland v. Christian, 69 Cal. 2d 108, 70 Cal. Rptr. 97, 443 P.2d 561, 32 A.L.R.3d 496 (1968) (extended rights granted to those on the land of another). See also Springrose v. Wilmore, 292 Minn. 23, 192 N.W.2d 826 (1971) (merger of assumption of risk into the comparative negligence system); accord, Bakke v. Rainbow Club, Inc., 306 Minn. 99, 235 N.W.2d 375 (1975).

[11]See Bielski v. Schulze, 16 Wis. 2d 1, 114 N.W.2d 105, 107–111 (1962). See also Dole v. Dow Chemical Co., 30 N.Y.2d 143, 331 N.Y.S.2d 382, 282 N.E.2d 288 (1972) (similar ruling).

[12]See Darling v. Charleston Community Memorial Hospital, 33 Ill. 2d 326, 211 N.E.2d 253, 14 A.L.R.3d 860 (1965).

[13]See cases cited in note 11 above; see also note 4, section 8.5, and accompanying text.

Hoffman v. Jones

The Supreme Court of Florida gave rather full retroactive effect to its landmark decision in *Hoffman v. Jones*, implementing comparative negligence.[14] The court's decision was made a bit complex because a lower court's decision had anticipated the change to comparative negligence and had already applied the new rule.[15] In these circumstances the court delineated the retroactivity of its rule as follows:

1. As to those cases in which the comparative negligence rule has been applied, this opinion shall be applicable.

2. As to those cases already commenced, but in which trial has not yet begun, this opinion shall be applicable.

3. As to those cases in which trial has already begun or in which verdict or judgment has already been rendered, this opinion shall not be applicable, unless the applicability of the comparative negligence rule was appropriately and properly raised during some stage of the litigation.

4. As to those cases on appeal in which the applicability of the comparative negligence rule has been properly and appropriately made a question of appellate review, this opinion shall be applicable.

5. This opinion shall be applicable to all cases commenced after the decision becomes final.[16]

The rules might be summarized by noting that the decision was applied, first, to all cases that had not come to trial, and second, to any other cases in which the applicability of comparative negligence had been properly raised and preserved.

---

[14]Hoffman v. Jones, 280 So. 2d 431, 78 A.L.R.3d 321 (Fla. 1973).

[15]See Jones v. Hoffman, 272 So. 2d 529 (Fla. App. 1973).

[16]Hoffman v. Jones, 280 So. 2d at 440. See also Williams v. Seaboard A. R. Co., 283 So. 2d 33 (Fla. 1973) (trial on basis of repealed railroad comparative negligence statute appropriately and properly raised issue of comparative negligence at trial); Thornton v. Elliott, 288 So. 2d 254 (Fla. 1973) (instruction to jury on prohibition against comparative negligence in response to a question from the jury appropriately and properly raised issue of comparative negligence); Orfaly v. Jeffries, 290 So. 2d 575 (Fla. App. 1974) (request for instruction on comparative negligence and objection to contributory negligence instruction preserved issue on appeal); accord, Jane v. Ubals, 296 So. 2d 593 (Fla. App. 1974); Horace Mann Ins. Co. v. Reed, 299 So. 2d 60 (Fla. App. 1974). See also Bonded Transp., Inc. v. Lee, 336 So. 2d 1132 (Fla. 1976) and Hartley v. Florida E. C. R. Co., 339 So. 2d 630 (Fla. 1976), which overruled Fitzsimmons v. Pensacola, 297 So. 2d 107 (Fla. App. 1974) (reasoning of issue in brief preserved issue on appeal). The 1976 *Hartley* decision affirmed Hartley v. Florida East Coast R. Co., 299 So. 2d 108 (Fla. App. 1974) (directed verdict that plaintiff was guilty of contributory negligence as a matter of law did not raise issue of applicability of comparative negligence). Accord, Hotaling v. Plantation Athletic League, 300 So. 2d 709 (Fla. App. 1974). But see Valdez v. Fesler, 298 So. 2d 512 (Fla. App. 1974) (discussion of comparative negligence issue at pretrial without subsequent action to preserve issue on appeal did not appropriately and properly raise issue).

Retroactivity of Judicial Change in Other States

In *Nga Li v. Yellow Cab Company*[17] the California Supreme Court adopted a rule of limited retroactivity. Pure comparative negligence applied to all cases in which trial had not begun prior to the final decision in *Li*, but did not apply in any case in which trial had begun before that date.[18] It did, however, apply to cases remanded for retrial.[19] In *Kaatz v. State*[20] the Alaska Supreme Court made comparative negligence broadly retroactive. Pure comparative negligence applied to any cases which had gone to trial prior to that date, but which had not been submitted to the jury, and to cases where the issue of the applicability of comparative negligence was raised at trial and preserved on appeal.[21]

In *Placek v. Sterling Heights*[22] the Michigan Supreme Court retroactively applied the pure comparative negligence doctrine, stating that adequate advance warning (one year and a half) had been given to lawyers and judges that the court intended to adopt comparative negligence principles. Initially, the Michigan court, in a split decision that failed to give effect to comparative negligence,[23] would have limited the applicability of the comparative negligence rule to cases filed after the date of that decision. However, in *Placek*, the court more fully extended retroactivity to its pure comparative negligence rule, holding the rule applicable to all cases pending on appeal (where the doctrine was requested at the trial court), all cases commenced but not yet submitted to the trier of fact, and all cases in which trial was to commence after the date of the opinion, provided counsel appropriately requested it.[24]

The West Virginia Supreme Court adopted a modified form of com-

---

[17]Nga Li v. Yellow Cab Co., 13 Cal. 3d 804, 119 Cal. Rptr. 858, 532 P.2d 1226, 78 A.L.R.3d 393 (1975); accord, Bachner v. Rich, 554 P.2d 430 (Alaska 1976) (retrial ordered of case originally tried under contributory negligence; comparative negligence principles to govern).

[18]Nga Li v. Yellow Cab Co., note 17 above, 532 P.2d at 1244; accord, Horn v. General Motors Corp., 17 Cal. 3d 359, 131 Cal. Rptr. 78, 551 P.2d 398 (1976) (citing this treatise); Spencer v. G.A. MacDonald Constr. Co., 63 Cal. App. 3d 836, 134 Cal. Rptr. 78 (1976) (no compelling reason to apply comparative negligence to case tried before California adopted comparative negligence).

[19]Nga Li v. Yellow Cab Co., note 17 above, 532 P.2d at 1244.

[20]Kaatz v. State, 540 P.2d 1037 (Alaska 1975).

[21]Id., at 1050. See also Leigh v. Lundquist, 540 P.2d 492 (Alaska 1975) (request for comparative negligence instruction and objection to instruction on contributory negligence preserved issue on appeal).

[22]Placek v. Sterling Heights, 405 Mich. 638, 275 N.W.2d 511 (1979); see also Smith v. O'Harrow Constr. Co., 95 Mich. App. 341, 290 N.W.2d 141 (1980) (comparative negligence doctrine held applicable to action filed in 1974 which had not yet been brought to trial); Rivers v. Ford Motor Co., 90 Mich. App. 94, 280 N.W.2d 875 (1979) (doctrine applicable where issues preserved on appeal); but see Wade v. State, 92 Mich. App. 234, 284 N.W.2d 522 (1979) (comparative negligence rule cannot apply retroactively where the doctrine was not requested at trial court).

[23]Kirby v. Larson, 400 Mich. 585, 256 N.W.2d 400 (1977).

[24]Placek v. Sterling Heights, note 22 above, 275 N.W.2d at 522.

parative negligence in *Bradley v. Appalachian Power Company*,[25] and analyzed the question of retroactivity as it was applied in those states which had adopted the "pure" form. The court decided that the new rule of comparative negligence in West Virginia would be fully retroactive.

The supreme courts of New Mexico,[26] Iowa,[27] and Kentucky[28] have made comparative negligence fully retroactive. The Illinois Supreme Court limited the doctrine to cases not yet tried or retried by the date of *Alvis v. Ribar*.[29] The Missouri Supreme Court limited application of the rule to cases not yet tried and "interim cases where the parties can mutually agree";[30] the court also chose as an effective date not the date of the decision but the date of its publication in the *South Western Reporter* advance sheets.[31]

8.3   Legislative intent to change prospectively

The statutory schemes of Colorado,[32] Hawaii,[33] Kansas,[34] Massachusetts,[35] New Hampshire,[36] New Jersey,[37] New York,[38] Oklahoma,[39]

---

[25]Bradley v. Appalachian Power Co., 163 W. Va. 332, 256 S.E.2d 879 (1979) (court held new rule of comparative negligence to be fully retroactive). See also Gaines v. Drainer, 289 S.E.2d 184 (W. Va. 1982) (*Bradley* held applicable to motion for summary judgment pending at the time of the decision).

[26]Scott v. Rizzo, 96 N.M. 682, 634 P.2d 1234, 1242 (1981).

[27]Goetzman v. Wichern, 327 N.W.2d 742, 754 (Iowa 1982), now superseded by Iowa Code Ann., ch. 668, effective July 1, 1984.

[28]Hilen v. Hays, 673 S.W.2d 713, 720 (Ky. 1984).

[29]Alvis v. Ribar, 85 Ill. 2d 1, 52 Ill. Dec. 23, 421 N.E.2d 886, 898 (1981). See Tonarelli v. Gibbons, 121 Ill. App. 3d 1042, 77 Ill. Dec. 408, 460 N.E.2d 464 (1984); Thompson v. Platt, 106 Ill. App. 3d 757, 62 Ill. Dec. 474, 436 N.E.2d 224 (1982).

[30]Gustafson v. Benda, 661 S.W.2d 11, 15 (Mo. 1983).

[31]January 31, 1984.

[32]Colo. Rev. Stat., § 41-2-14(4): "shall apply only to actions arising out of events which occur on or after ...."

[33]Hawaii Sess. Laws 1969, Act 227, § 2: "shall affect only those claims accruing after ...."

[34]Kan. Stat. Ann., § 60-258b; accord, Crutsinger v. Hess, 408 F. Supp. 548 (D. Kan. 1976).

[35]Mass. Acts 1969, ch. 761, § 2: "shall apply only to causes of action arising on or after ...."

[36]N.H. Rev. Stat. Ann., § 507:7-a: "shall govern all actions arising out of injuries ... sustained on and after ...."

[37]N.J. Laws 1973, ch. 146, § 4: "shall apply to causes of action arising on and after."

[38]N.Y. Civ. Prac. Law, § 1413. See also Quinlan v. Cecchini, 41 N.Y.2d 686, 394 N.Y.S.2d 872, 363 N.E.2d 578 (1977) (comparative negligence does not apply to cases accruing before September 1, 1975).

[39]Okla. Stat. Ann., tit. 23, § 11 was repealed in 1979. The new statute, tit. 23, § 13, stipulates that the doctrine controls in "all actions hereafter brought whether arising before or after the effective date of this act." See Amoco Pipeline Co. v. Montgomery, 487 F. Supp. 1268 (W.D. Okla. 1980).

Pennsylvania,[40] Texas,[41] Vermont[42] and Louisiana[43] clearly are to operate prospectively and to apply only to causes of action arising after their effective dates. The Arkansas 1961 statute[44] also clearly operated prospectively, but the 1973 law[45] replacing it omitted the key words "hereafter accruing." In spite of the precise language in those statutes, there has been some litigation in two of the states as to whether comparative negligence should be applied retroactively.

Judicial Change Before the Statute

The arguments made in favor of retroactivity go beyond statutory linguistics; plaintiffs have contended that courts should by common-law decision adopt comparative negligence as a rule of law with respect to cases that arose prior to the effective date of the statute. It has been suggested that this option is open to the court because the statute does not purport to govern cases that have arisen prior to its effective date; the legislature did not expressly state that contributory negligence had to be the rule prior to that time.

These assertions have not met with success.[46] In reply to such sophisticated arguments, courts have expressed the belief that judicial restraint required their honoring the prospective application of the rule as set forth by the statute. In addition, they have indicated that applying the rule by court-made decision when the statute was expressly prospective would add to confusion in the law.

There is merit in the position the courts have taken. For example, if the effective date of the statute is to be rendered meaningless, what new date of "effectiveness" is to be chosen? Is it to be the date the statute was published, or the date it was passed by the legislature? What of the case that arose prior to *that* time? What of the case that is on appeal at the time the legislation is passed? When the legislature has taken the care to be specific, unless the public need for retroactivi-

---

[40]Pa. Stat. Ann., tit. 17, § 2102 (1976), now tit. 42, § 7102; accord, Costa v. Lair, 241 Pa. Super. 517, 363 A.2d 1313 (1976); Garr v. Union Carbide Corp., 589 F.2d 147 (3d Cir. Pa. 1978).

[41]Tex. Gen. Laws 1973, ch. 28, § 4: "does not apply to any cause of action arising before . . . ." Accord, Conway v. Chemical Leaman Tank Lines, Inc., 610 F.2d 360 (5th Cir. Tex. 1980); Burkes v. Koppers Co., 567 S.W.2d 540 (Tex. Civ. App. 1978); Bellamy v. United States, 448 F. Supp. 790 (S.D. Tex. 1978).

[42]Vt. Stat. Ann., tit. 12, § 1036(b) as enacted by 1969 Vt. Acts (Adj. Sess.), No. 234: "shall apply to all causes of action arising after . . . ."

[43]La. Civ. Code Ann., art. 2323.

[44]Ark. Acts 1961 (1st Ex. Sess.), No. 61, § 2: "In all actions hereafter accruing. . . ."

[45]Ark. Stat. Ann., § 27-1764.

[46]See Heafer v. Denver-Boulder Bus Co., 176 Colo. 157, 489 P.2d 315 (en banc) (1971); Bissen v. Fujii, 51 Hawaii 636, 466 P.2d 429 (1970); accord, Silva v. Oishi, 52 Hawaii 129, 471 P.2d 524, 526 (1970).

ty is extraordinary, it would appear to this author that courts should follow the legislative mandate.[47]

8.4 Legislative change presumed prospective

In some comparative negligence statutes the legislature simply has not addressed itself in any direct way to the issue of retroactivity. Examples include the Arkansas 1973 statute[48] and the statutes of Connecticut,[49] Georgia,[50] Idaho,[51] Maine,[52] Montana,[53] Nebraska,[54] Nevada,[55] North Dakota,[56] Ohio,[57] Oregon,[58] South Dakota,[59] Utah[60] and Wisconsin.[61]

Of course, the legislature may indicate the effective date of the statute, or the effective date may be determined by general constitutional or statutory rules. It seems highly likely that the courts will apply the statute only to cases arising on or after this effective date.

Such holdings would apply a basic principle of statutory construction: that statutes are to have only a prospective operation unless the

---

[47]See Bissen v. Fujii, 51 Hawaii 636, 466 P.2d 429, 432 (1970) (dissenting opinion, Mr. Justice Levinson. The Justice's scholarly dissent would add a further confusion; even though the legislature adopted a modified comparative negligence system, he would apply pure comparative negligence prior to the date the statute became effective!)

[48]Ark. Stat. Ann., §§ 27–1763 to 27–1765.

[49]Conn. Acts 1973, No. 73–622.

[50]Ga. Code Ann., §§ 94–703, 105–603. In Georgia and some other states, of course, the statute is so old that retroactivity is no longer a live issue.

[51]Idaho Code, §§ 6–801, 6–802. Accord, Hunt v. Sun Valley Co., 561 F.2d 744 (9th Cir. Idaho 1977) (comparative negligence statute not to be applied retrospectively).

[52]Me. Rev. Stat. Ann., tit. 14, § 156.

[53]Mont. Code Ann., §§ 27-1-702, 27-1-703. See Dunham v. Southside Nat. Bank, 169 Mont. 466, 548 P.2d 1383 (1976) (Montana comparative negligence statute had only prospective effect); Penn v. Burlington Northern, Inc., 185 Mont. 223, 605 P.2d 600 (1980) (contributory negligence applied as accident occurred prior to effective date of statute).

[54]Neb. Rev. Stat., § 25–1151.

[55]Nev. Rev. Stat. 1973, ch. 787. Accord, Rice v. Wadkins, 92 Nev. 631, 555 P.2d 1232 (1976); Fennell v. Miller, 94 Nev. 528, 583 P.2d 455 (1978) (comparative negligence statute does not have retrospective application).

[56]N.D. Cent. Code, § 9–10–07.

[57]Ohio Rev. Code Ann., § 2315.19.

[58]Ore. Rev. Stat., § 18–470. The Oregon legislature enacted an amended version of the comparative negligence statute in 1975. Ore. Rev. Stat., §§ 18.470–18.510. The new statute applied retroactively to "all actions tried subsequent to its effective date." The Court of Appeals held that the version applied only to those cases actually litigated in the trial court after the effective date of the statute. Leigh v. United States, 586 F.2d 121 (9th Cir. Ore. 1978).

[59]S.D. Codified Laws, § 20–9–2.

[60]Utah Code Ann., §§ 78–27–37 to 78–27–43. See Smith v. Shreeve, 551 P.2d 1261 (Utah 1976).

[61]Wis. Stat. Ann., § 895.045.

legislature manifests clear intent to the contrary.[62] This rule of construction is based in part on the strong common-law tradition that while a court's pronouncements may apply to past conduct, a legislature's function is to declare law for the future.[63] It is also buttressed by the general assumption that a person should be able to plan his conduct with reasonable certainty of legal consequences.

The Wisconsin Decisions

This presumption of nonretroactivity has prevailed in the little litigation that has arisen with regard to comparative negligence statutes that do not specifically address themselves to the issue of retroactivity. For example in *Brewster v. Ludtke*,[64] the Supreme Court of Wisconsin barred plaintiff's claim under the contributory negligence defense because "the collision occurred before the enactment of the comparative negligence statute."[65] More recently, after the Wisconsin legislature amended the statute to provide that plaintiff could recover when his negligence was equal to that of defendant, the Supreme Court of Wisconsin declined to give retroactive effect to the amendment and barred a plaintiff who would have benefited from a retroactive change.[66]

When statutes are highly remedial in nature and retroactive application may aid in full effectuation of the legislative purposes, courts may find a legislative intent to give the statute such application.[67] Although a comparative negligence law might be characterized as remedial in nature, most courts have not built upon this to derive a legislative intent to give the law retroactive application. Thus, even though the Mississippi statute states that it is to be applied to "all actions hereafter brought," the supreme court of that state said in

---

[62]See J. Sutherland, *Statutes and Statutory Construction* § 2212 (F. Horack, Jr., 3d ed. 1943). Maine has reaffirmed this rule as late as 1963. See Stetson v. Johnson, 159 Me. 37, 187 A.2d 740 (1963). See also Smith v. Shreeve, 551 P.2d 1261 (Utah 1976) (contributory negligence operates as a complete defense to personal injury action where accident occurred prior to enactment of comparative negligence statute).

[63]See Smead, *The Rule Against Retroactive Legislation: A Basic Principle of Jurisprudence*, 20 Minn. L. Rev. 775, 789 (1936).

[64]Brewster v. Ludtke, 211 Wis. 344, 247 N.W. 449 (1933).

[65]Id., 247 N.W.2d at 450. See also Joseph v. Lowery, 261 Ore. 545, 495 P.2d 273 (1972), construing the Oregon statute in like manner.

[66]Holzem v. Mueller, 54 Wis. 2d 388, 195 N.W.2d 635 (1972). See also Lupie v. Hartzheim, 54 Wis. 2d 415, 195 N.W.2d 461 (1972) (declining to give the same statute retroactive power by "common law" decision). Accord, McGowan v. Story, 70 Wis. 2d 189, 234 N.W.2d 325 (1975).

[67]See Gleason v. Gleason, 26 N.Y.2d 28, 308 N.Y.S.2d 347, 256 N.E.2d 513 (1970) (dealing with divorce based on separation ground); Annot., "Retrospective effect of statute prescribing grounds of divorce," 23 A.L.R.3d 626, 630–632 (1969).

passing that it did not apply when the facts upon which the claim was based occurred prior to that date.[68]

The Ohio Supreme Court, on the other hand, in *Wilfong v. Batdorf*, decided that Ohio's comparative negligence statute is remedial or procedural in nature and should apply to all cases coming to trial after its effective date.[69] The Ohio Constitution forbids retroactive statutes,[70] but the Ohio courts have interpreted that provision to apply only to statutes affecting substantive, rather than procedural, rights.[71] The Ohio Supreme Court in an earlier case considered the comparative negligence statute substantive because of its impact on liability:

> Substantive rights ... include all privileges and obligations arising from the legal nature of transactions and relationships but separate from the means of effectuating those privileges and obligations.[72]

Only a year later the court reversed itself, stating that comparative negligence "does not alter a defendant's liability for his negligent acts, but merely changes the way a court is required to weigh a plaintiff's negligence."[73] The court added that it had the right to create a common-law comparative negligence rule to harmonize with the statute.[74] The second decision appears to have been based on eagerness to scrap the contributory negligence rule and as such was bitterly criticized by two dissenting justices of the court.[75]

Application of F.E.L.A.

An equally strong case for retroactive application arose under the Federal Employers' Liability Act. The comparative negligence section of that law begins "In all actions [hereafter] brought ...."[76] Nevertheless, the Supreme Court of the United States declined to construe the statute as having retroactive effect.[77] The court took this position in part because the modification of the contributory negligence defense could permit recovery where none was allowed before. In the Court's own words, the statute "introduced a new policy and quite radically changed the existing law."[78]

---

[68]See Fuller v. Illinois C. R. Co., 100 Miss. 705, 718, 56 So. 783 (1911). The parties had apparently assumed that the new statute would not apply, perhaps because the action had already been "brought" prior to enactment. In discussing an entirely different point, the court noted that the statute did not apply because enacted "subsequent to the injuries complained of." There is similar language in the Rhode Island statute. R.I. Gen. Laws, § 9-20-4.

[69]Wilfong v. Batdorf, 6 Ohio St. 3d 100, 6 Ohio B.R. 162, 451 N.E.2d 1185 (1983).

[70]Ohio Const., art. II, § 28.

[71]Wilfong v. Batdorf, note 69 above, 451 N.E.2d at 1188-1189 (citing cases).

[72]Viers v. Dunlap, 1 Ohio St. 3d 173, 1 Ohio B.R. 203, 438 N.E.2d 881 (1982); see also Straub v. Voss, 1 Ohio St. 3d 182, 1 Ohio B.R. 211, 438 N.E.2d 888 (1982) (decided the same day as *Viers*). The decisions are noted at 12 Cap. U.L. Rev. 639 (1983), 12 Cap. U.L. Rev. 321 (1982) and 10 Ohio N.U.L. Rev. 213 (1983).

[73]Viers v. Dunlap, 438 N.E.2d at 884.

[74]Wilfong v. Batdorf, note 69 above, 451 N.E.2d at 1189.

[75]Id., Locher, J., dissenting, at 1190-1191 and Holmes, J., dissenting, at 1191-1193.

[76]Act of April 22, 1908, ch. 149, § 3, 35 Stat. 66, 45 U.S.C. § 53.

[77]Winfree v. Northern P. R. Co., 227 U.S. 296, 57 L. Ed. 518, 33 S. Ct. 273 (1913).

[78]Id., 227 U.S. at 302, 33 S. Ct. at 274.

Of course, the F.E.L.A. did more to change the law than modify the contributory negligence defense; it also abolished the assumption of the risk defense and completely eliminated the contributory negligence defense when defendant violated a safety statute. These factors, plus the remote date of the case, should be borne in mind when considering its value as a precedent in other cases.

The Minnesota Statute

In a modern case, the Supreme Court of Minnesota gave that state's comparative negligence statute retroactive effect on the basis of the provision that it "shall be effective in any action the trial of which is commenced after July 1, 1969."[79] The court applied the new law to an action brought after that date even though the facts upon which it was based occurred prior to that time. The court was supported in its view by legislative history which evidenced that early versions of the bill had contained different provisions as to effective date, and that the language finally adopted was substituted by a conference committee.

As detailed in section 8.5, the court also held that retroactive application did not violate any provision of the state or federal constitution. This indicates that in the 1970's a change from contributory to comparative negligence is not as "radical" as it may have been in 1913—the date of the United States Supreme Court's decision under the F.E.L.A.

A final aspect of the Minnesota decision is most important in statutory construction in comparative negligence cases. The Supreme Court of Minnesota had acknowledged the precedential value of decisions of the Wisconsin Supreme Court on its comparative negligence statute;[80] nevertheless, Minnesota would depart from the Wisconsin precedents when required by differences in the wording of the statutes. It should be recalled that the Wisconsin statute says nothing about retroactivity,[81] in contrast to the Minnesota provision that the statute "shall be effective in any action the trial of which is commenced after July 1, 1969."

The Washington Statute

Washington followed the lead of Minnesota when it first enacted comparative negligence. The Washington comparative negligence statute provided for an effective date of "12:01 a.m. on April 1st, 1974."[82]

---

[79]Peterson v. Minneapolis, 285 Minn. 282, 173 N.W.2d 353, 355, 37 A.L.R.3d 1431 (1969). The statute in question was replaced by a new statute, effective April 15, 1978. 1978 Minn. Laws, ch. 738.

[80]See Olson v. Hartwig, 288 Minn. 375, 180 N.W.2d 870 (1970).

[81]See note 64 above, and accompanying text.

[82]Wash. Rev. Code Ann., § 4.22.010.

Nonetheless in *Godfrey v. State*[83] the Washington Supreme Court concluded that it was the intent of the legislature that the statute should operate retroactively, as prospective operation would result in the continued operation of the contributory negligence defense in cases which arose prior to the effective date of the statute, possibly for years after its official abandonment by the legislature. This would not comport, the court said, with the legislature's purpose in adopting comparative negligence: a fairer apportionment of damages when both parties are negligent.

In 1981 the Washington legislature enacted a comprehensive tort reform package that included a revised comparative fault law, effective July 26, 1981.[84] As an afterthought, the legislature passed a second bill making the old statute applicable to all causes of action arising before July 26, 1981 and the new statute applicable to all causes of action arising on or after that date.[85] A Washington appellate court upheld this arrangement based on the explicit wording of the statute.[86] The court's decision is reasonable in view of the fact that the new statute would not have substantially affected the case. Nonetheless, the case was peculiar because both the court and the defendant seemed to assume that if the old comparative negligence statute had expired, a contributory negligence instruction would have been appropriate.

8.5 Constitutionality of retroactive legislative change

If a court determines that the legislature intended to give a comparative negligence statute retroactive effect, it must then also determine whether the retroactivity deprives the defendant of any constitutionally protected right.[87] The Supreme Court of the United States long ago determined that the ex post facto clause applies only to retroactive criminal legislation.[88] Thus, where no impairment of obligation of contract is involved,[89] the focus is on the due process clause of the Fourteenth Amendment and whatever analogue might be contained in the state constitution. Since only four comparative negligence laws have been interpreted to have retroactive application, there have been only five decisions on the constitutional issues—those of the Supreme Court

---

[83]Godfrey v. State, 84 Wash. 2d 959, 530 P.2d 630 (1975); accord, McCrea v. Union P. R. Co., 15 Wash. App. 472, 550 P.2d 19 (1976); but see Ashcraft v. Wallingford, 16 Wash. App. 796, 558 P.2d 1383 (1977) (retroactivity of statute does not extend to actions arising more than three years prior to effective date of comparative negligence). The Court of Appeals subsequently affirmed the ruling, noting that the comparative negligence statute, operating retroactively, would have applied in this case, but that because the issue was not presented in trial court, plaintiff was not entitled to raise it for the first time on appeal. Ashcraft v. Wallingford, 17 Wash. App. 853, 565 P.2d 1224 (1977).

[84]Wash. Laws 1981, ch. 27, codified at Wash. Rev. Code Ann., §§ 4.22.005 and 4.22.015.

[85]Wash. Laws 1982, ch. 100.

[86]Mina v. Boise Cascade Corp., 37 Wash. App. 445, 681 P.2d 880 (1984).

[87]See Hochman, *The Supreme Court and the Constitutionality of Retroactive Legislation*, 73 Harv. L. Rev. 692 (1960) and references cited in note 1, section 8.1 above.

[88]See Calder v. Bull, 3 U.S. (3 Dall.) 386, 1 L. Ed. 648 (1798).

[89]See Hale, *The Supreme Court and the Contract Clause*, 57 Harv. L. Rev. 852 (1944).

of Minnesota, in *Peterson v. Minneapolis*,[90] and the Supreme Courts of Washington, Rhode Island, Oregon, and Michigan, which are discussed in the following paragraphs.

Vested Rights

The Minnesota court began its analysis of the isssue in traditional form. It recognized the general rule for determining the constitutionality of retroactive legislation under the due process clause—that a statute may not abrogate a "vested right."[91] Nevertheless, the court was wise enough to recognize that the term "vested right" is a mere conclusion. In effect, if a right is "vested," then it cannot be taken away by statute.[92] Then the court went on to examine whether in terms of fundamental fairness the comparative negligence rule could be applied to defendant's conduct even though comparative negligence was not the law at the time that conduct took place.

In making its determination that retroactive application of comparative negligence was indeed fair, the Minnesota court was persuaded by the fact that the legislative adoption of comparative negligence was no greater change than prior Minnesota judge-made changes in tort law which had been given limited retroactive application by the court. These prior court-made changes include abandonment of the rule imputing contributory negligence of a servant to the master, abolition of certain intrafamily immunities and extension to a wife of the right to recover for the loss of her husband's consortium.[93] In the words of the Peterson opinion, "the court has in a number of cases applied changes in laws similar to this in a retrospective manner, at least as to the parties-litigant who bring the matter before the court. If the court can do that, so can the legislature."[94]

In *Godfrey v. State*[95] the Supreme Court of Washington declared that the retroactive application of the comparative negligence statute would not violate a vested right. The negligent defendant could not be said to have planned his conduct in reliance on the common law of contributory negligence. Neither did the comparative negligence statute create any broad new liability which did not exist at common law. It merely abolished a bar to recovery in cases where the defendant had, in fact, engaged in tortious conduct.

A somewhat similar analysis was undertaken by the Supreme Court of Rhode Island in *Raymond v. Jenard*,[96] where the comparative negli-

---

[90]Peterson v. Minneapolis, 285 Minn. 282, 173 N.W.2d 353, 37 A.L.R.3d 1431 (1969).

[91]See, e.g., Federal Housing Administration v. Darlington, Inc., 358 U.S. 84, 3 L. Ed. 2d 132, 79 S. Ct. 141 (1958) (alternative holding).

[92]This has been recognized by legal scholars for many years. See 2 J. Austin, *Lectures on Jurisprudence* 856-857 (5th ed. 1875); Smith, *Retroactive Laws and Vested Rights*, 5 Tex. L. Rev. 231 (1927).

[93]See Peterson v. Minneapolis, 285 Minn. 282, 173 N.W.2d 353, 356 (1969).

[94]Id., 173 N.W.2d at 358.

[95]Godfrey v. State, 84 Wash. 2d 959, 530 P.2d 630 (1975).

[96]Raymond v. Jenard, 120 R.I. 634, 390 A.2d 358 (1978).

gence statute was held retroactively applicable to an action brought after enactment of the statute, based on an injury which had occurred prior to the legislation. The court, citing both the *Peterson* and *Godfrey* cases, found that the minimal harshness to the defendant by the statute's retroactive application was outweighed by the strong public interest in abolishing the effect of the traditional contributory negligence rule.

The Oregon Supreme Court, in *Hall v. Northwest Outward Bound School, Incorporated*,[97] declared that there is no constitutional bar (either federal or state) to a retroactive application of the comparative fault rule when determining the defendant's liability, notwithstanding the death of plaintiff's decedent prior to the statute's effective date.

In *In re Certified Questions from the United States Court of Appeals for the Sixth Circuit*,[98] the Michigan Supreme Court held that a product liability comparative fault statute applied to all cases that had not come to trial at the time of enactment and that retrospective application to a breach of warranty case was constitutional. The court first rejected the plaintiff's argument that application of the statute impaired contractual rights, on the ground that the cases cited by the plaintiff involved express contracts rather than an implied warranty.[99] The court then said that the statute did not take away vested rights— plaintiff still had his cause of action—but only improved and furthered a remedy.[1]

Weaknesses of the Minnesota Decision

The Minnesota court might have gone a few steps further in supporting its view that it was constitutional for the legislature to enact a retroactive comparative negligence law. Its basic argument is weakened by the strong common-law tradition that although a court's pronouncements may and usually do apply to past conduct, the legislature's function is to declare law for the future.[2] Further, the court itself had given only limited retroactivity to innovative judge-made rules in tort law; they had been applied only to the parties before the court. Finally, it is arguable that the change from contributory to comparative negligence was far more fundamental in tort law that any prior judicial change in Minnesota.[3]

---

[97]Hall v. Northwest Outward Bound School, Inc., 280 Ore. 655, 572 P.2d 1007 (1977).

[98]In re Certified Questions from the United States Court of Appeals for the Sixth Circuit (Karl v. Bryant Air Conditioning Co.), 416 Mich. 558, 331 N.W.2d 456 (1982) (air conditioner repairman injured when air conditioner terminal blew out found 95% at fault). See Karl v. Bryant Air Conditioning Co., 705 F.2d 164 (6th Cir. Mich. 1983).

[99]In re Certified Questions, 331 N.W.2d at 464.

[1]Id., at 466.

[2]See Smead, *The Rule Against Retroactive Legislation: A Basic Principle of Jurisprudence*, 20 Minn. L. Rev. 775, 789 (1936).

[3]See Haeg v. Sprague, Warner & Co., 202 Minn. 425, 291 N.W. 261 (1938) where the court had specifically declined to make the change from contributory to comparative negligence by judge-made rule because it thought a change of this dimension was for the legislature.

Nevertheless, there are considerations that support the Minnesota court's ruling. First, in weighing the legislature's power under the due process clause, consideration should be given to the fact that the legislation is broadly remedial in correcting a common-law rule that had served to produce great inequity in tort law. In considering whether retroactive application is unfair to defendants, it should be noted none of the parties places great reliance on the contributory negligence rule at the time of the negligent conduct. This is true, in part, because contributory negligence was a "common-law" rule, not a legislative one. More importantly, it is farfetched to suppose that defendants were negligent in reliance on the exonerating effect of plaintiff's contributory negligence. It is remotely possible that liability insurers might rely on the contributory negligence defense in setting their premiums, but this consideration is so speculative that, in the absence of specific proof on the matter, it should not bar retroactive application intended by the legislature.[4]

In sum, legislative retroactive application of comparative negligence should not be deemed contrary to the due process clause of the Fourteenth Amendment to the United States Constitution.

---

[4]See Morris, *Enterprise Liability and the Actuarial Process—The Insignificance of Foresight*, 70 Yale L.J. 554 (1961).

CHAPTER 9
ASSUMPTION OF RISK

Section

9.1   Assumption of risk and contributory negligence distinguished

The introduction of comparative negligence into a legal system may require courts to determine whether assumption of risk should continue as an absolute defense.[1] Indeed, the comparative negligence statute may serve as the trigger for a court's complete reexamination of the assumption of risk defense.[2] A number of courts[3] and authors[4] have

---

[1]See Blackburn v. Dorta, 348 So. 2d 287 (Fla. 1977); Springrose v. Willmore, 292 Minn. 23, 192 N.W.2d 826 (1971); McConville v. State Farm Mut. Automobile Ins. Co., 15 Wis. 2d 374, 113 N.W.2d 14 (1962), noted in 46 Marquette L. Rev. 119 (1962). See also 60 Mich. L. Rev. 819 (1962); 38 N.D. L. Rev. 599 (1962); 41 Tex. L. Rev. 459 (1963); 8 Wayne L. Rev. 451 (1962); Tiller v. Atlantic C. L. R. Co., 318 U.S. 54, 62 et seq., 87 L. Ed. 610, 63 S. Ct. 444, 143 A.L.R. 967 (1943) (describing the situation under the Federal Employers' Liability Act comparative negligence provisions, both before and after the 1939 Amendment which abolished the defense of assumption of risk); Note, *Contributory Negligence and Assumption of Risk—The Case for Their Merger*, 56 Minn. L. Rev. 47 (1971); Note, *Assumption of Risk as a Defense in Nebraska Negligence Actions Under the Comparative Negligence Statute*, 30 Neb. L. Rev. 608 (1951); Buford, *Assumption of Risk Under the Federal Employers' Liability Act*, 28 Harv. L. Rev. 163 (1914); and Peterson, *The Joker in the Federal Employers' Liability Act*, 80 Cent. L.J. 5 (1915). In regard to the general topic of assumption of risk, see W. P. Keeton et al., *Prosser and Keeton on the Law of Torts* § 68 (5th ed. 1984); 2 F. Harper & F. James, *The Law of Torts* § 21.1 (1956); Bohlen, *Voluntary Assumption of Risk*, 20 Harv. L. Rev. 14 (1906); James, *Assumption of Risk*, 61 Yale L.J. 141 (1952); Wade, "The Place of Assumption of Risk in The Law of Negligence," *in* Symposium: *Assumption of Risk*, 22 La. L. Rev. 5 (1961); Warren, *Volenti Non Fit Injuria in Actions of Negligence*, 8 Harv. L. Rev. 457 (1895); *Restatement (Second) of Torts* §§ 496A-496G (1965).

[2]See Parness v. Economics Laboratory, Inc., 284 Minn. 381, 386, 170 N.W.2d 554, 558 (1969) ("The question will be more meaningfully presented under the recently enacted statute abolishing contributory negligence as a complete defense.") and Springrose v. Willmore, 292 Minn. 23, 192 N.W.2d 826 (1971). See also Lyons v. Redding Constr. Co., 83 Wash. 2d 86, 515 P.2d 821 (1973).

[3]Hale v. O'Neill, 492 P.2d 101 (Alaska 1971); Frelick v. Homeopathic Hospital Assn., 51 Del. 568, 150 A.2d 17 (1959); Bulatao v. Kauai Motors, Ltd., 49 Hawaii 1, 406 P.2d 887 (1965); Fawcett v. Irby, 92 Idaho 48, 436 P.2d 714 (1968); Parker v. Redden, 421 S.W.2d 586 (Ky. 1967); Baltimore County v. State, 232 Md. 350, 193 A.2d 30 (1963); Felgner v. Anderson, 375 Mich. 23, 133 N.W.2d 136, 26 A.L.R.3d 531 (1965); Meistrich v. Casino Arena Attractions, Inc., 31 N.J. 44, 155 A.2d 90, 82 A.L.R.2d 1208 (1959); Ritter v. Beals, 225 Ore. 504, 358 P.2d 1080 (1961); Siragusa v. Swedish Hospital, 60 Wash. 2d 310, 373 P.2d 767 (1962). See also Blackburn v. Dorta, 348 So. 2d 287 (Fla. 1977); Blaw-Knox Food & Chemical Equipment Corp. v. Holmes, 348 So. 2d 604 (Fla. App. 1977), cert. dismissed 351 So. 2d 405 (Fla. 1977) (patent danger doctrine).

[4]See James, *Assumption of Risk: Unhappy Reincarnation*, 78 Yale L.J. 185 (1968); Symposium: *Assumption of Risk*, 22 La. L. Rev. 1 (1961).

called for the abandonment of "assumption of risk" even without a comparative negligence statute; therefore, in order to understand fully the problem of whether assumption of risk should survive as an absolute defense under comparative negligence, the nature of the defense itself must be considered.

Express or Implied Assumption of Risk

The root of the problem in analyzing the assumption of risk defense is that the term has been used to describe a number of very different legal concepts.[5] The form of assumption of risk that is easiest to understand is *express* assumption of risk. When a plaintiff expressly assumes a risk, he specifically agrees, prior to the time of the injury-causing event, to hold defendant blameless with regard to his negligence.[6] As indicated in section 9.2, this form of assumption of risk does not ordinarily present significant problems under comparative negligence.

The form of assumption of risk that presents the greatest confusion, with or without comparative negligence, is *implied* assumption of risk. This defense developed at common law in master-servant cases during the middle of the nineteenth century.[7] In effect, where an individual knowingly and voluntarily encounters a risk, he is treated as if he has agreed to look out for himself and to relieve the defendant of any duty toward him.

The defense has been analogized to consent, and that has been suggested as its basis.[8] In actual cases this basis is usually fictional because the injured party has not truly manifested his consent to hold the defendant blameless; rather, the law treats him as if he had done so.

Another basis underlying implied assumption of risk was suggested by Pound many years ago; he believed it was a device to give maximum freedom to expanding industry.[9] Today, because of workmen's compensation laws, the defense is applied less often in the area of its origin—work-related injuries. It does arise when workers bring product liability claims against manufacturers of machine tools, chemicals or other products used in the workplace. Assumption of risk appears more frequently today in other factual settings and may bar the claim of a plaintiff who falls on business premises, who accepts a ride with an automobile driver known to be incompetent, or who uses a consumer product that he knows to be defective.[10]

---

[5]See Tiller v. Atlantic C. L. R. Co., 318 U.S. 54, 87 L. Ed. 610, 63 S. Ct. 444, 143 A.L.R. 967 (1943); James, note 4 above, at 185.

[6]See W. P. Keeton et al., note 1 above, § 68 at 480–481.

[7]See Tiller v. Atlantic C. L. R. Co., 318 U.S. 54, 58–61, 87 L. Ed. 610, 63 S. Ct. 444, 143 A.L.R. 967 (1943).

[8]See W. P. Keeton et al., note 6 above, at 484–485.

[9]See Pound, *The Economic Interpretation and the Law of Torts*, 53 Harv. L. Rev. 365, 373 (1940).

[10]See W. P. Keeton et al., note 1 above, at 486. Assumption of risk in strict product liability is discussed more fully in Chapter 12.

Overlapping Contributory Negligence

Often when a plaintiff assumes a risk, he does not act as a reasonable person and therefore he is also contributorily negligent. When contributory negligence is an absolute defense, it usually is unnecessary for courts to distinguish carefully between that defense and assumption of risk.[11] But if a jurisdiction adopts comparative negligence and if the assumption of risk defense continues as a complete bar to a claim, the courts are

[I]mpel[led] ... to practice ... "the niceties, if not casuistries, of distinguishing between assumption of risk and contributory negligence, conceptions which never originated in clearly distinguished categories, but were loosely interchangeable until the [comparative negligence] statute attached such vital differences to them."[12]

Verbalizing the Distinction

The distinction between assumption of risk and contributory negligence can be verbalized and the *Restatement (Second) of Torts* has made a reasonable attempt to do so.[13] In general, assumption of risk bars the claim of

[A] plaintiff who fully understands a risk of harm to himself or his things caused by the defendant's conduct ... and who ... voluntarily chooses ... to permit that risk ....[14]

On the other hand, the contributory negligence defense bars the claim of a plaintiff whose conduct is unreasonable in that he does not adhere to "the standard to which he (as a reasonable man) should conform for his own protection...."[15] Obviously, an individual can be contributorily negligent without knowing of the risk that he incurs. For example, a person unfamiliar with a particular railroad crossing traverses it without seeing a stop sign or looking and is hit by a diesel engine.

---

[11]See Packard v. Quesnel, 112 Vt. 175, 22 A.2d 164, 167–168 (1941) ("the name to be applied to such conduct is of no great consequence. The result of the conduct is what counts and that result is preclusion from recovery").

[12]Tiller v. Atlantic C. L. R. Co., 313 U.S. 54, 63, 87 L. Ed. 610, 63 S. Ct. 444, 143 A.L.R. 967 (1943), quoting from Pacheco v. New York, N.H. & H. R. Co., 15 F.2d 467 (2d Cir. N.Y. 1926). See also Braswell v. Economy Supply Co., 281 So. 2d 669 (Miss. 1973) (as assumption of risk is a complete defense in Mississippi and contributory negligence is not, in cases where the two defenses overlap, comparative negligence principles shall apply).

[13]See *Restatement (Second) of Torts* §§ 496A through 496E (1965).

[14]Id., § 496C (1). See Curbo v. Harlan, 253 Ark. 816, 490 S.W.2d 467 (1973) (plaintiff, passenger of intoxicated driver, did not assume risk of another car backing onto highway); Shurley v. Hoskins, 271 So. 2d 439 (Miss. 1973) (hunter does not assume risk of being negligently shot by his companions); O'Brien v. Smith Bros. Engine Rebuilders, Inc., 494 S.W.2d 787 (Tenn. App. 1973) (customer does not assume risk of slipping on oil patch without actual knowledge of peril); Owens-Illinois, Inc. v. Bryson, 138 Ga. App. 78, 225 S.E.2d 475 (1976) (driver of extremely slow-moving vehicle does not assume risk of being struck from behind); but see Walker v. Hamby, 503 S.W.2d 118 (Tenn. 1973) (plaintiff, a passenger in dune buggy without doors, handholds, or seat belts, assumes risk of being thrown from vehicle).

[15]*Restatement (Second) of Torts* §§ 463, 464 (1965).

Although the distinctive aspects of implied assumption of risk can be verbalized in principle, such differentiations are extremely difficult to apply in the ordinary case where defendant's conduct is on the borderline of being unreasonable. This is demonstrated by the judicial experience under the Federal Employers' Liability Act during the period from 1908 to 1939, when that law embodied comparative negligence but was interpreted to retain assumption of risk as an absolute defense.[16]

Reasonable Implied Assumption of Risk

In the view of the *Restatement (Second) of Torts* and perhaps of some courts, the implied assumption of risk defense can bar plaintiff's claim when his conduct was *reasonable* so long as he voluntarily encountered a known risk.[17] This might occur, for example, where one makes a reasonable attempt to teach another to drive, and the latter has an accident in the course of instruction.[18] Professor James has vigorously argued that the assumption of risk defense should not be permitted to survive in this situation.[19] In recent years a number of courts have accepted James' position and have indicated that the implied assumption of risk defense applies only when a plaintiff's conduct is *unreasonable* and that, therefore, the defense is merged in or subsumed under contributory negligence.[20]

When a person voluntarily uses a product containing a defect known to him but his conduct could be regarded as reasonable under the circumstances, assumption of risk may totally bar his claim against the manufacturer. Some academics and a few courts and legislatures

---

[16]See Tiller v. Atlantic C. L. R. Co., 318 U.S. 54, 62–65, 87 L. Ed. 610, 63 S. Ct. 444, 143 A.L.R. 967 (1943) (the annotated codes "devote over thirty pages each of fine type merely to the citation and brief summary of the reported decisions and the number of unreported and settled cases in which the defense was involved must run into the thousands").

[17]See *Restatement (Second) of Torts* §§ 496A, 496C (1965); James, note 4 above, at 192 ("there was, of course, some judicial authority to support the *Restatement* position and a great deal of loose judicial language which could be construed to support it"). Compare Note, *Contributory Negligence and Assumption of Risk—The Case for Their Merger*, 56 Minn. L. Rev. 47, 53–58 (1971) (author attempts to show that cases relied on by *Restatement* do not support its position in this regard). The *Restatement* does allow limited consideration of reasonableness in determining whether conduct is *voluntary* in §§ 496D and 496E; thus no fault would attach to a pedestrian who must step off the sidewalk to get around an obstruction created by the defendant or to a driver who first notices a defective tire while driving through a dangerous neighborhood. The South Dakota Supreme Court recently suggested that reasonableness refers to "whether the plaintiff had a reasonable opportunity to elect whether or not to subject himself to the danger." Berg v. Sukup Mfg. Co., 355 N.W.2d 833, 835 (S.D. 1984).

[18]See Le Fleur v. Vergilia, 280 A.D. 1035, 117 N.Y.S.2d 244 (1952).

[19]See Halepeska v. Callihan Interests, Inc., 371 S.W.2d 368, 378 n. 3 (Tex. 1963) (describing the debate at the American Law Institute on the point which "the distinguished scholars refer to ... as 'The Battle of the Wilderness' ").

[20]E.g., Segoviano v. Housing Authority, 143 Cal. App. 3d 162, 191 Cal. Rptr. 578 (1983) (plaintiff injured by defect in playing field while playing flag football should have recovered full damages); Barstow v. Kroger Co., 730 F.2d 1058 (6th Cir. Ky. 1984) (whether plaintiff who slipped on wet floor near exit to grocery store acted reasonably was a question of fact for the jury).

have argued that "unreasonable conduct" should be added as an element to assumption of risk under comparative fault statutes.[21] The result is to make assumption of risk a "form" of contributory negligence and no longer a total bar to a product liability claim; presumably if a jury finds that the plaintiff acted "reasonably" despite knowing and voluntary assumption of the risk, e.g., if he consumed a bottle of lemon soda after observing a piece of metal in the bottle in the mistaken belief that he could strain the soda through his teeth, he could recover full damages. Another, and more logical, approach is to retain assumption of risk in its classic form, with knowledge and voluntary conduct as its only elements, and let the jury consider that conduct in reducing the *amount* of plaintiff's damages.

A complication arises when implied assumption of risk is "merged" into the contributory negligence defense. Courts on occasion have used "assumption of risk" in a very special sense—not to describe a defense but rather to explain a limitation on the duty owed by a defendant. For example, when an employer's business exposes an employee to dangers that *cannot* be removed by reasonable care, the employer may be immune from liability when one of those risks does in fact injure a worker. The worker "assumes the risk" of injury because the employer owes his employee no duty other than to warn him and make him aware of the risks.[22] This situation, which often looks like reasonable implied assumption of risk, is sometimes called "primary assumption of risk."[23] It can cause considerable confusion if the implied assumption of risk defense is merged into contributory negligence.[24]

9.2   Express assumption of risk

Parties may agree in advance that one of them is under no obliga-

---

[21]See Wade, *Product Liability and Plaintiff's Fault—The Uniform Compensation Fault Act*, 29 Mercer L. Rev. 373, 383 (1979); Gonzalez v. Garcia, 75 Cal. App. 3d 874, 142 Cal. Rptr. 503 (1977) (doctrine of contributory negligence and assumption of risk merged into comparative negligence doctrine when plaintiff's conduct was unreasonable); accord, Paula v. Gagnon, 81 Cal. App. 3d 680, 146 Cal. Rptr. 702 (1978); Kopischke v. First Continental Corp., 187 Mont. 471, 610 P.2d 668 (1980) (assumption of risk treated like any other form of contributory negligence), ovrld. Zahrte v. Sturm, Ruger & Co., 661 P.2d 17 (Mont. 1983); Idaho Code, § 6-1405(2); Minn. Stat. Ann., § 604.01(1a).

[22]See Martin v. Des Moines Edison Light Co., 131 Iowa 724, 732, 106 N.W. 359, 363 (1906), ovrld. on other grounds, Grismore v. Consolidated Products Co., 232 Iowa 328, 5 N.W.2d 646 (1942); Louisiana R. & N. Co. v. Eldridge, 293 S.W. 901, 903 (Tex. Civ. App. 1927); Modec v. Eveleth, 224 Minn. 556, 29 N.W.2d 453 (1947) (owner of hockey club owes no duty to safeguard patron from reasonable risks known to patron); Dobbins v. United Super Markets, 556 S.W.2d 387 (Tex. Civ. App. 1977) (comparative negligence does not abolish the no-duty concept of assumed risk).

[23]See Note, *Contributory Negligence and Assumption of Risk—The Case for Their Merger*, 56 Minn. L. Rev. 47, 48–50 (1971). See also Becker v. Beaverton School Dist., 25 Ore. App. 879, 551 P.2d 498 (1976) (citing this treatise).

[24]See Tiller v. Atlantic C. L. R. Co., 318 U.S. 54, 68–73, 87 L. Ed. 610, 63 S. Ct. 444, 143 A.L.R. 967 (1943) (concurring opinion of Mr. Justice Frankfurter expounding upon the distinction and the problem); Blackburn v. Dorta, 348 So. 2d 287 (Fla. 1977) (merging assumption of risk, a way of stating no-duty rules, with contributory negligence).

tion to use reasonable care for the benefit of the other and shall not be liable for the consequences of conduct that the law might otherwise deem negligent. When a plaintiff who has entered such a contract is injured by one of the risks on which he agreed to forego suit, courts may honor the agreement and bar his claim because he expressly assumed the risk.[25] On occasion, courts will decline to enforce such contracts, deeming them against public policy.[26]

It seems highly unlikely that a comparative negligence statute saying nothing about assumption of risk will be held to have any effect on the law of express assumption of risk. Cases which have arisen under such statutes have gone only so far as to merge *implied* assumption of risk into the contributory negligence defense and thus have apportioned damages only when based on *such* conduct. The courts have been crystal clear that express assumption of risk as a complete defense remains untouched.[27] Thus, in order to avoid having his claim completely barred by an expressed assumption of risk, plaintiff must convince a court that as a matter of social policy (e.g., because of inequality of bargaining power between the parties), the agreement to assume the risk should be deemed invalid. Precedents in the jurisdiction on the point will still apply.

Statutes Covering Assumption of Risk

When the comparative negligence statute indicates that assumption of risk is merged into the contributory negligence defense, the question arises whether express assumption of risk continues as a complete defense. As of 1985 the only comparative negligence statutes mentioning assumption of risk are the 1939 amendments to the F.E.L.A. [28] and

---

[25]See W. P. Keeton et al., *Prosser and Keeton on the Law of Torts* § 68, at 482–484 (5th ed. 1984).

[26]See Tunkl v. Regents of University of California, 60 Cal. 2d 92, 32 Cal. Rptr. 33, 383 P.2d 441, 6 A.L.R.3d 693 (1963) (invalidating a hospital patient's express agreement to assume risks of medical negligence); McCutcheon v. United Homes Corp., 79 Wash. 2d 443, 486 P.2d 1093 (1971) (lease agreement).

[27]See Springrose v. Willmore, 292 Minn. 23, 192 N.W.2d 826 (1971); Gilson v. Drees Bros., 19 Wis. 2d 252, 120 N.W.2d 63, 67 (1963) ("greater fairness will result if the claimed negligence of [plaintiff] is couched in terms of contributory negligence.... This will be true whenever the alleged assumption of risk arises by implication . . . as opposed to an express assumption of a known risk"); Lyons v. Redding Constr. Co., 83 Wash. 2d 86, 515 P.2d 821, 826 (1973); Blackburn v. Dorta, 348 So. 2d 287 (Fla. 1977); Wilson v. Gordon, 354 A.2d 398 (Me. 1976) (contractual assumption of risk not inconsistent with main comparative negligence statute) (dicta); Keegan v. Anchor Inns, Inc., 606 F.2d 35 (3d Cir. V.I. 1979) (assumption of risk charge should be given where there is express assumption of risk). The court indicated that assumption of risk would only be applied in cases where negligent conduct constitutes waiver or consent. Id., at 41, n. 8.

[28]See Act of April 22, 1908, ch. 149, § 4, 35 Stat. 66; August 11, 1939, ch. 685, § 1, 53 Stat. 1404, 45 U.S.C. § 54:

the statutes of Arizona,[29] Arkansas,[30] Connecticut,[31] Idaho (in product liability actions),[32] Indiana,[33] Iowa,[34] Massachusetts,[35] Minnesota,[36] New York,[37] Oklahoma,[38] Oregon,[39] Utah,[40] and Washington.[41]

In light of the general purpose of F.E.L.A. to assure that workmen recover at least some damages when their railroad-employer breaches a duty of reasonable care, it would seem that an attempt by an employer to subvert this purpose by contract would be deemed against public policy.[42]

The Oregon Statute

With respect to a former Oregon statute, there was a more difficult problem of legislative interpretation. Any legislative history would have been helpful. The statute said in part:

> Contributory negligence, including assumption of the risk, shall not bar recovery in an action ... if *such* negligence contributing to the injury was not as great as the negligence of the person against whom recovery is sought ... (emphasis added).[43]

The wording of the statute suggests that only the implied assumption of risk defense was referred to by the statute. This view is supported by the fact that the term "such negligence" was used in the second clause of the statute. The draftsmen were no doubt aware that the Supreme Court of Oregon had previously merged implied assumption of risk into contributory negligence.[44]

This interpretation of the statute was adopted by the Oregon Court

---

In any action brought against any common carrier under or by virtue of any of the provisions of this chapter to recover damages for injuries to, or the death of, any of its employees, such employee shall not be held to have assumed the risks of his employment in any case where such injury or death resulted in whole or in part from the negligence of any of the officers, agents, or employees of such carrier; and no employee shall be held to have assumed the risks of his employment in any case where the violation by such common carrier of any statute enacted for the safety of employees contributed to the injury or death of such employee.

See Norfolk S. R. Co. v. Rayburn, 213 Va. 812, 195 S.E.2d 860 (1973) (assumption of risk no defense under 1939 amendments to the F.E.L.A.; contributory negligence instruction which commingles elements of assumption of risk improper).

[29]Ariz. Rev. Stat. Ann., § 12–2505(A).
[30]Ark. Stat. Ann., § 27–1763.
[31]Conn. Gen. Stat. Ann., § 52–572h(c).
[32]Idaho Code, § 6–1405(2).
[33]Ind. Code, § 34–4–33–2.
[34]Iowa Code Ann., § 668.1.
[35]Mass. Gen. Laws Ann., ch. 231, § 85.
[36]Minn. Stat. Ann., § 604.1.
[37]N.Y. Civ. Prac. Law, § 1411.
[38]Okla. Stat. Ann., tit. 23, § 12.
[39]Ore. Rev. Stat., § 18.470.
[40]Utah Code Ann., § 78–27–37.
[41]Wash. Rev. Code Ann., § 4.22.015.
[42]See Tiller v. Atlantic C. L. R. Co., 318 U.S. 54, 66–67, 87 L. Ed. 610, 63 S. Ct. 444, 143 A.L.R. 967 (1943).
[43]Ore. Rev. Stat., § 18.470.
[44]See Ritter v. Beals, 225 Ore. 504, 358 P.2d 1080 (1961).

of Appeals in *Becker v. Beaverton School District*,[45] which held that assumption of risk was not barred absolutely, but that the statute applied to assumption of risk only in the secondary sense as contributory negligence. In 1975 the Oregon legislation rewrote the comparative negligence statute, abolishing implied assumption of risk and substituting "fault" for "negligence" in several places.[46]

The Oregon Supreme Court had a subsequent opportunity to rule on this issue. In *Thompson v. Weaver*[47] the revised Oregon statute was held to apply where the defendant denied any duty to a plaintiff who voluntarily participated in an activity where the dangers were known. The Court determined that the statute made no distinction as to whether "a plaintiff's implied assumption of the risk is regarded as a form of negligence on his part, or whether his implied assumption of the risk is claimed to excuse defendant for risks that would be his 'fault' vis-a-vis other persons in plaintiff's position."[48] A defense still remains, however, for consent or waiver that is verbally expressed.

The Utah Statute

The relevant section of the Utah statute is almost identical with that of Idaho, except that the Utah statute includes an additional sentence defining "contributory negligence" to include assumption of the risk.[49] There had been some question in Utah as to whether implied assumption of risk was a part of contributory negligence or was a separate defense.[50] The definition was apparently added to make it clear that implied assumption of risk is subject to comparison under the statute. It was questionable whether *express* assumption of risk is subject to comparison or remains as a separate complete defense.

The Utah Supreme Court, in *Rigtrup v. Strawberry Water Users Association*,[51] held the comparative negligence statute applicable when the plaintiff voluntarily assumed the risk of a known danger. The Court, indicating that a person should be made responsible for his conduct, declined to abolish the defense.

---

[45]Becker v. Beaverton School Dist., 25 Ore. App. 879, 551 P.2d 498 (1976) (citing this treatise).

[46]1975 Ore. Laws, ch. 599.

[47]Thompson v. Weaver, 277 Ore. 299, 560 P.2d 620 (1977). See also Kirby v. Sonville, 286 Ore. 339, 594 P.2d 818 (1979).

[48]Thompson v. Weaver, 560 P.2d at 623.

[49]Utah Code Ann., § 78–27–37.

[50]Contrast this statement from Foster v. Steed, 23 Utah 2d 148, 459 P.2d 1021, 1022 (1969):

The doctrines of contributory negligence and assumption of risk are different, but in some instances are interrelated.

with the following from Hindmarsh v. O. P. Skaggs Foodliner, 21 Utah 2d 413, 446 P.2d 410, 412 (1968):

The doctrine of assumption of risk is but a specialized aspect of the defense of contributory negligence.

[51]Rigtrup v. Strawberry Water Users Assn., 563 P.2d 1247 (Utah 1977) (plaintiff 90% at fault; therefore, no recovery permitted by Utah's 50% system).

The Utah Supreme Court may have pushed the distinction between primary and secondary implied assumption of risk to its limits in a ski injury case, *Meese v. Brigham Young University*.[52] The court held that the plaintiff, a beginning skier, had not assumed the risk that her instructor would fail to tell her to test the binding release mechanism on her equipment. The court upheld a comparative negligence finding that allowed the plaintiff to recover 75% of her damages.

The Connecticut Statute

The Connecticut statute expressly abolished "[t]he legal doctrines of last clear chance and assumption of risk."[53] The Connecticut courts had previously treated express assumption cases in terms of waiver, rather than assumption of risk.[54] Apparently, therefore, express assumption of risk remains a total defense in Connecticut, at least if the facts can be pleaded in terms of waiver or consent.

The Oklahoma Statute

The Oklahoma statute mentions assumption of risk only in a section guaranteeing jury trial on contributory negligence issues;[55] this provision merely repeats language embodied in the Oklahoma Constitution.[56] Although the Oklahoma Supreme Court has not yet been presented with a case arising under the statute, the court has suggested in dictum that comparative negligence will apply to assumption of risk.[57]

The New York Statute

The key section of the New York statute provides that "[T]he culpable conduct attributable to the claimant ... including contributory negligence and assumption of risk shall not bar recovery, but the amount of damages otherwise recoverable shall be diminished in the proportion which the culpable conduct attributable to the claimant ... bears to the culpable conduct which caused the damages."[58] The statute treats the two defenses interchangeably and it is clear that damages will be apportioned under implied assumption of risk. It is unclear whether express assumption of risk is subject to comparison.

The Uniform Comparative Fault Act

The Uniform Comparative Fault Act defines "fault" to include "unreasonable assumption of risk not constituting an enforceable express consent."[59] The Official Comment adds that there are many def-

---

[52]Meese v. Brigham Young University, 639 P.2d 720 (Utah 1981).

[53]1973 Conn. Acts, No. 73–622, § 1(c), codified at Conn. Gen. Stat. Ann., § 52–572(h)(c).

[54]See Panaroni v. Johnson, 158 Conn. 92, 256 A.2d 246, 254 (1969).

[55]Okla. Stat. Ann., tit. 23, § 12.

[56]Okla. Const., art. 23, § 6.

[57]Minor v. Zidell Trust, 618 P.2d 392 (Okla. 1980).

[58]N.Y. Civ. Prac. Law, § 1411. See Knieriemen v. Bache Halsey Stuart Shields, Inc., 74 A.D.2d 290, 427 N.Y.S.2d 10 (1980) (assumption of risk abandoned in New York; doctrine of comparative negligence applies).

[59]Unif. Comp. Fault Act, § 1(b), 12 U.L.A. 39, 41 (Supp. 1985). See Chapter 21.

initions of assumption of risk and that this definition covers only one of them:

> This is the case of unreasonable assumption of risk, which might be likened to deliberate contributory negligence and means that the conduct must have been voluntary and with knowledge of the danger. As used in this Act, the term does not include the meanings (1) of a valid and enforceable consent (which is treated like other contracts), (2) of a lack of violation of duty by the defendant (as in the failure of a landowner to warn a licensee of a patent danger on the premises), or (3) of a reasonable assumption of risk (which is not fault and should not have the effect of barring recovery).[60]

Iowa, Indiana and Minnesota have incorporated the Uniform Act definition of fault into their comparative fault statutes,[61] and the Supreme Court of Missouri has indicated that it would look to the Act for guidance in future cases.[62]

The Longshoremen and Harbor Workers' Compensation Act

The defense of assumption of risk was held to be precluded by the 1972 amendments to the Act in a 1977 federal court decision in the state of Washington.[63] The court announced that congressional intent to prohibit the defense in actions by longshoremen was unequivocal.

9.3 Implied assumption of risk as a complete defense

Courts in a number of states have, under comparative negligence, retained implied assumption of risk as a separate and complete defense

---

[60]Id., Official Comment to § 1.
[61]Ind. Code, § 34–4–33–2; Iowa Code Ann., § 668.1; Minn. Stat. Ann., § 604.1.
[62]Gustafson v. Benda, 661 S.W.2d 11, 15–16 (Mo. 1983).
[63]Davis v. Inca Compania Naviera S.A., 440 F. Supp. 448 (W.D. Wash. 1977).

to an action based on negligence. This appears true in Georgia,[64] Mississippi,[65] Nebraska,[66] Rhode Island[67] and South Dakota.[68]

Curiously, only in Rhode Island[69] did a court engage in a reasoned discussion of why the assumption of risk defense should continue after comparative negligence has been adopted. Perhaps plaintiffs' attorneys in other states did not press the point and the courts assumed that since the comparative negligence statute referred only to negligence, it was not intended to apply to assumption of risk. An additional argument in support of these decisions, developed in section 9.5, is that the assumption of risk defense is not based upon fault but upon consent, so that a comparative negligence statute apportioning damages on the basis of fault should not apply.

Mississippi Precedents

The Supreme Court of Mississippi did briefly address itself to this point in *Saxton v. Rose*.[70] There plaintiff's decedent was killed while riding in the cabin of a truck. Defendant's driver was intoxicated at

---

[64]Harris v. Star Service & Petroleum Co., 170 Ga. App. 816, 318 S.E.2d 239 (1984) (plaintiff assumed risk of falling in icy service station); Roberts v. King, 102 Ga. App. 518, 116 S.E.2d 885 (1960) (plaintiff-passenger in drag race deemed to assume risk in "all out" race which had more risks than an ordinary drag race); McChargue v. Black Grading Contractors, Inc., 122 Ga. App. 1, 176 S.E.2d 212 (1970) (defendant negligently used grading machine pushing down tree; plaintiff aware of activity; assumption of risk properly left to jury); Yankey v. Battle, 122 Ga. App. 275, 176 S.E.2d 714 (1970) (domestic servant fell on negligently maintained stairway); Wade v. Roberts, 118 Ga. App. 284, 163 S.E.2d 343 (1968) (although property owners may have been negligent in permitting gravel to accumulate on driveway, invitee or licensee who knew driveway was covered assumed risk).

[65]See Singleton v. Wiley, 372 So. 2d 272 (Miss. 1979) (instruction concerning plaintiff's assumption of risk in jumping on back of moving car held proper); Saxton v. Rose, 201 Miss. 814, 29 So. 2d 646 (1947) (plaintiff's claim barred by decedent's riding with driver he knew to be intoxicated); McDonald v. Wilmut Gas & Oil Co., 180 Miss. 350, 176 So. 395 (1937).

[66]See Fritchley v. Love-Courson Drilling Co., 177 Neb. 455, 129 N.W.2d 515 (1964) (employee knew of defects in ladder and used it anyway; insufficient to bar claim on ground of assumption of risk); Mason v. Western Power & Gas Co., 183 Neb. 392, 160 N.W.2d 204 (1968). W. Prosser, *Handbook of the Law of Torts* § 68, at 457 n. 71 (4th ed. 1971) indicates that damages are to be apportioned in Nebraska when there is negligent assumption of risk. The author of a note of some 35 years ago, *Assumption of Risk as a Defense in Nebraska Negligence Actions Under the Comparative Negligence Statute*, 30 Neb. L. Rev. 608 (1951) suggests the same conclusion. The apparent discrepancy between cases cited in this note and these authors is clarified in the text at note 81 below. See also McPherson v. Sunset Speedway, Inc., 594 F.2d 711 (8th Cir. Neb. 1979) (voluntary assumption of risk a complete defense in personal injury suit; plaintiff precluded from recovering damages for his resulting injury).

[67]Kennedy v. Providence Hockey Club, Inc., 119 R.I. 70, 376 A.2d 329 (1977). See text at notes 87a to 87c.

[68]See Bartlett v. Gregg, 77 S.D. 406, 92 N.W.2d 654 (1958) (court declined to find assumption of risk as a matter of law where employee had no opportunity to make an intelligent choice in his use of a stack mover on defendant's ranch); Myers v. Lennox Co-op Assn., 307 N.W.2d 863 (S.D. 1981) (plaintiff constructively knew of danger in stepping on loose lumber and assumed risk he would fall into garbage truck and get caught in rotating hopper).

[69]See note 67 above.

[70]Saxton v. Rose, 201 Miss. 814, 29 So. 2d 646 (1947); see note 65 above.

the time and the decedent was aware of this. In affirming the trial court's application of the assumption of risk defense, the Supreme Court stated that plaintiff's decedent "dared to accept the hazards of the adventure, fully aware of them, and the result of his risk was his untimely death."[71] In distinguishing between assumption of risk and contributory negligence the court followed traditional lines in stating that assumption of the risk

> [A]pplies when a party voluntarily and knowingly places himself in such a position, or submits himself to such a condition, appreciating that injury to himself on account thereof is liable to occur at any and all times so long as such position or condition continues. Contributory negligence arises when, but not until, the injured person by his own conduct has done something, or has omitted to do something, which contributes to the particular event, and at the particular time and place, which was the immediate cause of the injury.[72]

Continuation of assumption of the risk as a complete defense had a rather dramatic effect in the context of pure comparative negligence. The Supreme Court of Mississippi has "softened the blow" in two ways. First, it does not appear to permit the defense when plaintiff has *reasonably* assumed a known risk.[73] Second, the court is insistent that the issue be left to the jury.

The Mississippi court referred to the comparative negligence statute in a case leaving the issue of assumption of risk to the jury;[74] this suggested the court's awareness of the paradox of continuing assumption of risk of a complete defense. In that case, defendant was negligent in allowing a wet substance to accumulate in a refreshment area near its bowling alley. Plaintiff was a professional bowler and was aware of the danger of slipping when bowling with wet shoes, but he was injured in exactly that manner. Nevertheless, the court held that the jury could determine that plaintiff did not know there was a wet substance on his shoe.

---

[71]Id., 29 So. 2d at 648.

[72]Id., 29 So. 2d at 649.

[73]See McDonald v. Wilmut Gas & Oil Co., 180 Miss. 350, 176 So. 395 (1937); Saxton v. Rose, 201 Miss. 814, 29 So. 2d 646 (1947); Ideal Cement Co. v. Killingsworth, 198 So. 2d 248 (Miss. 1967) (decedent struck by automobile while he was pushing another auto across highway; court found no assumption of risk under facts); Elias v. New Laurel Radio Station, Inc., 245 Miss. 170, 146 So. 2d 558, 92 A.L.R.2d 1065 (1962) (plaintiff slipped on liquid left on floor in bowling alley); Shurley v. Hoskins, 271 So. 2d 439 (Miss. 1973) (hunter does not assume risk of being negligently shot by his companions).

[74]Elias v. New Laurel Radio Station, Inc., 245 Miss. 170, 146 So. 2d 558, 92 A.L.R.2d 1065 (1962).

In *Braswell v. Economy Supply Company*,[75] the Mississippi Supreme Court further limited the operation of implied assumption of risk by holding that in cases where the elements of assumption of risk and contributory negligence overlap, comparative negligence principles will apply. The Court expressly declined to abolish implied assumption of risk, but noted that the issue was whether the plaintiff had acted as a reasonably prudent man.[76] In view of the difficulty involved in distinguishing comparative negligence from assumption of risk, it is likely that most culpable behavior by plaintiffs will involve elements of both. Implied assumption of risk will likely be of limited future application in Mississippi.

Reluctant Application of Complete Defense

Nebraska[77] and South Dakota[78] seem to apply implied assumption of the risk as a complete defense only when plaintiff's conduct has been unreasonable, to give the jury wide latitude to reject the defense, and to admit only grudgingly that the "knowing" and "voluntary" elements of the defense have been established. Similarly, in a 1969 Arkansas case, a plaintiff injured his hand on dangerous machinery that he had utilized before; the majority of the court (over three dissents) left the issue of his knowledge of the risk to the jury.[79]

In Nebraska the courts have left the assumption of risk issue to the jury in the clearest of cases;[80] this may be why some authors assume

---

[75]Braswell v. Economy Supply Co., 281 So. 2d 669 (Miss. 1973); accord, Gordy v. Canton, 543 F.2d 558 (5th Cir. Miss. 1976) (assumption of risk instruction properly denied when plaintiff's decedent unwittingly unloaded a truck under power line); cf. McGowan v. St. Regis Paper Co., 419 F. Supp. 742 (S.D. Miss. 1976) (plaintiff injured while knowingly walking on slippery substance assumed the risk); Singleton v. Wiley, 372 So. 2d 272 (Miss. 1979) (see note 65 above; whether plaintiff who jumped on the back of a moving car knowingly and voluntarily assumed the risk was question of fact, but assumption of risk is still a complete defense).

[76]Braswell v. Economy Supply Co., 281 So. 2d 669, 677 (Miss. 1973).

[77]See note 66 above.

[78]See note 67 above.

[79]See Hudgins v. Maze, 246 Ark. 21, 437 S.W.2d 467 (1969). In Spradlin v. Klump, 244 Ark. 841, 427 S.W.2d 542 (1968) the injured party was experienced and admitted on cross-examination that he appreciated the danger. The court affirmed a directed verdict for defendant but observed that "assumption of risk is a harsh doctrine, not favored by the courts." See also Bugh v. Webb, 231 Ark. 27, 328 S.W.2d 379, 84 A.L.R.2d 444 (1959) (there plaintiff admitted on cross that he understood the risks involved in drag racing); Bartlett v. Gregg, 77 S.D. 406, 92 N.W.2d 654 (1958), where the court found that the plaintiff had no opportunity to make an "intelligent choice" between continuing the dangerous operation under the direction of his employer and stopping such activity, and Rone v. Miller, 257 Ark. 791, 520 S.W.2d 268 (1975) (evidence of the manner in which automobile was driven prior to accident in which both driver and plaintiff passengers were killed was admissible to prove assumption of risk).

[80]See Landrum v. Roddy, 143 Neb. 934, 12 N.W.2d 82, 149 A.L.R. 1041 (1943); Anthony v. Lincoln, 152 Neb. 320, 41 N.W.2d 147 (1950).

that the defense has been abandoned in Nebraska.[81] Nevertheless, the state retains the defense and permits an instruction that can bar plaintiff's claim if the jury decides to apply it.[82]

The Georgia Precedents

Georgia is the only state that has continued to apply the assumption of risk defense with any vigor under comparative negligence. There are cases in that state suggesting that *reasonable* implied assumption of risk may bar plaintiff's claim.[83] Also, Georgia courts have not been reluctant to grant defendant a summary judgment or directed verdict on the issue of assumption of risk.[84] Georgia also allows assumption of risk as an absolute defense to strict liability.[85] However, the Georgia cases should not be regarded as precedents in other comparative negligence jurisdictions. Georgia's system of comparative negligence is a unique court-created blend of two statutes, neither of which was a general comparative negligence law.[86] One of those statutes states that:

> If the plaintiff by ordinary care could have avoided the consequences to himself caused by the defendant's negligence, he is not entitled to recover. In other cases the defendant is not relieved, although the plaintiff may in some way have contributed to the injury sustained.[87]

Analysis of the wording of this unusual statute shows why assumption

---

[81]See note 66 above. Two cases which suggest the same conclusion are Jensen v. Hawkins Constr. Co., 193 Neb. 220, 226 N.W.2d 346 (1975) (plaintiff does not assume risk of falling on visibly wet surface) and Circo v. Sisson, 193 Neb. 704, 229 N.W.2d 50 (1975) (plaintiff does not assume risk of riding with intoxicated driver if reasonable minds could differ in determining whether he was too intoxicated to drive). See also Zrust v. Spencer Foods, Inc., 667 F.2d 760 (8th Cir. Neb. 1982) (harmless error not to give assumption of risk instruction where plaintiff was run over by a truck while inspecting it).

[82]See Munson v. Bishop Clarkson Memorial Hospital, 186 Neb. 778, 186 N.W.2d 492 (1971) (plaintiff fell from bed; case could be read to find no breach of duty by defendant) and cases cited in note 65 above. See also McPherson v. Sunset Speedway, Inc., 594 F.2d 711 (8th Cir. Neb. 1979) (plaintiff assumed the risk by entering infield area on racetrack knowing that there was no protective barrier between the track and the field).

[83]See Yankey v. Battle, 122 Ga. App. 275, 176 S.E.2d 714 (1970) (domestic servant entered a dark stairway when required to do so by her employment); Harris v. Star Service & Petroleum Co., 170 Ga. App. 816, 318 S.E.2d 239 (1984) (slip and fall in service station lot completely covered with ice).

[84]See Harris v. Star Service & Petroleum Co., 170 Ga. App. 816, 318 S.E.2d 239 (1984); Wade v. Roberts, 118 Ga. App. 284, 163 S.E.2d 343 (1968); Roberts v. King, 102 Ga. App. 518, 116 S.E.2d 885 (1960) (plaintiff's claim barred even if decedent did not know that defendant would engage in an "all out" race as opposed to a drag race). See also Mitchell v. Young Refining Corp., 517 F.2d 1036 (5th Cir. Ga. 1975) (plaintiff assumed risk of injury as a matter of law when he stepped on oily pipes at his place of employment). But see Tolar Constr. Co. v. Ellington, 137 Ga. App. 847, 225 S.E.2d 66 (1976) (trial court erred in not granting summary judgment on ground of assumption of risk when plaintiff construction worker walked backward across roof in which he knew there were holes. The Supreme Court of Georgia subsequently reversed this decision, finding genuine issues of material fact sufficient to preclude a summary judgment for the contractor. Ellington v. Tolar Constr. Co., 237 Ga. 235, 227 S.E.2d 336 (1976).

[85]Parzini v. Center Chemical Co., 136 Ga. App. 396, 221 S.E.2d 475 (1975).

[86]See section 1.5.

[87]Ga. Code Ann., § 51-11-7.

of risk has survived more vigorously in Georgia than in any other comparative negligence state.

Rhode Island

The Supreme Court of Rhode Island has discussed the assumption of risk defense at some length in two relatively recent decisions. In *Kennedy v. Providence Hockey Club*[87a] the court concluded that because a spectator at a hockey game voluntarily purchased a ticket for a seat in an area of the arena which was close to the ice, she knowingly encountered the risk of being injured by a puck. The court did not accept the premise that the principles of contributory negligence and assumption of risk overlapped, the key difference being "exercise of one's free will in encountering the risk."[87b] The court held that the comparative negligence statute did not affect the effectiveness of the defense of assumption of risk as a complete bar to recovery. The court elaborated on the distinction further in *Iadevaia v. Aetna Bridge Company*.[87c] In that case the court differentiated between comparative negligence and assumption of risk by explaining that comparative negligence was based on an objective standard, i.e., what the reasonable person would do, while assumption of risk was subjective, based on what the injured person actually knew and appreciated.

9.4 Implied assumption of risk as negligence subject to comparison

(A) STATUTORY MERGER INTO CONTRIBUTORY NEGLIGENCE

As indicated in section 9.2, the legislatures of Arizona,[88] Arkansas,[89] Connecticut,[90] Massachusetts,[91] New York,[92] Oregon,[93] Utah[94] and Washington[95] as well as the F.E.L.A.,[96] have eliminated implied assumption of risk as a separate defense within the context of their respective comparative negligence systems. Iowa,[97] Indiana,[98] Minneso-

---

[87a]Kennedy v. Providence Hockey Club, Inc., 119 R.I. 70, 376 A.2d 329 (1977).

[87b]Id., 376 A.2d at 333.

[87c]Iadevaia v. Aetna Bridge Co., 120 R.I. 610, 389 A.2d 1246 (1978).

[88]Ariz. Rev. Stat. Ann., § 12–2505(A).

[89]Ark. Stat. Ann., § 27–1763.

[90]Conn. Gen. Stat. Ann., § 52–572h(c); accord, DiIorio v. Tipaldi, 4 Mass. App. 640, 357 N.E.2d 319 (1976).

[91]Mass. Gen. Laws Ann., ch. 231, § 85.

[92]N.Y. Civ. Prac. Law, § 1411.

[93]See Ore. Rev. Stat., § 18.470. See also Becker v. Beaverton School Dist., 25 Ore. App. 879, 551 P.2d 498 (1976) (citing this treatise); Thompson v. Weaver, 277 Ore. 299, 560 P.2d 620 (1977); Ore. Rev. Stat., § 18.475.

[94]Utah Code Ann., § 78–27–37.

[95]Wash. Rev. Code Ann., § 4.22.015.

[96]See Act of April 22, 1908, ch. 149, § 4, 35 Stat. 66; August 11, 1939, ch. 685, § 1, 53 Stat. 1404, 45 U.S.C. § 54.

[97]Iowa Code Ann., § 668.1(1).

[98]Ind. Code, § 34–4–33–2.

ta,[99] and Missouri[1] have adopted a comparative fault definition that includes unreasonable implied assumption of risk.

The 1972 amendments to the Longshoremen's and Harbor Workers' Compensation Act were held to preclude the defense of assumption of risk in an action by an injured employee in *Davis v. Inca Compania Naviera S.A.*[2]

Unreasonable Assumption Reducing Damages

The language of the F.E.L.A. is clear that facts constituting implied assumption of risk have no materiality except as they might also constitute contributory negligence.[3] If they constitute negligence, plaintiff's conduct could be considered by the jury in making an apportionment of damages. Put another way, only facts that would constitute unreasonable implied assumption of risk (as contrasted with reasonable) can serve to reduce plaintiff's award.

The Connecticut statute appears to reach about the same result as the F.E.L.A. It completely abolishes the doctrine of assumption of risk.[4] Thus implied assumption of risk is no longer a complete defense, and the facts constituting implied assumption of risk can be used to reduce plaintiff's award only if they fit within the concept of contributory negligence. Translated into the language of negligence, only *unreasonable* implied assumption of risk is considered in apportioning damages.

The Oregon and Utah Statutes

The Oregon and Utah statutes are not so clear on this point. The Oregon statute provides:

> Contributory negligence, including assumption of the risk, shall not bar recovery ... if such negligence ... was not as great as the negligence of the [defendant], but any damages ... shall be diminished in the proportion to the amount of such negligence. ...[5]

This statute could be interpreted as indicating that *reasonable* implied assumption of risk brings about a reduction of the award. On the one

---

[99]Minn. Stat. Ann., § 604.1(1a).

[1]Gustafson v. Benda, 661 S.W.2d 11, 15-16 (Mo. 1983) (announcing that Uniform Comparative Fault Act principles would be applicable in future cases).

[2]Davis v. Inca Compania Naviera S.A., 440 F. Supp. 448 (W.D. Wash. 1977). The court referred to the legislative history of the amendments in its interpretation of congressional intent to prohibit assumption of risk as a defense. H.R. Rep. No. 1441, 92d Cong., 2d Sess. (1972), *reprinted in* 3 1972 U.S. Code Cong. & Ad. News 4698, 4705; S. Rep. No. 1125, 92d Cong., 2d Sess. 12 (1972).

[3]See note 28, section 9.2. See also Heater v. Chesapeake & O. R. Co., 497 F.2d 1243 (7th Cir. Ill. 1974) (giving instruction that assumption of risk is not a defense under comparative negligence when the defense is not maintained as harmless error). The provision of the F.E.L.A. abolishing the defense of assumption of risk was made applicable to seamen by the Jones Act, 46 U.S.C. § 688 (1946). In Rivera v. Farrell Lines, Inc., 474 F.2d 255 (2d Cir. N.Y. 1973) the court held that a voluntary encounter with a known risk (wet pantry floor) would be insufficient to charge a jury on contributory negligence as the court would be reviving the assumption of risk defense in another guise.

[4]See note 39, section 9.2, and accompanying text.

[5]Ore. Rev. Stat., § 18.470.

hand this result may be unlikely in Oregon since the Oregon Supreme Court had, prior to adoption of comparative negligence, abolished reasonable implied assumption of risk as a defense.[6] On the other hand, the court would be relieved of treating reasonable implied assumption of risk as a *complete* defense and could let the jury reduce the plaintiff's award in light of his knowledgeable conduct.

In 1976 the Oregon Court of Appeals adopted this statutory construction in *Becker v. Beaverton School District*,[7] holding that assumption of risk in its secondary sense as contributory negligence is barred by the comparative negligence statute. The Supreme Court of Oregon subsequently held that the defense of implied assumption of the risk has been abolished in any form, whether in its "primary" or "secondary" sense.[8]

The Utah comparative negligence statute is constructed somewhat differently:

> Contributory negligence shall not bar recovery ... if such negligence was not as great as the negligence ... of the [defendant], but any damages ... shall be diminished in the proportion to the amount of negligence.... As used in this act, "contributory negligence" includes "assumption of the risk."[9]

The language of the statute itself more clearly excludes reasonable assumption of risk as a ground for reducing the award than does the Oregon statute. The clause providing for diminution of damages specifies diminution proportionally "to the amount of negligence" (not "such negligence" or "contributory negligence"). Even if reasonable implied assumption of risk is included within the special definition of "contributory negligence," the argument runs, it is not included within the ordinary meaning of "negligence" as used in the clause providing for diminution of damages.

In 1977 the Utah Supreme Court declined to abolish the defense of assumption of risk in *Rigtrup v. Strawberry Water Users Association*.[10] The Court refused to repudiate the legislature's clear intent to include assumption of risk as an aspect of contributory negligence in Utah law. In subsequent cases, however, the court has treated implied assumption of risk as a form of comparative negligence.[11]

The best construction of the Oregon and Utah statutes would be to

---

[6]See Ritter v. Beals, 225 Ore. 504, 358 P.2d 1080 (1961).

[7]Becker v. Beaverton School Dist., 25 Ore. App. 879, 551 P.2d 498 (1976) (citing this treatise).

[8]Thompson v. Weaver, 277 Ore. 299, 560 P.2d 620 (1977). See Ore. Rev. Stat., § 18.475. See also Nylander v. State, 292 Ore. 254, 637 P.2d 1286 (1981) (applying comparative fault to accident on icy bridge); Christensen v. Murphy, 296 Ore. 610, 678 P.2d 1210 (1984) (abolition of assumption of risk removes justification for the "fireman's rule").

[9]Utah Code Ann., § 78–27–37.

[10]Rigtrup v. Strawberry Water Users Assn., 563 P.2d 1247 (Utah 1977).

[11]Meese v. Brigham Young University, 639 P.2d 720 (Utah 1981); Moore v. Burton Lumber & Hardware Co., 631 P.2d 865 (Utah 1981); Jacobsen Constr. Co. v. Structo-Lite Engineering, Inc., 619 P.2d 306 (Utah 1980).

allow the jury to reduce an award when a plaintiff has voluntarily encountered a known risk. While this conduct may not fit within classic "unreasonableness" in some cases it is significant because a plaintiff who truly knew the risk and truly voluntarily encountered it did in fact help in bringing about the very injury that befell him.

(B) JUDICIAL MERGER INTO CONTRIBUTORY NEGLIGENCE

To date, courts in ten states with general comparative negligence statutes have merged implied assumption of risk into contributory negligence even though the legislatures gave no specific direction to do so. The Supreme Court of Wisconsin took this step through a series of cases.[12] Minnesota accomplished the same result in one sweeping decision.[13] Washington abolished the remnants of its assumption of risk doctrine (except for express assumption) and its separate maxim of volenti non fit injuria in an opinion saying that comparative negligence would remove the necessity for implied assumption of risk except as one form of contributory negligence.[14] The Supreme Courts of North Dakota, Maine, Texas, Wyoming and Ohio merged assumption of risk into contributory negligence in single cases.[15] The Colorado Court of Appeals has held that it is error to give a separate assumption of risk instruction under Colorado's comparative negligence statute.[16]

---

[12]See McConville v. State Farm Mut. Automobile Ins. Co., 15 Wis. 2d 374, 113 N.W.2d 14 (1962) (host-guest automobile situation), noted in 46 Marq. L. Rev. 119 (1962), 60 Mich. L. Rev. 819 (1962), 38 N. Dak. L. Rev. 599 (1962), 41 Tex. L. Rev. 459 (1963) and 8 Wayne L. Rev. 451 (1962); Colson v. Rule, 15 Wis. 2d 387, 113 N.W.2d 21 (1962) (farm laborer-employer cases); Gilson v. Drees Bros., 19 Wis. 2d 252, 120 N.W.2d 63 (1963). Accord, Polsky v. Levine, 73 Wis. 2d 547, 243 N.W.2d 503 (1976) (assumption of risk instruction improper, should be couched in terms of contributory negligence).

[13]See Springrose v. Willmore, 292 Minn. 23, 192 N.W.2d 826 (1971). Cf. Alexander v. Fiftieth Street Heights, Co., 334 So. 2d 161 (Fla. App. 1976) (assumption of risk did not apply on the facts, but under proper circumstances could have been a basis for summary judgment for defendant). The Minnesota court made the abolition of assumption of risk prospective only. In causes of action which arose before the effective date of *Springrose*, but came to trial thereafter, Minnesota courts have been reluctant to apply assumptions of risk as a complete defense. See, e.g., Vanden Broucke v. Lyon County, 301 Minn. 399, 222 N.W.2d 792 (1974) (despite knowledge that bridges in area had been damaged by erosion, plaintiff did not assume risk of collapse without actual knowledge that that particular bridge was dangerous). See also Milloch v. Getty, 300 Minn. 442, 220 N.W.2d 481 (1974); Olson v. Hansen, 299 Minn. 39, 216 N.W.2d 124 (1974); Walsh v. Pagra Air Taxi, Inc., 282 N.W.2d 567 (Minn. 1979). But see Gottskalkson v. Canby, 296 Minn. 212, 207 N.W.2d 361 (1973) (plaintiff who interjected himself into scuffle assumed risk of injury against city). Minnesota has since codified the merger by adopting the fault definition of the Uniform Comparative Fault Act, which includes unreasonable implied assumption of risk.

[14]Lyons v. Redding Constr. Co., 83 Wash. 2d 86, 515 P.2d 821 (1973). See also Wash. Rev. Code Ann., § 4.22.015, making unreasonable assumption of risk a type of fault to be compared.

[15]Wentz v. Deseth, 221 N.W.2d 101 (N.D. 1974); Wilson v. Gordon, 354 A.2d 398 (Me. 1976); Farley v. M M Cattle Co., 529 S.W.2d 751 (Tex. 1975); Brittain v. Booth, 601 P.2d 532 (Wyo. 1979); Anderson v. Ceccardi, 6 Ohio St. 3d 110, 6 Ohio B.R. 170, 451 N.E.2d 780 (Ohio 1983).

[16]Loup-Miller v. Brauer & Associates–Rocky Mountain, Inc., 40 Colo. App. 67, 572 P.2d 845 (1977).

The Montana Supreme Court, in *Kopischke v. First Continental Corporation*, indicated that in the future it would follow the modern trend in treating assumption of risk as a form of contributory negligence to be apportioned on the basis of fault under the comparative negligence statute. However, a later decision held that the two defenses were distinct, but that both were controlled by the statute.[17]

In *Brittain v. Booth*[18] the Wyoming Supreme Court, using a "reasonable man of ordinary prudence" test to measure the plaintiff's conduct, declared that assumption of risk is not an absolute defense under comparative negligence. Rather, it would be a basis for the apportionment of fault.

In *Anderson v. Ceccardi*,[19] the Ohio Supreme Court merged implied assumption of risk with comparative negligence under Ohio's new comparative negligence statute in a case in which a tenant was injured when obviously dangerous front steps had collapsed under him. The court said that maintaining assumption of risk as a complete defense would produce "the anomalous situation where a defendant can circumvent the ... statute entirely by asserting the assumption of risk defense alone."[20]

Pennsylvania's law of assumption of risk is in transition at this writing. In 1981 the Pennsylvania Supreme Court rendered a 3-3 decision abolishing implied assumption of risk in the case of a high school student who lost his sight in one eye playing "jungle football" without protective equipment but also remanding the case for more factfinding on whether he knowingly and voluntarily assumed the risk at all.[21] The court said that the concept of implied assumption of risk was much like contributory negligence and noted that it would be appropriate to merge the rules in view of the comparative negligence statute.[22] In 1983 the court refused to apply comparative fault to a slip-and-fall case, saying the result was consistent with the earlier decision because a landowner has no duty to warn invitees of an obvious danger such as icy pavement.[23]

Mississippi, while expressly declining to abolish implied assumption of risk as a complete defense, has declared that in all cases where the defenses of assumption of risk and contributory negligence overlap, apportionment of damages will be allowed.[24]

---

[17]Kopischke v. First Continental Corp., 187 Mont. 471, 610 P.2d 668 (1980), ovrld. Zahrte v. Sturm, Ruger & Co., 661 P.2d 17 (Mont. 1983).

[18]Brittain v. Booth, 601 P.2d 532 (Wyo. 1979).

[19]Anderson v. Ceccardi, 6 Ohio St. 3d 110, 451 N.E.2d 780 (1983).

[20]Id., 451 N.E.2d at 783.

[21]Rutter v. Northeastern Beaver County School District, 496 Pa. 590, 437 A.2d 1198 (1981).

[22]Id., 437 A.2d at 1210, n.6.

[23]Carrender v. Fitterer, 503 Pa. 178, 469 A.2d 120 (1983).

[24]Braswell v. Economy Supply Co., 281 So. 2d 669 (Miss. 1973). See section 9.3.

In strong dicta, the Supreme Court of Vermont[25] acknowledged that the assumption of risk doctrine is a phase of contributory negligence, and that in a jury instruction on comparative negligence, it would be both confusing and irrelevant to use separate assumption of risk language.

Common-law comparative negligence states have also tended to abolish implied assumption of risk as a separate defense. In *Hoffman v. Jones*[26] the Florida Supreme Court declined to pass on the continued application of assumption of risk as a complete defense. Three divisions of the Florida Court of Appeals later held that assumption of risk merges into the comparative negligence scheme.[27] One division took the contrary view that assumption of risk continues as a complete defense.[28] Finally, clarification from the Florida Supreme Court was rendered in *Blackburn v. Dorta*.[29] The court held that implied assumption of risk no longer operated as a complete bar to recovery, but was merged with contributory negligence under the principles of comparative negligence.

In *Nga Li v. Yellow Cab Company*, the California Supreme Court merged assumption of risk where it is "no more than a variant of contributory negligence," thus retaining primary and express assumption of risk.[30]

It should be noted that several comparative negligence states had abolished implied assumption of risk as a separate defense or had severely limited its application many years before they adopted comparative negligence. Illinois, for example, had limited the defense to employment cases and strict product liability long before judicially adopting comparative negligence;[31] subsequently it was made subject to comparison in product liability.[32] Michigan and New Jersey both abolished the defense.[33] New Hampshire limited the rule to common-

---

[25]Sunday v. Stratton Corp., 136 Vt. 293, 390 A.2d 398 (1978). See also Green v. Sherburne Corp., 137 Vt. 310, 403 A.2d 278 (1979).

[26]Hoffman v. Jones, 280 So. 2d 431, 78 A.L.R.3d 321 (Fla. 1973).

[27]Parker v. Maule Industries, Inc., 321 So. 2d 106 (Fla. App. 1975), approved 348 So. 2d 287 (Fla. 1977); Rea v. Leadership Housing, Inc., 312 So. 2d 818 (Fla. App. 1975), approved 348 So. 2d 287 (Fla. 1977); accord, Trammel v. Reliance Ins. Co., 328 So. 2d 868 (Fla. App. 1976); Manassa v. New Hampshire Ins. Co., 332 So. 2d 34 (Fla. App. 1976).

[28]Dorta v. Blackburn, 302 So. 2d 450 (Fla. App. 1974), revd. 348 So. 2d 287 (Fla. 1977).

[29]Blackburn v. Dorta, 348 So. 2d 287 (Fla. 1977); see also Harley-Davidson Motor Co. v. Carpenter, 350 So. 2d 360 (Fla. App. 1977).

[30]Nga Li v. Yellow Cab Co., 13 Cal. 3d 804, 825, 119 Cal. Rptr. 858, 873, 532 P.2d 1226, 1241, 78 A.L.R.3d 393 (1975) (citing this treatise).

[31]Barrett v. Fritz, 42 Ill. 2d 529, 248 N.E.2d 111 (1969); Williams v. Brown Mfg. Co., 45 Ill. 2d 418, 261 N.E.2d 305, 46 A.L.R.3d 266 (1970).

[32]Coney v. J.L.G. Industries, Inc., 97 Ill. 2d 104, 73 Ill. Dec. 337, 454 N.E. 197. See section 12.5.

[33]Felgner v. Anderson, 375 Mich. 23, 133 N.W.2d 136, 26 A.L.R.3d 531 (1965); Meistrich v. Casino Arena Attractions, Inc., 31 N.J. 44, 155 A.2d 90, 82 A.L.R.2d 1208 (1959); McGrath v. American Cyanamid Co., 41 N.J. 272, 196 A.2d 238 (1963).

law actions for workplace accidents, thus effectively wiping out the defense.[34]

Most comparative negligence states have now established the same pattern with respect to the legal effect of the merger. Reasonable implied assumption of risk is no longer a defense.[35] The courts of these states apparently made the policy judgment that in a comparative negligence system, it would be untoward to reduce plaintiff's recovery when he reasonably assumed a known risk. As indicated above, under a contrary ruling plaintiff's conduct could be easily evaluated by the trier of fact and would give legal significance to conduct that helped produce the lawsuit.

(C) PRIMARY ASSUMPTION OF RISK

It should be noted, however, that some fact patterns that look like reasonable implied assumption of risk may still result in a verdict for defendant if they are recast under the duty concept. For example, in a New York case a spectator at a baseball game was struck by a foul ball while sitting in a box behind first base.[36] The court said that the comparative negligence statute made it necessary to define the duty of care that a baseball park owes to spectators. In another case the court had already determined that that duty was limited to providing a screen behind home plate;[37] the plaintiff was therefore barred from recovery.

Similarly, where the duty of a landowner to social guests is limited to warning them of known latent conditions, the abolition of the defense of reasonable implied assumption of risk does not necessarily change the result.[38] Plaintiff recovers full damages[39] only when it is clear that defendant had a duty to refrain from exposing plaintiff to a known risk and that plaintiff was reasonable in assuming the risk though unprotected.

---

[34]Brosor v. Sullivan, 99 N.H. 305, 109 A.2d 862 (1954).

[35]Springrose v. Willmore, 292 Minn. 23, 192 N.W.2d at 827 (1971) ("The doctrine of implied assumption of risk must ... be recast as an aspect of contributory negligence, meaning that the plaintiff's assumption of risk must be not only voluntary, but, under all the circumstances, unreasonable."); McConville v. State Farm Mut. Automobile Ins. Co., 15 Wis. 2d 374, 113 N.W.2d 14, 16-17 (1962). See also Farley v. M M Cattle Co., 529 S.W.2d 751 (Tex. 1975) ("[T]he reasonableness of an actor's conduct in confronting a risk will be determined under principles of contributory negligence."); Blaw-Knox Food & Chemical Equipment Corp. v. Holmes, 348 So. 2d 604 (Fla. App. 1977), cert. dismissed 351 So. 2d 405 (Fla. 1977) (patent danger doctrine, stated as assumption of risk as a matter of law, merged with contributory negligence).

[36]Davidoff v. Metropolitan Baseball Club, Inc., 61 N.Y.2d 996, 475 N.Y. S.2d 367, 463 N.E.2d 1219 (1984).

[37]Akins v. Glens Falls City School District, 53 N.Y.2d 325, 441 N.Y.S.2d 644, 424 N.E.2d 531 (1981). See Perkins, *The Liability of the Proprietor of a Baseball Park for Injuries to Spectators Struck by Batted or Thrown Balls*, 1951 Wash. U.L.Q. 434.

[38]See Keeton, *Assumption of Risk and the Landowner*, 20 Tex. L. Rev. 562 (1942).

[39]Cf. Hoar v. Sherburne Corp., 327 F. Supp. 570 (D. Vt. 1971), affd. Sherburne Corp. v. Hoar, 456 F.2d 1269 (2d Cir. Vt. 1972) (court held that defendant had a duty to take reasonable steps to obviate a danger and that plaintiff was reasonable in encountering a known risk).

This "no-duty" type of assumption of risk is known in some states as primary implied assumption of risk, as distinguished from secondary (unreasonable) implied assumption of risk or express waiver.[40] The concept has assumed more importance as comparative negligence jurisdictions have concluded that in some situations it would be inappropriate to allow any recovery, even under comparative fault. For example, the Florida courts have developed an exception to the merger of contributory negligence and assumption of risk for contact sports[41] and noncontact sports played in an "aberrant fashion,"[42] deeming these activities to involve an "express" assumption of risk. Plaintiffs engaging in sports are not considered to have assumed every possible risk: when a child was injured by a runaway horse in an amusement park ride, an appellate court held that the defendant had not proved knowing and voluntary assumption of the risk that the horse would be unsuitable for the ride and that the issue should have gone to the jury.[43] Similarly, a high school student injured in football training was held not to have assumed the risk of negligent supervision and improper equipment.[44] In a federal tort claims action, the United States was held to have breached a duty of care when the government negligently failed to warn plaintiff of an unknown risk in the waters of a recreational facility.[45] The plaintiff recovered full danages because the risk was a hidden one of which he had no awareness.

While the Florida courts have dealt with the issue most thoroughly, courts of several other states have also drawn the line between primary and secondary assumption of risk;[46] a number of state legislatures have enacted statutes protecting ski resort operators from liability for the inherent risks of skiing.[47]

The Fireman's Rule

Comparative fault appears to have had little impact on the "fire-

---

[40]W.P. Keeton et al., *Prosser and Keeton on the Law of Torts* § 68 at 496-497 (5th ed. 1984).

[41]Kuehner v. Green, 436 So. 2d 78 (Fla. 1983).

[42]Strickland v. Roberts, 382 So. 2d 1338 (Fla. App. 1980), review denied 389 So. 2d 1115 (Fla. 1980) (intentionally water skiing too close to dock); Gary v. Party Time Co., 434 So. 2d 338 (Fla. App. 1983) (skiing on roller skates).

[43]O'Connell v. Walt Disney World Co., 413 So. 2d 444 (Fla. App. 1982).

[44]Leahy v. School Board, 450 So. 2d 883 (Fla. App. 1984).

[45]Miller v. United States, 597 F.2d 614 (7th Cir. Ill. 1979), affirming 442 F. Supp. 555 (N.D. Ill. 1976).

[46]See, e.g., Frazier v. Norton, 334 N.W.2d 865 (S.D. 1983); Rieger v. Zackoski, 321 N.W.2d 16 (Minn. 1982) (duty found where racetrack failed to keep spectator from driving onto track and running over another spectator); Anderson v. Ceccardi, 6 Ohio St. 3d 110, 6 Ohio B.R. 170, 451 N.E. 2d 780 (1983) (distinguishing implied unreasonable assumption of risk from baseball spectator scenario); Sunday v. Stratton Corp., 136 Vt. 293, 390 A.2d 398 (1978) (skiing accident); Sherman v. Platte County, 642 P.2d 787 (Wyo. 1982) (obvious danger rule still bars recovery in slip and fall case notwithstanding comparative negligence statute).

[47]See, e.g., Utah Code Ann., §§ 78-27-51 to 78-27-54, barring recovery for the inherent risks of skiing, including weather, terrain, structures such as lift towers, collisions with other skiers, and failure to ski within one's own ability.

man's rule," which in its original form stated that a landowner owes no duty to a fireman to keep the premises in a safe condition.[48] The rule has been extended to include risks that are inherent in fire and police work and tends to be couched in assumption of risk language.[49] Now that assumption of risk and the licensee/invitee distinction underpinning the rule have been limited or abolished, the fireman's rule still survives in most jurisdictions that have considered the question, but it has become more limited in scope. The Minnesota Supreme Court has held that firemen assume only the risks that are reasonably apparent to them as a part of fire fighting; in that case a boiling liquid expanding vapor explosion at a liquified petroleum gas storage tank was held to be one of those risks.[50] In a California case, firemen were allowed to recover when a landowner negligently or intentionally represented to them that a boilover at a chemical plant did not involve toxic chemicals.[51] Oregon has abolished the rule altogether.[52]

Apportionment for Unreasonable Assumption

When plaintiff *unreasonably* assumes a known risk, his fault in that regard is negligence and his damage award may be subject to apportionment. Nevertheless, his unreasonableness in assuming the risk will not necessarily bar his claim, even in a 50% comparative negligence system.[53]

Both Wisconsin and Minnesota were under 50% comparative negligence when they abandoned assumption of risk as a separate defense. Neither considered that plaintiff's unreasonable assumption of the risk made him equally negligent as a matter of law; both left the question to the jury. In two of the cases plaintiff was a passenger in an automobile and had knowledge that defendant-driver was intoxicated or likely to drive dangerously.[54] A third decision upheld a verdict attributing

---

[48]See, e.g., Hamilton v. Minneapolis Desk Mfg. Co., 78 Minn. 3, 80 N.W. 693 (1899). See generally Annot., "Liability of owner or occupant of premises to fireman coming thereon in discharge of his duty," 11 A.L.R.4th 597 (1979).

[49]See, e.g., Los Angeles v. O'Brian, 154 Cal. App. 2d 904, 201 Cal. Rptr. 561 (1984) (city could not recover costs of worker's compensation and damage to police car from criminal suspect who intentionally backed van into police car); Armstrong v. Mailand, 284 N.W.2d 343, 11 A.L.R.4th 583 (Minn. 1979).

[50]Armstrong v. Mailand, 284 N.W.2d 343, 11 A.L.R.4th 583 (Minn. 1979).

[51]Lipson v. Superior Court, 31 Cal. 3d 362, 182 Cal. Rptr. 629, 644 P.2d 822 (1982).

[52]Christensen v. Murphy, 296 Ore. 610, 678 P.2d 1210 (1984).

[53]See section 9.3. Accord, Keegan v. Anchor Inns, Inc., 606 F.2d 35 (3d Cir. V.I. 1979) (assumption of risk not available as a bar to recovery when plaintiff's conduct amounts to negligence).

[54]See McConville v. State Farm Mut. Automobile Ins. Co., 15 Wis. 2d 374, 113 N.W.2d 14 (1962); Springrose v. Willmore, 292 Minn. 23, 192 N.W.2d 826 (1971).

only 35% contributory negligence to a farm laborer who knowingly stood on a weakened scaffold negligently maintained by his employer.[55]

Perhaps even more dramatic in this regard was *Gilson v. Drees Brothers*,[56] where a cattle buyer with wide experience in the propensities of animals was permitted to have the jury compare his "unreasonable" conduct with that of the defendant. The defendant's fault apparently was in negligently maintaining a bull who broke loose and injured the cattle buyer.

A Point of Difference

Wisconsin, Washington and Minnesota apparently differ in approach to assumption of risk on one point; only Minnesota retained the terminology of implied assumption of risk, and then only as an element of contributory negligence.[57] In that regard, the Supreme Court of Minnesota stated:

> The only question for submission in the usual case ... will be whether the particular plaintiff was, under the circumstances, negligent in regard to his own safety, for under that general issue counsel may fully argue the issue in all its aspects. There may be unusual cases, however, where contributory negligence and assumption of risk, in any distinctive aspects, may be separately submitted, subject, of course, to a single apportionment verdict.[58]

This limitation may serve only to create confusion. The court realized this and indicated that in the future it might reconsider the point.[59] The legislature subsequently enacted a new comparative fault statement making unreasonable implied assumption of risk a type of fault subject to comparison.[60]

Merger Under Comparative Negligence

The reasons for merger of implied assumption of risk into contributory negligence may become more persuasive once a state adopts comparative negligence. Minnesota specifically declined to abolish assumption of risk as a separate and distinct defense prior to the time comparative negligence was enacted.[61] Once comparative negligence is

---

[55]See Colson v. Rule, 15 Wis. 2d 387, 113 N.W.2d 21 (1962). See also Miles v. Ace Van Lines & Movers, Inc., 72 Wis. 2d 538, 241 N.W.2d 186 (1976) (customer who interjected himself into moving operation is guilty of causal negligence by voluntarily placing self in position of danger); Callan v. Peters Constr. Co., 94 Wis. 2d 225, 288 N.W.2d 146 (1979) (plaintiff's knowledge of prior accident at construction site did not require finding that her negligence was greater than subcontractors').

[56]Gilson v. Drees Bros., 19 Wis. 2d 252, 120 N.W.2d 63 (1963).

[57]See Springrose v. Willmore, 292 Minn. 23, 192 N.W.2d 826, 828 (1971).

[58]Id.

[59]Another distinct aspect of Minnesota's approach to merger is that it is to be applied prospectively only. This was somewhat ironic in that Minnesota is the only state whose comparative negligence statute was retroactive. See Peterson v. Minneapolis, 285 Minn. 282, 173 N.W.2d 353, 37 A.L.R.3d 1431 (1969) and section 8.4.

[60]Minn. Stat. Ann., § 604.01(1a).

[61]See Parness v. Economics Laboratory, Inc., 284 Minn. 381, 386, 170 N.W.2d 554, 558 (1969).

adopted, implied assumption of risk can take on new and extraordinary importance; if plaintiff's assumption of risk continues to provide a separate complete defense, defendant avoids paying any damages. Clearly, the Supreme Courts of Florida, Maine, Minnesota, North Dakota, Ohio, Texas, Washington, and Wisconsin did not believe that the policy underlying assumption of risk merited this drastic result. Thus, those courts treated conduct that amounted to implied assumption of risk as if it were contributory negligence and allowed the jury to apportion damages accordingly. Again, it is this author's view that it is unnecessary and inappropriate to add the element of "unreasonable conduct" to the defense in order to reach this result.

When the California Supreme Court in *Nga Li v. Yellow Cab Company*[62] judicially adopted comparative negligence, it also merged the defenses of assumption of risk and contributory negligence. In two subsequent decisions[63] the California Court of Appeals, following the *Li* decision, held that unreasonable conduct by the plaintiff fell within that area merged into the comparative negligence system, and therefore allowed apportionment of damages due to fault rather than completely barring recovery.

The Supreme Court of Wisconsin was also persuaded to merge the defenses because it had experienced over thirty years of futility in trying to determine precisely when defendant's contributory negligence became assumption of risk.[64]

Joint Tortfeasors

A final reason why comparative negligence may trigger abandonment of assumption of risk as a complete defense concerns contribution among joint tortfeasors. If assumption of risk is limited to consensual conduct between parties (as it was in Wisconsin), an automobile guest who knows his driver is intoxicated may be barred from a claim against him, but not barred against a third party negligent driver. The end result in a three-party suit is that the third party bears the entire

---

[62]Nga Li v. Yellow Cab Co., 13 Cal. 3d 804, 119 Cal. Rptr. 858, 532 P.2d 1226, 78 A.L.R.3d 393 (1975).

[63]Gonzalez v. Garcia, 75 Cal. App. 3d 874, 142 Cal. Rptr. 503 (1977) (citing this treatise); Paula v. Gagnon, 81 Cal. App. 3d 680, 146 Cal. Rptr. 702 (1978). Both cases pertained to auto accidents where the drivers were intoxicated. In the former, the passenger, knowing the driver to be drunk, nevertheless continued to ride; the decedent in the latter case chose to drive home rather than seeking assistance.

[64]See Colson v. Rule, 15 Wis. 2d 387, 113 N.W.2d 21, 23 (1962). See also Tiller v. Atlantic C. L. R. Co., 318 U.S. 54, 62-64, 87 L. Ed. 610, 63 S. Ct. 444, 143 A.L.R. 967 (1943) (referring to the same problem under pre-1939 F.E.L.A. law). The Wisconsin court found additional reasons in more specific contexts to abandon assumption of risk as a separate and complete defense. With respect to claims brought by farm workers, it would tend to immunize employers who were the greatest transgressors of the safe place statutes. The court realized that if a farm employee-worker refused to make use of defective equipment, it probably would cost him his job. See Colson v. Rule, 113 N.W.2d 21. In the context of automobile guests, the court was clearly thinking about the problems of general risk distribution in this specific area. See McConville v. State Farm Mut. Automobile Ins. Co., 15 Wis. 2d 374, 113 N.W.2d 14 (1962).

cost of an accident. This would not be in harmony with the general purpose of comparative negligence which is to apportion damages on the basis of fault.[65]

Conclusion

The courts in those comparative negligence states that have abandoned implied assumption of risk as a separate defense have found sufficient reasons for doing so in the introduction of comparative negligence into the law. As discussed at the beginning of this chapter in section 9.1, they did not have to engage in the general debate about the nature or worth of assumption of risk.

9.5　Probable future treatment of implied assumption of risk

Courts in a number of new comparative negligence states have not yet focused on the question considered in this chapter—whether damages will be apportioned when plaintiff has impliedly assumed the risk of defendant's negligent conduct.

It seems highly probable that states that have already abandoned implied assumption of risk as a separate and distinct defense prior to the adoption of comparative negligence will treat unreasonable conduct that might come within the erstwhile defense as subject to apportionment. Hawaii,[66] Idaho,[67] Kentucky,[68] New Jersey,[69] and probably New Hampshire[70] appear to be in this group. It is an easy matter of statutory construction to reach this result. The legislature has said in the statute that contributory negligence is to be apportioned. Prior to the enactment of the statute, the courts deemed unreasonable implied assumption of risk to be a form of contributory negligence. Therefore, unreasonable implied assumption of risk is also to be apportioned.

Question of Merger Open

A more difficult problem arises in those states that have not yet determined that assumption of risk should be merged into contributory negligence at the time their comparative negligence statute is adopted. Delaware, Nevada, and Oklahoma will have to determine on the merits whether implied assumption of risk is to remain as a complete defense and, if not, how it is to be handled, as will the seven remaining contributory negligence jurisdictions if they adopt comparative negligence.

---

[65]See 60 Mich. L. Rev. at 817.

[66]See Bulatao v. Kauai Motors, Ltd., 49 Hawaii 1, 406 P.2d 887 (1965). See also Burrows v. Hawaiian Trust Co., 49 Hawaii 351, 417 P.2d 816 (1966).

[67]See Fawcett v. Irby, 92 Idaho 48, 436 P.2d 714 (1968).

[68]Parker v. Redden, 421 S.W.2d 586 (Ky. 1967).

[69]See Meistrich v. Casino Arena Attractions, Inc., 31 N.J. 44, 155 A.2d 90, 82 A.L.R.2d 1208 (1959).

[70]See Bolduc v. Crain, 104 N.H. 163, 181 A.2d 641 (1962). Accord, Stevens v. Kanematsu-Gosho Co., 494 F.2d 367 (1st Cir. N.H. 1974). See also note 6, section 9.1 above, for other states that have merged the defense.

These are questions that a court should properly consider because assumption of risk is a judicially created doctrine.[71]

Arguments for Retention of Complete Defense

One of the most significant arguments for retention of assumption of risk as a complete defense is based on legislative intent, where a legislature did not specifically state that damages should be apportioned when plaintiff has impliedly assumed a risk. This argument is especially convincing where, as in Oklahoma, assumption of risk is separately mentioned in one section of the statute but not in the section providing for apportionment of damages.[72] In the absence of such an indication, however, courts should be hesitant to interpret the omission as a matter of legislative intent. In light of the fact that assumption of risk is judicially created, legislative intent on the matter should be expressed affirmatively.[73]

Probably the strongest argument for retention of assumption of risk as a complete defense is based on the generic difference between assumption of the risk and contributory negligence. In theory, it is based not so much on plaintiff's *fault* as on his agreement by his conduct to take the risk of the very consequences that befell him.[74] Viewed from that perspective, it is a close cousin of the consent defense to intentional torts.[75] Since consent would remain an absolute defense to intentional torts under a comparative negligence system, a fortiori, assumption of risk should keep its place as a bar to negligence.

Arguments for Merger

The best answer to this contention is that assumption of the risk differs from consent in one important respect. By consent to an intentional tort, plaintiff manifests his agreement to the actual invasion of his interest in person or property.[76] On the other hand, when plaintiff assumes a risk, he volunteers to be subject to a *possible* injury. This is a giant step away from consent when viewed from the perspective of whether plaintiff has *actually* agreed to hold defendant blameless for the risk.

In that light, facts constituting assumption of risk are as close to contributory negligence as they are to consent. The scores of cases that

---

[71]See Laugesen, *Colorado Comparative Negligence*, 48 Den. L.J. 469, 484-486 (1972) (suggesting no apportionment).

[72]Okla. Stat. Ann., tit. 23, §§ 11, 12.

[73]See section 21.4.

[74]See Keeton, "Assumption of Risk in Product Liability Cases," *in* Symposium: *Assumption of Risk*, 22 La. L. Rev. 1, 122, 164-165 (1961).

[75]See Wade, "The Place of Assumption of Risk in the Law of Negligence," *in* Symposium: *Assumption of Risk*, 22 La. L. Rev. 1, 5, 7-9 (1961).

[76]Id.

have attempted to characterize plaintiff's conduct as assumption of risk or contributory negligence demonstrate this.[77]

A rigorous application of implied assumption of risk as an absolute defense could serve to undermine seriously the general purpose of a comparative negligence statute to apportion damages on the basis of fault.[78] This is perhaps the reason that every commentator who has addressed himself to this specific problem has agreed that plaintiff should not have his claim barred if he has impliedly assumed the risk, but rather that this conduct should be considered in apportioning damages under the statute.[79]

The reasoning of the Wisconsin and Minnesota Supreme Courts, that *reasonable* implied assumption of risk should not serve to diminish the amount of plaintiff's recovery, is seriously flawed. When a person's conduct under the facts is truly voluntary and when he knows of the specific risk he is to encounter, this is a form of responsibility or fault that the jury should evaluate. Those who argue that the "jury cannot do this" have not met too many jurors. The true meaning of comparative fault is comparative responsibility.[80] When a plaintiff engages in classic assumption of risk conduct, he is *in part* responsible for his injury.

In some contexts, defendant may have discharged his duty in tort law by warning plaintiff of risks. In such cases the defendant has met his full responsibility to the plaintiff and the claim should be dismissed.

---

[77]See Tiller v. Atlantic C. L. R. Co., 318 U.S. 54, 62-64, 87 L. Ed. 610, 63 S. Ct. 444, 143 A.L.R. 967 (1943); McConville v. State Farm Mut. Automobile Ins. Co., 15 Wis. 2d 374, 113 N.W.2d 14 (1962).

[78]Georgia appears to be the only comparative negligence state that vigorously applies assumption of risk, and this phenomenon can be explained by the unique statutory basis of that state's comparative negligence system. See note 76, section 9.3 and accompanying text. See Blaw-Knox Food & Chemical Equipment Corp. v. Holmes, 348 So. 2d 604 (Fla. App. 1977), cert. dismissed 351 So. 2d 405 (Fla. 1977) (patent danger doctrine).

[79]See Note, *Assumption of Risk as a Defense in Nebraska Negligence Actions Under the Comparative Negligence Statute*, 30 Neb. L. Rev. 608 (1951) and other materials cited in note 1, section 9.1 above.

[80]See Chapter 12.

CHAPTER 10

THE GUEST STATUTES

Section

10.1 Nature of the guest statutes

10.2 Implied repeal or modification of the guest statute by comparative negligence

10.3 Comparison of negligence under the guest statute

10.1 Nature of the guest statutes

A few states that have enacted comparative negligence laws also have so-called "guest" statutes.[1] These statutes differ from each other in a number of important ways; in general, however, they limit the duty owed by a driver of an automobile (or pilot of a plane) to a gratuitous passenger with respect to risks of harm that might occur in the course of transportation.[2]

The guest statutes in most comparative negligence states reflect the variations that can be found in guest statutes generally. Some limit liability to acts of "wilful and wanton misconduct";[3] others draw the line at behavior that is "grossly negligent."[4]

Georgia and Massachusetts at one time had evolved case law limiting liability to guests,[5] but both states have overruled these limitations by statute.[6]

---

[1]Del. Code Ann., tit. 21, § 6101; Ill. Rev. Stat., ch. 95½, § 10-201 (hitchhikers only); Ind. Code, §§ 9-3-3-1 and 9-3-3-2; Neb. Rev. Stat., § 39-6, 191; Tex. Rev. Civ. Stat. Ann. (Vernon), art. 6701b (close relatives only).

[2]See 2 F. Harper & F. James, *The Law of Torts* § 16.15 (1956); W. P. Keeton et al., *Prosser and Keeton on the Law of Torts* § 34 at 211 (5th ed. 1984); Sanders, *Aviation Guest Laws: A Modern Anachronism*, 36 J. Air L. 185 (1970); Morrison and Arnold, *Automobile Guest Laws Today: Report of the Automobile Insurance Committee*, 27 Ins. Couns. J. 223, 225–236 (1960) (collecting statutes).

[3]See Ark. Stat. Ann., § 75-913 (repealed 1983).

[4]See Neb. Rev. Stat., § 39-740.

[5]See Caskey v. Underwood, 89 Ga. App. 418, 79 S.E.2d 558 (1953); Averette v. Oliver, 128 Ga. App. 54, 195 S.E.2d 925 (1973) (if passenger's presence was at owner's invitation and benefited the owner's economic interest, the duty owed the passenger is ordinary care); Massaletti v. Fitzroy, 228 Mass. 487, 118 N.E. 168 (1917) and Falden v. Crook, 342 Mass. 173, 172 N.E.2d 686 (1961) (a gratuitous passenger must show gross negligence to recover from his host).

[6]Ga. Code Ann., § 51-1-36; Mass. Gen. Laws Ann., ch. 231, § 85L. But the Massachusetts statute is limited to cases "in which the plaintiff was a passenger in the exercise of due care." Query: If the passenger was slightly negligent, does this remove the protection of the statute so that the common-law requirement of gross negligence returns before the passenger can have any recovery? If so, there is a limited return of the contributory negligence defense under the guise of "no duty" in the host. In any event, it is clear that there may be a recovery for wrongful death without a showing of gross negligence, based on the proposition that a wrongful death action is entirely statutory. Gallup v. Lazott, 271 Mass. 406, 171 N.E. 658 (1930).

Criticisms of the Guest Statutes

The guest statutes have brought a plethora of legal problems in and of themselves, and they have been criticized as being at variance with modern theories of risk distribution.[7] Their purported bases—that a guest should have no right to expect more than a limited degree of care from his host, and that applying the standard of ordinary care might foster collusion between host and guest—both seem less than satisfactory today than when the statutes were enacted in the 1920's and 1930's. As of early 1985, they remain on the books of only a few states.[8]

The supreme courts of thirteen states have struck down their state guest statutes on the ground that they violated the equal protection guarantees of the federal and state constitutions or other state constitutional provisions.[9] At least ten other states have repealed their guest statutes.[10]

Some legislatures that have enacted comparative negligence have not repealed the guest statutes. This has caused and will cause additional legal problems that are discussed in this chapter; they have only been touched upon elsewhere.[11]

10.2 Implied repeal or modification of the guest statute by comparative negligence

It could be logically contended that the general purpose of a comparative negligence statute to apportion damages on the basis of fault is seriously hampered by guest statutes which sharply limit the liability of culpable hosts. It might be deduced from this contention that a com-

---

[7]See materials cited in note 2 above and Georgetta, *The Major Issues in a Guest Case*, 1954 Ins. L.J. 583.

[8]Ala. Code, § 32-1-2 and the comparative fault states listed in note 1 herein. This count does not include statutes such as Virginia's, which states that drivers are liable to guest passengers for negligence. Va. Code, § 8.01-63.

[9]Brown v. Merlo, 8 Cal. 3d 855, 106 Cal. Rptr. 388, 506 P.2d 212, 66 A.L.R.3d 505 (1973); Thompson v. Hagan, 96 Idaho 19, 523 P.2d 1365 (1974); Bierkamp v. Rogers, 293 N.W.2d 577 (Iowa 1980); Henry v. Bauder, 213 Kan. 751, 518 P.2d 362 (1974); Ludwig v. Johnson, 243 Ky. 533, 49 S.W.2d 347 (1932); Manistee Bank & Trust Co. v. McGowan, 394 Mich. 655, 232 N.W.2d 636 (1975); Laakonen v. Eighth Judicial Dist. Court, 91 Nev. 506, 538 P.2d 574 (1975); McGeehan v. Bunch, 88 N.M. 308, 540 P.2d 238 (1975); Johnson v. Hassett, 217 N.W.2d 771 (N.D. 1974); Primes v. Tyler, 43 Ohio App. 2d 163, 72 Ohio Op. 2d 393, 335 N.E.2d 373 (1974) affd. 43 Ohio St. 2d 195, 72 Ohio Op. 2d 112, 331 N.E.2d 723 (1975); Ramey v. Ramey, 273 S.C. 680, 258 S.E.2d 883 (1979); Malan v. Lewis, No. 17606 (Utah May 1, 1984); Nehring v. Russell, 582 P.2d 67 (Wyo. 1978). Cf. Botsch v. Reisdorff, 193 Neb. 165, 226 N.W.2d 121 (1975) (holding auto guest statute constitutional).

[10]Arkansas, Colorado, Connecticut, Florida, Montana, Oregon, South Dakota, Vermont and Washington.

[11]See Annot., "Comparative negligence statute as applicable to actions under automobile guest statute," 149 A.L.R. 1050 (1944) (a one-page annotation); Dobbs, *Act 191 Comparative Negligence*, 9 Ark. L. Rev. 357, 371-373 (1955) (most thorough discussion to date); Gradwohl, *Comparative Negligence of an Automobile Guest—Apportionment of Damages Under the Comparative Negligence Statute*, 33 Neb. L. Rev. 54 (1953); Laugesen, *Colorado Comparative Negligence*, 48 Den. L.J. 469, 483-484 (1972); Spikes, *Gross Negligence Under the Guest Statute: A Collation of Nebraska Cases*, 22 Neb. L. Rev. 264 (1943); Sanders, note 2 above, at 235-236; Annot., "Liability to guest in airplane," 40 A.L.R.3d 1117 (1970).

parative negligence statute should be read as an implied repealer of the guest statute. However, no court has accepted this argument to date.[12] Since comparative negligence statutes, by their language, are limited to matters directly connected with the defense of contributory negligence, this would be too great a judicial leap.[13]

Strains on the Guest Statutes

Comparative negligence places an additional strain on the guest statute in either of two situations. A court might be persuaded to modify the effect of the guest statute, should one of the occasions arise.

Assume that a guest has been contributorily negligent while his host and the driver of another vehicle were both negligent to a greater extent than the guest but not grossly negligent. The injured guest can place the entire burden of liability upon the driver of the other vehicle. Because the host is insulated by the guest statute from liability to his guest, he may be safeguarded from any contribution claim by the other driver.[14] In this context, the court might hold that disallowing contribution would work such a serious dilution of the comparative negligence principle that "liability should be apportioned on the basis of fault"; it may, in turn, ignore the general rule that the right of contribution must arise out of a common liability.[15]

In a decision voiding a guest statute on equal protection grounds, the Utah Supreme Court discussed the contribution problem, noting that application of the guest statute would defeat the policy of the comparative negligence statute.[16]

Actions by Host Against Guest

The second situation in which the guest statute might be modified involves a suit by the host against the guest based on the latter's negligence in contributing to the accident.[17] A lawsuit of this kind would have been very unlikely when the contributory negligence defense was

---

[12]See, e.g., Nehring v. Russell, 582 P.2d 67 (Wyo. 1978), rejecting repeal by implication but voiding the statute on state constitutional grounds.

[13]In McConville v. State Farm Mut. Automobile Ins. Co., 15 Wis. 2d 374, 113 N.W.2d 14 (1962) the Supreme Court of Wisconsin abandoned its common-law rule in regard to the assumption of risk by an automobile guest. Nevertheless, the court did not rely on the state's comparative negligence statute in reaching this conclusion. Rather, the court based its decision on the fact that "Liability insurance is widely prevalent today." Id., at 19.

[14]See Troutman v. Modlin, 353 F.2d 382 (8th Cir. Ark. 1965); Beck v. Wessel, 90 S.D. 107, 237 N.W.2d 905 (1976) (although the defendant had recovered damages in a prior suit from the driver of the vehicle in which the plaintiff was riding, contribution was denied since the plaintiff's driver was insulated from liability under the guest statute). See also W. P. Keeton et al., *Prosser and Keeton on the Law of Torts* § 50 at 339-340 (5th ed. 1984).

[15]Cf. Bedell v. Reagan, 159 Me. 292, 192 A.2d 24 (1963); Weinberg v. Underwood, 101 N.J. Super. 448, 244 A.2d 538 (1968). Both decisions hold that family immunity does not prevent a husband from being liable to a third party for contribution on the ground that this is not the purpose of the immunity.

[16]Malan v. Lewis, No. 17606 (Utah May 1, 1984).

[17]See Dobbs, *Act 191 Comparative Negligence*, 9 Ark. L. Rev. 357, 371-373 (1955).

absolute because the host-driver's own negligence would have barred his claim against his guest. Of course, this is not the situation under comparative negligence and such suits are a distinct possiblity. For example, suppose the guest negligently assures his host-driver that the right lane is clear for a lane change, but there is in fact a vehicle in the driver's "blind spot." In such a circumstance, the host could assert a claim against the guest for his ordinary negligence.[18] On the other hand, the guest's counterclaim against the host would be barred under the guest statute because the host's conduct did not reach a sufficient degree of culpability.[19] Since this unusual consequence is brought about by the guest statute, the host's claim should be deemed a waiver of the guest statute protection and the guest should be allowed to cross-claim against the host on the basis of ordinary negligence or be permitted to show the host's negligence to reduce his claim.

10.3 Comparison of negligence under the guest statute

As is indicated in Chapter 5, most comparative negligence statutes operate with regard to claims based on "negligence." The question arises whether the statute applies when defendant host-driver's conduct constitutes the "gross negligence," "willful and wanton conduct," or "recklessness" that removes the protection of the guest statute. It seems highly unlikely that any court would hold in such a situation that contributory negligence remains an absolute defense;[20] rather, the question will be whether plaintiff's contributory negligence will serve to reduce his damages at all.

The overwhelming majority of American courts have ignored plaintiff's ordinary contributory negligence when defendant's conduct was reckless or willful or (in a few cases) grossly negligent.[21] Many courts have taken this same position when defendant's degree of culpability removed him from the protection of a guest statute.[22]

"Gross Negligence" Guest Statute

When the guest statute uses the words "grossly negligent" it is

---

[18]But see Delmore v. American Family Mut. Ins. Co., 118 Wis. 2d 510, 348 N.W.2d 151 (1984) (passenger can be liable to third persons by taking active control of the automobile, but acting as a lookout and giving directions are not enough).

[19]See 2 F. Harper & F. James, *The Law of Torts* § 16.15, at 957 (1956).

[20]See Landrum v. Roddy, 143 Neb. 934, 12 N.W.2d 82, 149 A.L.R. 1041 (1943), overruling Sheehy v. Abboud, 126 Neb. 554, 253 N.W. 683 (1934).

[21]See section 5.3 herein. See also Siders v. Gibbs, 39 N.C. App. 183, 249 S.E.2d 858 (1978) (owner's recovery not barred where owner/passenger is able to show that other motorist's conduct amounted to willful and wanton misconduct).

[22]See Zumwalt v. Lindland, 239 Ore. 26, 396 P.2d 205, 208 (1964) (applying contributory negligence defense because of clear legislative intent to give host-driver as much immunity from liability as constitutionally possible); 2 F. Harper & F. James, *The Law of Torts* § 22.6, at 1214, n. 8. Curiously, the assumption of risk defense might have barred plaintiff's claim in such a situation. See Pedrick, *Taken for a Ride: The Automobile Guest and Assumption of Risk*, 22 La. L. Rev. 90, 93-94 (1961); Rice, *The Automobile Guest and the Rationale of Assumption of Risk*, 27 Minn. L. Rev. 323, 324-34 (1943). For a discussion of how assumption of risk is handled under comparative negligence, see Chapter 9.

highly likely that a court will hold that a plaintiff's contributory negligence still diminishes damages under the comparative negligence statute. Precedents in existing comparative negligence jurisdictions suggest this result.[23] It is relatively easy for a court to characterize gross negligence as conduct that is merely different in degree from ordinary negligence and, therefore, subsumed under "negligence" in the comparative negligence statute.[24]

"Reckless" and "Wanton" Guest Statutes

Some of the guest statutes protect the driver-host from liability to his guest unless his conduct has been "reckless" or "willful and wanton." These statutes present no problem if the comparative negligence statute itself specifically applies to conduct of the kind described in the guest statute;[25]there, contributory negligence diminishes recovery regardless of the quality of the defendant's fault. In *Rone v. Miller*,[26] for example, the Arkansas Supreme Court admitted evidence of the passenger's negligence despite the driver's willful and wanton misconduct.

A more difficult question arises where the comparative negligence statute by its terms applies only to actions based on "negligence" but the guest statute requires recklessness or willfulness and wantonness before the host is liable. Arguably, the words of the act thus used in the guest statute create a liability base that is more closely akin to intent than to negligence. Therefore, the argument runs, contributory negligence is immaterial.[27]

A Difference in Kind?

There is an apparent trend to interpret words such as "reckless" and "wanton" as setting forth objective standards of fault that are dif-

---

[23]See Landrum v. Roddy, 143 Neb. 934, 12 N.W.2d 82, 149 A.L.R. 1041 (1943); Hess v. Holdsworth, 176 Neb. 774, 127 N.W.2d 487 (1964) (no contributory negligence found, but the court indicated comparative negligence statute would apply); Stukes v. Trowell, 119 Ga. App. 651, 168 S.E.2d 616 (1969) (Georgia applies limited host-duty rule by common-law decision); Wilson v. Swanson, 169 Mont. 328, 546 P.2d 990 (1976) (ordinary negligence will not bar passenger's claim under Montana guest statute); Johnson v. Tilden, 278 Ore. 11, 562 P.2d 1188 (1977) (comparative fault statute held applicable to actions brought under the guest-passenger statute).

[24]See 2 F. Harper & F. James, note 22 above, § 16.15, at 953; see also cases cited in note 23 above.

[25]Compare Ark. Stat. Ann., § 27-1763, requiring "willful and wanton conduct" with Ark. Stat. Ann., § 75-913, the now-defunct guest act, requiring "willfully and wantonly operating." In 1975 Ark. Acts 367, the Arkansas legislature deleted the specific inclusion of willful and wanton conduct in the state comparative negligence statute. However, the language of the new statute, "... any act, omission, conduct or risk assumed, breach of warranty or breach of any legal duty..." is plainly broad enough to cover willful and wanton conduct.

[26]Rone v. Miller, 257 Ark. 791, 520 S.W.2d 268 (1975). The Arkansas guest statute has since been repealed. See note 10 above.

[27]See section 5.3; Dobbs, *Act 191 Comparative Negligence*, 9 Ark. L. Rev. 357, 371–373 (1955).

ferent in kind, not just in degree, from negligence.[28] Nevertheless, courts may be reluctant to characterize these kinds of conduct, for purposes of the comparative negligence statute, "as something other than negligence."[29]

There is logic in the approach that treats recklessness or wantonness as simply a higher degree of fault than "ordinary" negligence. However, it does produce a result that may be unfair. The host's liability exposure is already severely limited by the guest statute; it can be logically argued that it is unjust, therefore, to reduce the award of a plaintiff whose conduct may just have crossed the threshold of ordinary negligence.

The Better Rule

On balance, however, it is probably best to consider plaintiff's contributory negligence as a basis for diminishing damages even when defendant's conduct has been so reckless or wanton as to remove him from the protection of the guest statute. This approach accords with the general purpose of comparative negligence, and it also facilitates the judicial administration of such laws. The Uniform Comparative Fault Act takes this approach by including reckless, willful or wanton conduct in the fault definition.[30]

In the host-guest context, the guest's unreasonable assumption of risk should not bar his claim but should merely subject him to apportionment.[31] This may serve to balance any disadvantage wrought by diminishing his award when he was guilty only of ordinary negligence.

---

[28]See *Restatement (Second) of Torts* § 500, Comment *g* at 590 (1965); 1 F. Harper & F. James, note 22 above, at 49-50.

[29]See Billingsley v. Westrac Co., 365 F.2d 619, 623 (8th Cir. Ark. 1966) (reckless conduct considered but guest statute not involved); Bielski v. Schulz, 16 Wis. 2d 1, 114 N.W.2d 105 (1962) (dealing with gross negligence, which had been interpreted under prior law as "recklessness"); Sorenson v. Allred, 112 Cal. App. 3d 717, 169 Cal. Rptr. 441, 10 A.L.R. 4th 937 (1980) (referring to defendant's conduct alternately as "gross negligence" and "willful and wanton" and characterizing the fault comparison as at most "oranges and lemons").

[30]Unif. Comp. Fault Act, § 1(b), Comment a, 12 U.L.A. 39, 41 (Supp. 1985).

[31]See section 9.4. Compare materials cited in note 22 above.

CHAPTER 11

ACTIONS BASED ON NUISANCE

Section

11.1 Introduction

11.2 Absolute nuisance and contributory negligence

11.3 Nuisance based on negligence

11.4 Basis of liability determining application of comparative negligence

11.1 Introduction

The topic of nuisance in the law of torts has never been known for clarity. Many authors, however, have attempted to make some sense of the subject.[1] Perhaps the best attempt at a definition was made by Professor Seavey some years ago. He says that a nuisance

[C]onnotes a condition or activity which unduly interferes with the use of land or of a public place. Conduct which interferes solely with the use of a relatively small area of private land is tortious but not criminal and is called a private nuisance. Conduct which interferes with the use of a public place or with the activities of an entire community is called a public nuisance.[2]

Since the task of defining tortious nuisance has given courts and legal writers some degree of difficulty, it might be expected that setting forth defenses to such a cause of action would work even more confusion. This has in fact occurred. In that regard, Chief Judge Crane of the New York Court of Appeals once wrote that "There has been so much written and said about the defense of negligence in an action of nuisance that the subject has become a mystery, smothered in verbiage."[3] Nevertheless, some careful attempts to set forth the defenses to an action of nuisance have been made and it is worthwhile to consult them in making a determination as to how comparative negligence will blend with the cause of action for nuisance.[4]

Bases of Liability for Nuisance

An exploration of those sources makes it clear that any of the full

---

[1]See, e.g., W. P. Keeton et al., *Prosser and Keeton on the Law of Torts*, ch. 15 at 616 (5th ed. 1984); 2 F. Harper & F. James, *The Law of Torts* § 1.23 (1956).

[2]See Seavey, *Nuisance: Contributory Negligence and Other Mysteries*, 65 Harv. L. Rev. 984 (1952).

[3]See Delaney v. Philhern Realty Holding Corp., 280 N.Y. 461, 468, 21 N.E.2d 507, 510 (1939) (concurring opinion).

[4]See W. P. Keeton et al., note 1 above, § 88B; 2 F. Harper & F. James, note 1 above, § 22.8; Berger, *Contributory Negligence as a Defense to Nuisance*, 29 Ill. L. Rev. 372 (1934); Prosser, *Private Action for Public Nuisance*, 52 Va. L. Rev. 997, 1023-1027 (1966); Seavey, *Nuisance: Contributory Negligence or Assumption of Risk as Defense*, 28 Tenn. L. Rev. 561 (1961); Annot., "Contributory negligence or assumption of risk as defense to action for damages from nuisance—modern views," 73 A.L.R.2d 1378 (1960).

variety of basic tort liability theories may underlie a cause of action for nuisance. A claim can be based on intentional wrong, negligence, or strict liability. For that reason, the *Restatement (Second) of Torts* discusses defenses to nuisance in light of the theory underlying defendant's interference with plaintiff's use and enjoyment of land. For example, the Tentative Draft sums up the place of contributory negligence by saying:

> In an action for nuisance, the contributory negligence of the plaintiff is a defense to the same extent as in other tort actions.[5]

The defense of assumption of risk is treated similarly.[6]

Whether these general principles will be applied in comparative negligence states is far from clear at this point. Nevertheless, cases in at least four such jurisdictions—Wisconsin,[7] Georgia,[8] Kansas,[9] and Michigan[10] —have accepted the proposition that when a nuisance arises out of mere negligence, in that defendant failed to take reasonable care to prevent the invasion, the ordinary contributory negligence defense applies and damages are apportioned.

Intentional Nuisances

By way of dictum, the Wisconsin and Georgia cases suggest that where a nuisance is predicated on intentional conduct, in that defendant desired to cause the wrong or at least knew that his conduct was substantially certain to bring about the harm that took place, contributory negligence is immaterial. The application of comparative negligence statutes in the law of nuisance can be more detailed and nuances can be more thoroughly explored. This is attempted in the present chapter.

At this juncture one potential problem should be laid to rest. Under the substantive law of private nuisance in some states, a court attempts to balance the harm to plaintiff against the harm to a defen-

---

[5]See *Restatement (Second) of Torts* § 840B (Tent. Draft 1979). The full text of the section is:
  (1) Where a nuisance results from negligent conduct of the defendant, the contributory negligence of the plaintiff is a defense to the same extent as in other actions founded on negligence.
  (2) Where the harm is intentional, or the result of recklessness, contributory negligence is not a defense.
  (3) Where the nuisance results from an abnormally dangerous condition or activity, contributory negligence is a defense only if the plaintiff has voluntarily and unreasonably subjected himself to the risk of harm.

[6]See *Restatement (Second) of Torts* § 840C (Tent. Draft 1979): "In an action for a nuisance, the plaintiff's assumption of risk is a defense to the same extent as in other tort actions."

[7]See Schiro v. Oriental Realty Co., 272 Wis. 537, 76 N.W.2d 355, 73 A.L.R.2d 1368 (1956) and the renewed appeal of same case reported at 7 Wis. 2d 556, 97 N.W.2d 385 (1959).

[8]See Floyd v. Albany, 105 Ga. App. 31, 123 S.E.2d 446, 449 (1961).

[9]See Sandifer Motors, Inc. v. Roseland Park, 6 Kan. App. 2d 308, 628 P.2d 239 (1981).

[10]See Melendres v. Soales, 105 Mich. App. 73, 306 N.W.2d 399 (1981).

dant before determining that there is a cause of action.[11] Moreover, when a plaintiff seeks an injunction, a court compares the injury plaintiff will suffer from letting the nuisance continue with the hardship defendant will endure if the injunction is granted. This balancing process is sometimes called "comparative injury," even in comparative negligence states.[12] This comparison has nothing to do with comparative negligence, although the terminology is similar. It is purely a part of the private law of nuisance which serves to determine whether an injunction should issue.

11.2 Absolute nuisance and contributory negligence

Some of the older cases in jurisdictions where contributory negligence was a complete defense contain general language to the effect that "contributory negligence cannot be a defense to an action based on a nuisance."[13] This is too broad a generalization today; modern cases show that contributory negligence is ignored only when there is an "absolute" nuisance.[14] There has been a good deal of uncertainty as to what constitutes an absolute nuisance.[15]

In spite of some confusion, cases find an absolute nuisance in two distinct situations. The first is where defendant commits an intentional wrong to plaintiff. In effect, he creates the nuisance for the purpose of causing harm to plaintiff or, at least, with the knowledge that such harm is substantially certain to occur. In a 1962 case involving an absolute nuisance,[16] defendant allowed sulphur dust to blow from his premises onto plaintiff's lot knowing that the substance was causing damage to steel stored there. The court characterized defendant's conduct as an "intentional invasion" and indicated that the doctrine of contributory negligence was of no help to the defendant.[17]

Intent in Creation of Nuisance

It should be kept in mind that "intent" in this context does not mean simply that a nuisance is intended (e.g., that a sidewalk is intended to be constructed with a particular degree of slope) but rather that

---

[11]See W. P. Keeton et al., note 1 above, § 88A, at 630.

[12]See Jost v. Dairyland Power Cooperative, 45 Wis. 2d 164, 172 N.W.2d 647, 653 (1969).

[13]See W. Prosser, *Handbook of the Law of Torts* § 91, at 608 (4th ed. 1971). The fifth edition, cited at note 11 above, has eliminated most of the discussion of plaintiff's conduct.

[14]See Annot., "Contributory negligence or assumption of risk as defense to action for damages from nuisance—modern views," 73 A.L.R.2d 1378 (1960).

[15]See Runnells v. Maine C. Railroad, 159 Me. 200, 190 A.2d 739, 743 (1963) ("We need not, nor do we, attempt to determine precisely where a line may be or ought to be drawn between nuisances characterized as absolute nuisances and negligence nuisances"); Beckwith v. Stratford, 129 Conn. 506, 29 A.2d 775 (1942).

[16]Associated Metals & Minerals Corp. v. Dixon Chemical & Research, Inc., 82 N.J. Super. 281, 197 A.2d 569 (1963).

[17]Id., 197 A.2d at 582. See also McFarlane v. Niagara Falls, 247 N.Y. 340, 160 N.E. 391, 57 A.L.R. 1 (1928) (Chief Judge Cardozo setting forth the distinction).

defendant intends the harm plaintiff suffered.[18] With this degree of fault, it is rational to bar contributory negligence as a defense.

The rule barring consideration of contributory negligence in absolute nuisance cases will probably apply under comparative negligence. Dicta in cases from three such states suggest this result.[19] A court's conclusion in this regard can be based in most comparative negligence states on explicit statutory language limiting the statute's operation to claims based on "negligence."[20]

Land Interference as Absolute Nuisance

The second instance in which a nuisance was deemed "absolute" and contributory negligence was ignored at common law was when the nuisance interfered with a person's activities in the use and enjoyment of his land. Thus, where an adjoining landowner piled straw unreasonably close to a railroad and the railroad negligently emitted sparks, the landowner's failure to use reasonable care did not bar his claim.[21]

The rationale of these cases is based on plaintiff's common-law right to use his land as he pleases so long as he doesn't cause harm to others. Allowing the contributory negligence defense in this specific context would, in effect, permit defendant to circumscribe plaintiff in his use and enjoyment of his own land.

The common law does not go so far as to allow plaintiff to aggravate his own damages once defendant's nuisance is operational. Thus, he cannot throw hay into an existing fire caused by a nuisance. This matter, however, was covered by the avoidable consequences rule—that once the nuisance is established and the interference with his rights has begun, plaintiff is required to take reasonable steps to guard against further harm.[22]

Contributory Negligence in Land Interference Cases

It is uncertain whether this second form of absolute nuisance will still totally eliminate the contributory negligence defense in a comparative negligence system. There is dictum in one Wisconsin decision that suggests it does, but this is very tenuous support.[23] In discussing whether or not plaintiff would have her damages apportioned when she fell on her own land as the result of a nuisance created by defendant's

---

[18]See Deane v. Johnston, 104 So. 2d 3, 65 A.L.R.2d 957 (Fla. 1958).

[19]See cases cited in notes 7 and 8, section 11.1. See also Houston v. Henderson, 506 S.W.2d 731 (Tex. Civ. App. 1974).

[20]See section 2.2, text and notes 6 to 8. States whose statutory language can be construed to limit applicability to cases based on negligence include Colorado, Connecticut, Idaho, Massachusetts, Nebraska, New Hampshire, New Jersey, North Dakota, Oklahoma, South Dakota, Texas, Vermont, and Wyoming, although some of these states have dealt separately with strict liability. See Chapter 12.

[21]See LeRoy Fibre Co. v. Chicago, M. & S. P. Ry., 232 U.S. 340, 58 L. Ed. 631, 34 S. Ct. 415 (1914) and cases collected in Annot., note 14 above, 73 A.L.R.2d at 1381-1383.

[22]See W. Prosser, note 13 above, § 91, at 610.

[23]See Schiro v. Oriental Realty Co., 272 Wis. 537, 76 N.W.2d 355, 361, 73 A.L.R.2d 1368 (1956).

defective retaining wall, the court said that "A party is not required to surrender a valuable use of his property merely because of defendant's wrongful conduct."[24] Nevertheless, in a later appeal of the same case the court upheld a jury's apportionment of 50% negligence to plaintiff on the ground that she had engaged in unreasonable conduct in stepping on an obvious hazard on her own land, even though it was created by defendant's nuisance.[25] Arguably, since this was a situation that was already in existence, the plaintiff's harm could be regarded as an avoidable consequence; but usually that doctrine does not serve to bar a tort action, only to mitigate damages.[26]

It may be anticipated that plaintiff's contributory negligence in the use of his own land in light of an existing nuisance will be taken into account under comparative negligence statutes, but common-law doctrine that he need not anticipate such wrongful conduct may prevail. In effect, in that context the plaintiff is not contributorily negligent at all. It is reasonable for him to use his land as he sees fit until an actual nuisance is in existence and the condition is affecting his land.

11.3 Nuisance based on negligence

Some texts and case law contain general statements that contributory negligence is never a defense to nuisance.[27] Nevertheless, when the underlying liability base of the nuisance is *negligence*, modern courts apply the defense.[28] The only possible exception to this general rule was discussed in section 11.2 above. When defendant's negligent nuisance has interfered with plaintiff's use and enjoyment of his own land, it may be deemed "absolute" and the contributory negligence defense may not apply.

It is clear, however, that when the negligence nuisance interferes with plaintiff's general right-of-way and causes an injury, his contributory negligence bars his claim where contributory negligence is a complete defense. Thus, in a 1969 Michigan case,[29] defendant created a nuisance in negligently maintaining signs on a highway right-of-way. A bicyclist was injured, in part because a sign blocked his view of the road. Nevertheless, when the bicyclist entered the adjacent highway he had failed to take reasonable precautions for his own welfare. The court barred his claim, even though it was properly predicated on nuisance.

---

[24]Id.

[25]Schiro v. Oriental Realty Co., 7 Wis. 2d 556, 97 N.W.2d 385 (1959).

[26]See W. Prosser, note 1 above, § 65, at 422.

[27]See W. Prosser, *Handbook of the Law of Torts* § 91, at 610 (4th ed. 1971) (collecting citations).

[28]See Annot., "Contributory negligence or assumption of risk as defense to action for damages from nuisance—modern views," 73 A.L.R.2d 1378, at 1379, 1387-1390 (1960).

[29]Young v. Groenendal, 382 Mich. 456, 169 N.W.2d 920 (1969).

Comparison in Negligent Nuisance Cases

This general rule will apply under comparative negligence. Thus, in a Georgia case,[30] defendant negligently permitted a penny weighing scale to remain in a dangerous position on a public sidewalk. Although the court deemed the scale a nuisance, plaintiff's contributory negligence was taken into account.

In *Sandifer Motors, Incorporated v. Roseland Park*[31] a Kansas appellate court held that the plaintiff's fault might be compared where the city's management of a dump damaged the plaintiff's drainage system. The court said that the city's conduct created a condition posing an undue risk of harm and did not rise to the level of a reckless act.

The same approach was taken in Wisconsin even when defendant had interfered with plaintiff's use and enjoyment of her own land. In *Schiro v. Oriental Realty Company*[32] plaintiff asserted that defendant maintained a nuisance in that it failed to repair a retaining wall after notice. The top of the wall had given way and moved laterally, thus permitting development of a dangerous incline on plaintiff's land. Plaintiff fell on the incline and brought suit based on nuisance. The court held that contributory negligence should be submitted to the jury, then in a later appeal affirmed a judgment for defendant based on a special verdict that plaintiff contributed 50% to her own injury. The court declined to find an intentional tort even though defendant had failed to repair the retaining wall after adequate notice.

The *Schiro* case indicates that in a close situation as to whether contributory negligence is material, a comparative negligence state is inclined to allow the defense and apportion damages on the basis of fault. This difference in attitude is understandable in light of the supposition by a number of authors that courts stretch both logic and fact to avoid applying the contributory negligence defense in actions of nuisance because of their discontent with a doctrine that would bar plaintiff's entire claim.[33] Thus, courts in comparative negligence states are likely to find defendant's conduct intentional (thus eliminating plaintiff's negligence from consideration) only when defendant has actually intended harmful results, not merely the creation of the nuisance itself.[34]

---

[30]Floyd v. Albany, 105 Ga. App. 31, 123 S.E.2d 446 (1961). Accord, Houston v. Henderson, 506 S.W.2d 731 (Tex. Civ. App. 1974) (city's negligent failure to install a "dead end" sign a nuisance, but evidence as to plaintiff's contributory negligence could go to the jury).

[31]Sandifer Motors, Inc. v. Roseland Park, 6 Kan. App. 2d 308, 628 P.2d 239 (1981).

[32]Schiro v. Oriental Realty Co., 272 Wis. 537, 76 N.W.2d 355, 73 A.L.R.2d 1368 (1956), later appealed, 7 Wis. 2d 556, 97 N.W.2d 385 (1959).

[33]See W. Prosser, note 27 above, § 91, at 610 ("decisions barring the defense have rested in reality upon a dislike of it; but the way to get rid of it is scarcely by resort to fictions transforming negligence into intent."); Denton, *Nuisance: Contributory Negligence or Assumption of Risk as Defense*, 28 Tenn. L. Rev. 561, 567 (1961).

[34]For a decision showing the distinction in what was then a contributory negligence state, see Deane v. Johnston, 104 So. 2d 3, 65 A.L.R.2d 957 (Fla. 1958).

Not all comparative negligence state courts that have considered the question have taken this view, however. A Michigan appellate court refused to apply comparative negligence to a case involving an unmarked dock in shallow, murky water, saying that this was an intentional nuisance.[35] In Michigan a nuisance is intentional if the landowner intended to bring about the conditions which caused the nuisance.[36]

Plaintiff's Reckless Conduct

Even when defendant's conduct is intentional, damages are apportioned if plaintiff recklessly encountered the nuisance.[37] The court may not call this "assumption of risk," but it is something akin to it and probably closer to a consent to the harm.[38]

It seems probable that comparative negligence states will apportion damages, even though defendant has created an absolute nuisance, where plaintiff has engaged in similar conduct and partially caused an inconvenience to himself.[39] The comparative negligence statute facilitates the accomplishment by the courts of what some jurisdictions have tried without such a statute: apportionment of damages according to the fault attributable to plaintiff and defendant.[40]

Strict Liability Cases

When the liability basis of defendant's nuisance is strict liability in that it is an "abnormally dangerous activity," there is uncertainty as to whether plaintiff's contributory negligence will be taken into account. As indicated in section 12.5, the general approach has been to disallow the contributory negligence defense in strict liability cases unless plaintiff unreasonably assumed the risk. The Tentative Draft of the *Restatement (Second) of Torts* has retained this approach in the area of nuisance.[41] Nevertheless, it seems probable that comparative negligence jurisdictions will find little benefit in drawing the distinction between contributory negligence and assumption of risk in this area; rather, they will simply permit apportionment if plaintiff's conduct unreasonably contributed to the harm he suffered.[42]

"Coming to the Nuisance"

The majority of American courts have held that a plaintiff who "comes to" the nuisance by buying land at a time when the nuisance is already in existence has not assumed the risk of the nuisance.[43] Coming

---

[35]Melendres v. Soales, 105 Mich. App. 73, 306 N.W.2d 399 (1981).

[36]Hall v. State, Michigan Dept. of Highways & Transp., 109 Mich. App. 592, 311 N.W.2d 813 (1981).

[37]See Schiro v. Oriental Realty Co., 7 Wis. 2d 556, 97 N.W.2d 385 (1959) (alternative holding).

[38]Id. See also, W. Prosser, note 27 above, § 91, at 610; Denton, note 33 above, at 564.

[39]See W. Prosser, note 27 above, § 91 at 611.

[40]Id.

[41]See note 5, section 11.1, and accompanying text.

[42]See sections 12.5 and 12.6.

[43]W. P. Keeton et al., note 27 above, § 88B, at 634-636.

to the nuisance is merely a factor to be considered in the balancing process.[44] So far no court appears to have rethought the doctrine in the light of comparative negligence, perhaps because many jurisdictions have abandoned it.[45]

11.4 Basis of liability determining application of comparative negligence

A helpful starting point for considering whether plaintiff's culpable conduct should be taken into consideration under comparative negligence when his claim is based on nuisance might be the *Restatement (Second) of Torts* focus on defenses to nuisance.[46] In effect, the court should determine the liability basis of the nuisance—intent, negligence, or strict liability—and apply the defense if it would be applied in actions directly predicated on the particular theory of recovery.

Adjustments Under Comparative Negligence

Nevertheless, some adjustment should be made for the comparative negligence system itself. Decisions that have taken an overbroad view of what was "intentional" conduct in nuisance cases should not be followed. These decisions were predicated, at bottom, on courts' dissatisfaction with the absolute nature of the contributory negligence defense. This problem is eliminated by comparative negligence.

It seems inappropriate to distinguish between contributory negligence and assumption of risk when defendant's nuisance is based on strict liability; rather, when plaintiff has unreasonably contributed to or assumed the risk of his own harm, fault should be apportioned.

Land Interference Cases

The most difficult problems in this general area will arise where defendant's nuisance has unreasonably interfered with plaintiff's use and enjoyment of his land. In certain factual contexts it may be inappropriate to allow the defendant through his nuisance to force plaintiff to act with special care on his own premises. It is suggested that such cases be handled by regarding plaintiff's conduct in failing to take special precautions against a potential nuisance as reasonable when it is appropriate to do so. This approach will avoid applying comparative negligence where reduction of damages is unwarranted.

---

[44]Id.

[45]See, e.g., Patrick v. Sharon Steel Corp., 549 F. Supp. 1259 (N.D. W.Va. 1982), in which the court refused to allow "coming to" as a defense to noxious emissions from a coke plant.

[46]See note 5, section 11.1.

CHAPTER 12

PRODUCT LIABILITY/STRICT LIABILITY AND COMPARATIVE NEGLIGENCE

12.1 The product liability revolution

When the first edition of this book was published in 1974, the United States was experiencing the first phase of a "product liability revolution." Between 1963 and the mid-1970's, most states adopted what courts labeled strict product liability in tort as an alternative to negligence or Uniform Commercial Code breach of warranty, usually in the language of *Restatement (Second) of Torts* § 402A,[1] as a theory of recovery for persons injured by defective products.[2] As of 1974 only a few scattered courts had considered or adopted comparative fault as a partial defense to strict product liability.[3]

In the mid-1970's the product liability revolution came to be perceived as a "product liability crisis" as successful claims mounted and some manufacturers and product sellers became concerned about their ability to obtain or afford liability insurance.[4] This perception brought about the second phase of the revolution: today many states have passed legislation creating new defenses to product liability actions, such as compliance with government standards,[5] conformance with the

---

[1] *Restatement (Second) of Torts* § 402A (1965). See Powers, *The Persistence of Fault in Products Liability*, 61 Tex. L. Rev. 777 (1983). Professor Powers has demonstrated that most states never really adopted strict liability in cases based on improper design or failure to warn.

[2] W. P. Keeton et al., *Prosser and Keeton on the Law of Torts* § 98, at 692–694 (5th ed. 1984).

[3] See, e.g., Hagenbuch v. Snap-On Tools Corp., 339 F. Supp. 676 (D. N.H. 1972) (attempting to anticipate New Hampshire law on this question); Chapman v. Brown, 198 F. Supp. 78 (D. Hawaii 1961), affd. 304 F.2d 149, 4 A.L.R.3d 490 (9th Cir. Hawaii 1962); Dippel v. Sciano, 37 Wis. 2d 443, 155 N.W.2d 55 (1967).

[4] See generally Interagency Task Force on Product Liability, U.S. Dept. of Commerce, *Final Report* (1977) reprinted in 5 L. Frumer & M. Friedman, *Products Liability* Appendix G (1984).

[5] See, e.g., Colo. Rev. Stat., § 13-21-403(1)(b), creating a rebuttable presumption of non-defectiveness if the product conformed to "any applicable code, standard or regulation adopted or promulgated by the United States or by this state, or by any agency of the United States or of this state."

state of the art,[6] or a statute of repose.[7] At the same time a majority of states have adopted comparative fault in product liability cases, allowing plaintiffs to recover where previously they might have been barred by assumption of risk, but reducing recovery in some instances. Comparative fault has been included in several model statutes, including the Uniform Comparative Fault Act[8] and the Model Product Liability Act,[9] and in federal product liability legislation now pending before the Congress of the United States.[10] One result of the "revolution" is that comparative fault in strict product liability, once purely a judge-made rule, has become statutory in many states.

12.2 Development of comparative fault in strict liability actions

As indicated in section 11.2, comparative negligence statutes in Wisconsin and a number of other states can be read as being limited to tort claims based on "negligence."[11] This should not prevent a court from using principles of comparative negligence in a strict liability case if the state's legislature has not specifically prohibited such application. Where reason and policy dictate that the principle of reducing plaintiff's recovery on the basis of his comparative fault would be helpful, it should be applied by the court.[12]

---

[6]See, e.g., Neb. Rev. Stat., § 25-21,182, making conformity with the prevailing state of the art at the time of first retail sale a defense. "State of the art" is defined as "the best technology reasonably available at the time." Id.

[7]See, e.g., Tenn. Code Ann., § 29-28-103, fixing a statute of limitations of 6 years after injury, 10 years after the first retail sale of the product, or 1 year after the end of the product's anticipated useful life, whichever comes first.

[8]12 U.L.A. 39 (Supp. 1985).

[9]Model Unif. Product Liability Act, reprinted in 44 Fed. Reg. 62,714-62,750 (Interagency Task Force on Product Liability, U.S. Dept. of Commerce, 1979).

[10]S. 100, 99th Cong., 1st Sess. § 9 (1985).

[11]See notes 6 to 8, section 11.2. The other states include Colorado, Connecticut, Hawaii, Idaho, Massachusetts, Minnesota, Nebraska, New Hampshire, New Jersey, North Dakota, Oklahoma, Oregon, South Dakota, Texas, Utah, Vermont, Washington and Wyoming. See also Ohio Rev. Code Ann., § 2315.19; Pa. Stat. Ann., tit. 42, § 7102; Kan. Stat. Ann., § 60-258a.

[12]See Hagenbuch v. Snap-On Tools Corp., 339 F. Supp. 676 (D. N.H. 1972) (attempting to anticipate New Hampshire case law on this point). Cf. Moragne v. States Marine Lines, Inc., 398 U.S. 375, 26 L. Ed. 2d 339, 90 S. Ct. 1772 (1970). The court created an action for wrongful death under federal maritime law. The late Mr. Justice Harlan, a man particularly sensitive to the respective roles of the legislature and the judiciary, stated in the opinion of the court that:
> It has always been the duty of the common-law court to perceive the impact of major legislative innovations and to interweave the new legislative policies with the inherited body of common-law principles—many of them deriving from earlier legislative exertions.

398 U.S. at 392, 90 S. Ct. at 1783.
See also Streatch v. Associated Container Transp., Ltd., 388 F. Supp. 935, 29 A.L.R. Fed. 771 (C.D. Cal. 1975) (plaintiff injured because of alleged defect in unloading vehicle; court held that strict liability is a part of federal maritime common law and is available despite the 1972 amendments to the Longshoremen's and Harbor-workers' Compensation Act which changed the theory of recovery from unseaworthiness to negligence).

Application of Comparative Negligence Statutes to Strict Liability

Included among the states which have used the above suggestion (put forth in the first edition of this treatise) and determined that their comparative negligence statutes apply to strict liability actions are: Kansas,[13] Montana,[14] New Jersey,[15] Oregon,[16] and Rhode Island.[17] See also case law in the Virgin Islands.[18]

The Supreme Court of Wisconsin took an extra step in order to apply its comparative negligence statute in a strict product liability case. The court said that conduct giving rise to liability under section 402A of the *Restatement (Second) of Torts* is in effect negligence per se and that, therefore, the comparative negligence statute for claims based on negligence should apply.[19]

In the view of this author, this additional and artificial step in reasoning is unnecessary; it is within the power of the judiciary to decide what defenses are appropriate in strict liability cases, and there is no reason why comparative negligence should not be selected in the appropriate situation. The court's role is not so adventurous as in a state that has not adopted comparative negligence at all;[20] since the legislature has endorsed comparative negligence, it is reasonable to apply it as a principle of common law where it would be helpful.[21]

Further, there is a growing recognition that strict liability and negligence are not narrow, exclusive concepts.[22] The *Restatement* itself requires that a product be "unreasonably dangerous" before a court can impose liability;[23] several courts have referred to the differences between the two rules as "semantic."[24] The California Supreme Court noted that "much overlapping and interweaving has developed in order

---

[13]Kennedy v. Sawyer, 228 Kan. 439, 618 P.2d 788 (1980). See also Schwartz, *Comparative Negligence in Kansas—Legal Issues and Probable Answers*, 13 Washburn L.J. 397 (1974).

[14]Zahrte v. Sturm, Ruger & Co., 661 P.2d 17 (Mont. 1983).

[15]Cartel Capital Corp. v. Fireco of New Jersey, 81 N.J. 548, 410 A.2d 674, 19 A.L.R.4th 310 (1980); Suter v. San Angelo Foundry & Machine Co., 81 N.J. 150, 406 A.2d 140 (1979) (citing this treatise).

[16]Sandford v. Chevrolet Div. of General Motors, 292 Ore. 590, 642 P.2d 624 (1982); Baccelleri v. Hyster Co., 287 Ore. 3, 597 P.2d 351 (1979).

[17]Fiske v. McGregor Div. of Brunswick, 464 A.2d 719 (R.I. 1983).

[18]Murray v. Fairbanks Morse, 610 F.2d 149 (3d Cir. V.I. 1979); Murray v. Beloit Power Systems, Inc., 450 F. Supp. 1145 (D. V.I. 1978).

[19]See Dippel v. Sciano, 37 Wis. 2d 443, 155 N.W.2d 55, 63-64 (1967). Wisconsin cases, also on the basis of somewhat tortured reasoning, treated cases under the state's strict liability dog-bite statute as predicated on negligence. See Nelson v. Hansen, 10 Wis. 2d 107, 102 N.W.2d 251 (1960); Wurtzler v. Miller, 31 Wis. 2d 310, 143 N.W.2d 27 (1966).

[20]See section 1.5.

[21]See Stone, *The Common Law in the United States*, 50 Harv. L. Rev. 4 (1936) and materials cited in note 12 above.

[22]See Powers, *The Persistence of Fault in Products Liability*, 61 Tex. L. Rev. 777 (1983).

[23]*Restatement (Second) of Torts* § 402A(1) (1965).

[24]Mulherin v. Ingersoll-Rand Co., 628 P.2d 1301, 1304 (Utah 1981); Daly v. General Motors Corp., 20 Cal. 3d 725, 735, 144 Cal. Rptr. 380, 385, 575 P.2d 1162, 1167 (1978).

to achieve substantial justice."[25] The court examined the policy reasons behind strict liability and said that the principal justification for it—easing the plaintiff's burden of proof—would not be compromised by the adoption of comparative fault; at the same time, making plaintiffs bear the cost of their own fault would promote fairness and equity.[26] Furthermore, Professor Powers has perceptively observed that in spite of some "judicial opinion" language to the contrary, fault has remained the essence of the test in product liability cases based on failure to design a product properly and failure to warn.[27]

It is important to remember that this problem of whether a court can utilize a comparative negligence statute in strict liability should not arise in states such as Arkansas, Maine, Mississippi, Nevada, Oregon, or Rhode Island where statutes do not contain any words of limitation such as "to recover damages for negligence."[28]

Adoption of Comparative Fault Rule

In addition to the states that have judicially applied a comparative negligence statute to strict liability or promulgated a rule over and above a statute, several of the common-law comparative negligence states have gone on to make the comparative negligence rule a comparative fault rule. Alaska took the lead in 1976 in *Butaud v. Suburban Marine and Sporting Goods, Incorporated,* a year after adopting comparative negligence.[29] In 1978, the California Supreme Court followed in *Daly v. General Motors Corporation.*[30] Since then, the question has

---

[25]Daly v. General Motors Corp., 20 Cal. 3d 725, 735, 144 Cal. Rptr. 380, 385, 575 P.2d 1162, 1167 (1978).

[26]Id., 144 Cal. Rptr. at 386-387.

[27]Powers, note 22 above, at 4.

[28]In Chapman v. Brown, 198 F. Supp. 78, 85, 86 (D. Hawaii 1961), affd. 304 F.2d 149, 4 A.L.R.3d 490 (9th Cir. Hawaii 1962), the Federal District Court suggested that comparative negligence be utilized in a strict liability case even in the absence of any statute endorsing the concept.

See N.Y. Civ. Prac. Law, § 1411, Comment C1411: 1 by Joseph M. McLaughlin, which states in part:

> By its terms, section 1411 is not limited to negligence actions. Thus, in an action for breach of warranty, strict liability in tort, or strict products liability, where it has become increasingly common to hold that contributory negligence or assumption of risk is a defense, CPLR 1411 now directs that the recovery be diminished by the proportion of the plaintiff's "culpable conduct." . . .

> In Codling v. Paglia, 1973, 32 N.Y.2d 330, 345 N.Y.S.2d 461, 298 N.E.2d 622, the Court of Appeals held that the use of a product for other than its intended purpose bars recovery in an action based upon strict products liability. This may be just another way of saying that contributory negligence is a defense; but the point is now academic since the new statute uses the broader phrase "culpable conduct." Thus, the culpable conduct of the plaintiff—regardless of how it was formerly termed—will henceforth diminish the plaintiff's recovery. So too, the "culpable conduct" of the defendant need not be negligence, but may be breach of warranty, a violation of a statute giving rise to liability, etc.

[29]Butaud v. Suburban Marine & Sporting Goods, Inc., 555 P.2d 42 (Alaska 1976), amending 543 P.2d 209, 81 A.L.R.3d 384 (Alaska 1975).

[30]Daly v. General Motors Corp., 20 Cal. 3d 725, 114 Cal. Rptr. 380, 575 P.2d 1162 (1978).

been considered and comparative fault rules adopted in Florida, West Virginia, Illinois and Missouri.[31]

States that have not yet dealt directly with strict liability and comparative fault include Kentucky, Mississippi and New Mexico. However, federal courts have predicted that Mississippi and New Mexico would allow comparison under their statutes.[32] Another federal court has assumed that Kentucky would not.[33]

Courts in Hawaii,[34] Louisiana,[35] New Hampshire,[36] North Dakota,[37] Texas,[38] and Utah[39] have found comparative negligence statutes inapplicable to strict liability but have created a common-law comparative fault rule instead.

States holding comparative negligence inapplicable in strict liability actions are: Indiana,[40] Massachusetts,[41] Nevada,[42] Oklahoma,[43] South Dakota,[44] and Vermont.[45] Federal courts considering Pennsylvania law have predicted that Pennsylvania would not apply comparative negligence to strict liability.[46]

---

[31]Martinez v. Clark Equipment Co., 382 So. 2d 878 (Fla. App. 1980); Star Furniture Co. v. Pulaski Furniture Co., 297 S.E.2d 854 (W. Va. 1982); Coney v. J.L.G. Industries, Inc., 73 Ill. Dec. 337, 454 N.E.2d 197 (1983); Gustafson v. Benda, 661 S.W.2d 11 (Mo. 1983) (dictum: Uniform Comparative Fault Act, which includes strict product liability in its fault definition, would serve as a guide in future cases).

[32]Edwards v. Sears, Roebuck & Co., 512 F.2d 726 (5th Cir. Miss. 1975); Herndon v. Seven Bar Flying Service, Inc., 716 F.2d 1322 (10th Cir. N.M. 1983), cert. denied 80 L. Ed. 2d 553, 104 S. Ct. 2170 (1984).

[33]Anderson v. Black & Decker, Inc., 597 F. Supp. 1298 (E.D. Ky. 1984), creating the anomalous result that contributory negligence is a complete defense to a product liability action, whether based on strict liability, negligence, or any other theory, while it may be compared in other personal injury cases. The federal court pronounced itself bound by Kentucky's product liability reform act, Ky. Rev. Stat., § 411.300 et seq., saying that the legislature must have been aware that comparative negligence was a possibility and therefore intended to make contributory negligence a complete defense regardless of other developments in the law.

[34]Kaneko v. Hilo Coast Processing, 65 Hawaii 447, 654 P.2d 343 (1982).

[35]Bell v. Jet Wheel Blast, Div. of Ervin Industries, No. 83-CQ-2158 (La. Jan. 14, 1985).

[36]Thibault v. Sears, Roebuck & Co., 118 N.H. 802, 395 A.2d 843 (1978).

[37]Day v. General Motors Corp., 345 N.W.2d 349 (N.D. 1984).

[38]Duncan v. Cessna Aircraft, 665 S.W.2d 414 (Tex. 1984).

[39]Mulherin v. Ingersoll-Rand Co., 628 P.2d 1301 (Utah 1981).

[40]Ind. Code, § 33-4-33-13, expressly ruling out comparative fault in strict liability or breach of warranty.

[41]Correia v. Firestone Tire & Rubber Co., 388 Mass. 342, 446 N.E.2d 1033 (1983), barring comparative negligence in breach of warranty. Massachusetts does not recognize strict product liability in tort. Swartz v. General Motors Corp., 375 Mass. 628, 378 N.E.2d 61, 24 U.C.C. Rep. Serv. (Callaghan) 1161 (1978).

[42]Young's Machine Co. v. Long, No. 15160 (Nev., Dec. 7, 1984).

[43]Kirkland v. General Motors Corp., 521 P.2d 1353 (Okla. 1974).

[44]Smith v. Smith, 278 N.W.2d 155 (S.D. 1979).

[45]Carr v. Case, 135 Vt. 524, 380 A.2d 91 (1977). This was a dog-bite case; the court applied comparative fault but said that the cause of action really sounded in negligence rather than strict liability.

[46]Bike v. American Motors Corp., 101 F.R.D. 77 (E.D. Pa. 1984); Conti v. Ford Motor Co., 578 F. Supp. 1429 (E.D. Pa. 1983), revd. on other grounds, 743 F.2d 195 (3d Cir. Pa. 1984).

Statutes Covering Strict Liability

Several state statutes specifically address strict and/or products liability in their comparative responsibility statutes[47] or have enacted separate statutes covering strict liability.[48] The Uniform Product Liability Act provides for comparative responsibility and apportionment of damages in product liability cases.[49]

12.3 Kinds of contributory negligence in strict liability actions

The question whether comparative negligence should apply to a claim based on strict liability is an extension of the more general and clearly unresolved problem of when plaintiff's conduct should bar his strict liability claim. There is a growing body of legal literature with respect to this more general issue.[50] The literature makes it clear that it is necessary to be precise in describing the kind of plaintiff misconduct that may either reduce or bar his strict liability claim.

---

[47] Ariz. Rev. Stat. Ann., § 12-2509 (comparative fault applies if the plaintiff alleges and proves negligence as well as strict liability, but not to strict liability alone); Ark. Stat. Ann., § 27-1763; Iowa Code Ann., § 668.1; Me. Rev. Stat. Ann., tit. 14, § 156; Minn. Stat. Ann., § 604.1; Neb. Rev. Stat., § 25-1151 (rejecting holding in Melia v. Ford Motor Co., 534 F.2d 795 (8th Cir. Neb. 1976)); N.Y. Civ. Prac. Law, § 1411 ("culpable conduct"); Wash. Rev. Code Ann., § 4.22.005.

[48] Colo. Rev. Stat., § 13-21-406; Conn. Gen. Stat. Ann., § 52-572o; Idaho Code, § 6-1404; Mich. Comp. Laws, § 600.2949 (enacted before the Michigan Supreme Court adopted a general comparative negligence rule).

[49] Model Unif. Product Liability Act §§ 111 & 112, reprinted in 44 Fed. Reg. 62,735-39 (Interagency Task Force on Product Liability, U.S. Dept. of Commerce, 1979).

[50] See 2 L. Frumer & M. Friedman, *Products Liability* § 16.01 (1984); R. Hursh, *American Law of Products Liability* § 3:9 (1961); W. P. Keeton et al., *Prosser and Keeton on the Law of Torts* § 79, at 565-567, and § 102, at 748 (5th ed. 1984); 2 F. Harper & F. James, *The Law of Torts* § 22.7 (1956); Epstein, *Products Liability: Defenses Based on Plaintiff's Conduct*, 1968 Utah L. Rev. 267; Levine, *Buyer's Conduct as Affecting the Extent of Manufacturer's Liability in Warranty*, 52 Minn. L. Rev. 627 (1968); Groark, *Contributory Negligence—An Integral Part of Product Liability Cases*, 56 Ill. B.J. 904 (1968); Horsley, *Products Liability Defenses*, 15 Def. L. J. 399 (1966); Postillion, *Strict Liability and Contributory Negligence: The Two Just Don't Mix*, 57 Ill. B.J. 26 (1968); Noel, *Defective Products: Abnormal Use, Contributory Negligence, and Assumption of Risk*, 25 Vand. L. Rev. 93 (1972); Comment, *Products Liability: For the Defense—Contributory Fault*, 33 Tenn. L. Rev. 464 (1966); Annot., "Products liability: Contributory negligence or assumption of risk as defense under doctrine of strict liability in tort," 46 A.L.R.3d 240 (1972); Freedman, *Comparative Negligence Doctrine Under Strict Liability: Defendant's Conduct Becomes Another "Proximate Cause" of the Injury, Damage or Loss*, 1975 Ins. L.J. 468; Schwartz, *Strict Liability and Comparative Negligence*, 42 Tenn. L. Rev. 171 (1974); Epstein, *Plaintiff's Conduct in Product Liability Actions: Comparative Negligence, Automatic Division and Multiple Parties*, 45 J. Air L. 87 (1979); Fischer, *Products Liability—Applicability of Comparative Negligence*, 43 Mo. L. Rev. 431 (1978); Kroll, *Comparative Fault: A New Generation in Products Liability*, 1977 Ins. L.J. 492; Richardson, *Some Observations on Comparative Negligence and Strict Products Liability*, 67 Ill. B.J. 582 (1979); Sales, *Assumption of the Risk and Misuse in Strict Tort Liability—Prelude to Comparative Fault*, 11 Tex. Tech. L. Rev. 729 (1980); Twerski, *Many Faces of Misuse: An Inquiry Into the Emerging Doctrine of Comparative Causation*, 29 Mercer L. Rev. 403 (1978), 22 Trial Law. Guide 289 (1978); Wade, *Products Liability and Plaintiff's Fault—The Uniform Comparative Fault Act*, 29 Mercer L. Rev. 373 (1978); Westra, *Restructuring the Defenses to Strict Products Liability—An Alternative to Comparative Negligence*, 19 Santa Clara L. Rev. 355 (1979); Greenlee & Rochelle, *Comparative Negligence and Strict Tort Liability—A Marriage of Necessity*, 18 Land & Water L. Rev. 643

Before discussing in detail the question of whether comparative negligence should apply in strict liability cases, one must isolate the precise patterns of plaintiff misconduct that might bar his claim in a state that has retained contributory negligence as a complete defense. These patterns of behavior include a plaintiff's

(1) misuse or alteration of a product;

(2) contributory negligence that is the equivalent of unreasonable assumption of risk;

(3) contributory negligence based on a failure to discover or foresee dangers which an ordinary person would have discerned.

There are now many reported decisions in which courts have attempted to apply comparative negligence to claims ostensibly based on strict liability. These can be misleading if not analyzed within the guidelines of existing product liability law. The cases are placed within that framework in the remainder of this chapter, and a possible approach to blending strict liability and comparative negligence is suggested with respect to each general type of plaintiff misconduct.

12.4 Unintended unforeseeable misuse or alteration by plaintiff

When a user makes an unforeseeable misuse of a product and is injured, the supplier of the product is not deemed liable under either section 402A of the *Restatement (Second) of Torts* or under implied warranty.[51] Thus, plaintiff's placement of an improper size tire on his vehicle, keeping the tire at an improper pressure and driving on it at an excessive speed over unpaved roads is an unforeseeable misuse or alteration of the product and plaintiff can recover no damages.[52] Similarly, where a seller reasonably expects that a buyer will follow directions in administering a product, a lack of compliance with such directions may

---

(1983); Mitchell, *Examining the Plaintiff's Conduct Under the Model Uniform Product Liability Act*, 46 J. Air L. & Com. 419 (1981); Colley & Thomas, *Comparative Negligence Principles and Strict Liability: Theoretical Confluence or Confusion?*, 19 Trial 58 (1983); Razook, *Merging Comparative Negligence and Strict Products Liability: The Case for Judicial Innovation*, 20 Am. Bus. L.J. 511 (1983).

[51]Noel, *Defective Products: Abnormal Use, Contributory Negligence and Assumption of Risk*, 25 Vand. L. Rev. 93, 95 (1972); Daly v. General Motors Corp., 20 Cal. 3d 725, 144 Cal. Rptr. 380, 575 P.2d 1162, 1168 (1978) (manufacturer not responsible for unforeseeable use).

[52]See McDevitt v. Standard Oil Co., 391 F.2d 364 (5th Cir. Tex. 1968).

relieve the seller of liability.[53] Courts will take the plaintiff's capacity into account if the misuse was foreseeable.[54]

No Duty, No Liability

Although unforeseeable misuse is sometimes called a form of contributory negligence,[55] the denial of plaintiff's claim is better placed on the ground that the product simply was not "defective" or that defendant breached no warranty at all.[56] Thus, when a plaintiff uses a bottle to hammer a nail or uses a product designed for automatic dishwashers as a water softener,[57] the product has not been proved defective and defendant has not breached a warranty. In tort law terms, where a user makes an unintended and unforeseeable misuse of a product, the supplier has breached no duty to the user.

A comparative negligence statute should not apply to unintended unforeseeable misuse of a product by plaintiff; there is simply no duty breached and no liability. It should apply when a defendant has violated a duty to plaintiff. Most reported decisions support this result and do not apply comparative negligence statutes to a plaintiff who clearly has made an unintended and unforeseeable misuse of a product. Courts agree that when such a case does arise, the comparative negligence statute should have no application and plaintiff's claim should be dis-

---

[53]See Magee v. Wyeth Laboratories, Inc., 214 Cal. App. 2d 340, 29 Cal. Rptr. 322 (1963). But see Jagmin v. Simonds Abrasive Co., 61 Wis. 2d 60, 211 N.W.2d 810, 825 (1973). See also D'Arienzo v. Clairol, Inc., 125 N.J. Super. 224, 310 A.2d 106 (1973) (lack of compliance will not bar the claim if directions are inadequate). In Sun Valley Airlines, Inc. v. Avco-Lycoming Corp., 411 F. Supp. 598 (D. Idaho 1976) the court found that an unforeseeable misuse of an aircraft (improper maintenance) was not an absolute bar to recovery under products liability, but was subject to causal comparison. While it is arguable that the misuse was unforeseeable, it was not an unintended use. The airplane was being used for the purpose for which it was intended. Thus, it may be important to distinguish between misuses where such conduct arises out of upkeep or maintenance of a product and those which arise where the product itself is used for an unintended purpose.

[54]Bellotte v. Zayre Corp., 116 N.H. 52, 352 A.2d 723 (1976) (five-year-old child's capacity will be taken into account in determining if playing with matches was an unforeseeable misuse).

[55]See McDevitt v. Standard Oil Co., 391 F.2d 364 (5th Cir. Tex. 1968).

[56]See *Restatement (Second) of Torts* § 5, Comment *j* at 331 (1965); Williams v. Brown Mfg. Co., 45 Ill. 2d 418, 261 N.E.2d 305, 310, 46 A.L.R.3d 226 (1970). Many cases require a breach of duty which may not exist if the product is not defective. Murray v. Fairbanks Morse, 610 F.2d 149 (3d Cir. V.I. 1979); General Motors Corp. v. Hopkins, 548 S.W.2d 344, 351 (Tex. 1977) (misuse not a defense when not a proximate cause of injury). Accord, Southwestern Bell Tel. Co. v. Griffith, 575 S.W.2d 92 (Tex. Civ. App. 1978); Sun Valley Airlines, Inc. v. Avco-Lycoming Corp., 411 F. Supp. 598 (D. Idaho 1976) (violation of duty).

[57]See also Shaw v. Calgon, Inc., 35 N.J. Super. 319, 332, 114 A.2d 278, 285 (1955); Carlson v. American Safety Equipment Corp., 528 F.2d 384 (1st Cir. Mass. 1976) (plaintiff wore unstrapped safety helmet); Cepeda v. Cumberland Engineering Co., 138 N.J. Super. 344, 351 A.2d 22 (1976) (operation of industrial machine without guard with which it was equipped an unforeseeable misuse). The *Cepeda* decision was reversed with regard to its factual determination that such misuse was unforeseeable in Cepeda v. Cumberland Engineering Co., 76 N.J. 152, 386 A.2d 816 (1978), and it was overruled as a matter of law for permitting contributory negligence to be a defense in a product design case in Suter v. San Angelo Foundry & Machine Co., 81 N.J. 150, 406 A.2d 140, 153 (1979). See section 12.5.

missed. The legislatures that have dealt specifically with the strict liability defenses have generally taken this position.[58]

Some legislatures and courts, however, have not excluded unforeseeable misuse from the defenses to be included in the comparative fault calculation.[59] There may be some reluctance to foreclose recovery altogether in an area where there has been no precise test for foreseeability: even where the plaintiff has disregarded a warning, questions may remain about the adequacy of that warning.[60] Defendants in these jurisdictions may still properly argue that the plaintiff's conduct constituted 100% of the fault because the product was not defective or the plaintiff's conduct was a superseding cause of the injury. In a scenario such as that in a recent Illinois case, where the plaintiff's decedent held one end of an extension cord attached to an electric facial sauna in her mouth and attempted to plug in the other end while sitting in a bathtub full of water, it is highly unlikely that a jury would have found for the plaintiff, even if the manufacturer had not warned against using the appliance in the tub.[61]

12.5 Unintended foreseeable misuse by plaintiff

There are some relatively unusual uses of a product against which a manufacturer may have a duty to guard or at least supply a warning. Thus, a chair manufacturer was held liable when plaintiff was injured while standing upon it,[62] and the manufacturer of a hula skirt was held liable for plaintiff's burns when the garment caught flame as plaintiff danced near a fire.[63]

The Model Uniform Product Liability Act defines misuse as con-

---

[58]Ariz. Rev. Stat. Ann., § 12-683 (strict product liability statute; comparative fault statute leaves statutory defenses intact); Conn. Gen. Stat. Ann., § 52-572p; Iowa Code Ann., § 668.1 ("fault" includes "misuse of a product for which the defendant otherwise would be liable").

[59]Idaho Code, § 6-1405(3); Minn. Stat. Ann., § 601.01(1a); Wash. Rev. Code Ann., § 4.22.005; Coney v. J.L.G. Industries, 97 Ill. 2d 104, 73 Ill. Dec. 337, 454 N.E.2d 197 (1983), citing to Williams v. Brown Mfg. Co., 45 Ill. 2d 418, 261 N.E.2d 305, 46 A.L.R.3d 226 (1970) on the misuse definition; Mauch v. Manufacturers Sales & Services, Inc., 345 N.W.2d 338 (N.D. 1984); Mulherin v. Ingersoll-Rand Co., 628 P.2d 1301 (Utah 1981). In each of these cases the plaintiff's misuse was arguably foreseeable: in Mulherin's case there was technically inadmissible evidence that standing on the winch was a standard practice in the mining industry.

[60]See, e.g., Ferebee v. Chevron Chemical Co., 552 F. Supp. 1293 (D. D.C. 1982) (adequacy of manufacturer's warnings on use of paraquat where worker relied on on-the-job instructions concerning safe handling); Smith v. United States Gypsum Co., 612 P.2d 251, 7 A.L.R.4th 147 (Okla. 1980) (warnings concerning explosive flammability of adhesive inadequate when fan used for ventilation caused the explosion); Parks v. Allis Chalmers Corp., No. 48629 (Minn., Nov. 2, 1979) (jury could find farm machine defective in spite of warnings not to unclog the machine with the power on when it was much easier and faster to do it that way and safety devices were feasible).

[61]Lindsey v. Schick, No. 83-1010 (Ill. App., June 19, 1984). It is not clear in this case whether comparative fault might have been applicable.

[62]See Phillips v. Ogle Aluminum Furniture, Inc., 106 Cal. App. 2d 650, 235 P.2d 857 (1951).

[63]See Brown v. Chapman, 304 F.2d 149, 4 A.L.R.3d 490 (9th Cir. Hawaii 1962).

duct that occurs "when the product user does not act in a manner that would be expected of an ordinary reasonably prudent person who is likely to use the product in the same or similar circumstances."[64] To the extent such product misuse caused claimant's harm, damages shall be reduced.[65]

The line between an unforeseeable misuse (for which defendant is not responsible) and a foreseeable misuse (which may impose liability on defendant) is much easier to state than to apply.[66] For example, drawing the line was once very controversial in determining whether an automobile manufacturer should be liable for injuries caused by the so-called "second collision" of a passenger, although today most jurisdictions consider automobile collisions a foreseeable misuse.[67] In other types of cases, courts have allowed plaintiff a total recovery on finding foreseeable though unintended misuse of a product;[68] this may explain why some judges have been reluctant to find "foreseeability" in the automobile collision cases.

Second Collisions

When courts determine liability in an automobile accident involving "second collisions," they look at the negligence of the driver of the automobile that caused the first collision and the fault of the manufacturer whose defective design aggravated injuries in the so-called second collision.[69] The second collision occurs when plaintiff-passenger is impacted against the interior of the automobile or otherwise harmed as a result of the force of the first collision. In *Austin v. Ford Motor Company*,[70] for example, the court instructed the jury to compare both the negligence of the driver who caused the first collision and that of the manufacturer of the defective seat belt. In *Day v. General Motors Corporation*, the North Dakota Supreme Court held that damages might be reduced for plaintiff's negligence in falling asleep at the wheel and not locking the door or using the seat belt.[71]

Now that the second collision theory is almost universally accepted, in the interests of fairness courts should have the power to reduce a

---

[64]Model Uniform Product Liability Act § 112(c), reprinted in 44 Fed. Reg. 62,737 (Interagency Task Force on Product Liability, U.S. Dept. of Commerce, 1979).

[65]Id.

[66]See Noel, *Defective Products: Abnormal Use, Contributory Negligence and Assumption of Risk*, 25 Vand. L. Rev. 93, 96 (1972). See, generally, Butaud v. Suburban Marine & Sporting Goods, Inc., 555 P.2d 42 (Alaska 1976) (critique of foreseeability as a practical concept).

[67]Compare Evans v. General Motors Corp., 359 F.2d 822 (7th Cir. Ind. 1966) (unforeseeable) with Larsen v. General Motors Corp., 391 F.2d 495 (8th Cir. Minn. 1968) (foreseeable). The *Larsen* view is now accepted everywhere except in Mississippi and West Virginia. R. Goodman, *Automobile Design Liability* § 1.4, at 8-9 (2d ed. 1983).

[68]See cases cited in notes 62 and 63 above. See also Daly v. General Motors Corp., 20 Cal. 3d 725, 144 Cal. Rptr. 380, 575 P.2d 1162, 1168 (1978) (dicta).

[69]Fietzer v. Ford Motor Co., 590 F.2d 215 (7th Cir. Wis. 1978).

[70]Austin v. Ford Motor Co., 86 Wis. 2d 628, 273 N.W.2d 233 (1979).

[71]Day v. General Motors Corp., 345 N.W.2d 349 (N.D. 1984).

plaintiff's award for his share of fault in causing his injuries when that fault consists of negligent driving. Comparative fault also increases fairness in cases like *Day* or *Daly v. General Motors Corporation.*[72] In both cases the plaintiff might not have been thrown from the car if the door latch button had not protruded from the handle, but the plaintiff could have prevented his injuries by availing himself of standard safety features designed into the car. In *Day*, one North Dakota judge advocated assigning the driver full responsibility for the "accident producing fault" and reducing damages further for his share of the "injury enhancing fault."[73] In *Daly* the California Supreme Court approached the problem by allowing the fact finder to consider the presence of safety devices in determining whether the automobile is defective in the first place.[74]

Fairness of Comparative Negligence

Comparative negligence statutes can provide a predicate of fairness in some cases of foreseeable misuse, thus making easier the task of a court resolving such matters. If the defendant should have foreseen the misuse and should bear some responsibility for it, but if plaintiff also is responsible for the misuse (as in the case of standing on a chair instead of a ladder), it seems appropriate to reduce plaintiff's award by the amount which a jury deems him at fault in bringing about the injury.

The Supreme Court of Wisconsin appears to have applied this principle in *Netzel v. State Sand and Gravel Company.*[75] Plaintiff, who should have known that concrete could cause burns, allowed defective material to fall inside his shoes and remain lodged against his legs for a considerable period of time. This was a misuse of the product although it was foreseeable. The court held as a matter of law that the jury should reduce the amount of plaintiff's award; nevertheless, it deemed defendant strictly liable for furnishing defective materials.

---

[72]Daly v. General Motors Corp., 20 Cal. 3d 725, 144 Cal. Rptr. 380, 575 P.2d 1162 (1978).

[73]Day v. General Motors Corp., note 71 above, 345 N.W.2d at 358 (Vande Walle, J., concurring).

[74]Daly v. General Motors Corp., note 72 above, 144 Cal. Rptr. at 393.

[75]Netzel v. State Sand & Gravel Co., 51 Wis. 2d 1, 186 N.W.2d 258 (1971). See also Ford Motor Co. v. Matthews, 291 So. 2d 169 (Miss. 1974) (starting tractor in gear not a misuse of product but a proper use performed in a negligent manner); Rice v. Hyster Co., 273 Ore. 191, 540 P.2d 989 (1975) (use of forklift to carry construction workers a foreseeable misuse of product); Powers v. Hunt-Wesson Foods, Inc., 64 Wis. 2d 532, 219 N.W.2d 393 (1974) (light tapping of catsup bottle to open top foreseeable).

12.6 Plaintiff's assumption of risk

Traditionally, in cases predicated on strict liability, plaintiff's conduct amounting to an assumption of risk will bar his claim.[76]

The assumption of risk defense has been applied in strict liability cases based on warranty, on section 402A of the *Restatement (Second) of Torts* and on abnormally dangerous or ultrahazardous activities.[77] A great many cases have relied on language in a Comment to the *Restatement* to the effect that in strict liability cases

> [T]he form of contributory negligence which consists in voluntarily and unreasonably proceeding to encounter a known danger, and commonly passes under the name assumption of risk, is a defense. . . .[78]

Actual Knowledge as Issue

Since the *Restatement* and many courts have taken the position that ordinary contributory negligence "is not a defense when such negligence consists merely in a failure to discover the defect in the product, or to guard against the possibility of its existence,"[79] the assumption of risk defense has taken on extraordinary importance in strict liability cases.[80] In that connection, close questions have arisen as to whether plaintiff actually knew of the risk and whether he voluntarily encoun-

---

[76]See Williams v. Brown Mfg. Co., 45 Ill. 2d 418, 261 N.E.2d 305, 46 A.L.R.3d 226 (1970); Annot., "Products liability: Strict liability in tort," 13 A.L.R.3d 1057, 1100-1103 (1967); Annot., "Products liability: Contributory negligence or assumption of risk as defense under doctrine of strict liability in tort," 46 A.L.R.3d 240, 253-256 (1972) (citing cases from nineteen jurisdictions). But see Blaw-Knox Food & Chemical Equipment Corp. v. Holmes, 348 So. 2d 604 (Fla. App. 1977), cert. dismissed 351 So. 2d 405 (Fla. 1977) (patent danger doctrine).

[77]See W. P. Keeton et al., *Prosser and Keeton on the Law of Torts* § 79 at 565-566 and § 103 at 712 (5th ed. 1984).

[78]*Restatement (Second) of Torts* § 402A, Comment *n* at 356 (1965).

[79]Id.

[80]See Noel, *Defective Products: Abnormal Use, Contributory Negligence and Assumption of Risk*, 25 Vand. L. Rev. 93, 121-128 (1972); Keeton, *Assumption of Risk in Products Liability Cases*, 22 La. L. Rev. 122 (1961).

tered it.[81] There is a need to resolve these questions in jurisdictions that have held the contributory negligence defense inapplicable to strict liability cases unless plaintiff unreasonably assumed the risk.

Comparing Assumption of Risk

There may be no need to draw these shadowy lines in a comparative negligence jurisdiction; rather, assumption of risk can be treated as a form of contributory negligence constituting a basis for apportionment under the comparative negligence statutes. All the comparative fault statutes that enumerate types of fault include assumption of risk as a partial, not a complete, defense,[82] and state courts have generally taken the same approach. For example, in *Netzel v. State Sand and Gravel Company*[83] plaintiff suffered second and third degree burns from contact with defendant's defective concrete. He had worked before as a "puddler" and knew that ordinary concrete could inflict burns on prolonged personal contact; therefore, it could be said that he assumed the risk of being burned by defendant's product. Nevertheless, his assumption of risk did not bar his claim but only reduced it.

A federal district court in New Hampshire, interpreting the state's law, held that assumption of risk does not bar a plaintiff's claim in

---

[81]See Williams v. Brown Mfg. Co., 45 Ill. 2d 418, 261 N.E.2d 305, 46 A.L.R.3d 226 (1970); Keener v. Dayton Elec. Mfg. Co., 445 S.W.2d 362 (Mo. 1969); Parzini v. Center Chemical Co., 136 Ga. App. 396, 221 S.E.2d 475 (1975) (while negligent failure to discover defect might bar plaintiff's recovery on a negligence theory, it does not constitute assumption of risk); Devaney v. Sarno, 125 N.J. Super. 414, 311 A.2d 208 (1973), affd. 65 N.J. 235, 323 A.2d 449 (1974) (operation of vehicle with inoperable seat belt not unreasonable assumption of risk); Ellithorpe v. Ford Motor Co., 503 S.W.2d 516 (Tenn. 1973) (operation of vehicle with three sharp spikes on steering wheel not unreasonable assumption of risk); but see Baker v. Chrysler Corp., 55 Cal. App. 3d 710, 127 Cal. Rptr. 745 (1976) (when injury to pedestrian is aggravated when struck by negligently designed front end of automobile, for assumption of risk defense to operate plaintiff need only knowingly assume risk of being struck by an automobile, and need not have actual knowledge of the claimed defect in design); Houston-New Orleans, Inc. v. Page Engineering Co., 353 F. Supp. 890 (E.D. La. 1972) (sluggish operation of machinery alerted plaintiff to defect; assumption of risk defense allowed and damages apportioned). However, even when the plaintiff voluntarily encounters a known danger, that encounter might still not be unreasonable assumption of risk. See, e.g., Brooks v. Dietz, 218 Kan. 698, 545 P.2d 1104 (1976) (plumber's action in returning to source of known gas leak not unreasonable assumption of risk).

[82]Idaho Code, § 6-1405(2) ("use of a product with a known defective condition"); Iowa Code Ann., § 668.1; Minn. Stat. Ann., § 604.01(1a); Wash. Rev. Code Ann., § 4.22.015; Unif. Comparative Fault Act § 1(b); Model Unif. Product Liability Act, § 112(B); S. 100, 99th Cong., 1st Sess. § 9(e)(2) (1985); Martinez v. Clark Equipment Co., 382 So. 2d 878 (Fla. App. 1980); Wenzel v. Rollins Motor Co., 598 S.W.2d 895 (Tex. Civ. App. 1980) (plaintiff's recovery reduced to extent misuse was proximate cause of accident). See also Cartel Capital Corp. v. Fireco of New Jersey, 81 N.J. 548, 410 A.2d 674, 19 A.L.R.4th 310 (1980) (dicta); Suter v. San Angelo Foundry & Machine Co., 81 N.J. 150, 406 A.2d 140 (1979) (citing this treatise); Sowles v. Urschel Laboratories, Inc., 595 F.2d 1361 (8th Cir. Minn. 1979); Murray v. Beloit Power Systems, Inc., 450 F. Supp. 1145 (D. V.I. 1978); Daly v. General Motors Corp., 20 Cal. 2d 725, 144 Cal. Rptr. 380, 575 P.2d 1162 (1978); Hamilton v. Motor Coach Industries, Inc., 569 S.W.2d 571 (Tex. Civ. App. 1978). See section 9.4 in regard to the general problem of changing assumption of risk into contributory negligence in a comparative negligence jurisdiction.

[83]Netzel v. State Sand & Gravel Co., 51 Wis. 2d 1, 186 N.W.2d 258 (1971).

product liability under a comparative negligence statute, but serves only to mitigate his damages.[84] In that case, plaintiff was injured when a chip from defendant's defectively manufactured hammer flew into his eye. The hammer had chipped previously while plaintiff was using it; because of that, it could be said he had assumed risk of the harm that befell him. Nevertheless, the court allowed the defense, applied the comparative negligence statute and reduced the damages by twenty percent.

As a general rule, New Jersey courts apply the Comparative Negligence Act when the plaintiff's conduct is unreasonable and voluntary,[85] even though New Jersey has abolished assumption of risk as a separate defense in negligence actions.[86] The courts have made an exception to this rule when an employee is working at an assigned task on a plant machine. The courts believed that policy reasons demand that the employee's fault, even if voluntary and unreasonable, should not be considered in the apportionment of damages.[87]

Cases applying comparative fault in this context are congruent with policies underlying product liability. When plaintiff (acting voluntarily and unreasonably) is injured and defendant *has* engaged in unreasonable conduct in making a *defective* product or *has* engaged in abnormally dangerous activity, responsibility for the accident is partially plaintiff's and partially defendant's.[88]

Obvious Hazards

One situation in product liability cases that may look like assumption of risk needs to be distinguished. In some jurisdictions product manufacturers have not been held liable for "obvious" hazards or risks;[89] plaintiff's claim is barred when he is injured by an obvious or patent defect in a product regardless of whether he subjectively knew of it. The obvious danger rule may continue to be a complete defense,[90]

---

[84]Hagenbuch v. Snap-On Tools Corp., 339 F. Supp. 676 (D. N.H. 1972). The New Hampshire Supreme Court later found the statute inapplicable to strict liability. Thibault v. Sears, Roebuck & Co., 118 N.H. 802, 395 A.2d 843 (1978).

[85]Cartel Capital Corp. v. Fireco of New Jersey, 81 N.J. 548, 410 A.2d 674, 19 A.L.R.4th 310 (1980); Suter v. San Angelo Foundry & Machine Co., 81 N.J. 150, 406 A.2d 140 (1979) (citing this treatise).

[86]See Chapter 9.

[87]Green v. Sterling Extruder Corp., 95 N.J. 263, 471 A.2d 15 (1984); Suter v. San Angelo Foundry & Machine Co., 81 N.J. 150, 406 A.2d 140, 141-148 (1979) (overruling Cepeda v. Cumberland Engineering Co., 76 N.J. 152, 386 A.2d 816 (1978) insofar as the case held contributory negligence to be a defense in a design defect action).

[88]See Calabresi & Hirschoff, *Toward a Test for Strict Liability in Torts*, 81 Yale L.J. 1055 (1972); Levine, *Buyer's Conduct as Affecting the Extent of Manufacturer's Liability in Warranty*, 52 Minn. L. Rev. 627, 648 (1968). See also Chapter 9.

[89]See, e.g., Jamieson v. Woodward & Lothrop, 101 App. D.C. 32, 247 F.2d 23 (D.C. Cir. 1957) (rubber exercise rope snapped back and hit user in the eye); Hagans v. Oliver Machinery Co., 576 F.2d 97 (5th Cir. Tex. 1978) (industrial table saw; pre-comparative negligence case); Sherk v. Daisy-Heddon, 498 Pa. 594, 450 A.2d 615 (1982) (air rifle).

[90]Mach v. General Motors Corp., 112 Mich. App. 158, 315 N.W.2d 561 (1982) (no liability where plaintiff attempted to jumpstart bulldozer and was thrown from it and run over).

especially when the "defect" is what makes the product useful to begin with,[91] as with guns and matches. Some courts have reexamined the rule as it applies to industrial machinery that might have been equipped with safety devices;[92] in comparative fault states there may be a trend toward merging the obvious hazard rule with assumption of risk and negligence in the fault calculation.[93] The practitioner should bear in mind that the result may be ultimately the same: no liability.[94]

12.7 Plaintiff's failure to discover or foresee dangers

A growing number of courts and legislatures have followed the position of the *Restatement (Second) of Torts*[95] that in cases predicated on strict liability, contributory negligence based solely on a failure to discover or foresee danger is not a defense even though the ordinary person would have discerned the danger.[96] The *Restatement* position in this regard has been a rule in search of a rationale.[97] One purported rationale is that it is illogical to have a fault-based defense when the predicate of liability is non-fault.[98] This line of reasoning relies on a non sequitur; there seems no reason why a negligent plaintiff should not be made to bear a loss which is due only in part to the defendant's defective product or abnormally dangerous activity.[99] The disregard of

---

[91]Sherk v. Daisy-Heddon, 498 Pa. 594, 450 A.2d 615 (1982).

[92]Micallef v. Miehle Co., 39 N.Y.2d 376, 384 N.Y.S.2d 115, 348 N.E.2d 571, 95 A.L.R.3d 1055 (1976); De Medeiros v. Koehring Co., 709 F.2d 734, 13 Fed. R. Evid. Serv. (Callaghan) 959 (1st Cir. Mass. 1983), citing Uloth v. City Tank Corp., 376 Mass. 874, 384 N.E.2d 1188 (1978). See also Banks v. Iron Hustler Corp., 59 Md. App. 408, 475 A.2d 1243 (1984) (refusing to extend negligence-based patent danger rule to strict liability).

[93]Campos v. Firestone Tire & Rubber Co., 98 N.J. 198, 485 A.2d 305 (1984) (obviousness of danger is just one factor to be considered in determining whether duty to warn exists).

[94]See, e.g., Bishop v. Interlake, Inc., 121 Mich. App. 397, 328 N.W.2d 643 (1982) (upholding jury finding of zero percent liability and zero percent fault on the part of the plaintiff where plaintiff stapled her finger in industrial stapler).

[95]*Restatement (Second) of Torts* § 402A, Comment n at 356 (1965) (strict product liability) and § 524 (Tent. Draft No. 10, 1964) (abnormally dangerous activities).

[96]See Annot., "Products liability: Contributory negligence or assumption of risk as defense under doctrine of strict liability in tort," 46 A.L.R.3d 240, 248-253 (1972) (collecting cases from thirteen jurisdictions); Annot., "Products liability: Strict liability in tort," 13 A.L.R.3d 1057, 1100-1103 (1967); W. P. Keeton et al., *Prosser and Keeton on the Law of Torts* § 79, at 565 (abnormally dangerous activities) and § 102, at 710-712 (product liability) (5th ed. 1984). See also Henderson v. Ford Motor Co., 519 S.W.2d 87 (Tex. 1974) (contributory negligence either in failure to discover defect or in failure to use reasonable means of escape from peril following discovery not a defense to a products liability action); Busch v. Busch Constr., Inc., 262 N.W.2d 377 (Minn. 1977) (negligent failure to inspect not a defense in strict liability suit). See Model Unif. Product Liability Act § 112(A)(1), reprinted in 44 Fed. Reg. 62,736 (Interagency Task Force on Product Liability, U.S. Dept. of Commerce, 1979) (claimant's failure to inspect). But see Buttrick v. Arthur Lessard & Sons, Inc., 110 N.H. 36, 260 A.2d 111 (1969) (broad dictum that contributory negligence is always a defense in product liability cases).

[97]See Noel, *Defective Products: Abnormal Use, Contributory Negligence and Assumption of Risk*, 25 Vand. L. Rev. 93, 107-114 (1972).

[98]See Sandy v. Bushey, 124 Me. 320, 128 A. 513 (1925).

[99]See Maiorino v. Weco Products Co., 45 N.J. 570, 214 A.2d 18 (1965); Lowndes, *Contributory Negligence*, 22 Georgetown L.J. 674 (1934).

the defense with respect to abnormally dangerous activities has been explained by the fact that liability itself is based in part on defendant's

> [W]ilful creation of an unreasonable risk to others by abnormal conduct ... and in part in the policy which places the absolute responsibility for preventing the harm upon the defendant, whether his conduct is regarded as fundamentally anti-social, or he is considered merely to be in a better position to transfer the loss to the community.[1]

Risk Distribution Policy

Nevertheless, risk distribution arguments are conclusory. Today over 80% of accident victims *have* health and accident insurance and have been reimbursed for a substantial portion of their medical costs. Moreover, in terms of social policy, why should the community at large absorb a loss due in part to plaintiff's fault? With respect to strict product liability based on implied warranty, there is some logic to the suggestion that plaintiff has relied on the manufacturer to produce a product without defect and that therefore his failure to discover imperfections should not bar his claim.[2] Nevertheless, such cases are better explained on the ground that plaintiff has not been negligent at all. When a reasonable man under the circumstances would have discovered the defect and avoided the harm, contributory negligence in a meaningful sense returns.

Probably the best explanation of why the *Restatement* and the courts have not applied the defense of contributory negligence based on failure to discover in strict liability cases focuses on the modern distrust of the defense as a complete bar to an injured plaintiff's claim.[3] As has been pointed out in section 12.6, however, these authorities have not abandoned the contributory negligence defense altogether; unreasonable assumption of risk (a form of contributory negligence) remains. The result has been a tremendous amount of litigation attempting to characterize plaintiff's conduct as one form of contributory negligence or the other.

Comparing Failure to Discover Hazards

A comparative negligence state can avoid the necessity for characterization of contributory negligence and can reach a conclusion based on sound public policy. When plaintiff in a strict liability case has been negligent in failing to foresee or discover a danger, his claim need not be either barred or paid in full; rather, his damages can be reduced by

---

[1]W. P. Keeton et al., note 96 above, § 79, at 565.

[2]See, e.g., West v. Caterpillar Tractor, 336 So. 2d 80, 24 U.C.C. Rep. Serv. (Callaghan) 1154 (Fla. 1976), certified from the Fifth Circuit, 504 F.2d 967 (1974), answer conformed to, 547 F.2d 885 (5th Cir. Fla. 1977): "[I]t is unreasonable to require the noncommercial consumer to make any sort of detailed or expert inspection ... The consumer or user is entitled to believe that the product will do the job for which it was built. On the other hand, the consumer, user, or bystander is required to exercise ordinary due care."

[3]Noel, note 97 above, at 117-119.

an amount a jury believes is appropriate in the specific case. One federal district court struggled to reach this result even when the jurisdiction had not yet adopted comparative negligence.[4] Further, the Supreme Court of Wisconsin[5] and a federal court interpreting New Hampshire law[6] reached this result. The initial Wisconsin case has been cited favorably in Minnesota[7] and Rhode Island.[8]

A federal circuit court decision interpreting New Hampshire law also held that the plaintiff's negligence would limit recovery.[9] A similar result obtained in an admiralty case where the defect was discovered but the full extent of the danger was not due to the plaintiff's negligence.[10] The Florida Supreme Court, answering a question certified to it by the Fifth Circuit,[11] has also held that comparative negligence, as a want of ordinary due care, is a defense to both breach of implied warranty and strict liability actions.[12] The Illinois Supreme Court, however, has held that comparative fault does not include failure to discover a defect or guard against its existence.[12a]

The drafters of the Model Uniform Product Liability Act[13] and proposed federal product liability legislation[14] also have attempted to deal with contributory negligence in failing to observe a defective condition. Both provide for reduction of damages when the claimant has been injured by a defective condition that would have been apparent, without inspection, to a reasonably prudent person.[15] The drafters give as an example eating a candy bar with bright green worms crawling all over it;[16] this example is based on a pre-comparative fault California case. In *Kassouf v. Lee Brothers, Incorporated*,[17] brought on an implied

---

[4]See Chapman v. Brown, 198 F. Supp. 78, 85 (D. Hawaii 1961), affd. 304 F.2d 149, 4 A.L.R.3d 490 (9th Cir. Hawaii 1962). The point was not adverted to on appeal. A few years later the state of Hawaii adopted a comparative negligence statute. See Hawaii Rev. Stat., § 663-31. See also Model Unif. Product Liability Act, note 96 above, § 112(A)(a) (claimant's failure to observe an apparent defective condition).

[5]See Dippel v. Sciano, 37 Wis. 2d 443, 155 N.W.2d 55 (1967); Netzel v. State Sand & Gravel Co., 51 Wis. 2d 1, 186 N.W.2d 258 (1971).

[6]See Hagenbuch v. Snap-On Tools Corp., 339 F. Supp. 676 (D. N.H. 1972).

[7]See Haney v. International Harvester Co., 294 Minn. 375, 201 N.W.2d 140, 146 (1972). But see Busch v. Busch Constr., Inc., 262 N.W.2d 377 (Minn. 1977) (negligent failure to inspect not a defense to strict liability actions).

[8]Ritter v. Narragansett Electric Co., 109 R.I. 176, 283 A.2d 255, 263 (1971).

[9]Cyr v. B. Offen & Co., 501 F.2d 1145 (1st Cir. N.H. 1974).

[10]Houston-New Orleans, Inc. v. Page Engineering Co., 353 F. Supp. 890 (E.D. La. 1972).

[11]West v. Caterpillar Tractor Co., 504 F.2d 967 (5th Cir. Fla. 1974), certified question answered 336 So. 2d 80, 24 U.C.C. Rep. Serv. (Callaghan) 1154 (Fla. 1976), answer conformed to 547 F.2d 885 (5th Cir. Fla. 1977).

[12]Id., 336 So. 2d 80; on remand, 547 F.2d 967.

[12a]Simpson v. General Motors Corp. (Ill., July 17, 1985).

[13]Model Uniform Product Liability Act, note 93 above, § 112(A)(1), 44 Fed. Reg. 62736.

[14]S. 100, 99th Cong., 1st Sess. § 9(e)(1) (1985).

[15]See notes 13 and 14 above.

[16]Model Uniform Product Liability Act, note 96 above, § 112, Analysis.

[17]Kassouf v. Lee Bros., Inc., 209 Cal. App. 2d 568, 26 Cal. Rptr. 276 (1962) (holding that contributory negligence would not bar a claim in implied breach of warranty).

warranty theory, the plaintiff began eating a candy bar and noticed at once that it tasted peculiar but assumed that this was because she had not eaten all day. After she had eaten about one-third of the candy she noticed that it was covered with eggs, webbing, and crawling worms. No one would suggest that the candy manufacturer should escape all liability in this case, but there is no reason why the manufacturer should have to bear the damages flowing from the plaintiff's carelessness. Under comparative fault the jury can evaluate the extent to which a reasonably prudent person would have noticed the worms and allocate damages accordingly.

Strict Liability as Negligence Per Se

The Supreme Court of Wisconsin has tried to force strict liability into negligence terminology by describing strict product liability under section 402A of the *Restatement* as "negligence per se,"[18] and by treating violation of a dog-bite statute, which would give rise to a strict liability claim in other states,[19] as a form of "negligence."[20] The state's comparative negligence law addresses itself to "claims based on negligence."[21] Apart from this, perhaps the reason is a rather difficult conceptual problem of comparing the conduct of a negligent plaintiff with that of one who is strictly liable. As a practical matter, this conceptual difficulty is not insuperable; a federal judge in a New Hampshire case was able to overcome it and he set forth his reasoning.[22] Juries have been able to handle the "problem" with ease in the many states that have applied comparative fault in product liability actions.

Obviously, there are certain elements of fault that creep into strict liability cases.[23] If defendant has committed acts that would objectively characterize his conduct as wrongful, the trier of fact should be permitted to consider that. The Supreme Court of Wisconsin has clearly seen this.[24] As has been indicated, it has been pointed out, with persuasive force, that most courts have actually applied fault principles in design and duty to warn cases.[25] Nevertheless, even when defendant's liability

---

[18]Dippel v. Sciano, 37 Wis. 2d 443, 155 N.W.2d 55, 64 (1967); Black v. General Electric Co., 89 Wis. 2d 195, 278 N.W.2d 224 (1979). See also Thomas v. Board of Township Trustees, 224 Kan. 539, 582 P.2d 271 (1978); Sun Valley Airlines, Inc. v. Avco-Lycoming Corp., 411 F. Supp. 598 (D. Idaho 1976).

[19]See Hallen, *Liability of Dog Owners*, 12 Ohio St. L.J. 343 (1951).

[20]Nelson v. Hansen, 10 Wis. 2d 107, 102 N.W.2d 251 (1960). The statute allows an injured plaintiff a claim although defendant has no reason to know that the dog has a vicious temperament; Wis. Stat. Ann., § 174.02. Accord, Carr v. Case, 135 Vt. 524, 380 A.2d 91 (1977) (dog-bite cause of action is really based on negligence).

[21]This issue is discussed in section 12.2.

[22]Hagenbuch v. Snap-On Tools Corp., 339 F. Supp. 676, 683 (D. N.H. 1972). The courts refer to the concept of comparative causation in comparing the claimant's fault to the defendant's strict liability.

[23]See Wade, *Strict Tort Liability of Manufacturers*, 19 Sw. L.J. 5 (1965).

[24]Nelson v. Hansen, 10 Wis. 2d 107, 102 N.W.2d 251, 258-259 (1960).

[25]See note 27 above and accompanying text.

is based entirely on strict liability in its true sense, a jury can take plaintiff's contributory negligence into account and reduce his recovery.

The concept of comparative causation focuses on responsibility to pay rather than on negligence.[26] The term "causation" can be misleading to the extent that it suggests physical force rather than blameworthiness;[27] "fault" and "responsibility" are better words. Some courts use their equity powers to provide for a fair and just result.[28]

Impairing Risk Distribution Policy

A fundamental argument against the comparative causation approach is that it might create poor risk distribution. The plaintiff may have to absorb part of a loss that defendant might otherwise distribute on a wide scale.[29] First, plaintiff is likely to have *already* been at least partially compensated for his injuries through workers' compensation or health or accident insurance. On a more fundamental policy level, obviously, when risks are distributed, they increase the cost of the product or the activity. It is a question of policy whether the user of the service or consumer of the product should bear the total cost of an accident which is due, in part, to plaintiff's fault. Comparative negligence allows a just and simple way of placing a part of the cost where it belongs—on the individual plaintiff.[30]

The only danger that might arise from this approach occurs in modified comparative negligence states which bring back the entire defense of contributory negligence when plaintiff has been equally negligent or, in some states, more negligent than defendant. Since defendant's liability is "strict" and based in part upon principles of "risk distribution," the contributory negligence defense should not return as an absolute bar even under a statute providing for modified comparative negligence. Rather, pure comparative negligence should be utilized.[31]

Certainly a court would have the power to do this, since the legisla-

---

[26]Murray v. Fairbanks Morse, 610 F.2d 149 (3d Cir. V.I. 1979) (causative contribution); Thibault v. Sears, Roebuck & Co., 118 N.H. 802, 395 A.2d 843 (1978); Busch v. Busch Constr., Inc., 262 N.W.2d 377 (Minn. 1977); General Motors v. Hopkins, 548 S.W.2d 344 (Tex. 1977); Duncan v. Cessna Aircraft Co., 665 S.W.2d 414 (Tex. 1984); Kennedy v. Sawyer, 4 Kan. App. 2d 545, 608 P.2d 1379 (1980), revd. 228 Kan. 439, 618 P.2d 788 (1980).

[27]See Chapter 4. To translate the motorcycle accident hypothetical into product liability terms, if a plaintiff is injured by a flying champagne cork after a lifetime of New Year's Eves, his injury may be caused 100% by the pressure within the bottle, but the fault may be 100% his.

[28]Cline v. Sawyer, 600 P.2d 725 (Wyo. 1979) (special finding); Daly v. General Motors Corp., 20 Cal. 3d 725, 144 Cal. Rptr. 380, 575 P.2d 1162 (1978) (courts have broad discretion).

[29]See Calabresi & Hirschoff, *Toward a Test for Strict Liability in Torts,* 81 Yale L.J. 1055 (1972).

[30]See Epstein, *Products Liability: Defenses Based on Plaintiff's Conduct,* 1968 Utah L. Rev. 267, 284. See generally Model Unif. Product Liability Act, note 96 above, §§ 111 and 112, 44 Fed. Reg. 62,735-37 (analysis); Murray v. Fairbanks Morse, 610 F.2d 149 (3d Cir. V.I. 1979) (comparative causation); Daly v. General Motors Corp., 20 Cal. 3d 725, 144 Cal. Rptr. 380, 575 P.2d 1162 (1978) (equitable apportionment/allocation of loss).

[31]See section 3.5.

ture in a comparative negligence state often has not addressed itself to the strict liability case.[32] Several state supreme courts have.[33] As was suggested in section 12.2, courts have the opportunity to adjust the principles of comparative negligence as appropriate to strict liability.

12.8 The advantages of comparative negligence in strict liability cases

Courts are still developing the relationship between comparative negligence and strict liability. Nevertheless, it is already evident that comparative negligence principles may be particularly helpful in resolving a problem that has caused great confusion in the states where contributory negligence is a complete defense—the problem of plaintiff's misconduct in the strict or product liability cases.

As is suggested in section 12.2 above, courts in comparative negligence jurisdictions need not forego the benefits of comparative negligence simply because the statute appears to be restricted to claims based on "negligence." Rather, the principles of comparative negligence should be developed by the courts and applied as they may be appropriate in strict liability cases.

Unintended Unforeseeable Misuse

It is suggested that plaintiff's unintended unforeseeable misuse of a product should constitute a complete defense and comparative negligence should have no bearing. Defendant has violated no duty to plaintiff and, therefore, should pay no penalty.

Unintended Foreseeable Misuse

On the other hand, when plaintiff makes an unintended but reasonably anticipated or truly foreseeable misuse of a product that is defective as to that use, his claim should be reduced by the amount he is at fault.

Assumption of Risk

Where plaintiff has assumed the risk of a defect or hazard in a product or engaged in similar conduct with respect to an abnormally dangerous activity, his damages should be reduced by the amount a jury finds him at fault.

Failure to Discover Risks

When, in regard to a product or unusually dangerous activity, plaintiff has been contributorily negligent in failing to discover or foresee dangers that a reasonable man would have discovered, his damages should be reduced by the jury.

It is, at best, extremely difficult to justify the distinction made in

---

[32]See notes in section 12.2.
[33]Day v. General Motors Corp., 345 N.W.2d 349 (N.D. 1984); Duncan v. Cessna Aircraft Co., 665 S.W.2d 414 (Tex. 1984); Mulherin v. Ingersoll-Rand Co., 628 P.2d 1301 (Utah 1981). But see Thibault v. Sears, Roebuck & Co., 118 N.H. 802, 395 A.2d 843 (1978).

contributory negligence states between, on the one hand, assumption of risk as an absolute defense to strict liability, and, on the other hand, ordinary contributory negligence as no defense. This troublesome dichotomy need not and should not be retained under comparative negligence.

It is true that the jury might have some difficulty in making the calculation required under comparative negligence when defendant's responsibility is based on strict liability. Nevertheless, this obstacle is more conceptual than practical. Juries have shown that they are capable, when the plaintiff has been objectively at fault, of taking into account how much bearing that fault had on the amount of damage suffered and of adjusting and reducing the award accordingly. Triers of fact are able to do this, and the benefits from the approach suggest that it be applied in all comparative negligence jurisdictions.

Pure Comparison Under Modified Statutes

The conceptual difficulty in strict liability cases does preclude a return of contributory negligence as a complete defense under the modified comparative negligence statutes. An attempt to apply the modification in this way would seriously undermine policies of risk distribution that underlie strict liability. In light of the fact that courts are in fact utilizing comparative negligence principles from their respective states' comparative negligence statutes rather than applying the letter of that legislation itself, it would seem that they have the power to apply whatever comparative negligence system is appropriate to strict liability. Comparative negligence will enhance and facilitate the development of strict liability theory, rather than cause additional problems.

The Supreme Courts of North Dakota,[34] Texas,[35] and Utah[36] have followed the suggestion in the first edition of this text and have taken this approach, stating in each case that because the comparative negligence statute was limited to "negligence," the court was free to fashion a new rule. The Texas Supreme Court cited the "relative inefficiency and reduced deterrent effect of modified comparative apportionment."[37] The North Dakota Supreme Court said that while strict liability was not absolute liability, it was greater than liability for negligence; therefore the modified form was unacceptable.[38]

---

[34]Day v. General Motors Corp., 345 N.W.2d 349 (N.D. 1984).
[35]Duncan v. Cessna Aircraft Co., 665 S.W.2d 414 (Tex. 1984).
[36]Mulherin v. Ingersoll-Rand Co., 628 P.2d 1301 (Utah 1981).
[37]Duncan v. Cessna Aircraft Co., 665 S.W.2d 414, 428 (Tex. 1984).
[38]Day v. General Motors Corp., 345 N.W.2d 349, 357 (N.D. 1984).

CHAPTER 13

WRONGFUL DEATH AND SURVIVAL STATUTES

Section

13.1 Survival statutes

Survival statutes are enacted to preserve the remedy for personal injury in cases where the injured person dies as the result of defendant's wrong.[1] Today, virtually every state permits personal injury actions to survive regardless of the cause of death.[2] The decedent's personal representative is permitted to recover on behalf of his estate the damages that the decedent would have been able to obtain had he lived.[3]

Since a survival statute merely continues the decedent's *own* cause of action beyond his death, it is clear that any defenses which might have been set up against the decedent if he had lived are still available to the defendant.[4] This should continue under comparative negligence, except that decedent's contributory negligence will serve only to reduce damages rather than to bar a claim.

Statutory Coverage of Survival Actions

It seems clear that all existing comparative negligence statutes are intended to embrace survival actions. Such a claim is "for injuries" received by decedent prior to his demise, and all comparative negligence statutes contain specific language covering this kind of claim.

In a few instances, survival statutes go beyond awarding damages

---

[1] See W. P. Keeton et al., *Prosser and Keeton on The Law of Torts* § 126, at 942 (5th ed. 1984).

[2] Id., § 126 at 942. See S. Speiser, *Recovery for Wrongful Death*, Appendix A (2d ed. 1975), listing all statutes.

[3] See S. Speiser, note 2 above, § 14:1.

[4] See W. P. Keeton et al., note 1 above, § 127, at 954. Motor Transit Co. v. Hutchinson, 154 Fla. 798, 19 So. 2d 57 (1944) (contributory negligence); Freyermuth v. Lutfy, 376 Mass. 612, 382 N.E.2d 1059 (1978) (decedent 40% negligent, therefore plaintiff beneficiary's recovery was reduced by that amount).

for decedent's injuries and permit an award for death itself.[5] The comparative negligence statutes in Connecticut,[6] Georgia,[7] Nebraska,[8] Ohio,[9] and South Dakota,[10] do not specifically include damages for "death." Nevertheless, as set out in more detail in section 13.2, cases in those states have uniformly *interpreted* their comparative negligence statutes to include claims for wrongful death.[11] Therefore, unless the legislature expressly *excludes* damages for death (an unlikely event), comparative negligence statutes will always be deemed applicable to that element of damages.

Negligence of Beneficiaries

It is important to note that in survival actions, negligence of the party who brings the claim or of ultimate beneficiaries is immaterial; in theory, the cause being prosecuted is that of the decedent himself.[12] This principle is deeply embedded in the law of survival actions and is unlikely to be altered by the advent of comparative negligence.[13]

13.2 Wrongful death statutes and comparative negligence

All existing general comparative negligence statutes except those in Connecticut, Georgia, Nebraska, Ohio and South Dakota specifically mention causes of action to recover damages for "death."[14] The courts

---

[5]See S. Speiser, note 2 above, § 14:3 (indicating statutes of this type are found in Connecticut, Iowa, New Hampshire and Tennessee). See Freyermuth v. Lutfy, note 4 above. Here, an automobile accident precipitated the recurrence of decedent's involutional psychosis causing her to commit suicide. The defendant was found liable for conscious pain and suffering as well as wrongful death.

[6]1973 Conn. Acts No. 73-622.

[7]Ga. Code Ann., §§ 94-703, 105-603.

[8]Neb. Rev. Stat., § 25-1151.

[9]Ohio Rev. Code Ann., § 2315.19. Language allowing an action by "a person or his legal representative" seems to contemplate actions for wrongful death, however.

[10]S.D. Codified Laws, § 20-9-2.

[11]See notes 14 to 16 below.

[12]See Mitchell v. Akers, 401 S.W.2d 907, 20 A.L.R.3d 1385 (Tex. Civ. App. 1966); Koehler v. Waukesha Milk Co., 190 Wis. 52, 208 N.W. 901 (1926) (contributory negligence case); Note, *The Contributory Negligence of a Beneficiary Does Not Bar Recovery Under the Texas Survival Statute*, 4 Hous. L. Rev. 534 (1966); Note, *Survival Statute—Parents' Contributory Negligence*, 19 Baylor L. Rev. 153 (1967).

[13]See Potter v. Potter, 224 Wis. 251, 272 N.W. 34 (1937).

[14]See Ariz. Rev. Stat. Ann., § 12-2505; Ark. Stat. Ann., §§ 27-1764, 27-1765; Colo. Rev. Stat., § 13-21-111; Del. Code Ann., tit. 10, § 8132; Hawaii Rev. Stat., § 663-31; Idaho Code, § 6-801; Ind. Code, § 34-4-33-1; Iowa Code Ann., § 668.3; Kan. Stat. Ann., § 60-258a; La. Code, § 2323; Me. Rev. Stat. Ann., tit. 14, § 156; Mass. Gen. Laws Ann., ch. 231, § 85; Minn. Stat. Ann., § 604.01; Miss. Code Ann., § 11-7-15; Mont. Code Ann., § 27-1-702; Nev. Rev. Stat., § 41.141; N.H. Rev. Stat. Ann., § 507:7-a; N.J. Stat. Ann., § 2A:15-5.1; N.Y. Civ. Prac. Law, § 1411; N.D. Cent. Code, § 9-10-07; Okla. Stat. Ann., tit. 23, § 13; Ore. Rev. Stat., § 18.470; Pa. Stat. Ann., tit. 17, § 2101; R.I. Gen. Laws, § 9-20-4; Tex. Rev. Civ. Stat. Ann. (Vernon), art. 2212a; Utah Code Ann., § 78-27-37; Vt. Stat. Ann., tit. 12, § 1036; Wash. Rev. Code Ann., § 4.22.005; Wis. Stat. Ann., § 895.045; Wyo. Stat., § 1-1-109.

of Georgia[15] and Nebraska[16] have always assumed that comparative negligence applied in wrongful death actions even though the word "death" is not specifically mentioned in the text of the statutes.

The Lone Reported Case on Wrongful Death

The issue of whether comparative negligence statutes apply in wrongful death actions has been discussed in a reported opinion only once. In *Stone v. Hinsvark*,[17] decided by the Supreme Court of South Dakota, the claim was for the wrongful death of plaintiff's child. There was evidence that the decedent had darted into the path of defendant's vehicle. Defendant contended that the child's contributory negligence should totally bar plaintiff's claim because the statute specifically authorized comparison of fault only in an action between the injured person and a defendant. A claim for wrongful death, defendant argued, was a creature of statute, brought by a legal representative and not "an action brought to recover damages for injuries" within the meaning of the state's comparative negligence statute.[18]

The court made short shrift of defendant's contention. It said that defendant's construction would give too technical a reading to the statute and decided that it was intended that the comparative negligence statute apply to actions by an executor or administrator for injuries or death to a husband, wife or children as authorized by the wrongful death statute.[19] The court bolstered its conclusion by noting that the legislature had copied the comparative negligence statute from Nebraska after the courts in that state had construed the words to include actions for death.[20]

Summary

In sum, it seems highly likely that any comparative negligence statute will be read to include actions for wrongful death unless the legislature specifically excludes such claims. Some discussion is merited as to the precise way in which comparative negligence and wrongful death statutes mesh. The basic problems created by the nexus are considered in the remainder of this chapter.

13.3 Comparison of decedent's negligence

Traditionally, the overwhelming majority of states have indicated

---

[15]See Georgia S. & F. R. Co. v. Overstreet, 17 Ga. App. 629, 87 S.E. 909 (1916); Huell v. Southeastern Stages, Inc., 78 Ga. App. 311, 50 S.E.2d 745 (1948); King v. Adams, 113 Ga. App. 708, 149 S.E.2d 548 (1966); Jordan v. Ellis, 148 Ga. App. 286, 250 S.E.2d 859 (1978); Harden v. United States, 485 F. Supp. 380 (S.D. Ga. 1980).

[16]See Spomer v. Allied Electric & Fixture Co., 120 Neb. 399, 232 N.W. 767 (1930); Huckfeldt v. Union P. R. Co., 154 Neb. 873, 50 N.W.2d 110 (1951); Wieck v. Blessin, 165 Neb. 282, 85 N.W.2d 628 (1957). See also Hrabik v. Gottsch, 198 Neb. 86, 251 N.W.2d 672 (1977).

[17]Stone v. Hinsvark, 74 S.D. 625, 57 N.W.2d 669 (1953).

[18]See S.D. Codified Laws, § 20-9-2.

[19]Stone v. Hinsvark, 74 S.D. 625, 57 N.W.2d 669, 673 (1953).

[20]Id.; and see note 16 above.

that the contributory negligence of a decedent that would be sufficient to bar his own action will bar a claim for his wrongful death.[21] The wrongful death action has been treated as derivative because most statutes contain the language of Lord Campbell's Act which conditioned liability upon conduct that "would, if death had not ensued, have entitled the party to maintain an action and recover damages . . . therefor."[22] Further, this requirement has been read into most wrongful death statutes by implication even where it is not expressly set out.[23]

Some commentators have argued that the wrongful death statute should be reinterpreted as creating a separate and independent cause of action for the designated beneficiaries and that decedent's contributory negligence should be ignored.[24] However, it is unlikely that enactment of comparative negligence will cause courts to undertake this change. This has been borne out by decisions in Arkansas,[25] Alaska,[26] Georgia,[27] Louisiana,[28] Michigan,[29] Mississippi,[30] Nebraska,[31] New

---

[21]See 2 F. Harper & F. James, *The Law of Torts* § 24.4 (1956); W. P. Keeton et al., *Prosser and Keeton on the Law of Torts* § 127, at 954 (5th ed. 1984); S. Speiser, *Recovery for Wrongful Death* § 5.01 (2d ed. 1975). See also Velasquez v. Levingston, 598 S.W.2d 346 (Tex. Civ. App. 1980) (plaintiff's recovery barred as decedent 75% negligent and defendant only 25% negligent).

[22]See 9 and 10 Vict., ch. 93, 1846.

[23]See W. P. Keeton et al., note 21 above, § 127 at 954 and n. 7; S. Speiser, note 21 above, § 5:1 (collecting cases).

[24]See 2 F. Harper & F. James, note 21 above, at 1289-1290; Nourse, *Is Contributory Negligence of Deceased a Defense to a Wrongful Death Action?*, 42 Calif. L. Rev. 310 (1954); Wettach, *Wrongful Death and Contributory Negligence*, 16 N.C. L. Rev. 211 (1938). But see Phillips, *Contributory Negligence—A Defense for Wrongful Death in California?*, 29 S. Cal. L. Rev. 344 (1956).

[25]See J. Paul Smith Co. v. Tipton, 237 Ark. 486, 374 S.W.2d 176 (1964).

[26]State v. Guinn, 555 P.2d 530 (Alaska 1976) (where conduct of both decedent and defendant was negligent, principles of comparative negligence should apply; trial judge left to apportion the negligence).

[27]See Huell v. Southeastern Stages, Inc., 78 Ga. App. 311, 50 S.E.2d 745, 752 (1948) and cases cited in note 15 above. See Harden v. United States, 485 F. Supp. 380 (S.D. Ga. 1980) (under Georgia's wrongful death statute, the right of action for negligent homicide of a child is vested in the parents).

[28]Simmons v. Whittington, 444 So. 2d 1357 (La. App. 1984) (court refused to apply comparative negligence because child decedent was not negligent in view of his age).

[29]Wigginton v. City of Lansing, 129 Mich. App. 53, 341 N.W.2d 228 (1983) (instruction on comparative negligence was erroneous because decedent had no duty to retreat from her home to avoid being shot by off-duty police officer).

[30]See Ideal Cement Co. v. Killingsworth, 198 So. 2d 248 (Miss. 1967) (overturning jury award where court believed jury disregarded instructions to take decedent's contributory negligence into account); Proctor & Gamble Defense Corp. v. Bean, 146 F.2d 598 (5th Cir. Miss. 1945) (dictum, applying Mississippi law).

[31]See note 16, section 13.2, and Huckfeldt v. Union P. R. Co., 154 Neb. 873, 50 N.W.2d 110 (1951).

York,[32] South Dakota,[33] Washington,[34] and Wisconsin,[35] as well as in admiralty.[36] It seems highly likely that other comparative negligence states will follow these decisions unless the language of either the comparative negligence statute or the wrongful death statute is to the contrary.

It should be noted that a plaintiff beneficiary obtains the basic benefit that comparative negligence provides. His decedent's negligence does not necessarily bar the claim; rather, he may recover an award reduced to allow for decedent's contributory negligence.[37]

In *Davies v. Butler*[38] the Nevada Supreme Court, in a wrongful death action, held decedent's mere negligence would not bar the plaintiff beneficiary's claim when the defendant was guilty of willful and wanton misconduct. Such behavior was left outside the purview of the comparative negligence statute.

13.4 Comparison of beneficiary's negligence

Most wrongful death statutes are deemed to create a cause of action that inures directly to the benefit of statutorily listed beneficiaries; for that reason, the contributory negligence of the beneficiaries can bar their claim.[39] In that regard, a wrongful death claim differs from a survival action, where damages for injury and death are recovered for the benefit of decedent's estate. As indicated in section 13.1 herein,[40] negligence of the *ultimate* beneficiary of a survival claim does not bar recovery.

The rule that deems a beneficiary's contributory negligence material in wrongful death actions is well entrenched[41] and is based on the

---

[32]Horne v. Metropolitan Transit Authority, 82 A.D.2d 909, 440 N.Y.S.2d 695 (1981).

[33]See Pleinis v. Wilson Storage & Transfer Co., 75 S.D. 397, 66 N.W.2d 68 (1954) (plaintiff's decedents' negligence more than slight; claim barred); Audiss v. Peter Kiewit Sons Co., 190 F.2d 238 (8th Cir. S.D. 1951) (jury questioned on whether decedent was guilty of more than "slight negligence").

[34]Griffin v. Gehret, 17 Wash. App. 546, 564 P.2d 332 (1977) (parent's recovery under wrongful death statute reduced by child decedent's contributory negligence) (citing this treatise).

[35]See Browne v. Bark River Culvert & Equipment Co., 425 F.2d 3 (7th Cir. Wis. 1970) (applying Wisconsin law and sustaining a 25/75 apportionment where plaintiff was killed underneath defendant's elevator).

[36]Doty v. United States, 508 F. Supp. 250 (N.D. Ill. 1981).

[37]See cases cited in notes 25 to 35 above.

[38]Davies v. Butler, 95 Nev. 763, 602 P.2d 605 (1979). See also Ewing v. Cloverleaf Bowl, 20 Cal. 3d 389, 143 Cal. Rptr. 13, 572 P.2d 1155 (1978) (court decided a jury could conclude that a bartender who continually served patron after he was manifestly intoxicated was guilty of willful and wanton misconduct, thus permitting plaintiff beneficiary's recovery in a wrongful death action).

[39]See W. P. Keeton et al., *Prosser and Keeton on The Law of Torts* § 127, at 958 (5th ed. 1984); 2 F. Harper & F. James, *The Law of Torts* § 23.8 (1956); S. Speiser, *Recovery for Wrongful Death* §§ 5:6 and 5:7 (2d ed. 1975); Wigmore, *Contributory Negligence of the Beneficiary as a Bar to an Administrator's Action for Death*, 2 Ill. L. Rev. 487 (1908).

[40]See final paragraph, section 13.1; S. Speiser, note 39 above, § 5:6.

[41]See S. Speiser, note 39 above, § 5.7, at 588–590 (collecting decisions for 28 states and the Virgin Islands).

policy that "no one should profit from his own wrong." The rule is an interpretation of the respective states' wrongful death statutes, and the enactment of a comparative negligence law is unlikely to do more than modify it in accordance with comparative negligence principles. Thus, a beneficiary may have his individual award reduced if his negligence contributed to the death.[42] If the beneficiary's negligence goes beyond the threshold point of the applicable comparative negligence statute, his claim may be barred entirely.[43]

The Innocent Benficiary

Complications can arise when only one of several beneficiaries is contributorily negligent. What happens to the claim of the innocent beneficiary? Courts that have dealt with this problem under comparative negligence have developed a rule that is analogous to what has come to be the "prevailing view"[44] in contributory negligence states; contributory negligence is material as a defense only against the beneficiary whose conduct contributed to the decedent's death. The innocent beneficiary's claim will not be reduced.[45]

Conduct of beneficiaries whose negligence helped to cause the death can be so interrelated that a court may decline to treat the negligence of each separately. For example, in *Reber v. Hanson*[46] a mother and father brought a wrongful death action against the driver of a truck who negligently ran over their child. The jury found that the parents' failure to supervise their child was 75% of the culpable cause of the accident. The Supreme Court of Wisconsin indicated that while it would not *impute* the negligence of one beneficiary to the other, the wrongful conduct of beneficiaries could be so intertwined that it would be meaningless to separate it. Under these circumstances, a jury may

---

[42]See Nelson v. Northern Leasing Co., 104 Idaho 185, 657 P.2d 482 (1983); Minners v. State Farm Mut. Automobile Ins. Co., 284 Minn. 343, 170 N.W.2d 223, 224 n.2 (1969); Rudelson v. United States, 431 F. Supp. 1101 (C.D. Cal. 1977), affd. 602 F.2d 1326 (9th Cir. Cal. 1979).

[43]See Reber v. Hanson, 260 Wis. 632, 51 N.W.2d 505 (1951) (jury found parents 75% negligent and driver who killed child 25% negligent); Wieck v. Blessin, 165 Neb. 282, 85 N.W.2d 628 (1957) (husband's negligence found more than slight barred his claim for wrongful death of his child).

[44]See W. P. Keeton et al., note 39 above, § 127, at 958-959.

[45]See Walden v. Coleman, 217 Ga. 599, 124 S.E.2d 265, 95 A.L.R.2d 579 (1962); Herring v. R. L. Mathis Certified Dairy Co., 118 Ga. App. 132, 162 S.E.2d 863 (1968), affd. in part and revd. in part, Bourn v. Herring, 225 Ga. 67, 166 S.E.2d 89 (1969) (alleged negligence of father did not bar or affect mother's claim); Nichols v. United States Fidelity & Guaranty Co., 13 Wis. 2d 491, 109 N.W.2d 131, 135 (1961) (cause of action belongs to the particular beneficiary); Nosser v. Nosser, 161 Miss. 636, 137 So. 491 (1931) (contributory negligence of one statutory beneficiary not imputed to the others so as to reduce damages recoverable from tortfeasor); Hines v. McCullers, 121 Miss. 666, 83 So. 734, 736 (1920); Harden v. United States, 485 F. Supp. 380 (S.D. Ga. 1980); Singletary v. National Railroad Passenger Corp., 376 So. 2d 1191 (Fla. App. 1979) (negligence of parent/driver did not affect recovery of other parent). Cf. Williams v. Steves Industries, Inc., 678 S.W.2d 205 (Tex. App. 1984) (negligence of one parent will not be imputed to innocent parent to reduce recovery for loss of children's companionship).

[46]Reber v. Hanson, 260 Wis. 632, 51 N.W.2d 505 (1951).

treat beneficiaries as one unit in apportioning fault between them and defendant. Such cases are unusual, and the typical approach will be to reduce a beneficiary's claim only if he himself has negligently contributed to the death.

13.5 Combining decedent's and beneficiary's negligence

What will occur under comparative negligence if both the decedent and the plaintiff beneficiary were negligent? For example, suppose plaintiff's decedent, his wife, was driving an automobile at the time of the accident and negligently failed to watch the road. Plaintiff husband was a passenger and had a reasonable opportunity but failed to warn his spouse about defendant's negligently driven automobile. How much is the husband's claim reduced? This problem does not arise in contributory negligence jurisdictions because the culpable conduct of the decedent herself bars the claim.[47]

Decisions in comparative negligence states have shied away from deciding the question.[48] In the closest case on point, *Bachman v. Lieser*,[49] the Supreme Court of Minnesota appears to have combined the negligence of the beneficiary with that of the decedent in a single figure and weighed that against the negligence of the defendant. In that case, a father sued for the wrongful death of his eleven-year-old son, who was killed while operating a motorbike. The jury found the plaintiff father 20% negligent because he allowed his son to use the motorbike on a highway and failed to instruct him adequately as to its proper use. Further, the jury found the child himself 80% at fault because of the manner in which he handled the motorbike. Thus, by its allocation of percentages, the jury determined that the defendant was not negligent at all!

Combined Negligence as Measure

Nevertheless, the *Bachman* case provided an approach in wrongful death actions under comparative negligence, where both the beneficiary and the decedent have engaged in culpable conduct that contributed to the death. Plaintiff's claim should be reduced by the combined percentage of his own negligence and that of his decedent. Other non-negligent beneficiaries should not bear the burden of the negligent beneficiary's culpable conduct;[50] their claims against the third-party

---

[47]See S. Speiser, *Recovery for Wrongful Death* § 5:5, at 585 (2d ed. 1975) (in discussing whether a beneficiary's negligence bars his claim, the author "assume[d] for the purpose of...discussion that the decedent himself was not guilty of 'contributory' negligence... since, if he was guilty of such contributory negligence, under the terms of the various death statutes no right of action would be capable of successful prosecution...").

[48]Bachman v. Lieser, 289 Minn. 298, 184 N.W.2d 11, 13 (1971) ("The question of how comparative negligence should be allocated between drivers and third persons, whose negligence may have also contributed to the happening of the accident, is an issue which it is not necessary to resolve in this litigation.")

[49]Id.

[50]See note 42, section 13.4, and accompanying text.

wrongdoer should be reduced only by the amount that decedent was at fault.[51]

13.6 Apportionment of wrongful death damages subject to statutory limit

Wrongful death statutes in a few jurisdictions contain a limitation or ceiling on the amount of damages plaintiff may collect.[52] As Stewart M. Speiser, the noted authority on wrongful death actions has indicated, there has been a significant trend toward increasing the amount of the limitation or abolishing it altogether.[53] As of 1985, no state limits total recovery in all cases. Kansas,[54] Maine,[55] Massachusetts,[56] New Hampshire[57] and Wisconsin[58] have limitations on certain elements of recovery or limits that apply in special circumstances.

The arguments in favor of keeping the restraints have been that they keep insurance rates down and prevent excessive verdicts based on passion.

These arguments have been demolished by experience and by commentators. They note that "[t]he function of insurance is to shift the risk of loss and if it is necessary to raise insurance rates to protect the public adequately from such serious consequences, then the public should insist that such protection be provided."[59] Commentators have noted that the curbing of jury passion can be performed less arbitrarily by careful use of remittitur by trial and appellate court judges.[60] This is an important element in making the entire system work and should be exercised in cases of excessive damage awards.

Reduction of Award Subject to Statutory Limitation

The limitations can create a special problem under comparative negligence if the jury is not informed about the restriction. For example, in *Olson v. Hartwig*[61] plaintiff's decedent was killed in a collision

---

[51]See section 13.2.

[52]See S. Speiser, *Recovery for Wrongful Death* §§ 7:1 to 7:6 (2d ed. 1975).

[53]Id., § 7:2 and 1984 Supp.

[54]Kan. Stat. Ann., § 60-1903 (1975 amendment removing monetary limits on recovery for pecuniary loss; maximum recovery of $25,000 for all other loss). See also Benton v. Union P. R. Co., 430 F. Supp. 1380 (D. Kan. 1977) (discussion of wrongful death statute's limitation on recoverable damages; procedural interaction with the comparative negligence statute); Kleibrink v. Missouri-Kansas-Texas R. Co., 224 Kan. 437, 581 P.2d 372 (1978) (comparative negligence applicable; recovery limited to $50,000).

[55]Me. Rev. Stat. Ann., tit. 18-A, § 2-804(b) ($10,000 for consortium of minor child).

[56]Mass. Gen. Laws Ann., ch. 229, § 1 ($4000 where recovery based on highway defect).

[57]N.H. Rev. Stat. Ann., § 556:13 ($50,000 where no close dependent relative).

[58]Wis. Stat. Ann., § 895.04 ($5000 for loss of society).

[59]See Nageley, *Wrongful Death Limitation in Oregon—A Rational Result or an Historical Mistake*, 1 Willamette L.J. 616, 624 (1961) quoted in S. Speiser, note 52 above, § 7:4 at 694. Speiser also notes that the experience in jurisdictions that do not have limitations shows that the effect upon rates is minimal.

[60]See Note, *Wrongful Death Recovery Limitations—R.I.P.*, 17 De Paul L. Rev. 385 (1968).

[61]Olson v. Hartwig, 288 Minn. 375, 180 N.W.2d 870 (1970).

between a bakery delivery van that he was driving and a semitrailer truck driven by defendant. The jury found the plaintiff's decedent had contributed 40% to the cause of the collision and the defendant driver 60%. It found damages of $65,000. The trial court deducted 40% from $65,000, leaving plaintiff with $39,000. All of this would seem to present no problem, except that the wrongful death statute then applicable limited recovery in such an action to only $35,000.[62] The trial court gave only passing acknowledgment to the limitation provision and simply reduced plaintiff's award to $35,000. Defendant contended that the trial court should have begun with the $35,000 figure and reduced that by 40%.

The Supreme Court of Minnesota upheld the trial court. It noted that the statute's limitation was explicitly on the recovery amount—and not on the assessment of damages. The comparative negligence statute, on the other hand, did use the word "damages." Using a rather tight linguistic analysis, the court concluded that the trial judge had proceeded correctly.

Reliance on Wisconsin History

The Minnesota Supreme Court also relied on the Wisconsin case of *Mueller v. Silver Fleet Trucking Company*,[63] where that Supreme Court reached the same conclusion, even though its wrongful death statute limitation used the word "damages." It should be noted that the Wisconsin legislature later amended its wrongful death statute to overrule *Mueller*.[64] Nevertheless, the Minnesota court reasoned that "if [its] legislature had intended to follow the amendment of Wisconsin's death by wrongful act statute, it would have adopted the statute as amended, either by appropriate provision in [the] comparative negligence statute or by amending [the] death by wrongful act statute."[65]

The Kansas Solution

In *Benton v. Union Pacific Railroad Company*[66] a federal district court applying Kansas law and citing the Minnesota[67] and Wisconsin[68] cases held that in a wrongful death action arising out of incidents occurring between the effective date of Kansas' comparative negligence statute and an amendment to its wrongful death statute removing the monetary limits on recovery for pecuniary loss, the jury would not be informed of the total recovery limitation of $50,000. If damages, as

---

[62]Minn. Stat. Ann., § 573.02; the limitation has since been abolished.

[63]Mueller v. Silver Fleet Trucking Co., 254 Wis. 458, 37 N.W.2d 66 (1949) (a 4-3 decision).

[64]See Wis. Stat. Ann., § 895.04(7).

[65]See Olson v. Hartwig, 288 Minn. 375, 180 N.W.2d 870, 872 (1970).

[66]Benton v. Union P. R. Co., 430 F. Supp. 1380 (D. Kan. 1977); accord, Kleibrink v. Missouri-Kansas-Texas R. Co., 224 Kan. 437, 581 P.2d 372 (1978); McCart v. Muir, 230 Kan. 618, 641 P.2d 384 (1982).

[67]Olson v. Hartwig, 288 Minn. 375, 180 N.W.2d 870 (1970).

[68]Mueller v. Silver Fleet Trucking Co., 254 Wis. 458, 37 N.W.2d 66 (1949) (a three-to-four decision).

reduced proportionately to the plaintiff's negligence, were still more than $50,000, the plaintiff would recover only $50,000.

The Better Policy

In light of the emptiness of policy reasons underlying the limitation on wrongful death statutes,[69] comparative negligence states should follow *Olson v. Hartwig*[70] where the legislature has not specifically addressed itself to the problem. If the jury finds damages above the maximum in an action for wrongful death, decedent's contributory negligence should be deducted from the damages found, not from the statutory maximum.

---

[69]See notes 59 and 60 above, and accompanying text.
[70]Olson v. Hartwig, 288 Minn. 375, 180 N.W.2d 870 (1970).

CHAPTER 14

STANDARD OF CONDUCT MODIFIED FOR PARTY'S CAPACITY

Section

14.1 Children and comparative negligence
14.2 Aged persons and comparative negligence
14.3 Reduced mental capacity and comparative negligence
14.4 Higher standard of conduct for specially qualified plaintiffs

14.1 Children and comparative negligence

Tort law traditionally has not held children to the same standard of care as adults. As Prosser has indicated, "the standard which is ordinarily applied, and which is customarily given to the jury, is to measure the child's conduct against what would be 'reasonable to expect of children of like age, intelligence and experience.' "[1]

In some jurisdictions a series of "presumptions" have given children additional protection. For example, sometimes children below seven years of age are *conclusively* presumed incapable of any negligence.[2] In some jurisdictions, children between seven and fourteen are *presumed* incapable of negligence—a presumption which can be rebutted.[3] The Minnesota Supreme Court, considering an attractive nuisance case, has suggested that courts should not set arbitrary age limits but consider each child as an individual.[4]

---

[1]See W. P. Keeton et al., *Prosser and Keeton on the Law of Torts* § 32, at 179 (5th ed. 1984). Accord, Wentz v. Deseth, 221 N.W.2d 101 (N.D. 1974).

[2]See Baker v. Alt, 374 Mich. 492, 132 N.W.2d 614 (1965). Accord, Gault v. Tablada, 400 F. Supp. 136 (S.D. Miss. 1975), affd. without published opinion 526 F.2d 1405 (5th Cir. Miss. 1976); Kopera v. Moschella, 400 F. Supp. 131 (S.D. Miss. 1975), affd. without published opinion 526 F.2d 1405 (5th Cir. Miss. 1976); see also Metropolitan Dade County v. Dillon, 305 So. 2d 36 (Fla. App. 1974); MacConnell v. Hill, 569 S.W.2d 524 (Tex. Civ. App. 1978) (child under 5 is presumptively incapable of negligence); Barrett v. Carter, 248 Ga. 389, 283 S.E.2d 609 (1981) (child under 13 is immune from tort liability); Fromenthal v. Clark, 442 So. 2d 608 (La. App. 1983) (two year old who bit newborn baby is incapable of negligence or intentional tort); but see Korbelik v. Johnson, 193 Neb. 356, 227 N.W.2d 21 (1975) (although a five-year-old child is incapable of contributory negligence as a matter of law, if the child's conduct is the sole proximate cause of the accident there can be no recovery); Toetschinger v. Ihnot, 312 Minn. 59, 250 N.W.2d 204 (1977) (child 5 years, 8 months can be held 80% contributorily negligent); Yun Jeong Koo v. St. Bernard, 89 Misc. 2d 775, 392 N.Y.S.2d 815 (1977) (infant plaintiff of 4 years, 10 months can be found contributorily negligent).

[3]See Kuhns v. Brugger, 390 Pa. 331, 135 A.2d 395, 68 A.L.R.2d 761 (1957). See also Hoyem v. Manhattan Beach City School Dist., 22 Cal. 3d 508, 150 Cal. Rptr. 1, 585 P.2d 851 (1978) (where student-truant's negligence was a proximate cause of his injuries, school district's liability may be diminished on basis of comparative negligence). Accord, Balart v. Michel's Kartway, Inc., 364 So. 2d 90 (Fla. App. 1978); Harden v. United States, 485 F. Supp. 380 (S.D. Ga. 1980) (negligence of fifteen-year-old child permissible for comparison under comparative negligence statute).

[4]Hughes v. Quarve & Anderson Co., 338 N.W.2d 422 (Minn. 1983) (upholding 40% reduction in award where plaintiff dove into a shallow, murky quarry pool).

Prosser has noted that "the great bulk of the decisions in which all these questions have been considered have involved the contributory negligence of child plaintiffs."[5] Professor Fleming James of Yale has contended that when a child is a defendant, no allowance should be made for his age.[6] Professor James's argument is based on the assumption that a child does not actually pay a judgment and that, therefore, allowing a softer standard for a child defendant results in a poor economic distribution of risk.

The Restatement Position

The Second *Restatement*[7] has taken a middle-of-the-road position and would hold a child to adult standards whenever he engages "in an activity which is normally undertaken only by adults, and for which adult qualifications are required."[8] The compromise position appears to be predicated on the reasonable expectation by other persons affected that the child defendant engaged in such activities *would* adhere to adult standards.

If the child is of sufficient age and experience to understand fully the dangers involved in an activity, the child should be held to an adult standard of care.[9]

If a minor has had special training, such as a hunting safety course prior to the purchase of a rifle, and if the minor is older and has had experience with firearms, a higher standard of care may be imposed upon him by the finder of fact.[10]

For the most part, courts have not addressed themselves to the question of how comparative negligence should (or should not) affect the standard of care applied to a child defendant.[11] It is this author's view that the reasons for holding a child defendant to an adult stan-

---

[5]See W. P. Keeton et al., note 1 above, § 32 at 181.

[6]See James, *Accident Liability Reconsidered: The Impact of Liability Insurance*, 57 Yale L.J. 549, 554-556 (1948).

[7]*Restatement (Second) of Torts* § 283A (1965).

[8]Id., § 283A, Comment *c* at 16; Dellwo v. Pearson, 259 Minn. 452, 107 N.W.2d 859, 97 A.L.R.2d 866 (1961); Wollaston v. Burlington Northern, Inc., 188 Mont. 192, 612 P.2d 1277 (1980) (minor held to same standard of care as adult in operation of motor vehicle); Demeri v. Morris, 194 N.J. Super. 554, 477 A.2d 426 (1983) (twelve year old operating dirt bike on public roadway is held to an adult standard of care). But see Mahon v. Heim, 165 Conn. 251, 332 A.2d 69 (1973) (declining to adopt rule holding child to an adult standard of care when engaged in an activity normally only undertaken by adults).

[9]Kushnir v. Benson, 520 P.2d 134 (Colo. App. 1973) (child of fifteen capable of understanding peril involved in sitting on bumper of moving car, and held to adult standard of care); Dorais v. Paquin, 113 N.H. 187, 304 A.2d 369 (1973) (child of seventeen held to adult standard of care when accident resulted from walking in highway under conditions of poor visibility); Garrison v. Funderburk, 262 Ark. 711, 561 S.W.2d 73 (1978) (negligence of minor driver, who was found to be 72% at fault, imputed to mother in her counterclaim for damages in an automobile accident case). But see Holcomb v. Gilbraith, 257 Ark. 32, 513 S.W.2d 796 (1974) (whether child of fourteen was contributorily negligent per se for violating jaywalking statute was a question for jury).

[10]Arredondo v. Duckwall Stores, Inc., 227 Kan. 842, 610 P.2d 1107 (1980).

[11]See Fromenthal v. Clark, 442 So. 2d 608 (La. App. 1983), refusing to find a two-year-old defendant liable under comparative negligence.

dard are persuasive and go beyond the compass of comparative negligence. Therefore, it would seem proper under comparative negligence to treat a child defendant as an adult when proper risk distribution requires it or when, as suggested by the Comment to the *Restatement*, the child is engaged in adult activities creating a risk to others.

The Child Plaintiff

Many decisions in comparative negligence states have dealt with a negligent child plaintiff. Most of the development has occurred in Wisconsin. That state has evolved a doctrine in which the child's age is treated as a mitigating factor — twice.[12]

The jury is instructed to consider the age of the child in determining whether he was negligent at all.[13] If the jury determines that in spite of the plaintiff's youthful age he was contributorily negligent, it then must *again* consider the child's age and experience in comparing his negligence with that of the defendant.

In *Blahnik v. Dax*[14] plaintiff, an eight year old, attempted to cross a highway on her bicycle. Defendant automobile driver collided with plaintiff at a point ten to fifteen feet from the edge of a driveway. The jury was instructed that it should consider the child's youthful "age, capacity, discretion, knowledge and experience" in determining whether she generally "failed to exercise reasonable care for her own safety."[15] If the jury found the young plaintiff contributorily negligent, it was again to consider her youth in comparing relative fault. The court instructed:

In answering this comparative negligence question, if you are to answer it, you should take into consideration that the [defendant] was an adult and [plaintiff] was a child, and consider and weigh the credible evidence bearing upon the inquiries presented, in the light of the difference in the rules which you were previously instructed, to apply in determining whether the conduct of the parties was negligence.[16]

Contributory negligence of a thirteen-year-old child was held not a bar to recovery in *Scott v. Independent School District*.[17] There, a statute enacted specifically to protect youngsters from their own inexperience and lack of judgment was violated when the school district neglected to enforce the wearing of protective safety glasses by the plaintiff in an industrial arts class. Although this conduct constituted negligence per se, the court allowed the issue of the minor's contributory negligence to go to the jury.

---

[12]See Brice v. Milwaukee Automobile Ins. Co., 272 Wis. 520, 76 N.W.2d 337 (1956); Gremban v. Burke, 33 Wis. 2d 1, 146 N.W.2d 453 (1966).

[13]See Blahnik v. Dax, 22 Wis. 2d 67, 125 N.W.2d 364 (1963).

[14]Id.

[15]Id., 125 N.W.2d at 368.

[16]Id., 125 N.W.2d at 369.

[17]Scott v. Independent School Dist., 256 N.W.2d 485 (Minn. 1977).

Consider Age Twice?

Other comparative negligence states such as Nebraska[18] and Mississippi[19] have recognized that plaintiff's immaturity may be material in determining whether he was contributorily negligent. However, it is less clear that those states would consider the factor a second time when a *comparison* of negligence is made. Nevertheless, it is submitted that taking account of plaintiff's immaturity a second time in apportioning negligence is appropriate; it is in harmony with the basic purpose of comparative negligence to allocate the award on the basis of fault.

At least in Wisconsin there is a trend to allow the principle of considering a child's age in determining whether he was contributorily negligent to be utilized to assure at least some recovery when a child has been injured by a negligent defendant. For example, in *Cirillo v. Milwaukee*[20] a fourteen-year-old high school student was injured when his physical education teacher left the gym class unsupervised. Plaintiff was pushed to the floor and injured during a "roughhouse" in the teacher's absence. The trial court entered a summary judgment for defendant, finding as a matter of law that the plaintiff's negligence was at least 50% of the total. The Supreme Court of Wisconsin reversed, stating that

> [T]he age of the respective parties is a relevant consideration in comparing their negligence. When the negligence of a youth is being compared with that of an adult, this court is particularly reluctant to interfere.[21]

A Texas court followed the Wisconsin approach in *MacConnell v. Hill*.[22] A six-year-old boy who accompanied his father to a service station was observing the repairs when water gushed out of the automobile radiator, scalding him. The appellate court overturned a finding of 60% negligence on the part of the child, saying that the jury should have been instructed not only that the plaintiff was a child but that they should take into consideration that one party was a child and the other an adult.

---

[18]See Vacanti v. Montes, 180 Neb. 232, 142 N.W.2d 318, 322 (1966) (nine-year-old pedestrian struck by defendant's automobile; trier of fact could take into account plaintiff's immaturity in determining whether his negligence was slight in comparison with defendant's); Gadeken v. Langhorst, 193 Neb. 299, 226 N.W.2d 632 (1975) (trier of fact may take age into account in determining whether eleven-year-old child was guilty of negligence sufficient to bar recovery).

[19]See Moak v. Black, 230 Miss. 337, 92 So. 2d 845 (1957) (jury could not consider nine-year-old plaintiff's contributory negligence because no proof was presented that showed he could comprehend risk); Johnson v. Howell, 213 Miss. 195, 56 So. 2d 491 (1952) (similar). But see Davis v. Waterman, 420 So. 2d 1063 (Miss. 1982) (adult standard applies to anyone operating a motor vehicle).

[20]Cirillo v. Milwaukee, 34 Wis. 2d 705, 150 N.W.2d 460 (1967).

[21]Id., 150 N.W.2d at 465, 466.

[22]MacConnell v. Hill, 569 S.W.2d 524 (Tex. Civ. App. 1978).

Child Distinguished from Adult Plaintiff

In *Brice v. Milwaukee Automobile Insurance Company*[23] a ten-year-old child was injured by defendant's negligent driving. The trial court entered judgment on a jury finding that the child was 35% negligent as to lookout and yielding the right-of-way. In a memorandum decision, the trial judge indicated that if the plaintiff had been an adult, he would have directed a judgment for defendant. The Supreme Court of Wisconsin appeared to accept this premise and affirmed.

The court was even more explicit on the point in *Kohler v. Dumke*.[24] There a six year old stepped out between two parked cars, saw defendant's truck coming and "froze." The jury found the child 30% at fault. In denying defendant's request to overturn this determination, the court said:

> If [plaintiff] had been an adult, we would have little difficulty in holding that his causal negligence, in stepping out into traffic lane of the truck from between two parked cars without first making any attempt to make an observation as to whether he could do so with safety, was at least equal to the causal negligence of [the defendant.][25]

The Supreme Court of Wisconsin seemed to come close to showing sympathy for a child plaintiff in *Hanson v. Binder*.[26] There, the court upheld the grant of a new trial after the jury found the child plaintiff more at fault than the defendant. In that case a five year old ran into the path of defendant's automobile. In the course of its opinion, the court made a statement that potentially could always permit a very young but negligently injured child *some* recovery:

> The mere fact that, in this collision between the two, the jury found that the child was more negligent than the adult demonstrated to the court's satisfaction that the jury did not appreciate that different standards of ordinary care apply to these different actors.[27]

The court's position in this regard seems at variance with its often expressed view that it will make every effort to uphold a jury's apportionment of negligence between the parties.[28]

Contrast with Older Children

Again in *Gremban v. Burke*[29] the Wisconsin Supreme Court affirmed a trial court decision overturning a verdict for defendant and ordering a new trial. The court said:

> [W]hile the act of plaintiff in running across the street into the path of an oncoming car would be extremely negligent conduct on the

---

[23]Brice v. Milwaukee Automobile Ins. Co., 272 Wis. 520, 76 N.W.2d 337 (1956).

[24]Kohler v. Dumke, 13 Wis. 2d 211, 108 N.W.2d 581 (1961).

[25]Id., 108 N.W.2d at 583.

[26]Hanson v. Binder, 260 Wis. 464, 50 N.W.2d 676 (1952).

[27]Id., 50 N.W.2d at 678.

[28]See note 20 above, and accompanying text.

[29]Gremban v. Burke, 33 Wis. 2d 1, 146 N.W.2d 453 (1966).

part of an older child, plaintiff's tender age tends to somewhat mitigate this.[30]

On the other hand, the same Supreme Court has sometimes been unwilling to stretch its apparent sensitivity for children to the length of overturning a verdict for defendant when the trial court decided not to do so. Thus, in *Metcalf v. Consolidated Badger Cooperative*,[31] a seven year old was injured playing on defendant's conveyor belt. The jury found plaintiff 70% negligent, thus barring his claim under the Wisconsin statute. Although the trial court had used "may" instead of "should" in instructing on consideration of plaintiff's youth, the verdict was affirmed because the Supreme Court was satisfied that the jurors knew that they were "continually to take account of [plaintiff's] age whenever they considered his actions...."[32]

Negligent Supervision

In cases where a child has been injured partly through its own action, the parents' derivative causes of action, such as wrongful death,[33] may be subject to reduction of damages for the parents' negligent failure to supervise the child, even if the child itself is too young to be legally at fault. The parents will not, however, be found negligent if the child did nothing that would be negligent if done by an adult.[34]

14.2 Aged persons and comparative negligence

It has been a relatively open question in tort law whether advanced age can be considered as a mitigating factor in determining whether plaintiff has been contributorily negligent.[35]

At least one decision under comparative negligence has allowed the jury to take the matter into consideration in apportioning negligence. In *Helms v. Fox Badger Theatres Corporation*[36] an elderly plaintiff fell in exiting from a restroom in a dimly lighted theater. The jury found plaintiff 35% negligent as to lookout and the theater 65% negligent for inadequate lighting. In upholding the plaintiff's verdict the court said:

> In considering the extent to which there was contributory negligence on [plaintiff's] part, the jury could take into consideration the facts that at the time of the accident [plaintiff] was about 74 to 76

---

[30]Id., 146 N.W.2d at 459.

[31]Metcalf v. Consolidated Badger Cooperative, 28 Wis. 2d 552, 137 N.W.2d 457 (1965).

[32]Id., 137 N.W.2d at 461. See also Rangel v. Graybar Elec. Co., 70 Cal. App. 3d 943, 139 Cal. Rptr. 191 (1977) (court refused to overturn jury verdict holding fourteen-year-old plaintiff 95% negligent).

[33]Nelson v. Northern Leasing Co., 104 Idaho 185, 657 P.2d 482 (1983) (one year old crawled under truck in parking lot and was killed when truck started up).

[34]Owen v. Burcham, 100 Idaho 441, 599 P.2d 1012 (1979) (parents' award not reduced because there was no evidence to support finding that twelve year old was riding bicycle negligently).

[35]See W. P. Keeton et al., *Prosser and Keeton on the Law of Torts* § 32, at 182 (5th ed. 1984).

[36]Helms v. Fox Badger Theatres Corp., 253 Wis. 113, 33 N.W.2d 210 (1948).

years of age, and had been suffering from high blood pressure, and senile dementia of long standing.[37]

Since the infirmities and physical disabilities of advanced age can be comprehended by jurors and do serve to mitigate plaintiff's fault, there appears no reason why advanced age should not be taken into account when plaintiff's contributory negligence is at issue.

14.3 Reduced mental capacity and comparative negligence

A rule has evolved from very early tort law[38] that diminished mental capacity, even amounting to insanity, does not excuse a defendant from responsibility for invasion of the physical integrity of another or for destruction of property.[39] In spite of arguments that it is unjust to hold a man responsible for wrong that he was unable to avoid,[40] the general rule has been applied both to batteries[41] and to negligent conduct.[42] Rather than inquire into the individual's mental capacity, the law holds the insane or mentally deficient person to the standard required of a reasonable man.

It seems unlikely that comparative negligence will have any effect on this deeply embedded rule of tort law. However, in *Breunig v. American Family Insurance Company*[43] the Wisconsin Supreme Court, while upholding a jury finding that defendant driver had forewarning of an incapacitating mental illness, said by way of dictum:

> [T]he statement that insanity is no defense is too broad when it is applied to a negligence case where the driver is suddenly overcome without forewarning by a mental disability or disorder which incapacitates him from conforming his conduct to the standards of a reasonable man under like circumstances.[44]

The *Breunig* dictum alters traditional tort law to make it comport more honestly with a true fault system. However, the decision did not appear to be prompted in any way by comparative negligence.

Incompetent Plaintiffs

Traditional tort law has been more lenient to the insane when their

---

[37]Id., 33 N.W.2d at 212.

[38]See Weaver v. Ward, Hobart 134, 80 Eng. Rep. 284 (1616) ("if a lunatick hurt a man, he shall be answerable in trespass . . .").

[39]See W. P. Keeton et al., *Prosser and Keeton on the Law of Torts* § 135, at 1072-1073 (5th ed. 1984); Bohlen, *Liability in Tort of Infants and Insane Persons*, 23 Mich. L. Rev. 9 (1924).

[40]See Wilkinson, *Mental Incompetency As a Defense to Tort Liability*, 17 Rocky Mtn. L. Rev. 38 (1944).

[41]See McGuire v. Almy, 297 Mass. 323, 8 N.E.2d 760 (1937).

[42]See Sforza v. Green Bus Lines, 150 Misc. 180, 268 N.Y.S. 446 (1934).

[43]Breunig v. American Family Ins. Co., 45 Wis. 2d 536, 173 N.W.2d 619, 49 A.L.R.3d 179 (1970).

[44]Id., 173 N.W.2d at 624. See also Buckley & Toronto Transp. Comms. v. Smith Transport Ltd., [1946] Ont. L. Rep. 798, 4 Dom. L. Rep. 721.

contributory negligence was at issue.[45] In some jurisdictions, in order to excuse what would otherwise be contributory negligence, the plaintiff must be "absolutely insane" or "totally devoid of intellect" so as to be unable to apprehend danger and avoid exposure to it.[46] In one comparative negligence case, this requirement was met, with the result that plaintiff's objectively negligent conduct was not taken into account and there was no apportionment of damages.[47] In a recent Texas case[48] a jury refused to find an incompetent nursing-home patient negligent at all, either as a plaintiff or as a defendant, where the patient had wandered out of the institution and onto the highway, knocking down a motorcyclist. The jury found the nursing home 75% at fault because the staff knew about the patient's tendency to wander and attributed the rest of the fault to the motorcyclist.

There is some pre-comparative negligence judicial authority in comparative negligence states that would not require absolute or total insanity to permit a jury to take into consideration plaintiff's mental capacity. Some courts have held that diminished mental capacity not amounting to outright insanity may be taken into account by the jury in determining whether plaintiff has exercised the requisite degree of care for his own safety.[49] In *Warner v. Kiowa County Hospital Authority*[50] a patient suffering from "alcohol psychosis" and requiring restraint, while not insane, was held of such diminished mental capacity to permit the jury to take his condition into account in determining the issue of contributory negligence. This approach might be criticized because it introduces into civil litigation the very difficult task of determining what is or is not mental illness. It also might provide too ready an excuse for the accident-prone victim. Nevertheless, because of the flexibility inherent in comparative negligence, it would seem appropriate to permit a plaintiff to present to the jury facts bearing on his mental capacity that might serve to diminish his fault.

14.4 Higher standard of conduct for specially qualified plaintiffs

In at least one case, a specially qualified plaintiff's duty of care was modified so as to exceed "ordinary care." In *Nimmer v. Purtell*[51] a plaintiff osteopath was negligently treated by another osteopath. The jury barred his claim, finding him 57% contributorily negligent. The

---

[45]See Annot., "Contributory negligence of mentally incompetent or mentally or emotionally disturbed person," 91 A.L.R.2d 392 (1963); W.P. Keeton et al., note 39 above, § 32, at 178 (suggesting that policy reasons cause courts to consider incapacity as one of many contributing factors).

[46]Annot., note 45 above, 91 A.L.R.2d at 399.

[47]See Emory University v. Lee, 97 Ga. App. 680, 104 S.E.2d 234 (1958).

[48]Golden Villa Nursing Home, Inc. v. Smith, 674 S.W.2d 343 (Tex. App. 1984).

[49]See Snider v. Callahan, 250 F. Supp. 1022 (W.D. Mo. 1966); Feldman v. Howard, 5 Ohio App. 2d 65, 34 Ohio Op. 2d 163, 214 N.E.2d 235 (1966), revd. 10 Ohio St. 2d 189, 39 Ohio Op. 2d 228, 226 N.E.2d 564 (1967).

[50]Warner v. Kiowa County Hospital Authority, 551 P.2d 1179 (Okla. App. 1976).

[51]Nimmer v. Purtell, 69 Wis. 2d 21, 230 N.W.2d 258 (1975).

Supreme Court of Wisconsin upheld an instruction that the plaintiff's duty of care was that usually exercised by an osteopath under the same or similar circumstances.

CHAPTER 15

CHOICE OF LAW AND COMPARATIVE NEGLIGENCE

Section

15.1 Introduction

As the *Restatement of Conflict of Laws* has indicated:

Each state has rules to determine which law (its own local law or the local law of another state) shall be applied by it to determine the rights and liabilities of parties resulting from an occurrence involving foreign elements.[1]

The myriad problems in the rather volatile area of choice of law are considerably beyond the scope of this text. Nevertheless, it is worthwhile to explore some major choice-of-law cases that have involved comparative negligence.

Categories of Choice-of-Law Questions

It is not surprising that there has been a good number of such cases. When a tort case has some connection with a jurisdiction that applies comparative negligence and the injured plaintiff was partly at fault, it is natural that his attorney will attempt to develop a choice-of-law theory that will persuade the court to apply comparative negligence rather than the traditional contributory negligence defense. The principal occasions for this may be categorized as follows:

1. Where the forum applies the contributory negligence defense but another jurisdiction with which the case has some connection applies comparative negligence.

2. Where the forum applies comparative negligence but another jurisdiction with which the case has some connection considers contributory negligence a complete bar to recovery.

3. Where the action is in a federal court sitting in either a comparative or contributory negligence jurisdiction.

This chapter explores these basic situations and may provide some perspective about the legal picture of choice of law today. Nevertheless, an exploration of the broader field of conflicts of laws is necessary

---

[1]See *Restatement of the Law (Second) Conflict of Laws* § 2, Comment *a* (3) (1971).

for a complete understanding of any specific problem; other sources offer a place to derive that important overview.[2]

15.2 State courts in a contributory negligence forum

When a case is brought in a jurisdiction that recognizes the contributory negligence defense, but all other basic connections of the action are to a jurisdiction that has comparative negligence, it is almost certain that the court will apply comparative negligence. The result is reached under traditional choice-of-law rules by a process of legal characterization.[3] The law that determines whether contributory fault on the part of the plaintiff bars his recovery in whole or merely reduces it is regarded as substantive, and not procedural.[4]

Under traditional choice-of-law rules, the *forum's* law always governs procedural matters. Oddly enough, the current edition of Corpus Juris Secundum says there is some authority that comparative negligence "pertains merely to the remedy"[5] and is, therefore, "procedural" for the purposes of choice-of-law rules. The only authority cited is an Iowa decision[6] declining to apply comparative negligence even though the accident occurred in Illinois, which then had a comparative negligence doctrine,[7] and even though both parties were Illinois residents. The Iowa decision was expressly overruled in 1936.[8]

Lex Loci Delicti

It is easy to understand the prevailing doctrine that applies comparative negligence, under traditional choice-of-law rules, when that is the law of the place where the accident occurred. Comparative negligence "does more than touch or affect a matter of procedure."[9] Rather, it "gives a right to recover not recognized by the common law"[10] and is therefore regarded as substantive for choice-of-law purposes.

---

[2]See in addition to the *Restatement* cited in note 1 above: A. Ehrenzweig, *Conflict of Laws* (1962) (a somewhat personalized and now outdated view); H. Goodrich, *Handbook of the Conflict of Laws* (E. Scoles, 4th ed. 1964) (more objective but also outdated); R. Leflar, *American Conflicts Law* (rev. ed. 1968) (balanced and objective but somewhat outdated); R. Weintraub, *Commentary on the Conflicts of Laws* (2d ed. 1980) (most up-to-date but also the most subjective).

[3]See *Restatement (Second) of Conflict of Laws* § 7 and accompanying comments (1971).

[4]See Tepel v. Thompson, 359 Mo. 1, 220 S.W.2d 23 (1949); Fitzpatrick v. International R. Co., 252 N.Y. 127, 169 N.E. 112, 68 A.L.R. 801 (1929); Snyder v. Missouri P. R. Co., 183 Tenn. 471, 192 S.W.2d 1008 (1946).

[5]65A C.J.S. *Negligence* § 173 at 283 (1966).

[6]Johnson v. Chicago & N. W. R. Co., 91 Iowa 248, 59 N.W. 66 (1894), ovrld. Kingery v. Donnell, 222 Iowa 241, 268 N.W. 617 (1936).

[7]See notes 76 and 77, section 1.5, and accompanying text.

[8]Kingery v. Donnell, 222 Iowa 241, 268 N.W. 617, 623 (1936). Iowa has now adopted comparative negligence. Goetzman v. Wichern, 327 N.W.2d 742 (Iowa 1982); Iowa Code Ann., ch. 668.

[9]Fitzpatrick v. International R. Co., 252 N.Y. 127, 169 N.E. at 115, 68 A.L.R. 801 (1929).

[10]Id. Accord, Dertz v. Pasquina, 59 Ill. 2d 68, 319 N.E.2d 12 (1974) (applying Wisconsin comparative negligence as substantive law).

On substantive matters, traditional choice-of-law theory selects lex loci delicti; the substantive rights of parties to a tort action are governed by the law of the place of the wrong. If this approach is taken when the choice is between comparative and contributory negligence, the forum court applies comparative negligence if that is the law in the jurisdiction where the accident took place.[11] Courts that still follow traditional conflicts doctrine will continue to take this approach.

The lex loci delicti approach to selecting governing tort law has, however, come under severe criticism and has been rejected by a good number of courts,[12] the *Restatement*[13] and commentators.[14] The fundamental criticism of the traditional rule rests on the fact that the place of the wrong may be purely adventitious; there may be other more meaningful connections to another jurisdiction sufficient to justify application of that jurisdiction's law. Nevertheless, it should be noted that even the modern *Restatement* begins with the assumption that the substantive law of the place of the wrong will govern.[15]

Modern Choice-of-Law Theory

Modern choice-of-law theory does not automatically apply comparative negligence simply because the accident occurred in a state that has that doctrine. For example, in *Frummer v. Hilton Hotels International,*

---

[11]See, e.g., Frost v. Whitfield, 353 So. 2d 1154 (Ala. 1977) (court held that comparative negligence law of Mississippi applied to an accident which occurred in Mississippi). Cf. Olsen v. State Farm Auto. Ins. Co., 386 So. 2d 600 (Fla. App. 1980), certified question answered and decision quashed, 406 So. 2d 1109 (Fla. 1981). The plaintiff, a resident of Florida, was killed in an accident in Illinois. The insurer asked for a declaratory judgment that Illinois law, which was then contributory negligence, would apply. The lower court found that although the Florida rule was lex loci delicti, contributory negligence was so contrary to public policy that it should not apply. 386 So. 2d at 601. The Florida Supreme Court said that lex loci delicti had priority unless another state had a stronger interest: in this case Illinois was not only the locus of the accident but had an interest in citizens subject to the insurer's subrogation rights against an uninsured motorist. 406 So. 2d at 1111. The court also cited reasons of uniformity and ease in the determination and application of law.

[12]See Annot., "Modern status of rule that substantive rights of parties to a tort action are governed by the law of the place of the wrong," 29 A.L.R.3d 603 (1970). See, e.g., Blazer v. Barrett, 10 Ill. App. 3d 837, 295 N.E.2d 89 (1973) (declining to apply Wisconsin comparative negligence even though accident occurred in Wisconsin, since both parties were Illinois residents and plaintiff's medical treatment took place in Illinois); but see Cardin v. Cardin, 14 Ill. App. 3d 82, 302 N.E.2d 238 (1973) (applying rule of lex loci delicti to suit arising out of accident in Wisconsin when application of Illinois law would work hardship on plaintiff who filed suit believing Wisconsin comparative negligence would apply). See also Mulcahy v. Harris Corp., 487 F. Supp. 499 (N.D. Ill. 1980) (as plaintiff resides in Illinois and injury occurred there, court applied Illinois law).

[13]See *Restatement (Second) of Conflict of Laws* §§ 6, 145, and 164 (1971).

[14]See, e.g., Cheatham & Reese, *Choice of the Applicable Law*, 52 Colum. L. Rev. 959 (1952); Symposium, *Comments on Babcock v. Jackson: A Recent Development in Conflict of Laws*, 63 Colum. L. Rev. 1212 (1963) (featuring Professors Cavers, Cheatham, Currie, Ehrenzweig, Leflar and Resses).

[15]See *Restatement (Second) of Conflict of Laws* § 164 (1971) ("Contributory fault . . . (2) The applicable law will usually be the local law of the state where the injury occurred"). See also §§ 6 and 145.

Incorporated[16] a New York resident sustained injuries when he slipped in a bathtub while taking a shower at defendant's hotel in England. New York applied the contributory negligence defense, but England had a form of comparative negligence.

The court in *Frummer* was required by New York choice-of-law doctrine to take a modern approach rather than simply to apply lex loci delicti. Using this approach, the court

1. Isolated the particular tort issue—contributory versus comparative negligence.

2. Identified the policies underlying the substantive law principles in potential conflict.

3. Made a selection in light of those policies as well as the interests of the respective states in having their local substantive law applied.

The court found it difficult to find *any policy* that supported contributory negligence. The only rational basis for the rule was that it would limit the liability exposure of insurance companies.[17] The court also noted that contributory negligence "protects defendants who neglect to purchase sufficient insurance or perhaps are unable to obtain adequate amounts."[18]

In light of all this, the court could find no New York interest in having its own doctrine applied because defendant was not a New York resident. The court speculated that if New York had any interest, it would be in applying English law because if the "plaintiff [became] permanently disabled he might well become a burden on New York's public and private facilities if his contributory negligence barred all recovery."[19] On the other hand, the *Frummer* court noted that the rationale of comparative negligence was that a person who was "principally responsible for injuries to another should not escape liability completely because the injured party was also in part at fault."[20] Since plaintiff might have borne costs in England that would have to be paid, it saw that jurisdiction as having an interest in applying its own law.

Better Law as an Indicium

The *Frummer* court went further and found that it might have a case before it in which "no state has a compelling interest in having its law applied in order to vindicate some relevant policy."[21] Therefore,

---

[16]Frummer v. Hilton Hotels International, Inc., 60 Misc. 2d 840, 304 N.Y.S.2d 335 (1969).

[17]Even with respect to this rationale, the court noted that it was "a highly debatable proposition." Id., 304 N.Y.S.2d at 342.

[18]Id.

[19]Id., 304 N.Y.S.2d at 343. Accord, Knieriemen v. Bache Halsey Stuart Shields, Inc., 74 A.D.2d 290, 427 N.Y.S.2d 10 (1980) (New York law did not apply to a negligence cause of action brought by a Louisiana resident, notwithstanding existence of a contract between the parties which stipulated that New York law should govern).

[20]Frummer v. Hilton Hotels International, Inc., note 16 above, 304 N.Y.S.2d at 342.

[21]Id., 304 N.Y.S.2d at 344.

resort could be had to another modern choice-of-law indicium—the "better law."[22]

As pointed out in section 21.2, a number of persuasive arguments can be developed that comparative negligence is better law than the contributory negligence defense. Courts that acknowledge the "better law" choice-of-law indicium may be persuaded to apply comparative negligence rather than their local law of contributory negligence, even when the case's contacts with the comparative negligence jurisdiction are less substantial than they were in the *Frummer* case.[23]

Summary of Choice of Substantive Law

In sum, in traditional choice-of-law analysis, a contributory negligence state will always apply comparative negligence if the wrong occurred in a jurisdiction where that doctrine is extant. Under modern choice-of-law theories, the same result will be reached in most instances, in part because comparative negligence is better law than contributory negligence.

Thus, today there may be instances where contributory negligence states will apply comparative negligence even though the wrong occurred in its own jurisdiction. For example, if both parties and defendant are residents of a comparative negligence jurisdiction and their respective vehicles are licensed and insured in their home state, but they have an accident in a contributory negligence state, even the contributory negligence state might, utilizing modern choice-of-law theory, apply comparative negligence. The basic rationale would be that the forum jurisdiction had no interest in applying its own contributory negligence law and that it would be wiser to choose comparative negligence because that is a better rule of law.

In a recent case involving the application of comparative contribution among joint tortfeasors, a federal court sitting in Washington, D.C. found that under the "governmental interests" test there was no true conflict between the District of Columbia and Virginia, both equal share jurisdictions, and Florida, Texas, and Washington, all pure comparative contribution states.[24] While the case involved comparative contribution among joint tortfeasors and not comparative negligence on the part of a plaintiff, its approach is instructive in regard to comparative negligence cases. An Air Florida plane manufactured by Boeing had taken off in a snowstorm from National Airport in Virginia and had crashed in the Potomac River, hitting a major arterial bridge. The District of Columbia was the forum and the crash site. The District and

---

[22]Id. See also R. Leflar, *American Conflicts of Law* § 110 (rev. ed. 1968). Accord, Schwartz v. Consolidated Freightways Corp., 300 Minn. 487, 221 N.W.2d 665 (1974) (applying Minnesota comparative negligence to a suit brought by a Minnesota plaintiff arising out of an accident in Indiana as the better rule of law).

[23]Cf. Decker v. Fox River Tractor Co., 342 F. Supp. 1089 (E.D. Wis. 1971) (discussed in section 15.3 below; court may also have been influenced by fact that it was applying law of its own jurisdiction).

[24]In re Air Crash Disaster at Washington, 559 F. Supp. 333 (D. D.C. 1983).

Virginia had incurred substantial costs in rescue operations and the ensuing transportation crisis.[25] Most of the passengers were citizens of the District, Maryland, and Virginia, although some were from Florida and Massachusetts. Boeing was located in the State of Washington, Air Florida in Florida, and American Airlines, which allegedly had taken part in inadequate de-icing procedures, in Texas. The court identified the District's and Virginia's relevant policies as encouraging conformance to due care and facilitating determination of each share of the judgment. The court found that the three comparative contribution jurisdictions had an interest in ensuring fair treatment of defendants. The court also found that comparative contribution would not contravene the District's and Virginia's interest in encouraging due care but on the contrary would enhance it, whereas the equal share rule would "offend the legitimate and profound interests of the defendants' home states."[26] The court therefore ruled that comparative contribution would apply.

Choice of Procedural Law

Assuming that a court in a contributory negligence jurisdiction selects comparative negligence in a choice-of-law case, a problem may arise as to how the court will apply this foreign law. For example, if the comparative law jurisdiction couples its rule with the use of special interrogatories, will the forum court use this procedure? An Illinois court in *Millsap v. Central Wisconsin Motor Transport Company*,[27] held that it should. The court determined that the Wisconsin special interrogatory process was so intimately tied with the correct application of that state's comparative negligence doctrine that it was, in effect, part of the substantive law of the state. The court reached this conclusion because special interrogatories are used in Wisconsin to enable jurors to make a fair comparison of the negligence of the parties as well as to facilitate a court's role in reviewing the jury's determination.[28] Also the court adopted the Wisconsin procedural policy of not informing the jury of the effect of their answers respecting percentages of negligence.

The *Millsap* decision shows that matters that are on their face procedural may become substantive for choice-of-law purposes when sufficiently enmeshed with the basic purposes of a substantive rule as to become virtually a part of it. The *Millsap* case is close with respect to

---

[25]By sheer coincidence, a subway train had derailed the same day, paralyzing the subway system for several days. Id., at 339.

[26]Id. at 352.

[27]Millsap v. Central Wisconsin Motor Transport Co., 41 Ill. App. 2d 1, 189 N.E.2d 793 (1963).

[28]Id., 189 N.E.2d at 802.

this issue.[29] There is a substantial burden on a counsel who is trying to show the forum that what would appear to be procedural devices are so linked with the basic goals and purposes of a particular foreign state's comparative negligence statute that they should be treated as substantive and therefore applied. Under modern choice-of-law rules, the forum might be persuaded to apply such procedural devices if it would be relatively easy for it to do so.[30]

15.3 State courts in a comparative negligence forum

When action is brought in a state that has comparative negligence, arising out of an accident which occurred in a contributory negligence state, traditional choice-of-law analysis selects contributory negligence as the applicable law.[31] Thus, in *Tri-State Transit Company v. Mondy*[32] a former Louisiana resident brought action in Mississippi on a claim from an accident occurring in Louisiana. The forum court had comparative negligence as the law, but held that it would "apply the substantive law of Louisiana, including that of contributory negligence. ..."[33]

The lex loci delicti rule also prevailed in an early Wisconsin case, *Kane v. Loyd's American Line*.[34] There, both the plaintiff and the principal defendant were Wisconsin residents. The accident occurred in Minnesota, but only seven miles from the Wisconsin border, and its connection with Minnesota did not appear to be great. Nevertheless, Wisconsin applied the traditional choice-of-law rules and declined to apply its own comparative negligence rule. The Supreme Court of Wisconsin simply said:

> The accident in question having occurred in the state of Minnesota, any contributory negligence of the decedent is a defense to the action and is for the jury.[35]

Modern Choice-of-Law Theory

Under modern conflict-of-law analysis, the *Kane* case would not be

---

[29]Cf. Lang v. Rogney, 201 F.2d 88, 97 (8th Cir. Minn. 1953) (declining to reverse a district court that had failed to utilize interrogatories because they were discretionary under Federal Rule of Civil Procedure 49 (a)) with Erie R. Co. v. Tompkins, 304 U.S. 64, 82 L. Ed. 1188, 58 S. Ct. 817, 11 Ohio Op. 246, 114 A.L.R. 1487 (1938), discussed at notes 60 to 70, section 15.4, and accompanying text.

[30]See R. Weintraub, *Commentary on the Conflict of Laws* 55 (2d ed. 1980) ("the proper standard is one that balances the difficulty to the forum in finding and applying the foreign rule against the likelihood that the outcome will be affected").

[31]See Tri-State Transit Co. v. Mondy, 194 Miss. 714, 12 So. 2d 920 (1943); Kane v. Loyd's American Line, 247 Wis. 145, 19 N.W.2d 296 (1945). As reflected in notes 36 to 44 herein and accompanying text, both Wisconsin and Mississippi today would apply a modern conflict-of-laws analysis.

[32]Tri-State Transit Co. v. Mondy, 194 Miss. 714, 12 So. 2d 920 (1943).

[33]Id., 12 So. 2d at 922. Louisiana has since adopted comparative negligence. La. Civ. Code Ann., art. 2323.

[34]Kane v. Loyd's American Line, 247 Wis. 145, 19 N.W.2d 296 (1945).

[35]Id., 19 N.W.2d at 298. At the time of this decision, Minnesota had not yet enacted comparative negligence. Today, of course, the same problem would not arise. See Minn. Stat. Ann., § 604.01.

so simple to decide. A modern court would look with considerably more circumspection at the various contacts of the parties and the accident with the two jurisdictions in question, before making its final choice of law.

In *Mitchell v. Craft*,[36] the Supreme Court of Mississippi had before it a case that would have been relatively simple to decide under traditional conflict-of-laws theory. The accident had occurred in Louisiana, a contributory negligence state; under the lex loci delicti rule, Louisiana's substantive law would apply. The court did not take this approach, but attempted to apply a modern conflict-of-laws analysis. It noted that both plaintiff's decedent and defendant's decedent were domiciled in Mississippi and their estates were being administered there. Although the accident had occurred in Louisiana, it took place only two miles from the Mississippi border and the parties were both, at the time of the accident, traveling to their respective homes in Mississippi.

The court indicated that the traditional rule relied on a "purely adventitious" relationship between the entire transaction and Louisiana.[37] Further, the court noted, the "only virtue of invariably applying the rule of the place of the injury is that it is easy for a court to apply. Nevertheless, in many cases ... it bears no relation to any rational criteria for choosing one law as against another in a tort-conflicts case."[38]

Advancement of Governmental Interests

In deciding that it would apply its own rule of comparative negligence, the Mississippi court in *Mitchell* took the position that "[a] primary consideration in determining applicable law is the advancement of the forum's governmental interests."[39] Since both parties were residents of Mississippi, no Louisiana interest would be advanced by the application of Louisiana law. On the other hand, there was a Mississippi concern "with the protection of its injured domiciliaries and their families, and the distribution of its domiciliaries' estates."[40]

Better Law Criterion

The Mississippi court also was influenced by its belief that comparative negligence was "the better rule of law."[41] While the court discussed a number of other "choice-influencing considerations,"[42] balancing governmental interests and looking to "the better rule of law" were the primary factors that led to its decision to apply Mississippi law.

---

[36]Mitchell v. Craft, 211 So. 2d 509 (Miss. 1968).
[37]Id., 211 So. 2d at 513.
[38]Id.
[39]Id., at 514.
[40]Id.
[41]Id.
[42]Id., at 515. At 516, the court cited all of the general choice-of-law considerations embodied in *Restatement (Second) of Conflict of Laws* § 6 (1971).

An Extreme Case

A modern choice-of-law approach was also applied in a Wisconsin case that arose in federal court.[43] The decision is of note because comparative negligence was applied where the contacts with the forum were thinner than those in *Mitchell.*[44] Plaintiff brought his action in Wisconsin for injuries received in Pennsylvania from a harvester machine purchased in Pennsylvania. The only Wisconsin contact was that the harvester had been manufactured in that state by the defendant. The court traced through five factors that are "choice-influencing" considerations in modern conflict-of-laws theory:

1. Predictability of results.
2. Maintenance of interstate and international order.
3. Simplification of judicial task.
4. Advancement of the forum's governmental interests.
5. Application of the better rule of law.

Apparently the parties agreed that the first two factors were not significant considerations in the case before the court. The court itself found the third factor "not decisive," for its own "greater familiarity with Wisconsin's comparative negligence law [was] balanced by the arguably easier application of a rule of law in which a plaintiff's negligence acts as a bar to recovery and in which the need for special verdicts presumably is negated."[45]

In *Schwartz v. Consolidated Freightways Corporation*[46] the Supreme Court of Minnesota applied Minnesota comparative negligence to an accident occurring in Indiana. The plaintiff was a Minnesota resident and both defendants were corporations doing business in Minnesota. The court advanced a Minnesota governmental interest in that Minnesota residents would bear the economic brunt of the injury.[47] Further, the court found a strong state policy supporting the application of comparative negligence as the better rule of law.[48]

Decisive Considerations

With respect to the fourth factor, advancement of the forum's governmental interests, the court concluded that the forum's interests

---

[43]Decker v. Fox River Tractor Co., 324 F. Supp. 1089 (E.D. Wis. 1971). The court applied what it thought to be Wisconsin choice-of-law rules. A federal court in a diversity of citizenship case must take this approach because choice-of-law rules are regarded as substantive for purposes of Erie R. Co. v. Tompkins, 304 U.S. 64, 82 L. Ed. 1188, 58 S. Ct. 817, 11 Ohio Op. 246, 114 A.L.R. 1487 (1938). See Klaxon Co. v. Stentor Electric Mfg. Co., 313 U.S. 487, 85 L. Ed. 1477, 61 S. Ct. 1020 (1941).

[44]See notes 36 to 42 above, and accompanying text.

[45]Decker v. Fox River Tractor Co., 324 F. Supp. 1089, 1091 (E.D. Wis. 1971).

[46]Schwartz v. Consolidated Freightways Corp., 300 Minn. 487, 221 N.W.2d 665 (1974).

[47]Id., 221 N.W.2d at 668.

[48]See also Sabell v. Pacific Intermountain Express Co., 36 Colo. App. 60, 536 P.2d 1160 (1975) (applying Colorado comparative negligence to an accident occurring in Iowa); Fells v. Bowman, 274 So. 2d 109 (Miss. 1973) (applying Mississippi comparative negligence to an accident occurring in Louisiana).

would be *damaged* by the adoption of a rule under which no apportionment of fault is possible. Finally, the most decisive consideration appeared to be the court's belief that comparative negligence was the better rule of law. Defendant had argued that Pennsylvania's law was the better rule and stressed that comparative negligence was only a minority view in the United States.[49] The court answered this contention by noting that "the fact that most states do not have comparative negligence statutes is not persuasive, nor is Wisconsin's law 'obsolete or senseless.' "[50] To the contrary, the court expressed its belief that contributory negligence was a "discredited doctrine."

Critique of the Decker Case

Although the Wisconsin federal court noted that it was "perhaps too easy to let the 'better rule of law' factor dominate the other four [considerations] and be solely determinative of the choice of law,"[51] its opinion suggests that it committed that very sin. There was no consideration of Pennsylvania's interests in having its law applied nor any apparent thought given as to why it was fair to defendant to apply Wisconsin law simply because the harvester had been manufactured in that state.

Arguably, Pennsylvania had little interest in the decision; it would have no concern about protecting a Wisconsin corporation. Further, the decision may have been fair to the defendant in that it operated in a state that had comparative negligence and defendant no doubt was aware of it. Nevertheless, the decision does stand near the outer limit of what a comparative negligence jurisdiction might do in reaching to apply its own rule of law. Although the Supreme Court of the United States has permitted a wide latitude to the states in the area of conflict of laws,[52] a party could be deprived of due process within the meaning of the Fourteenth Amendment if a court decided "a lawsuit by rules of law that [were] unconnected with the transaction sued on. ..."[53]

Necessary Considerations in Choice of Law

It is this author's view that although a forum with comparative negligence has the better rule of law on contributory fault,[54] a court in that forum has an obligation of careful consideration both of unfairness to the defendant and of competing state interests when the acci-

---

[49]Now, however, comparative negligence has been adopted by forty-four states, an overwhelming majority. See section 1.1.

[50]Decker v. Fox River Tractor Co., 324 F. Supp. 1089, 1091 (E.D. Wis. 1971).

[51]Id.

[52]See Richards v. United States, 369 U.S. 1, 15, 7 L. Ed. 2d 492, 82 S. Ct. 585 (1962) ("Where more than one State has sufficiently substantial contact with the activity in question, the forum State, by analysis of the interests possessed by the States involved, could constitutionally apply to the decision of the case the law of one or another state having such an interest in the multistate activity"). Comment, *States' Rights in Conflict of Laws*, 19 Ark. L. Rev. 142 (1965).

[53]See R. Leflar, *American Conflicts of Law* § 56, at 122 (rev. ed. 1968).

[54]See section 21.2.

dent occurred in a jurisdiction that still applies the contributory negligence defense. Where the forum's only contact is that plaintiff is a resident of that state, it is unfair and perhaps unconstitutional to apply its own "better rule of law."[55]

15.4 Choice of law in the federal courts

Federal courts may have a problem in choosing between comparative and contributory negligence when it is uncertain whether a case arises under admiralty or state law.[56] A choice-of-law problem may also arise in federal courts when a case is clearly predicated upon state substantive law. This may include cases arising under federal diversity and pendent claim jurisdiction.

In diversity and pendent claim cases, federal courts apply the appropriate state substantive law. Federal courts treated comparative negligence as a substantive rule even before the historic decision in *Erie R. Co. v. Tompkins*.[57] This was because federal courts applied state substantive statutory law even prior to *Erie*. The *Erie* case of course made it clear that federal courts would be required to apply state substantive common law also.

Comparative Negligence Substantive

The important practical point to remember is that both before and after *Erie*, the federal courts have treated comparative negligence as substantive and not procedural law.[58] Since the comparative negligence doctrine relates to the basic rights and obligations between parties,[59] this does not seem surprising. Federal courts also apply the state inter-

---

[55]Cf. Neumeier v. Kuehner, 31 N.Y.2d 121, 335 N.Y.S.2d 64, 286 N.E.2d 454 (1972) (only forum contact with the transaction was defendant's decedent's residence and registration of his vehicle; the Ontario guest statute was applied). However, if both plaintiff and defendant are residents of the forum state, some courts have followed their own "better rule of law." See, e.g., Sabell v. Pacific Intermountain Express Co., 36 Colo. App. 60, 536 P.2d 1160 (1975).

[56]See, e.g., In re Dearborn Marine Service, Inc., 499 F.2d 263, 30 A.L.R.Fed. 499 (5th Cir. Tex. 1974) (in an action for wrongful death resulting from an explosion on an oil platform which engulfed a vessel on which decedent was working, the suit against the operator of the platform was governed by the then applicable Texas rule of contributory negligence, but the action against the owner of the vessel was in admiralty); Jig the Third Corp. v. Puritan Marine Ins. Underwriters Corp., 519 F.2d 171 (5th Cir. Tex. 1975) (when injury occurs at sea as a result of negligence during the shipbuilding process, maritime law applies); Lopez v. Delta S.S. Lines, Inc., 387 F. Supp. 955 (D. P.R. 1974) (state law applies to an action arising out of accident on pier caused by shore-based equipment); Ross v. Moak, 388 F. Supp. 461 (M.D. La. 1975) (barge moored permanently on river bank and used as a place of business not a vessel in navigation for purposes of admiralty jurisdiction).

[57]Erie R. Co. v. Tompkins, 304 U.S. 64, 82 L. Ed. 1188, 58 S. Ct. 817, 11 Ohio Op. 246, 114 A.L.R. 1487 (1938). See Mississippi Power & Light Co. v. Whitescarver, 68 F.2d 928 (5th Cir. Miss. 1934).

[58]See Railway Express Agency v. Mallory, 168 F.2d 426 (5th Cir. Miss. 1948); Greenwood v. McDonough Power Equipment, Inc., 437 F. Supp. 707 (D. Kan. 1977) (citing this treatise).

[59]See Fitzpatrick v. International R. Co., 252 N.Y. 127, 169 N.E. 112, 68 A.L.R. 801 (1929); Jones v. Petroleum Carrier Corp., 483 F.2d 1369 (5th Cir. Ga. 1973).

pretation of comparative negligence statutes since this is part of the substantive law.[60] If the substantive question is one of first impression, the federal court is bound to decide it as would a court of the state whose substantive law is applied.[61] Thus, if state courts in a comparative negligence jurisdiction treat assumption of risk as a form of contributory negligence for the purpose of apportionment of damages, the federal courts will follow that guideline in cases in which that state's law applies.[62]

A federal court sitting in a diversity jurisdiction case must also apply the choice-of-law rules of the forum, although modern choice-of-law rules give federal courts quite a bit of leeway. This is especially true when the forum state courts have not made a ruling on the general subject.[63]

Federal Procedure Applied

The federal courts may, however, apply their own rules on matters they regard as procedural implementations of comparative negligence. This is likely to occur when a Federal Rule of Civil Procedure specifically governs a procedure.

An extreme example refusing to apply state procedural law was *Lang v. Rogney*.[64] There the Eighth Circuit Court of Appeals affirmed a lower court's refusal to require special verdicts in a case where Wisconsin's comparative negligence statute was applicable. Wisconsin has long treated the special verdict procedure as mandatory on timely request,[65] and the federal court was aware of this.[66] On the other hand, under Federal Rule of Civil Procedure 49(a) the use of special verdicts is within the discretion of the district court. The Court of Appeals applied the Federal Rule.

The *Lang* court did indicate that it thought the failure of the district court to require special verdicts was "unfortunate" because the procedure was of "material assistance to any court in cases involving the Wisconsin comparative negligence statute."[67] However, it concluded that the matter was in the procedural realm and was thus controlled

---

[60]See Lang v. Rogney, 201 F.2d 88, 95-96 (8th Cir. Minn. 1953).

[61]See, e.g., Wright v. Standard Oil Co., 470 F.2d 1280 (5th Cir. Miss. 1972) (in an action for personal injury to a child under Mississippi law, if only one of the parents is contributorily negligent, only that parent's proportional share of the award for the child's loss of wages is reduced by the percentage of negligence attributable to the parent).

[62]See Decker v. Fox River Tractor Co., 324 F. Supp. 1089, 1090 (E.D. Wis. 1971).

[63]Turcotte v. Ford Motor Co., 494 F.2d 173 (1st Cir. R.I. 1974) (applying modern choice of law principles over lex loci delicti); Meyer v. Chicago, R. I. & P. R. Co., 508 F.2d 1395 (8th Cir. Minn. 1975) (applying Minnesota comparative negligence to an accident occurring in Iowa); but see Tiedeman v. Chicago, M., S. P. & P. R. Co., 513 F.2d 1267 (8th Cir. Iowa 1975) (Minnesota comparative negligence applies to an action resulting from an accident occurring in Minnesota brought by an Iowa resident).

[64]Lang v. Rogney, 201 F.2d 88 (8th Cir. Minn. 1953).

[65]See Pearson v. Kelly, 122 Wis. 660, 100 N.W. 1064 (1904).

[66]See Lang v. Rogney, 201 F.2d 88, 97 (8th Cir. Minn. 1953).

[67]Id.

by federal law. A later United States Supreme Court decision[68] could be read to indicate that the *Lang* court was correct and that, applying the Federal Rule, the matter of whether special interrogatories should be used by a federal court applying comparative negligence was a matter of choice rather than necessity.

Special Verdicts Appropriate Where Required by State

It may be that as a general matter it is fair and reasonable to allow federal courts to conduct cases through their own procedural mechanisms. Nevertheless, it seems inappropriate to ignore the mandatory special verdict procedure used by a state such as Wisconsin in connection with a modified comparative negligence system. In effect, the procedure allows comparative negligence to work properly in that it:

1. Enables jurors to make a conscientious comparison of the fault between the parties.

2. Permits the court to make an honest appraisal of the jury's determinations.

For these reasons, an Illinois court in a state choice-of-law case indicated that the "Wisconsin interrogatory process is so intimately tied to the correct application of the comparative negligence doctrine as to constitute an integral part of the *substance* of that doctrine."[69] The criteria for characterizing a matter as "substantive" in the context of federal-state choice-of-law problems may not be precisely the same as those involved in an interstate choice-of-law question, so that the Illinois decision is not wholly congruent precedent for the federal courts. Nevertheless, it is relatively easy for the federal courts to utilize the special verdict procedure in comparative negligence cases.[70] When the state courts would do so, the federal courts should as well, regardless of the precise way the *Erie* issue might be decided. It is interesting to note that a number of federal courts apparently have taken this approach without much discussion.[71]

A Multiple Tortfeasor Problem

In *Hefley v. Textron, Inc.*[72] the Tenth Circuit held that the Kansas "phantom party" rule, which allows allocation of fault to nonparties, would not be applied to allow impleading of parties who were immune from liability under federal law. The plaintiffs were members of the

---

[68]Hanna v. Plumer, 380 U.S. 460, 14 L. Ed. 2d 8, 85 S. Ct. 1136 (1965); not followed, Walker v. Armco Steel Corp., 592 F.2d 1133 (10th Cir. Okla. 1979), affd. 446 U.S. 740, 64 L. Ed. 2d 659, 100 S. Ct. 1978 (1980).

[69]See Millsap v. Central Wisconsin Motor Transport Co., 41 Ill. App. 2d 1, 189 N.E.2d 793, 802 (1963) (emphasis added). See also section 17.4 herein.

[70]Fed. R. Civ. P. 49 (a) provides for the special verdict procedure. It should not be an overwhelming burden on the federal courts to apply it in comparative negligence cases when the state courts would do so.

[71]See Odekirk v. Sears, Roebuck & Co., 274 F.2d 441 (7th Cir. Ill. 1960); Decker v. Fox River Tractor Co., 324 F. Supp. 1089 (E.D. Wis. 1971).

[72]Hefley v. Textron, Inc., 713 F.2d 1487 (10th Cir. Kan. 1983).

Kansas National Guard who were injured in a helicopter crash. They sued the helicopter manufacturer, who brought a third-party action for contribution and indemnity against the federal and Kansas governments. The court found that the claim against the United States was barred by the *Feres* doctrine[73] and the claim against the state was barred by the Eleventh Amendment. The manufacturer wanted to include the governmental parties as defendants for purposes of apportionment only, because as parties they were subject to broader discovery than they would be as nonparties. The court found that refusal to allow inclusion as defendants would not be outcome determinative because fault of "phantom parties" would be assessed in any case; the effect of narrower discovery would be slight, and Textron would be liable only for its proportionate share of damages.

Other Federal-State Questions

The special verdict procedure seems the major federal-state choice-of-law uncertainty in regard to comparative negligence. The characterization of most of the other matters discussed in this text as "substantive" or "procedural" for federal-state conflicts purposes is relatively clear.

---

[73]Feres v. United States, 340 U.S. 135, 95 L. Ed. 152, 71 S. Ct. 153 (1950) (the United States is immune from lawsuits by servicemen who are injured in the course of military service).

CHAPTER 16

MULTIPLE PARTIES

Section

16.1 Comparison of imputed negligence

There are two basic situations in which the law imputes the negligence of one party to another. The more familiar of the two is vicarious liability, wherein a non-negligent party is held liable for the acts of another.

The reasons for vicarious liability are manifold and have shifted over time. Today, there is sometimes given as a reason the right of control exercised by the person who is not at fault over the negligent individual.[1] Perhaps a more realistic basis is that the person not at fault set in motion an enterprise which is profitable to him and which involves the negligent party. Thus the enterpriser, rather than an innocent party, should bear the cost of accidents which occur in the course of the business.[2]

Imputed Contributory Negligence

The second form of imputed negligence involved contributory fault. Here, the party who is not at fault may have his claim barred because of the fault-laden conduct of another.[3] At one time, there were numerous situations in which A's negligence would be imputed to B so as to bar B's claim for damages against a third person, even though B would not have been vicariously liable for injury to the third person resulting from A's negligence.[4] For example, the negligence of a husband-driver

---

[1] 2 F. Harper & F. James, *The Law of Torts* § 26.3 (1956); see W. P. Keeton et al., *Prosser and Keeton on the Law of Torts* § 69 (5th ed. 1984).

[2] See 2 F. Harper & F. James, note 1 above, § 26.5; W. P. Keeton et al., note 1 above, § 69.

[3] See 2 F. Harper & F. James, note 1 above, § 23.1; W. P. Keeton et al., note 1 above, § 74.

[4] 2 F. Harper & F. James, note 1 above, § 23.1 at 1265; W. P. Keeton et al., note 1 above, § 74 at 529.

might be imputed to a passenger-wife and bar her claim against a third party.[5]

Today, excluding some exceptions in a few community property states, contributory negligence of one person is not imputed to another unless there would be vicarious liability for injury to a third person caused by the negligent person.[6] Conversely, in most situations in most states today, if A would be vicariously liable for the acts of B, B's contributory negligence is imputed to A. This general principle was called by the late Dean Prosser "the both ways test."[7]

In some jurisdictions a spouse's claim for loss of consortium and medical expenses will be reduced or barred by the injured spouse's negligence.[8] If both spouses are negligent, their negligence will be combined to reduce the recovery.[9] This is not an imputation of negligence

---

[5]2 F. Harper & F. James, note 1 above, § 23.4; W. P. Keeton et al., note 1 above, § 74 at 531-532. Other examples of such imputed contributory negligence occurred between driver and passenger, parent and child, and bailee and bailor. See 2 F. Harper & F. James, above, §§ 23.2, 23.3, 23.5; W. P. Keeton et al., above, § 74.

[6]In some community property states the claim of an innocent spouse is barred to prevent the negligent spouse from benefiting from a share of the damages. See 2 F. Harper & F. James, note 1 above, § 23.4; W. P. Keeton et al., note 1 above, § 74 at 531; Cox, *Comparative Negligence: Tort Damage Relief for the Marital Community,* 9 Idaho L. Rev. 56, 57 (1972). For other minor exceptions see W. P. Keeton et al., above.

The Louisiana Supreme Court abolished imputation of negligence from wife to husband because under community property theory it operated only from wife to husband and thus involved unlawful gender-based discrimination under the state constitution. Lewis v. Till, 395 So. 2d 737 (La. 1981).

See also DeLozier v. Smith, 22 Ariz. App. 136, 524 P.2d 970 (1974); but see Schwing v. Bluebonnet Express, Inc., 489 S.W.2d 279 (Tex. 1973) (the contributory negligence of a surviving spouse will not bar an action by other beneficiaries under the Texas wrongful death statute). In Wisconsin by statute, an automobile or motorboat owner who brings a claim for damages to his vehicle must bear the consequences of the negligence of his child or spouse if that person was operating the vehicle at the time of the accident. In other words, the contributory negligence of the spouse or child is imputed to the owner in this limited situation. See Wis. Stat. Ann., § 895.048. See also Thomas Oil, Inc. v. Onsgaard, 298 Minn. 465, 215 N.W.2d 793 (1974) (negligence of truck driver imputable to corporate employer so as to bar employer's claim; such imputation held constitutional since a corporation can act only through its agents or employees).

[7]See W. P. Keeton et al., note 1 above, § 74 at 529; Prosser, Wade & Schwartz, *Cases and Materials on Torts* 703 (7th ed. 1982); Gregory, *Vicarious Responsibility and Contributory Negligence,* 41 Yale L.J. 831 (1932). But see Nowak v. Nowak, 30 Conn. Supp. 233, 309 A.2d 259 (1973) (refusing to impute contributory negligence of student to driving instructor despite criminal statute imposing vicarious liability on instructor).

[8]See, e.g., Victorson v. Milwaukee & Suburban Transport Co., 70 Wis. 2d 336, 234 N.W.2d 332 (1975); White v. Lunder, 66 Wis. 2d 563, 225 N.W.2d 442 (1975); but see Macon v. Seaward Constr. Co., 555 F.2d 1 (1st Cir. N.H. 1977) (wife's recovery for loss of consortium not reduced in relation to husband's degree of comparative negligence; court observed that the action should not be deemed derivative in nature).

The majority rule also applies to a parent's derivative action for medical expenses. See, e.g., Welter v. Curry, 260 Ark. 287, 539 S.W.2d 264 (1976). However, the contributory negligence of one spouse will not be imputed to the other to reduce his or her share of an award for loss of a minor's services or mental anguish. Wright v. Standard Oil Co., 470 F.2d 1280 (5th Cir. Miss. 1972); Stull v. Ragsdale, 273 Ark. 277, 620 S.W.2d 264 (1981).

[9]White v. Lunder, 66 Wis. 2d 563, 225 N.W.2d 442 (1975). However, the claim will not be barred unless the negligence of either spouse exceeded that of the defendant compared separately.

since the action is derivative: the plaintiff's right is deemed wholly based on the injured spouse's right.[10]

The Effect of Comparative Negligence

Comparative negligence, in and of itself, has not changed these basic principles. When negligence is apportioned in the presence of vicarious liability, the master bears the burden of his servant's negligence.[11] If the master has been partially at fault, the percentage of negligence attributed to the servant is added to the percentage attributed to the master.[12]

The same approach is taken in imputing contributory negligence. Thus, in *Johnsen v. Pierce*[13] a mother and son on a mutually agreed upon journey in a jointly owned car were found to be engaged in a joint venture. The negligence of the driver-son was imputed to the mother and barred her claim against a third party. Similarly, in *Stuart v. Winnie*[14] when a son was found to be driving as his mother's agent, his negligence was imputed to bar her claim. Other comparative negli-

---

[10]Id.

[11]See Dearing v. Ferrell, 165 F. Supp. 508 (W.D. Ark. 1958); Pennebaker v. Parker, 232 Miss. 725, 100 So. 2d 363 (1958); Sears, Roebuck & Co. v. Creekmore, 199 Miss. 48, 23 So. 2d 250 (1945); Loper v. Yazoo & M. V. R. Co., 166 Miss. 79, 145 So. 743 (1933); Hall v. McDonald, 229 Wis. 472, 282 N.W. 561 (1938) (cases under comparative negligence in which employers are subject to vicarious liability for actions of employees within the scope of their employment). In determining whether a negligent shipowner is entitled to indemnity from the employer of a contributorily negligent longshoreman, the longshoreman's negligence will be imputed to his employer. Santiago Martinez v. Compagnie Generale Transatlantique, 517 F.2d 371 (1st Cir. P.R. 1975). However, the longshoreman's negligence will not be imputed to the stevedore if it did not arise out of a breach of the employer's warranty of workmanlike performance. Carrillo v. Samaeit Westbulk, 385 F. Supp. 119 (D. P.R. 1974), affd. in part and vacated in part, 514 F.2d 1214 (1st Cir. P.R. 1975) (modified only as to award of fees to counsel).

[12]See Ismil v. L. H. Sowles Co., 295 Minn. 120, 203 N.W.2d 354 (1972) (error of trial court in holding master vicariously liable despite loaned servant doctrine was not prejudicial when master was independently liable for direct negligence in furnishing an incompetent operator, and plaintiff was not contributorily negligent).

[13]Johnsen v. Pierce, 262 Wis. 367, 55 N.W.2d 394 (1952). But see Edlebeck v. Hooten, 20 Wis. 2d 83, 121 N.W.2d 240 (1963), confining the concept of "joint adventure" to business enterprises.

[14]Stuart v. Winnie, 217 Wis. 298, 258 N.W. 611 (1935).

gence states have also continued to impute contributory negligence.[15] However, Washington saw fit, when it adopted pure comparative negligence, to abolish interspousal imputed contributory negligence.[16]

Florida continues to impute contributory negligence in some situations.[17] New York has abolished imputed negligence for all practical purposes,[18] although in some situations one may achieve the same result through respondeat superior or statutory remedies.[19]

Dissatisfaction with the "Both Ways" Test

It should be noted that in general tort law there has been considerable dissatisfaction with the "both ways" test.[20] This is because the reasons underlying vicarious liability do not always support the imputation of contributory negligence. For example, in *Weber v. Stokely-Van Camp, Incorporated*[21] the Supreme Court of Minnesota declined to impute a servant's contributory negligence to bar his master's claim for damage to an automobile. The court indicated that a basic reason for

---

[15]See, e.g., Hass v. Kessell, 245 Ark. 361, 432 S.W.2d 842 (1968) (dictum) (driver's negligence not imputed to occupant but might have been if occupant had directed driver in commission of the negligent acts); Petersen v. Schneider, 154 Neb. 303, 47 N.W.2d 863 (1951) (dictum) (negligence of driver not imputed to owner-passenger but would be in cases of agency or joint enterprise, or where the owner is the operator's employer or directs or exercises control over the operation of the automobile); Schoenrock v. Sisseton, 78 S.D. 419, 103 N.W.2d 649 (1960) (by implication) (negligence of husband-driver not imputed to wife-passenger in absence of evidence that the wife exercised control or was engaged in a joint enterprise; implies that if one of these factors had been present, the result would be different); Helton v. Missouri P. R. Co., 260 Ark. 342, 538 S.W.2d 569 (1976) (dicta) (driver's negligence not imputable to passenger on theory of joint enterprise unless passenger shared responsibility of control); Beck v. Wessel, 90 S.D. 107, 237 N.W.2d 905 (1976) (the negligence of a passenger may not be imputed to the driver simply because they are husband and wife); Dimond v. Kling, 221 N.W.2d 86 (N.D. 1974) (two minors may not be members of a joint enterprise for the purpose of imputing contributory negligence); Central of G. R. Co. v. Luther, 128 Ga. App. 178, 196 S.E.2d 149 (1973); Steedley v. Snowden, 138 Ga. App. 155, 225 S.E.2d 703 (1976); Jones v. Petroleum Carrier Corp., 483 F.2d 1369 (5th Cir. Ga. 1973); Martinez v. Union P. R. Co., 714 F.2d 1028 (10th Cir. Wyo. 1983); Thomas Oil, Inc. v. Onsgaard, 298 Minn. 465, 215 N.W.2d 793 (1974). Cf. Hover v. Clamp, 40 Colo. App. 410, 579 P.2d 1181 (1978) (husband/driver's negligence will be imputed to wife/passenger in her claim against him because she was the owner of the car).

[16]Wash. Rev. Code Ann., § 4.22.020.

[17]Acevedo v. Acosta, 296 So. 2d 526 (Fla. App. 1974) (negligence of driver imputable to owner). However, there is no interspousal imputed contributory negligence. See, e.g., Gilmore v. Morrison, 314 So. 2d 5 (Fla. App. 1975).

[18]State v. Popricki, 89 A.D.2d 391, 456 N.Y.S.2d 850 (1982) (imputed negligence has been abolished both in master/servant and agent/principal relationships). See also Bibergal v. McCormick, 101 Misc. 2d 794, 421 NY.S.2d 978 (1979), citing legislative history indicating that imputed negligence is to be applied narrowly, if at all, under the comparative fault act.

[19]State v. Popricki, 89 A.D.2d 391, 456 N.Y.S.2d 850 (1982) (state is obligated by statute to compensate victims for the negligence of its employees).

[20]See 2 F. Harper & F. James, note 1 above, § 23.6; *Restatement (Second) of Torts* § 485, Comment a at 541 (1965); Gregory, *Vicarious Responsibility and Contributory Negligence*, 41 Yale L.J. 831 (1932); Comment, *Imputed Contributory Negligence—Not Imputed under Automobile Owner's Liability When Passenger in Car—Imputed Contributory Negligence*, 1 Willamette L.J. 528 (1961).

[21]Weber v. Stokely-Van Camp, Inc., 274 Minn. 482, 144 N.W.2d 540 (1966).

vicarious liability of a master is to reach a financially responsible party, and that this does not justify imputing the servant's negligence to bar a master's claim against a third person.[22] The abandonment of the "both ways" test has proceeded apace in Minnesota and has had some minor impact in other states.[23]

Weber v. Stokely-Van Camp, Incorporated was given prospective effect only; however, in a case arising before the effective date of *Weber*, the Minnesota Supreme Court declined to find the necessary agency relationship to impute negligence.[24]

It should be noted that neither in Minnesota nor in other states has comparative negligence been cited as a reason for or against abandoning the "both ways" rule. The Minnesota decision occurred before that state adopted comparative negligence. Further, a number of comparative negligence states have continued to apply the "both ways" test.[25] Thus, today, reconsideration and change in the imputing of contributory negligence has taken place independently of comparative negligence. Nevertheless, a state might find the inception of comparative negligence a stimulus for examining the continued viability of the "both ways" test and whether contributory negligence should continue to be imputed. Comparative negligence is predicated on the general idea that damages should be allocated on the basis of fault; the "both ways" test does not serve that purpose.

16.2 Joinder of defendants

Comparative negligence may have significant effect in many ways when the liability of joint and several tortfeasors is involved. This is an area of substantive law and should be kept separate from procedural joinder of parties.[26] Procedural joinder rules present few, if any, problems under comparative negligence.

Under broad rules of joinder persons may be brought in as defen-

---

[22]Id., 274 Minn. at 487-488, 144 N.W.2d at 543, citing Christensen v. Hennepin Transp. Co., 215 Minn. 394, 413, 10 N.W.2d 406, 417, 147 A.L.R. 945 (1943). The negligence of the servant will still be imputed to the master in other situations. See Clay County v. Burlington Northern, Inc., 296 Minn. 463, 209 N.W.2d 420 (1973) (*Weber* rule will not be extended to municipal corporations); Thomas Oil, Inc. v. Onsgaard, 298 Minn. 465, 215 N.W.2d 793 (1974) (employee's negligence will be imputed to corporation); but see Smedsrud v. Brown, 303 Minn. 330, 227 N.W.2d 572 (1975) (negligence of bailee of automobile not imputable to bailor).

[23]Pinaglia v. Beaulieu, 28 Conn. Supp. 90, 250 A.2d 522 (1969) (contributory negligence of driver of family car not imputed to bar claim of owner); Johnson v. Los Angeles-Seattle Motor Express, Inc., 222 Ore. 377, 352 P.2d 1091 (1960) (justification for imputing negligence of driver to car owner is not present in owner's action against third party; owner's claim is not barred in absence of actual negligence).

[24]Bray v. Chicago, R. I. & P. R. Co., 305 Minn. 31, 232 N.W.2d 97 (1975) (passenger gratuitously aided plaintiff in cornshelling).

[25]See, e.g., Wilson v. Great N. R. Co., 83 S.D. 207, 157 N.W.2d 19 (1968); notes 13 to 15 above.

[26]See W. P. Keeton et al., *Prosser and Keeton on the Law of Torts* § 47 (5th ed. 1984). Accord, Gilson v. Mitchell, 131 Ga. App. 321, 205 S.E.2d 421 (1974), affd. 233 Ga. 453, 211 S.E.2d 744 (1975).

dants against whom there is asserted any right to relief arising out of
the same transaction, occurrence or series of transactions and occurrences, if a question of law or fact is common to all defendants.[27] This
is more inclusive than the common-law rule permitting only joint
tortfeasors to be joined by the plaintiff.[28] Comparative negligence has
not and will not necessitate any change in the new broad procedural
joinder rules.

The Kansas comparative negligence statute specifically provides for
the joinder of any other person whose causal negligence is claimed to
have contributed to the injury. This procedure can be implemented by
motion of any person against whom a claim is asserted.[29] At the same
time, a potential party's fault will be assessed whether or not he is
joined.[30] The Kansas Supreme Court has held that once a party is
joined, failure to assert a claim against any party so joined causes the
claim to be forever barred. A person not a party is not so bound.[31] California also allows defendants to bring in co-defendants but allows the
trial judge discretion to sever claims.[32]

Value of Joinder Under Comparative Negligence

On occasion the procedural safety valve that appears in a number of
state codes permitting the court to "order separate trials or make other
orders to prevent delay or prejudice" may be utilized to avoid joinder in
a particular action.[33] In general, however, joinder will be helpful in
comparative negligence. The defendants may be joined and negligence

---

[27]E.g., Fed. R. Civ. P. 20(a).

If a joint tortfeasor is not joined as a defendant, a party joined may bring him in on a
third-party complaint if that third party"... is or may be liable ... to them for all or part
of the plaintiff's claim...." See Fed. R. Civ. P. 14(a); Gerrard v. Larsen, 517 F.2d 1127
(8th Cir. N.D. 1975); Dawn v. Essex Conveyors, Inc., 379 F. Supp. 1342 (E.D. Tenn. 1973);
Shiver v. Burnside Terminal Co., 392 F. Supp. 1078 (E.D. La. 1975); Markey v. Skog, 129
N.J. Super. 192, 322 A.2d 513 (1974); see also Mihoy v. Proulx, 113 N.H. 698, 313 A.2d 723
(1973) (a defendant may not implead a party for purposes of apportioning liability who
has received a covenant not to sue from the plaintiff); Zerby v. Warren, 297 Minn. 134,
210 N.W.2d 58 (1973) (a defendant held strictly liable under a statute prohibiting the sale
of glue to minors may not implead as third party defendants the manufacturer or a
minor companion of the deceased to establish a right to contribution or indemnity). But
see Greenwood v. McDonough Power Equipment, Inc., 437 F. Supp. 707 (D. Kan. 1977)
(refusal to join parties whose inclusion would destroy diversity jurisdiction; reconciliation
of federal with state jurisdiction by considering negligence of nonparties in allocating
liability for damage award) (citing this treatise).

[28]F. James & G. Hazard, *Civil Procedure* § 10.7 (1977).

[29]Kan. Stat. Ann., § 60-258a. See Miles v. West, 224 Kan. 284, 580 P.2d 876 (1978);
Brown v. Keill, 224 Kan. 195, 580 P.2d 867 (1978). See also Albertson v. Volkswagen
Aktiengesellschaft, 230 Kan. 368, 634 P.2d 1127 (1981) (product liability claim against
auto manufacturer must be brought at the same time as claims against other parties to
the accident), noted, 21 Washburn L.J. 725 (1982).

[30]McGraw v. Sanders Co. Plumbing & Heating, Inc., 233 Kan. 766, 667 P.2d 289 (1983);
accord, Hefley v. Textron, Inc., 713 F.2d 1487 (10th Cir. Kan. 1983).

[31]Eurich v. Alkire, 224 Kan. 236, 579 P.2d 1207 (1978).

[32]American Motorcycle Assn. v. Superior Court of Los Angeles County, 20 Cal. 3d 578,
146 Cal. Rptr. 182, 578 P.2d 899, 901 (1978).

[33]E.g., Fed. R. Civ. P. 20(b).

may be apportioned so that a multiplicity of lawsuits is avoided. When there is more than one transaction or occurrence involving more than one defendant and resulting in separate injuries, the negligence is apportioned separately for each transaction.[34]

In *Dulman v. Seaboard Coast Line Railroad Company*,[35] a Florida case, the trial court went so far as to dismiss a complaint without prejudice for failure to join a possible tortfeasor. The court of appeals, however, reversed, holding the plaintiff had a right to sue any or all of the possible joint tortfeasors.[36]

16.3 Joint tortfeasors under comparative negligence

The substantive law category of joint tortfeasors has been enlarged in recent times. It once consisted only of those tortfeasors who acted in concert. Today it includes any defendants whose tortious conduct has made a substantial contribution to the cause of a single, indivisible injury.[37] Traditionally, a number of legal consequences may flow from characterization of parties as joint tortfeasors.

First, there is the rule that the release of one joint tortfeasor releases all.[38] Most states have modified this doctrine by allowing covenants not to sue as a way around it or by making statutory provision for settlements with one of several joint tortfeasors not acting as a release of the other.[39] Some comparative negligence jurisdictions have enacted release statutes allowing the effect of a settlement to be based on proportionate fault as well as cash amount.[40]

Second, there is the rule prohibiting contribution between joint tortfeasors.[41] Rules regarding contribution will not necessarily be changed by the introduction of comparative negligence, but, as shown

---

[34]For example, the negligence which caused plaintiff to contract a disease could be the subject of one apportionment. A second apportionment could be made of negligence which aggravated the disease some time later. See Poster v. Central Gulf S.S. Corp., 25 F.R.D. 18 (E.D. Pa. 1960).

[35]Dulman v. Seaboard C. L. R. Co., 308 So. 2d 53 (Fla. App. 1975).

[36]Id.

[37]F. James & G. Hazard, *Civil Procedure* § 10.8, at 469 (1977). See Leib v. Tampa, 326 So. 2d 52 (Fla. App. 1976) (designer of intersection and grossly negligent driver characterized as joint tortfeasors); but see Welter v. Curry, 260 Ark. 287, 539 S.W.2d 264 (1976) (if the injured party has no legal remedy against a party whose tortious conduct contributed to an injury, that party is not a joint tortfeasor). See also Johnson v. Heintz, 73 Wis. 2d 286, 243 N.W.2d 815 (1976); Sims v. Bryan, 140 Ga. App. 69, 230 S.E.2d 39 (1976) (multiple collisions resulting in a single indivisible injury make individual negligent parties joint tortfeasors).

[38]1 F. Harper & F. James, *The Law of Torts* § 10.1, at 711 (1956); W. P. Keeton et al., *Prosser and Keeton on the Law of Torts* § 49 (5th ed. 1984).

[39]W. P. Keeton et al., note 38 above, § 49, at 333-334.

[40]See, e.g., Idaho Code Ann., § 6-805 (remaining claim reduced by either dollar amount or proportionate share of fault); Utah Code Ann., § 78-27-42 (proportionate share or amount of consideration paid for settlement).

[41]1 F. Harper & F. James, note 38 above, § 10.2; W. P. Keeton et al., note 38 above, § 50.

in section 16.7, many comparative negligence states allow contribution.

Third, there is the rule providing that each joint tortfeasor is jointly and severally liable for plaintiff's entire loss.[42] This rule may create complications under comparative negligence. Some comparative negligence statutes are specific in stating that, "joint tortfeasor means one of two or more persons jointly or severally liable in tort for the same injury to person or property, whether or not judgment has been recovered against all or some of them."[43] The Maine statute provides for joint and several liability, but permits any defendant to have the percentage of his fault determined in the principal action by a special interrogatory to the jury.[44] Other state statutes are not so specific.[45] In all states problems may arise as to precisely how joint and several liability is to be handled. They will be considered in section 16.4.

16.4 Joint and several liability of joint tortfeasors

The concept of joint and several liability of tortfeasors has been retained under comparative negligence, unless the statute specifically abolishes it, in most states that have been called upon to decide the question. As mentioned in section 16.3, some comparative negligence statutes expressly provide that joint tortfeasors shall remain severally liable to the plaintiff for the whole award.[46]

There is a minority trend in the direction of abrogating the common-law doctrine of joint and several liability. A Wisconsin federal district court held a manufacturer-defendant responsible only for his own

---

As of 1985 only a few states, other than those that have abolished joint and several liability under comparative negligence, retained the common-law rule. See, e.g., Sherman Concrete Pipe Machinery, Inc. v. Gadsden Concrete & Metal Pipe Co., Inc., 335 So. 2d 125 (Ala. 1976); Knight v. Autumn Co., 271 S.C. 112, 245 S.E.2d 602 (1978); Ind. Code, § 34-4-33-7.

[42]1 F. Harper & F. James, note 38 above, § 10.1; W. P. Keeton et al., note 38 above, § 47. Accord, Echeverria v. Barczak, 308 So. 2d 633 (Fla. App. 1975); Little v. Miller, 311 So. 2d 116 (Fla. App. 1975); Randle-Eastern Ambulance Service, Inc. v. Millens, 294 So. 2d 38 (Fla. App. 1974); Walker v. U-Haul Co., 300 So. 2d 289 (Fla. App. 1974); Winzler & Kelly v. Superior Court of Humboldt County, 48 Cal. App. 3d 385, 122 Cal. Rptr. 259 (1975).

[43]See, e.g., Idaho Code, § 6-803(4); Utah Code Ann., § 78-27-40(3); Wyo. Stat., § 1.7.3(d). Some statutes provide for contribution between jointly liable persons with each remaining jointly and severally liable for the whole award. Minn. Stat. Ann., § 604.01, subd. 1; N.J. Stat. Ann., § 2A:15-5.3; N.D. Cent. Code, § 9-10-07. Texas provides for joint and several liability, except that a defendant who was less negligent than plaintiff may be held for no more than his proportionate share. Tex. Rev. Civ. Stat. Ann. (Vernon), art. 2212a, § 2(c).

The North Dakota Supreme Court determined in Bartels v. Williston, 276 N.W.2d 113, 121 (N.D. 1979) that joint and several liability is for the benefit of an injured party and may be waived by the injured party.

[44]Me. Rev. Stat. Ann., tit. 14, § 156.

[45]For example, in providing for contribution, some statutes do not mention joint and several liability. N.H. Rev. Stat. Ann., § 507:7-a; Vt. Stat. Ann. 1959, tit. 12, § 1036.

[46]See notes 43 and 44, section 16.3 above.

causal negligence.[47] The Wisconsin comparative negligence statute does not, however, specifically abolish joint and several liability.[48] Oklahoma courts apply joint and several liability when the plaintiff has not been negligent; otherwise, each defendant is severally liable.[49] The Oklahoma comparative negligence statute is silent on the issue.[50]

The comparative negligence statutes of Kansas,[51] New Hampshire,[52] Pennsylvania,[53] and Vermont[54] all use similar language that may be construed to abolish joint and several liability.[55] However, the New Hampshire courts, while generally refusing to impose joint liability on multiple tortfeasors, do place the entire liability on remaining defendants when the plaintiff cannot recover from a defendant because of immunities or other procedural bars.[56] Courts in both Pennsylvania[57] and Vermont[58] have upheld joint and several liability, while Kansas courts have done the reverse.[59] The Ohio statute, which uses slightly different language, appears to abolish joint and several liability.[60]

A few states have modified joint and several liability by limiting it to defendants who were more at fault than the plaintiff.[61] In other

---

[47]Soeldner v. White Metal Rolling & Stamping Corp., 473 F. Supp. 753 (E.D. Wis. 1979) (court applied dicta from May v. Skelly Oil Co., 83 Wis. 2d 30, 264 N.W.2d 574 (1978)). In the *Soeldner* decision, the court limited its holding to those instances in which a plaintiff has a separate remedy against his employer by way of a workmen's compensation claim. Id., at 756.

[48]Wis. Stat. Ann., § 895.045.

[49]Anderson v. O'Donoghue, 677 P.2d 648 (Okla. 1983); Laubach v. Morgan, 588 P.2d 1071 (Okla. 1978).

[50]Okla. Stat. Ann., tit. 23, §§ 12 to 14.

[51]Kan. Stat. Ann., § 60-258a(d).

[52]N.H. Rev. Stat. Ann., § 507.7a.

[53]Pa. Stat. Ann., tit. 42, § 7102.

[54]Vt. Stat. Ann., tit. 12, § 1036.

[55]E.g., Kan. Stat. Ann., § 60-658a(d):
[E]ach such party shall be liable for that portion of the total dollar amount awarded as damages to any claimant in the proportion that the amount of his or her causal negligence bears to the amount of the causal negligence attributed to all parties against whom such recovery is allowed.

[56]Simonsen v. Barlo Plastics Co., 551 F.2d 469 (1st Cir. N.H. 1977); Mihoy v. Proulx, 113 N.H. 698, 313 A.2d 723 (1973).

[57]Sirianni v. Nugent Bros., Inc., 480 A.2d 285 (Pa. Super. 1984); Reilly v. Southeastern Pennsylvania Transp. Auth., 479 A.2d 973 (Pa. Super. 1984), clarified 484 A.2d 1390 (Pa. Super. 1984).

[58]English v. Myers, 142 Vt. 144, 454 A.2d 251 (1982).

[59]Brown v. Keill, 224 Kan. 195, 580 P.2d 867 (1978). The court cited this treatise and, at p. 873, cited Schwartz, *Comparative Negligence in Kansas—Legal Issues and Probable Answers*, 13 Washburn L.J. 397, 416 (1974). See also Geier v. Wikel, 4 Kan. App. 2d 188, 603 P.2d 1028 (1979).

[60]Ohio Rev. Code Ann., § 2315.19(A)(2). See Stearns v. Johns-Manville Sales Corp., No. C79-2088 (N.D. Ohio February 17, 1984), citing this treatise. See also Note, *Ohio's Comparative Negligence Statute: The Effect on Joint and Several Liability, Absent Defendants and Joinder*, 50 U. Cin. L. Rev. 342 (1981).

[61]Nev. Rev. Stat., § 41.141(3)(a); Ore. Rev. Stat., § 18.485; Tex. Rev. Civ. Stat. Ann. (Vernon), art. 2212a, § 2(c). Iowa goes further and limits joint and several liability to a defendant who bears at least 50% of the total fault. Iowa Code Ann., § 668.4.

states, such as Wisconsin,[62] Mississippi[63] and Georgia,[64] courts have determined that each joint tortfeasor remains severally liable to the plaintiff for the entire award. In operation this means that if plaintiff was 20% negligent, defendant A was 25% liable and defendant B was 55% liable, plaintiff could recover 80% of his damages from defendant A. If forced to pay the full 80%, defendant A's remedy against B, if any, would be through contribution. That is why it is vital in any comparative negligence system to permit contribution among joint tortfeasors.[65]

New Mexico judicially abolished joint and several liability shortly after adopting comparative negligence.[66] The court said that the "indivisible wrong" concept was obsolete, as it was based on common-law pleading rules, and that there was no good reason to favor the plaintiff in a situation where the identity of the plaintiff in a multiple-party case might be determined by a race to the courthouse.

Since 1973, the following state courts have indicated that tortfeasors remain jointly and severally liable: Arkansas,[67] Colorado,[68] Oregon,[69] Idaho,[70] Washington,[71] California[72] and West Virginia.[73] However, the courts do allow some equitable adjustments approaching

---

[62]Caldwell v. Piggly Wiggly Madison Co., 32 Wis. 2d 447, 145 N.W.2d 745 (1966); Walker v. Kroger Grocery & Baking Co., 214 Wis. 519, 252 N.W. 721, 92 A.L.R. 680 (1934); Dertz v. Pasquina, 59 Ill. 2d 68, 319 N.E.2d 12 (1974) (Wisconsin law). The courts in Wisconsin are recognizing limited exceptions to the general rule of joint and several liability for the purpose of avoiding unfair and inequitable results. E.g., Soeldner v. White Metal Rolling & Stamping Corp., 473 F. Supp. 753 (E.D. Wis. 1979); May v. Skelly Oil Co., 83 Wis. 2d 30, 264 N.W.2d 574 (1978); but see Reiter v. Dyken, 95 Wis. 2d 461, 290 N.W.2d 510 (1980) and Wisconsin Natural Gas Co. v. Ford, Bacon & Davis Constr. Corp., 96 Wis. 2d 314, 291 N.W.2d 825 (1980). See section 16.6.

[63]Saucier v. Walker, 203 So. 2d 299 (Miss. 1967); Gillespie v. Olive Branch Bldg. & Lumber Co., 174 Miss. 154, 164 So. 42 (1935).

[64]Gazaway v. Nicholson, 190 Ga. 345, 9 S.E.2d 154 (1940); Hightower v. Landrum, 109 Ga. App. 510, 136 S.E.2d 425 (1964); Akin v. Randolph Motors, Inc., 95 Ga. App. 841, 99 S.E.2d 358 (1957).

[65]See section 16.7.

[66]Bartlett v. New Mexico Welding Supply, Inc., 98 N.M. 152, 646 P.2d 579 (App. 1982), cert. den. 98 N.M. 336, 648 P.2d 794 (1982).

[67]Wheeling Pipe Line, Inc. v. Edrington, 259 Ark. 600, 535 S.W.2d 225 (1976).

[68]Dunham v. Kampman, 37 Colo. App. 233, 547 P.2d 263 (1975), affd. 192 Colo. 448, 560 P.2d 91 (1977).

[69]Rice v. Hyster Co., 273 Ore. 191, 540 P.2d 989 (1975).

[70]Tucker v. Union Oil Co., 100 Idaho 590, 603 P.2d 156 (1979). See Idaho Code, § 6-804.

[71]Seattle First Nat. Bank v. Shoreline Concrete Co., 91 Wash. 2d 230, 588 P.2d 1308 (1978). See also Wash. Rev. Code Ann., § 4.22.030.

[72]Mattschei v. United States, 600 F.2d 205 (9th Cir. Cal. 1979); Adams v. Cerritos Trucking Co., 79 Cal. App. 3d 957, 145 Cal. Rptr. 310 (1978); American Motorcycle Assn. v. Superior Court of Los Angeles County, 20 Cal. 3d 578, 146 Cal. Rptr. 182, 578 P.2d 899 (1978) (citing this treatise).

[73]Bradley v. Appalachian Power Co., 163 W.Va. 332, 256 S.E.2d 879, 886 (1979).

apportionment,[74] such as comparative contribution. Florida's legislature has adopted a rule preserving joint and several liability and allowing contribution based on proportionate fault.[75]

The Minnesota Supreme Court has held that a defendant will only be jointly and severally liable when the plaintiff is free from negligence that would bar his recovery under that state's modified comparative negligence doctrine.[76] Thus, a plaintiff who was 10% negligent could not recover from a defendant who was also 10% negligent. His only recovery would be against a defendant whose negligence exceeded his own.

16.5 Comparison of negligence of tortfeasors not joined as defendants

Where one or more joint tortfeasors are not parties to a negligence action under comparative negligence, it is important to determine whether the comparison will include the negligence of the absent tortfeasors or will be made solely with regard to the parties to the action. Most present comparative negligence statutes do not answer this question with precision.

The Absent Tortfeasor Shielded from Liability

The question was determined in Wisconsin in *Walker v. Kroger Grocery and Baking Company.*[77] There the plaintiff-passengers' host driver was effectively absent from the action because plaintiffs' claim against him was barred by the then extant Wisconsin doctrine of assumption of risk. In the passengers' action against the driver of another vehicle, the trial court instructed the jury to compare the passengers' negligence against the combined negligence of the two drivers. The Supreme Court held that this was proper even though the host driver was shielded by the assumption of risk defense from liability for contribution. The Supreme Court regarded this result as merely an application

---

[74]In an effort to prevent unfair results and unjust enrichment, the courts will, in many instances, modify the harsh joint and several liability rule. When a plaintiff has already recovered workmen's compensation benefits, the courts will deduct the amount of such benefits from judgments rendered against other tortfeasors. See, e.g., Tucker v. Union Oil Co., 100 Idaho 590, 603 P.2d 156 (1979). Courts typically suggest an equitable action for partial indemnification in the same suit determining negligence and liability; Seattle First Nat. Bank v. Shoreline Concrete Co., 91 Wash. 2d 230, 588 P.2d 1308 (1978); American Motorcycle Assn. v. Superior Court of Los Angeles County, 20 Cal. 3d 578, 146 Cal. Rptr. 182, 578 P.2d 899 (1978) (partial indemnity based on comparative negligence); Mattschei v. United States, 600 F.2d 205 (9th Cir. Cal. 1979). See also Adams v. Cerritos Trucking Co., 79 Cal. App. 3d 957, 145 Cal. Rptr. 310 (1978) (equitable modification of judgment).

[75]Fla. Stat. Ann., § 768.31, as amended in 1976, superseding Lincenberg v. Issen, 318 So. 2d 386 (Fla. 1975); Moore v. St. Cloud Utilities,, 337 So. 2d 982 (Fla. App. 1976), cert. den. 337 So. 2d 809 (Fla. 1976), revd. 355 So. 2d 446 (Fla. App. 1978); Warn Industries v. Geist, 343 So. 2d 44 (Fla. App. 1977); see also Blocker v. Wynn, 425 So. 2d 166 (Fla. App. 1983).

[76]Kowalske v. Armour & Co., 300 Minn. 301, 220 N.W.2d 268 (1974).

[77]Walker v. Kroger Grocery & Baking Co., 214 Wis. 519, 252 N.W. 721, 92 A.L.R.2d 680 (1934).

of the Wisconsin doctrine of joint and several liability of each tortfeasor for all damages recoverable by plaintiff.

In *Ross v. Koberstein,*[78] a passenger brought action against the driver of another vehicle but did not join the driver of his own vehicle as a defendant. The trial court instructed the jury to compare the plaintiff's negligence with that of the in-court defendant only. Although this was wrong, the Supreme Court of Wisconsin said, *defendant* was not prejudiced by it. If plaintiff's negligence had been properly compared with the combined negligence of the two drivers, the result could not have been less favorable to the plaintiff and might even have been more favorable. Wisconsin has long taken the position that all tortfeasors are jointly and severally liable. Therefore, the addition of the out-of-court tortfeasor's percentage of negligence would not reduce the amount of defendant's liability.

In a state where joint tortfeasors are not jointly and severally liable under comparative negligence, the defendant would be prejudiced and defendant's argument in *Ross v. Koberstein* would be more persuasive. Under those conditions, if the other tortfeasor were brought in and the jury had an opportunity to look at the case as a whole, it might find defendant only 60% at fault instead of 95%. If defendant is liable only for a part of the damages proportionate to his own negligence, the amount of damages for which he is liable would be reduced.

A result more compatible with the goals of comparative negligence is reached by determining the negligence of all concurrent tortfeasors irrespective of whether they are parties to the suit. The Kansas Supreme Court has held that the negligence of all defendants must be determined whether one or more defendants has a valid defense.[79] A Kansas lower court has stated that "the proportionate fault of all parties to the occurrence is to be determined even though one or more of them is not a party to the action and is unable to pay, or cannot be required for any reason to pay his or her proportionate fault."[80] The Supreme Court of California similarly holds that the negligence of all tortfeasors should be determined whether or not joined as defendants,[81] as does the Supreme Court of Minnesota.[82] A federal district court in Hawaii held that the comparative fault of the United States government could be ascertained under the Federal Tort Claims Act even though the plaintiff's employer, a contractor to the Navy, was immune

---

[78]Ross v. Koberstein, 220 Wis. 73, 264 N.W. 642 (1936).

[79]Brown v. Keill, 224 Kan. 195, 580 P.2d 867 (1978) (valid defense of sovereign immunity and covenant not to sue).

[80]Geier v. Wikel, 4 Kan. App. 2d 188, 603 P.2d 1028, 1030 (1979) (release).

[81]American Motorcycle Assn. v. Superior Court of Los Angeles County, 20 Cal. 3d 578, 589 n.2, 146 Cal. Rptr. 182, 189 n.2, 578 P.2d 899, 902 (1978). See also Transit Casualty Co. v. Spink Corp., 94 Cal. App. 3d 124, 156 Cal. Rptr. 360 (1979).

[82]Lines v. Ryan, 272 N.W.2d 896 (Minn. 1978).

from suit for contribution under worker's compensation law.[83] This results in the determination of the negligence of a "phantom" defendant, a defendant who is not a party to the suit, but whose negligence contributed to the injury, a strategy sometimes called the "empty chair" defense.

The new Indiana comparative negligence statute makes specific provisions for consideration of the fault of "nonparties." The statute creates a "nonparty defense," in which a defendant may plead and prove that the damages were caused by someone else.[84] Special verdicts must include the name and amount of fault charged to a nonparty found to be at fault.[85] The nonparty's fault counts in determining whether the plaintiff's fault is greater than that of all defendants.[86]

Many courts do not recognize a "phantom" defendant. Florida permits only the negligence of parties joined to be considered.[87] A similar rule applies in Oregon[88] and Montana.[89] In South Dakota, an immune party's negligence will not be considered in the apportionment of negligence.[90] The Uniform Comparative Fault Act limits allocation of fault to parties to the lawsuit.[91]

Settlement by Joint Tortfeasor

Failure to consider the causal negligence of a joint tortfeasor who has settled and been released by plaintiff may be ground for a successful appeal by the nonsettling defendant. This is true where the release provides for discharge of that percentage of plaintiff's damages attributable to the causal negligence of the settling tortfeasor. The Supreme Court of Wisconsin considered this problem in *Pierringer v. Hoger*.[92] The court noted that the issue between the plaintiff and the nonsettling tortfeasor was the percentage of that tortfeasor's negligence, but that this percentage could be determined only by an allocation of *all* the causal negligence of all the tortfeasors. The judgment against the nonsettling defendant would be in proportion to the percentage of negli-

---

[83]Barron v. United States, 473 F. Supp. 1077, 1088 (D. Hawaii 1979), affd. in part and revd. in part 654 F.2d 644 (9th Cir. Hawaii 1981). The court distinguished Sugue v. F. L. Smithe Machine Co., 56 Hawaii 598, 546 P.2d 527 (1976), supp. op. 57 Hawaii 78, 549 P.2d 1150 (1978) a case disallowing the "empty chair" defense, by saying it was really assessing the fault of the defendant, not that of the absent tortfeasor!

[84]Ind. Code, § 34-4-33-5.

[85]Ind. Code, § 34-4-33-6.

[86]Ind. Code, § 34-4-33-4(2).

[87]See, e.g., Kapchuck v. Orlan, 332 So. 2d 671 (Fla. App. 1976); Blocker v. Wynn, 425 So. 2d 166 (Fla. App. 1983).

[88]Conner v. Mertz, 274 Ore. 657, 548 P.2d 975 (1976).

[89]Consolidated Freightways Corp. v. Osier, 185 Mont. 439, 605 P.2d 1076 (1979).

[90]Beck v. Wessel, 90 S.D. 107, 237 N.W.2d 905 (1976).

[91]Unif. Comparative Fault Act, § 2, Comment, 12 U.L.A. 39, 43 (Supp. 1985).

[92]Pierringer v. Hoger, 21 Wis. 2d 182, 124 N.W.2d 106 (1963). Accord, Connar v. West Shore Equipment, Inc., 68 Wis. 2d 42, 227 N.W.2d 660 (1975); Reddington v. Beefeaters Tables, Inc., 72 Wis. 2d 119, 240 N.W.2d 363 (1976), modified 243 N.W.2d 401 (Wis. 1976). Heathcote v. Sturgeon, Docket No. 47915 (Cal. App. 1977).

gence attributed to him, as the balance of plaintiff's claim had been satisfied by the release of the other tortfeasors.

When, as in *Pierringer*, plaintiff has settled with some of the tortfeasors, has given releases protecting those tortfeasors against subsequent liability for contribution, and proceeds to trial against nonsettling tortfeasors, it is in the plaintiff's interest to obtain a verdict attributing a high percentage of the causal negligence to defendants. Plaintiff's strategy, therefore, is not only to show that his own negligence was slight or absent but also to show that the negligence of the settling tortfeasors constituted only a small percentage of the total causal negligence. In this respect, plaintiff is stepping into the shoes of the tortfeasors with whom he has settled.

When a plaintiff has settled with a defendant, the courts adjust the judgment in one of two ways: (1) the remaining defendants are entitled to a reduction in the damages by the amount of consideration paid by the settling defendant(s) for the release or covenant not to sue;[93] or (2) there is a reduction in the verdict by the percentage of the causal negligence attributed to the settling defendant(s), thereby limiting the plaintiff's recovery to the percentage of negligence attributed to the remaining nonsettling tortfeasors.[94]

In some states the plaintiff may elect which method to use and stipulate a proportional reduction in the remaining judgment in the settlement agreement.[95] The dollar-for-dollar method sometimes results in inequities if the settlement turns out to be larger than the judgment: the loss is placed entirely on the tortfeasor who settled, a result which goes against the public policy of rewarding settlements. On the other hand, under the percentage method, the plaintiff may receive a windfall if he negotiates a large settlement but then obtains a large judgment and a heavy allocation of fault to the remaining defendants.[96] A New Mexico court, considering this result, said that the plaintiff should receive the benefit of his bargain and that the proportional fault rule would encourage settlements.[97] Of course, it is possible that a plaintiff may accept a small settlement and end up with much less than he would have under the dollar-for-dollar rule.[98]

---

[93]Geier v. Wikel, 4 Kan. App. 2d 188, 603 P.2d 1028 (1979); Deal v. Madison, 576 S.W.2d 409, 420 (Tex. Civ. App. 1978). See also Johnson v. Heintz, 73 Wis. 2d 286, 243 N.W.2d 815 (1976); Arkansas Kraft Corp. v. Johnson, 257 Ark. 629, 519 S.W.2d 74 (1975).

[94]Bartels v. Williston, 276 N.W.2d 113 (N.D. 1979); American Motorcycle Assn. v. Superior Court of Los Angeles County, 20 Cal. 3d 578, 146 Cal. Rptr. 182, 578 P.2d 899 (1978) (citing this treatise); Rogers v. Spady, 147 N.J. Super. 274, 371 A.2d 285 (1977); Simon v. Lambert, 115 N.H. 242, 340 A.2d 101 (1975).

[95]Ark. Stat. Ann., § 34-1004; Del. Code Ann., tit. 6, § 304; Idaho Code, § 6-803; R.I. Gen. Laws, § 10-6-7; S.D. Codified Laws, § 15-8-17. In all five states the claim is reduced dollar for dollar if the consideration for the settlement turns out to be higher than the proportion stipulated.

[96]See, e.g., Wilson v. Galt, 100 N.M. 227, 668 P.2d 1104 (App. 1983).

[97]Id., 668 P.2d at 1109.

[98]See, e.g., Kizer v. Peter Kiewit Sons' Co., 489 F. Supp. 835 (N.D. Calif. 1980) (plaintiff settled what turned out to be two-thirds of a $234,000 claim for $40,000).

In dollar-for-dollar jurisdictions courts have also had to decide whether a settlement should be subtracted before or after the plaintiff's share of fault is applied to the damages. For example, suppose plaintiff's total damages are found to be $100,000, plaintiff is 20% at fault, defendants A and B are each 40% at fault, and defendant A has settled for $50,000. If plaintiff's share of fault is applied first, he receives $80,000 less $50,000, or $80,000 total. If the settlement is subtracted first, he receives 80% of $50,000, or $90,000 total. If defendant A had settled for $30,000 instead of $50,000, the plaintiff would still receive $80,000 under the first method but $86,000 under the second. The first method—subtracting the settlement after deducting for plaintiff's fault—produces more accurate results and reflects the assumption that plaintiff's fault is a factor in settlement negotiations; most states that have considered the question have adopted this calculation method.[99] Michigan appears to be the only state to have adopted the other method, on the ground that it encourages settlements.[1] The Michigan rule may be fairer when the jury is not allowed to consider an absent tortfeasor's fault.[2]

Workers' Compensation

Treatment of multiple defendant cases where one tortfeasor is a statutorily immune employer has become an increasingly vexing problem, especially in the product liability context. Typically, an employee has been injured by a machine, such as a punch press, for which safety devices were feasible but were not used through a combination of manufacturer and employer fault; the employee may also be partly at fault for ignoring instructions or overlooking an obvious danger. Under traditional rules, the employee makes an administrative claim against the employer for workers' compensation benefits consisting of medical expenses and an allowance for lost income, which are granted without regard to fault.[3] At the same time, the employee sues the machine manufacturer through the tort system. In most states the employer may join in the suit through subrogation and is reimbursed for benefits paid if the employee wins.[4] When contributory negligence was the law, a negligent employee would be unable to recover on a negligence cause of action. In most states, the employer's fault would not bar recovery, but in some jurisdictions the negligent employer would be unable to

---

[99]See Lemos v. Eichel, 83 Cal. App. 3d 110, 147 Cal. Rptr. 603 (1978); Peterson v. Multnomah County School Dist., 64 Ore. App. 81, 668 P.2d 385 (1983); Dongo v. Banks, 448 A.2d 885 (Me. 1982); Scott v. Cascade Structures, 100 Wash. 2d 537, 673 P.2d 179 (1983).

[1]See Jackson v. Barton Malow Co., 131 Mich. App. 719, 346 N.W.2d 591 (1984); Rittenhouse v. Erhart, 126 Mich. App. 674, 337 N.W.2d 626 (1983).

[2]Gagnon v. Dresser Industries Corp., 130 Mich. App. 452, 344 N.W.2d 582 (1983); Scott v. Cascade Structures, 100 Wash. 2d 537, 673 P.2d 179, 183-184 (1983) (Utter, J., dissenting).

[3]A. Larson, *Workmen's Compensation* § 1.10 (1984).

[4]A. Larson, note 3 above, § 75.20.

exercise his subrogation right.[5] Almost every state still bars contribution claims by the manufacturer against the employer.[6] Wisconsin makes no provision for a credit for workers' compensation benefits in the judgment against a third-party tortfeasor and requires the third party to pay the full amount of the damages, regardless of the employer's fault.[7]

With the advent of comparative negligence and increasing focus on product liability policy issues,[8] courts have begun reconsidering loss allocation in cases involving an employer. In the wake of Li[9] the California Supreme Court adopted a rule crediting the manufacturer with the employer's proportionate share of damages, not to exceed worker's compensation benefits.[10] In Minnesota the employer is liable in contribution, but only to the extent of worker's compensation benefits.[11] In New York, the court applies a rule of "equitable indemnity," in which the employee recovers full damages from the third party and reimburses the employer for benefits paid; at the same time, the third party collects a proportional share of damages from the employer.[12] Some reformers have been reluctant to tamper with the workers' compensation system,[13] but others have suggested deduction of benefits from damages together with the elimination of contribution and subrogation.[14] Although no method is likely to be perfect in reconciling the policy goals of reasonable compensation for injured workers, fair treatment of all defendants, and minimal transaction costs, this proposal is sound because it eliminates double recoveries and shifts some of the burden to an employer tortfeasor without necessarily making compensation an all-or-nothing proposition for one tortfeasor.

---

[5]E.g., Fireman's Fund Indem. Co. v. United States, 110 F. Supp. 937 (N.D. Fla. 1953), affd. 211 F.2d 773 (5th Cir. Fla. 1954).

[6]A. Larson, note 3 above, § 76.20; Annot., "Modern status of effect of state workmen's compensation act on right of third-person tortfeasor to contribution or idemnity from employer of injured or killed workman," 100 A.L.R.3d 350 (1977).

[7]Mulder v. Acme-Cleveland Corp., 95 Wis. 2d 173, 290 N.W.2d 276 (1980).

[8]See section 12.1.

[9]Nga Li v. Yellow Cab Co., 13 Cal. 3d 804, 119 Cal. Rptr. 858, 532 P.2d 1226, 78 A.L.R.3d 393 (1975).

[10]Associated Constr. & Engineering Co. v. Workers' Compensation Appeals Board, 22 Cal. 3d 829, 150 Cal. Rptr. 888, 587 P.2d 684 (1978); accord, Tucker v. Union Oil Co., 100 Idaho 590, 603 P.2d 156 (1979).

[11]Lambertson v. Cincinnati Corp., 312 Minn. 114, 257 N.W.2d 679, 100 A.L.R.3d 335 (1977); Bjerk v. Universal Engineering Corp., 552 F.2d 1314 (8th Cir. Minn. 1977).

[12]Dole v. Dow Chemical Co., 30 N.Y.2d 143, 331 N.Y.S.2d 382, 282 N.E.2d 288, 53 A.L.R.3d 175 (1972).

[13]See Comment to Unif. Comparative Fault Act, § 6, 12 U.L.A. 48 (Supp. 1985) (see section 21.4), describing several possible approaches but abstaining from the endorsement of any one of them because of substantial variation in the policies behind workers' compensation in the states.

[14]Model Unif. Product Liability Act § 114, reprinted in 44 Fed. Reg. 62,740 (Interagency Task Force on Product Liability, U.S. Dept. of Commerce, 1979); S. 100, 99th Cong., 1st Sess., § 10 (1985); A. Larson, note 3 above, § 76.92(c).

Absent Tortfeasors: Insolvency

At least one comparative negligence state has adopted a provision of the Uniform Comparative Fault Act that attempts to reconcile equitable apportionment and joint liability where one defendant is insolvent at the time of judgment.[15] Within one year after judgment, a party may move to have the share of the insolvent defendant reapportioned among the remaining parties, *including a claimant at fault,* for purposes of contribution and payment of the claim.[16] California has judicially adopted a rule reallocating damages among all defendants according to their percentage of fault.[17]

Denial of Joinder Sought by Plaintiff

The Wisconsin cases have suggested in dictum that plaintiff might have a ground for appeal if he were refused the right to join a tortfeasor in an action.[18] It was suggested in *Ross v. Koberstein* that if plaintiff had joined the additional tortfeasor, the jury would possibly have found that the plaintiff's negligence was less than when it was compared with the negligence of one driver alone. While the court's assumption may be more speculation than precise mathematical logic, obviously the case is important should the problem arise for a plaintiff in any comparative negligence jurisdiction.

Both Kansas[19] and California[20] allow parties to a suit to bring anyone into the action whose negligence might have caused the injury. A party not joined may have his causal negligence determined; however, he is not bound by the action.[21] Failure to make a claim bars all future claims against any party to the suit.[22]

16.6 Comparison of negligence of tortfeasors joined as defendants

It should be understood how negligence is compared between plaintiff and two or more joint tortfeasors who are defendants in the action. Is plaintiff's negligence to be compared with that of each individual defendant? Or should the comparison be made between plaintiff's negligence and the aggregate negligence of all defendants combined?

The determination of this question is especially significant under the 50% system or one of its derivatives. For example, if plaintiff's negligence is 30% and the negligence attributed to three defendants is 25%,

---

[15]Minn. Stat. Ann., § 604.02(2).

[16]Unif. Comparative Fault Act, § 2(d), 12 U.L.A. 43 (Supp. 1985).

[17]Paradise Valley Hospital v. Schlossman, 143 Cal. App. 3d 87, 191 Cal. Rptr. 531 (1983).

[18]Hardware Mut. Cas. Co. v. Harry Crow & Son, Inc., 6 Wis. 2d 396, 94 N.W.2d 577, 583 (1959); Patterson v. Edgerton Sand & Gravel Co., 227 Wis. 11, 277 N.W. 636, 641 (1938); Gross v. Midwest Speedways, Inc., 81 Wis. 2d 129, 260 N.W.2d 36, 40 (1977).

[19]Eurich v. Alkire, 224 Kan. 236, 579 P.2d 1207 (1978).

[20]American Motorcycle Assn. v. Superior Court of Los Angeles County, 20 Cal. 2d 578, 146 Cal. Rptr. 182, 578 P.2d 899, 901 (1978).

[21]Eurich v. Alkire, 224 Kan. 236, 579 P.2d 1207, 1208 (1978).

[22]Id.

25% and 20% respectively, plaintiff cannot recover in a 50% system *if* his negligence is compared with each defendant individually. On the other hand, if plaintiff's negligence is compared with the aggregate negligence of all the tortfeasors, he can recover 70% of his damages.

Statutory Comparison with Combined Negligence

In the states with a modified form of comparative negligence, the statutes of Connecticut,[23] Delaware,[24] New Jersey, [25] Nevada,[26] Ohio,[27] Oklahoma,[28] and Oregon[29] specifically provide for comparison of plaintiff's negligence with the "combined negligence" of multiple defendants.[30] Texas[31] probably achieves the same result by permitting recovery if plaintiff's negligence is "not greater than the negligence of the person or party or persons or parties against whom recovery is sought."

The Arkansas,[32] Kansas,[33] Massachusetts,[34] Pennsylvania,[35] and Vermont[36] comparative negligence statutes, through the use of language similar to the Texas statute, also imply that the plaintiff's negligence will be compared to the combined negligence of all defendants.

Legislation in other modified comparative negligence states has not been precise on this problem. Some statutes prescribe a comparison of plaintiff's negligence with that of "the person against whom recovery is sought"[37] or "the defendant."[38]

---

[23]Conn. Gen. Stat. Ann., § 52-572h(a).

[24]Del. Code Ann., tit. 10, § 8132.

[25]New Jersey Stat. Ann., § 2A:15-5.1.

[26]Nev. Rev. Stat., § 41.141, Subd. 2(a).

[27]Ohio Rev. Code Ann., § 2315.19(A)(1).

[28]Okla. Stat. Ann., tit. 23, § 13.

[29]Ore. Rev. Stat., § 18.470.

[30]See also Hawaii Rev. Stat., § 663-31 ("aggregate negligence"); Ind. Code, § 34-4-33-4(b) ("the fault of all persons"); Iowa Code Ann., § 668.3 ("combined percentage").

[31]Tex. Rev. Civ. Stat. Ann. (Vernon), art. 2212a, § 1.

[32]Ark. Stat. Ann., § 27-1765.

[33]Kan. Stat. Ann., § 60-258a (". . . party or parties against whom claim for recovery is made"). See also Greenwood v. McDonough Power Equipment, Inc., 437 F. Supp. 707 (D. Kan. 1977) (citing this treatise).

[34]Mass. Gen. Laws Ann., ch. 231, § 85.

[35]Pa. Stat. Ann., tit. 17, § 2102 ("defendant or defendants against whom recovery is sought").

[36]Vt. Stat. Ann., tit. 12, § 1036.

[37]Colo. Rev. Stat. Ann., § 41-2-14(1); Hawaii Rev. Stat., § 663-31(a); Idaho Code, § 6-801; Mass. Gen. Laws Ann., ch. 231, § 85; Minn. Stat. Ann., § 604.01, Subd. 1; N.J. Rev. Stat. Ann., § 2A:15-5.1; N.D. Cent. Code, § 9-10-07; Ore. Rev. Stat., § 18.470; Utah Code Ann., § 78-27-37; Wis. Stat. Ann., § 895.045; Wyo. Stat., § 1-7.2(a).

[38]Neb. Rev. Stat., § 25-1151; N.H. Rev. Stat. Ann., § 507:7-a; S.D. Codified Laws, § 20-9-2.

The Wisconsin Rule Against Combining Negligence

Wisconsin,[39] Georgia,[40] Idaho,[41] and Wyoming[42] have interpreted their respective statutes to bar recovery from a joint defendant if, under the state's modified system, plaintiff would have been barred by contributory negligence in an action against that defendant alone. They find it against the spirit of the 50% system (or the slight-gross system) to hold a defendant liable to a plaintiff more negligent than himself. Finally, if each defendant is severally liable for the entire damages, the opposite holding could cause a defendant to whom a small percentage of negligence is attributed to be liable for the entire recovery.

The states taking this general position may be induced to treat defendants as an aggregate if they find that defendants have breached an indivisible preexisting duty and that the opportunity to discharge the duty was equal for all. By analogy, in *Reber v. Hanson*,[43] a Wisconsin wrongful death action for a child, the contributory negligence of two parents was combined and compared with that of defendant.

More in point perhaps is the Minnesota decision in *Krengel v. Midwest Automatic Photo, Incorporated*,[44] an action against joint venturers. Although a legislative committee comment to the Minnesota statute specified that "In cases involving more than one defendant the plaintiff's negligence is [to be] compared to that of each defendant separately and he can recover only from the defendant or defendants whose negligence exceeds his own,"[45] the court held that where the duty of the tortfeasors was joint and preexisting, substantive law required that their negligence be treated in the aggregate.[46] On the other hand, Minnesota compares each tortfeasor's negligence separately where their negligence is merely concurrent and there is no joint venture.[47]

In *Rawson v. Lohsen*,[48] the Superior Court of New Jersey adopted the Wisconsin rule against combining negligence. The plaintiff motorcyclist was found 45% negligent, which exceeded the negligence of any

---

[39]Walker v. Kroger Grocery & Baking Co., 214 Wis. 519, 252 N.W. 721, 92 A.L.R. 680 (1934).

[40]Mishoe v. Davis, 64 Ga. App. 700, 14 S.E.2d 187 (1941). The continuing vitality of the rule in Georgia is in doubt. See Banks v. Brunswick, 529 F. Supp. 695, 700 (S.D. Ga. 1981), affd. 667 F.2d 97 (5th Cir. Ga. 1982).

[41]Odenwalt v. Zaring, 102 Idaho 1, 624 P.2d 383 (1980).

[42]Board of County Comrs. v. Ridenour, 623 P.2d 1174 (Wyo. 1981).

[43]Reber v. Hanson, 260 Wis. 632, 51 N.W.2d 505 (1951).

[44]Krengel v. Midwest Automatic Photo, Inc., 295 Minn. 200, 203 N.W.2d 841 (1973).

[45]Minn. Stat. Ann., § 604.01, Committee Comment, 1969, at 137 (Supp. 1973).

[46]Krengel v. Midwest Automatic Photo, Inc., note 44 above, 302 N.W.2d at 847.

[47]Marier v. Memorial Rescue Service, Inc., 296 Minn. 242, 207 N.W. 2d 706 (1973) (relying on Wisconsin cases). Minnesota will not find joint liability in situations where other jurisdictions might. See, e.g., Cambern v. Sioux Tools, Inc., 323 N.W.2d 795 (Minn. 1982) (although employer can be impleaded by machine manufacturer, they are not joint tortfeasors because one owed plaintiff a safe workplace, the other a safe machine).

[48]Rawson v. Lohsen, 145 N.J. Super. 71, 366 A.2d 1022 (1976). See also Van Horn v. William Blanchard Co., 173 N.J. Super. 280, 414 A.2d 265 (1980).

individual defendant. The court held that this barred his recovery as the negligence of multiple defendants will not be combined unless a joint enterprise exists between them. The New Jersey legislature subsequently amended the statute to allow recovery in this situation.[49]

Dicta in *May v. Skelly Oil Company*[50] and the decision of a Wisconsin federal district court[51] both indicated that Wisconsin might abolish the rule against combining negligence because it led to harsh and inequitable results. The Wisconsin Supreme Court in *Reiter v. Dyken*,[52] however, reaffirmed the Wisconsin rule by refusing to combine negligence of joint tortfeasors to permit recovery by the plaintiff against the tortfeasors.

Maine's comparative negligence statute says only that "[I]f such claimant is found by the jury to be equally at fault, the claimant shall not recover."[53] Although litigants have proceeded on the assumption that the Wisconsin rule is in effect, the Maine courts have not decided this issue.[54]

States Permitting Comparison with Combined Negligence

Under the Texas statute, plaintiff's negligence is compared with the total negligence of all the defendants.[55] A defendant whose negligence is equal to or greater than that of plaintiff can be held jointly and severally liable for the entire award, but a defendant whose negligence is less than plaintiff's can be held only for that portion of the award attributable to his own negligence.[56] This rule avoids the unfair possibility that a defendant whose negligence was only a small percentage of the total might eventually have to pay all or most of the award, although it can cause other problems.[57]

At least one state, Arkansas, has held that the negligence of multiple tortfeasors should always be considered in the aggregate, even though they may not have shared a joint duty.[58] Thus, if plaintiff's neg-

---

[49]N.J. Laws 1982, Ch. 191.

[50]May v. Skelly Oil Co., 83 Wis. 2d 30, 264 N.W.2d 574 (1978). The court was unable to invoke the new rule of aggregating the negligence of all defendants because the second defendant was not negligent.

[51]Soeldner v. White Metal Rolling & Stamping Corp., 473 F. Supp. 753 (E.D. Wis. 1979).

[52]Reiter v. Dyken, 95 Wis. 2d 461, 290 N.W.2d 510 (1980). Accord, Wisconsin Natural Gas Co. v. Ford, Bacon & Davis Constr. Corp., 96 Wis. 2d 314, 291 N.W.2d 825 (1980).

[53]Me. Rev. Stat. Ann., tit. 14, § 156.

[54]Otis Elevator Co. v. F. W. Cunningham & Sons, 454 A.2d 335 (Me. 1983).

[55]Tex. Rev. Civ. Stat. Ann. (Vernon), art. 2212a, § 2(b).

[56]Id., § 2(c).

[57]See section 16.8.

[58]Walton v. Tull, 234 Ark. 882, 356 S.W.2d 20, 8 A.L.R.3d 708 (1962). The Arkansas legislature amended its comparative negligence statute in 1975 to provide that the negligence of multiple defendants shall be aggregated in comparing their negligence with that of the plaintiff. See Ark. Stat. Ann., § 27-1765: "If the fault chargeable to a party claiming damages is of less degree than the fault chargeable to the party or parties from whom the claiming party seeks to recover damages, then the claiming party is entitled to recover the amount of his damages after they have been diminished in proportion to his own fault."

ligence is 20% and that of three defendants 10%, 20% and 50%, plaintiff can hold any of the defendants—even the one whose negligence was only 10%—jointly and severally liable for 80% of his damages.

The Supreme Court of Arkansas recognized that its holding may not be perfectly congruent with the legislative language. However, the court has found that this construction comports with the legislative purpose[59] to distribute the cost of an accident among those who were at fault and caused it. The court believes that the legislature did not intend to deny recovery to a plaintiff when his negligence was less than 50% of the cause of his own damages, as could happen under the non-aggregate approach if those joint tortfeasors who were more negligent than plaintiff are also judgment-proof.

Eighteen states in addition to Texas and Arkansas aggregate the negligence of all defendants when compared with the negligence of the plaintiff: Colorado,[60] Connecticut,[61] Delaware,[62] Hawaii,[63] Indiana,[64] Iowa,[65] Kansas,[66] Massachusetts,[67] Nevada,[68] New Hampshire,[69] New Jersey,[70] Ohio,[71] Oklahoma,[72] Oregon,[73] Pennsylvania,[74] Utah,[75] Vermont,[76] and West Virginia.[77]

Fairness of the Arkansas Rule

The Arkansas approach can be commended on the ground that plaintiff's chance of recovery is not jeopardized by the fact that several tortfeasors happen to be involved. Under the nonaggregate Wisconsin approach, for example, if plaintiff is 30% negligent, the likelihood of his recovery may be reduced if three or four joint defendants are involved. The jury could, as a practical matter, reduce the amount of negligence attributed to each defendant with the result that plaintiff would be more negligent than any one of the defendants.

---

[59]Walton v. Tull, 234 Ark. 882, 891-893, 356 S.W.2d 20, 25, 26 (1962).

[60]Mountain Mobile Mix, Inc. v. Gifford, 660 P.2d 883 (Colo. 1983).

[61]Conn. Gen. Stat. Ann., § 52-572h.

[62]Del. Code Ann., tit. 10, § 8132.

[63]Hawaii Rev. Stat., § 663-31(a). See Wong v. Hawaiian Scenic Tours, Ltd., 64 Hawaii 401, 642 P.2d 930 (1982).

[64]Ind. Code, § 34-4-33-4.

[65]Iowa Code, § 668.3(1).

[66]Kan. Stat. Ann., § 60-258a(a).

[67]Mass. Gen. Laws Ann., ch. 231, § 85. See Graci v. Damon, 6 Mass. App. 160, 374 N.E.2d 311 (1978), affd. 376 Mass. 931, 383 N.E.2d 842 (1978).

[68]Nev. Rev. Stat., § 41.141(1).

[69]Hurley v. Public Service Co., 123 N.H. 750, 465 A.2d 1217 (1983).

[70]N.J. Stat. Ann., § 2A:15-5.1.

[71]Ohio Rev. Code Ann., § 2315.19(A)(1).

[72]Okla. Stat. Ann., tit. 23, § 13. See Amoco Pipeline Co. v. Montgomery, 487 F. Supp. 1268 (W.D. Okla. 1980) (applied statute, citing this treatise); Laubach v. Morgan, 588 P.2d 1071 (Okla. 1978).

[73]Ore. Rev. Stat., § 18.470.

[74]Pa. Stat. Ann., tit. 42, § 7102. See subsection 3.5(C), note 1.

[75]Jensen v. Intermountain Health Care, Inc., 679 P.2d 903 (Utah 1984).

[76]Vt. Stat. Ann., tit. 12, § 1036.

[77]Bradley v. Appalachian Power Co., 163 W. Va. 332, 256 S.E.2d 879 (1979).

The aggregate approach was challenged in the Supreme Court of Arkansas in 1972 on the ground that it was contrary to the general principle that plaintiff should not recover from a defendant whose negligence was less than his own.[78] Nevertheless, the court reaffirmed its endorsement of the aggregate approach, observing "that several intervening sessions of the legislature have not deemed it necessary to amend the statute to correct the asserted misinterpretation. . . ."[79] This argument has since been strengthened by the fact that in 1975 the Arkansas legislature replaced its comparative negligence statute with a new law expressly comparing plaintiff's fault with that of the "party or parties" from whom he seeks to recover damages.[80]

The Practical Approach

Under modified comparative negligence, practical and theoretical justice may conflict on the question whether plaintiff's negligence should be compared with defendants' negligence separately or in the aggregate. This author subscribes to the more practical Arkansas approach and would compare plaintiff's negligence with the combined negligence of the defendants.

The concept of joint and several liability may of course produce some unfairness to particular defendants if the aggregate approach is used. In theory, a defendant with a small percentage of negligence may become liable for a large portion of the damages.[81] The Texas statute has merit as a means of avoiding this unfair result. Under the statute, plaintiff's negligence is compared with the total negligence of all the defendants.[82] A defendant whose negligence is equal to or greater than that of plaintiff can be held jointly and severally liable for the entire award, but a defendant whose negligence is less than plaintiff's can be held liable only for that portion of the award attributable to his own negligence.[83] Iowa and Nevada have enacted similar provisions.[84] It is also suggested that joint and several liability not be utilized unless the contribution of a particular tortfeasor was *very* substantial in producing the plaintiff's harm.

---

[78]Riddell v. Little, 253 Ark. 686, 488 S.W.2d 34 (1972).

[79]Id., 488 S.W.2d at 36; Larson Machine, Inc. v. Wallace, 268 Ark. 192, 600 S.W.2d 1 (1980) (plaintiff entitled to recover when his negligence is less than combined negligence of three defendants).

[80]Ark. Stat. Ann., §§ 27-1763 to 27-1765.

[81]See, e.g., Gannon Personnel Agency, Inc. v. New York, 103 Misc. 2d 60, 425 N.Y.S.2d 446 (1979), involving 43 consolidated suits arising out of a gas explosion in a commercial building where the owner of a new restaurant had left a pipe unconnected and city inspectors had failed to notice it. The Appellate Division upheld a finding of liability against the city and Con Ed, notwithstanding the likelihood that based on their 8% combined fault they would end up paying all of the damages. The finding against the city was later reversed on the ground that there was no special relationship between the city and the plaintiffs. O'Connor v. New York, 58 N.Y.2d 184, 460 N.Y.S.2d 485, 447 N.E.2d 33 (1983).

[82]Tex. Rev. Civ. Stat. Ann. (Vernon), art. 2212a, § 2(b).

[83]Id., § 2(c).

[84]Iowa Code Ann., § 668.4; Nev. Rev. Stat., § 41.141(3)(a).

Once again the importance of contribution among joint tortfeasors is demonstrated. The operation of contribution under comparative negligence is discussed in section 16.7.

16.7 Contribution among tortfeasors

Under the older common-law rule, a tortfeasor who pays a judgment for which he and other tortfeasors are jointly and severally liable has no enforceable right to contribution from the others. If comparative negligence is to fulfill its role of apportioning damages on the basis of fault, this rule must be abolished. If the legislature fails to modify the common-law rule, the change should be made by the courts.

Thirteen states provide for contribution among joint tortfeasors as part of their comparative negligence or tort reform statutes.[85] Many comparative negligence states retain separate contribution statutes, most of them based on either the 1939 or 1955 version of the former Uniform Contribution Among Tortfeasors Act.[86] Two states' comparative negligence statutes lay a basis for contribution if there is joint and several liability but, ironically, may have abolished joint and several liability itself![87] The New Mexico courts have explicitly overridden a contribution statute in abolishing joint and several liability.[88]

There is a right to contribution between joint tortfeasors in noncollision maritime cases.[89] In adopting this rule the Supreme Court of the United States did not decide if the contribution should be based on

---

[85]Ariz. Rev. Stat. Ann., §§ 12-2501 to 12-2509; Conn. Gen. Stat. Ann., § 52-572m-o; Mont. Code Ann., §§ 604.01 to 604.04; Idaho Code, § 6-803(1); Minn. Stat. Ann., § 604.01, subd. 1; N.J. Stat. Ann., § 2A:15-5.3; N.D. Cent. Code, § 9-10-07; Pa. Stat. Ann., tit. 42, § 7102; Tex. Rev. Civ. Stat. Ann. (Vernon), art. 2212a, § 2(b); Utah Code Ann., § 78-27-39; Wash. Rev. Code Ann., §§ 4.22.005 to 4.22.060; Wyo. Stat., §§ 1-1-109 to 1-1-114.

[86]Alaska Code, §§ 09.16.010 to 09.16.060; Ark. Stat. Ann., §§ 34-1001 to 34-1009; Calif. Civ. Proc. Code, §§ 13-50.5-101 to 13-50.5-106; Del. Code Ann., tit. 10, §§ 6302 to 6308; Fla. Stat. Ann., § 768.31; Ga. Code Ann., §§ 23-2-71 and 23-2-72; Hawaii Rev. Stat., §§ 663-11 to 663-17; Ill. Rev. Stat., ch. 70, §§ 301 to 305; Ky. Rev. Stat., §§ 412.030 to 412.050; Mass. Gen. Laws Ann., ch. 231B; Mich. Comp. Laws, §§ 600.2925a to 600.2925d; Miss. Code Ann., § 85-5-5; Mo. Rev. Stat., § 537.060; Ohio Rev. Code Ann., § 2307.31; Okla. Stat. Ann., tit. 12, §§ 831 to 832; Ore. Rev. Stat., §§ 18.440 to 18.455; N.Y. Civ. Prac. Law, §§ 1401 to 1404; N.D. Cent. Code, §§ 32-38-01 to 32-38-04; R.I. Gen. Laws, §§ 10-6-1 to 10-6-11; S.D. Codified Laws, §§ 15-8-11 to 15-8-22; W. Va. Code, § 55-7-13. Pennsylvania has retained the Uniform Act, Pa. Stat. Ann., tit. 42, § 8327, while making additional provisions for contribution in its comparative negligence statute. Pa. Stat. Ann., tit. 42, § 7102.

[87]N.H. Rev. Stat. Ann., § 507:7a; Vt. Stat. Ann., tit. 12, § 1036. See text at notes 20-23 below.

[88]Bartlett v. New Mexico Welding Supply, Inc., 98 N.M. 152, 646 P.2d 579 (App. 1982), cert. den. 98 N.M. 336, 648 P.2d 794 (1982).

[89]Cooper Stevedoring Co. v. Fritz Kopke, Inc., 417 U.S. 106, 40 L. Ed. 2d 694, 94 S. Ct. 2174 (1974), affirming Sessions v. Fritz Kopke, Inc., 479 F.2d 1041 (5th Cir. Tex. 1973); Dugas v. Pelican Constr. Co., 481 F.2d 773 (5th Cir. La. 1973); Lockheed Aircraft Corp. v. United States, 460 U.S. 190, 74 L. Ed. 2d 911, 103 S. Ct. 1033 (1983) (third-party indemnification claim allowed against the federal government notwithstanding the exclusive remedy provisions of the Federal Employees' Compensation Act).

equal division or on relative degrees of fault.[90] Since the Supreme Court's decision in *Reliable Transfer*,[91] it should be clear that contribution should be based on degrees of relative fault.

Common-Law Rule of Equal Division of Liability

If there is a right of contribution among tortfeasors, then a system of apportionment must be devised. The majority rule in the absence of statute has been equal division among all the tortfeasors,[92] subject to some equitable modification noted by the late Dean Prosser:

> [W]here the owner and the driver of a car are joined as defendants, equity may require treating the two together as liable for a single share, or that the share of a tortfeasor who is insolvent or absent from the jurisdiction be borne by the others.[93]

Nevertheless, until the late 1970's the basic rule remained that each joint defendant pays a pro rata share of the damages.

The Idaho court in *Tucker v. Union Oil Company* [94] held that each defendant had a right to contribution from other joint tortfeasors based on pro rata shares. The court adhered to the common-law rule of equal division of liability. Massachusetts also adheres to this common-law rule.[95]

The equal division system has the virtue of simplicity and ease of application. Nevertheless, it is not congruent with the general comparative negligence goal of apportioning damages according to fault.

The 1939 Uniform Act

There have been inroads on the equal division rule both by case law and by statute. Section 2 of the 1939 Uniform Contribution Among Tortfeasors Act contained an optional subsection (4), reading:

> When there is such a disproportion of fault among joint tortfeasors as to render inequitable an equal distribution among them of the common liability by contribution, the relative degrees of fault of the joint tortfeasors shall be considered in determining their pro rata shares.[96]

This provision does not require apportionment of damages strictly

---

[90]Cooper Stevedoring Co. v. Fritz Kopke, Inc., 417 U.S. 106, 108 n.3, 40 L. Ed. 2d 694, 94 S. Ct. 2174 (1974). See Western Tankers Corp. v. United States, 387 F. Supp. 487 (S.D. N.Y. 1975) (equal division); but see Seeley v. Red Star Towing & Transp. Co., 396 F. Supp. 129 (S.D. N.Y. 1975) (relative degrees of fault).

[91]United States v. Reliable Transfer Co., 421 U.S. 397, 44 L. Ed. 2d 251, 85 S. Ct. 1708 (1975). See Croshaw v. Koninklijke Nedlloyd, B.V. Rijswijk, 398 F. Supp. 1224 (D. Ore. 1975) (awarding contribution on basis of relative degrees of fault).

[92]See W. P. Keeton et al., *Prosser and Keeton on the Law of Torts* § 50 (5th ed. 1984). See also Note, *Adjusting Losses Among Joint Tortfeasors in Vehicular Collision Cases*, 68 Yale L.J. 964 (1959) (collection of jurisdictions).

[93]See W. P. Keeton et al., note 92 above, § 50, at 340.

[94]Tucker v. Union Oil Co., 100 Idaho 590, 603 P.2d 156 (1979). But see Idaho Code Ann., § 6-803(3).

[95]Graci v. Damon, 6 Mass. App. 160, 374 N.E.2d 311 (1978), affd. 376 Mass. 931, 383 N.E.2d 842 (1978).

[96]Reprinted at 12 U.L.A. 57.

according to the percentage of fault found, but it does recognize fault as a primary factor in apportioning liability. Obviously, under this act a joint tortfeasor would have to present enough evidence to support a finding that equal division would be "inequitable." It is even more apparent that such a standard presents a most uncertain gauge for determining when apportionment should vary from equal division. The vagueness of the words "disproportionate" and "inequitable" in the optional subsection of the 1939 Uniform Act recalls the words "slight" and "gross" used in the Nebraska and South Dakota statutes and the difficulties encountered in applying them.[97]

Although Hawaii adopted the 1939 version of the Uniform Contribution Among Tortfeasors Act, a federal court applying Hawaii law in *Barron v. United States*[98] seemed to ignore the statutory requirement to apportion "disproportionate fault." The court stated that the comparative fault of the tortfeasors should be determined to ascertain the proportion of damages assessed against each tortfeasor.[99] The Hawaii Supreme Court has recently stated that pure comparative negligence would apply in contribution actions.[1]

The 1955 Uniform Act

When the 1939 Uniform Contribution Among Tortfeasors Act was revised in 1955, degree of fault was abandoned as one of the factors to be considered in apportioning liability. Instead, there was inserted a provision that "their relative degrees of fault shall not be considered."[2] Only three of the comparative negligence states—Alaska,[3] Massachusetts[4] and North Dakota[5]—have retained the 1955 version of the Uniform Act. In North Dakota this clause appears to have been superseded, at least in part, by the provision in the comparative negligence statute that "contributions to awards shall be in proportion to the percentage of negligence attributable to each."[6] In Florida[7] and Michigan[8] the legislature simply amended the 1955 Act to delete the word "not,"

---

[97]See subsection (B), section 3.4. There is a difference, however. In Nebraska and South Dakota, if plaintiff and defendant are equally negligent or nearly so, both are barred from recovery and each bears his own damages. On the other hand, under the 1939 Uniform Act, if two tortfeasors are equally at fault or nearly so, the damages are divided equally between them and one who has paid more than half has a right to contribution from the other.

[98]Barron v. United States, 473 F. Supp. 1077 (D. Hawaii 1979), affd. in part and revd. in part 654 F.2d 644 (9th Cir. Hawaii 1981). (Federal Tort Claims Act states that plaintiff's right to recover and right to damages is to be governed by law of place where tort occurred—in this case, Hawaii).

[99]Id., 473 F. Supp. at 1088 (plaintiff was not contributorily negligent).

[1]Liberty Mut. Ins. Co. v. General Motors Corp., 65 Hawaii 428, 653 P.2d 96 (1982).

[2]Uniform Contrib. Among Tortfeasors Act § 2(a), 12 U.L.A. 87 (1955).

[3]Alaska Stat., § 09.16.020.

[4]Mass. Gen. Laws Ann., ch. 231B.

[5]N.D. Cent. Code, §§ 32-38-01 to 32-38-04.

[6]Id., § 9-10-07.

[7]Fla. Stat. Ann., § 768.31(3).

[8]Mich. Comp. Laws, § 600.2925b.

so that the statute now reads, "Their relative degrees of fault shall be considered."

Statutory Provisions for Apportionment

Of the seventeen statutes providing for contribution among tortfeasors in comparative negligence states, eight contain the language of the optional provision in the 1939 Uniform Act.[9] Two other states with statutes other than either version of the Uniform Act have incorporated the equal division rule in their statutes.[10]

Pure Comparative Negligence Among Tortfeasors

Many states have provided in their comparative negligence statutes for the application of pure comparative negligence in questions of contribution among tortfeasors. The Minnesota statute provides:

> When there are two or more persons who are jointly liable, contributions to awards shall be in proportion to the percentage of negligence attributable to each, provided, however, that each shall remain jointly and severally liable for the whole award.[11]

The New Jersey statute is even more specific. It requires a finding of fact as to "[T]he extent, in the form of a percentage, of each party's negligence,"[12] and then provides that

> Any party who is so compelled to pay more than such party's percentage share may seek contribution from the other joint tortfeasors.[13]

Texas recognizes the same basic principle in providing that "contribution to the damages awarded to the claimant shall be in proportion to the percentage of negligence attributable to each defendant."[14] The Texas statute also requires contribution claims between named defendants to be determined in the primary suit but permits later proceedings against a tortfeasor who was not a party to the primary suit and has not settled with plaintiff.[15]

A New York case has held that comparative apportionment is per-

---

[9]Ark. Stat. Ann., § 34-1002; Colo. Rev. Stat., § 13-50.5-103; Del. Code Ann., tit. 10, § 6302; Hawaii Rev. Stat., § 663-12; Idaho Code, § 6-803(3); R.I. Gen. Laws, § 10-6-3; S.D. Codified Laws, § 15-8-15; Utah Code Ann., § 78-27-40(2).

[10]Ga. Code Ann., § 23-2-71; Miss. Code Ann., § 85-5-5.

[11]Minn. Stat. Ann., § 604.01, subd. 1. See, e.g., Lametti v. Peter Lametti Constr. Co., 305 Minn. 72, 232 N.W.2d 435 (1975). But see Lambertson v. Cincinnati Corp., 312 Minn. 114, 257 N.W.2d 679, 100 A.L.R.3d 335 (1977) (third-party tortfeasor, a manufacturer, entitled to contribution from employer in amount not to exceed worker compensation benefits paid to employee by employer as a result of accident).

[12]N.J. Stat. Ann., § 2A:15-5.2, subd. b. See Rogers v. Spady, 147 N.J. Super. 274, 371 A.2d 285 (1977).

[13]N.J. Stat. Ann., § 2A:15-5.3.

[14]Tex. Rev. Civ. Stat. Ann. (Vernon), art. 2212a, § 2(b). In Cartel Capital Corp. v. Fireco of New Jersey, 81 N.J. 548, 410 A.2d 674, 19 A.L.R.4th 310 (1980) the New Jersey Supreme Court held that the effect of this language on the existing contribution statute was to redefine "pro rata" as "percentage."

[15]Tex. Rev. Civ. Stat. Ann. (Vernon), art. 2212a, § 2(h).

mitted among joint tortfeasors when their respective degrees of responsibility for the accident are not equal.[16]

The North Dakota comparative negligence statute[17] provides for pure comparative negligence in contribution actions, and that state's highest court has held each defendant liable for his proportionate share of negligence.[18]

The release of one or more persons who might be liable for a proportionate share of claimant's damages under the Kansas statute has no effect on the claimant's right to recover from other persons.[19]

Abolish Joint Liability?

New Hampshire and Vermont appear to have accomplished the same end but with one important difference. The pertinent portion of both their statutes states that:

> [W]here recovery is allowed against more than one defendant, each such defendant shall be liable for that proportion of the total dollar amount awarded as damages in the ratio of the amount of his causal negligence to the amount of causal negligence attributed to all defendants against whom recovery is allowed.[20]

This approach allows pure comparative negligence similar to that in Minnesota, New Jersey and Texas; the apparent difference in the statutes centers on the possiblity that the New Hampshire and Vermont laws could be interpreted to abolish the concept of joint liability. Subsequent judicial interpretation bears out this possibility.[21] New Hampshire and Vermont also are among the few states that have not enacted a statute abrogating the common-law rule against contribution among joint tortfeasors. The New Hampshire Supreme Court has rejected contribution under the comparative negligence statute.[22] The Vermont Supreme Court refused to allow contribution even under the comparative negligence statute in 1974,[22a] but a federal court recently

---

[16]Graphic Arts Mut. Ins. Co. v. Bakers Mut. Ins. Co., 58 A.D.2d 397, 397 N.Y.S.2d 66 (1977), affd. 45 N.Y.2d 551, 410 N.Y.S.2d 571, 382 N.E.2d 1347 (1978); Dole v. Dow Chemical Co., 30 N.Y.2d 143, 331 N.Y.S.2d 382, 282 N.E.2d 288, 53 A.L.R.3d 175 (1972), codified at N.Y. Civ. Prac. Law, § 1402.

[17]N.D. Cent. Code, § 9-10-07.

[18]Bartels v. Williston, 276 N.W.2d 113 (N.D. 1979).

[19]Geier v. Wikel, 4 Kan. App. 2d 188, 603 P.2d 1028 (1979); Stueve v. American Honda Motors Co., 457 F. Supp. 740 (D. Kan. 1978); Brown v. Keill, 224 Kan. 195, 580 P.2d 867 (1978); Eurich v. Alkire, 224 Kan. 236, 579 P.2d 1207 (1978).

[20]N.H. Rev. Stat. Ann., § 507:7-a; Vt. Stat. Ann., tit. 12, § 1036. See Howard v. Spafford, 132 Vt. 434, 321 A.2d 74 (1974) (Vermont comparative negligence statute abolishes joint and several liability and contribution); Heathcote v. Sturgeon, Docket No. 47915 (Cal. App. 1977) (discussion of abolition of joint and several liability).

[21]Simonsen v. Barlo Plastics Co., 551 F.2d 469, 472 (1st Cir. N.H. 1977); Stannard v. Harris, 135 Vt. 544, 380 A.2d 101 (1977) (adopts the dicta of Howard v. Spafford, 132 Vt. 434, 321 A.2d 74 (1974)). But see Eagle Star Ins. Co. v. Metromedia, Inc., 578 F. Supp. 184 (D. Vt. 1984).

[22]Consolidated Utility Equipment Services, Inc. v. Emhart Mfg. Corp., 123 N.H. 258, 459 A.2d 287 (1983).

[22a]Howard v. Spafford, 132 Vt. 434, 321 A.2d 74 (1974).

questioned the viability of the common-law rule against contribution in the light of the adoption of comparative negligence.[23]

The statutes of many states, while establishing a means of considering fault in apportioning liability among tortfeasors, still make it clear that any of the tortfeasors may be held liable for the entire award.[24] Texas, Nevada, Iowa, and Oregon apply the same rule except against those tortfeasors whose negligence was less than plaintiff's.[25] In this respect, these statutes are an improvement over those of New Hampshire and Vermont, which left the concept of joint and several liability in doubt.

Idaho[26] retains joint and several liability but allows apportionment for contribution on the basis of fault. In Minnesota[27] and Colorado,[28] the courts hold their comparative negligence statutes did not abolish joint and several liability. See also section 16.4.

Common-Law Right to Contribution?

In the absence of a statute, is there a right to contribution among joint tortfeasors? A minority of states, including two comparative negligence states, have held that there is.[29] Wisconsin[30] and Maine[31] both reached this result before enactment of their respective comparative negligence statutes.

In the absence of governing statute, how is liability among tortfeasors to be apportioned in determining contribution rights? The same two comparative negligence states of Wisconsin and Maine apportion liability according to percentage of negligence found.[32] In neither

---

[23]Eagle Star Ins. Co. of America v. Metromedia, Inc., 578 F. Supp. 184 (D. Vt. 1984).

[24]Ark. Stat. Ann., § 34-1002; Ariz. Rev. Stat. Ann., § 12-2501(A); Conn. Gen. Stat. Ann., § 52-572o (product liability statute, but cites "common law joint and several liability of joint tortfeasors:") Idaho Code, § 6-804; Iowa Code, § 668.4 (applies only to tortfeasors who bear at least 50% of the total fault); Me. Rev. Stat. Ann., tit. 14, § 156; Minn. Stat. Ann., § 604.02(1); Mont. Code Ann., § 27-1-703(1); Nev. Rev. Stat., § 41.141(3)(a) (similar to Iowa rule supra); N.J. Stat. Ann., § 2A:15-5.3; N.D. Cent. Code, § 9-10-07; Pa. Stat. Ann., tit. 42, § 7102(b); Tex. Rev. Civ. Stat. Ann. (Vernon), art. 2212a, § 2(c) (similar to Iowa statute supra); Utah Code Ann., § 78-27-41(1); Wash. Rev. Code Ann., § 4.22.30; Wyo. Stat., § 1-1-110(h).

[25]Tex. Rev. Civ. Stat. Ann. (Vernon), art. 2212a, § 2(c); Nev. Rev. Stat., § 41.141(3)(a); Iowa Code, § 668.4; Ore. Rev. Stat., § 18.485.

[26]Tucker v. Union Oil Co., 100 Idaho 590, 603 P.2d 156 (1979).

[27]Johnson v. United States Fire Ins. Co., 586 F.2d 1291 (8th Cir. Minn. 1978).

[28]Martinez v. Stefanich, 195 Colo. 341, 577 P.2d 1099 (1978); Kampman v. Dunham, 192 Colo. 448, 560 P.2d 91 (1977).

[29]See Note, *Adjusting Losses Among Joint Tortfeasors in Vehicular Collision Cases*, 68 Yale L.J. 964, 981-984 (1959).

[30]Ellis v. Chicago & N. W. R. Co., 167 Wis. 392, 167 N.W. 1048 (1918).

[31]Hobbs v. Hurley, 117 Me. 449, 104 A. 815 (1918).

[32]Bielski v. Schulze, 16 Wis. 2d 1, 114 N.W.2d 105 (1962); Packard v. Whitten, 274 A.2d 169 (Me. 1971). Accord, Valiga v. National Food Co., 58 Wis. 2d 232, 206 N.W.2d 377 (1973); Franklin v. Badger Ford Truck Sales, Inc., 58 Wis. 2d 641, 207 N.W.2d 866 (1973); Dickens v. Kensmoe, 61 Wis. 2d 211, 212 N.W.2d 484 (1973); see also Hartford Fire Ins. Co. v. Osborn Plumbing & Heating, Inc., 66 Wis. 2d 454, 225 N.W.2d 628 (1975) (for purposes of statute of limitations the cause of action for contribution accrues when one joint tortfeasor pays more than his proportional share of the common liability).

case does a statute specifically require this rule, but in both cases the existence of a comparative negligence statute influenced the court in reaching the result.

In *Dole v. Dow Chemical Company*,[33] the Court of Appeals of New York judicially adopted a rule of contribution among joint tortfeasors based on relative degrees of fault. This preceded New York's statutory adoption of pure comparative negligence.

Connecticut noted its unique common-law rule against contribution among joint tortfeasors and stated that the comparative negligence statute did not modify that rule.[34]

The Montana Supreme Court adhered to the common-law rule against contribution among joint tortfeasors when the comparative negligence statute permitting contribution did not apply to the facts of the case.[35]

Bielski v. Schulze

The Supreme Court of Wisconsin discussed this issue fully in *Bielski v. Schulze*.[36] First, the court pointed out that the comparative negligence statute has "no application to the doctrine of contribution."[37] This is true in other states that have, like Wisconsin, adopted comparative negligence statutes that do not specifically mention apportionment of liability among defendants.[38] Therefore, the right to contribution, if it exists, is not barred by the fact that the negligence of the tortfeasor seeking contribution may have been greater than that of the tortfeasor from whom contribution is sought.

The court then discussed

[W]hether the present automatic method of determining the number of equal shares between the number of joint tortfeasors involved is as equitable and as just a determination of contribution as determining the amount of the shares in proportion to the percentage of causal negligence attributable to each tortfeasor.[39]

The court found it

[D]ifficult to justify, either on a layman's sense of justice or on natural justice, why a joint tortfeasor who is 5% causally negligent should only recover 50% of the amount he paid to the plaintiff from

---

[33]Dole v. Dow Chem. Co., 30 N.Y.2d 143, 331 N.Y.S.2d 382, 282 N.E.2d 288, 53 A.L.R.3d 175 (1972); see also Smart v. Wozniak, 86 Misc. 2d 940, 385 N.Y.S.2d 498 (1976), affd. 58 A.D.2d 993, 397 N.Y.S.2d 489 (1977); Yun Jeong Koo v. St. Bernard, 89 Misc. 2d 775, 392 N.Y.S.2d 815 (1977) (defendant may recover contribution from infant plaintiff's parents if their actions were an active, competent, producing cause of plaintiff's accident).

[34]Gomeau v. Forrest, 176 Conn. 523, 409 A.2d 1006 (1979). A Connecticut statute now allows contribution in product liability claims. Conn. Gen. Stat. Ann., § 52-572o.

[35]Consolidated Freightways Corp. v. Osier, 185 Mont. 439, 605 P.2d 1076 (1979).

[36]Bielski v. Schulze, 16 Wis. 2d 1, 114 N.W.2d 105 (1962).

[37]Id., 114 N.W.2d at 107.

[38]Arkansas, Colorado, Connecticut, Delaware, Georgia, Hawaii, Massachusetts, Oklahoma and Oregon.

[39]Bielski v. Schulze, note 36 above, 114 N.W.2d at 108.

a co-tortfeasor who is 95% causally negligent, and conversely why the defendant who is found 5% causally negligent should be required to pay 50% of the loss by way of reimbursement to the co-tortfeasor who is 95% negligent.[40]

The injustice of the prior rule was sufficient to free the court from the shackles of long established precedent. It discounted an argument that pure comparative negligence as applied to joint tortfeasors would discourage settlement. The court stated that in settling under a pure comparative negligence approach, one "whose potential causal negligence is greater than 50% should be more willing to contribute a greater amount to a settlement than formerly."[41]

Royal Indemnity v. Aetna Casualty and Surety

In *Royal Indemnity Company v. Aetna Casualty and Surety Company*,[42] the Supreme Court of Nebraska judicially abrogated the common-law rule of no contribution among negligent joint tortfeasors. The right to contribute accrues when one tortfeasor discharges more than his "proportionate share" of the common liability.[43] It is unclear whether contribution will be based on comparative fault or equal division.

Packard v. Whitten

In *Packard v. Whitten*,[44] the Supreme Judicial Court of Maine followed the same line of reasoning as in *Bielski v. Schulze* and relied heavily on that precedent. The court found additional support in a sentence in the Maine statute permitting defendants to obtain a jury finding as to "the percentage of fault contributed by each defendant."[45] This sentence, the court said, "would appear to have little purpose except, to lay the basis for a comparative contribution."[46]

It should be noted that in neither *Bielski* nor the *Packard* case was plaintiff contributorily negligent. Thus, strictly speaking, the comparative negligence statute did not apply to either. Nevertheless, the existence of comparative negligence statutes made the decisions easier for both courts, partly through legislative approval of the principle of apportioning liability according to fault, and partly by establishing a procedure for determining the relative fault of the tortfeasors.

Kohr v. Allegheny Airlines

In *Kohr v. Allegheny Airlines, Incorporated*,[47] the United States Court of Appeals for the Seventh Circuit imposed a federal "common

---

[40]Id., 114 N.W.2d at 109.

[41]Id., 114 N.W.2d at 111.

[42]Royal Indem. Co. v. Aetna Cas. & Surety Co., 193 Neb. 752, 229 N.W.2d 183 (1975).

[43]Id., 193 Neb. at 764, 229 N.W.2d at 190.

[44]Packard v. Whitten, 274 A.2d 169 (Me. 1971).

[45]Me. Rev. Stat. Ann., tit. 14, § 156.

[46]Packard v. Whitten, note 44 above, 274 A.2d at 180.

[47]Kohr v. Allegheny Airlines, Inc., 504 F.2d 400 (7th Cir. Ind. 1974).

law" rule of contribution among joint tortfeasors based on pure comparative negligence to actions arising out of mid-air collisions over national air space. The court found pure comparative negligence to be the "better rule."[48]

Comparative Fault Among Tortfeasors Under Contributory Negligence

That application of comparative fault principles between tortfeasors is not dependent on comparative negligence between plaintiff and defendant is shown by the Third Circuit decision in *Gomes v. Brodhurst.*[49] That case arose in the Virgin Islands, which had not at that time adopted comparative negligence. Nevertheless, the Third Circuit Court of Appeals abandoned the equal division rule and declared instead that, as between tortfeasors, contributions to plaintiff's award should be based on jury findings as to the relative fault of the tortfeasors. The decision is unusual, but it could be followed in any jurisdiction, with or without comparative negligence between plaintiff and defendant, unless (as in Massachusetts, Mississippi and Georgia[50]) there is a statute specifically prohibiting consideration of fault.[51] Missouri adopted pure comparative fault among joint tortfeasors[52] five years before adopting pure comparative negligence.[53]

Encouraging Settlement

A most important practical effect of using comparative fault rather than equal division in determining contribution among joint tortfeasors is in the area of settlement. The Third Circuit speculated in *Gomes v. Brodhurst* that it would make little difference,[54] and the Wisconsin Supreme Court indulged in the same hypothesis in *Bielski.*[55] These judicial speculations were based on the premise that "defendants generally contribute to the settlement in some rough proportion to what they think their negligence is...."[56] Nevertheless, the conscientious attorney representing a joint defendant should be careful in settlement negotiations to point out how much "less at fault" his client was than

---

[48]Id., at 405.

[49]Gomes v. Brodhurst, 394 F.2d 465 (3d Cir. V.I. 1967). Accord, DeLaval Turbine, Inc. v. West India Indus., Inc., 502 F.2d 259 (3d Cir. V.I. 1974) (allocation of liability according to the proportionate share of the joint tortfeasor's responsibility).

[50]See text at notes 4 and 10 above.

[51]Cf. George's Radio, Inc. v. Capital Transit Co., 75 App. D.C. 187, 126 F.2d 219 (1942), followed in McKenna v. Austin, 77 App. D.C. 228, 134 F.2d 659, 148 A.L.R. 1253 (1943). Accord, Hawkeye-Security Ins. Co. v. Lowe Constr. Co., 251 Iowa 27, 99 N.W.2d 421 (1959); Iowa Power & Light Co. v. Abild Constr. Co., 259 Iowa 314, 144 N.W.2d 303 (1966); Blunt v. Brown, 225 F. Supp. 326 (S.D. Iowa 1963) (applying Iowa law); Cage v. New York C. R. Co., 276 F. Supp. 778 (W.D. Pa. 1967), affd. 386 F.2d 998 (3d Cir. Pa. 1967) (citing precedent case, Goldman v. Mitchell-Fletcher Co., 292 Pa. 354, 141 A. 231 (1928)). See also, Annot., "Contribution between negligent tortfeasors at common law," 60 A.L.R.2d 1354 (1958).

[52]Missouri P. R. Co. v. Whitehead & Kales Co., 566 S.W.2d 466 (Mo. 1978).

[53]Gustafson v. Benda, 661 S.W.2d 11 (Mo. 1983).

[54]Gomes v. Brodhurst, 394 F.2d 465 (3d Cir. V.I. 1967).

[55]Bielski v. Schulze, 16 Wis. 2d 1, 114 N.W.2d 105, 111 (1962).

[56]Id.

any other defendant in settlement negotiations. The difference in systems is important.

It is clear that pure comparative negligence is fairer to all concerned than the equal division rule in determining contribution among joint tortfeasors. Nevertheless, the equal division method must be taken into account as a matter of strategy both in the area of settlement and trial.

16.8 Contribution among tortfeasors under modified comparative negligence

Under modified comparative negligence, either one of the 50% systems or the slight-gross system, assuming that there is joint liability with a right of contribution, there are at least three basic possibilities for apportioning damages among joint tortfeasors:

1. The common-law "majority rule," embodied in the 1955 Uniform Contribution Among Tortfeasors Act.[57] Damages are divided equally among the tortfeasors without considering relative fault.

2. Pure comparative negligence, or the approach to it contained in the optional subsection (4) of Section 2 of the 1939 Uniform Contribution Among Tortfeasors Act.[58] Each tortfeasor who has paid more than his share may enforce contribution from any who has paid less than his share.

3. Modified comparative negligence. Liability is apportioned according to fault, but no tortfeasor may enforce contribution from another whose fault was less than his own (or under the slight-gross system, from another whose fault was slight in comparison with his own).

Summary of Statutory Treatment

As of 1985, twenty-nine states had adopted one or another of the various forms of modified comparative negligence.

In two of these states, joint tortfeasors are apparently jointly and severally liable for the entire award but there is no right of contribution among them except perhaps in certain special relationships between tortfeasors.[59]

Two of the modified comparative negligence states follow the common-law equal division principle. Georgia's statute providing for contribution among joint judgment debtors incorporates the equal division rule.[60] Massachusetts has the 1955 Uniform Contribution Among

---

[57]See notes 92 to 8, section 16.7, and accompanying text.

[58]See notes 96 to 1, section 16.7, and accompanying text.

[59]Connecticut and Indiana. See Note, *Adjusting Losses Among Joint Tortfeasors in Vehicular Collision Cases,* 68 Yale L.J. 964, 982 (1959).

[60]Ga. Code Ann., §§ 105-2011, 105-2012.

Tortfeasors Act, including the clause prohibiting consideration of fault in determining contributions.[61]

Pure Comparative Negligence Applied

The other states with modified comparative negligence all apply some form of pure comparative negligence to the apportionment of damages between tortfeasors and the right of contribution. Seven have the language of the optional subsection from the 1939 Uniform Contribution Among Tortfeasors Act permitting consideration of fault.[62] The difficulties in applying this language have been noted in section 16.7 above.[63]

Thirteen of the states with modified comparative negligence— Arizona,[64] Minnesota,[65] Montana,[66] Nevada,[67] New Hampshire,[68] New Jersey,[69] North Dakota,[70] Ohio,[71] Pennsylvania,[72] Texas,[73] Vermont,[74] Washington,[75] and Wyoming[76] —provide in their comparative negligence statutes for apportionment of liability among joint tortfeasors on the basis of comparative negligence. The language varies, but the effect is the same: pure comparative negligence.

The Kansas comparative negligence statute[77] seems to indicate that if joint and several liability continues, contribution will be based on relative degrees of fault. The Kansas courts have decided that the statute abolishes joint and several liability, and with it, contribution.[78] A rule of "comparative implied indemnity" is available when one defendant has settled for more or less than his proportionate share,[79] but only in product liability cases involving a chain of distribution.[80] Minnesota creates an exception to comparative contribution under its worker compensation system: a manufacturer is entitled only to contribution

---

[61]Mass. Gen. Laws Ann., ch. 231B, § 2. See also text accompanying note 92, section 16.7.

[62]Arkansas, Delaware, Hawaii, Idaho, South Dakota, Utah and Wyoming. See notes 96 to 1, section 16.7, and accompanying text.

[63]Id.

[64]Ariz. Rev. Stat. Ann., § 12-2502.

[65]Minn. Stat. Ann., § 604.01, subd. 1.

[66]Mont. Code Ann., § 27-1-703(2).

[67]Nev. Rev. Stat., § 41.141(3).

[68]N.H. Rev. Stat. Ann., § 507:7-a. See text accompanying note 20, section 16.7.

[69]N.J. Stat. Ann., § 2A:15-5.3. See text accompanying notes 12, 13, section 16.7.

[70]N.D. Cent. Code, § 9-10-07. See text accompanying notes 17, 18, section 16.7.

[71]Ohio Rev. Code Ann., § 2315.19.

[72]Pa. Stat. Ann., tit. 17, § 2101.

[73]Tex. Rev. Civ. Stat. Ann. (Vernon), art. 2212a, § 2(b). See text accompanying note 56, section 16.7.

[74]Vt. Stat. Ann., tit. 12, § 1036. See text accompanying note 20, section 16.7.

[75]Wash. Rev. Code Ann., § 4.22.040.

[76]Wyo. Stat., § 1-1-111.

[77]Kan. Stat. Ann., § 60-258a.

[78]Brown v. Keill, 224 Kan. 195, 580 P.2d 867 (1978).

[79]Kennedy v. Sawyer, 228 Kan. 439, 618 P.2d 788 (1980).

[80]Ellis v. Union P. R. Co., 213 Kan. 182, 643 P.2d 158 (1982).

from an employer in an amount not to exceed benefits payable to the employee as a result of the accident.[81]

Judicially Adopted Pure Comparative Negligence

As noted in section 16.7,[82] five other states with modified comparative negligence—Hawaii, Maine, Nebraska, West Virginia and Wisconsin—have, by judicial decision, applied pure comparative negligence to contribution among tortfeasors. The Wisconsin court flatly refused to apply between tortfeasors the 50% principle that might have barred a negligent plaintiff:

> The right of one tortfeasor to contribution is not barred because his negligence may be equal to or greater than the negligence of his co-tortfeasor.[83]

Indeed, the tortfeasor seeking contribution in the Wisconsin case had been found 95% negligent. Despite this, even though he did not obtain the 50% contribution he sought, he did obtain a 5% contribution.

In *Royal Indemnity Company v. Aetna Casualty and Surety Company*[84] the Supreme Court of Nebraska judicially abolished the common-law rule of no contribution among negligent joint tortfeasors. The right to contribution accrues when one joint tortfeasor discharges more than his proportionate share of the common liability.[85] It is unclear whether contribution is based on comparative fault or equal division.

The West Virginia Supreme Court adopted pure comparative contribution in *Sitzes v. Anchor Motor Freight.*[86] The court explicitly considered whether a defendant who was 70% at fault should be barred from contribution and concluded that the equitable nature of the contribution action supported a pure comparative contribution rule.[87]

Arguments Against Barring Contribution

Use of the 50% principle to bar contribution claims between tortfeasors would result in marked unfairness. The basic premise used to support the 50% rule between plaintiff and defendant—that "no one who is more at fault should recover damages from another"[88]—is simply inapplicable among tortfeasors. In contribution actions, no one is recov-

---

[81]Lambertson v. Cincinnati Corp., 312 Minn. 114, 257 N.W.2d 679, 100 A.L.R.3d 335 (1977).

[82]See text accompanying notes 29 to 53, section 16.7.

[83]Bielski v. Schulze, 16 Wis. 2d 1, 114 N.W.2d 105, 108 (1962). Accord, Johnson v. Heintz, 73 Wis. 2d 286, 243 N.W.2d 815 (1976); Hartford Fire Ins. Co. v. Osborn Plumbing & Heating, Inc., 66 Wis. 2d 454, 225 N.W.2d 628 (1975); Valiga v. National Food Co., 58 Wis. 2d 232, 206 N.W.2d 377 (1973); Brown v. Wisconsin Natural Gas Co., 59 Wis. 2d 334, 208 N.W.2d 769, 71 A.L.R.3d 1159 (1973) (dicta).

[84]Royal Indem. Co. v. Aetna Cas. & Surety Co., 193 Neb. 752, 229 N.W.2d 183 (1975).

[85]Id., 193 Neb. at 764, 229 N.W.2d at 190.

[86]Sitzes v. Anchor Motor Freight, Inc., 289 S.E.2d 679 (W. Va. 1982).

[87]Id., at 689.

[88]Ghiardi & Hogan, *Comparative Negligence—The Wisconsin Rule and Procedures,* 18 Def. L.J. 537 (1969).

ering anything on a net basis; what is being determined is the portion of the cost of plaintiff's award to be borne by each tortfeasor.

Barring contribution claims by use of the 50% principle could create almost insurmountable confusion in multi-party actions and would open the door to collusive abuses, especially in intrafamily cases or other cases involving both a passenger and his driver. Suppose, for example, a passenger injured in a two-vehicle collision (or an insurer by subrogation after payments under a medical coverage) brings an action against both his own driver and the driver of the other vehicle. The driver of the vehicle in which the passenger was riding (perhaps a member of the family) is found 40% negligent and the driver of the other vehicle 60%. The passenger then proceeds to execution and recovers his full judgment from the driver of the other vehicle. If contribution from the driver who was 40% negligent is barred, then the plaintiff's own driver goes scot-free, simply because plaintiff chose to execute against the other driver first.

When all of these things are considered, it is easy to see why no state with modified comparative negligence has applied the 50% principle to claims for contribution and why the overwhelming majority have applied pure comparative negligence to contributions among tortfeasors.

Similar difficulties may arise in the states that have abolished joint and several liability as to defendants who bear less than 50% of the total fault or are less negligent than the plaintiff.[89] When plaintiff is not at fault at all, the effect will be exactly the same as the application of modified comparative negligence to contribution. When plaintiff is partly at fault, a sort of sliding scale of unfairness would apply. The Texas Supreme Court acknowledged the problems inherent in this system when it adopted a rule of unmodified joint and several liability in cases where at least one defendant is liable on a theory other than negligence.[90]

Contribution Under the "Wisconsin Rule"

Maine appears to be the only state to have discussed whether contribution is available from a tortfeasor who is not liable to the plaintiff because he, the defendant, was less negligent. This occurred in a jurisdiction where the plaintiff's fault is compared with *each* individual defendant rather than with all defendants. The question arose in *Otis Elevator Company v. F. W. Cunningham and Sons*.[91] The court said that in Maine the controlling question was not common liability but

---

[89]Tex. Rev. Civ. Stat. Ann. (Vernon), art. 2212a, § 2(c); Nev. Rev. Stat., § 41.141(3)(a); Iowa Code Ann., § 668.4; Ore. Rev. Stat., § 18.485.

[90]Duncan v. Cessna Aircraft Co., 665 S.W.2d 414, 429 (Tex. 1984).

[91]Otis Elevator Co. v. F. W. Cunningham & Sons, 454 A.2d 335 (Me. 1983). The court noted that it was still an open question whether Maine in fact followed the Wisconsin rule—the parties here had stipulated that it did—but refused to decide that question because it had not been raised or briefed. Id., at 336 n. 3.

equity, and that the personal defense of one tortfeasor should make no difference as to his liability to other tortfeasors. The court noted that the contributory neglience rule was based not on defendant's lack of liability but on policy grounds; under the comparative negligence rule the unfairness of making the other tortfeasor pay the whole amount would outweigh other considerations.

16.9 Indemnity of tortfeasors

Causes of action for indemnity differ sharply from contribution claims, in that damages are not in any way apportioned between the parties. In the successful indemnity action, the plaintiff-indemnitee recovers from the defendant-indemnitor the *entire* loss he has sustained.[92]

Common-Law Indemnity

The common-law duty of indemnity is not easy to detail, as the late Dean Prosser noted,[93] but the categories were reasonably well stated in an American Law Reports annotation.[94] There it was indicated that indemnity may be granted in the following situations:

1. Where the indemnitee has only an imputed or vicarious liability for damage caused by the indemnitor.

2. Where the indemnitee has incurred tort liability by performing, at the direction of and in reliance upon the indemnitor, an act not manifestly wrong.

3. Where the indemnitee has incurred liability for failure to correct a hazardous condition which, as between the indemnitor and the indemnitee, it was the duty of the indemnitor to correct.[95]

4. Where the indemnitee has incurred liability by reason of his reliance, even negligent reliance, upon the duty of care which the indemnitor owes as a supplier of goods.[96]

In categories 1 and 2 above, the indemnitee is simply not at fault and the law of indemnity is not modified under comparative negli-

---

[92]See W. P. Keeton et al., *Prosser and Keeton on the Law of Torts* § 51 (5th ed. 1984).

[93]Id., § 51, at 343.

[94]Annot., "Right of tortfeasor guilty of only ordinary negligence to be indemnified by one guilty of intentional wrongdoing, wanton misconduct, or gross negligence," 88 A.L.R.2d 1355, 1356 (1963).

[95]See, e.g., Saalfrank v. O'Daniel, 390 F. Supp. 45 (N.D. Ohio 1974) (a negligent provider of medical services, secondarily liable, may recover indemnity from the negligent party causing the original injury), revd. 533 F.2d 325 (6th Cir. Ohio 1976) (held that no right to indemnification existed in this action).

[96]88 A.L.R.2d, note 94 above, at 1356. Accord, Allison Steel Mfg. Co. v. Superior Court of Arizona, 20 Ariz. App. 185, 511 P.2d 198 (1973) (indemnity denied negligent concurrent tortfeasor but granted retailer against manufacturer whose defective product caused the injury).

gence.[97] This conclusion also will hold with regard to category 3, for in that situation the indemnitor is primarily liable. The basis for the last category is really that there is a sufficient differentiation between the passive negligence of the receiver of goods and the active negligence of a supplier.[98]

The common law imposed a duty of indemnification upon the supplier at a time when contribution was not allowed between joint tortfeasors. The general principle permitting indemnity to a passive joint tortfeasor from an active one was applied by courts in new and other contexts, probably because of the harshness of the "no contribution among joint tortfeasors" rule. In comparative negligence states that permit contribution, it is likely that this principle will be curbed.

Federal Adoption of Contribution in Lieu of Indemnity

In *Cooper Stevedoring Company v. Fritz Kopke, Incorporated*[99] the Supreme Court of the United States denied indemnity but granted contribution to a shipowner against a stevedoring company in an action brought against it by a longshoreman employee of the stevedoring company. The shipowner based his claim for indemnity on the implied warranty of workmanlike performance which exists between the stevedoring company and the shipowner. Many previous cases indicated that this warranty created a duty of indemnity from the stevedoring company to the shipowner when a judgment is rendered in favor of a long-

---

[97]See Brown v. Wisconsin Natural Gas Co., 59 Wis. 2d 334, 208 N.W.2d 769, 71 A.L.R.3d 1159 (1973); Welter v. Curry, 260 Ark. 287, 539 S.W.2d 264 (1976) (both cases denied indemnity but recognized the continued validity of common-law indemnity based on vicarious liability).

[98]See American Pecco Corp. v. Concrete Bldg. Systems Co., 392 F. Supp. 789 (N.D. Ill. 1975); Beaunit Corp. v. Volunteer Natural Gas Co., 402 F. Supp. 1222 (E.D. Tenn. 1975) (all granting indemnity on a theory of active/passive negligence). Cf. Becker v. Black & Veatch Consulting Engineers, 509 F.2d 42 (8th Cir. S.D. 1974) (failure of consulting engineer to properly inspect gas line pursuant to contractual agreement is active negligence barring indemnity); Morrissette v. Sears, Roebuck & Co., 114 N.H. 384, 322 A.2d 7 (1974); Ruvolo v. United States Steel Corp., 139 N.J. Super. 578, 354 A.2d 685 (1976) (dicta); Cochran v. B. & O. R.R., 41 Ohio App. 2d 186, 70 Ohio Ops. 2d 352, 324 N.E.2d 759 (1974) (no common-law indemnity on theory of active/passive negligence unless both parties share a common duty to the plaintiff); Leesburg Hosp. Assn. v. Carter, 321 So. 2d 433 (Fla. App. 1975) (indemnity denied hospital against physician on theory of active/passive negligence); Mize v. Atchison, T. & S. F. R. Co., 46 Cal. App. 3d 436, 120 Cal. Rptr. 787 (1975) (sending a railroad switch engine into construction area without a prior inspection may constitute active negligence). All these cases recognize that indemnity may be granted on a theory of active/passive negligence.

[99]Cooper Stevedoring Co. v. Fritz Kopke, Inc., 417 U.S. 106, 40 L. Ed. 2d 694, 94 S. Ct. 2174 (1974), affirming Sessions v. Fritz Kopke, Inc., 479 F.2d 1041 (5th Cir. Tex. 1973).

shoreman against a shipowner.[1] In holding that there could be no indemnity based on the implied warranty of workmanlike performance, the court distinguished the case of *Ryan Stevedoring Company v. Pan-Atlantic Steamship Corporation*,[2] which had been used as precedent for the indemnity cases, as that case had been decided prior to the 1972 amendments to the Longshoremen's and Harbor Workers' Compensation Act. The court found that *Ryan Stevedoring* had been legislatively overruled and that since the longshoreman's recovery against the shipowner was now based on negligence rather than strict liability, the shipowner's remedy against the employer should lie in contribution. This result is consistent with the tendency to limit the availability of common-law indemnity under comparative negligence. However, indemnity may still be available to shipowners in longshoreman cases, based not on a theory of breach of warranty, but of active/passive negligence.[3]

Wisconsin Erosion of Common-Law Indemnity

An interesting series of Wisconsin cases illustrates the way in which the common-law right to indemnity may be modified by comparative negligence. In *Pachowitz v. Milwaukee and Suburban Transport Corporation*,[4] a bus driver discharged a passenger at a place where the curb was defective but failed to warn her of the defect. The passenger fell and sustained injuries. When she brought action against the bus company, it filed a third-party complaint against the city, seeking indemni-

---

[1]See, e.g., Lamar v. Admiral Shipping Corp., 476 F.2d 300 (5th Cir. Fla. 1973); Julian v. Mitsui O. S. K. Lines, Ltd., 479 F.2d 432 (5th Cir. Tex. 1973) (longshoreman's contributing negligence to be considered in determining if stevedore has breached warranty of workmanlike performance); King v. Deutsche Dampfs-Ges, 523 F.2d 1042 (2d Cir. N.Y. 1975) (shipowner entitled to indemnity from marine carpenter's employer); Sousa v. M/V Caribia, 360 F. Supp. 971 (D. Mass. 1973); Maritime Fruit Carriers v. Luckenbach S.S. Co., 294 So. 2d 671 (Fla. App. 1974); Henderson v. S. C. Loveland Co., 381 F. Supp. 1102 (N.D. Fla. 1974); Scalafani v. Moore McCormack Lines, Inc., 388 F. Supp. 897 (E.D. N.Y. 1975), affd. without published opinion 535 F.2d 1242, 1243 (2d Cir. N.Y. 1975); cf. Castellano v. Oetker, Polarstein, 392 F. Supp. 668 (E.D. N.Y. 1975), affd. without published opinion 538 F.2d 308 (2d Cir. N.Y. 1976) (if shipowner hinders stevedore in fulfilling warranty of workmanlike performance, indemnity unavailable); Parker v. S/S Dorothe Olendorff, 483 F.2d 375 (5th Cir. La. 1973); Arthur v. Flota Mercante Gran Centro Americana S.A., 487 F.2d 561 (5th Cir. La. 1973); Williams v. Brasea, Inc., 497 F.2d 67 (5th Cir. Tex. 1974), mod. 513 F.2d 301 (5th Cir. Tex. 1975) (plaintiff must show breach of warranty of workmanlike performance on part of stevedoring company to obtain indemnity); but see Nye v. A/S D/S Svendborg, 501 F.2d 376 (2d Cir. N.Y. 1974) (indemnity denied shipowner due to contributing active negligence); Santiago Martinez v. Compaignie Generale Transatlantique, 517 F.2d 371 (1st Cir. P.R. 1975) (longshoreman's contributory negligence does not automatically establish breach of warranty of workmanlike performance); Stranahan v. A/S Atlantica & Tinfos Papirfabrik, 521 F.2d 700 (9th Cir. Ore. 1975) (no warranty of workmanlike performance extends to the charterer of a vessel).

[2]Ryan Stevedoring Co. v. Pan-Atlantic S.S. Corp., 350 U.S. 124, 100 L. Ed. 133, 76 S. Ct. 232 (1956).

[3]See, e.g., Kelloch v. S & H Subwater Salvage, Inc., 473 F.2d 767 (5th Cir. La. 1973) (shipowner recovers full indemnity from employer of harbor worker on a theory of active/passive negligence).

[4]Pachowitz v. Milwaukee & Suburban Transport Corp., 56 Wis. 2d 383, 202 N.W.2d 268 (1972).

ty. The bus company argued that its driver's negligence was passive and the city's was active in building an uneven and defective curb or in permitting it to continue in that condition.

Conceivably, the Wisconsin Supreme Court might have denied the bus company's claim to indemnity on traditional grounds—that the bus driver's negligence was not merely "passive," that the city's negligence was not "active," or that the bus driver's failure to warn was a separate contributing cause. However, the court chose instead to base its denial of indemnity on the policy of the comparative negligence statute. The granting of indemnity, the court said, was a choice of judicial policy; however, the policy manifested in the comparative negligence statute and in *Bielski v. Schulze*[5] favored contribution between tortfeasors over indemnity. Therefore, the court held, the bus company's only remedy against the city was for contribution based on findings as to the relative negligence of the parties.

Indemnity Under Product Liability

Three months after the *Pachowitz* case, *Gies v. Nissen Corporation*[6] came before the Wisconsin Supreme Court. There a college student was injured while performing on a trampoline belonging to the college under supervision of one of the college's instructors. The student brought action against the college, alleging improper supervision and failure to warn of inherent dangers. The college then filed a third-party complaint against the seller of the trampoline, alleging failure to warn and negligence per se on strict product liability, and seeking indemnity.

Once again the Wisconsin Supreme Court relied on the policy of the comparative negligence statute and, citing the *Pachowitz* case, held that the college's only remedy was for contribution—a remedy which, under the state of the pleadings in the particular case, had been foreclosed as *res judicata*. Thus was the policy denying common-law indemnity extended to a product liability case, at least as between seller and user.

Indemnity of Dealer by Manufacturer

Less than four months after the decision in the *Gies* case, the Wisconsin Supreme Court denied indemnity in another product liability case.[7] In that case, a defective wheel caused a city fire truck to upset while turning a corner. The city brought action against the dealer which had sold the truck to the city, the company that had assembled the chassis and the company that had manufactured the defective wheel. After judgment for the city, the dealer sought indemnity from the chassis maker and the wheel maker, and the chassis maker sought indemnity from the wheel maker.

---

[5]Bielski v. Schulze, 16 Wis. 2d 1, 114 N.W.2d 105 (1962). See text accompanying notes 36 to 41, section 16.7.

[6]Gies v. Nissen Corp., 57 Wis. 2d 371, 204 N.W.2d 519 (1973).

[7]Franklin v. Badger Ford Truck Sales, Inc., 58 Wis. 2d 641, 207 N.W.2d 866 (1973).

The Wisconsin Supreme Court once more denied indemnity, citing the *Gies* and *Pachowitz* decisions. The dealer's only remedy was for contribution based on jury findings as to the relative fault of the defendants. Thus, indemnity was denied—even as between sellers in the chain of production and distribution—in a case falling squarely within category 4 of the instances reviewed above[8] where the common law would have granted indemnity.

Indemnity of Negligent Parties Unlikely

In sum, traditional common-law duties of indemnity which allowed a non-negligent party to recover full damages from a party who caused him to suffer liability to a third party will doubtless remain under comparative negligence. However, cases that enlarged the indemnity remedy and allowed negligent tortfeasors to make an end run around the no-contribution-among-joint-tortfeasors rule will be suspect. They certainly will not be expanded.

Several courts have considerably limited the availability of common-law indemnity under comparative negligence. Some have found that a claim for indemnity against an employer by a negligent third party who is found liable to an injured employee is barred by the exclusive remedy provisions of workers' compensation laws.[9] In *Lockheed Aircraft Corporation v. United States*,[10] however, the Supreme Court of the United States ruled that the Federal Employees' Compensation Act does not directly bar third-party indemnity actions; the FECA exclusive liability provision, the Court held, was intended to govern only the rights of employees, their relatives, and people claiming through them or on their behalf.

Many courts have declined to adopt,[11] or have limited the application of,[12] the active/passive negligence theory as a basis for common-law indemnity. In *Dole v. Dow Chemical Company*[13] the Court of

---

[8]See text accompanying note 96 above.

[9]Herman v. United States, 382 F. Supp. 818 (E.D. Wis. 1974); Coleman v. General Motors Corp., 386 F. Supp. 87 (N.D. Ga. 1974); cf. Galimi v. Jetco, Inc., 514 F.2d 949 (2d Cir. N.Y. 1975).

[10]Lockheed Aircraft Corp. v. United States, 460 U.S. 190, 74 L. Ed. 2d 911, 103 S. Ct. 1033 (1983).

[11]Zaleskie v. Joyce, 133 Vt. 150, 333 A.2d 110 (1975) (dicta) (declining to adopt indemnity based on active/passive negligence); cf. Ryan v. New Bedford Cordage Co., 421 F. Supp. 794 (D. Vt. 1976), affd. without published opinion 559 F.2d 1205 (2d Cir. Vt. 1977) (indemnity denied user against supplier of rope used in scaffolding which collapsed as both parties were actively negligent. The court appeared to have been unaware of *Zaleskie*, supra, which should have foreclosed the indemnity question).

[12]See E. B. Wills Co. v. Superior Court of Merced County, 56 Cal. App. 3d 650, 128 Cal. Rptr. 541 (1976) (employer's active negligence no longer entitles passively negligent third party to indemnity for a recovery by an injured employee).

[13]Dole v. Dow Chem. Co., 30 N.Y.2d 143, 331 N.Y.S.2d 382, 282 N.E.2d 288, 53 A.L.R.3d 175 (1972); but see Bass v. United States, 379 F. Supp. 1208 (D. Colo. 1974) (Colorado comparative negligence statute does not preclude claim for indemnity against a joint tortfeasor who is "sole or primary" cause of the injury; Colorado comparative negligence statute does not provide for apportionment of recovery among negligent joint tortfeasors).

Appeals of New York rejected the theory of complete indemnity based on active/passive negligence prior to that state's legislature's adoption of pure comparative negligence. The court found that the rule of indemnity based on a theory of active/passive negligence was adopted to ameliorate the harshness of the common-law rule of no contribution among joint tortfeasors. The court concluded that the purpose would be better served by a rule based on degrees of relative fault rather than the "artificial distinction" of active/passive negligence. Had New York not adopted pure comparative negligence, an anomaly would have existed in that state's tort law—negligence would have been apportioned between defendants, but not between plaintiff and defendant.

The Supreme Court of California took a leaf from the *Dole* decision. It created an "end run" around the state's limited *pro rata* division contribution statute by modifying the law of common-law indemnity. The court held that the "all or nothing" approach of common-law indemnity should be modified in appropriate cases to permit a right of *partial* indemnity among multiple tortfeasors.[14] Damages would be apportioned on a comparative fault basis, not on a *pro rata* basis. This result is in keeping with the spirit of the *Li* decision, which adopted comparative negligence in California.[15]

It should be noted that in an action for indemnity, the issue of apportionment of fault among defendants can be decided in the initial action brought by plaintiff. Under California's contribution statute, the right to bring an action does not arise until a judgment has been imposed on the party seeking to bring such a claim.

The Kansas Supreme Court, which has for practical purposes abolished contribution,[16] has created a rule of comparative implied indemnity where one defendant has settled for more than his share of damages[17] but has limited it to product liability chain-of-distribution cases.[18]

In *Southern Railway Company v. Brunswick Pulp and Paper Company*,[19] a court applied comparative negligence principles to a *contractual* indemnity agreement. An agreement between two negligent par-

---

[14]American Motorcycle Assn. v. Superior Court of Los Angeles County, 20 Cal. 3d 578, 146 Cal. Rptr. 182, 578 P.2d 899 (1978) (citing this treatise). See generally Mattschei v. United States, 600 F.2d 205 (9th Cir. Cal. 1979); Safeway Stores, Inc. v. Nest-Kart, 21 Cal. 3d 322, 146 Cal. Rptr. 550, 579 P.2d 441 (1978) (extending rule to situation where one or more defendants is strictly liable); Arbaugh v. Procter & Gamble Mfg. Co., 80 Cal. App. 3d 500, 145 Cal. Rptr. 608 (1978); Sears, Roebuck & Co. v. International Harvester Co., 82 Cal. App. 3d 492, 147 Cal. Rptr. 262 (1978).

[15]Nga Li v. Yellow Cab Co., 13 Cal. 3d 804, 119 Cal. Rptr. 858, 532 P.2d 1226, 78 A.L.R.3d 393 (1975).

[16]Brown v. Keill, 224 Kan. 195, 580 P.2d 867 (1978).

[17]Kennedy v. Sawyer, 228 Kan. 439, 618 P.2d 788 (1980).

[18]Ellis v. Union P. R. Co., 213 Kan. 182, 643 P.2d 158 (1982).

[19]Southern R. Co. v. Brunswick Pulp & Paper Co., 376 F. Supp. 96 (S.D. Ga. 1974). See also Dugas v. Pelican Constr. Co., 481 F.2d 773 (5th Cir. La. 1973) (refusing to enforce express agreement to indemnify against subcontractor as party seeking indemnity was sole negligent actor).

ties that one should indemnify the other for all damages resulting from its negligence was interpreted as entitling the indemnitee to recover the percentage of his damages not attributable to his own negligence. The rule to be applied was not indemnity, but a form of contribution based on degrees of relative fault. Most courts, however, continue to treat express indemnity agreements as a matter of contract between the parties.[20]

---

[20]See, e.g., Shell Oil Co. v. Brinkerhoff-Signal Drilling Co., 658 P.2d 1187 (Utah 1983) (express indemnity contract unaffected by comparative negligence or workers' compensation immunity statute).

CHAPTER 17

FACT FINDING UNDER COMPARATIVE NEGLIGENCE

Section

17.1 The basic difficulty in comparing negligence

Comparative negligence becomes operative only when evidence has been presented which would support a jury finding that a plaintiff negligently contributed to his own injury.[1] Defendant is required to plead and prove facts supporting this finding.[2] All comparative negligence systems require the trier of fact to determine the extent to which plaintiff's fault contributed to the accident. How can this be done? It is not easy to articulate precisely why a plaintiff was a particular percentage at fault in a particular accident.[3]

Under most comparative negligence systems, the jury is asked to apportion fault as if it were a tangible and measurable commodity. For example, in Wisconsin, the jury is given a special interrogatory questioning "to what extent each party is to blame for the accident in question."[4] This is part of the process of implementing the comparative negligence goal of holding each party responsible for the damage he negligently caused.

Guilt, Not Causation

The process is *not* allocation of physical causation, which could be scientifically apportioned, but rather of allocating *fault*, which cannot be scientifically measured. For example, suppose an intoxicated motorcyclist speeds at eighty miles an hour down a highway with a 55 mile speed limit. He loses control of his vehicle and crosses over into the opposite lane where he collides with a large truck traveling 65 miles per hour. The point of collision is the left fender of the truck. As a result of the impact, the motorcyclist is killed and his vehicle is a total

---

[1]See Gardner v. Morrison, 427 F.2d 654 (5th Cir. Ga. 1970) (applying Georgia law).

[2]Railway Express Agency v. Mallory, 168 F.2d 426 (5th Cir. Miss. 1948); McGuiggan v. Hiller Bros., 214 Wis. 388, 253 N.W. 403 (1934).

[3]Aiken, *Proportioning Comparative Negligence—Problems of Theory and Special Verdict Formulation*, 53 Marq. L. Rev. 293, 294-297 (1970).

[4]Ghiardi & Hogan, *Comparative Negligence—The Wisconsin Rule and Procedure*, 18 Def. L. J. 537, 561 (1969).

loss. The truck, however, is only slightly damaged and the truckdriver is not hurt at all.

In terms of pure physical causation, perhaps an expert could testify that the truck supplied 95% of the force that killed the motorcyclist, based on formulae combining the relative weights, speeds and directions of the vehicles. Even without expert assistance, the jurors might, by instinct, regard the truck as the more substantial cause. Nevertheless, the jury's line of inquiry under comparative negligence does not focus on physical causation; rather, it considers and weighs culpability.[5] In Nebraska and South Dakota, the question is whether plaintiff's negligence was "slight" and defendant's "gross" in comparison. In many other states, the jury must determine the percentage of fault to be allocated to the plaintiff when the accident is considered as a whole.

Different juries and different jurors will often give dissimilar answers. Some might say the motorcyclist in our hypothetical case was 5% at fault, others 60%, even 90%. Nevertheless, in a particular trial, all jurors (or a legal majority if the state permits a less-than-unanimous verdict) must agree on a fixed percentage of fault attributable to the plaintiff. The trial lawyer can readily observe that the system creates a greater temptation for the jury to render a quotient verdict; nevertheless, jurors are not legally permitted to average out their respective guesses as to plaintiff's fault and agree to call that their verdict.[6]

The Need for Joinder of Parties

Another significant problem with the inexact nature of fault apportionment is that if multiple trials are held concerning the same accident, different juries may produce dissimilar results with regard to the percentage of a particular individual's contribution to the accident. Legal scholars note that under comparative negligence, the need for compulsory joinder is almost self-evident. However, not all states with comparative negligence have compulsory joinder.[7]

---

[5]See Houston-New Orleans, Inc. v. Page Engineering Co., 353 F. Supp. 890 (E.D. La. 1972); accord, Pan-Alaska Fisheries v. Marine Constr. & Design Co., 402 F. Supp. 1187 (W.D. Wash. 1975) (citing this treatise) (vacated on other grounds in 565 F.2d 1129 (9th Cir. Wash. 1977)); State v. Kaatz, 572 P.2d 775 (Alaska 1977) (citing this treatise). See also Danculovich v. Brown, 593 P.2d 187 (Wyo. 1979) (jury should consider evidence on issues of willful and wanton misconduct).

[6]See McNamee v. Woodbury Congregation of Jehovah's Witnesses, 193 Conn. 15, 475 A.2d 262 (1984); Jackowska-Peterson v. D. Reik & Sons Co., 240 Wis. 197, 199, 2 N.W.2d 873, 874 (1942).

[7]States with both comparative negligence and compulsory joinder (usually in the pattern of Fed. R. Civ. P., 19(a)) include Arizona (Ariz. R.Civ.P., Rule 19(a)), Arkansas (Ark. Stat. Ann., § 27-808), Colorado (Colo. R.Civ.P., Rule 19(a)), Delaware (Del. Super. Ct. Civ. L., Rule 19(a)), Georgia (Ga. Code Ann., § 9-11-19), Hawaii (Hawaii R.Civ.P., Rule 19), Idaho (Idaho R.Civ.P., Rule 19a), Indiana (Ind. R. Tr. Proc., Rule 19(a)), Maine (Me. R.Civ.P., Rule 19(a)), Minnesota (Minn. Stat. Ann., Tit. 27, Rule 19.01), Nebraska (Neb. Rev. Stat., § 25-318), Nevada (Nev. R.Civ.P., Rule 19(a)), New Jersey (N.J. R.Civ.P., Rule 3:19-1), North Dakota (N.D. R.Civ.P., Rule 19(a)), Oklahoma (Okla. Stat. Ann., tit. 12, §§ 230, 231), Oregon (Ore. Rev. Stat., § 13.110), Rhode Island (R.I. R.Civ.P., Rule 19(a)), South Dakota (S.D. Codified Laws, § 15-6-19(a)), Texas (Tex. R.Civ.P., Rule 39), Utah (Utah R.Civ.P., Rule 19(a)) and Wyoming (Wyo. R.Civ.P., Rule 19(a)). States with comparative negligence but not compulsory joinder include Florida, Massachusetts, Mississippi, New Hampshire, Vermont, Washington and Wisconsin.

Because of these untoward possibilities, the comparative negligence states are very hesitant to overturn a jury determination judicially,[8] and they are also reluctant to allow jurors to impeach their own verdict.[9] The courts know that the jury's determination is inexact at best. When the apportionment of negligence is determined by a judge sitting as the trier of fact, the appellate court may be more likely to set aside the apportionment, particularly if the trial judge does not state the factual bases of his apportionment.[10]

Jury Selection

The Wyoming Supreme Court has found that comparative negligence has had an impact on jury selection. In *Distad v. Cubin*[11] the court held that joint defendants were each entitled to a full allocation of peremptory challenges because each had an interest in increasing the other's liability and therefore had antagonistic interests with regard to one another. It should be noted that this theory applies with special force in a jurisdiction like Wyoming which compares the fault of the plaintiff to each defendant in deciding whether the plaintiff is more than half at fault; a defendant who succeeds in assigning enough fault to a co-defendant will not have to pay any damages at all.

Guidelines for Jury Determination

Comparative negligence systems have had to allow for the fact that comparisons of fault cannot be made scientifically. Nevertheless, the trial lawyer and the court can provide a jury with guidelines that may assist it in making a responsible determination.

First, the jury might be asked to focus on the probability, from the negligent party's point of view, that the particular kind of harm would occur which in fact did occur. If the risk was high, he may have been significantly at fault. In the hypothetical involving the motorcyclist, it would appear that the risk of physical injury was quite high. The truckdriver, on the other hand, did not take as great a risk; certainly it could be persuasively argued that the probability that a motorcyclist from the opposite lane would cross in front of him was quite low.

Second, the jury might focus on the extent to which either the plaintiff or the defendant, as an ordinary reasonable person, would real-

---

[8]See, e.g., Elias v. New Laurel Radio Station, Inc., 245 Miss. 170, 146 So. 2d 558, 92 A.L.R.2d 1065 (1962); Presser v. Siesel Constr. Co., 19 Wis. 2d 54, 119 N.W.2d 405 (1963); Campbell, *Ten Years of Comparative Negligence*, 1941 Wis. L. Rev. 289; Prosser, *Comparative Negligence*, 51 Mich. L. Rev. 482-483 (1953). Accord, Cullinan v. Burlington Northern, Inc., 522 F.2d 1034 (9th Cir. Mont. 1975); Renzaglia v. Chipman, 298 Minn. 384, 215 N.W.2d 477 (1974); Riley v. Lake, 295 Minn. 43, 203 N.W.2d 331 (1972); Hudson v. Columbus, 139 Ga. App. 789, 229 S.E.2d 671 (1976); but see Jones v. Jones, 113 N.H. 553, 311 A.2d 522 (1973) (withdrawal from jury of issue of passenger's contributory negligence was proper); Dertz v. Pasquina, 59 Ill. 2d 68, 319 N.E.2d 12 (1974) (proper for judge to direct verdict as to comparison of negligence; plaintiff not contributorily negligent as a matter of law); Powell v. Ouray, 32 Colo. App. 44, 507 P.2d 1101 (1973).

[9]Jackowska-Peterson v. D. Reik & Sons Co., 240 Wis. 197, 2 N.W.2d 873 (1942).

[10]See, e.g., Williams v. Brasea, Inc., 497 F.2d 67 (5th Cir. Tex. 1974), mod. 513 F.2d 301 (5th Cir. Tex. 1975).

[11]Distad v. Cubin, 633 P.2d 167 (Wyo. 1981).

ize that the particular harm might indeed occur. It would be important, in making this determination, for the jury to know what facts which the plaintiff and defendant had gained from their prior experience that would aid them in realizing the dangers at hand.

Third, the jury might evaluate what, if anything, of value was to be gained by either party's taking the risk. If, for example, the motorcyclist was a doctor rushing to attend a critical patient, his negligence might be reduced.

Fourth, if something of significant value was to be gained by taking the risk, might there have been more reasonable ways to obtain that value? If the motorcyclist was a doctor on an errand of mercy, could he have taken an automobile instead?

These considerations are not dissimilar from those utilized to measure negligence in general.[12] Nevertheless, they can be distilled from opinions that attempt to review a jury's effort in comparing negligence.[13] Courts have shied away from giving more specific formulas, and most have declined even to attempt to list the considerations presented here.[14] Nevertheless, the four factors will be helpful to the attorney who wishes to present his final argument in an organized and persuasive manner. The four considerations present a method of putting a difficult process, that of comparing fault, into practice.

17.2 Pleading and burden of proof

The states' comparative negligence statutes have not, with four exceptions,[15] dealt with the problems of pleading and burden of proof.

In Wisconsin, questions in this area have been resolved by case law. There, as in the majority of contributory negligence states, plaintiff need not plead or produce evidence of his own freedom from contributory negligence in order to obtain a full recovery. The burden of coming forward with the evidence of the plaintiff's negligence rests with

---

[12]See United States v. Carroll Towing Co., 159 F.2d 169 (2d Cir. N.Y. 1947) (admiralty case in which Judge Learned Hand applied negligence principles); Davison v. Snohomish County, 149 Wash. 109, 270 P. 422 (1928) (stressing social utility of defendant's road-building activity).

[13]See Associated Engineers, Inc. v. Job, 370 F.2d 633, 641 (8th Cir. S.D. 1967) (applying South Dakota law).

[14]The case cited in note 13 above is one of the few decisions to make the attempt. But see State v. Kaatz, 572 P.2d 775 (Alaska 1977) (citing this treatise) (court lists four items which make apportionment process more concrete for trier of fact).

[15]New Hampshire's comparative negligence statute provides that "the burden of proof as to the existence or amount of causal negligence alleged to be attributable to a party shall rest upon the party making such allegation." N.H. Rev. Stat. Ann., § 507:7-a. See, e.g., Jones v. Jones, 113 N.H. 553, 311 A.2d 522 (1973). The New York comparative negligence statute provides that negligence ascribed in diminution of damages "shall be an affirmative defense to be pleaded or proved by the party ascribing the defense." N.Y. Civ. Prac. Law, § 1412. See Woods v. J.R. Liquors, Inc., 86 A.D.2d 546, 446 N.Y.S.2d 64 (1982). The Massachusetts statute places the burden of proof on the defense and states that there is a presumption of due care on the part of the plaintiff. Mass. Gen. Laws Ann., ch. 231, § 85. The Iowa statute also places the burden of pleading and proving contributory fault on the defendant. Iowa Code Ann., § 619.17.

the defendant.[16] Once defendant introduces enough evidence to support a finding that the plaintiff was negligent in some degree, plaintiff has the burden of persuasion to show that defendant's negligence was at least as great as his own.[17]

In the overwhelming majority of states where contributory negligence is or was a complete defense, defendant has or had the burden of coming forward with evidence and the burden of persuasion as to plaintiff's negligence.[18] It seems proper, when comparative negligence is adopted, to leave these burdens with the defendant,[19] and those state courts that have dealt with the issue have done so.[20] Contributory negligence returns as a complete bar in the majority of comparative negligence states when plaintiff is as negligent as or more negligent than defendant. This seems all the more reason to allocate the burdens of pleading and proof as they were before comparative negligence.

In *Crocker v. Coombs*,[21] the Supreme Court of Maine held that the advent of comparative negligence in Maine required a shifting of the burden of proof on the issue of the plaintiff's contributory negligence. Prior to Maine's adoption of comparative negligence, plaintiffs in that state were required to plead and prove their own freedom from contributory negligence. The Crocker court held that the humanitarian rationale underlying comparative negligence required that "the burden of proving the causal negligence of a tortiously injured party now falls on his adversary, who must support this burden by a fair preponderance of the evidence."[22]

---

[16]See, e.g., Guderyon v. Wisconsin Tel. Co., 240 Wis. 215, 2 N.W.2d 242 (1942); Fjelstad v. Walsh, 244 Wis. 295, 12 N.W.2d 51 (1943); Potter v. Potter, 224 Wis. 251, 272 N.W. 34 (1937); McGuiggan v. Hiller Bros., 214 Wis. 388, 253 N.W. 403 (1934).

[17]See Vogel v. Vetting, 265 Wis. 19, 60 N.W.2d 399 (1953) (intersection collision; jury found both parties negligent as to lookout and control; on motions after verdict, trial court found plaintiff negligent for failing to yield right-of-way; held, where plaintiff was negligent as a matter of law regarding right-of-way, he failed to carry burden of proof on 50% issue, and so was barred). Smith v. Green Bay, 223 Wis. 427, 271 N.W. 28 (1937) (presumption of due care for one's own safety disappears once defendant has introduced evidence of negligence).

[18]See, e.g., Comment, *Comparative Negligence: Some New Problems for the Maine Courts*, 18 Me. L. Rev. 65, 92-93 (1966); W. Prosser, *Handbook of the Law of Torts* § 65 (4th ed. 1971).

[19]Comment, note 18 above, 18 Me. L. Rev. at 92-93.

[20]See, e.g., Browning v. Kahle, 106 Ga. App. 353, 126 S.E.2d 892 (1962); McGraw v. Sanders Co. Plumbing & Heating, Inc., 233 Kan. 766, 667 P.2d 289 (1983); Mileur v. Briggerman, 110 Ill. App. 3d 721, 66 Ill. Dec. 443, 442 N.E.2d 1356 (1982); Addair v. Bryant, 284 S.E.2d 374, 378 n.3 (W. Va. 1981) (dictum). The Vermont Supreme Court has stated that the defendant has the burden not only of proving that the plaintiff was negligent but of showing that the plaintiff was more negligent than he. Frost v. Tisbert, 135 Vt. 345, 376 A.2d 748 (1977).

[21]Crocker v. Coombs, 328 A.2d 389 (Me. 1974).

[22]Id., at 392; accord, Ginn v. Penobscot Co., 334 A.2d 874 (Me. 1975), mod. 342 A.2d 270 (Me. 1975). In Iadevaia v. Aetna Bridge Co., 120 R.I. 610, 389 A.2d 1246 (1978) the Rhode Island Supreme Court noted in dictum that Rhode Island placed the burden of proof on the plaintiff but that the instant case had arisen before Rhode Island adopted comparative negligence.

17.3 Summary judgment and directed verdict

Appellate courts are very reluctant to uphold a trial court's direction of summary judgment in comparative negligence cases when the issue could be construed as focusing on a factual determination of plaintiff's negligence. For example, in *Cirillo v. Milwaukee*[23] an action by a student against his teacher and the city, the trial court granted summary judgment on the ground that as a matter of law, the teacher could not have foreseen plaintiff's injury, so was not negligent in leaving a class unsupervised. The Supreme Court of Wisconsin reversed, stating that "Summary judgment is a poor device for deciding questions of comparative negligence."[24]

Under the comparative negligence statute the totality of causal negligence in the case must be examined for the jury to apportion negligence.[25] The *Cirillo* court reiterated that comparison of negligence is a jury function, and that only in rare cases may a court hold as a matter of law that the negligence of one party is equal to or greater than that of the other.[26]

Similarly, a federal court applying Colorado law pointed out that comparative fault would preclude summary judgment, even where the defendant had run a red light, because it was still necessary to determine the degree of fault on both sides.[27] In *Taylor v. Bolton*[28] the Court of Appeals of Georgia affirmed the lower court's denial of summary judgment for defendant in a farmhand's negligence action against his employer. The court stated:

> It is also well settled that ordinarily issues of negligence and proximate cause, including defenses ... are jury questions and that a court should not take the place of a jury in solving them except in plain and indisputable cases.[29]

Thus the court may very rarely decide comparative negligence ques-

---

[23]Cirillo v. Milwaukee, 34 Wis. 2d 705, 150 N.W.2d 460 (1967). See also C. C. Natvig's Sons, Inc. v. Summers, 198 Neb. 741, 255 N.W.2d 272 (1977); Cincinnati Ins. Co. v. Schneider, 349 So. 2d 728 (Fla. App. 1977) (grant of partial summary judgment for plaintiff when defendant raised defenses of contributory negligence and assumption of risks constitutes reversible error).

[24]Cirillo v. Milwaukee, note 23 above, 150 N.W.2d at 466. See also Plant v. Lowman, 134 Ga. App. 752, 216 S.E.2d 631 (1975) (issue of comparison of negligence does not lend itself to summary adjudication).

[25]Cirillo v. Milwaukee, note 23 above, 150 N.W.2d at 466. This does not preclude the trial court from ruling, if the circumstances so warrant after all the evidence, that plaintiff's negligence is at least as great as defendant's.

[26]Id., 150 N.W.2d at 465, citing Baumgarten v. Jones, 21 Wis. 2d 467, 471, 124 N.W.2d 609, 611 (1963); Rewolinski v. Harley-Davidson Motor Co., 32 Wis. 2d 680, 146 N.W.2d 485, 487 (1966); Mix v. Farmers Mut. Automobile Ins. Co., 6 Wis. 2d 38, 41, 93 N.W.2d 869, 871 (1959). See also McClain v. Seaboard C. L. R. Co., 490 F.2d 863 (5th Cir. Ga. 1974) (directed verdict for defendant improper when twelve-year-old boy injured when attempting to crawl under train).

[27]McCormick v. United States, 539 F. Supp. 1179 (D. Colo. 1982).

[28]Taylor v. Bolton, 121 Ga. App. 141, 173 S.E.2d 96 (1970).

[29]Id., 173 S.E.2d at 98.

tions without submitting them to the jury. Three states provide in their comparative negligence statutes that plaintiff's negligence is *always* a jury question.[30]

The 50% Bar

In all jurisdictions with 50% comparative negligence, the courts have been troubled in determining when plaintiff's negligence has, as a matter of law, reached the vital point (either equal to or greater than defendant's negligence) that will bar the claim. In 1953, the late Dean Prosser collected many cases from Georgia and Wisconsin and demonstrated inconsistency even in the same jurisdiction.[31] Prosser noted a trend away from the recitation of predictable principles in this area,[32] and this trend has developed even further in the years since. That plaintiff has committed more acts of negligence than has defendant, thus, does not automatically ensure victory for the defendant.[33]

When plaintiff and defendant have been guilty of the same kind of negligence, a verdict for the plaintiff may be upheld on the ground that the jury could have found that the negligence of the parties differed in degree.[34] On the other hand, where different kinds of negligence were involved, a jury finding that plaintiff's negligence equaled that of defendant may well be upheld.[35]

It seems more and more difficult for a defendant to secure a directed verdict on the ground that plaintiff's negligence was equal to or greater than his.[36] It is probably even harder to obtain a summary judgment for defendant on this issue.[37] Likewise, the judgment n.o.v. is

---

[30]Ariz. Rev. Stat. Ann., § 12-2505(A); Neb. Rev. Stat., § 25-1151; Okla. Stat. Ann., tit. 23, § 12.

[31]See Prosser, *Comparative Negligence*, 51 Mich. L. Rev. 465, 491-492 (1953), citing 69 cases demonstrating lack of consistency in this area. See also Note, *Comparative Negligence: Some New Problems for the Maine Courts*, 18 Me. L. Rev. 65, 75 (1966), posing the problem in terms of the Maine statute.

[32]Prosser, note 31 above, at 493.

[33]See, e.g., Maus v. Cook, 15 Wis. 2d 203, 112 N.W.2d 589 (1961); Sailing v. Wallestad, 32 Wis. 2d 435, 145 N.W.2d 725 (1966); Jensen v. Rural Mut. Ins. Co., 41 Wis. 2d 36, 163 N.W.2d 158 (1968).

[34]See, e.g., Jensen v. Rural Mut. Ins. Co., 41 Wis. 2d 36, 163 N.W.2d 158 (1968); Winkler v. State Farm Mut. Auto. Ins. Co., 11 Wis. 2d 170, 105 N.W.2d 302 (1960); Strupp v. Farmers Mut. Auto. Ins. Co., 14 Wis. 2d 158, 109 N.W.2d 660 (1961). See also Hansberry v. Dunn, 230 Wis. 626, 284 N.W. 556 (1939).

[35]Ernst v. Karlman, 242 Wis. 516, 8 N.W.2d 280 (1943).

[36]See Bourassa v. Gateway Erectors, Inc., 54 Wis. 2d 176, 194 N.W.2d 602, 604 (1972); Huettl v. Huettl, 278 Ore. 701, 565 P.2d 752 (1977) (plaintiff's directed verdict motion properly denied since jury would still have to decide percentage of fault if defendant were negligent); Farley v. M M Cattle Co., 529 S.W.2d 751 (Tex. 1975) (trial court erred when it directed a verdict for the defendant at the end of plaintiff's case, as sufficient evidence existed to raise a fact issue of negligence and for case to go to the jury). But see Vasquez v. Clubb, 531 P.2d 978 (Colo. App. 1975) (directed verdict for defendant upheld).

[37]Cf. Arnstein v. Porter, 154 F.2d 464 (2d Cir. N.Y. 1946) (limitation on use of summary judgment procedure). See McGuire v. Ford Motor Co., 360 F. Supp. 447 (E.D. Wis. 1973) (summary judgment denied; issue of whether intervening negligence relieved defendant of liability is for jury); Jordan v. Coos-Curry Electric Cooperative, Inc., 267 Ore. 164, 515 P.2d 913 (1973) (generally, apportionment of negligence is for jury).

available to set aside a jury verdict when there is no credible evidence supporting it.[38] The popularity of statutes permitting a plaintiff who was 50% at fault to recover half his damages, including a 1971 change in the Wisconsin statute, will probably accelerate these trends.[39]

Pure Comparative Negligence

Pure comparative negligence makes it more difficult for defendants to obtain directed verdicts and summary judgments. As no 50% bar exists, the jury is permitted to make its comparison of negligence unless it is clear as a matter of law that one party's negligence was the sole proximate cause of the injury.[40]

17.4 Special verdicts and jury interrogatories

The comparative negligence statutes of sixteen states specifically provide for the use of special verdicts. In seven of those states the special verdict is required in every case where contributory negligence is an issue.[41] In nine other states, a special verdict may be used at the discretion of the court and must be provided on timely request by any party.[42] In Nevada, the jury need not find specific percentages if it finds that plaintiff's negligence was greater than defendant's, thus barring his recovery.[43] The specificity of these statutes avoids the clumsiness and difficulty that have affected the special verdict device.

The statutes indicate that the jury is to return a special verdict stating:

---

[38]See, e.g., Heater v. Chesapeake & O. R. Co., 497 F.2d 1243 (7th Cir. Ill. 1974).

[39]But see Schuh v. Fox River Tractor Co., 63 Wis. 2d 728, 218 N.W.2d 279 (1974) (finding plaintiff who stood in dangerous position on crop blower guilty of negligence greater than defendants as a matter of law); Jacobs v. Stack, 63 Wis. 2d 672, 218 N.W.2d 364 (1974) (directed verdict appropriate in absence of any evidence of defendant's negligence); see also Riley v. Lake, 295 Minn. 43, 203 N.W.2d 331 (1972) (adoption of "not greater than" version of comparative negligence supports need for a jury apportionment of negligence).

[40]See, e.g., Pritchett v. Jacksonville Auction, Inc., 449 So. 2d 364 (Fla. App. 1984) (summary judgment is appropriate only if plaintiff could not recover "under any reasonable view of the evidence"); Rea v. Leadership Housing, Inc., 312 So. 2d 818 (Fla. App. 1975), affd. 348 So. 2d 287 (Fla. 1977); Goldberg v. McCabe, 313 So. 2d 47 (Fla. App. 1975); cf. Santiesteban v. McGrath, 320 So. 2d 476 (Fla. App. 1975) (jury apportionment of negligence necessary even when one party is negligent as a matter of law); Martin v. Hertz Corp., 104 Ill. App. 3d 592, 60 Ill. Dec. 363, 432 N.E.2d 1262 (1982); Williams v. New York, 101 A.D.2d 835, 475 N.Y.S.2d 495 (1984).

[41]Colo. Rev. Stat., § 13-21-111(2); Hawaii Rev. Stat., § 663-31(b); Ind. Code, § 34-4-33-6; Iowa Code Ann., § 668.3(2); Kan. Stat. Ann., § 60-258a(b); N.J. Stat. Ann., § 2A:15-5.2; Ohio Rev. Code Ann., § 2315.19(B). The 1973 amendment of the Massachusetts statute, Mass. Gen. Laws Ann., ch. 231, § 85, deleted the provision for special verdicts, but special verdicts are still allowed within the discretion of the trial judge. Kettinger v. Black & Decker Mfg. Co., 13 Mass. App. 993, 432 N.E.2d 736 (1982).

[42]Idaho Code, § 6-802; La. Code Civ. Proc., art. 1812; Me. Rev. Stat. Ann., tit. 14, § 156 (interrogatories); Minn. Stat. Ann., § 604.01, subd. 1; Nev. Rev. Stat., § 41.141(2)(b); N.D. Cent. Code, § 9-10-07; Ore. Rev. Stat., § 18.480(1); Utah Code Ann., § 78-27-38; Wyo. Stat., § 1-1-109(b).

[43]Nev. Rev. Stat., § 41.141(2)(b).

1. The amount of damages which would have been recoverable if there had been no contributory negligence; and

2. The degree of negligence of each party, expressed as a percentage.

The court then is required to reduce the amount of coverage in proportion to the amount of contributory negligence. In 50% jurisdictions, the court is empowered to enter judgment for the defendant if the jury has found that plaintiff's negligence has reached the percentage required to bar his recovery.

Comparative negligence statutes dealing directly with special verdicts usually provide that in a nonjury case, the court shall make findings of fact.[44] This is in effect a refined substitute for the special verdict.

Additional Questions Submitted

There seems to be nothing to prevent a court from requiring from the jury special verdicts beyond the basic two set forth in the statute. This may be necessary to achieve clarity in a multiparty case. Further, if in a particular case, more jury control is desirable, the special verdict procedure could be supplemented by special interrogatories.

The comparative negligence statutes of eighteen states[45] leave open the type of verdict to be rendered and who shall reduce the damages if plaintiff is found contributorily negligent. The special verdict is authorized, however, in nearly all states by either statute or common law.[46]

The Supreme Court of Florida, overruling a prior system of trial court discretion, held in *Lawrence v. Florida East Coast Railway Com-*

---

[44]See statutes cited in notes 41 and 42 above. See also Lawrence v. Florida E. C. R. Co., 346 So. 2d 1012 (Fla. 1977).

[45]Arizona, Arkansas, Connecticut, Delaware, Georgia, Massachusetts, Mississippi, Montana, Nebraska, New York, Oklahoma, Pennsylvania, Rhode Island, South Dakota, Texas, Vermont, Washington and Wisconsin. See Bradley v. Maurer, 17 Wash. App. 24, 560 P.2d 719 (1977) (failure to give special verdict form not error). The Oklahoma Constitution allows only a general verdict; however, as long as the jury finds in favor of either party, special findings of fact do not deprive the verdict of its generality. Smith v. Gizzi, 564 P.2d 1009 (Okla. 1977).

[46]Prosser, *Comparative Negligence*, 51 Mich. L. Rev. 465, 499 (1953). See, for example, Colo. R.Civ.P., Rule 49; Conn. Gen. Stat. Ann., § 52-224; Ga. Code Ann., § 7-11-49; Hawaii Rev. Stat., § 635-19; Idaho R.Civ.P., Rule 49; Mass. Gen. Laws Ann., ch. 231, § 124; Minn. Stat. Ann., § 546.19; Neb. Rev. Stat., §§ 25-1120 to 25-1122; N.D. R.Civ.P., Rule 49; Okla. Stat. Ann., tit. 12, § 587; Ore. Rev. Stat., §§ 17.405, 17.415; S.D. Codified Laws, § 15-6-49; Tex. R.Civ.P., Rule 291; Utah R.Civ.P., Rule 49; Vt. R.Civ.P., Rule 49; Wis. Stat. Ann., § 270.27. See generally W. Barron & A. Holtzoff, *Federal Practice and Procedure* § 1051, (Rules ed. 1961); F. James & G. Hazard, *Civil Procedure* § 7.15 (1977); C. Wright, *The Law of Federal Courts* § 94 (4th ed. 1983).

In Arkansas, a provision of the original comparative negligence statute (Ark. Acts 1955, No. 191) provided for mandatory submission on special issues when requested, but since that provision was repealed (Ark. Acts 1957, No. 296), the trial court has had discretion whether to submit a case for general or special verdicts. Cobb v. Atkins, 239 Ark. 151, 388 S.W.2d 8 (1965). See also Carlson v. Hanson, 166 Neb. 96, 88 N.W.2d 140 (1958), holding it proper to dismiss the complaint after the jury returned special verdicts that defendant's negligence was less than gross and plaintiff's negligence was more than slight in comparison.

pany[47] that special verdicts were required in all jury trials involving comparative negligence, as did the Supreme Court of New Mexico.[48]

California, in judicially adopting pure comparative negligence, approved the use of special verdicts, but left their use to the discretion of the trial court.[49] Oregon also leaves the question of the use of special verdicts to the discretion of the trial judge.[50]

When the West Virginia Supreme Court adopted comparative negligence in *Bradley v. Appalachian Power Company*,[51] it provided that the jury would be required to state the gross amount of damages of each party by general verdict and the percentage of fault attributable to each party via special interrogatory. The trial court would then calculate the net amount by deducting the party's percentage of fault from the gross award.

Wisconsin Special Verdict

It is surprising to learn that Wisconsin, the state that has done the most to develop and popularize the use of special verdicts in comparative negligence cases, does not have the procedure spelled out in its comparative negligence statute. Rather, the Supreme Court of Wisconsin looked to the state's general statute on special verdicts and indicated that they should always be used in jury-tried comparative negligence cases.

Wisconsin has developed a rather elaborate set of special verdict questions which inquire as to the component factual issues upon which the ultimate issues of fact are determined. First, inquiry is made as to whether any of the parties was negligent, then as to whether such negligence was a cause of the accident, then as to the respective percentages of causal negligence, and finally as to the damages sustained. An example follows:[52]

QUESTION NO. 1

At and just prior to the collision, was the defendant _____negligent with respect to:

(a) speed? Answer: _____
(b) racing? Answer: _____
(c) overtaking and passing? Answer: _____

---

[47]Lawrence v. Florida E. C. R. Co., 346 So. 2d 1012 (Fla. 1977). See also Florida E. C. R. Co. v. Lawrence, 328 So. 2d 249 (Fla. App. 1976) (when contributory negligence is at issue, special verdict should be given on timely request by any party) (citing this treatise).

[48]Armstrong v. Industrial Electric & Equipment Service, 97 N.M. 272, 639 P.2d 81 (1981) citing N.M. Sup. Ct. Order No. 8000, Misc. (March 30, 1981).

[49]Nga Li v. Yellow Cab Co., 13 Cal. 3d 804, 824 n.18, 119 Cal. Rptr. 858, 532 P.2d 1226, 1246 n.18, 78 A.L.R.3d 393 (1975).

[50]Hammagren v. Wald Constr., Inc., 274 Ore. 267, 545 P.2d 859 (1976) (citing this treatise).

[51]Bradley v. Appalachian Power Co., 163 W. Va. 332, 256 S.E.2d 879 (1979).

[52]From Ghiardi & Hogan, *Comparative Negligence—The Wisconsin Rule and Procedure*, 18 Def. L.J. 537, App. II at 564-566 (1969).

QUESTION NO. 2

If you answer any subdivision of Question No. 1 "Yes," then answer the corresponding subdivision of this question: Was such negligence on the part of the defendant _____ a cause of the collision with respect to:

(a) speed?   Answer: _____
(b) racing?   Answer: _____
(c) overtaking and passing?   Answer: _____

QUESTION NO. 3

At and just prior to the collision, was the defendant _____ negligent with respect to:

(a) speed?   Answer: _____
(b) racing?   Answer: _____

QUESTION NO. 4

If you answer any subdivision of Question No. 3 "Yes," then answer the corresponding subdivision of this question: Was such negligence on the part of the defendant _____ a cause of the collision with respect to:

(a) speed?   Answer: _____
(b) racing?   Answer: _____

QUESTION NO. 5

At and just prior to the collision, was the plaintiff _____ negligent with respect to:

(a) the manner of making his left turn?   Answer: _____
(b) directional signals?   Answer: _____

QUESTION NO. 6

If you answer any subdivision of Question No. 5 "Yes," then answer the corresponding subdivision of this question: Was such negligence on the part of the plaintiff _____ a cause of the collision with respect to:

(a) the manner of making his left turn?   Answer: _____
(b) directional signals?   Answer: _____

QUESTION NO. 7

If you find by your answers to any subdivisions of Questions No. 1 and 3 that either the defendant _____ or the defendant _____, or both, were negligent, and if you further find by your answers to any subdivision of Questions No. 2 and 4 that negligence of either the defendant _____ or the defendant _____, or both, was a cause of the collision, and if you find by your answer to any subdivision of Question No. 5 that the plaintiff _____ was negligent, and if you further find by your answer to any subdivision of Question No. 6 that the negligence of the plaintiff _____ was a cause of the collision, then answer this question: Taking the combined negligence which caused the collision as a 100%, what percentage of such negligence is attributable to:

(a) the defendant _____?   Answer: _____%

303

(b) the defendant _____?   Answer: _____%
(c) the plaintiff _____?   Answer: _____%
                                                       Total: 100%

QUESTION NO. 8

What sum of money will fairly and reasonably compensate the plaintiff _____ with respect to:

(a) personal injuries to date?   Answer: $_____
(b) past medical and hospital expenses?   Answer: $_____
(c) loss of earnings to date?   Answer: $_____
(d) damage to his automobile?   Answer: $_____

Wisconsin has not required this elaborate form of special verdict procedure in all cases. Parties may stipulate to a simplified special verdict form that states only the percentage of negligence of each party and the amount of plaintiff's damages.

In *Jahnke v. Smith*[53] the jury found the defendants not causally negligent, but nonetheless in the apportionment of damages reduced the defendant's recovery on his counterclaim by 10%. The court refused to order a new trial on the ground that the plaintiff had not been prejudiced by the inconsistency and the defendant had waived the issue by a motion for judgment for 90% of the damages in his counterclaim.

In *Reiter v. Dyken*[54] the Wisconsin Supreme Court reversed a lower court ruling which had permitted the combination of the negligence of both defendants enabling recovery by the plaintiffs. The jury had apportioned the causal negligence as follows: plaintiff, 50%; one defendant, 30%; and the other defendant, 20%. By combining the defendants' negligence, plaintiff was allowed to recover from the one defendant not immune under the Workers' Compensation Act. The Supreme Court held this combination to be improper, and suggested the legislature would be the appropriate place to effectuate such a significant change in the statute in order to allow a plaintiff to recover from a less negligent defendant.

Colorado Form

Another example of a form of verdict, approved for use as a guideline by the Supreme Court of Colorado, is as follows:[55]

We, the jury, present our Answers to Questions submitted by the court, to which we have unanimously agreed:

QUESTION NO. 1: Was the defendant, _____, negligent? (yes or no)

ANSWER NO. 1:

---

[53]Jahnke v. Smith, 56 Wis. 2d 642, 203 N.W.2d 67 (1973).
[54]Reiter v. Dyken, 95 Wis. 2d 461, 290 N.W.2d 510 (1980).
[55]From Laugesen, *Colorado Comparative Negligence*, 48 Den. L.J. 469, App. at 495 (1972).

QUESTION NO. 2: Was the defendant's negligence, if any, a proximate cause of the plaintiff's claimed (injuries) (damages) (losses)? (yes or no)

ANSWER NO. 2

QUESTION NO. 3: Was the plaintiff, _____, contributorily negligent? (yes or no)

ANSWER NO. 3:

QUESTION NO. 4: Was the plaintiff's contributory negligence, if any, a proximate cause of (his) (her) claimed (injuries) (damages) (losses)? (yes or no)

ANSWER NO. 4:

QUESTION NO. 5: If you have answered all the four foregoing questions "yes," then you are to answer this question:

Taking the combined negligence that proximately caused the (injuries) (damages) (losses) as 100 percent, what percentage of that negligence was attributable to the defendant and what percentage was attributable to the plaintiff?

ANSWER NO. 5:
Percentage of combined negligence attributable
to defendant, _____: _____%
Percentage of combined negligence attributable
to plaintiff, _____: _____%
                                        Total: 100 %

QUESTION NO. 6: If you have answered Questions 1 and 2 "yes," state the amount of damages, if any, sustained by the plaintiff and proximately caused by the (accident) (occurrence), without regard to the contributory negligence of the plaintiff, if any.

ANSWER NO. 6: $_____

General Verdict Required

The Wisconsin precedents might be relied on in states whose comparative negligence statutes take no position on special verdicts.[56] In two states and the Virgin Islands, however, comparative negligence statutes specifically provide that damages be diminished "by general verdict."[57] In that connection, the reporter's notes to the Vermont statute state that the special verdict procedure outlined in the general rules of civil procedure of the state is not to supersede the provision of

---

[56]See note 45 above.
[57]See N.H. Rev. Stat. Ann., § 507:7-a; Vt. Stat. Ann., tit. 12, § 1036; V.I. Code Ann., tit. 5, § 1451(c).

the comparative negligence statute.[58] The reporter suggests, however, that special interrogatories might be used in conjunction with the general verdict.

The Ohio comparative negligence statute requires a jury to return a general verdict accompanied by answers to interrogatories, specifying the total amount of damages that would have been recovered by the complainant but for his negligence and the percentage of negligence attributable to each party to the action.[59]

The comparative negligence statutes in Mississippi and Rhode Island specify that the jury is to reduce plaintiff's damages on the basis of the percentage he was at fault.[60] In Maine the jury is specifically instructed to reduce the damages "to the extent deemed equitable" and to return both amounts.[61] These statutes preclude separate special verdicts on the issues of damages and percentage of fault. Even though the jury makes the calculation, a court *might* permit jury interrogatories on the underlying issues to determine percentage of fault and amount of damages.

Difficulties in Framing Special Verdicts

A special verdict procedure removes from the jury the power to render a general legal conclusion at the end of a case. As stated by Professor James, "the verdict has to include findings upon all material facts and issues, and it must do so by stating without ambiguity facts, not evidence or conclusions of law."[62]

Special verdict questions are generally rendered in written form. They are not easy to frame, and for that reason have not been popular in American courts.[63] By accident or design, the special verdict may fail to cover all the issues in the case or may contain incorrect terminology.[64]

Federal Rule 49

Federal Rule of Civil Procedure 49(a) has attempted to avoid some of the pitfalls of common-law special verdicts and has been a much more popular device.[65] For example, if the federal court omits "any issue of fact raised by the pleadings or by the evidence" in its special

---

[58]Vt. R.Civ.P., Rule 49 is identical to Fed. R.Civ.P. 49 on special verdicts and special interrogatories.

[59]Ohio Rev. Code Ann., § 2315.19.

[60]Miss. Code Ann., § 11-7-15; R.I. Gen. Laws, § 9-20-4.

[61]Me. Rev. Stat. Ann., tit. 14, § 156.

[62]F. James & G. Hazard, note 46 above, § 7.15 at 296.

[63]Id.

[64]See Missouri P. R. Co. v. Cross, 501 S.W.2d 868 (Tex. 1973) for an example of the difficulties inherent in framing and correcting errors in jury interrogatories. See also Dunham v. Kampman, 37 Colo. App. 233, 547 P.2d 263 (1975), affd. 192 Colo. 448, 560 P.2d 91 (1977) (submission to jury of special verdict form used in comparing negligence in action by passenger/wife for damages not error even though none of the 99% causal negligence attributed to her driver/husband could be imputed to her).

[65]J. Moore, 5A *Federal Practice* ¶ 49.03 (1984).

verdict "each party waives his right to a trial by jury of the issue so omitted unless before the jury retires he demands its submission to the jury."[66]

In spite of the improvements in the federal rule, the special verdict procedure may still be awkward. A newer procedural device, jury interrogatories, captures most of the advantages of the special verdict procedure but avoids its disadvantages. In this procedure the jury returns a general verdict but also answers questions upon one or more issues of fact the decision of which is necessary to its general verdict. By the very nature of the general verdict, it is clear that the jury has passed upon all issues; nevertheless, the interrogatories allow the court and attorneys to have a better perspective on precisely how the jury arrived at its more general finding.

Advantages of Special Verdicts and Interrogatories

The special verdict and interrogatory procedures can be of special value in comparative negligence jurisdictions.[67] First, they may make it more difficult for a jury to avoid applying rules they disagree with—especially the requirement of reducing plaintiff's award because of his contributory negligence. Next, they may allow a court to isolate an issue on which the jury has floundered and thus to provide for a limited reversal. Finally, the special verdict (but not jury interrogatories) makes possible less cumbersome instructions.[68]

Obviously, there are policy arguments both for and against use of special verdicts or jury interrogatories. It is important to understand these whenever the permissible use of either special verdicts or special interrogatories is left open by the comparative negligence statute.

At first blush it is difficult to see why the application of a special verdict procedure to comparative negligence should be criticized. If the special verdicts are spelled out in the statute, the awkwardness that compromised the common-law special verdict system is eliminated. If they are not spelled out, recourse can be had to the useful forms developed in Wisconsin and other states.

Control of Jury by Special Verdict

The special verdict will tend to ensure that comparative negligence law achieves its basic goal of apportioning damages on the basis of fault. The procedure causes the jury to separate in its mind the question of the amount of damages plaintiff suffered from the question of

---

[66]Fed. R.Civ.P. 49. See, e.g., Carrillo v. Samaeit Westbulk, 385 F. Supp. 119 (D. P.R. 1974) (special verdict form on comparison of negligence need not require finding on which acts constituted plaintiff's negligence), affd. 514 F.2d 1214 (1st Cir. P.R. 1975) (modified only as to award of counsel's fees).

[67]See Lawrence v. Florida E. C. R. Co., 346 So. 2d 1012 (Fla. 1977) (citing this treatise).

[68]See Ferguson v. Northern States Power Co., 307 Minn. 26, 239 N.W.2d 190 (1976) for good example of how the special verdict can expose jury error.

the percentage of his fault.[69] Those who criticize the special verdict procedure acknowledge this, but prefer the general verdict because it allows for jury "flexibility" in dealing with law that may not be generally popular.[70] In effect, critics of the special verdict prefer the general verdict because it makes it easier for the jury to ignore plaintiff's contributory negligence.

This line of argument is particularly inappropriate in comparative negligence jurisdictions. The unpopular contributory negligence defense has been eliminated. Comparative negligence usually is the result of comparatively recent legislative judgment. Therefore, the law should be applied as a legislature intended it, or it should be changed at that level.

Facilitating Judicial Review

Aside from assuring that the jury performs its proper function in applying comparative negligence, the special verdict provides a means for more efficient review of jury findings. Special verdicts (or jury interrogatories) localize error and allow a court to find the remaining portion of the verdict valid. For example, if the jury has been in error with respect to the amount of damages plaintiff suffered, the court might use additur or remittitur and correct that mistake. Further, as indicated in section 18.3, if the court believes the jury's allocation of fault was totally unreasonable, it might set aside the finding on that issue.[71]

Special verdicts and jury interrogatories may also show whether an error in an instruction to the jury played any part in the verdict. For example, if an error is committed in instructing on the effect of contributory negligence, it will be harmless if the jury found no negligence on the part of the defendant. All of these advantages are secured by the use of jury interrogatories.

Simplification of Instructions

The final advantage of a special verdict procedure under comparative negligence is that it can result in simpler jury instructions. The jury need not be told the legal consequences of its findings. Thus, in Wisconsin the jury must find the amount of plaintiff's damages and the relative degrees of plaintiff's and defendant's fault. The jury is not told the effect of its findings on the legal issues of the case; in fact, it is

---

[69]See generally F. James & G. Hazard, note 46 above, § 7.15 at 298-299. But see Downum v. Muskogee Stockyards & Livestock Auction, Inc., 565 P.2d 368 (Okla. 1977) (refusal to grant new trial on basis of jury foreman's affidavit that verdict finding plaintiff 45% and defendant 55% negligent with damages of $17,000 was intended to give plaintiff $17,000 not error).

[70]F. James & G. Hazard, note 46 above, at § 7.15; C. Wright, note 46 above, § 94 at 631-633.

[71]See Orwick v. Belshan, 304 Minn. 338, 231 N.W.2d 90 (1975) (court may set aside a special verdict when evidence requires a different apportionment of causal negligence as a matter of law).

reversible error to inform the jury of that effect.[72] The approach is considered worthwhile because it may draw forth the jury's unbiased opinion.

Special Verdicts and Multiple Defendants

In a negligence action involving multiple defendants, a California appeals court concluded that the lower court may not direct the jury to apportion comparative fault among the defendants and other nonparties by special verdict.[73] The court may direct the jury to find a special verdict only upon those issues being litigated. As the proportionate fault of the defendants and another nonparty was not in issue in the instant case, it was not a proper subject for a special verdict.

17.5 Informing jury as to effect of apportionment

On the face of most mandatory special verdict statutes the jury's role in comparative negligence cases is restricted to apportioning negligence and fixing the total amount of damages the plaintiff suffered.[74] The court then synthesizes these jury findings and determines:

1. Whether the defendants are liable to plaintiff, and, if they are liable,

2. The extent of their liability after the plaintiff's damages are reduced according to his fault.

In these states the courts must decide whether it would be reversible error to inform the jury of the consequences of its findings.[75] The rationale is that if the jury does not know, its determinations will be logical and defendants will be protected against verdicts based on sympathy rather than on the facts. Wisconsin judicially adopted the rule against ultimate outcome instructions while contributory negligence

---

[72]Pecor v. Home Indem. Co., 234 Wis. 407, 291 N.W. 313 (1940) (statements of counsel had effect of conveying to jury information that if they answered yes to certain questions plaintiff would be out of court). See Blahnik v. Dax, 22 Wis. 2d 67, 125 N.W.2d 364 (1963) (court properly refused to give jury information as to the effect of apportionment of negligence on ultimate recovery); De Groot v. Van Akkeren, 225 Wis. 105, 273 N.W. 725 (1937) (admonishes court to avoid telling jury the effect of their answers). See also Brown v. Keaton, 232 Ark. 12, 334 S.W.2d 676 (1960); Laugesen, note 55 above, at 473 n.24 ("There is obviously no necessity to tell the jury the effect of their findings and it would seem violative of the spirit of the clear legislative mandate to possibly prejudice their function or encourage speculation by unneeded knowledge of judicial implementation of the statute").

[73]Klemme v. Hoag Memorial Hosp. Presbyterian, 103 Cal. App. 3d 640, 163 Cal. Rptr. 109 (1980).

[74]See, e.g., Colo. Rev. Stat., § 41-2-14(2); Hawaii Rev. Stat., § 663-31(b); Mass. Gen. Laws Ann., ch. 231, § 85; N.J. Stat. Ann., § 2A:15-5.2.

[75]See De Groot v. Van Akkeren, 225 Wis. 105, 273 N.W. 725, 730 (1937). But see Roman v. Mitchell, 82 N.J. 336, 413 A.2d 322 (1980) (citing this treatise) (court holding jury should be given an ultimate outcome charge in a comparative negligence situation in order for it better to fulfill its fact-finding function). See generally Comment, *Informing the Jury of the Legal Effect of Special Verdict Answers in Comparative Negligence Actions*, 1981 Duke L.J. 824 (1981).

was still in effect,[76] and this was the majority rule until the mid 1970's.[77]

When the Supreme Court of Utah first considered the question in 1974, it adopted a rule that the jury should not be informed of the legal effect of its apportionment of negligence.[78] The court later found that withholding the instruction was more likely to confuse the jury and adopted a new rule allowing an ultimate outcome instruction at the request of the parties.[79] Under the new Utah rule, the trial court still has discretion to deny the instruction in "the unusual or complex case where it would lead to confusion or improper jury deliberations."[80]

In *Christiansen v. Robertson*[81] the Court of Appeals of Georgia held that the submission of questions concerning the finding of negligence and instruction as to the general verdict based thereon was not error.

In *Simpson v. Anderson*[82] the Colorado Court of Appeals held that it was permissible to inform the jury of the legal effect of their apportionment of negligence as the application of law to fact is within the province of the jury. The court reasoned that since the law of comparative negligence is not secret, it will probably become known to at least some members of the jury. The Supreme Court of Colorado reversed,[83] holding that such a revelation would tend to influence jury verdicts and usurp the function of the trial judge.

The Colorado legislature restored the holding of the Colorado Court of Appeals. The applicable statute states that:

> In a jury trial in any civil action in which contributory negligence is an issue for determination by the jury, the trial court shall instruct the jury on the effect of its findings as to the degree of negligence of each party. The attorneys for each party shall be allowed to argue the effect of the instruction on the facts which are before the jury.[84]

Even in the states that still refuse to allow an ultimate outcome instruction, the rule has been weakened by exceptions, such as inference from other information in the courtroom or conditional special verdicts.[85]

---

[76]Ryan v. Rockford Ins. Co., 77 Wis. 611, 46 N.W. 885 (1890). Wisconsin still adheres to the rule. McGowan v. Story, 70 Wis. 2d 189, 234 N.W.2d 325 (1975).

[77]See Comment, note 75 above, at 832.

[78]McGinn v. Utah Power & Light Co., 529 P.2d 423 (Utah 1974).

[79]Dixon v. Stewart, 658 P.2d 591 (Utah 1982).

[80]Id. at 596.

[81]Christiansen v. Robertson, 139 Ga. App. 423, 228 S.E.2d 350 (1976), revd. on other grounds 237 Ga. 711, 229 S.E.2d 472 (1976). See also National Trailer Convoy, Inc. v. Sutton, 136 Ga. App. 760, 222 S.E.2d 98 (1975).

[82]Simpson v. Anderson, 33 Colo. App. 134, 517 P.2d 416 (1973), revd. 186 Colo. 163, 526 P.2d 298 (1974).

[83]Id., 186 Colo. 163, 526 P.2d 298 (1974). For a full discussion of the court's reasoning see Avery v. Wadlington, 186 Colo. 158, 526 P.2d 295 (1974); accord, Shuey v. Hamilton, 540 P.2d 1122 (Colo. App. 1975).

[84]Colo. Rev. Stat., § 13-21-111(4).

[85]Comment, note 75 above, at 833-835.

Permitting Jury to Know

Four states that have adopted 50% systems now require an ultimate outcome instruction in all cases.[86] Four others require the instruction if a party requests it.[87] Minnesota leaves the instruction to the discretion of the trial judge.[88] Four of these eight states expressly allow attorneys to mention the instruction in argument to the jury.[89] In some modified comparative negligence states, use of the special verdict is optional;[90] in those states there should be no bar to informing the jury of the effect of its finding.

Courts in Arkansas,[91] Idaho,[92] Kansas,[93] New Jersey,[94] Oklahoma,[95] Pennsylvania,[96] Texas,[97] and West Virginia[98] have permitted the ultimate outcome instruction in the absence of an express statutory prohibition.[99]

In *Roman v. Mitchell*[1] the New Jersey Supreme Court held that a jury in a comparative negligence situation should thereafter be given an "ultimate outcome charge" in order to be made fully aware of the legal effect of its findings as to percentages of negligence.

The Kansas Supreme Court ruled it permissible to inform the jury as to the legal effect of its special verdict.[2] By advising the jury on both the theory and legal effect of its comparative negligence, the court reasoned that the jury would be better informed and less likely to speculate as to the effects of its findings. A Kansas appeals court subsequently held that this rule should be applied only to those cases

---

[86]Colo. Rev. Stat., § 13-21-111; Conn. Gen. Stat. Ann., § 52-572h; Iowa Code Ann., § 668.3(5); Ore. Rev. Stat. § 18-480(e).

[87]Nev. Rev. Stat., § 41.141(2)(a); N.D. Cent. Code, § 9-10-07; Wyo. Stat., § 1-1-109(b)(iii); Dixon v. Stewart, 658 P.2d 591 (Utah 1982).

[88]Minn. R.Civ.P., Rule 49.01(2).

[89]Colo. Rev. Stat., § 13-21-111; Iowa Code Ann., § 668.3(5); Minn. R.Civ.P., Rule 49.01(2); N.D. Cent. Code, § 9-10-07.

[90]See section 17.4, note 42.

[91]Cobb v. Atkins, 239 Ark. 151, 388 S.W.2d 8 (1965).

[92]See Seppi v. Betty, 99 Idaho 186, 579 P.2d 683 (1978), construing Idaho Code, § 6-801. The Idaho Supreme Court concluded that the jury should be informed as to the effect of its answers in a special verdict when applied to the state's 50% system of comparative negligence. However, in a complex case, where such instructions may confuse or mislead the jury, a trial court should have the discretion to withhold an ultimate outcome instruction.

[93]Thomas v. Board of Township Trustees, 224 Kan. 539, 582 P.2d 271 (1978).

[94]Roman v. Mitchell, 82 N.J. 336, 413 A.2d 322 (1980) (citing this treatise).

[95]Smith v. Gizzi, 564 P.2d 1009 (Okla. 1977).

[96]Peair v. Home Assn. of Enola Legion No. 751, 287 Pa. Super. 400, 430 A.2d 665 (1981).

[97]Cruthirds v. RCI, Inc., 624 F.2d 632 (5th Cir. Tex. 1980).

[98]Adkins v. Whitten, 297 S.E.2d 881 (W. Va. 1982).

[99]No state comparative fault statute expressly forbids an ultimate outcome instruction.

[1]Roman v. Mitchell, 82 N.J. 336, 413 A.2d 322 (1980).

[2]Thomas v. Board of Township Trustees, 224 Kan. 539, 582 P.2d 271 (1978).

pending and untried when the rule was announced, and in all cases filed thereafter.[3]

It would appear that in Vermont and New Hampshire the jury may be so informed, although the courts in those states have not ruled on the question.[4]

There is also authority supporting the view that the jury is entitled to know the legal effect of its apportionment in admiralty cases decided under the optional special verdict procedure of Rule 49(a).[5]

The Maine statute is unique in directing that the jury "reduce the total damages by dollars and cents, and not by percentage, to the extent deemed just and equitable, having regard to the claimant's share in the responsibility for the damages."[6] Further, the Maine jury is instructed "to return both amounts with the knowledge that the lesser figure is the final verdict in the case."[7]

In a Minnesota case,[8] however, a jury found a plaintiff 35% causally negligent and found damages in the amount of $75,000. When informed that this would require a 35% reduction in the award, the jury "rede-liberated" and returned a verdict of $116,000. The Supreme Court of Minnesota found this to be jury misconduct and gave the plaintiff the option of a new trial on damages or accepting the original verdict.

The 50% Negligent Plaintiff

The controversy as to whether the jury should be informed as to the legal effect of its findings may be a tempest in a teapot in many situations; frequently, the jurors will be able to conjecture correctly as to the result of the findings. In one situation, however, the jurors may conjecture incorrectly; they may believe that a plaintiff whose negligence is 50% of the total recovers 50% of his damages. As has been indicated in section 3.5, however, the 50% negligent plaintiff is barred from all recovery in thirteen of the twenty 50% states, including three states with a mandatory special verdict procedure.

On this particular aspect of special verdicts, critics of the procedure have a sound point. When the jury is not aware that a plaintiff who is 50% negligent recovers nothing, it may casually return a 50-50 verdict as a compromise. The jury does not realize the very devastating impact of its decision. Further, it will have devoted unnecessary time computing plaintiff's damages.

---

[3]Cook v. Doty, 4 Kan. App. 2d 499, 608 P.2d 1028 (1980).

[4]Vt. Stat. Ann., tit. 12, § 1036; N.H. Rev. Stat. Ann., § 507:7-2. See Flynn, *Comparative Negligence: The Debate*, 8 Trial 49, 50 (1972).

[5]Porche v. Gulf Mississippi Marine Corp., 390 F. Supp. 624 (E.D. La. 1975) (jury may be informed whether named damage figure will be reduced by plaintiff's percentage of fault).

[6]Me. Rev. Stat. Ann., tit. 14, § 156.

[7]Id.

[8]Rosenthal v. Kolars, 304 Minn. 378, 231 N.W.2d 285 (1975).

Better to Inform the Jury

These factors persuade this author that the jury should be informed of the legal effect of the apportionment of fault. Although this would call for a longer instruction and it might compromise the "control" virtue of special verdicts, the jury, at least in 50% systems, should be made aware of the consequences of its own judgment.

CHAPTER 18

JUDICIAL CONTROL OF THE FINDERS OF FACT

Section

18.1 Jury discretion in apportioning fault

Courts in comparative negligence states are usually circumspect about altering determinations made by the jury. The courts will rarely disturb the jury's apportionment of negligence between parties or reverse findings for the plaintiff or defendant.

Martin v. Bussert

The Supreme Court of Minnesota said in *Martin v. Bussert*[1] that it would not substitute its own judgment for a jury's apportionment of negligence "unless there is no evidence reasonably tending to sustain the apportionment or the apportionment is manifestly and palpably against the weight of the evidence."[2]

Martin was a consolidation of reciprocal actions arising out of an intersection collision. The Minnesota Supreme Court affirmed a jury apportionment of 20% of the causal negligence to one driver and 80% to the other. The court noted that it might appear inconceivable that the driver who failed to yield the right-of-way and entered the intersection

---

[1]Martin v. Bussert, 292 Minn. 29, 193 N.W.2d 134 (1971).

[2]Id., 292 Minn. at 38, 193 N.W.2d at 139. Accord, Sandhofer v. Abbott-Northwestern Hospital, 283 N.W.2d 362 (Minn. 1979); Wovcha v. Mattson, 296 Minn. 538, 209 N.W.2d 422 (1973); Bray v. Chicago, R. I. & P. R. Co., 305 Minn. 31, 232 N.W.2d 97 (1975); Campion v. Knutson, 307 Minn. 263, 239 N.W.2d 248 (1976); Dugan v. Sears, Roebuck & Co., 73 Ill. Dec. 320, 454 N.E.2d 64 (App. 1983); Magnone v. Chicago & North Western Transp. Co., 126 Ill. App. 3d 170, 81 Ill. Dec. 459, 466 N.E.2d 1261 (1984); but see Martineau v. Nelson, 311 Minn. 92, 247 N.W.2d 409 (1976) (jury apportionment of 50% of causal negligence to plaintiff plainly against weight of evidence when only inference of negligence raised by plaintiff's failure to use other birth control methods when improperly performed tubal ligation resulted in unwanted pregnancy); Stapleman v. St. Joseph the Worker, 295 Minn. 406, 205 N.W.2d 677 (1973) (jury apportionment of negligence reversed; plaintiff who tripped on coat-rack in plain sight guilty of negligence equaling or exceeding that of defendant as a matter of law); see also Ramfjord v. Sullivan, 301 Minn. 238, 222 N.W.2d 541 (1974) (jury award of medical expenses in amount less than stipulated an obvious clerical error which properly could be corrected by court-ordered redeliberation); Dehn v. Otter Tail Power Co., 251 N.W.2d 404 (N.D. 1977) (jury award of $30,000 general and $350,000 special damages in apparent confusion over the two terms was construed by the court as $350,000 general and $30,000 special damages).

without ever having seen the other vehicle was only one-fourth as negligent as the other driver. Nevertheless, there was evidence to support the jury findings. The court in the Martin case relied on analogous case law from Wisconsin.

The Wisconsin Approach

The Supreme Court of Wisconsin has refrained from reassessing the percentages of negligence determined by the jury. In 1972, the court said that the jury apportionment "will be sustained ... if there is any credible evidence which under any reasonable view supports the jury's findings."[3] When the verdict is against the great weight of the evidence, the most the court has been willing to do is to find the negligence of one party at least equal to that of the other.[4]

In *Britton v. Hoyt*[5] the Wisconsin Supreme Court held that when a jury verdict is against the weight or clear preponderance of the evidence, the trial court may not fix the exact percentages of negligence. The proper procedure is to grant a new trial.[6] However, in cases where judges believe that no reasonable juror could avoid the conclusion that the plaintiff's negligence equaled or exceeded the defendant's, they will so find and disregard the jury's attempt at apportionment.[7]

Most comparative negligence jurisdictions adhere to the principle expressed by the Supreme Court of Wisconsin in the first case[8] it decid-

---

[3]Bourassa v. Gateway Erectors, Inc., 54 Wis. 2d 176, 194 N.W.2d 602, 604 (1972). Accord, Werner Transp. Co. v. Barts, 57 Wis. 2d 714, 205 N.W.2d 394 (1973); Gould v. Allstar Ins. Co., 59 Wis. 2d 355, 208 N.W.2d 388 (1973); Krauth v. Quinn, 69 Wis. 2d 280, 230 N.W.2d 839 (1975); Lapierre v. Maltais, 119 N.H. 610, 406 A.2d 123 (1979); Weber v. New York, 101 A.D.2d 757, 475 N.Y.S.2d 401 (1984); cf. Jagmin v. Simonds Abrasive Co., 61 Wis. 2d 60, 211 N.W.2d 810 (1973); DeGroff v. Schmude, 71 Wis. 2d 554, 238 N.W.2d 730 (1976) (if jury's apportionment of negligence is insupportable, new trial should be held); but see Schuh v. Fox River Tractor Co., 83 Wis. 2d 728, 218 N.W.2d 279 (1974); Jacobs v. Stack, 63 Wis. 2d 672, 218 N.W.2d 364 (1974) (if plaintiff is clearly guilty of negligence barring recovery, as a matter of law, the jury verdict will be upset).

[4]See text accompanying notes 10 and 11, section 18.7.

[5]Britton v. Hoyt, 63 Wis. 2d 688, 218 N.W.2d 274 (1974) (the court found that the jury verdict was supported by credible evidence).

[6]Jagmin v. Simonds Abrasive Co., 61 Wis. 2d 60, 211 N.W.2d 810 (1973).

[7]Britton v. Hoyt, 63 Wis. 2d 688, 218 N.W.2d 274 (1974).

[8]Brown v. Haertel, 210 Wis. 345, 244 N.W. 630 (1933). Accord, Haynes v. Moore, 14 Wash. App. 668, 545 P.2d 28 (1975); Vinson v. Glenn, 338 So. 2d 385 (Miss. 1976); Standard Furniture Co. v. Wallace, 288 So. 2d 461 (Miss. 1974) (Mississippi courts will only upset jury apportionment on evidence of bias, passion or prejudice); Kinsey v. Kelly, 312 So. 2d 461 (Fla. App. 1975) (jury verdict will be upset if against "manifest weight" of the evidence); Model v. Rabinowitz, 313 So. 2d 59 (Fla. App. 1975) (jury verdict upset as improper application of comparative negligence); Dunham v. Kampman, 37 Colo. App. 233, 547 P.2d 263 (1975), affd. 192 Colo. 448, 560 P.2d 91 (1977); Transamerica Ins. Co. v. Pueblo Gas & Fuel Co., 33 Colo. App. 92, 519 P.2d 1201 (1973) (Colorado courts will not upset jury apportionment unless it is against manifest weight of evidence or reasonable minds could not have arrived at it); Fargason v. Pervis, 138 Ga. App. 686, 227 S.E.2d 464 (1976) (jury may apportion damages "as they see fit" if there is evidence to support finding that plaintiff's negligence contributed in less degree than defendant's); Masterson v. P & H Harnischfeger Corp., 55 A.D.2d 570, 389 N.Y.S.2d 612 (1976) (New York courts will not upset verdict if there is evidence to support it); Shea v. Peter Glenn Shops, Inc., 132 Vt. 317, 318 A.2d 177 (1974) (Vermont courts will not upset jury apportionment unless "unreasonable or a product of jury misconduct"); see also Bowe v. Willis, 323 A.2d 593 (Me. 1974) (jury apportionment upheld despite strong physical evidence indicating a contrary result as that evidence could conceivably be interpreted to support a fact pattern consistent with jury verdict).

ed under the state's general comparative negligence statute. The opinion recognized that it might be within the province of the court to say that plaintiff was guilty of contributory negligence as a matter of law, but found the comparison quite another matter:

> When two persons are negligent and injury to one proximately results from the combined negligence of both, it must often be a very delicate and difficult question to decide whether the negligence of one was greater than that of the other, and contributed in a greater degree to produce the injury.[9]

Thus the comparison was left to be decided by the jury.

The Alaska Supreme Court, in *State v. Kaatz*,[10] refused to vacate the apportionment of negligence made by the trial judge at the initial trial. The court expressed confidence that in this particular instance the judge could properly apportion the negligence himself based on evidence received at the initial trial, and that it was unnecessary to submit this question to the jury.

Counting and Measuring

Subsequent Wisconsin cases have set forth more specific principles which demonstrate the scope of the jury's discretion in apportionment. For example, negligent acts of two parties need not be regarded as equal because the acts are within the same category of negligence or the parties are negligent in the same respects. Accordingly, in *Hansberry v. Dunn*[11] the Supreme Court of Wisconsin affirmed a judgment for plaintiff, stating that the apportionment of negligence was within the province of the jury and that "the court may not adopt a rule of thumb that will check off automatically lookout against lookout, control against control, etc., holding these items equal as a matter of law in every case."[12]

Further, in *Taylor v. Western Casualty and Surety Company*,[13] the Wisconsin Supreme Court stated that the degree of negligence is not to be measured by the number of respects in which a party is found to have been at fault. In affirming the jury verdict for plaintiff by declining to find that plaintiff's negligence was, as a matter of law, equal to or greater than that of the defendant, the court noted that the jury must weigh the conduct of the parties considered as a whole to deter-

---

[9]Brown v. Haertel, 210 Wis. 345, 350–351, 244 N.W. 630, 632 (1933), quoting Dohr v. Wisconsin C. R. Co., 144 Wis. 545, 553–554, 129 N.W. 252, 255 (1911) (dissenting opinion). See also Riley v. Lake, 302 Minn. 120, 223 N.W.2d 413 (1974) (apportionment of negligence is for jury even when one party is negligent as a matter of law); accord, Santiesteban v. McGrath, 320 So. 2d 476 (Fla. App. 1975).

[10]State v. Kaatz, 572 P.2d 775 (Alaska 1977) (citing this treatise); State v. Guinn, 555 P.2d 530 (Alaska 1976) (trial judge who presided at initial trial could properly apportion the negligence).

[11]Hansberry v. Dunn, 230 Wis. 626, 284 N.W. 556 (1939). See also State v. Kaatz, 572 P.2d 775 (Alaska 1977).

[12]Hansberry v. Dunn, note 11 above, 284 N.W. at 559; see, e.g., Jensen v. Rural Mut. Ins. Co., 41 Wis. 2d 36, 163 N.W.2d 158 (1968); Strupp v. Farmers Mut. Auto. Ins. Co., 14 Wis. 2d 158, 109 N.W.2d 660 (1961).

[13]Taylor v. Western Casualty & Surety Co., 270 Wis. 408, 71 N.W.2d 363 (1955).

mine liability and apportionment.[14] The court pointed out in *Lovesee v. Allied Development Corporation*[15] that, although the character and number of elements of negligence may be considered in determining apportionment, there is no mathematical formula by which to make the comparison.

Jury Favoring Defendant

The latitude given to the jury may serve to the disadvantage of a plaintiff. In a 1972 Wisconsin case, that state's Supreme Court upheld a 36% apportionment of fault to a plaintiff guest-passenger for failing to keep a lookout or warn the driver.[16] The court quoted a prior case, saying:

> In the absence of patent unreasonableness of the apportionment, we will not substitute our judgment for that of the jury. We adhere to the rule that a jury's apportionment ... will be set aside only when the "percentages of negligence ... are ... grossly disproportionate."[17]

Special Verdict as Check on Jury

One check on the jury's determinations of comparative fault is the special verdict procedure. When this is applied, the jury only apportions fault on a percentage basis and finds the total amount of damages plaintiff suffered. As indicated in section 17.4, a significant number of comparative negligence states follow this procedure in all cases.[18]

Nine states provide for the mandatory use of the special verdict by statute or case law.[19] In at least nine other states,[20] the parties have a

---

[14]Id., 270 Wis. at 411, 71 N.W.2d at 365. Accord, DeGroff v. Schmude, 71 Wis. 2d 554, 238 N.W.2d 730 (1976).

[15]Lovesee v. Allied Development Corp., 45 Wis. 2d 340, 345, 173 N.W.2d 196, 199 (1970). But see Line v. Nourie, 298 Minn. 269, 215 N.W.2d 52 (1974) (reversible error to fail to instruct on plaintiff's possible negligent failure to keep a proper lookout, even though instruction given on two other alleged acts of negligence. However, the case does not require a "counting and measuring" approach: merely that all possible acts of negligence be considered by the jury).

[16]Davis v. Allstate Ins. Co., 55 Wis. 2d 56, 197 N.W.2d 734 (1972). See also Downum v. Muskogee Stockyards & Livestock Auction, Inc., 565 P.2d 368 (Okla. 1977) (refusal to grant new trial in face of jury foreman's affidavit that verdict finding plaintiff 45% negligent and defendant 55% negligent with damages $17,000 was intended to allow plaintiff to recover the full $17,000 not error).

[17]Davis v. Allstate Ins. Co., 55 Wis. 2d 56, 197 N.W.2d 734, 736, quoting Hillstead v. Smith, 44 Wis. 2d 560, 567, 171 N.W.2d 315, 318 (1969).

[18]See notes 41 to 52 and accompanying text, section 17.4.

[19]Colorado, Florida, Hawaii, Indiana, Iowa, Kansas, New Jersey, Ohio and Wisconsin. See section 17.4

[20]Idaho, Louisiana, Maine, Minnesota, Nevada, North Dakota, Oregon, Utah and Wyoming. See note 42, section 17.4. See Steinhaus v. Adamson, 304 Minn. 14, 228 N.W.2d 865, 88 A.L.R.3d 613 (1975) (court may order redeliberation on the apportionment of negligence if special verdicts reveal that the jury misapplied comparative negligence); see also Florida E. C. R. Co. v. Lawrence, 328 So. 2d 249 (Fla. App. 1976) (when comparative negligence is at issue, either party has a right to a special verdict on timely request) (citing this treatise). In answering certified questions in this case, the Florida Supreme Court subsequently held that special verdicts were required in all jury trials involving comparative negligence. Lawrence v. Florida E. C. R. Co., 346 So. 2d 1012 (Fla. 1977).

statutory or common law right to special verdicts or interrogatories on timely request, and in almost all states the attorney can invoke the discretion of the trial court either to require special verdicts or to pose special interrogatories. The results may assist the attorney on appeal in arguing that the ultimate award was not supported by the evidence.

Storey v. Madsen[21] is a good example of the difficulties which can result if the jury is not controlled by special verdict. The jury used an optional general verdict form and found the defendant 5% more negligent than the plaintiff. Rather than award the plaintiff 55% of his damages, the jury multiplied the 5% figure times the general damages alleged and the special damages provided. The verdict was reversed on appeal and a remand resulted. Had the special verdict form been used, the defective verdict could have been cured by redeliberation.[22]

Reducing Number of Appeals

The general trend to give the jury more latitude in apportioning fault goes far to mitigate a basic criticism of the 50% system. That criticism is that the system fosters numerous appeals by parties arguing that the negligence of plaintiff did not hit the vital point completely barring him from recovery.[23] It is reasonable to believe that as it becomes clear to attorneys that an appellate court is most reluctant to overturn jury apportionment, the number of appeals will, ultimately, decline.

Court-Imposed Reapportionment

Another problem may explain the hesitancy of courts to overturn jury apportionment of negligence. Most of the courts in cases contesting the jury apportionment see only two choices for disposition if the jury apportionment is reversed: to grant a new trial, or (in a modified comparative negligence system) to direct a verdict for defendant if, as a matter of law, plaintiff's negligence is sufficient to bar his recovery.

Chief Justice Hallows of the Wisconsin Supreme Court suggests a third method of disposing of a case in which a court finds the jury's apportionment of negligence unsupported by the evidence.[24] This would be to order the party favored by the unsupported apportionment *either* to accept the court's reapportionment *or* to suffer a new trial. This procedure would be analogous to but different in principle from the famil-

---

[21]Storey v. Madsen, 276 Ore. 181, 554 P.2d 500 (1976).

[22]See, e.g., Steinhaus v. Adamson, 304 Minn. 14, 228 N.W.2d 865, 88 A.L.R.3d 613 (1975).

[23]See, e.g., Comment, *Comparative Negligence: Some New Problems for the Maine Courts,* 18 Me. L. Rev. 65, 75 (1966); Prosser, *Comparative Negligence,* 51 Mich. L. Rev. 465, 491–492 (1953).

[24]See Bourassa v. Gateway Erectors, Inc., 54 Wis. 2d 176, 194 N.W.2d 602 (1972). In note 2 at 605, Hallows cites Powers v. Allstate Ins. Co., 10 Wis. 2d 78, 102 N.W.2d 393 (1960) (a case requiring remittitur of excessive damages); Lawver v. Park Falls, 35 Wis. 2d 308, 151 N.W.2d 68 (1967) (concurring opinion); Pruss v. Strube, 37 Wis. 2d 539, 155 N.W.2d 650 (1968).

iar devices of additur and remittitur. Here, the purpose is not to correct the jury's unreasonable award of damages but rather to correct its unreasonable apportionment of fault. Perhaps appellate courts have been reluctant to use the device suggested by the Chief Justice because this would inevitably bring about more appeals.

There is variation between the different forms of comparative negligence under specific circumstances; nevertheless, it is certain that the role of the finders of fact is significant in all comparative negligence jurisdictions. However, a number of approaches to "jury control" may be utilized. Among these are limited reversal on the basis of apportionment and limited reversal by additur or remittitur. These will be discussed in sections 18.3 and 18.4.

18.2 Quotient verdicts

One situation in which the court may intervene is when the jury has improperly apportioned negligence by a quotient verdict. This issue was raised in *Schiro v. Oriental Realty Company*,[25] where the jury found plaintiff 50% negligent, thus barring her recovery. The plaintiffs in that case contended that the jury arrived at its answers to the apportionment questions of the special verdict by an invalid quotient verdict method. The court used the traditional definition of a quotient verdict as to amount of damages:

> [A] verdict resulting from an agreement whereby each juror writes down the amount of damages to which he thinks the party is entitled, and these several amounts are added together and divided by the number of jurors, the quotient thereby obtained being accepted as the amount of the verdict.[26]

Plaintiffs contended that this method was used by the jury to reach the percentages of negligence attributed to each party. The Supreme Court of Wisconsin stated that, to invalidate the verdict, there must be proof that the jurors agreed to be bound by the quotient result *before* each communicated his apportionment.[27]

When Averaging Permitted

There is nothing wrong with the jurors averaging their different estimates, either as to damages or as to apportionment of fault, in the course of their deliberations.[28] That procedure is acceptable so long as each juror personally concurs with the final figure after it is known. Proof was clear in the *Schiro* case that the jurors had used averaging

---

[25]Schiro v. Oriental Realty Co., 7 Wis. 2d 556, 97 N.W.2d 385 (1959).

[26]Id., 7 Wis. 2d at 564, 97 N.W.2d at 389, quoting Annot., "Quotient verdicts," 52 A.L.R. 41 (1928).

[27]Id., 7 Wis. 2d at 566, 97 N.W.2d at 390; accord, Index Drilling Co. v. Williams, 242 Miss. 775, 137 So. 2d 525, 8 A.L.R. 3d 323 (1962) (verdict not shown to be quotient verdict, but reversed because damages found were grossly excessive).

[28]Id., 7 Wis. 2d at 564, 97 N.W.2d at 389. Accord, McNamee v. Woodbury Congregation of Jehovah's Witnesses, 193 Conn. 15, 475 A.2d 262 (1984); Papp v. Cantrell, 96 Idaho 751, 536 P.2d 746 (1975).

in the course of their deliberations. Nevertheless, circumstances indicated that they did not commit themselves to the figures before it was produced. For example, one juror refused to go along with the final figure.

Prevention of Quotient Verdicts

Obviously, in light of the general rule preventing jurors from impeaching their own verdict,[29] a party will be able only rarely to prove that there was an illegal quotient verdict apportioning negligence. Careful instruction to the jury may help prevent a quotient verdict, and polling after announcement of the jury's decision may help discover it.

The very nature of comparative negligence encourages what was apparently done by jurors in the *Schiro* case, that is, averaging during the course of deliberations. Nevertheless, the flexibility in the system is more likely to lead to an honest group result than the all-or-nothing contributory negligence rule.

18.3 Limited reversal on apportionment of negligence

In an appropriate comparative negligence case, a court may determine as a matter of law that the jury was incorrect in returning a verdict for plaintiff or defendant. For example, a court in a 50% system state may, in an extraordinary situation, hold that a jury's determination for plaintiff cannot stand because, as a matter of law, plaintiff's negligence equaled or exceeded that of the defendant.[30]

New Trial on Apportionment Only

It is, of course, possible for a court in a comparative negligence

---

[29]There are cases that would permit a juror to testify as to the existence of conditions, occurrences or events calculated to influence the verdict improperly. See Wright v. Illinois & Mississippi Tel. Co., 20 Iowa 195 (1866); Perry v. Bailey, 12 Kan. 539 (1874); State v. Kociolek, 20 N.J. 92, 118 A.2d 812, 58 A.L.R.2d 545 (1955). Many modern evidence scholars believe that there is no harm in allowing jurors to testify as to improper conduct in the jury room and that only questions directed to the jurors' own mental operations should be excluded. See Fed. R. Evid. 606 and Advisory Committee Notes.

In Chenell v. Westbrook College, 324 A.2d 735 (Me. 1974) (upholding grant of new trial by trial judge on the basis of quotient verdict and inadequacy of damages) the court stated that, since jury deliberations cannot ordinarily be the subject of testimony by jurors, a quotient verdict may be proved by the result produced if it can be done with some approximation of accuracy; cf. Ramfjord v. Sullivan, 301 Minn. 238, 222 N.W.2d 541 (1974) (upholding trial court's denial of new trial based on compromise verdict). The question appears to be very much within the discretion of the trial judge.

[30]Rewolinski v. Harley-Davidson Motor Co., 32 Wis. 2d 680, 146 N.W.2d 485 (1966); Schwarz v. Winter, 272 Wis. 303, 75 N.W.2d 447 (1956). See section 18.7. Accord, Krauth v. Quinn, 69 Wis. 2d 280, 230 N.W.2d 839 (1975) (dicta); Stapleman v. St. Joseph the Worker, 295 Minn. 406, 205 N.W.2d 667 (1973); see also Orwick v. Belshan, 304 Minn. 338, 231 N.W.2d 90 (1975) (the jury entered inconsistent answers to special verdicts finding that the plaintiff's negligence was a proximate cause as a matter of law and entered a judgment based on the jury's apportionment); Hands v. Arkon, 489 S.W.2d 633 (Tex. Civ. App. 1972) (trial court struck down jury's verdict of plaintiff's causal negligence and entered judgment n.o.v. in accordance with remaining answers of jury; unclear from opinion what percentage of negligence was apportioned to the plaintiff).

state to exercise slightly less control. The court might determine that the jury was justified in finding a particular party or parties negligent but that its apportionment of negligence was improper. For a court to reach this decision, it would have to know how the jury made its apportionment; a special verdict procedure may be necessary for the court to have this information.[31] Assuming the court has been so informed, it could set a new trial restricted to the issue of apportionment of causal negligence.

The Supreme Court of Wisconsin has, on occasion, utilized this device. For example, in *Caldwell v. Piggly Wiggly Madison Company*[32] the plaintiff was injured when she exited from a supermarket. The foot treadle on the door had been left in a state of disrepair. One defendant in the case was a repairman who knowingly left the area unattended and unguarded. The other defendant was the supermarket, which had constructive knowledge of the hazard but did nothing to alleviate it. The jury apportioned 5% of negligence to the plaintiff, 25% to the repairman, and 70% to the supermarket.

The Supreme Court of Wisconsin held that while both defendants were indeed negligent,

> [A] fair reading of the record [led] to the inevitable conclusion that a finding of almost triple the negligence on [the part of the supermarket] constitute[d] a probable miscarriage of justice.[33]

The court upheld the jury's finding of 5% negligence on the part of the plaintiff and ordered a retrial in which the jury was to allocate the remaining 95% of negligence between the two defendants. The finding of causal negligence on the part of each was to stand, but evidence was to be introduced for the purpose of determining the apportionment.

A Washington appellate court allowed a new trial on liability but not on damages where liability had not been tried.[34] The plaintiff had obtained summary judgment on defendant's negligence; the trial judge then ruled that plaintiff was not negligent as a matter of law and directed a verdict on liability. The appellate court said that the facts regarding plaintiff's location in the crosswalk when the light changed supported reversal and a new trial on plaintiff's negligence, but that a new trial on damages would not be necessary.

Reapportionment Between Plaintiff and Defendant

The Supreme Court of Wisconsin has also made limited reversals of this kind where it disagreed with allocation of damages between plaintiff and defendant. For example, in *Firkus v. Rombalski*,[35] the defendant drove his car into the right side of plaintiff's vehicle. The evidence

---

[31]See section 17.4.

[32]Caldwell v. Piggly Wiggly Madison Co., 32 Wis. 2d 447, 145 N.W.2d 745 (1966).

[33]Id., 32 Wis. 2d at 459, 145 N.W.2d at 752.

[34]Clements v. Blue Cross of Washington & Alaska, Inc., 37 Wash. App. 544, 682 P.2d 942 (1984).

[35]Firkus v. Rombalski, 25 Wis. 2d 352, 130 N.W.2d 835 (1964).

also showed that defendant was driving at a considerably higher speed than plaintiff. The jury apportioned negligence in the amount of 30% to plaintiff, 35% to defendant, and 35% to a third-party defendant. The court determined that defendant's

> [N]egligence [was] so disproportionate to [plaintiff's] in any view of the facts as not to be fairly reflected by ascribing only 5 percent more negligence to [the defendant].[36]

The court ordered "a new trial on the issue of the apportionment of causal negligence."[37]

Minnesota Reluctance

In light of the Wisconsin cases, it is somewhat surprising that the Supreme Court of Minnesota in *Juvland v. Mattson*[38] held that a trial court should not have ordered a new trial limited to the single issue of the percentage of causal negligence attributable to each tortfeasor. The Supreme Court did this even though Minnesota practice permits a partial new trial.[39]

In the *Juvland* case, the trial court had held those special verdicts improper which attributed 90% of the negligence to defendant and 10% to plaintiff. The Supreme Court of Minnesota held that the issue of *how much* each party was at fault could not fairly be separated from the issue of *whether* each party was negligent. It therefore declined to endorse a new trial limited to the apportionment issue, saying:

> [O]n retrial, if the ultimate fact issue of causal negligence of each driver were to be given binding effect, the trial court would be limited to merely declaring that the causal negligence of each driver had been previously established without specifying in what particular respect each was causally negligent. It is thus clear that the issue of the percentage of negligence attributable to each driver is not separate and distinct from the issues of the particular negligence claimed and its causal effect. In our opinion, therefore, the order limiting the retrial to this narrow issue is neither feasible nor practical, in the sense of saving litigation time and expense.[40]

The Minnesota Supreme Court found it "conceivable" that a new trial could be limited to the issue of apportionment of negligence if the

---

[36]Id., 25 Wis. 2d at 362, 130 N.W.2d at 840.

[37]Id., 25 Wis. 2d at 362, 130 N.W.2d at 840. Accord, Miles v. Ace Van Lines & Movers, Inc., 72 Wis. 2d 538, 241 N.W.2d 186 (1976) (new trial ordered as apportionment against clear preponderance of evidence; liability issue to be retried in full).

[38]Juvland v. Mattson, 289 Minn. 365, 184 N.W.2d 423 (1971).

[39]Id., 289 Minn. at 369, 184 N.W.2d at 425, quoting Minn. R. Civ. P. 59.01. Accord, Begin v. Weber, 305 Minn. 441, 234 N.W.2d 192 (1975); cf. Martineau v. Nelson, 311 Minn. 92, 247 N.W.2d 409 (1976) (new trial on all issues granted for improper apportionment of negligence); but see Riley v. Lake, 302 Minn. 120, 223 N.W.2d 413 (1974). New trial granted for improper apportionment of negligence. Instructions to be given to jury that plaintiff was negligent as a matter of law; jury to determine percentages of negligence. The Supreme Court of Minnesota upheld this instruction as not invading the province of the jury.

[40]Juvland v. Mattson, note 38 above, 184 N.W.2d at 425.

special verdicts in the first trial had determined "each respect in which the tortfeasors were alleged to be negligent...."[41] In *Juvland*, however, the findings on the first trial were only on the ultimate issues of negligence and causation and the Supreme Court thought the jury in the new trial might be prejudiced by a judge's instruction that negligence had been established. The court speculated that it would be natural for jurors to treat the parties as "equally" at fault when instructed that they were to deem each party negligent.[42]

Critique of the Minnesota Ruling

The Minnesota court appears unduly concerned with a possibility of prejudice, and it unnecessarily rejected what Wisconsin has found to be a very useful procedure. In that regard, prejudice might be avoided if the jury at the second trial were instructed:

> You are to assume that each of the parties in this case was negligent to some degree. Nevertheless, you are to apportion the amount of negligence attributable to each party. You should not assume that the parties were equally at fault or that one has been more at fault than the other. Allocation of amount of negligence is to be your concern and decision-making responsibility.

The Minnesota Supreme Court is correct, however, that limiting a new trial to the issue of apportionment may not represent a great saving of litigation time. Probably, facts relating to the general liability issue will have to be introduced on the issue of apportionment of fault. Nevertheless, the resolution of the case as a whole will be advanced by a reversal based solely on apportionment; the finding of negligence is closed once the highest appellate court in the state has made the determination. This can be true regardless of whether the jury has rendered its verdict in terms of ultimate facts, or by answering specific questions concerning each particular respect in which the evidence would support a finding of negligence.

Complications in 50% System

In pure comparative negligence states the limited reversal on the basis of apportionment should present no complications. In 50% jurisdictions, however, problems can occur because the issue of liability can become entwined with allocation of fault; if plaintiff is more than 50%

---

[41]Id., 289 Minn. at 369, 184 N.W.2d at 425.

[42]Id., 289 Minn. at 370, 184 N.W.2d at 425. In a case where the New Jersey Supreme Court could have ordered a new trial limited to the apportionment of negligence issue, a full trial on the issue of liability was ordered. Pappas v. Santiago, 66 N.J. 140, 329 A.2d 337 (1974). See also Rekiec v. Zuzio, 132 N.J. Super. 71, 332 A.2d 222 (1975). In State v. Kaatz, 572 P.2d 775 (Alaska 1977) (citing this treatise), the court refused to allow retrial on the issue of apportionment of negligence, even though the case was remanded for a new trial on damages. This decision was based partly on the notion that the apportionment of negligence is part of the liability phase of the case rather than the damages phase, and that these issues may be considered separately. The court ruled that in this instance it was permissible for the trial judge to make the apportionment of negligence himself, rather than submit this question to the jury.

at fault (or equally at fault with defendant in some jurisdictions), there can be no recovery.

Confusion can be avoided if the court which overrules the original jury allocation is specific in its determination. For example, if a jury has determined that plaintiff is only 5% at fault and defendant is 95% at fault, an appellate court might decide that this is grossly unfair to defendant and also that a reasonable jury could find plaintiff more at fault than defendant. In such case the trial court should instruct the second jury that each party is to be deemed negligent but that the jury is to apportion fault. The jury will have the option to make a finding that will result in a judgment for defendant.

On the other hand, if the appellate court believes that the first jury's verdict must permit at least some recovery for plaintiff, the trial court should instruct the second jury that it is to apportion fault but should not deem plaintiff more at fault than defendant.

Value of Limited Reversal

It is this author's view that courts could utilize reversal "solely on the basis of apportionment" to provide additional jury control and to expedite trials. They should treat the procedure in the same manner that remittitur and additur are handled in many states. If the court finds that the jury's apportionment of fault improperly favors plaintiff, it could indicate the most favorable allocation with regard to plaintiff that it would uphold. Then, plaintiff could either accept that apportionment or run the gauntlet of a new trial.

Similarly, if the court believed that the jury's allocation of fault was grossly unfair to the plaintiff, it could indicate the most favorable allocation with regard to defendant that it could uphold. It would then be up to defendant either to accept that allocation or to face a new trial.

Again, it should be noted that this approach has not been used to date; it is merely suggested.[43] Its advantages in terms of jury control and economy of judicial time are clear. Its only disadvantage is that it might tempt appellate courts to exercise too much control over a jury. The drafters of the Uniform Comparative Fault Act have suggested use of this procedure.[44]

In *Bohlman v. American Family Mutual Insurance Company*,[45] the Wisconsin Supreme Court noted that since the remittitur/additur approach is limited to the issue of inadequate or excessive damages, and not the apportionment of negligence, the only remedy lay in a new trial.

---

[43]Cf. Lawver v. Park Falls, 35 Wis. 2d 308, 315, 151 N.W.2d 68, 71 (1967) (concurring opinion).

[44]Unif. Comparative Fault Act §2, Comment, 12 U.L.A. 43 (Supp. 1985). See section 21.4.

[45]Bohlman v. American Family Mut. Ins. Co., 61 Wis. 2d 718, 722 n.2, 214 N.W.2d 52, 58 n.2 and accompanying text (1974).

18.4 Reversal by remittitur and additur

Remittitur and additur are procedural devices whereby a court may avoid a new trial even though the jury has returned a verdict that is improper as to damages. When a jury has given an excessively high award to plaintiff, remittitur may be used.[46] The court determines the highest jury verdict that it would uphold and allows plaintiff the option of taking that amount in judgment or undergoing a new trial on all the issues.[47] The judge may not simply substitute his judgment for the jury verdict without granting plaintiff the option of a new trial.[48]

Conversely, when the jury has awarded an unreasonably low amount in damages, additur may be used.[49] The court sets a damage award which is the lowest that it could possibly uphold.[50] Defendant is then given the option of paying that amount or undergoing a new trial.

Blurring of Issues Under Comparative Negligence

In their normal operations in contributory negligence states, remittitur and additur do not deal with the issues of liability or relative fault of the parties. They deal solely with the damage issue. When comparative negligence is introduced, however, the separation between the issues of fault and liability and the issue of damages may blur.

This is highly likely to occur in states such as Mississippi where it is the duty of the jury to reduce damages in proportion to the amount of contributory negligence it attributes to the plaintiff. For example, if a plaintiff suffers $100,000 damages and obtains an award from the jury in the full amount of his claim, yet was clearly contributorily negligent, an appellate court might utilize the remittitur device and reduce damages, giving plaintiff an option either to take that award or to face a

---

[46]F. James & G. Hazard, *Civil Procedure* §7.21 (1977). Accord, Smith v. Bullington, 499 S.W.2d 649 (Tenn. App. 1973).

[47]F. James & G. Hazard, note 46 above, at 331. In Wisconsin a remittitur may be ordered in accordance with the "Powers" variation in which the court allows plaintiff the option of an amount fixed by the court as reasonable, or a new trial. Powers v. Allstate Ins. Co., 10 Wis. 2d 78, 102 N.W.2d 393 (1960); Spleas v. Milwaukee & Suburban Transport Corp., 21 Wis. 2d 635, 124 N.W.2d 593 (1963); Leibl v. St. Mary's Hosp., 57 Wis. 2d 227, 203 N.W.2d 715 (1973). Previous Wisconsin practice had offered the plaintiff the least amount considered reasonable. Gennrich v. Schrank, 6 Wis. 2d 87, 93 N.W.2d 876 (1959).

[48]Staplin v. Maritime Overseas Corp., 519 F.2d 969 (2d Cir. N.Y. 1975); Hanson v. Chicago, R. I. & P. R. Co., 345 N.W.2d 736 (Minn. 1984).

[49]F. James & G. Hazard, note 46 above, §7.21. Granting additur: Labree v. Major, 111 R.I. 657, 306 A.2d 808 (1973); Hamrick v. Yellow Cab Co. of Providence, 111 R.I. 515, 304 A.2d 666 (1973).

[50]F. James & G. Hazard, note 46 above, at 332. In Wisconsin the "Powers" variation has also been adopted for additur cases to provide defendant with the option of accepting an amount set by the court as reasonable or undergoing a new trial. Parchia v. Parchia, 24 Wis. 2d 659, 130 N.W.2d 205 (1964); Helleckson v. Loiselle, 37 Wis. 2d 423, 155 N.W.2d 45 (1967).

new trial. The Supreme Court of Mississippi has done just that and has been rather explicit on the issue.[51]

Maine requires that additur be offered a defendant before a new trial is ordered on the basis of inadequacy of damages,[52] unless the inadequacy is the result of a quotient verdict.[53]

There appears to be nothing inherently wrong with such a procedure, so long as the court is clear as to why it has reduced damages. The court should indicate whether it is reducing the award because plaintiff has not suffered that much damage (the ordinary remittitur situation in contributory negligence states), or because plaintiff is not entitled to his full damages because of his own contributory negligence.[54]

The Small Verdict

Confusion can be compounded in comparative negligence states when a jury returns a general verdict for markedly less than the amount of damages plaintiff clearly suffered. Did the jury reduce the award because plaintiff was at fault? Or did the jury fail to make a proper estimate of plaintiff's damages? The Supreme Court of Mississippi has recognized this problem and refrained from using an additur device when there is evidence of plaintiff's contributory negligence that would justify reduction of the award to that extent.[55] Of course, if an appellate court in such a situation finds *no* contributory negligence or that contributory negligence was insufficient to account for such a low award of damages, it can properly use additur to increase plaintiff's award to a reasonable level or, in the alternative, to award a new trial.

Georgia courts flatly refuse to set aside small verdicts in compara-

---

[51]Ideal Cement Co. v. Killingsworth, 198 So. 2d 248 (Miss. 1967) (as size of verdict indicated that the jury did not comply with instruction to reduce it in proportion to the contributory negligence, thus evincing bias, passion or prejudice, the court ordered a remand on the question of damages or a remittitur); Gulf & S. I. R. Co. v. Bond, 181 Miss. 254, 179 So. 355 (1938) (remittitur or remand ordered because jury had not reduced plaintiff's damages sufficiently in view of contributory negligence). Accord, Dorris v. Carr, 330 So. 2d 872 (Miss. 1976) (even more emphatic: the trial court ordered an additur, but set it aside and ordered a new trial on the question of damages. The Supreme Court of Mississippi reinstated the original order for additur); Stockton v. Lamberth, 278 So. 2d 423 (Miss. 1973); but see Powers v. Malley, 302 So. 2d 262 (Miss. 1974) (new trial ordered on damages as damages clearly inadequate; defendant not given option of additur).

[52]Me. R. Civ. P. 59(a).

[53]Chenell v. Westbrook College, 324 A.2d 735 (Me. 1974) (dicta).

[54]See Ginn v. Penobscot Co., 334 A.2d 874 (Me. 1975), mod. 342 A.2d 270 (Me. 1975). Both the questions of blurring of issues and excessive award were raised on appeal. The Supreme Court of Maine granted remittitur, specifying that the remittitur was granted on the basis of the plaintiff's failure to prove sufficient damage.

[55]See Ramsey v. Price, 249 Miss. 192, 161 So. 2d 778 (1964) (although the court stated that damages were inadequate, it would not substitute its judgment for that of the jury when the jury was the sole judge of plaintiff's contributory negligence, and the evidence was in conflict).

tive negligence cases,[56] on the ground that the court has no way of reviewing the basis for the finding.[57]

Advantages of Special Verdict

In Wisconsin[58] and a number of other states,[59] the jury in a comparative negligence case is always required to return a special verdict stating the full amount of damage sustained by plaintiff. In nine other states,[60] any party is entitled to demand such a special verdict. In nearly every state it is within the discretion of the trial court to seek that information either by special verdict or by special interrogatory.[61]

When the special verdict procedure is used, the merger of the issues of fault and damages is avoided. The devices of remittitur and additur can be confined to situations where the jury has made an improper estimate of the plaintiff's damages. Remittitur and additur thus remain damage-cleansing devices.[62]

In a particular case, one special verdict may be that plaintiff suffered $10,000 damage and a second may be that plaintiff was 50% at fault. If the court believes that the $10,000 estimate of damage is not supported by the evidence, it can reduce the amount to the highest figure supported by the evidence (perhaps $5000), and then reduce that amount by 40%. At first blush, this might appear to result in too low a recovery for plaintiff. However, it must be remembered that the jury, in determining the amount plaintiff was damaged, is not supposed to take into account plaintiff's fault; that is dealt with in a separate question. Similarly, the court in arriving at the $5000 figure is to consider only plaintiff's damage and not his fault.

Remittitur, Additur and Special Verdicts

In sum, remittitur and additur are helpful procedural devices that can certainly survive the advent of comparative negligence. Special verdicts should be utilized to keep reasonable control over the jury and, as well, to confine remittitur and additur to their traditional functions of adjusting damages in relation to the amount plaintiff actually suffered. Of course, as suggested in section 18.3 a device analogous to remittitur and additur could be used to correct a jury's improper allocation of fault. Nevertheless, if courts are to keep reasonable control of the jury and ascertain what in fact it has done, it is helpful to use

---

[56]See, e.g., Young v. Southern Bell Tel. & Tel. Co., 168 Ga. App. 40, 308 S.E.2d 49 (1983); Powers v. Pate, 107 Ga. App. 25, 129 S.E.2d 193 (1962).

[57]Atlanta Recycled Fiber Co. v. Tri-Cities Steel Co., 152 Ga. App. 259, 262 S.E.2d 554 (1979).

[58]See section 17.4; see also Wis. Stat. Ann., § 270.27.

[59]Colorado, Florida, Hawaii, Indiana, Iowa, Kansas, Massachusetts, New Jersey and Ohio. See note 41, section 17.4. In Maine, also, the jury is required to find and return both the full amount of damages and the amount of the reduced award plaintiff should receive in view of his contributory fault. Me. Rev. Stat. Ann., tit. 14, §156. This accomplishes the same purpose of separating the issues as does the special verdict.

[60]Idaho, Louisiana, Maine, Minnesota, Nevada, North Dakota, Oregon, Utah and Wyoming. See note 42, section 17.4

[61]See note 46, section 17.4 and accompanying text.

[62]See, e.g., Boyce v. Herzberg, 296 Minn. 52, 206 N.W.2d 548 (1973).

special verdicts or special questions. The operation of these devices is considered in section 17.4.

18.5 Judicial review under pure comparative negligence

F.E.L.A.

The Federal Employers' Liability Act[63] applies a pure form of comparative negligence. The specific purpose of the F.E.L.A. and its policy basis strongly favor plaintiff-railroad workers. For this reason the standards used in review of jury verdicts under F.E.L.A. are suspect as precedent for cases arising under state comparative negligence statutes of general application.

The Supreme Court of the United States pointed out in *Rogers v. Missouri Pacific Railroad Company*[64] that "the special features of this statutory negligence action ... make it significantly different from the ordinary common-law negligence action." The court also stated that the statute supplants the common-law duty of the master to his servant "with the far more drastic duty of paying damages for injury or death at work due in whole or part to the employer's negligence."[65]

Viewed in this light, a very liberal standard of sufficiency of evidence to support a jury verdict for plaintiff is consistent with F.E.L.A. Thus, in the *Rogers* case, the Supreme Court reversed a ruling below "that the evidence was insufficient to support the jury's verdict for plaintiff." The Supreme Court stated that:

> Under this statute the test of a jury case is simply whether the proofs justify with reason the conclusion that employer negligence played any part, even the slightest, in producing the injury or death for which damages are sought.[66]

The standard established in *Rogers* has been generally applied in other F.E.L.A. cases.[67] Thus, solicitude for plaintiffs and a willingness

---

[63]Federal Employers' Liability Act of April 22, 1908, ch. 149, §3, 35 Stat. 66, 45 U.S.C. § 53.

[64]Rogers v. Missouri P. R. Co., 352 U.S. 500, 509-510, 1 L. Ed. 2d 493, 77 S. Ct. 443, 450 (1957).

[65]Id., 352 U.S. at 507, 77 S. Ct. at 449.

[66]Id., 352 U.S. at 506, 77 S. Ct. at 448.

[67]See, e.g., Arnold v. Panhandle & S. F. R. Co., 353 U.S. 360, 1 L. Ed. 2d 889, 77 S. Ct. 840 (1957); Webb v. Illinois C. R. Co., 352 U.S. 512, 1 L. Ed. 2d 503, 77 S. Ct. 451 (1957); Kelly v. Illinois C. G. R. Co., 552 F. Supp. 399 (W.D. Mo. 1982). The standard was also applied in Jones Act cases to determine the sufficiency of evidence as to both negligence and contributory negligence. See, e.g., Ferguson v. Moore-McCormack Lines, Inc., 352 U.S. 521, 1 L. Ed. 2d 511, 77 S. Ct. 457 (1957); Fleming v. American Export Isbrandtsen Lines, Inc., 451 F.2d 1329, 1331 (2d Cir. N.Y. 1971), citing Lavender v. Kurn, 327 U.S. 645, 653, 90 L. Ed. 916, 66 S. Ct. 740 (1946) and McBride v. Loffland Bros. Co., 422 F.2d 363 (5th Cir. La. 1970). See also Stobie v. Potlatch Forests, Inc., 95 Idaho 666, 518 P.2d 1 (1973) (review of jury verdict in maritime case will be governed by more liberal federal standard of sufficiency of evidence to support a verdict). A similar solicitude for the plaintiff appears in actions arising under the Jones Act. See, e.g., Landry v. Two R. Drilling Co., 511 F.2d 138 (5th Cir. La. 1975).

to uphold jury verdicts for them are found time and again.[68] Hence, this group of cases is not a representative sample on which to construct standards for judicial review under pure comparative negligence statutes of general application.

State Pure Comparative Negligence Laws

Fourteen states now apply pure comparative negligence in negligence actions generally: six by statute[69] and eight by judicial decision.[70] Because Mississippi has had pure comparative negligence longer than any of the other states, its body of case law on judicial review is well developed and serves to illustrate issues that arise.

The statutory and case law of Mississippi begins with the assumption that all questions of negligence and contributory negligence are for the jury to determine.[71] This assumption has been followed in the case law of California.[72] Where the trial court has properly instructed the jury in accord with the comparative negligence statute, though the defendant might contend that the verdict is excessive, appellate courts may assume that the jury considered the effect of any contributory negligence in reaching the amount of its verdict.[73] On the other hand, where there is evidence warranting a finding of contributory negli-

---

[68]See Powell, *Contributory Negligence: A Necessary Check on the American Jury,* 43 A.B.A. J. 1005, 1061 n.31 (1957) ("The general solicitude for plaintiffs under this law is further illustrated by the fact that of the forty-eight FELA cases decided by the Supreme Court in the past twenty years (through the term ending in June, 1957), involving sufficiency of the evidence to support a verdict, the plaintiffs won forty-two cases or 88 per cent").

[69]Ariz. Rev. Stat. Ann., § 12-2505; La. Civ. Code Ann., art. 2323; Miss. Code Ann., § 11-7-15; N.Y. Civ. Prac. Law, § 1411; R.I. Gen. Laws, § 9-20-4; Wash. Rev. Code Ann., § 4.22.10.

[70]Hoffman v. Jones, 280 So. 2d 431, 78 A.L.R.3d 321 (Fla. 1973); Nga Li v. Yellow Cab Co., 13 Cal. 3d 804, 119 Cal. Rptr. 858, 532 P.2d 1226, 78 A.L.R.3d 393 (1975); Kaatz v. State, 540 P.2d 1037 (Alaska 1975); Placek v. Sterling Heights, 405 Mich. 638, 275 N.W.2d 511 (1979); Scott v. Rizzo, 96 N.M. 682, 634 P.2d 1234 (1981); Alvis v. Ribar, 85 Ill. 2d 1, 52 Ill. Dec. 23, 421 N.E.2d 886 (1981); Gustafson v. Benda, 661 S.W.2d 11 (Mo. 1983); Hilen v. Hays, 673 S.W.2d 713 (Ky. 1984).

[71]Miss. Code Ann., §11-7-17. See Medley v. Carter, 234 So. 2d 334 (Miss. 1970) (under comparative negligence statute, all questions of negligence are for the jury); Southeastern Constr. Co. v. Dependent of Dodson, 247 Miss. 1, 153 So. 2d 276 (1963) (apportionment of damages under the comparative negligence act is for the jury in the light of the circumstances and within reasonable bounds); Gaskin v. Davis, 246 Miss. 166, 149 So. 2d 850 (1963) (verdict for defendants could not be set aside where evidence was conflicting and credibility of witnesses was open to question); Schumpert v. Watson, 241 Miss. 199, 129 So. 2d 627 (1961) (verdict based on conflicting evidence in a negligence case will be set aside only if clearly against the weight of evidence or if the jury was mistaken or influenced by passion, prejudice or corruption).

[72]See Wittenbach v. Ryan, 63 Cal. App. 3d 712, 134 Cal. Rptr. 47 (1976).

[73]Bill Hunter Truck Lines, Inc. v. Jernigan, 384 F.2d 361 (5th Cir. Miss. 1967).

gence, the appellate court will often affirm a judgment even though the plaintiff has contested it as inadequate.[74]

Removal of Issues from Jury

Nevertheless, as in other general comparative negligence systems, it is possible for the issues to be removed from the jury. Thus the Supreme Court of Mississippi has stated:

> The verdict of the jury will not be disturbed on appeal when a mere preponderance of the evidence is against it, but will be set aside when it is palpably against the weight of the evidence.[75]

Of course, defendant rarely achieves a complete reversal of a jury verdict under this standard in a pure comparative negligence system. The appellate court would have to find that no causal negligence is attributable to him.

Defendant may, however, achieve a partial victory; he may convince the appellate court that the jury ignored evidence of plaintiff's negligence when it computed damages.[76] Thus, in *Dendy v. Pascagoula*,[77] plaintiff was injured when he dived into shallow water from a city pier. It was clear that he had not used reasonable care with regard to his own safety. The Supreme Court of Mississippi found that the jury's failure to reduce the damages evidenced "bias, passion, and preju-

---

[74]Carr v. Cox, 255 So. 2d 317 (Miss. 1971) (although jury wasn't given an instruction on contributory negligence, it was justified in reducing plaintiff's damages in proportion to the amount of negligence attributable to her; the otherwise inadequate verdict was justified under the comparative negligence statute); Ramsey v. Price, 249 Miss. 192, 161 So. 2d 778 (1964) (although court stated that damages were inadequate, it could not substitute its judgment for that of the jury, which was the sole judge of whether plaintiff was guilty of contributory negligence); Gore v. Patrick, 246 Miss. 715, 150 So. 2d 169 (1963) (court not justified in reversing on ground of inadequate damages as issue of contributory negligence was for the jury).

[75]Vaughan v. Bollis, 221 Miss. 589, 595-596, 73 So. 2d 160, 162 (1954), citing Flournoy v. Brown, 200 Miss. 171, 26 So. 2d 351 (1946). Accord, Kinsey v. Kelly, 312 So. 2d 461 (Fla. App. 1975). See also Model v. Rabinowitz, 313 So. 2d 59 (Fla. App. 1975) (jury verdict will be set aside if answers to interrogatories indicate improper application of comparative negligence).

[76]Under Mississippi's comparative negligence system, the jury is given the role of reducing damages in proportion to plaintiff's fault. The jury returns a general verdict reflecting this calculation, but an appellate court can only speculate as to how the apportionment was made. See also Huser v. Santa Fe Pomeroy, Inc., 513 F.2d 1298 (9th Cir. Cal. 1975) (admiralty; trial judge has discretion to reduce award by percentage of negligence attributable to plaintiff if jury ignores evidence of that negligence). Such review can also work to the defendant's disadvantage. In Benson v. American Export Isbrandtsen Lines, Inc., 478 F.2d 152 (3d Cir. Pa. 1973), the court overturned a jury finding of negligence on the part of the plaintiff longshoreman and entered a judgment in the full amount of his damages.

[77]Dendy v. Pascagoula, 193 So. 2d 559 (Miss. 1967); accord, Ideal Cement Co. v. Killingsworth, 198 So. 2d 248 (Miss. 1967).

dice."[78] A new trial was ordered unless the plaintiff was willing to accept a remittitur.[79]

Inadequate Verdicts

A verdict may also be deemed so inadequate as to evince passion or prejudice, and be reversed to the advantage of plaintiff. For example, in *Swartzfager v. Southern Bell Telephone and Telegraph Company*[80] an award of $3000 damages to plaintiff, who had sustained permanent and painful injuries in an automobile collision and had already expended $3564, was held "grossly disproportionate" to any contributory negligence imputable to plaintiff. The case arose from an intersection collision, and the evidence suggested that the parties were equally at fault. The Mississippi Supreme Court concluded that the verdict resulted either from passion or prejudice, or from failure to evaluate plaintiff's damages properly.[81]

Pure comparative negligence may give plaintiff an opportunity to overturn a verdict for defendant. If defendant's negligence contributed to the accident, plaintiff is entitled to recover at least some damages. Thus, in *Moak v. Black*[82] the Supreme Court of Mississippi reversed a verdict for defendant in an action for the death of a nine-year-old bicyclist. The court found the verdict contrary to the overwhelming weight of the evidence, as the defendant had testified that he saw the deceased several hundred feet before the point of the accident but neither sounded his horn nor applied his brakes until within twelve to fifteen feet of the deceased. The court noted that the power of the court to set aside the verdict in such a case was a necessary incident of the right of trial by jury.[83]

In sum, determinations concerning the respective fault of the parties are usually a function of the jury, but sometimes they may be reversed under pure comparative negligence. When the jury does the mathematics of reducing damages according to the relative negligence, such reversals are likely to be based on extremes in the size of recov-

---

[78]Dendy v. Pascagoula, note 77 above, 193 So. 2d at 564.

[79]Id. Accord, Stockton v. Lamberth, 278 So. 2d 423 (Miss. 1973) (remittitur ordered); but see Standard Furniture Co. v. Wallace, 288 So. 2d 461 (Miss. 1974) (verdict upheld as not excessive, not against weight of evidence, and not so large as to evince jury passion or prejudice).

[80]Swartzfager v. Southern Bell Tel. & Tel. Co., 236 Miss. 322, 110 So. 2d 380 (1959).

[81]Accord, Winstead v. Hall, 251 Miss. 800, 171 So. 2d 354 (1965); Dickey v. Parham, 295 So. 2d 284 (Miss. 1974); Kinne v. Burgin, 311 So. 2d 695 (Fla. App. 1975). See also Smith v. Washam, 288 So. 2d 20 (Miss. 1974) (reinstating trial court's original order of additur in an adequate verdict case rather than the trial court's subsequent order of a new trial). But see Wittenbach v. Ryan, 63 Cal. App. 3d 712, 134 Cal. Rptr. 47 (1976) (jury verdict adequate when in accordance with one rational view of conflicting evidence); West v. Food Fair Stores, Inc., 305 So. 2d 280 (Fla. App. 1974) (verdict not inadequate if it could be reached rationally: jury may properly attribute plaintiff's damage to congenital condition).

[82]Moak v. Black, 230 Miss. 337, 92 So. 2d 845 (1957).

[83]Id., 230 Miss. at 348, 92 So. 2d at 850.

ery. Under other systems the bases for reversal may be somewhat different.

18.6 Judicial review under the slight-gross system

Nebraska and South Dakota are the only states with a slight-gross system of comparative negligence.[84] Under this system, the general rule once again is that it is for the jury to determine questions of negligence and contributory negligence.[85] As said by the Supreme Court of Nebraska,

> Where reasonable minds may differ as to conclusions or inferences to be drawn from the evidence, and where there is a conflict in the evidence as to whether or not it establishes negligence or contributory negligence and the degree thereof, such issues must be submitted to a jury.[86]

Conversely, where, under the evidence, reasonable minds can arrive at only one conclusion, the court may decide the negligence issue as a matter of law.[87]

Reversal on the Evidence

A reversal may be founded on the jury's faulty comparison of negligence between the parties. In this regard, there appears to be little difference in the standards for judicial review used in Nebraska and South Dakota despite the material difference in the wording of the two statutes.[88]

There are cases which demonstrate a willingness of courts to reverse jury findings for the plaintiff when, as a matter of law, the plaintiff is guilty of negligence "more than slight" in comparison with defendant. Thus, in *Haffke v. Grinnell*[89] the Nebraska Supreme Court upheld the trial court's dismissal of the action though the jury had entered a verdict for the plaintiff. Plaintiff-motorcyclist had observed a turn signal on defendant's automobile preceding him, but failed to

---

[84]Neb. Rev. Stat., § 25-1151; S.D. Codified Laws, § 20-9-2. See section 3.4.

[85]Neb. Rev. Stat., § 25-1151; Pexa v. Clark, 85 S.D. 37, 176 N.W.2d 497 (1970).

[86]Speedway Transp., Inc. v. De Turk, 183 Neb. 629, 631, 163 N.W.2d 283, 285 (1968). See, e.g., Holly v. Mitchell, 213 Neb. 203, 328 N.W.2d 750 (1982); Schutz v. Hunt, 212 Neb. 228, 322 N.W.2d 414 (1982); Johnson v. Riecken, 185 Neb. 78, 173 N.W.2d 511 (1970); Zucker v. Monohan, 183 Neb. 686, 163 N.W.2d 786 (1969).

[87]E.g., Gerhardt v. McChesney, 210 Neb. 351, 314 N.W.2d 258 (1982); Jarosh v. Van Meter, 171 Neb. 61, 105 N.W.2d 531, 82 A.L.R.2d 714 (1960); Johnson v. Riecken, 185 Neb. 78, 173 N.W.2d 511 (1970); Hrabik v. Gottsch, 198 Neb. 86, 251 N.W.2d 672 (1977).

[88]The Nebraska comparative negligence statute provides that contributory negligence is not a bar to recovery when it was slight and the negligence of defendant was gross in comparison. Neb. Rev. Stat., § 25-1151. However, the South Dakota statute does not require a finding of gross negligence on the part of defendant in order for plaintiff to recover, but only that plaintiff's negligence was slight in comparison with that of defendant. S.D. Codified Laws, § 20-9-2.

[89]Haffke v. Grinnell, 188 Neb. 323, 196 N.W.2d 390 (1972). Accord, Blum v. Brichacek, 191 Neb. 457, 215 N.W.2d 888 (1974) (affirming judgment n.o.v. for defendant. Plaintiff who stepped in front of defendant's moving car following an altercation guilty of negligence more than slight as a matter of law).

maintain sufficient control over his vehicle to enable him to avoid collision. The defendant was negligent in failing to maintain a proper lookout and in failing to approach the intersection in the turn lane as
required by ordinance; however, the plaintiff was traveling too fast and
too close, and was, as a matter of law, guilty of contributory negligence
which was "more than slight" and was sufficient to bar his recovery.
Such cases seem to demonstrate unwillingness of the court to allow a
sympathetic jury to award a recovery which should be barred under the
slight-gross statutory scheme.

New Trial on Damages

Nebraska and South Dakota differ on whether a new trial may be
granted solely on the issue of damages. This may be done in Nebraska
where liability has been determined fairly.[90] The Supreme Court of
South Dakota has not thus far allowed a new trial on "damages
only."[91] Possibly a new trial on damages will be allowed in some future
South Dakota case where it is clear that liability was fairly determined
but damages are incorrect and the error in damages does not result
from a compromise on liability.[92]

18.7 Judicial review under the 50% system and its derivatives

Under the comparative negligence statutes of nine states, plaintiff is
barred from recovery if his negligence equals or is greater than that of
the defendant.[93] One state now applies the "50%" modified form of comparative negligence by judicial decision.[94] In nineteen other jurisdictions
plaintiff may receive part of his damages if his negligence exactly equals
that of the defendant but is barred if his negligence is greater.[95]

In *Reiter v. Dyken*[96] the Supreme Court of Wisconsin refused to
combine the negligence of the defendants for purposes of determining
whether plaintiffs were entitled to recover. In reversing the lower
court's ruling, the Supreme Court reasoned that it would be improper
to combine the negligence after the case had already been tried and
then submit it to the jury on the assumption that the parties would be

---

[90]Schaffer v. Bolz, 181 Neb. 509, 149 N.W.2d 334 (1967); Scofield v. Haskell, 180 Neb.
324, 142 N.W.2d 597 (1966); Caster v. Moeller, 176 Neb. 446, 126 N.W.2d 485 (1964). However, where it appears that the verdict was the result of a compromise under the comparative negligence system, a new trial should be granted on all issues. Schaffer v. Bolz, 181
Neb. at 511, 149 N.W.2d at 337.

[91]Hanisch v. Body, 77 S.D. 265, 90 N.W.2d 924 (1958) (new trial solely on the issue of
damages cannot be granted in personal injury actions where the jury may mitigate damages according to comparative negligence law).

[92]See Pexa v. Clark, 85 S.D. 37, 176 N.W.2d 497 (1970) (two judges believed that a
new trial limited to the issue of damages should be granted, but the majority thought the
record reflected a compromise and did not jusify a limited remand; a new trial was granted on all issues).

[93]Arkansas, Colorado, Georgia, Idaho, Kansas, Maine, North Dakota, Utah and Wyoming. See section 3.5.

[94]Bradley v. Appalachian Power Co., 163 W. Va. 332, 256 S.E.2d 879 (1979).

[95]Connecticut, Delaware, Hawaii, Indiana, Iowa, Massachusetts, Minnesota, Montana,
Nevada, New Hampshire, New Jersey, Ohio, Oklahoma, Oregon, Pennsylvania, Texas,
Vermont, the Virgin Islands and Wisconsin. See subsection 3.5(B).

[96]Reiter v. Dyken, 95 Wis. 2d 461, 290 N.W.2d 510 (1980). See subsection 3.5(C).

compared individually. Rather, the court indicated that the legislature would be the appropriate forum for the solution of problems in situations involving multiple tortfeasors.

As in the other two systems,[97] the courts have, under the 50% system or its derivative, been hesitant to disturb jury findings. Determination of the degree of negligence of the parties is within the province of the jury. This is reflected in the standards courts have articulated for court disturbance of jury findings. Thus, courts have stated that they will overturn verdicts only when "apportionment is manifestly and palpably against the weight of the evidence"[98] or "it is manifest as a matter of law that allocation is unreasonably disproportionate."[99] In sum, courts are reluctant to set aside the percentages found if any credible evidence would support the jury determination.[1]

---

[97]See sections 18.5 and 18.6.

[98]Martin v. Bussert, 292 Minn. 29, 193 N.W.2d 134 (1971); Duchene v. Wolstan, 258 N.W.2d 601 (Minn. 1977).

[99]Hollie v. Gilbertson, 38 Wis. 2d 245, 250, 156 N.W.2d 462, 465 (1968). See, e.g., Frederick v. Hotel Investments, Inc., 48 Wis. 2d 429, 180 N.W.2d 562 (1970) (jury's findings as to apportionment of negligence will be sustained if there is any credible evidence which under any reasonable view supports the finding, especially where the trial judge has approved the findings); Holzem v. Mueller, 54 Wis. 2d 388, 195 N.W.2d 635 (1972) (evidence supports jury apportionment of 50% negligence each to defendant motorist and decedent bicyclist; it could not be concluded, as a matter of law, that the motorist's negligence was greater); Young v. Anaconda American Brass Co., 43 Wis. 2d 36, 168 N.W.2d 112 (1969) (it could not be said as a matter of law that negligence of the employee, whose foot slipped on grease on the owner's overhead crane, equaled or exceeded that of the owner in the situation; jury finding of 10% of the causal negligence attributable to employee was affirmed); Bruno v. Biesecker, 40 Wis. 2d 305, 162 N.W.2d 135 (1968) (left-turning driver's negligence in turning in the path of an automobile approaching from the opposite direction is not as a matter of law at least 50% of fault, and the apportionment of negligence is peculiarly within the province of the jury); Browne v. Bark River Culvert & Equipment Co., 425 F.2d 3 (7th Cir. Wis. 1970); Schuster v. St. Vincent Hosp., 45 Wis. 2d 135, 172 N.W.2d 421, 36 A.L.R.3d 1227 (1969); Crotty v. Bright, 42 Wis. 2d 440, 167 N.W.2d 201 (1969); Neider v. Spoehr, 41 Wis. 2d 610, 165 N.W.2d 171 (1969); Lautenschlager v. Hamburg, 41 Wis. 2d 623, 165 N.W.2d 129 (1969); Bash v. Employers Mut. Liability Ins. Co., 38 Wis. 2d 440, 157 N.W.2d 634 (1968); Pruss v. Strube, 37 Wis. 2d 539, 155 N.W.2d 650 (1968); Chapman v. Keefe, 37 Wis. 2d 315, 155 N.W.2d 13 (1967); Ernst v. Greenwald, 35 Wis. 2d 763, 151 N.W.2d 706 (1967); Barber v. Oshkosh, 35 Wis. 2d 751, 151 N.W.2d 739 (1967); Lawver v. Park Falls, 35 Wis. 2d 308, 151 N.W.2d 68 (1967); Britton v. Hoyt, 63 Wis. 2d 688, 218 N.W.2d 274 (1974) (reinstating jury apportionment of negligence set aside by trial judge); Bohlman v. American Family Mut. Ins. Co., 61 Wis. 2d 718, 214 N.W.2d 52 (1974); Gould v. Allstar Ins. Co., 59 Wis. 2d 355, 208 N.W.2d 388 (1973) (apportionment of 15% of negligence to plaintiff who dived into shallow water without determining depth and 85% to defendant pier owner upheld); Steinhaus v. Adamson, 304 Minn. 14, 228 N.W.2d 865, 88 A.L.R.3d 613 (1975) (it could not be said that negligence of plaintiff who collided with defendant at an uncontrolled intersection equaled defendant's as a matter of law).

[1]E.g., Werner Transp. Co. v. Barts, 57 Wis. 2d 714, 205 N.W.2d 394 (1973); Smith v. St. Paul Fire & Marine Ins. Co., 56 Wis. 2d 752, 203 N.W.2d 34 (1973); Kenwood Equipment, Inc. v. Aetna Ins. Co., 48 Wis. 2d 472, 180 N.W.2d 750 (1970); Johnson v. Chemical Supply Co., 38 Wis. 2d 194, 156 N.W.2d 455 (1968); see note 93 above. See also Dehn v. Otter Tail Power Co., 251 N.W.2d 404 (N.D. 1977) (no error in construing verdict which reversed amounts of general and special damages); Jordan v. Ellis, 148 Ga. App. 286, 250 S.E.2d 859 (1978) (even though mother's and father's verdicts were inconsistent, court not prepared to find inference of gross mistake or undue bias, as mother's case on appeal was based upon the proper legal theory); Lonardo v. Litvak Meat Co., 676 P.2d 1229 (Colo. App. 1983) (special verdict finding plaintiff not negligent and assessing no damages was harmless error because it was equivalent to finding plaintiff as negligent as defendant).

Errors of Law by Trial Court

There are two categories of cases in which the courts will overturn a verdict. The first is obvious—when the verdict may have resulted from an error of law by the trial judge. For example, in *Turk v. H. C. Prange Company*[2] the trial judge instructed the jury that plaintiff could not rely on res ipsa loquitur if his negligence contributed to the happening of the accident. This was erroneous under the comparative negligence statute according to the Supreme Court. The jury returned a verdict for defendant and the Supreme Court ordered a new trial because of the error in the instruction.

Reversals on the Evidence

The second category of cases in which a court under the 50% system might reverse a jury finding is more difficult to define. It is the cases where it would be unreasonable to find that defendant was guilty of greater negligence than plaintiff.

A jury finding of greater negligence in defendant might be reversed, for example, where defendant was clearly trying to avoid a consequence of plaintiff's negligence. For example, in *Robertson v. Johnson*[3] the Supreme Court of Minnesota reversed the jury findings of 10% negligence to plaintiff, 50% to defendant, and 40% to a third party. Defendant, driving a five-ton truck in his own lane of traffic on the freeway, was suddenly confronted by plaintiff's oncoming vehicle crossing the median of the highway. The court found that, as a matter of law, defendant was not guilty of a greater degree of negligence than plaintiff in failing to avoid the accident. The court noted, "We cannot escape the conclusion that the jury was influenced by the severity of plaintiff's injuries."[4]

In *Seppi v. Betty*[5] the Idaho Supreme Court affirmed the lower court's granting of a new trial based upon the trial judge's decision that the jury was not justified in finding the plaintiff guilty of 50% negligence. The Court stressed that a trial court has broad discretion to order a new trial when it believes that the verdict is a product of either jury misunderstanding or failure to follow instructions properly.

---

[2]Turk v. H. C. Prange Co., 18 Wis. 2d 547, 119 N.W.2d 365 (1963). Accord, Thoen v. Lanesboro School Dist., 296 Minn. 252, 209 N.W.2d 924 (1973) (instruction that plaintiff's failure to wear a hard hat while installing telephone line could be considered improper in apportioning negligence in an action that arose when plaintiff was struck by a school bus); see also Johnson v. Serra, 521 F.2d 1289 (8th Cir. Minn. 1975) (remittitur ordered; error to allow evidence of inflationary trends in distant future in determining damages); but see Hughes v. Keller, 302 Minn. 8, 224 N.W.2d 738 (1974) (verdict apportioning 65% of negligence to plaintiff upheld despite improper instruction on last clear chance and superseding cause).

[3]Robertson v. Johnson, 291 Minn. 154, 190 N.W.2d 486 (1971).

[4]Id., 291 Minn. at 158, 190 N.W.2d at 488. Of course, defendants are also subject to reversals on the evidence. See, e.g., Olson v. Hansen, 299 Minn. 39, 216 N.W.2d 124 (1974); Cuozzo v. Ronan & Kunzl, Inc., 453 So. 2d 902 (Fla. App. 1984); Trinity River Authority v. Williams, 659 S.W.2d 714 (Tex. App. 1983); Witt v. Martin, 672 P.2d 312 (Okla. App. 1983).

[5]Seppi v. Betty, 99 Idaho 186, 579 P.2d 683 (1978).

Railroad Cases

Similarly, in a wrongful death action[6] arising out of a collision of decedent's truck with defendant's train at a crossing, the evidence was deemed insufficient to support a finding that the causal negligence of the railroad in its failure to avoid the accident was greater than that of plaintiff's decedent.

Again, in *Atlantic Coast Line Railroad Company v. Street*[7] a Georgia appellate court reversed a verdict for plaintiff in a wrongful death action where decedent was struck by a train while attempting to rescue a dog. There was ample evidence that decedent knew the train was approaching but simply misjudged its distance and speed. The court was aided in its decision by the unique wording of the Georgia statute barring all recovery if the plaintiff "by ordinary care could have avoided the consequences to himself."[8] This clause was applied by the court in a sort of amalgamation of plaintiff's last clear chance and assumption of risk. However, the same result could probably have been reached in any of the 50% states by considering decedent's stepping in front of the train as a form of contributory negligence that was obviously greater than the railroad's negligence.

Reversal Under the New Hampshire Variant

The number of reversals of verdicts unreasonably favoring plaintiffs in a 50% system may be sharply reduced if the state adopts or converts to the New Hampshire approach permitting recovery by a plaintiff whose negligence exactly equals defendant's.[9] For example, in the Wisconsin case of *Rewolinski v. Harley-Davidson Motor Company*[10] the jury found plaintiff 30% and defendant 70% negligent. Because plaintiff had violated his employer's safety rules and unnecessarily exposed himself to the danger of the harm that befell him, the trial court was convinced that his negligence was at least "equal" to that of defendant. This determination was upheld on appeal.[11]

Today in Wisconsin the judge would have had to go further before holding for defendant against a verdict for plaintiff. He would have to decide that no reasonable juror could find other than that plaintiff was more negligent than defendant. This is a much more difficult determination to justify. It is easier to conclude, as a number of old Wisconsin decisions did,[12] that the parties must be deemed equally at fault.

---

[6]Gagnier v. Bendixen, 439 F.2d 57 (8th Cir. Minn. 1971). Accord, Tiedeman v. Chicago, M., S. P. & P. R. Co., 513 F.2d 1267 (8th Cir. Iowa 1975).

[7]Atlantic C. L. R. Co. v. Street, 116 Ga. App. 465, 157 S.E.2d 793 (1967).

[8]Ga. Code Ann., § 51-11-7.

[9]See note 94 above and subsection 3.5(B).

[10]Rewolinski v. Harley-Davidson Motor Co., 32 Wis. 2d 680, 146 N.W.2d 485 (1966).

[11]Id., 32 Wis. 2d at 684, 146 N.W.2d at 487.

[12]E.g., Rewolinski v. Harley-Davidson Motor Co., note 10 above; see Schwarz v. Winter, 272 Wis. 303, 75 N.W.2d 447 (1956); Crawley v. Hill, 253 Wis. 294, 34 N.W.2d 123 (1948); Gross v. Denow, 61 Wis. 2d 40, 212 N.W.2d 2 (1973) (case arose before adoption of New Hampshire variant).

CHAPTER 19

COUNTERCLAIMS

Section

19.1 The complication of setoff
19.2 Setoff in the 50% and slight-gross systems
19.3 Setoff under pure comparative negligence

19.1 The complication of setoff

Counterclaims—claims asserted by defendants against plaintiffs in the same action[1]—present fewer problems than do cross-claims, wherein defendants seek contribution from each other.[2] The only complication under comparative negligence is when a counterclaim results in a setoff of damages. That is the situation discussed in this chapter.

At one time, a counterclaim had to relate to the occurrence upon which plaintiff's action was based.[3] Today it may arise from a separate occurrence. Such counterclaims are rarely made, however, except perhaps in product liability cases where there may be a continuing commercial relationship of buyer and seller; in any event, no special problem is presented by comparative negligence when such a counterclaim is made.

19.2 Setoff in the 50% and slight-gross systems

It is rare that the assertion of a counterclaim will lead to a setoff in either a 50% comparative negligence system or a slight-gross system. Under the majority rule a party can recover only from another party whose negligence was greater than his own.[4] When reciprocal claims are asserted in the same action, the jury finding of negligence will usually support recovery by one of the claimants, but will bar recovery by the other.

There are two situations under 50% comparative negligence in which there might be setoff of a plaintiff's award and an award to a counterclaiming defendant:

1. In a state following the New Hampshire variant of the 50% sys-

---

[1]F. James & G. Hazard, *Civil Procedure* § 10.16 (1977).

[2]See section 16.7.

[3]F. James & G. Hazard, note 1 above, § 10.15.

[4]Kirchen v. Tisler, 255 Wis. 208, 38 N.W.2d 514 (1949); Hahn v. Smith, 215 Wis. 277, 254 N.W. 750 (1934).

tem,[5] when plaintiff and counterclaiming defendant are found equally negligent.

2. In a state following the Arkansas rule as to comparison between plaintiff and the combined negligence of multiple defendants,[6] when there are multiple parties and the jury finds that the negligence of neither claimant is as much as 50% of the total.

In *Amoco Pipeline Company v. Montgomery*[7] an Oklahoma district court ruled that the defendant counterclaimants were entitled to an award of punitive damages without any setoff, notwithstanding that state's comparative negligence statute.

Equally Negligent Parties

In New Hampshire and seventeen other states[8] and the Virgin Islands, a plaintiff may recover half his damages in a two-party action if his negligence exactly equals defendant's. If the defendant has counterclaimed, obviously he will, on a verdict apportioning negligence equally, recover half of his damages, to be set off against plaintiff's award. Suppose, for example, plaintiff has $10,000 in damages, counterclaiming defendant has $5000 in damages, and the jury finds the parties equally at fault. Under these circumstances,

1. Plaintiff's award is $5000.

2. Defendant's award is $2500.

3. Net recovery for plaintiff is $2500 after setting off defendant's award.

Setoff in Multiparty Actions

In some 50% states, a plaintiff is barred from recovery from a defendant whose negligence is less than his own, even if the combined negligence of all the defendants exceeds plaintiff's negligence.[9] However, in most of the 50% states, a negligent plaintiff may recover from a defendant who is less negligent than he, provided his own negligence is less than that of all the defendants combined.[10]

Suppose that after a three-vehicle collision, driver A brings action against B and C for his damages. C counterclaims against A and cross-claims against B for his damages. The jury apportions fault 10% to A,

---

[5]Conn. Gen. Stat. Ann., § 52-572h; Del. Code Ann., tit. 10, § 8132; Hawaii Rev. Stat., § 663.31; Ind. Code, § 34-4-33-4; Iowa Code Ann., § 668.3; Mass. Gen. Laws Ann., ch. 231, § 85; Minn. Stat. Ann., § 604.01; Mont. Code Ann., § 27-1-702; Nev. Rev. Stat., § 41.141 (1); N.H. Rev. Stat. Ann., § 507:7a; N.J. Stat. Ann., § 2A:15-5.1; Ohio Rev. Code Ann., § 2315.19(A)(1); Okla. Stat. Ann., tit. 23, § 13; Ore. Rev. Stat., § 18.470; Pa. Stat. Ann., tit. 42, § 7102; Tex. Rev. Civ. Stat. Ann. (Vernon), art. 2212a; Vt. Stat. Ann., tit. 12, § 1036; Wis. Stat. Ann., § 895.045.

[6]See text accompanying notes 58 to 80, section 16.6.

[7]Amoco Pipeline Co. v. Montgomery, 487 F. Supp. 1268 (W.D. Okla. 1980).

[8]Connecticut, Delaware, Indiana, Iowa, Massachusetts, Minnesota, Montana, Nevada, New Hampshire, New Jersey, Ohio, Oklahoma, Oregon, Pennsylvania, Texas, Vermont and Wisconsin. See note 5 above.

[9]See notes 39 to 54 and accompanying text, section 16.6

[10]See notes 58 to 80 and accompanying text, section 16.6.

60% to B and 30% to C. It assesses A's damages at $10,000 and C's at $5000. B is uninsured and judgment-proof.

Under the above set of facts, in states that compare plaintiff's fault with that of each defendant, if there is joint and several liability, A can recover 90% of his damages, or $9000, from C. C is barred by his own negligence from recovery from A, so there is no setoff.

In states where each plaintiff's claim is compared with the combined negligence of the defendants,[11] and where there is joint and several liability, A could recover 90% of his damages, or $9000, from C. C, in turn, could recover 70% of his damages, or $3500, from A. C's award would be set off, leaving A a net recovery of $5500.

Texas and several other states apply the same basic rule for comparing fault,[12] but limit joint liability to those who were at least as much at fault as the claimant.[13] Under that statute, A could recover 90% of his damages, or $9000, from C. On the other hand, C could recover no more than 10% of his damages, or $500, from A. After applying setoff, A's net recovery from C would be $8500. Texas expressly grants setoff to the claimant liable for the higher amount.[14]

19.3 Setoff under pure comparative negligence

Under pure comparative negligence, there is a broad potential for uses of claims and counterclaims with setoffs in cases where both parties were at fault and both suffered damages. The courts have recognized this in affirming verdicts.

In a 1959 Mississippi case[15] the evidence was sharply conflicting as to negligence of the parties and might have supported almost any finding from entire fault in the plaintiff to entire fault in the defendant. There were no special verdicts or special interrogatories—only a general verdict of $20,000 for defendant-counterclaimant. The Supreme Court of Mississippi affirmed without really knowing whether the jury had found any negligence at all on defendant's part, saying it was "inescapable that the amount of the verdict constituted the excess of [the defendant's] claim over [the plaintiff's], if he had any, as measured by the jury."[16]

The Mississippi case demonstrates the ease of affirmance of verdicts under pure comparative negligence, especially when no use is made of jury-control devices such as special verdicts or special interrogatories. When the evidence is conflicting, there may be almost no way that an appellate court can effectively review a verdict for consistency with the weight of the evidence, unless the verdict is excessive in amount.

---

[11]See text above at note 10.

[12]Tex. Rev. Civ. Stat. Ann. (Vernon), art. 2212a(1).

[13]Id., art. 2212a(2)(c). See section 16.4, note 61, section 16.6, notes 55 and 56, and section 16.7, note 25.

[14]Tex. Rev. Civ. Stat. Ann. (Vernon), art. 2212a(2)(f).

[15]Johnson v. Richardson, 234 Miss. 849, 108 So. 2d 194 (1959).

[16]Id., 234 Miss. at 861, 108 So. 2d at 199.

Setoff Barred to Insurers

One commentator has suggested that comparative negligence statutes should prohibit casualty insurance companies from applying judgments for their insured as setoffs against judgments against their insured.[17] That author believes that the use of setoffs which mutually cancel damages awarded to seriously injured parties impairs the general goal of fairness that is hoped for under a comparative negligence system.

Similarly, the Uniform Comparative Fault Act provides that if an insurance carrier's liability is reduced by reason of a setoff, the insured is entitled to recover from the carrier the amount of the reduction.[18] The authors of the Act believe that this system produces fairer results when one party is insolvent.[19]

Neither proposal has had general approval in comparative negligence jurisdictions. The Rhode Island statute does contain a provision that "There shall be no set-off of damages between the respective parties."[20] Apparently, however, the Rhode Island statute is not limited to insurance company cases; it appears to prevent even an individual party from applying for a setoff. While as a practical matter the statute may be involved only when liability insurance companies are paying the verdict, its phraseology is overly broad. It could unfairly deprive an uninsured private party of the benefits of his successful counterclaim.[21]

In *Bournazian v. Stuyvesant Insurance Company*[22] plaintiff and his wife brought an action for personal injury against the owner and operator of the other vehicle and their insurer. The defendants filed a counterclaim against plaintiff-husband and his insurer. Both parties were found liable and damages were apportioned. The trial court set off the total of personal injury verdicts for one side against total personal injury verdicts for the other side. The Appellate Court reversed on the ground that the plaintiff's wife's verdict was wiped out even though she was not a party to the counterclaim. The only parties to benefit from the setoff would be the insurance companies, and this would not comport with the policy of encouraging compensation for accident victims who can prove fault.[23] The court, however, indicated that setoffs would be allowed when there was an identity of parties in the claim and the counterclaim.

---

[17]Flynn, *Comparative Negligence: The Debate*, 8 Trial 49, 52 (May/June 1972).

[18]Unif. Comp. Fault Act, § 3, 12 U.L.A. 45 (Supp. 1985). See section 21.4.

[19]Id., Comment to § 3.

[20]R.I. Gen. Laws, § 9-20-4.1. This could mean simply that defendant must bring a separate action for his damages.

[21]The statute does not specify what procedure is followed if both plaintiff and defendant are awarded damages.

[22]Bournazian v. Stuyvesant Ins. Co., 303 So. 2d 71 (Fla. App. 1974), affd. 342 So. 2d 471 (Fla. 1976).

[23]Id., 303 So. 2d at 73.

The California Supreme Court in *Jess v. Herrmann*[24] similarly reasoned that insurance companies would unreasonably benefit from a setoff. This court held, therefore, that the setoff statute would not be applied in those comparative negligence cases where both parties were insured.

The Arizona legislature, adopting a comprehensive comparative negligence statute, included a provision that setoff is to be allowed only by agreement of both parties.[25]

It is highly unlikely that a court would, on its own, bar setoffs when the state's comparative negligence system mathematically permits them. The proposal of disallowing setoffs when casualty insurance companies are parties is thoughtful, but has obvious earmarks of invidious discrimination. Nevertheless, its potential benefit suggests that the proposal be given careful consideration by legislatures.

---

[24]Jess v. Herrmann, 26 Cal. 3d 131, 161 Cal. Rptr. 87, 604 P.2d 208 (1979) (citing this treatise).

[25]Ariz. Rev. Stat. Ann., § 12-2507.

CHAPTER 20

STRATEGIC CONSIDERATIONS FOR THE ADVOCATE

Section

20.1 Introduction

An attorney who manages and litigates tort cases in a comparative negligence system will eventually have to delve into all of the areas of the law covered by the various chapters in this text. Indeed, to be best prepared for such cases the lawyer must become familiar with the basic arguments on both sides of all of the issues discussed herein.

Nevertheless, it seems appropriate here to segregate some of the more important issues and to synthesize them in the framework of practical advocacy. What are some of the basic legal arguments that a plaintiff (or a defendant) can make to a court to secure favorable rulings on motions, favorable instructions to the jury, favorably framed special interrogatories, or advantageous treatment of jury findings? How can the facts be presented and argued before the jury to produce the most favorable jury findings? What are the special considerations under pure comparative negligence? Under modified comparative negligence?

These matters are considered in this chapter, first from the plaintiff's point of view, and then from that of the defendant.

20.2 General considerations for the plaintiff

The advent of comparative negligence is generally considered a boon for the injured plaintiff. No longer is he completely barred from recovery by the fact that his own negligence may have been one of the causes of his injury. Rather, he has a good chance of recovering a substantial portion, though not all, of his damages.

Plaintiff's attorneys, however, should not overlook the possibility that, in a particular case, there may be legal precedents in the jurisdiction that will cause a court to ignore plaintiff's negligence and to permit him recovery of his full damages. For example, if defendant acted with reckless disregard for plaintiff's safety, plaintiff's contributory

345

negligence might be considered immaterial.[1] The same result might be reached if defendant had the last clear chance to avoid the accident.[2]

Reckless Disregard—Last Clear Chance

This author believes, and a number of states have ruled, that contributory negligence, under the comparative negligence statutes, should reduce plaintiff's recovery, even when defendant acted in "reckless disregard" or had the last clear chance. Nevertheless, proper representation of a plaintiff in a jurisdiction where either of these questions is still open demands that the argument for ignoring contributory negligence be asserted. Basically the argument is as follows:

1. That the comparative negligence statute is intended to apply only to situations where under the common law plaintiff's recovery would have been barred by contributory negligence;

2. That under the common law (citing precedents in the jurisdiction), contributory negligence would have been immaterial where defendant acted in "reckless disregard" (or had the last clear chance) and plaintiff could have recovered his full damages;

3. That, therefore, the statute does not apply where defendant acted in "reckless disregard" (or had the last clear chance) and the common-law rule allowing full recovery still applies.

Strict Liability in Product Cases

It has been noted previously[3] that in jurisdictions where comparative negligence has not yet been adopted, certain types of contributory negligence may not constitute a defense in product liability cases based on strict liability in tort. When similar facts are presented under a comparative negligence statute, the plaintiff's attorney should try to have the precedents which were established under the common law carried over under the comparative negligence system; that is, the argument should be that contributory negligence is ignored in strict liability cases. The argument is analogous to that detailed above with respect to "reckless disregard" and "last clear chance" cases. One can also add the argument that fault-based defenses should not be utilized when the basis of liability is not fault. This is the so-called "you should not mix the apples of fault with the oranges of non-fault" argument.

Again, this author believes that it is much sounder policy to compare contributory negligence in product liability cases based on strict liability.[4] But there is precedent the other way and counsel for plaintiff should make the argument if the question is still open in his jurisdiction.

---

[1]See section 5.1 at notes 2 to 5, and section 5.3 at notes 40 and 41.
[2]See section 7.2 especially at notes 30 to 33, 62 to 64 and 77 to 79.
[3]See sections 12.5 and 12.7.
[4]See final two paragraphs, section 12.5 and text beginning at note 4, section 12.7.

Joinder of Defendants

Plaintiff's attorney generally should join as defendants all persons who may have had a part in the accident. In most situations, as a practical matter, the more culpable parties there are before the jury, the better chance there will be to spread the apportionment of fault around and thus to reduce the percentage attributed to plaintiff. If there is joint and several liability, as there is in most states,[5] the primary defendant's potential liability will not be reduced by the fact that some portion of the fault may be attributed to a codefendant rather than to him. The courts have suggested that a trial court ruling preventing plaintiff from joining all participants in the accident would be error.[6]

The one situation where caution should be exercised on joinder occurs where a state does not have joint and several liability, operates under a 50% system, and compares the plaintiff's fault with each individual defendant instead of with defendants as a group.[7] In such a situation plaintiff's fault may be found to be less than a single in-court defendant, but may be found to be greater than each of a number of in-court defendants.

Argument to Jury

Plaintiff's attorney will want to wrap his final argument to the jury around the court's instruction on comparative negligence. The nature of this instruction will vary between pure and modified comparative negligence jurisdictions as is shown in sections 20.3 and 20.4.

20.3 Representing the plaintiff under pure comparative negligence

Under pure comparative negligence, the court will usually instruct the jury in statutory language that contributory negligence shall not bar a recovery.[8] An attorney representing a plaintiff who has clearly been negligent is remiss in his duty if he does not stress these statutory words in his closing argument.

Once the jurors clearly understand that they are not to bar plaintiff's claim, the attorney can then go to work on the facts and show that plaintiff's negligence was minor in comparison to that of defendant. If the defendant has shown plaintiff's lack of care only with respect to his own safety, the jury may well find that a defendant's disregard for the safety of others is considerably worse and more culpable. Finally, if plaintiff has done his job in conveying to the jury the extent and nature of his injury, the jury may be reluctant to make more than a slight reduction in the final verdict.

---

[5] See section 16.4.

[6] See text at note 18, section 16.5.

[7] See section 16.6.

[8] See section 3.2.

20.4 Representing the plaintiff under modified comparative negligence

Under modified comparative negligence, the plaintiff's attorney faces the danger that his client will, because of his own negligence, leave the courtroom with no damages at all.[9] If the plaintiff was negligent, therefore, his attorney must plan his strategy with utmost care to show that the defendant was considerably more culpable in regard to the accident than was the plaintiff.

In some states a plaintiff who is equally at fault with defendant is allowed to recover half his damages.[10] But even in those states, the jury finding of equal culpability should be considered an alternative that is barely acceptable to plaintiff. The attorney should carefully assemble the evidence to support the argument that "The facts make it clear that my client *was less* at fault than defendant with respect to this accident."

Weighing Fault

Plaintiff's attorney may be helped by language in Wisconsin opinions suggesting that plaintiff need not be found equally at fault with defendant merely because he committed a greater number of negligent acts.[11] Further, assistance may be found in opinions saying that plaintiff need not be found equally at fault with defendant simply because he was guilty of the same kind of negligence.[12] It is suggested that language from these cases be abstracted and offered as instructions to the jury in order that plaintiff may make the utmost use of them in appropriate situations.

Joinder of Defendants

Apart from the exceptional situation noted in section 20.2 above, plaintiff should be particularly diligent in 50% system states to join as defendants all who may have contributed to the accident. As a practical matter, from the juror's perspective, this may reduce plaintiff's role of culpability in the total accident.

If the issue is unsettled in the jurisdiction, plaintiff should cite and rely on the Arkansas cases which compare plaintiff's negligence with that of multiple defendants in the aggregate.[13] Thus, if plaintiff is 40% at fault, defendant A 30%, defendant B 20% and defendant C 10%, plaintiff would be entitled to a recovery under the Arkansas rule. As section 16.6 makes clear, however, a few states would not permit plaintiff this advantage.

---

[9]See text at notes 2 to 4, section 3.1.

[10]See text at notes 69 to 75, section 3.5.

[11]See Taylor v. Western Casualty & Surety Co., 270 Wis. 408, 71 N.W.2d 363 (1955); Lovesee v. Allied Development Corp., 45 Wis. 2d 340, 345, 173 N.W.2d 196, 199 (1970).

[12]See Hansberry v. Dunn, 230 Wis. 626, 284 N.W. 556 (1939).

[13]See Riddell v. Little, 253 Ark. 686, 488 S.W.2d 34 (1972), discussed in section 16.6.

20.5 General considerations for the defendant

Assuming that defendant has negligently caused injury to a plaintiff, defendant's main goal under comparative negligence is to establish plaintiff's culpability and to use that culpability as a basis for reducing the amount of plaintiff's award. He should argue that reduction should always occur when plaintiff was at fault.

Defendant may encounter cases decided in the jurisdiction before comparative negligence was adopted to the effect that plaintiff's negligence is ignored when defendant was reckless[14] or had the last clear chance to prevent the harm.[15] When faced with such precedents, defendant should argue that these decisions were intended to provide an escape from the harsh common-law rule completely barring recovery when there is contributory negligence. Now that comparative negligence has replaced the harsh rule of the common law, the argument runs, the reason for escape no longer exists and plaintiff's negligence should be considered and compared.[16] If there are precedents eliminating contributory negligence under strict products liability, these too should be treated as no longer applicable once comparative negligence or comparative fault is the law. The arguments for this position are more fully developed in Chapter 12 and are supported by the Model Uniform Product Liability Act.[17]

Argument to Jury

In arguing to the jury, defense counsel should stress the statutory language providing for reduction of the award when plaintiff was negligent. The jury should be impressed by the fairness of the comparative negligence principle. "Why should defendant bear the entire cost of this accident when it was not all his fault?" The fairness of comparative negligence may cause a jury to apply it more strictly against a plaintiff than it would have applied the common-law contributory negligence rule. The defense must stress the practical, commonsense fairness of the system.

Assumption of Risk

Defendant may be able to escape all liability in some cases when plaintiff has assumed the risk. In all states, express assumption of risk remains a complete defense, even under comparative negligence, unless barred by public policy in certain special instances.[18]

As indicated in section 9.5[19] this author believes that implied assumption of risk should be merged into contributory negligence and

---

[14]See text at notes 2 to 5, section 5.1 and notes 40 and 41, section 5.3.

[15]See section 7.1.

[16]See text at notes 47 to 58, section 5.3 and notes 65 to 76, section 7.2.

[17]Model Unif. Product Liability Act, reprinted in 44 Fed. Reg. 62,714 (Interagency Task Force on Product Liability, U.S. Dept. of Commerce, 1979).

[18]See section 9.2.

[19]See text beginning at note 76, section 9.5.

should, under comparative negligence, no longer constitute a complete defense; the conduct should be compared with defendant's negligence. However, not all states follow this approach.[20] Defense counsel should explore whether in his state, it may still be possible to assert implied assumption of risk as a complete defense.

The effect of implied assumption of risk is not entirely a legal question. Even if the law of the state prevents assertion of assumption of risk as a complete defense, it still may be the basis of a most effective argument to the jury. Common sense dictates and a jury may be convinced that a plaintiff who has *voluntarily* and *knowingly* assumed a *known* risk should have his award substantially reduced. This should be stressed in final argument. In a 50% state, the result may even be an apportionment of fault that will push the plaintiff past the "vital point," barring his recovery.

Joinder of Additional Defendants

In most situations, the joinder of additional defendants will tend to reduce the percentage of fault attributed to plaintiff. This in turn would tend to increase the amount for which defendant is potentially liable under joint and several liability. In some factual contexts, the addition of new defendants might even cast a different light on the evidence, so that plaintiff is found less culpable than any of the defendants though he might not have been so found had his fault been compared against that of only one defendant.

For these reasons, defendant must be circumspect about bringing in new defendants. Though the addition of defendants might reduce the percentage of fault attributed by the jury to the first defendant, this will not help *unless there is a right of contribution among tortfeasors* and the added defendants are either solvent or adequately insured. Or it could be of help in 50% states that do not have joint and several liability if the court compares plaintiff's fault with that of each individual defendant. The net result of adding defendants may be to minimize the result against your client so that plaintiff's fault will be greater than your client's fault.[21] Of course, this may not be necessary if the jurisdiction permits the "empty chair" argument and lets you introduce evidence of the fault of a party who is not in court.[22] There are no arithmetic formulas; judgment must be exercised.

Comparing Combined Negligence of Defendants

In 50% states that follow the Arkansas rule on comparing plaintiff's negligence against the combined negligence of all the defendants,[23] bringing in additional defendants could have adverse consequences for the first defendant, especially if plaintiff's negligence was substantial.

---

[20]See section 9.3.

[21]See section 16.6.

[22]See section 16.5.

[23]See text at notes 58 to 80, section 16.6.

Under the Arkansas rule, the addition of defendants could convert the case from one in which plaintiff is barred because his negligence is greater than that of a single defendant to one in which plaintiff could recover because his negligence is less than the combined negligence of all the defendants. In a context of joint and several liability, this could be disastrous.

20.6 Representing the defendant under pure comparative negligence

Pure comparative negligence can be frightening to a defense attorney. A negligent plaintiff may recover as long as he was not totally at fault with regard to the accident. Nevertheless, careful advocacy can reduce the impact of pure comparative negligence.

Assumption of Risk

First, as indicated above in section 20.5, the assumption of risk defense should not be forgotten.

Proximate Cause

Second, perhaps more importantly, defense attorneys should remember their old friend from law school, "proximate cause." As indicated in section 4.4,[24] defendant has prevailed in a number of cases under pure comparative negligence by successfully arguing to either a court or a jury that plaintiff's conduct was the sole proximate cause of the harm that befell him.

Sometimes these arguments are really based on cause in fact; even if defendant had done everything he should, plaintiff still would have suffered the same injury. But other cases are more to the point that defendant's negligence is so remote or minute, in relation to that of plaintiff, that it was not a proximate cause of the accident. This author disagrees with some of those cases when they subvert the basic axiom of pure comparative negligence. However, they are there for the defendant's advocate to use.

Defendant's attorney should put across to the jury that pure comparative negligence is *not supposed to be a total giveaway*. The jury must diminish plaintiff's award by the amount he is at fault. In final argument, defendant's attorney should stress the common sense and fairness of this approach and wrap himself in the words of the statute calling for reduction of the award.

If the jury fails to take legal prescription into account, there is precedent for a limited reversal on the ground that the jury ignored the court's instruction.[25]

---

[24]See especially the text at notes 39 to 47, section 4.4.

[25]See text at notes 76 to 79, section 18.5.

20.7 Representing the defendant under modified comparative negligence

Modified comparative negligence gives the defense attorney a sledge hammer. He may be able to convince the jury that plaintiff's negligence has reached the point totally barring his recovery. As a practical matter, the defense is aided if the state follows the Wisconsin rule that the jury is not to be informed that plaintiff will be barred if he is found more at fault than (or equally at fault with) defendant.[26] The jury will more readily reach a 50-50 apportionment in such a situation.

Equal Apportionment

In a great many cases under modified comparative negligence, the best defense strategy is to strive for a 50-50 apportionment of fault. In complex accident cases, equal apportionment is often a very comfortable position for the trier of fact. One might argue along these lines:

It is clear under the facts that two people failed to act as reasonable persons. Who is to say that plaintiff was more at fault than defendant, or that defendant was more at fault than plaintiff? With due respect to my opponent in this case, it might take a power greater than any of us to make such a judgment. Unless we try to make judgments that are beyond human capability, we should find that these persons are both at fault and equally so.

In several states, of course, a 50-50 apportionment of fault would permit plaintiff to recover half his damages. Nevertheless, assuming that defendant was clearly negligent,[27] that is not so bad—especially if defendant is counterclaiming for his own damages!

---

[26]See text at notes 76 and 77, section 17.5.
[27]See text at notes 69 to 77, section 3.5.

CHAPTER 21

THE BEST MEANS OF DEALING WITH PLAINTIFF'S NEGLIGENCE

Section

21.1 The arguments for contributory negligence as a bar

Those who have argued to retain the contributory negligence defense,[1] an ever-shrinking group,[2] have relied on five basic arguments to support their position.

Difficulty in Measuring Fault

First, it is asserted that comparative negligence is theoretically unsound because fault cannot be measured on a scientific basis.[3] As indicated in section 17.1, this argument has some logic behind it. Nevertheless, in states that have adopted comparative negligence, juries have been able to make a rough apportionment of fault. While such verdicts are not at all scientific, they come closer to the realities in negligence cases than does the all-or-nothing approach of the contributory negligence rule. Those who favor comparative negligence therefore are correct in observing that although their system is not scientifically accu-

---

[1]See, e.g., Benson, *Comparative Negligence—Boon or Bane*, 23 Ins. Couns. J. 204 (1956); Gilmore, *Comparative Negligence from a Viewpoint of Casualty Insurance*, 10 Ark. L. Rev. 82 (1955); Harkavy, *Comparative Negligence: The Reflections of a Skeptic*, 43 A.B.A. J. 1115 (1957); Lipscomb, *Comparative Negligence*, 1951 Ins. L.J. 667; Powell, *Contributory Negligence: A Necessary Check on the American Jury*, 43 A.B.A. J. 1005 (1957); Varnum, *Comparative Negligence in Automobile Cases*, 24 Ins. Couns. J. 60 (1957).

[2]See text at notes 10 to 12, section1.1.

[3]See, e.g., American Motorcycle Assn. v. Superior Court of Los Angeles County, 20 Cal. 3d 578, 146 Cal. Rptr. 182, 206-207, 578 P.2d 899 (1978) (Clark, J., dissenting).

rate in the individual case, it comes closer to justice than does contributory negligence.[4]

Contributory Negligence as Deterrent

Second, those who oppose comparative negligence contend that contributory negligence has a helpful deterrent effect, in that it prevents people from being careless of their own safety. There is no empirical evidence to support this conclusion. It is doubtful whether most laymen even know of the contributory negligence defense. Even if some do, all systems of comparative negligence reduce plaintiff's award when his fault has contributed to the happening of an accident. Therefore, deterrent impact is not completely abolished.

Finally, as Dean Prosser has reminded the critics of comparative negligence, tort law also seeks to deter wrongful conduct by defendants.[5] If people are aware of the rule, the contributory negligence defense works contrary to the goal of reasonable care for the safety of others.

Judicial Administration of Comparative Negligence

Third, those in favor of the contributory negligence defense contend that comparative negligence will be difficult for the courts to administer. The critics speculate that the complexity of third-party claims renders comparative negligence systems very vulnerable.

Here there is empirical evidence and it tends to abate such concerns. Mississippi has functioned well with comparative negligence for over seventy years,[6] and Wisconsin has weathered any untoward complications for more than fifty years.[7] No state that has adopted comparative negligence has abandoned it and retreated to the contributory negligence rule.[8] Further, courts in all states have been able to apply comparative negligence under the Federal Employers' Liability Act.[9]

It is true that third-party cases may present difficult problems of

---

[4]See, e.g., C. Gregory, *Legislative Loss Distribution in Negligence Actions—A Study in Administrative Aspects of Comparative Negligence and Contribution in Tort Litigation* 173-176 (1936); Maloney, *From Contributory to Comparative Negligence: A Needed Law Reform*, 11 U. Fla. L. Rev. 135 (1958); Pound, *Comparative Negligence*, 13 N.A.C.C.A. L.J. 195 (1954); Philbrick, *Loss Apportionment in Negligence Cases*, 99 U. Pa. L. Rev. 572, 766 (1951); Prosser, *Comparative Negligence*, 51 Mich. L. Rev. 465 (1953).

[5]Prosser, note 4 above, at 468.

[6]See 1910 Miss. Laws, ch. 135, now Miss. Code Ann., § 11-7-15.

[7]The Wisconsin general comparative negligence statute, Wis. Stat. Ann., § 895.045, was enacted in 1931. See Whelan, *Comparative Negligence*, 1938 Wis. L. Rev. 289.

[8]Arkansas modifed the kind of comparative negligence system that it first adopted. See Rosenberg, *Comparative Negligence in Arkansas: A "Before and After" Survey*, 13 Ark. L. Rev. 89 (1959). Several other states have switched from a "49%" to a "50%" modified system. See section 3.5. After the Iowa Supreme Court adopted pure comparative negligence, the Iowa legislature enacted a comprehensive modified comparative negligence statute. Goetzman v. Wichern, 327 N.W.2d 742 (Iowa 1982); Iowa Code Ann., ch. 668.

[9]See annotations to 45 U.S.C.A § 53.

damage apportionment.[10] But, as Dean Prosser has indicated, these cases are few in number.[11] As pointed out in Chapter 16, such cases can be rationally resolved.

Encouraging Settlement

Critics also contend that comparative negligence creates administrative problems in that it discourages settlement and the courts will have an even greater flood of litigation than they do with contributory negligence. This contention is refuted by a careful study, conducted by the Columbia University Project for Effective Justice in cooperation with the Arkansas Bar Association, of the experience in Arkansas before and after the state adopted comparative negligence. Settlements occurred with the same degree of frequency under comparative as under the contributory negligence rule.[12] In general, the study concluded that the administrative factor should neither persuade nor dissuade a state from changing from contributory to comparative negligence.[13]

Effect on Insurance Rates

Fourth, the critics of comparative negligence contend that it will be too costly because it will push insurance rates to extraordinary heights. The North Carolina study discussed in section 2.4 and the Arkansas study mentioned above,[14] as well as a most painstaking survey conducted by Professor Cornelius Peck of the University of Washington School of Law,[15] refute this supposition. The effect of comparative negligence on insurance rates has been minimal. This is because insurance adjusters,[16] juries,[17] and sometimes even courts[18] actually practice comparative negligence in contributory negligence states.

It should be recalled that comparative negligence is not purely a plaintiff's doctrine. The doctrine of last clear chance and other limitations to the contributory negligence defense may make a defendant pay

---

[10]C. Gregory, note 4 above, at 181-186; Gowan, *Admiralty—Texas Wrongful Death and Survival Statutes—Unseaworthiness and Comparative Negligence*, 16 Sw. L.J. 675 (1962); Sirkin, *Torts—Contribution Determined by Percentage of Causal Negligence; Gross Negligence No Longer Bars Contribution*, 14 Syracuse L. Rev. 140 (1962).

[11]Prosser, note 4 above, at 507.

[12]Rosenberg, note 8 above.

[13]Id.

[14]See text at note 12 above. See also *Panel on Comparative Negligence and Liability Insurance*, 11 Ark. L. Rev. 71 (1956-57).

[15]Peck, *Comparative Negligence and Automobile Liability Insurance*, 58 Mich. L. Rev. 689, 726-728 (1960). See also Todd, *The Prospect for Automobile Insurance Rate Changes under Comparative Negligence*, 36 Tex. B.J. 1153 (1973).

[16]Peck, note 15 above, at 726-728.

[17]See Alibrandi v. Helmsley, 63 Misc. 2d 997, 314 N.Y.S.2d 95 (1970); Anderson v. Muniz, 21 Ariz. App. 25, 515 P.2d 52 (1973); Washington Metropolitan Area Transit Authority v. Jones, 443 A.2d 45, 53 (D.C. App. 1982) (Ferren, J., concurring).

[18]See Layton v. Rocha, 90 Ariz. 369, 368 P.2d 444 (1962); Karcesky v. Laria, 382 Pa. 227, 234, 114 A.2d 150 (1955).

more under contributory negligence than he would under a comparative negligence system in which these limitations are not applied.[19]

Jury-Fashioned Comparative Negligence

Finally, defenders of contributory negligence argue that since juries do apply comparative negligence sub silentio, no change is needed.[20] The answer to this contention is twofold. First, at times the juries do not apply comparative negligence, or they are denied the opportunity to apply it by courts which take the contributory negligence defense seriously. More importantly, in a democratic society, ostensible law should reflect what is actually being done. This is especially desirable in negligence cases, which are among the most frequent points of contact for the ordinary person with the judicial system. The law as contained in instructions by the court should be the law applied in fact.

Constitutionality of Comparative Negligence

Critics of comparative negligence have not gone so far as to argue that it is unconstitutional.[21] It would be useless for them to do so since judicial authority has upheld the constitutionality of across-the-board comparative negligence laws in both state[22] and federal courts.[23]

It should be noted, however, that in at least two states, a comparative negligence law that applied only to a limited class of defendants has been held an unconstitutional denial of equal protection of the law.[24] The rationale is that it is unfair to subject any particular class of defendants to comparative negligence when there is no proof that they engage in negligent conduct more frequently than any other group.[25]

---

[19]See, e.g., Cushman v. Perkins, 245 A.2d 846 (Me. 1968) (rejecting application of last clear chance).

[20]Powell, *Contributory Negligence: A Necessary Check on the American Jury*, 43 A.B.A. J. 1005 (1957).

[21]See materials cited in note 1 above.

[22]Natchez & S. R. Co. v. Crawford, 99 Miss. 697, 55 So. 596 (1911).

[23]In re Second Employers' Liability Cases, 223 U.S. 1, 56 L. Ed. 327, 32 S. Ct. 169, 38 L.R.A. (N.S.) 44 (1912).

[24]Georgia, S. & F. R. Co. v. Seven-Up Bottling Co., 175 So. 2d 39 (Fla. 1965), noted in 18 U. Fla. L. Rev. 166 (1965). The immediate effect of the decision has since been effectively nullified by Florida's judicial adoption of comparative negligence for all negligence actions. Hoffman v. Jones, 280 So. 2d 431 (Fla. 1973). See also Marley v. Kirby, 271 S.C. 122, 245 S.E.2d 604 (1978), invalidating a statute applying only to motor vehicle accidents.

[25]The Florida statute protected "any person" who endured physical injuries negligently caused by a railroad. In the case, the injustice stood out in sharp relief as comparative negligence would have allowed partial recovery against the railroad while contributory negligence completely barred the railroad's counterclaim against plaintiff, the corporate owner of a truck. It is probable that comparative negligence statutes that protect only employees of railroads or common carriers will continue to be upheld as reasonable because such employees are subject to a higher degree of danger as a class than are other persons. See St. Louis, I. M. & S. R. Co. v. Ingram, 118 Ark. 377, 176 S.W. 692 (1915); Loftin v. Crowley's, Inc., 150 Fla. 836, 8 So. 2d 909, 142 A.L.R. 626 (1942), cert. den. 317 U.S. 661, 87 L. Ed. 531, 63 S. Ct. 60 (1942); Indianapolis Traction & Terminal Co. v. Kinney, 171 Ind. 612, 85 N.E. 954, 23 L.R.A. (N.S.) 711 (1908); Kiley v. Chicago, M. & S. P. R. Co., 138 Wis. 215, 120 N.W. 756 (1909).

21.2 The arguments for comparative negligence

The most significant arguments raised in favor of comparative negligence are based on the rationale that as a system of distributing the costs of accidents, it is superior to that which has evolved under the contributory negligence defense.[26] Modern defendants do not need to be protected from the harms they negligently cause as did the infant industries of the early nineteenth century days of *Butterfield v. Forrester*. Today in light of the fact that most enterprises are insured against liability, the need to protect enterprise does not justify putting the entire cost of the accident on the contributorily negligent plaintiff.

Better Distribution of Risk

Comparative negligence achieves better risk distribution without abandoning the fault system. To some extent, plaintiff must still pay for the fact that he was careless. In reality, comparative negligence allows for a full implementation of the fault principle. It may even help a defendant in cases in which, under exceptions to the contributory negligence defense, loss was shifted entirely back to him.[27]

Flexibility of Comparative Negligence

Second, comparative negligence provides needed flexibility in the law of negligence. The absolute nature of the contributory negligence defense has pushed courts into arbitrary resolutions when they have been faced with problems such as how to give fair treatment to a plaintiff who negligently fails to wear a seat belt[28] or carelessly uses a defective product.[29] Comparative negligence provides a mechanism for dividing loss in these difficult situations.

Salvaging the Fault System

Finally, comparative negligence at least gives the fault system a chance to work.[30] The contributory negligence rule has given adherents of no-fault compensation systems a strong argument that the fault system does not work at present. Adherents of no-fault systems have charged that some injured parties recover nothing, in part because of antiquated common-law doctrines.[31] While Professors Keeton and

---

[26]See C. Gregory, *Legislative Loss Distribution In Negligence Actions—A Study in Administrative Aspects of Comparative Negligence and Contribution in Tort Legislation* 173-179 (1936); Note, 43 Notre Dame Law. 442 (1968).

[27]See note 19, section 21.1, and accompanying text.

[28]See Miller v. Haynes, 454 S.W.2d 293, 299 (Mo. App. 1970) (without comparative negligence, no seat belt defense); Annot., "Automobile occupant's failure to use seat belt as contributory negligence," 92 A.L.R.3d 1025 (1974).

[29]See Epstein, *Products Liability: Defenses Based on Plaintiff's Conduct*, 1968 Utah L. Rev. 267, 268.

[30]See Turk, *Comparative Negligence on the March, Part II*, 28 Chi.-Kent L. Rev. 304, 343-344 (1950).

[31]R. Keeton & J. O'Connell, *Basic Protection for the Traffic Victim; A Blueprint for Reforming Automobile Insurance* 1 (1965).

O'Connell in their book[32] chose "to omit [comparative negligence] from the scope of [their] study," [33] they agreed that "a further study of this area would be useful."[34]

It is interesting to note that pressures for no-fault caused development of the Wisconsin comparative negligence system in the 1930's.[35] And Wisconsin has not seriously considered a no-fault system since then.[36] Further, it has been speculated that the operation of comparative negligence in Mississippi staved off that state's adoption of a workmen's compensation system until the late 1940's.[37]

It may be that the fault system is unsalvageable in the area of low-cost automobile accidents. But both in that limited situation and more importantly elsewhere in tort law,[38] jurists[39] and other legal scholars[40] believe that comparative negligence should be tried in order to give the fault system a chance to work.

21.3 The best comparative negligence system

The search for the best comparative negligence system has proceeded in a number of directions for more than fifty years.[41] As early as 1936 a treatise was written on legislative systems of distributing losses

---

[32]Id.

[33]Id., at 522.

[34]Id., at 520. The problems Professors Keeton and O'Connell suggested for study are among those considered in this text.

[35]Hayes, *Rule of Comparative Negligence and Its Operation in Wisconsin*, 23 Ohio St. B.A. Rep. 233, 234 (1950).

[36]New York Times, Oct. 7, 1971, at 69, cols. 4-5 ("legislators took a halfhearted look"). As of 1984 Wisconsin still had not enacted a no-fault system. W. P. Keeton et al., *Prosser and Keeton on the Law of Torts* § 84 at 607, note 46 (5th ed. 1984).

[37]Note, *Effect of Mississippi's Comparative Negligence Statute on Other Rules of Law*, 39 Miss. L.J. 493, 497 (1968).

[38]Such as slip and fall cases and product liability cases.

[39]See Vincent v. Pabst Brewing Co., 47 Wis. 2d 120, 177 N.W.2d 513, 521 (1970) (Justice Hallows dissenting in favor of a pure comparative negligence system); Henry, "Why Not Comparative Negligence in Washington?" *in* American Trial Lawyers Association, *Comparative Negligence* 1-24 (ATL Monograph, W. Schwartz ed. 1970).

[40]See materials cited in note 1, section 21.1.

[41]General References: Flynn, *Comparative Negligence: The Debate*, 8 Trial 49 (1972); Mole & Wilson, *A Study of Comparative Negligence*, 17 Cornell L.Q. 333, 604 (1932); Maloney, *From Contributory to Comparative Negligence: A Needed Law Reform*, 11 U. Fla. L. Rev. 135 (1958); Philbrick, *Loss Apportionment in Negligence Cases*, 99 U. Pa. L. Rev. 572, 766 (1951); Prosser, *Comparative Negligence*, 51 Mich. L. Rev. 465 (1953); Turk, *Comparative Negligence on the March*, 28 Chi.-Kent L. Rev. 189, 304 (1950); C. Gregory, *Legislative Loss Distribution in Negligence Actions—A Study in Administrative Aspects of Comparative Negligence and Contribution in Tort Litigation* (1936).

For Pure Comparative Negligence: Juenger, *Brief for Negligence Law Section of the State Bar of Michigan in Support of Comparative Negligence as Amicus Curiae*, 18 Wayne L. Rev. 3 (1972); American Trial Lawyers Association, *Comparative Negligence* (ATL Monograph Series, W. Schwartz ed. 1970); Prosser, *Comparative Negligence*, 51 Mich. L. Rev. 465 (1953); Campbell, *Recent Developments of the Law of Negligence in Wisconsin*, 1955 Wis. L. Rev. 5 and 1958 Wis. L. Rev. 4; Symposium, *Comments on Maki v. Frelk—Comparative v. Contributory Negligence: Should the Court or Legislature Decide?*, 21 Vand. L. Rev. 889; Keeton, *Comments* at 906; Leflar, *Comments* at 918 (1968).

due to negligence.[42] Comparative negligence has been the subject of many legislative fact-finding efforts; for example, in 1970 an Advisory Committee appointed by the Wisconsin legislature held hearings for several days on the matter.[43] Unfortunately, each such exploration of this very important question appears to begin as if it were proceeding on uncharted waters. Here we will consider the arguments that have appeared over these many years and, in light of this analysis, arrive at an opinion as to the best comparative negligence system.

The Principal Contenders

There appears to be no question that the two principal contenders for being the best system are pure comparative negligence[44] and the 50% system, including its derivatives.[45] Other modified systems of comparative negligence have not attracted much support.

Equal Division

Probably the reason the equal division system has been largely abolished is because of its arbitrariness. As indicated in section 3.3, it was applied principally in American maritime law, but only in a limited area of that law. Finally, where it was applicable, a number of escapes were derived to avoid its full application. Obviously, the rule is fair only when in fact the parties to the lawsuit have been equally negligent. While this is often the case, in a greater number of situations one party is substantially more negligent than the other. In such situations, the equal division rule fails.

The Slight-Gross System

The other principal modified system, the "slight-gross" system, has had no following as a rule of general comparative negligence law outside the states of Nebraska and South Dakota.[46] Those states have derived methods of living with their respective forms of this system. However, the struggles each state has had in formulating standards of what is "slight" negligence should deter other states from adopting that system.[47] As illustrated in section 3.4, both South Dakota and

---

For Modified Comparative Negligence: Decker, *Some Random Observations About Comparative Negligence and the Trial Process in Wisconsin*, 1 Conn. L. Rev. 56 (1968); Ghiardi, *Comparative Negligence, The Case Against a Mississippi Type Statute*, 10 For the Def. 61 (1969).

Other Approaches: Parkhill, *A Better Comparative Negligence Rule*, 56 A.B.A. J. 263 (1970); Note, *Comparative Negligence Statute*, 18 Vand. L. Rev. 327 (1964).

Overall Evaluation: Peck, *Comparative Negligence and Automobile Liability Insurance*, 58 Mich. L. Rev. 689 (1960); Rosenberg, *Comparative Negligence in Arkansas: A "Before and After" Survey*, 13 Ark. L. Rev. 89 (1959).

[42]C. Gregory, note 41 above.

[43]Wisconsin Legislative Council, Minutes of Judiciary Committee on Automobile Accident Liability (July 16, 1970) (hereinafter cited as Wis. Leg. Council Comm.).

[44]See works listed for pure comparative negligence, note 41 above; see also section 3.2.

[45]See works listed for modified comparative negligence, note 41 above; see also section 3.5.

[46]See section 3.4.

[47]Id.

Nebraska courts have, de facto, been treating their system as if it were a form of the 50% system in one important respect: the state courts tend not to direct a verdict for defendant when the negligence of plaintiff is equal to or less than that of the defendant.

The Forms of 50% Systems

The "best" comparative negligence system is either pure comparative negligence or some form of the 50% system. Before finally choosing between these two, one must determine which form of the 50% system is the best. At one time a majority of the 50% states barred plaintiff's claim when his negligence was either equal to or greater than that of the defendant's.[48] Beginning with New Hampshire's 1969 statute, some states decided to honor plaintiff's claim when his negligence was equal to the defendant's and let him recover 50% of his damages.[49] The Wisconsin Legislative Council advisory committee decided in 1970 that this latter form of the 50% system is superior.[50] The Wisconsin legislature agreed and amended its statute accordingly in 1971;[51] several other modified comparative negligence states followed suit.[52] That decision is difficult to question.

This variant, which permits partial recovery by the plaintiff who is equally at fault, still does not permit plaintiff to recover if he has been more culpable than defendant. It therefore precludes any theoretical moral impropriety involved in awarding damages to someone more at fault. Further, it allows compensation in a situation that occurs with some frequency in the minds of jurors—that in which plaintiff and defendant are equally blameworthy. It is against this New Hampshire form of the 50% system that pure comparative negligence should be tested.

Moral Basis for 50% System

The principal argument in favor of the New Hampshire variant (Wisconsin's present 50% system) as against pure comparative negligence centers on the moral impropriety of allowing a party who is more at fault in an accident to recover from one whose blameworthiness is less.[53] Advocates of the 50% system often hypothesize a case to demonstrate the "unfairness" of pure comparative negligence: a 90% negligent plaintiff who suffered $100,000 in damage recovers $10,000 from a 10% negligent defendant; if the defendant suffered only $1000 in damage and a setoff is allowed, $9100 will still flow to plaintiff.

---

[48]See section 3.5, at note 51.

[49]Id., at note 52.

[50]See note 43 above; see also Wisconsin Legislative Council, Report of Judiciary Committee on Automobile Accident Liability, Vol. 1, Subchapter 2: Conclusions and Recommendations of the Committee 107 (1971).

[51]Wis. Laws 1971, ch. 47, amending Wis. Stat. Ann., § 895.045.

[52]See subsection 3.5(B).

[53]See e.g., Ghiardi, note 41 above; Ghiardi and Hogan, *Comparative Negligence—The Wisconsin Rule and Procedure*, 18 Def. L. J. 537 (1969).

On the surface, the result of this hypothetical case seems unfair. Nevertheless, there are convincing arguments in justification of it. First, making a judgment about an entire comparative negligence system based on an unusual hypothetical case is a classic example of a hard case making bad law. Mississippi has had pure comparative negligence since 1910 in all personal injury actions; yet a search of the pages of annotations to that statute will not reveal any cases in which a 90% at fault plaintiff obtained a substantial recovery from a defendant.[54]

Even if this hypothetical case were to occur, the fault of the plaintiff is not ignored under pure comparative negligence. He has been made to bear 90% of his costs and 90% of the defendant's costs from an accident for which he was 90% at fault. Requiring him to bear 100% of all costs, or even all of his own costs plus 90% of defendant's, would tax him beyond his culpability.

Finally, proximate cause rules may bar the claims of plaintiffs whose negligence was the substantial cause of the accident,[55] further reducing the likelihood of an unfair result in applying pure comparative negligence.

Insurance and Administrative Costs

A second principal contention of those who favor a 50% system is that pure comparative negligence will substantially increase the costs both of insurance and of administering the judicial system.[56] It is argued that insurance costs will rise because of the need to make more payoffs in more cases.[57]

This contention was made by insurance company representatives who appeared before the 1970 Wisconsin Legislative Council advisory committee which had the responsibility of considering whether that state should change from its 50% system to pure comparative negligence.[58] But these representatives presented no statistical evidence to support their contention. In fact, the representative from the American Family Insurance Company indicated that although he had some information regarding costs, it "probably would not stand close scrutiny because of the difficulty involved in predicting costs."[59] In point of fact, the most thorough and conscientious study of the question concluded

---

[54]See Miss. Code Ann., § 11-7-15; see also section 3.2.

[55]See section 4.4. See also Menden v. Wisconsin Elec. Power Co., 240 Wis. 87, 2 N.W.2d 856 (1942) (application of proximate cause rule to defeat recovery under a modified system).

[56]See, e.g., McKinnon, *The Case Against Comparative Negligence*, 28 Cal. St. B.J. 23 (1953); Gilmore, *Comparative Negligence From a Viewpoint of Casualty Insurance*, 10 Ark. L. Rev. 82 (1955); Ghiardi, note 41 above.

[57]See Gilmore, note 56 above.

[58]See Wis. Leg. Council Comm., note 43 above, at 10-13.

[59]Id., at 11.

that the difference in liability insurance costs would be inconsequential.[60]

Judicial Costs

There are few data to support the contention that pure comparative negligence would substantially increase court costs over and above those in a 50% system. The assertion is based on speculation that plaintiffs, knowing that they will be able to recover "something," will decline to settle cases in order to have a crack at the jury.[61] This argument ignores the possibility that defendants under pure comparative negligence might be more inclined to settle their case since they cannot rely on the 50% "drop off" rule to protect them.

The one careful study done on this issue—a study of the experience of Arkansas lawyers, first under pure comparative negligence operative and subsequently under a 50% system—showed a slight decrease in the number of settlements under the 50% system.[62] One of the speakers before the Wisconsin Legislative advisory committee predicted that the adoption of pure comparative negligence would result in a 25% increase in the state's judicial budget,[63] but neither that speaker nor anyone else has proved that such costs would in fact occur. The experiences in Mississippi, various Canadian provinces and England indicate that pure comparative negligence does not increase judicial costs.[64] There has been no indication that the system increases costs in California, Florida, Michigan, or New York, states that have adopted pure comparative negligence.

To determine definitively whether pure comparative negligence would increase either insurance or judicial costs in a particular state, extensive empirical studies would be required. It is interesting to note that in Wisconsin six members of the Supreme Court who declined to make a judicial change from a 50% system to pure comparative negligence[65] gave as a reason for their reluctance that the legislature was better able to make a thorough study of the subject. In point of fact, however, from the available data, it appears that the Legislative Council advisory committee considered only generalized arguments by various witnesses—arguments that could have been made to the court through amicus curiae briefs.

---

[60]See Peck, note 41 above, at 727-728 ("The choice then between the two rules would not be one involving a question of substantially higher insurance rates for everyone, but a question of the justness of results in a limited number of cases"). See also Fuchsberg, *Comparing Comparative Negligence*, 1970 A.B.A. Sect. Ins. N. & C. L. 522, 525.

[61]See Wis. Leg. Council Comm., note 43 above, at 15.

[62]See Rosenberg, note 41 above. See also Heft & Heft, *The Two-Layer Cake: No Fault and Comparative Negligence*, 58 A.B.A. J. 933, 935 (1972).

[63]Remarks of Judge Decker in Wis. Leg. Council Comm., note 43 above, at 5, 6.

[64]See American Trial Lawyers Association, note 41 above.

[65]Vincent v. Pabst Brewing Co., 47 Wis. 2d 120, 177 N.W.2d 513, 517-518 (1970).

Fair Distribution of Responsibility

This author agrees with those who contend that the 50% system "distorts the very principle it recognizes."[66] Only pure comparative negligence truly distributes responsibility according to fault of the respective parties. The contributory negligence defense has been one of the great failures of the fault system simply because it did not distribute responsibility according to fault, but rather forced one party to bear the entire costs of the accident.

Omissions from the Statutory Systems

Although this author concludes that pure comparative negligence is better than the 50% approach, pure comparative negligence without more is not the best comparative negligence system. The simple pure comparative negligence statutes of Mississippi, Rhode Island and Washington and in the Federal Employers' Liability Act leave too many important questions unanswered. Rhode Island does deal with the rather sticky problem of setoff;[67] but all of these statutes leave attorneys at a loss concerning the following issues:

1. whether old modifications of the contributory negligence system remain in effect;

2. how comparative negligence works in tandem with co-existing legal doctrines such as the assumption of the risk defense;

3. how comparative negligence is to be applied to complex cases involving multiple parties;

4. whether and how the finders of fact are to be controlled under pure comparative negligence.

Section 21.4 suggests guidelines for legislative solutions to the important legal problems raised by a comparative negligence system.

21.4 A model comparative negligence statute

Since the publication of the first edition of this treatise a committee of the National Conference on Uniform State Laws has drafted a Uniform Comparative Fault Act. The committee was chaired by Professor John W. Wade of the Vanderbilt School of Law. The author of the present treatise served as legal consultant to the committee.

The act was adopted by the Conference on August 5, 1977. Section 3 was amended in 1979.

While there are a number of aspects of it about which reasonable persons might vigorously disagree, it is the most thoroughly researched comparative negligence law to be presented as a public document in the United States. As the reader will discern, it resolves a number of major issues that have been discussed in this treatise.

A number of states have adopted the act in part, but of equal (per-

---

[66]Juenger, note 41 above, at 50.
[67]R.I. Gen. Laws, § 9-20-4.1.

haps greater) importance is the fact that courts have utilized it as a resource to create a comparative negligence system or to provide answers to important questions not covered by existing statutes. This utilization can occur, not only in states that have judicially adopted comparative negligence, but also in those that have adopted it legislatively.

We have set forth both the statute and the comments. This has been done to provide the reader with the rationale underlying the choices made in the statute.

UNIFORM COMPARATIVE FAULT ACT

Section 1. [Effect of Contributory Fault]

(a) In an action based on fault seeking to recover damages for injury or death to person or harm to property, any contributory fault chargeable to the claimant diminishes proportionately the amount awarded as compensatory damages for an injury attributable to the claimant's contributory fault, but does not bar recovery. This rule applies whether or not under prior law the claimant's contributory fault constituted a defense or was disregarded under applicable legal doctrines, such as last clear chance.

(b) "Fault" includes acts or omissions that are in any measure negligent or reckless toward the person or property of the actor or others, or that subject a person to strict tort liability. The term also includes breach of warranty, unreasonable assumption of risk not constituting an enforceable express consent, misuse of a product for which the defendant otherwise would be liable, and unreasonable failure to avoid an injury or to mitigate damages. Legal requirements of causal relation apply both to fault as the basis for liability and to contributory fault.

COMMENT

This Section states the general principle, that a plaintiff's contributory fault does not bar his recovery but instead apportions damages according to the proportionate fault of the parties.

Harms Covered. The specific application of that principle, as provided for in this Act, is confined to physical harm to person or property. But it necessarily includes consequential damages deriving from the physical harm, such as doctor's bills, loss of wages or costs of repair or replacement of property. It does not include matters like economic loss resulting from a tort such as negligent misrepresentation, or interference with contractual relations, or injurious falsehood, or harm to reputation resulting from defamation. But failure to include these harms specifically in the Act is not intended to preclude application of the general principle to them if a court determines that the common law of the state would make the application.

Conduct Covered. (a) Defendant's Conduct. The Act applies to "acts or omissions that are in any measure negligent or reckless toward the person or property . . . of others." This includes the traditional action for negligence but covers all negligent conduct, whether it comes within the traditional negligence action or not. It includes negligence as a matter of law, arising from court decision or criminal statute. "In any measure" is intended to cover all degrees and kinds of negligent conduct without the need of listing them specifically.

In some states reckless conduct goes by a different name, such as willful or wanton misconduct. The decision must be made in the particular state whether the language used is sufficiently broad for the purpose or if additional language is needed.

Although strict liability is sometimes called absolute liability or liability without fault, it is still included. Strict liability for both abnormally dangerous activities and for products bears a strong similarity to negligence as a matter of law (negligence per se), and the fact finder should have no real difficulty in setting percentages of fault. Putting out a product that is dangerous to the user or the public or engaging in an activity that is dangerous to those in the vicinity involves a measure of fault that can be weighed and compared, even though it is not characterized as negligence.

An action for breach of warranty is held to sound sometimes in tort and sometimes in contract. There is no intent to include in the coverage of the Act actions that are fully contractual in their gravamen and in which the plaintiff is suing solely because he did not recover what he contracted to receive. The restriction of coverage to physical harms to person or property excludes these claims.

The Act does not include intentional torts. Statutes and decisions have not applied the comparative fault principle to them. But a court determining that the general principle should apply at common law to a case before it of an intentional tort is not precluded from that holding by the Act.

For certain types of torts, such as nuisance, the defendant's conduct may be intentional, negligent or subject to strict liability. In the latter two instances the Act would apply, but not in a case in which the defendant intentionally inflicts the injury on the plaintiff.

A tort action based on violation of a statute is within the coverage of the Act if the conduct comes within the definition of fault and unless the statute is construed as intended to provide for recovery of full damage irrespective of contributory fault.

(b) Plantiff's Conduct. "Fault," as defined in Subsection (b), includes conduct of the plaintiff or other claimant, as well as a defendant.

"Contributory fault chargeable to the claimant" includes legally imputed fault as in the cases of principal and agent and of an action for loss of services of a spouse. It also covers a situation in which fault is not imputed but would still have barred recovery prior to passage of the Act—as, for example, a wrongful-death action in which the decedent's contributory negligence would have barred recovery even though it was not imputed to the person bringing the action.

Contributory fault diminishes recovery whether it was previously a bar or not, as for example, in the case of ordinary contributory negligence in an action based on strict liability or recklessness. Last clear chance is expressly included with its variations.

"Assumption of risk" is a term with a number of different meanings—only one of which is "fault" within the meaning of this Act. This is the case of unreasonable assumption of risk, which might be likened to deliberate contributory negligence and means that the conduct must have been voluntary and with knowledge of the danger. As used in this Act, the term does not include the meanings (1) of a valid and enforceable consent (which is treated like other contracts), (2) of a lack of violation of duty by the defendant (as in the failure of a landowner to warn a licensee of a patent danger on the premises), or (3) of a reasonable assumption of risk (which is not fault and should not have the effect of barring recovery).

"Misuse of a product" is a term also with several meanings. The meaning in this Section is confined to a misuse giving rise to a danger that could have been reasonably anticipated and guarded against. The Act does not apply to a misuse giving rise to a danger that could not reasonably have been anticipated and guarded against by the manufacturer, so that the product was therefore not defective or unreasonably dangerous.

The doctrine of avoidable consequences is expressly included in the coverage.

Causation. For the conduct stigmatized as fault to have any effect under the provisions of this Act it must have had an adequate causal relation to the claimant's damage. This includes the rules of both cause in fact and proximate cause.

"Injury attributable to the claimant's contributory fault" refers to the requirement of a causal relation for the particular damage. Thus, negligent failure to fasten a seat belt would diminish recovery only for damages in which the lack of a seat-belt restraint played a part, and not, for example, to the damage to the car. A similar rule applies to a defendant's fault; a physician, for example, negligently setting a broken arm, is not liable for other injuries received in an automobile accident.

1979 Addition to Comment: *Adaptation of the Act to Modified Form of Comparative Negligence.* If a state now using the modified form of comparative negligence should decide that in the light of its experience it is wedded to that form and not willing to change to the pure form, the Act may be adopted for this purpose, as indicated below, by adding the words in italics:

Section 1. [Effect of Contributory Fault]

(a) In an action based on fault seeking to recover damages for injury or death to person or harm to property, any contributory fault chargeable to the claimant, *if not greater than the combined fault of all other parties to the claim, including third-party defendants and persons released under Section 6,* diminishes proportionately the amount awarded as compensatory damages for an injury attributable to the claimant's contributory fault, but does not bar recovery. This rule applies whether or not under prior law the claimant's contributory fault constituted a defense or was disregarded under applicable legal doctrines, such as last clear chance.

(b) *Whenever both parties to a claim and counterclaim have sustained damage caused by fault or both, each party can recover from the other in proportion to their relative fault in accordance with Section 3, regardless of whose fault is the greater.*

(c) "Fault" includes acts or omissions that are in any measure negligent or reckless toward the person or property of the actor or others, or that subject a person to strict tort liability. The term also includes breach of warranty, unreasonable assumption of risk not constituting an enforceable express consent, measure of a product for which the defendant otherwise would be liable, and unreasonable failure to avoid an injury or to mitigate damages. Legal requirements of causal relation apply both to fault as the basis for liability and to contributory fault.

Section 2. [Apportionment of Damages]

(a) In all actions involving fault of more than one party to the action, including third-party defendants and persons who have been released under Section 6, the court, unless otherwise agreed by all parties, shall instruct the jury to answer special interrogatories or, if there is no jury, shall make findings, indicating:

(1) the amount of damages each claimant would be entitled to recover if contributory fault is disregarded; and

(2) the percentage of the total fault of all of the parties to each claim that is allocated to each claimant, defendant, third-party defendant, and person who has been released from liability under Section 6. For this purpose the court may determine that two or more persons are to be treated as a single party.

(b) In determining the percentages of fault, the trier of fact shall consider both the nature of the conduct of each party at fault and the extent of the causal relation between the conduct and the damages claimed.

(c) The court shall determine the award of damages to each claimant in accordance with the findings, subject to any reduction under Section 6, and enter judgment against each party liable on the basis of rules of joint-and-several liability. For purposes of contribution under Sections 4 and 5, the court also shall determine and state in the judgment each party's equitable share of the obligation to each claimant in accordance with the respective percentages of fault.

(d) Upon motion made not later than [one year] after judgment is entered, the court shall determine whether all or part of a party's equitable share of the obligation is uncollectible from that party, and shall reallocate any uncollectible amount among the other parties, including a claimant at fault, according to their respective percentages of fault. The party whose liability is reallocated is nonetheless subject to contribution and to any continuing liability to the claimant on the judgment.

COMMENT

Parties. It is assumed that the state procedure provides for bringing in third-party defendants as parties. If not, the procedural statutes or rules may need to be amended to permit it, at least for purposes of contribution.

The limitation to parties to the action means ignoring other persons who may have been at fault with regard to the particular injury but who have not been joined as parties. This is a deliberate decision. It cannot be told with certainty whether that person was actually at fault or what amount of fault should be attributed to him, or whether he will ever be sued, or whether the statute of limitations will run on him, etc. An attempt to settle these matters in a suit to which he is not a party would not be binding on him. Both plaintiff and defendants will have significant incentive for joining available defendants who may be liable. The more parties joined whose fault contributed to the injury, the smaller the percentage of fault allocated to each of the other parties, whether plaintiff or defendant.

In situations such as that of principal and agent, driver and owner of a car, or manufacturer and retailer of a product, the court may under appropriate circumstances find that the two persons should be treated as a single party for purposes of allocating fault.

Percentages of fault. In comparing the fault of the several parties for the purpose of obtaining percentages there are a number of implications arising from the concept of fault. The conduct of the claimant or of any defendant may be more or less at fault, depending upon all the circumstances including such matters as (1) whether the conduct was mere inadvertence or engaged in with an awareness of the danger involved, (2) the magnitude of the risk created by the conduct, including the number of persons endangered and the potential seriousness of the injury, (3) the significance of what the actor was seeking to attain by his conduct, (4) the actor's superior or inferior capacities, and (5) the particular circumstances, such as the existence of an emergency requiring a hasty decision.

A rule of law that a particular defendant owes a higher degree of care (as in the case of a common carrier of passengers) or a lesser degree of care (as in the case of an automobile host in a state having a valid automobile-guest statute) or that no negligence is required (as in the case of conducting blasting operations in an urban area) is important in determining whether he is liable at all. If the liability has been established, however, the rule itself does not play a part in determining the relative proportion of fault of this party in comparison with the others. But the policy behind the rule may be quite important. An error in driving on the part of a bus driver with a load of passengers may properly produce an evaluation of greater fault than the same error on the part of a housewife gratuitously giving her neighbor a ride to the shopping center; and an automobile manufacturer putting out a car with a cracked brake cylinder may, even in the absence of proof of negligence in failing to discover the crack, properly be held to a greater measure of fault than another manufacturer producing a mechanical pencil with a defective clasp that due care would have discovered.

In determining the relative fault of the parties, the fact finder will also give consideration to the relative closeness of the causal relationship of the negligent conduct of the defendants and the harm to the plaintiff. Degrees of fault and proximity of causation are inextricably mixed, as a study of last clear chance indicates, and that common-law doctrine has been absorbed in this Act. This position has been followed under statutes making no specific provision for it.

Joint and Several Liability and Equitable Shares of the Obligation. The common law rule of joint-and-several liability of joint tortfeasors continues to apply under this Act. This is true whether the claimant was contributorily negligent or not. The plaintiff can recover the total amount of his judgment against any defendant who is liable.

The judgment for each claimant also sets forth, however, the equitable share of the total obligation to the claimant for each party, based on his established percentage of fault. This indicates the amount that each party should eventually be responsible for as a result of the rules of contribution. Stated in the judgment itself, it makes the information available to the parties and will normally be a basis for contribution without the need for a court order arising from motion or separate action.

Reallocation. Reallocation of the equitable share of the obligation of a party takes place when his share is uncollectible.

Reallocation takes place among all parties at fault. This includes a claimant who is contributorily at fault. It avoids the unfairness both of the common law rule of joint-and-several liability, which would cast the total risk of uncollectibility upon the solvent defendants, and of a rule abolishing joint-and-several liability, which would cast the total risk of uncollectibility upon the claimant.

Control by the court. The total of the several percentages of fault for the plaintiff and all defendants, as found in the special interrogatories, should add up to 100%. Whether the court will inform the jury of this will depend upon the local practice.

The court should be able to exercise any usual powers under existing law of setting aside or modifying a verdict if it is internally inconsistent or shows bias or prejudice, etc. On the same basis as the remittitur principle, a court might indicate its intent to set aside a percentage allocation unless the parties agreed to a somewhat different one.

Illustration No. 1. (Simple 2-party situation).

A sues B. A's damages are $10,000.

A is found 40% at fault.

B is found 60% at fault.

A recovers judgment for $6,000.

Illustration No. 2. (Multiple-party situation).

A sues B, C and D. A's damages are $10,000.

A is found 40% at fault.

B is found 30% at fault.

C is found 30% at fault.

D is found 0% at fault.

A is awarded judgment jointly and severally against B & C for $6,000. The court also states in the judgment the equitable share of the obligation of each party:

A's equitable share is $4,000 (40% of $10,000).

B's equitable share is $3,000 (30% of $10,000).

C's equitable share is $3,000 (30% of $10,000).

Illustration No. 3. (Reallocation computation under Subsection (d)).

Same facts as in Illustration No. 2.

On proper motion to the court, C shows that B's share is uncollectible. The court orders that B's equitable share be reallocated beween A and C. The court orders that B's equitable share be allocated between A and C.

A's equitable share is increased by $1,714 ($\frac{4}{7}$ of $3,000).

C's equitable share is increased by $1,286 ($\frac{3}{7}$ of $3,000).

Section 3. [Set-off]

A claim and counterclaim shall not be set off against each other, except by agreement of both parties. On motion, however, the court, if it finds that the obligation of either party is likely to be uncollectible, may order that both parties make payment into court for distribution. The court shall distribute the funds received and declare obligations discharged as if the payment into court by either party had been a payment to the other party and any distribution of those funds back to the party making payment had been a payment to him by the other party.

COMMENT

A set-off involves a single claim and counterclaim. If there are multiple defendants, separate set-off issues may arise between a claimant and each of several defendants, but each set-off would be a separate issue, determined independently of the others. The same principle applies in case of a cross-claim subject to a counterclaim.

Whether the rule is for or against set-off, if it should be applied categorically to all situations it would produce unfair results in some of them. In attaining a fair application to a particular factual situation, consideration needs to be given to the circumstances of whether each party is able to pay his obligation and whether the payment comes from his own pocket or from liability insurance covering him. The provisions of this Section provide a fair solution to each situation, as illustrated below.

Illustration No. 4. (Parties fully covered by liability insurance.) A sues B. B counterclaims. Each is found to have suffered $100,000 in damage. Each is fully covered by liability insurance. A is found 30% at fault. B is found 70% at fault. Under the statutory provision there is no set-off except by agreement of the parties, and it would not be in their best interests here to agree to a set-off. A recovers $70,000 from B, and B recovers $30,000 from A.

Illustration No. 5. (No insurance but both parties able to pay judgments.) The same facts as in Illustration 4, but there is no liability insurance. Each is able to pay the judgment against him. If the parties do not agree to a set-off, A receives $70,000 from B, and B receives $30,000 from A. For their own convenience they may find it simpler to agree on a set-off, with A receiving $40,000 from B.

Illustration No. 6. (No insurance; B is able to pay and A is not.) As in Illustration 4, each party has $100,000 damages, A is 30% at fault and B is 70% at fault. Neither party has liability insurance coverage. B moves the court to require both parties to make payment into court for distribution. Finding it likely that A's obligation will be uncollectible the court issues the order. B pays into court $70,000; A can pay nothing. The court distributes $40,000 to A and $30,000 back to B. This is treated as if B had directly paid A

$70,000 and A had directly paid B $30,000 and the obligations of both parties are extinguished.

Illustration No. 7. (A has insurance; B does not and is unable to pay.) The same facts as in Illustration 6, but B has no insurance and cannot pay, while A has full liability insurance. A's motion that both parties pay into court is granted. A's insurance company pays $30,000. A pays nothing. The court distributes the $30,000 to A. This extinguishes the liability of A and his insurance company under the liability coverage, and B's liability to A reduced from $70,000 to $40,000. For application of any uninsured-motorist coverage contained in A's insurance policy, the court's delivery of the $30,000 to A is treated as a direct payment by B to A.

Illustration No. 8. (Both parties have inadequate insurance coverage and no other available funds.)

A is 30% negligent, has damages of $50,000 and carries liability insurance of $20,000. B is 70% negligent, has damages of $100,000 and carries liability insurance of $30,000.

A therefore owes B $30,000 and has a claim against B of $35,000; and B owes A $35,000 and has a claim against A of $30,000.

On granting of a motion to pay into court, A's carrier pays $20,000 which is initially allocated to B as payment to him of $20,000 and reduces A's debt to B to $10,000 and

B's carrier pays $30,000, which is initially allocated to A as payment to him of $30,000 and reduces B's debt to A to $5,000.

The court now reallocates to B $10,000 from A's initial allocation of $30,000, leaving $20,000 for A. It also reallocates to A $5,000 from B's initial allocation of $20,000, leaving $15,000 for B.

A is thus entitled to the $20,000 remaining in the initial allocation, plus $5,000 from the subsequent allocation, making a total of $25,000; and

B is entitled to the $15,000 remaining in the initial allocation, plus $10,000 from the subsequent allocation, making a total of $25,000.

Of the $50,000 paid in, A receives $25,000 and B receives $25,000. All obligations are discharged.

For a complex illustration like No. 8, the process of tracking literally the language of the Section is somewhat laborious and difficult to work out. Fortunately, it is possible to reach exactly the same result much more simply and easily by using the formula, $D = C - O + P$ to determine the amount each claimant is entitled to receive. D signifies the amount to be distributed to the particular claimant from the funds paid into court; C signifies the amount of his claim after it has been reduced by the court because of his own negligence; O signifies the amount that he is found by the court to owe to the other party; and P signifies the amount that he has paid into court.

Use of this formula in each of illustrations above will reach exactly the same result as that which is stated in the illustration. Thus, in Illustration 8, the formula $D = C - O + P$ operates like this: For A: $35,000-$30,000+$20,000=$25,000. For B: $30,000-$35,000+$30,000=$25,000.

Observe that if use of the formula produces a negative number for one of the two parties, it corresponds with a number larger by that figure than the amount of deposit with the court and indicates that the party with the negative figure continues to owe that amount to the other party. This occurs, for example, in Illustration No. 7.

The system for distributing the funds outlined by the section is not the only one that could be utilized but it appears to be the fairest and most equitable. It gives due consideration to the relative amounts owed by each party and the relative amounts paid by each; and their relative fault is of course already taken into consideration in determining the amounts of their enforceable claims.

Section 4. [Right of Contribution]

(a) A right of contribution exists between or among two or more persons who are jointly and severally liable upon the same indivisible claim for the same injury, death, or harm, whether or not judgment has been recovered against all or any of them. It may be enforced either in the original action or by a separate action brought for that purpose. The basis for contribution is each person's equitable share of the obligation, including the equitable share of a claimant at fault, as determined in accordance with the provisions of Section 2.

(b) Contribution is available to a person who enters into a settlement with a claimant only (1) if the liability of the person against whom contribution is sought has been extinguished and (2) to the extent that the amount paid in settlement was reasonable.

COMMENT

Sections 4, 5 and 6 are expected to replace the Uniform Contribution Among Tortfeasors Act (1955) in a state following the principle of comparative fault. The three sections, however, apply whether the plaintiff was contributorily at fault or not.

Section 4 is in general accord with the provisions of the 1955 Uniform Act, but the test for determining the measure of contribution and thus establishing the ultimate responsibility is no longer on a pro rata basis. Instead, it is on a basis of proportionate fault determined in accordance with the provisions of Section 2. A plaintiff who is contributorily at fault also shares in the proportionate responsibility.

Joint-and-several liability under the common law means that each defendant contributing to the same harm is liable to him for the whole amount of the recoverable damages. This is not changed by the Act. Between the defendants themselves, however, the apportionment is in accordance with the equitable shares of the obligation, as established under Section 2.

If the defendants cause separate harms or if the harm is found to be divisible on a reasonable basis, however, the liability may become several for a particular harm, and contribution is not appropriate. See Restatement (Second) of Torts § 433A (1965).

Section 5. [Enforcement of Contribution]

(a) If the proportionate fault of the parties to a claim for contribution has been established previously by the court, as provided by Section 2, a party paying more than his equitable share of the obligation, upon motion, may recover judgment for contribution.

(b) If the proportionate fault of the parties to the claim for contribution has not been established by the court, contribution may be enforced in a separate action, whether or not a judgment has been rendered against either the person seeking contribution or the person from whom contribution is being sought.

(c) If a judgment has been rendered, the action for contribution must be commenced within [one year] after the judgment becomes final. If no judgment has been rendered, the person bringing the action for contribution either must have (1) discharged by payment the common liability within the period of the statute of limitations applicable to the claimant's right of action against him and commenced the action for contribution within [one year] after payment, or (2) agreed while action was pending to discharge the common liability and, within [one year] after the agreement, have paid the liability and commenced an action for contribution.

COMMENT

Illustration No. 9. (Equitable shares previously established by court).

A sues B and C. His damages are $20,000.

A is found 40% at fault.

B is found 30% at fault.

C is found 30% at fault.

A, with a joint-and-several judgment for $6,000 against B and C, collects the whole amount from B.

On proper motion to the court, B is entitled to contribution from C in the amount of $3,000.

Illustration No. 10. (Equitable shares not established).

A sues B. His damages are $20,000.

A is found 40% at fault.

B is found 60% at fault.

Judgment for A for $12,000 is paid by B.

B then brings a separate action seeking contribution from C, who was not a party to the original action.

C is found to be liable for the same injury, and as between B and C, C is found to be 50% at fault.

Judgement for contribution for $6,000 is awarded to B.

If A had voluntarily joined or been brought in as a party to this second action, proportionate fault would have been determined for all parties, including A and B, and contribution against C would have been awarded on that basis.

Section 6. [Effect of Release]

A release, covenant not to sue, or similar agreement entered into by a claimant and a person liable discharges that person from all liability for contribution, but it does not discharge any other persons liable upon the same claim unless it so provides. However, the claim of the releasing person against other persons is reduced by the amount of the released person's equitable share of the obligation, determined in accordance with the provisions of Section 2.

COMMENT

Effect of release on liability of other tortfeasors. The provision that release of one tortfeasor does not release the others unless the release so provides is taken from the Uniform Contribution Among Tortfeasors Act (1955). It is a common statutory provision.

Effect of release on right of contribution. The question of the contribution rights of tortfeasors A and B against tortfeasor C, who settled and obtained a release or covenant not to sue admits of three answers: (1) A and B are still able to obtain contribution against C, despite the release, (2) A and B are not entitled to contribution unless the release was given not in good faith but by way of collusion, and (3) the plaintiff's total claim is reduced by the proportionate share of C. Each of the three solutions has substantial disadvantages, yet each has been adopted in one of the uniform acts. The first solution was adopted by the 1939 Uniform Contribution Act. Its disadvantage is that it discourages settlements; a tortfeasor has no incentive to settle if he remains liable for contribution. The second solution was adopted by the 1955 Contribution Act. While it theoretically encourages settlements, it may be unfair to the other defendants and if the good-faith requirement is conscientiously enforced settlements may be discouraged.

The third solution is adopted in this Section. Although it may have some tendency to discourage a claimant from entering into a settlement, this solution is fairly based on the proportionate-fault principle.

"Discharges . . . from all liability for contribution." A reallocated share of contribution, as provided in Section 2(d), comes within the meaning of this phrase, and the discharge of the released person under this Section applies to that liability as well. Since the claim is reduced by the amount of the released person's equitable share, the increased amount of that share as a result of the reallocation is charged against the releasing person.

Illustration No. 11. (Effect of release).

A was injured through the concurrent negligence of B, C and D. His damages are $20,000. A settles with B for $2,000.

The trial produces the following results:

A, 40% at fault (equitable share, $8,000)

B, 30% at fault (equitable share, $6,000)

C, 20% at fault (equitable share, $4,000)

D, 10% at fault (equitable share, $2,000)

A's claim is reduced by B's equitable share ($6,000). He is awarded a judgment against C and D, making them jointly and severally liable for $6,000.

Their equitable shares of the obligation are $4,000 and $2,000 respectively.

Illustration No. 12. (Release to one tortfeasor; another's share is uncollectible).

Same facts as in Illustration No. 11.

It is now found that D's share of $2,000 is uncollectible. Upon proper motion to the court that share is reallocated as follows:

A's equitable share is increased by $4/9$ (his own proportionate fault), plus $3/9$ (B's proportionate fault), or $1,556.

C's equitable share is increased by $2/9$ or $444.

Immunities. The problem of a wrongdoer who is entitled to a legal immunity could be treated like a released tortfeasor in this Section—join him to the action to determine his equitable share of the obligation and subtract it from the amount of the claimant's recovery. But this would unfairly cast the whole loss on the claimant. This might be adjusted by spreading the immune party's obligation among all of the parties at fault, including the claimant, as in Subsection 2(d). But this same result is also accomplished by leaving the immune party out of the action altogether; a far easier and simpler solution. This Act therefore makes no provision for immunities. It must be borne in mind, however, that some states treat some immunities as not applying to a suit for contribution. This raises different problems, which can be handled under third-party practice.

Worker's compensation. An injured employee who has received or is entitled to worker's compensation benefits from his employer may ordinarily bring a tort action against a third party, such as the manufacturer of the machine that injured him, and recover for his injury in full. Under the rule in most states, the defendant is not entitled to contribution from the employer, even though the employer was negligent in maintaining the machine or instructing the employee in its use. This casting of the whole loss on the tort defendant may be unfair and greatly in need of legislative adjustment. It is so affected by the policies underlying the worker's compensation systems, however, and these policies vary so substantially in the several states that it was felt inappropriate to include a section on the problem in a uniform act.

Several solutions are possible. Thus, contribution against the employer may be provided for. Or the recovery by the employee may be reduced by the proportionate share of the employer. Or the amount of that proportionate share may be divided evenly between the employer and employee, so that the compensation system bears responsibility for it. Provision also needs to be made for the relation of the tort defendant to the compensation benefits. In any event, contributory negligence on the part of the employee will come within the scope of this Act and will affect the amount of recovery.

Section 7. [Uniformity of Application and Construction]

This Act shall be applied and construed so as to effectuate its general purpose to make uniform the law with respect to the subject of this Act among states enacting it.

Section 8. [Short Title]

This Act may be cited as the Uniform Comparative Fault Act.

Section 9. [Severability]

If any provision of this Act or application of it to any person or circumstances is held invalid, the invalidity does not affect other provisions or applications of the Act that can be given effect without the invalid provision or application, and to this end the provisions of this Act are severable.

Section 10. [Prospective Effect of Act]

This Act applies to all [claims for relief] [causes of action] accruing after its effective date.

Section 11. [Repeal]

The following acts and parts of acts are repealed:

COMMENT

A state that has adopted either of the two Uniform Contribution Among Tortfeasors Acts will of course plan to repeal it. This is also true of other statutory provisions on contribution for tortfeasors.

This Act does not necessitate any changes in the statutory language of Article 2 of the Uniform Commercial Code, but it may have the effect of slightly modifying some of the Comments to §§ 2-314 to 2-316 and 2-715 on proximate cause and the effect of contributory fault.

21.5 The controversy over judicial adoption of comparative negligence

Many arguments, some of them quite sophisticated,[68] have been advanced for and against the proposition that comparative negligence can and should be implemented by the judiciary in the absence of legislative action. The high degree of interest that the issue has provoked is probably based upon the fact that neither courts nor lawyers nor law professors have "any agreed upon theory on the limits of the powers of common law courts."[69]

In sections 21.1 and 21.2, the arguments for and against comparative negligence as a substitute for the contributory negligence defense have been considered. It is only when the decision is made, as this author advocates, that comparative negligence is indeed a better system than the common-law contributory negligence defense, that one reaches the question discussed in sections 21.6 and 21.7: whether comparative negligence can or should be introduced by judicial decision. In sections 21.6 and 21.7, the arguments considered in sections 21.1 and 21.2 are not repeated; rather, it is assumed that comparative negligence has been judged to be the better system.

21.6 The arguments against judicial adoption of comparative negligence

At first, the arguments against introduction of comparative negligence by the judiciary met with some success in the courts themselves[70] but with almost total failure in law review commentaries. [71] Since the publication of the first edition of this treatise there has been a major

---

[68]See Symposium, *Comments on Maki v. Frelk—Comparative v. Contributory Negligence: Should the Court or Legislature Decide?*, 21 Vand. L. Rev. 889 (1968); Comment, *Judicial Adoption of a Comparative Negligence Rule in Illinois*, 1967 U. Ill. L. F. 351; Note, *Torts—Comparative Negligence—A Court Moves to Strike the Arbitrary Doctrine of Contributory Negligence*, 17 Buffalo L. Rev. 573 (1968); Phillips, *Maki v. Frelk: The Rise and Fall of Comparative Negligence in Illinois*, 57 Ill. B.J. 10 (1968); Note, 43 Notre Dame Law. 422 (1968); Note, *Torts—Contributory Negligence*, 20 S.C. L. Rev. 146 (1968); Annot., "Comment Note.—The doctrine of comparative negligence and its relation to the doctrine of contributory negligence," 32 A.L.R.3d 463, 482-487 (1970).

[69]Symposium, *Comments on Maki v. Frelk*, note 66 above, at 897.

[70]Harrison v. Montgomery County Bd. of Education, 295 Md. 442, 456 A.2d 894 (1983); McGraw v. Corrin, 303 A.2d 641 (Del. 1973); Loui v. Oakley, 50 Hawaii 260, 50 Hawaii 272, 438 P.2d 393 (1968); Maki v. Frelk, 40 Ill. 2d 193, 239 N.E.2d 445, 32 A.L.R.3d 452 (1968); Haeg v. Sprague, Warner & Co., 202 Minn. 425, 281 N.W. 261 (1938); Rossman v. La Grega, 28 N.Y.2d 300, 321 N.Y.S.2d 588, 270 N.E.2d 313 (1971); Krise v. Gillund, 184 N.W.2d 405 (N.D., 1971); Peterson v. Culp, 255 Ore. 269, 465 P.2d 876 (1970). Accord, Chandler v. Mattox, 544 S.W.2d 85 (Mo. App. 1976) (rejecting comparative negligence without discussion); but see Street v. Calvert, 541 S.W.2d 576 (Tenn. 1976) (amicus brief by Dean John W. Wade). Although it declined to address the question of a change to comparative negligence because the issue was not reached in the trial court, the Tennessee Supreme Court noted the impetus that had gathered behind comparative negligence and that contributory negligence was in disrepute with leading scholarly writers. Id., at 586-587.

[71]See materials cited in note 68, section 21.5.

change in the attitude of the courts, very much as the treatise predicted and suggested.[72]

The first decision occurred in 1973 in Florida.[73] Soon after, Alaska,[74] and California[75] made the change. In 1977 the Supreme Court of Michigan came right to the borderline of adopting comparative negligence. Three justices believed that adoption should take place; three believed that the particular case before the court was an inappropriate vehicle for adoption because the issue was not briefed. The seventh justice, new to the court, did not participate in the decision.[76]

In 1979, the Michigan Supreme Court, in *Placek v. Sterling Heights*,[77] finally resolved this issue by judicially adopting the comparative negligence rule. In a thorough opinion, the court concluded that the pure form of comparative negligence was the most appropriate system. Justice Williams noted that while courts may not be the primary agencies for the adoption of principles of comparative negligence, they are "certainly in as good, if not better, a position to evaluate the need for change, and to fashion that change."[78] Since 1979 state supreme courts in West Virginia,[79] New Mexico,[80] Illinois,[81] Iowa,[82] Missouri[83] and Kentucky[84] have adopted comparative negligence.

Preference for Legislative Action

The most common argument against judicial implementation is that the matter is better left to the legislature.[85] Although contributory negligence was introduced by common-law decision, the argument runs, it has been with us so long and is so deeply engrained in the law that it has become a fundamental part of our jurisprudence, and only the legislature can change it.[86] Moreover, it is arguable that legislative inac-

---

[72]See V. Schwartz, *Comparative Negligence* § 21.7 (1974).

[73]Hoffman v. Jones, 280 So. 2d 431, 78 A.L.R.3d 321 (Fla. 1973).

[74]Kaatz v. State, 540 P.2d 1037 (Alaska 1975).

[75]Nga Li v. Yellow Cab Co., 13 Cal. 3d 804, 119 Cal. Rptr. 858, 532 P.2d 1226, 78 A.L.R.3d 393 (1975).

[76]Kirby v. Larson, 400 Mich. 585, 256 N.W.2d 400 (1977).

[77]Placek v. Sterling Heights, 405 Mich. 638, 275 N.W.2d 511 (1979) (citing this treatise).

[78]Id., 275 N.W.2d at 518.

[79]Bradley v. Appalachian Power Co., 256 S.E.2d 879 (W.Va. 1979).

[80]Scott v. Rizzo, 96 N.M. 682, 634 P.2d 1234 (1981).

[81]Alvis v. Ribar, 85 Ill. 2d 1, 52 Ill. Dec. 23, 421 N.E.2d 886 (1981).

[82]Goetzman v. Wichern, 327 N.W.2d 742 (Iowa 1982).

[83]Gustafson v. Benda, 661 S.W.2d 11 (Mo. 1983).

[84]Hilen v. Hays, 673 S.W.2d 713 (Ky. 1984).

[85]Harrison v. Montgomery County Bd. of Education, 295 Md. 442, 456 A.2d 894 (1983); McGraw v. Corrin, 303 A.2d 641 (Del. 1973); Loui v. Oakley, 50 Hawaii 260, 50 Hawaii 272, 438 P.2d 393 (1968); Maki v. Frelk, 40 Ill. 2d 193, 239 N.E.2d 445, 32 A.L.R.3d 452 (1968); Haeg v. Sprague, Warner & Co., 202 Minn. 425, 281 N.W.261 (1938); Krise v. Gillund, 184 N.W.2d 405 (N.D. 1971); Peterson v. Culp, 255 Ore. 269, 465 P.2d 876 (1970).

In all of these states except Maryland the legislatures subsequently enacted comparative negligence statutes. See section 1.4.

[86]See Maki v. Frelk, 40 Ill. 2d 193, 239 N.E.2d 445, 32 A.L.R.3d 452 (1968).

tion, especially outright failure to pass comparative negligence statutes, evinces a legislative intention to retain contributory negligence.[87]

Precedent for Judicial Changes in Tort Law

In recent years the judiciary in many states have weeded many anachronistic doctrines out of the law of torts. These include the rule protecting charities from their negligence,[88] the doctrine that the plaintiff must have suffered physical impact before he can recover for negligent infliction of emotional harm[89] and decisions that prevented an infant from recovering for injuries received while in the womb.[90] Nevertheless, it has been suggested by courts that the change from contributory to comparative negligence is so pervasive—it potentially affects every negligence case—that the courts should be very hesitant to make a change.[91] Further, it is contended that the need for the change is lessened by the fact that the contributory negligence doctrine has been ameliorated in almost every state.[92]

The most important distinction between judicial adoption of comparative negligence and a number of the other major judge-made changes of the past two decades is the very difficult problem of formulating an alternative rule.[93] What form of comparative negligence is to be chosen? Is it to be pure comparative negligence as in Florida, Mississippi, California and eleven other states?[94] If it is to be modified comparative negligence—the approach taken by the majority of states with legislation on the subject—[95] which type should be selected: the simple equal division system,[96] or the rule that precludes the plaintiff from any recovery if his negligence equals that of defendant?[97] Or should the rule that requires abrogation of plaintiff's claim only when he is *more* negligent than defendant be adopted?[98]

Adoption of Entire System

The choice before the court involves more than selecting case law from another jurisdiction. Comparative negligence is usually statutory. The court must do more than reason from a statute, a judicial practice

---

[87]See Henthorne v. Hopwood, 218 Ore. 336, 338 P.2d 373, 378 (1959) (concurring opinion of Justice O'Connell).

[88]See W. P. Keeton et al., *Prosser and Keeton on the Law of Torts* § 133 (5th ed. 1984).

[89]Id., at § 54.

[90]Id., at § 55.

[91]See Maki v. Frelk, 40 Ill. 2d 193, 239 N.E.2d 445, 32 A.L.R.3d 452 (1968). See also cases cited in note 77 above.

[92]See section 1.2, outlining ways in which courts have mitigated the contributory negligence defense.

[93]See Krise v. Gillund, 184 N.W.2d 405 (N.D. 1971) (explicitly relying on difficulty in selecting an alternative system in declining to make the change).

[94]See section 3.2.

[95]See sections 3.3 to 3.5.

[96]See section 3.3.

[97]See section 3.5.

[98]Id. Once a legislature has spoken, courts are reluctant to change to another form. See Vincent v. Pabst Brewing Co., 47 Wis. 2d 120, 177 N.W.2d 513 (1970).

that has received carefully articulated support.[99] Rather, the court must adopt an entire statutory system, an act that goes beyond the traditional bounds of case-law decision.[1]

The choice before the court is even more complicated, in the long run, than a selection from the numerous forms of comparative negligence. Once a system is selected, the court will be faced with many questions in future decisions. For example, should the change be retroactive?[2] Should assumption of the risk still be a defense?[3] How are cases involving third parties to be handled?[4]

Up until the mid-1970's the overwhelming majority of courts saw the abyss and left the role of change to the legislature,[5] but that trend has been reversed.

21.7 The arguments for judicial adoption of comparative negligence

Arguments in favor of judicial implementation of a comparative negligence system begin with the fundamental fact that the contributory negligence defense was created by the courts. Therefore, it is argued, it can be judicially excised or modified.

Judicial Origins of Contributory Negligence as Bar

Statements like that of the Minnesota Supreme Court that "the rule of contributory negligence, through no fault of ours, remains in our law"[6] are simply in contravention of documented legal history. The contributory negligence defense began with *Butterfield v. Forrester*[7] and was implemented in this country by judicial decision, sometimes with little thought or discussion.[8] In 1984 the South Carolina Court of Appeals attempted to adopt comparative negligence and abolish the contributory negligence defense.[8a] The court noted that *Freer v. Cameron*,[8b] the first South Carolina opinion to mention contributory negligence, held it to be *inapplicable* to the facts of that case. Despite this holding, *Freer*—an 1850 case—was "applied unchallenged"[8c] thereafter, as if it were a fountainhead of the defense. In 1985 the state's supreme

---

[99]See Landis, "Statutes and the Sources of Law," *Harvard Legal Essays* 213 (R. Pound ed. 1934); Stone, *The Common Law in the United States*, 50 Harv. L. Rev. 4 (1936).

[1]Symposium, *Comments on Maki v. Frelk—Comparative v. Contributory Negligence: Should the Court or Legislature Decide?*, 21 Vand. L. Rev., at 899.

[2]See section 8.2.

[3]See Chapter 9.

[4]See Chapter 16.

[5]See cases cited in note 78 above. But see Hoffman v. Jones, 280 So. 2d 431, 78 A.L.R.3d 321 (Fla. 1973).

[6]Haeg v. Sprague, Warner & Co., 202 Minn. 425, 429, 281 N.W. 261, 263 (1938).

[7]Butterfield v. Forrester, 11 East 60, 103 Eng. Rep. 926 (1809).

[8]See Juenger, *Brief for Negligence Law Section of the State Bar of Michigan in Support of Comparative Negligence as Amicus Curiae*, 18 Wayne L. Rev. 3, 9 (1972), citing Smith v. Smith, 19 Mass. 621 (1824).

[8a]Langley v. Boyter, 325 S.E.2d 550 (S.C. App. 1984).

[8b]Freer v. Cameron, 38 S.C.L. (4 Rich.) 228, 232 (1850).

[8c]Langley v. Boyter, 325 S.E.2d at 561.

court, in quashing the appellate court's adoption of comparative negligence on jurisdictional grounds, once again characterized the contributory negligence rule as "a basic, well-established law."[8d] The common-law doctrine of stare decisis places value on judicial precedent. Nevertheless, when the reasons for a judge-made rule fail, courts adopt rational alternatives.

Contributory Negligence Defense Outmoded

It is almost universally agreed,[9] even by courts that have declined to implement comparative negligence,[10] that the contributory negligence defense is outmoded.

In shifting from contributory negligence to a system of comparative negligence, the Supreme Court of West Virginia in *Bradley v. Appalachian Power Company*[11] chose to adopt the modified rather than the pure form, thus becoming the first high court to adopt the "equal to or greater than" 50% system. The court deemed the pure comparative negligence rule "permissive," "extreme" and having "basic inequities;" it was unwilling to abandon the idea that a party who substantially contributes to his injury should not be permitted to recover for any part of them. The court defined a substantially negligent plaintiff as one whose "contributory negligence is equal to or above 50% of the combined negligence of the parties to the accident."[12] This intermediate position was preferred by the court because it would not involve a radical change in the state's fault-based system.

The Supreme Court of New Mexico in *Scott v. Rizzo*[13] adopted in toto the opinion of Judge Walters of the New Mexico Court of Appeals, thereby adopting comparative negligence as the law of the state. The opinion provides an excellent analysis of the issue of comparative negligence. In answer to the argument that its adoption should be made by the legislature, Judge Walters concluded that contributory negligence

---

[8d]Langley v. Boyter, 332 S.E.2d 100, 101 (S.C. 1985).

[9]See American Trial Lawyers Association, *Comparative Negligence* (ATL Monograph Series, W. Schwartz ed. 1970); Prosser, *Comparative Negligence*, 51 Mich. L. Rev. 465, 469 (1953); F. Harper & F. James, *The Law of Torts* 1193-1209 (1956). Even defense counsel does not oppose comparative negligence. See Defense Research Institute, *Pamphlet No. 8, Responsible Reform: An Update* 15 (1972) (recommending it as a matter for local option, but expressing a preference for the Wisconsin system).

[10]Haeg v. Sprague, Warner & Co., 202 Minn. 425, 429-430, 281 N.W. 261, 263 (1938). See also Street v. Calvert, 541 S.W.2d 576, 586-87 (Tenn. 1976); Wenatchee Wenoka Growers Assn. v. Krack Corp., 89 Wash. 2d 847, 576 P.2d 388 (1978) (comparative negligence system represents attempt to achieve greater fairness); State v. Kaatz, 572 P.2d 775 (Alaska 1977) (citing this treatise). But see Harrison v. Montgomery County Bd. of Education, 295 Md. 442, 456 A.2d 894, 905 (1983) ("we are unable to say that the circumstances of modern life have so changed as to render contributory negligence a vestige of the past, no longer suitable to the needs of the people of Maryland").

[11]Bradley v. Appalachian Power Co., 163 W. Va. 332, 256 S.E.2d 879 (1979) (citing this treatise).

[12]Id., 256 S.E.2d at 887, n.19.

[13]Scott v. Rizzo, 96 N.M. 682, 634 P.2d 1234 (N.M. 1981).

is a "rule peculiarly for the courts to change if it is no longer validly justified."

There is no longer a need to protect infant industry. As the Illinois Supreme Court, when it adopted pure comparative negligence, pointed out, most workplace accidents now come under workers' compensation, in which the victim's conduct is not an issue.[14] In light of the fact that most defendants are insured against their acts of negligence, the contributory negligence defense produces a very poor allocation of costs in negligence cases. In fact, the unjust results worked by the contributory negligence defense have provided one of the most signficant arguments on behalf of those in favor of a no-fault system for apportioning the costs of automobile accidents.[15]

Justice Black, speaking for the Supreme Court of the United States in *Pope and Talbot, Incorporated v. Hawn*[16] stated that:

> The harsh rule of the common law under which contributory negligence wholly barred an injured person from recovery is completely incompatible with modern admiralty policy and practice.[17]

Judge Hallows of Wisconsin has said that "perhaps the doctrine of contributory negligence has done more to deny justice to the injured person than any other one legal concept."[18] This is why advocates of no-fault systems place such reliance on the doctrine in arguing for abolition of the entire fault system in automobile negligence cases.

Ineffectiveness of Modifications

The injustice of the contributory negligence defense can manifest itself in spite of modifications. In the cases where plaintiff sought to have the court change from contributory to comparative negligence, there apparently was no safety device by which to allow a seriously injured negligent plaintiff any recovery.[19] Commonsense judgments have suggested that juries almost always modify the contributory negligence defense and apply a de facto comparative negligence system;[20]

---

[14]Alvis v. Ribar, 85 Ill. 2d 1, 52 Ill. Dec. 23, 421 N.E.2d 886, 893 (1981).

[15]See R. Keeton & J. O'Connell, *Basic Protection for the Traffic Victim; A Blueprint for Reforming Automobile Insurance* 1 (1965).

[16]Pope & Talbot, Inc. v. Hawn, 346 U.S. 406, 98 L. Ed. 143, 74 S. Ct. 202 (1953).

[17]Id., 346 U.S. at 408, 409, 74 S. Ct. at 204.

[18]Hallows, *Comparative Negligence: Is It the Answer?*, 19 Fed'n Ins. Couns. Q. 71, 72 (Spring 1969).

[19]See Loui v. Oakley, 50 Hawaii 260, 50 Hawaii 272, 438 P.2d 393 (1968); Maki v. Frelk, 40 Ill. 2d 193, 239 N.E.2d 445, 32 A.L.R.3d 452 (1968); Haeg v. Sprague, Warner & Co., 202 Minn. 425, 281 N.W. 261 (1938); Krise v. Gillund, 184 N.W.2d 405 (N.D. 1971).

[20]See Alibrandi v. Helmsley, 63 Misc. 2d 997, 314 N.Y.S.2d 95 (1970) ("... as every trial lawyer knows, the jury would likely have ignored its instructions on contributory negligence and applied a standard of comparative negligence"; judge, acting as the trier of fact, felt compelled to apply the contributory negligence defense); J. Ulman, *A Judge Takes the Stand* 30-34 (1933).

but serious studies of the American jury suggest that they often respect the judge's charge and apply the defense to preclude recovery.[21]

Legislative Endorsement by Inaction

Some judges apparently still believe that legislative action is the answer. They may believe that legislative inaction is tantamount to endorsement of the contributory negligence defense. To the contrary, it is arguable that unless the current legislature has specifically rejected a comparative negligence law, there is no legislative imprimatur on the issue. Until the legislature does enact a statute endorsing contributory negligence, the area is open for judicial decision.

In the early 1980's state supreme courts began to interpret legislative inaction not as an endorsement of the contributory negligence defense but as stalemate. The Illinois Supreme Court noted that six comparative negligence bills had been introduced in the legislature between 1976 and 1979 and interpreted inaction on them as the legislature's deferral to the judiciary.[22] The Missouri Supreme Court, citing Professor James, suggested that legislative inaction "reflects inertia rather than community sentiment."[23]

Precedents for Judicial Change in Tort Law

As Professor Robert Keeton has suggested, courts of last resort have not failed in the past ten years to rid tort law of outmoded and unjust common-law rules.[24] A number of such changes are less complex and pervasive than the shift from contributory to comparative negligence; nevertheless, several recent decisions represent very fundamental changes. For example, the Supreme Court of California in *Rowland v. Christian*[25] rejected the common-law categories of trespasser, licensee and invitee as the ultimate vehicle for formulating the duty of a landholder to persons who come on his property. This decision, as would be the case in a change from contributory to comparative negligence, creates a problem of fashioning an alternative rule. Nevertheless, it has gained growing acceptance by courts.[26]

Similarly, many courts have abolished intrafamily immunities,[27] even though this creates special problems in defining the obligations of

---

[21]See Symposium, *Comments on Maki v. Frelk—Comparative v. Contributory Negligence: Should the Court or Legislature Decide?*, 21 Vand. L. Rev. 889, 897, 902-903 (1968). See also the *Alibrandi* case, note 20 above, where a judge acting as trier of fact felt compelled to apply the defense.

[22]Alvis v. Ribar, 85 Ill. 2d 1, 52 Ill. Dec. 23, 421 N.E.2d 886, 895-896 (1981).

[23]Gustafson v. Benda, 661 S.W.2d 11, 15 (Mo. 1983).

[24]Keeton, *Creative Continuity in the Law of Torts*, 75 Harv. L. Rev. 463 (1962) (collecting more than ninety overruling decisions on more than thirty separate rules of tort law).

[25]Rowland v. Christian, 69 Cal. 2d 108, 70 Cal. Rptr. 97, 443 P.2d 561, 32 A.L.R.3d 496 (1968).

[26]See Pickard v. City and County of Honolulu, 51 Hawaii 134, 452 P.2d 445 (1969).

[27]See *Restatement (Second) of Torts* § 895 G and H (1979).

family members toward one another.[28] In fact, almost every rejection of a deep-seated common-law rule forces a court to fashion an alternative approach. This need to develop a new rule occurred with the adoption of the last clear chance doctrine; nevertheless, some form was selected and evolved in almost every jurisdiction in the United States.[29]

Statute Underlying Judicial Change

A court adopting a new rule may use a statute, rather than a case, as the basis for it. This has been done in the area of contribution among joint tortfeasors without creating a serious crisis;[30] it could also be done in judicially adopting comparative negligence.

An even more persuasive precedent is a decision of the Supreme Court of the United States.[31] The late Mr. Justice Harlan, a man who was particularly sensitive to the precise roles of courts and legislatures, held for a unanimous court that the judiciary could create an action for wrongful death under federal maritime law. In order to do this, the federal courts had to look to legislation in other areas to fashion a remedy. This did not trouble Justice Harlan. He said:

> It has always been the duty of the common-law court to perceive the impact of major legislative innovations and to interweave the new legislative policies with the inherited body of common-law principles—many of them deriving from earlier legislative exertions.[32]

The number of issues requiring consideration in wrongful death actions is certainly as great as in comparative negligence.[33] Nevertheless, the court was not troubled by problems such as who should be the beneficiaries or how damages should be formulated or how a statute of limitations should be founded. The court said it would not be "without persuasive [statutory] analogy for guidance."[34] The same approach could be taken by a court in dealing with the topic of comparative negligence. In effect, the Supreme Court of Hawaii appeared ready to do so if the legislature did not act.[35]

Two state courts have relied at least in part on the Uniform Comparative Fault Act, set out in section 21.4, in shaping a comparative negligence doctrine. The Kentucky Supreme Court adopted the Uniform Act's jury instructions but explicitly made only that portion of

---

[28]See Cole v. Sears, Roebuck & Co., 47 Wis. 2d 629, 177 N.W.2d 866 (1970); Lemmen v. Servais, 39 Wis. 2d 75, 158 N.W.2d 341 (1968).

[29]See W. Prosser, *Handbook of the Law of Torts* § 66, at 429 (4th ed. 1971).

[30]Moyses v. Sparton Asphalt Paving Co., 383 Mich. 314, 174 N.W.2d 797, 806 (1970).

[31]Moragne v. States Marine Lines, Inc., 398 U.S. 375, 26 L. Ed. 2d 339, 90 S. Ct. 1772 (1970).

[32]Id., 398 U.S. at 392, 90 S. Ct. at 1783.

[33]See Speiser, *Recovery for Wrongful Death* (2d ed. 1975).

[34]Moragne v. States Marine Lines, Inc., note 31 above, 398 U.S. at 408, 90 S. Ct. at 1792.

[35]Loui v. Oakley, 50 Hawaii 260, 265 n.5, 50 Hawaii 272, 438 P.2d 393, 397 n.5 (1968). The legislature did act the following year. 1969 Hawaii Laws, ch. 227, § 1, codified at Hawaii Rev. Stat., § 663-31.

the Act applicable in Kentucky at that time.[36] The Missouri Supreme Court, however, directed that all future cases would be decided according to the Act except where it conflicted with an existing contribution statute.[37]

Precedent for Judicial Adoption of Comparative Negligence

As of early 1985, ten state supreme courts had adopted comparative negligence.[38] Even before the Florida decision introducing comparative negligence,[39] there was strong precedent for implementation of such a system by the judiciary. For over a hundred years the courts of Georgia have fashioned their own workable comparative negligence system.[40] Those courts originally relied on two statutes (one dealing exclusively with railroads) to fashion their decisions.[41] Dean Prosser has properly called the original cases a "remarkable tour de force of construction."[42]

Finally, it should be noted that the federal courts have, by pure case-law decision, fashioned two comparative negligence systems in the area of admiralty law.[43] Those courts have been able to implement the rules by judicial decision and are unlikely ever to retreat from the "fairer and more flexible rule which allows such consideration of contributory negligence in mitigation of damages as justice requires."[44]

Collateral Legal Problems

It is true that once a comparative negligence system is adopted, many new and challenging legal problems may arise. For example, it must be determined whether assumption of the risk is ground for apportionment,[45] or whether the doctrine of last clear chance will survive.[46] Existence of these problems does not suggest, however, that implementation of comparative negligence must await legislative action. In the majority of cases where the legislature has implemented comparative negligence, it has not chosen to resolve these problems.[47] The courts still must resolve these matters on the basis of common-law

---

[36]Hilen v. Hays, 673 S.W.2d 713, 720 (Ky. 1984).

[37]Gustafson v. Benda, 661 S.W.2d 11, 16-17 (Mo. 1983).

[38]See section 1.5.

[39]Hoffman v. Jones, 280 So. 2d 431, 78 A.L.R.3d 321 (Fla. 1973).

[40]See Macon & W. R. Co. v. Winn, 26 Ga. 250, 254 (1858); Flanders v. Meath, 27 Ga. 358, 361-362 (1859); Seagraves v. Abco Mfg. Co., 118 Ga. App. 414, 164 S.E.2d 242 (1968); Hilkey, *Comparative Negligence in Georgia*, 8 Georgia B.A.J. 51 (1945).

[41]See cases cited in note 40 above. Currently, the statutes are Ga. Code Ann., §§ 46-8-291 and 51-11-7.

[42]W. P. Keeton et al., *Prosser and Keeton on the Law of Torts* § 67, at 471 (5th ed. 1984).

[43]See section 3.3.

[44]Pope & Talbot, Inc. v. Hawn, 346 U.S. 406, 409, 98 L. Ed. 143, 74 S. Ct. 202, 205 (1953).

[45]See section 9.4.

[46]See section 7.1.

[47]Federal Employers' Liability Act of April 22, 1908, ch. 149, § 3, 35 Stat. 66, 45 U.S.C. 53; Miss. Code Ann., § 11-7-15; Wis. Stat. Ann., § 895.045.

decision. Since this is the case, the courts should not hesitate to adopt a comparative negligence system that they believe to be just.

21.8 Judicial change from modified to pure comparative negligence

Just as there is authority for judicial abolition of the contributory negligence defense and substitution of comparative negligence, so it can be argued that a court can adopt pure comparative negligence even though a previous court or a legislature has adopted a modified form, whether the 50% form, the slight-gross form or equal division.[48] In *United States v. Reliable Transfer Company*[49] the Supreme Court of the United States changed the judicially adopted equal division system[50] in admiralty to one of pure comparative negligence.

Statutory Construction Argument

The argument begins with the premise that all the legislature has done is to eliminate the contributory negligence defense in certain specified cases when, in the terms of the statute, plaintiff's negligence was less than, no greater than, or slight in comparison with defendant's negligence. This premise is supported by the fact that the operative language in a number of the statutes is "Contributory negligence shall not bar recovery in an action . . . if . . .".[51]

Arguably, the modified comparative negligence statutes that are framed in this way leave other cases—where plaintiff's negligence exceeded the statutory measure—subject to the common law. The courts then have the same power to adopt pure comparative negligence as if the legislature had not acted.

This argument based on statutory construction would not be available, of course, under a statute like Maine's, which specifically provides, "If each claimant is found by the jury to be equally at fault, the claimant shall not recover,"[52] or the Georgia statute stating that "If the plaintiff by ordinary care could have avoided the consequences . . . he is not entitled to recover."[53] But the curious fact is that most modified comparative negligence statutes are not so explicit.

---

[48]See Vincent v. Pabst Brewing Co., 47 Wis. 2d 120, 177 N.W.2d 513 (1970).

[49]United States v. Reliable Transfer Co., 421 U.S. 397, 44 L. Ed. 2d 251, 95 S. Ct. 1708 (1975).

[50]The Schooner Catharine v. Dickinson, 58 U.S. (17 How.) 170, 15 L. Ed. 233 (1855).

[51]Colo. Rev. Stat., § 13-21-111; Conn. Gen. Stat. Ann., § 52-572h; Del. Code Ann., tit. 10, § 8132; Hawaii Rev. Stat., § 663-31 (a); Idaho Code, § 6-801; Iowa Code Ann., § 668.3; Mass. Gen. Laws Ann., ch. 231, § 85; Minn. Stat. Ann., § 604.01, subd. 1; Nev. Rev. Stat., § 41.141; N.H. Rev. Stat. Ann., § 507:7-a; N.J. Stat. Ann., § 2A:15-5.1; N.D. Cent. Code, § 9-10-07; Ohio Rev. Code Ann., § 2315.19; Okla. Stat. Ann., tit. 23, § 11; Ore. Rev. Stat., § 18.470; Pa. Stat. Ann., tit. 42, § 7102; Tex. Rev. Civ. Stat. Ann. (Vernon), art. 2212a, § 1; Utah Code Ann., § 78-27-37; Vt. Stat. Ann., tit. 12, § 1036; Wis. Stat. Ann., § 895.045; Wyo. Stat., § 1-7.2. See also Ark. Stat. Ann., § 27-1764 ("Fault chargeable to a party claiming damages shall not bar recovery of damages . . . where . . ."); Neb. Rev. Stat., § 25-1151 and S.D. Codified Laws, § 20-9-2 ("the fact that the plaintiff may have been guilty of contributory negligence shall not bar a recovery when . . .").

[52]Me. Rev. Stat. Ann., tit. 14, § 156.

[53]Ga. Code Ann., § 51-11-7.

Vincent v. Pabst Brewing Company

In *Vincent v. Pabst Brewing Company*[54] this line of argument was presented in an attempt to persuade the Wisconsin Supreme Court to adopt pure comparative negligence by judicial decision. Four of the seven justices agreed that the court had the power to make the change despite legislative adoption of modified comparative negligence. However, three of the four thought it best to refrain from making the change because the Wisconsin legislature was then studying the question; they therefore concurred in the result reached by the other three justices who thought the legislature had pre-empted the question.[55] Chief Justice Hallows strongly dissented, however, arguing that the court ought to adopt pure comparative negligence then and there.[56]

In 1971, as a result of the study that was in process when *Vincent* was decided, the Wisconsin legislature amended that state's statute.[57] However, that amendment did not adopt pure comparative negligence. All it did was substitute "not greater than" for "not as great as," so that a plaintiff whose negligence was exactly 50% would not be barred.[58]

Lupie v. Hartzheim

In 1972, after the Wisconsin legislature had concluded its study and taken its limited action, the Wisconsin Supreme Court was again presented the basic question decided in *Vincent*, but in a somewhat different context. In *Lupie v. Hartzheim*,[59] the jury found the parties equally at fault, so that either under pure comparative negligence or under the 1971 amendment of the statute, plaintiff would have been able to recover half his damages. However, the accident in *Lupie* took place before the 1971 amendment, and it was conceded that the 1971 amendment was not intended to be retroactive.

The plaintiff in *Lupie* wanted the Wisconsin Supreme Court to use its inherent judicial power to extend recovery beyond the statutory requirement at least far enough to cover the 50% negligent plaintiff. Chief Justice Hallows reasserted his position that the court ought to adopt pure comparative negligence.[60] However, the other six justices declined to extend recovery beyond the former statutory requirements, which were in force at the time of the accident. They deferred to the legislature *as a matter of judicial discretion*.

Judicial Prerogative Asserted

It should be noted that although the Wisconsin Supreme Court declined in *Vincent* and *Lupie* to adopt pure comparative negligence

---

[54]Vincent v. Pabst Brewing Co., 47 Wis. 2d 120, 177 N.W.2d 513 (1970).
[55]Id.; opinions of Heffernan and Wilkie (Beilfuss concurring) 177 N.W.2d at 517-518.
[56]Id., 177 N.W.2d at 518-523.
[57]1971 Wis. Laws, ch. 47, amending Wis. Stat. Ann., § 895.045.
[58]See section 3.5, at note 71.
[59]Lupie v. Hartzheim, 54 Wis. 2d 415, 195 N.W.2d 461 (1972).
[60]Id., at 195 N.W.2d 462, citing his dissent in *Vincent* at 177 N.W.2d 518.

judicially, or even to extend recovery retroactively to the 50% negligent plaintiff, the writer of the majority opinion in *Lupie* was careful to note that

> [T]he majority of the court reasserts the authority to make such change and adheres to its position that passage of the comparative negligence act has not divested this court of its inherent common-law prerogative of reconsidering matters that stem from judicial decision.[61]

Even though the court in *Vincent* and *Lupie* declined, in view of the legislative activity at the time, to adopt pure comparative negligence, the concurring and dissenting opinions in *Vincent* and *Lupie* provide good authority that a court has the *power* to adopt pure comparative negligence even after the legislature has enacted a modified rule.

21.9 Comparative negligence as a legislative-judicial enterprise

Even though a court may have the power to adopt comparative negligence by judicial decision, the policy considerations involved in selection of the best system, as well as the problems of adjusting collateral legal doctrines, suggest that the legislature is best equipped to make the change. The legislature has the power, and probably better resources, to make a concerted study of the growing number of legislative alternatives in the various states and foreign countries. It may be able to determine the effect of comparative negligence on insurance rates in the state.[62] It can put lawyers' minds at ease with respect to such uncertainties as retroactivity and the handling of third-party practice.

Obviously, the legislature cannot anticipate and resolve every legal problem that may arise under comparative negligence. Some questions will inevitably be left for the courts. Nevertheless, the legislature can take advantage of the long experience of states such as Wisconsin and Mississippi and can provide some guidelines. An example of a model statute which does this is set out in section 21.4.

Ideally, the implementation of comparative negligence should be a joint legislative-judicial enterprise. The legislature should take the initiative and should provide the basic policy and guidelines for collateral issues. The courts then should fill in the gaps as they become apparent in the cases and should reconcile the new principles with the existing jurisprudence. However, the need for comparative negligence is great; if a legislature fails to act, a court should take the initiative in order to preserve the fault system as a means of distributing loss.

---

[61]Id., at 195 N.W.2d 462.

[62]See Rosenberg, *Comparative Negligence in Arkansas: A "Before and After" Survey,* 13 Ark. L. Rev. 89 (1959); Peck, *Comparative Negligence and Automobile Liability Insurance,* 58 Mich. L. Rev. 689 (1960).

The Hawaiian History

A method by which a court concerned with this problem might take the initiative is suggested by the action of the Supreme Court of Hawaii in *Loui v. Oakley*.[63] On its facts, that case did not directly involve the contributory negligence defense; rather, the issues concerned proximate cause and responsibility for injuries aggravated by subsequent accidents. The court nevertheless appended to its opinion a gratuitous footnote saying:

> It may be time to reconsider the applicability of the doctrine of contributory negligence, a judge-made rule, in light of the mores of the day. Perhaps it should be judicially replaced by a comparative negligence standard, as an Illinois court has done after concluding that the doctrine of contributory negligence is "unsound and unjust under present conditions," and that courts have "not only the right, but the duty to abolish the defense."[64]

After the decision in *Loui v. Oakley*, the legislature of Hawaii took the hint and enacted a modified comparative negligence statute[65] which resolved a few of the major problems and left others for the judiciary. The general approach taken by the Supreme Court of Hawaii suggests a method of initiating action to abolish the contributory negligence defense in other states.

The Iowa Direct Action Approach

The Iowa Supreme Court chose a more direct approach: after hinting strongly at the need for comparative fault,[66] the court adopted pure comparative negligence in 1982.[67] Two years later the Iowa legislature adopted a comprehensive modified comparative negligence statute dealing with strict liability, assumption of risk, control of fact finding and multiple defendants.[68]

21.10 Conclusion

This book is primarily for practicing lawyers and is intended to be practical. Nevertheless, it provides empirical evidence of the very delicate nature of the common law. The book demonstrates how the modification of one basic principle—that a plaintiff's claim for negligence is

---

[63]Loui v. Oakley, 50 Hawaii 260, 50 Hawaii 272, 438 P.2d 393 (1968).

[64]Id., 50 Hawaii at 265 n.5, 438 P.2d at 397 n.5, citing the intermediate court decision in Maki v. Frelk, 85 Ill. App. 2d 439, 229 N.E.2d 284 (1967), which was later reversed at 40 Ill. 2d 193, 239 N.E.2d 445, 32 A.L.R.3d 452 (1968). See subsection 1.5(C). See also Peterson v. Culp, 255 Ore. 269, 465 P.2d 876, 878 (1970), concurring opinion of Mr. Justice Denecke: "If the legislature is inactive on this subject I would favor reexamining the problem."

[65]Hawaii Rev. Stat., § 663-31. See Bissen v. Fujii, 51 Hawaii 636, 466 P.2d 429 (1970).

[66]Fuller v. Buhrow, 292 N.W.2d 672 (Iowa 1980); Stewart v. Madison, 278 N.W.2d 284 (Iowa 1979).

[67]Goetzman v. Wichern, 327 N.W.2d 742 (Iowa 1982).

[68]1984 Iowa Laws, H.B. 2487, codified at Iowa Code Ann., ch. 668.

barred when he is at fault—may well require substantial changes throughout the entire law of torts.

It has taken many pages and hundreds of citations to show this total picture. Still, it must be recognized that it is impossible to predict in detail all of the changes in tort law that may be brought about by comparative negligence. As was true after the publication of the first edition of this treatise, courts will find new problems with comparative negligence in contexts that have not been covered here with absolute precision. This is why, as a modified version of the old saying goes, there are erasers on pencils and supplements to treatises. However, the reader should find guidelines that will help resolve most problems. It is hoped that this second edition will enjoy the good fortune of the first and that courts and practitioners will look to it for guidance to the resolution of new and unforeseen problems.

APPENDIX A

SUMMARY OF COMPARATIVE NEGLIGENCE SYSTEMS OF GENERAL APPLICATION IN AMERICAN JURISDICTIONS

State	Year of Adoption/Amendment	Current Code or Other Authority
Alaska	1975	Kaatz v. State, 540 P.2d 1037

Pure comparative negligence

| Arizona | 1984 | Ariz. Rev. Stat. Ann., §§ 12-2501 to 12-2509 |

Pure comparative negligence

| Arkansas | 1955/1957/ 1973/1975 | Ark. Stat. Ann., §§ 27-1763 to 27-1765 |

"fault ... is of less degree than the fault chargeable to the party or parties from whom the claiming party seeks to recover damages"

| California | 1975 | Nga Li v. Yellow Cab Co., 532 P.2d 1226 |

Pure comparative negligence

| Colorado | 1971/1975 | Colo. Rev. Stat., § 13-21-111 |

"not as great as the negligence of the person against whom recovery is sought"

| Connecticut | 1973/1977/1982 | Conn. Gen. Stat. Ann., § 52-572h |

"not greater than the combined negligence of the person or persons against whom recovery is sought"

| Delaware | 1984 | Del. Code Ann., tit. 10, § 8132 |

"not greater than the negligence of the defendant or the combined negligence of all defendants against whom recovery is sought"

| Florida | 1973 | Hoffman v. Jones, 280 So. 2d 431 |

Pure comparative negligence

| Georgia | 1855 (court decision); 1863 (stat.) | Macon & W. R. Co. v. Davis, 18 Ga. 679; Ga. Code Ann., §§ 46-8-291, 51-11-7 |

"by ordinary care could have avoided the consequences to himself caused by the defendant's negligence ... not entitled to recover ... other cases the defendant is not relieved, although the plaintiff may in some way have contributed to the injury sustained"

| Hawaii | 1969/1972/ 1975/1976 | Hawaii Rev. Stat., § 663-31 |

"not greater than the negligence of the person or ... the aggregate negligence of such persons against whom recovery is sought"

| Idaho | 1971 | Idaho Code, §§ 6-801 to 6-806 |

"not as great as the negligence or gross negligence of the person against whom recovery is sought"

| Illinois | 1981 | Alvis v. Ribar, 421 N.E.2d 886 |

Pure comparative negligence

Indiana   1983/1984   Ind. Code, §§ 34-4-33-1 to 34-4-33-
                          eff. 1/1/85   13
"claimant is barred from recovery if his contributory fault is greater than the fault of all persons whose fault proximately contributed to the claimant's damages"

Iowa   1982 (court decision);   Goetzman v. Wichern, 372 N.W.2d
                          1984 (stat.)   742; Iowa Code Ann., §§ 668.1 to
                                                   668.10
"Contributory fault shall not bar recovery . . . unless the claimant bears a greater percentage of fault than the combined percentage of fault attributed to the defendants, third party defendants, and persons who have been released"

Kansas   1974/1976   Kan. Stat. Ann., §§ 60-258a, 60-
                                                 258b
"was less than the causal negligence of the party or parties against whom claim for recovery is made"

Kentucky   1984   Hilen v. Hays, 673 S.W.2d 713
Pure comparative negligence

Louisiana   1979   La. Civ. Code Ann., art. 2323
                          eff. 8/1/80
Pure comparative negligence

Maine   1965/1969/1971   Me. Rev. Stat. Ann., tit. 14, § 156
"equally at fault . . . shall not recover"

Massachusetts   1969/1973   Mass. Gen. Laws Ann., ch. 231,
                                                 § 85
"not greater than the total amount of negligence attributable to the person or persons against whom recovery is sought"

Michigan   1979   Placek v. Sterling Heights, 275
                                                 N.W.2d 511
Pure comparative negligence

Minnesota   1969/1978   Minn. Stat. Ann., §§ 604.01, 604.02
"contributory fault was not greater than the fault of the person against whom recovery is sought"

Mississippi   1910/1920   Miss. Code Ann., § 11-7-15
Pure comparative negligence

Missouri   1983   Gustafson v. Benda, 661 S.W.2d 11
Pure comparative negligence

Montana   1975/1977/1981   Mont. Code Ann., §§ 27-1-702, 27-
                                                 1-703
"not greater than the negligence of the person against whom recovery is sought"

Nebraska   1913/1978   Neb. Rev. Stat., § 25-1151
"contributory negligence of the plaintiff was slight and the negligence . . . of the defendant was gross in comparison"

Nevada   1973/1979   Nev. Rev. Stat., § 41.141
"not greater than the negligence or gross negligence of the person or persons against whom recovery is sought"

New Hampshire   1969/1970   N.H. Rev. Stat. Ann., § 507:7-a "not greater than the causal negligence of the defendant"

New Jersey   1973/1982   N.J. Stat. Ann., §§ 2A:15-5.1 to
2A:15-5.3

"not greater than the negligence of the person against whom recovery is sought"

New Mexico   1981   Scott v. Rizzo, 634 P.2d 1234
Pure comparative negligence

New York   1975   N.Y. Civ. Prac. Law, §§ 1411 to
1413

Pure comparative negligence

North Dakota   1973   N.D. Cent. Code, § 9-10-07
"not as great as the negligence of the person against whom recovery is sought"

Ohio   1980   Ohio Rev. Code Ann., § 2315.19
"no greater than the combined negligence of all other persons from whom recovery is sought"

Oklahoma   1973/1979   Okla. Stat. Ann., tit. 23, §§ 12 to
14
"shall not bar a recovery, unless any negligence of the person ... is of greater degree than the combined negligence of any persons ... causing such damage"

Oregon   1971/1975/1981   Ore. Rev. Stat., §§ 18.470 to 18.510
"not greater than the combined fault of the person or persons against whom recovery is sought"

Pennsylvania   1976/1978/   Pa. Stat. Ann., tit. 42, § 7102
1980/1982
"not greater than the causal negligence of the defendant or defendants against whom recovery is sought"

Puerto Rico   1956   P.R. Laws Ann., tit. 31, § 5141
Pure comparative negligence

Rhode Island   1971/1972   R.I. Gen Laws, §§ 9-20-4, 9-20-4.1
Pure comparative negligence

South Dakota   1941/1964   S.D. Codified Laws, § 20-9-2
"contributory negligence shall not bar recovery when ... slight in comparison with the negligence of the defendant"

Texas   1973   Tex. Rev. Civ. Stat. Ann.
(Vernon), art. 2212a
"not greater than the negligence of the person or party or persons or parties against whom recovery is sought"

Utah   1973   Utah Code Ann., §§ 78-27-37 to 78-27-43
"not as great as the negligence or gross negligence of the person against whom recovery is sought"

Vermont   1969/1979   Vt. Stat. Ann., tit. 12, § 1036
eff. 1970
"not greater than the causal total negligence of the defendant or defendants"

Virgin Islands   1973   V.I. Code Ann., tit. 5, § 1451
"claimant ... more at fault than the defendant, or, in the case of multiple defendants, more at fault than the combined fault of the defendants, the claimant may not recover"

Washington   1973/1981   Wash. Rev. Code Ann., §§ 4.22.005 to 4.22.020

Pure comparative negligence

West Virginia   1979   Bradley v. Appalachian Power Co., 256 S.E.2d 879
"negligence ... does not exceed or equal combined negligence ... of the other parties"

Wisconsin   1931/1949/   Wis. Stat. Ann., § 895.045
                      1965/1971
"not greater than the negligence of the person against whom recovery is sought"

Wyoming   1973/1977   Wyo. Stat., §§ 1-1-109 to 1-1-113
"not as great as the negligence of the person against whom recovery is sought"

TEXT OF COMPARATIVE NEGLIGENCE STATUTES

ARIZONA
Ariz. Rev. Stat. Ann., §§ 12-2501 to 12-2509 (S.L. 1984, ch. 237, § 1)

12-2501. Right to contribution.

A. Except as otherwise provided in this article, if two or more persons become jointly or severally liable in tort for the same injury to person or property or for the same wrongful death, there is a right of contribution among them even though judgment has not been recovered against all or any of them.

B. The right of contribution exists only in favor of a tortfeasor who has paid more than his pro rata share of the common liability, and his total recovery is limited to the amount paid by him in excess of his pro rata share. No tortfeasor is compelled to make contribution beyond his own pro rata share of the entire liability.

C. There is no right of contribution in favor of any tortfeasor who the trier of fact finds has intentionally, wilfully or wantonly caused or contributed to the injury or wrongful death.

D. A tortfeasor who enters into a settlement with a claimant is not entitled to recover contribution from another tortfeasor whose liability for the injury or wrongful death is not extinguished by the settlement nor in respect to any amount paid in a settlement which is in excess of what was reasonable.

E. A liability insurer, which by payment has discharged in full or in part the liability of a tortfeasor and has thereby discharged in full its obligation as insurer, is subrogated to the tortfeasor's right of contribution to the extent of the amount it has paid in excess of the tortfeasor's pro rata share of the common liability. This subsection does not limit or impair any right of subrogation arising from any other relationship.

F. This article does not impair any right of indemnity under existing law. If one tortfeasor is entitled to indemnity from another, the right of the indemnity obligee is for indemnity and not contribution, and the indemnity obligor is not entitled to contribution from any obligee for any portion of his indemnity obligation.

G. This article does not apply to breaches of trust or of other fiduciary obligation.

H. This article does not create a right of contribution against an employer or other person who has paid or who is liable for workmen's compensation in connection with an injury or death pursuant to title 23, chapter 6, unless the employer or other person is subject to direct suit under § 23-1022. For purposes of determining the amount of pro rata shares under this article, any employer or other person who has paid or who is liable for workmen's compensation shall not be considered unless the employer or other person is subject to direct suit under § 23-1022.

12-2502. Pro rata shares. In determining the pro rata share of tortfeasors in the entire liability:

1. Their relative degrees of fault are the basis for allocation.

2. If equity requires, the collective liability of some as a group constitutes a single share.

3. Principles of equity applicable to contribution generally apply.

12-2503. Enforcement.

A. Whether or not judgment has been entered in an action against two or more tortfeasors for the same injury or wrongful death, contribution may be enforced by separate action.

B. If a judgment has been entered in an action against two or more tortfeasors for the same injury or wrongful death, contribution may be enforced in that action by judgment in favor of one against other judgment defendants by motion on notice to all parties to the action.

C. If there is a judgment for the injury or wrongful death against the tortfeasor seeking contribution, any separate action by him to enforce contribution must be commenced within one year after the judgment has become final by lapse of time for appeal or after appellate review.

D. If there is no judgment for the injury or wrongful death against the tortfeasor seeking contribution, his right of contribution is barred unless he has either:

1. Discharged by payment the common liability within the statute of limitations period applicable to the claimant's right of action against him and has commenced his action for contribution within one year after payment.

2. Agreed while action is pending against him to discharge the common liability and has within one year after the agreement paid the liability and commenced his action for contribution.

E. The recovery of a judgment for an injury or wrongful death against one tortfeasor does not of itself discharge the other tortfeasors from liability for the injury or wrongful death unless the judgment is satisfied. The satisfaction of the judgment does not impair a right of contribution.

F. The judgment of the court in determining the liability of the several defendants to the claimant for an injury or wrongful death is binding as among the defendants in determining their right to contribution. If the claimant's case is tried, the trier of fact shall apportion and determine the respective degrees of fault of the defendants to the action.

12-2504. Release or convenant not to sue. If a release or a covenant not to sue or not to enforce judgment is given in good faith to one of two or more persons liable in tort for the same injury or the same wrongful death both of the following apply:

1. It does not discharge any of the other tortfeasors from liability for the injury or wrongful death unless its terms so provide, but it reduces the claim against the others to the extent of any amount stipulated by the release or the covenant or in the amount of the consideration paid for it, whichever is the greater.

2. It discharges the tortfeasor to whom it is given from all liability for contribution to any other tortfeasor.

12-2505. Comparative negligence; definition.

A. The defense of contributory negligence or of assumption of risk is in all cases a question of fact and shall at all times be left to the jury. If the jury applies either defense, the claimant's action is not barred, but the full damages shall be reduced in proportion to the relative degree of the claimant's fault which is a proximate cause of the injury or death, if any. There is no right to comparative negligence in favor of any claimant who has intentionally, wilfully or wantonly caused or contributed to the injury or wrongful death.

B. In this section, "claimant's fault" includes the fault imputed or attributed to a claimant by operation of law, if any.

12-2506. Apportionment of degrees of fault.

A. The relative degree of fault of the claimant under § 12-2505 and the relative degrees of fault of all defendants under § 12-2503, subsection F shall be determined and apportioned as a whole at one time by the trier of fact.

B. If two or more claimants have independent claims, a separate determination and apportionment of the relative degrees of fault of the respective parties shall be made with respect to each of the independent claims.

12-2507. Treatment of counterclaims and cross claims. A counterclaim or cross claim for injury to person or property or for wrongful death shall be treated as an independent claim for purposes of § 12-2506. A claim and counterclaim shall not be set off against each other except by agreement of both parties.

12-2508. Redetermination of contribution shares. On motion made not later than one year after a judgment determining contribution rights is entered, the court shall determine whether all or part of a tortfeasor's contribution share under § 12-2502 is uncollectible from that tortfeasor. If a contribution share is totally or partially uncollectible, the court shall redetermine the contribution shares of the other tortfeasors so that the uncollectible contribution amount is paid, based on the ratio of the percentages of the contribution shares of the other tortfeasors. The court's order redetermining the contribution shares shall include a judgment for the uncollectible amount against the tortfeasor whose share is totally or partially uncollectible and in favor of the other tortfeasors.

12-2509. Scope of contribution and comparative negligence.
A. The right to contribution under §§ 12-2501 through 12-2504 applies to all tortfeasors whose liability is based on negligence, strict liability in tort or any product liability action, as defined in § 12-681, including warranty.
B. If an action involves claims for relief alleging both negligence and strict liability in tort, and if § 12-2505 is applied with respect to the negligence claims for relief, the reduction in damages under § 12-2505 shall be applied to the damages awarded against all defendants, except that contributory negligence, as distinguished from assumption of risk, is not a defense to a claim alleging strict liability in tort, including any product liability action, as defined in § 12-681, except claims alleging negligence.
C. For purposes of § 12-2502, § 12-2503, subsection F and § 12-2505 with respect to cases involving assumption of risk, the relative degree of fault of a person strictly liable in tort is the defect causing injury to the claimant. Among two or more persons strictly liable in tort who are entitled to claim contribution against each other, the relative degree of fault of each is the degree to which to each contributed to the defect causing injury to the claimant.

ARKANSAS
Ark. Stat. Ann., §§ 27-1763 to 27-1765 (as am. Acts 1975, No. 367, §§ 1-3)

27-1763. "Fault" defined. The word "fault" as used in this Act includes any act, omission, conduct, risk assumed, breach of warranty or breach of any legal duty which is a proximate cause of any damages sustained by any party.

27-1764. Liability determined by comparing fault. In all actions for damages for personal injuries or wrongful death or injury to property in which recovery is predicated upon fault, liability shall be determined by comparing the fault chargeable to a claiming party with the fault chargeable to the party or parties from whom the claiming party seeks to recover damages.

27-1765. Comparative fault to determine amount of recovery. If the fault chargeable to a party claiming damages is of less degree than the fault chargeable to the party or parties from whom the claiming party seeks to recover damages, then the claiming party is entitled to recover the amount of his damages after they have been diminished in proportion to the degree of his own fault. If the fault chargeable to a party claiming damages is equal to or greater in degree than any fault chargeable to the party or parties from whom the claiming party seeks to recover damages, then the claiming party is not entitled to recover such damages.

COLORADO
Colo. Rev. Stat., § 13-21-111 (as am. L. 1975, p. 570, § 1)

13-21-111. Negligence cases—comparative negligence as measure of damages. (1) Contributory negligence shall not bar recovery in any action by any person or his legal representative to recover damages for negligence resulting in death or in injury to person or property, if such negligence was not as great as the negligence of the person against whom recovery is sought, but any damages allowed shall be diminished in proportion to the amount of negligence attributable to the person for whose injury, damage, or death recovery is made.

(2) (a) In any action to which subsection (1) of this section applies, the court, in a nonjury trial, shall make findings of fact or, in a jury trial, the jury shall return a special verdict which shall state:

(b) The amount of the damages which would have been recoverable if there had been no contributory negligence; and

(c) The degree of negligence of each party, expressed as a percentage.

(3) Upon the making of the finding of fact or the return of a special verdict, as is required by subsection (2) of this section, the court shall reduce the amount of the verdict in proportion to the amount of negligence attributable to the person for whose injury, damage, or death recovery is made; but if the said proportion is equal to or greater than the negligence of the person against whom recovery is sought, then, in such event, the court will enter a judgment for the defendant.

(4) In a jury trial in any civil action in which contributory negligence is an issue for determination by the jury, the trial court shall instruct the jury on the effect of its finding as to the degree of negligence of each party. The attorneys for each party shall be allowed to argue the effect of the instruction on the facts which are before the jury.

CONNECTICUT
Conn. Gen. Stat. Ann., § 52-572h (as am. 1982, P.A. 82-160, § 241)

52-572h. Negligence actions; Doctrines applicable.

(a) In causes of action based on negligence, contributory negligence shall not bar recovery in an action by any person or his legal representative to recover damages resulting from injury to persons or damage to property, if the negligence was not greater than the combined negligence of the person or persons against whom recovery is sought. Any damages allowed shall be diminished in the proportion of the percentage of negligence attributable to the person recovering.

(b) In any action to which this section is applicable, the instructions to the jury given by the court shall include an explanation of the effect on awards and liabilities of the percentage of negligence found by the jury to be attributable to each party.

(c) The legal doctrines of last clear chance and assumption of risk in actions to which this section is applicable are abolished.

(d) The family car doctrine shall not be applied to impute contributory or comparative negligence pursuant to this section to the owner of any motor vehicle or motor boat.

DELAWARE
Del. Code Ann., tit. 10, § 8132 (L. 1984, S.B. No. 381)

Tit. 10, § 8132. Comparative negligence. In all actions brought to recover damages for negligence which results in death or injury to person or property, the fact that the plaintiff may have been contributorily negligent shall not bar a recovery by the plaintiff or his legal representative where such negligence was not greater than the negligence of the defendant or the combined negligence of all defendants against whom recovery is sought, but any damages awarded shall be diminished in proportion to the amount of negligence attributed to the plaintiff.

GEORGIA
Ga. Code Ann., § 46-8-291 (former § 94-703 renumbered and modified by 1981 Code); § 51-11-7 (former § 105-603 renumbered by 1981 Code)

46-8-291. Damages from railroad; consent and contributory negligence as defenses; comparative negligence as affecting amount of recovery. No person shall recover damages from a railroad company for injury to himself or his property where the same is done by his consent or is caused by his own negligence, provided that if the complainant and the agents of the company are both at fault, the former may recover, but the damages shall be diminished by the jury in proportion to the amount of fault attributable to him.

51-11-7. Plaintiff's failure to avoid consequences of defendant's negligence. If the plaintiff by ordinary care could have avoided the consequences to himself caused by the defendant's negligence, he is not entitled to recover. In other cases the defendant is not relieved, although the plaintiff may in some way have contributed to the injury sustained.

HAWAII
Hawaii Rev. Stat., § 663-31 (as am. L. 1976, ch. 161, § 1)

663-31. Contributory negligence no bar; comparative negligence; findings of fact and special verdicts. (a) Contributory negligence shall not bar recovery in any action by any person or his legal representative to recover damages for negligence resulting in death or in injury to person or property, if such negligence was not greater than the negligence of the person or in the case of more than one person, the aggregate negligence of such persons against whom recovery is sought, but any damages allowed shall be diminished in proportion to the amount of negligence attributable to the person for whose injury, damage or death recovery is made.

(b) In any action to which subsection (a) of this section applies, the court, in a nonjury trial, shall make findings of fact or, in a jury trial, the jury shall return a special verdict which shall state:

(1) The amount of the damages which would have been recoverable if there had been no contributory negligence; and

(2) The degree of negligence of each party, expressed as a percentage.

(c) Upon the making of the findings of fact or the return of a special verdict, as is contemplated by subsection (b) above, the court shall reduce the amount of the award in proportion to the amount of negligence attributable to the person for whose injury, damage or death recovery is made; provided that if the said proportion is greater than the negligence of the person or in the case of more than one person, the aggregate negligence of such persons against whom recovery is sought, the court will enter a judgement for the defendant.

(d) The court shall instruct the jury regarding the law of comparative negligence where appropriate.

IDAHO
Idaho Code Ann., §§ 6-801 to 6-806 (L. 1971, ch. 186, §§ 1 to 6)

6-801. Comparative negligence—Effect of contributory negligence. Contributory negligence shall not bar recovery in an action by any person or his legal representative to recover damages for negligence or gross negligence resulting in death or in injury to person or property, if such negligence was not as great as the negligence or gross negligence of the person against whom recovery is sought, but any damages allowed shall be diminished in the proportion to the amount of negligence attributable to the person recovering.

6-802. Verdict giving percentage of negligence. The court may, and when requested by any party shall, direct the jury to find separate special verdicts determining the amount of damages and the percentage of negligence attributable to each party; and the court shall then reduce the amount of such damages in proportion to the amount of negligence attributable to the person recovering.

6-803. Contribution among joint tortfeasors. (1) The right of contribution exists among joint tortfeasors, but a joint tortfeasor is not entitled to a money judgment for contribution until he has by payment discharged the common liability or has paid more than his pro rata share thereof.

(2) A joint tortfeasor who enters into a settlement with the injured person is not entitled to recover contribution from another joint tortfeasor whose liability to the injured person is not extinguished by the settlement.

(3) When there is such a disproportion of fault among joint tortfeasors as to render inequitable an equal distribution among them of the common liability by contribution, the relative degrees of fault of the joint tortfeasors shall be considered in determining their pro rata shares solely for the purpose of determining their rights of contribution among themselves, each remaining severally liable to the injured person for the whole injury as at common law.

(4) As used herein, "joint tortfeasor" means one (1) of two (2) or more persons jointly or severally liable in tort for the same injury to person or property, whether or not judgment has been recovered against all or some of them.

6-804. Common law liabilities preserved. Nothing in this act affects:

(1) The common law liability of the several joint tortfeasors to have judgment recovered and payment made from them individually by the injured person for the whole injury. However, the recovery of a judgment by the injured person against one (1) joint tortfeasor does not discharge the other joint tortfeasors.

(2) Any right of indemnity under existing law.

6-805. Effect of release of one tortfeasor on liability of others. A release by the injured person of one (1) joint tortfeasor, whether before or after judgment, does not discharge the other tortfeasors unless the release so provides, but reduces the claim against the other tortfeasors in the amount of the consideration paid for the release, or in any amount or proportion by which the release provides that the total claim shall be reduced, if such amount or proportion is greater than the consideration paid.

6-806. Effect of release of one tortfeasor on his liability for contribution. A release by the injured person of one (1) joint tortfeasor does not relieve him from liability to make contribution to another joint tortfeasor unless the release is given before the right of the other tortfeasor to secure a money judgment for contribution has accrued, and provides for a reduction, to the extent of the pro rata share of the released tortfeasor, of the injured person's damages recoverable against all the other tortfeasors. This section shall apply only if the issue of proportionate fault is litigated between joint tortfeasors in the same action.

INDIANA
Ind. Code, §§ 34-4-33-1 to 34-4-33-13 (as am. 1984, P.L. 174, §§ 1 to 8)

34-4-33-1. Application of chapter; causation. (a) This chapter governs any action based on fault that is brought to recover damages for injury or death to person or harm to property.

(b)   In an action brought under this chapter, legal requirements of causal relation apply to:

(1)   fault as the basis for liability; and

(2)   contributory fault.

34-4-33-2.   Definitions; defendant as single party.   (a) As used in this chapter:

"Fault" includes any act or omission that is negligent, willful, wanton, or reckless toward the person or property of the actor or others, but does not include an intentional act. The term also includes unreasonable assumption of risk not constituting an enforceable express consent, incurred risk, and unreasonable failure to avoid an injury or to mitigate damages.

"Nonparty" means a person who is, or may be, liable to the claimant in part or in whole for the damages claimed but who has not been joined in the action as a defendant by the claimant. A nonparty shall not include the employer of the claimant.

(b)   For purposes of sections 4 and 5 of this chapter, a defendant may be treated along with another defendant as a single party where recovery is sought against that defendant not based upon his own alleged act or omission but upon his relationship to the other defendant.

34-4-33-3.   Effect of contributory fault.   In an action based on fault, any contributory fault chargeable to the claimant diminishes proportionately the amount awarded as compensatory damages for an injury attributable to the claimant's contributory fault, but does not bar recovery except as provided in section 4 of this chapter.

34-4-33-4.   Barring of recovery; degree of contributory fault.   (a) In an action based on fault that is brought against:

(1)   one (1) defendant; or

(2)   two (2) or more defendants who may be treated as a single party;

the claimant is barred from recovery if his contributory fault is greater than the fault of all persons whose fault proximately contributed to the claimant's damages.

(b)   In an action based on fault that is brought against two (2) or more defendants, the claimant is barred from recovery if his contributory fault is greater than the fault of all persons whose fault proximately contributed to the claimant's damages.

34-4-33-5.   Instructions to jury; award of damages.   (a) In an action based on fault that is brought against one (1) defendant or two (2) or more defendants who may be treated as a single party, and that is tried to a jury, the court, unless all the parties agree otherwise, shall instruct the jury to determine its verdict in the following manner:

(1)   The jury shall determine the percentage of fault of the claimant, of the defendant, and of any person who is a nonparty. The percentage of fault figures of parties to the action may total less than one hundred percent (100%) if the jury finds that fault contributing to cause the claimant's loss has also come from a nonparty or nonparties.

(2)   If the percentage of fault of the claimant is greater than fifty percent (50%) of the total fault involved in the incident which caused the claimant's death, injury, or property damage, the jury shall return a verdict for the defendant and no further deliberation of the jury is required.

(3)   If the percentage of fault of the claimant is not greater than fifty percent (50%) of the total fault, the jury then shall determine the total

amount of damages the claimant would be entitled to recover if contributory fault were disregarded.

(4) The jury next shall multiply the percentage of fault of the defendant by the amount of damages determined under subdivision (3) and shall then enter a verdict for the claimant in the amount of the product of that multiplication.

(b) In an action based on fault that is brought against two (2) or more defendants, and that is tried to a jury, the court, unless all the parties agree otherwise, shall instruct the jury to determine its verdict in the following manner:

(1) The jury shall determine the percentage of fault of the claimant, of the defendants, and of any person who is a nonparty. The percentage of fault figures of parties to the action may total less than one hundred percent (100%) if the jury finds that fault contributing to cause the claimant's loss has also come from a nonparty or nonparties.

(2) If the percentage of fault of the claimant is greater than fifty percent (50%) of the total fault involved in the incident which caused the claimant's death, injury, or property damage, the jury shall return a verdict for the defendants and no further deliberation of the jury is required.

(3) If the percentage of fault of the claimant is not greater than fifty percent (50%) of the total fault, the jury shall then determine the total amount of damages the claimant would be entitled to recover if contributory fault were disregarded.

(4) The jury next shall multiply the percentage of fault of each defendant by the amount of damages determined under subdivision (3) and shall enter a verdict against each such defendant (and such other defendants as are liable with the defendant by reason of their relationship to such defendant) in the amount of the product of the multiplication of each defendant's percentage of fault times the amount of damages as determined under subdivision (3).

(c) In an action based on fault that is tried by the court without a jury, the court shall make its award of damages according to the principles specified in subsections (a) and (b) for juries.

34-4-33-6. Forms of verdicts; disclosure requirements. The court shall furnish to the jury forms of verdicts that require the disclosure of:

(1) the percentage of fault charged against each party; and

(2) the calculations made by the jury to arrive at their final verdict.

If the evidence in the action is sufficient to support the charging of fault to a nonparty, the form of verdict also shall require a disclosure of the name of the nonparty and the percentage of fault charged to the nonparty.

34-4-33-7. Contribution; indemnity. In an action under this chapter, there is no right of contribution among tortfeasors. However, this section does not affect any rights of indemnity.

34-4-33-8. Government entities or public employees excepted. This chapter does not apply in any manner to tort claims against governmental entities or public employees under IC 34-4-16.5.

34-4-33-9. Verdict; inconsistent award with determinations of total damages and percentages of fault. In actions brought under this chapter, whenever a jury returns verdicts in which the ultimate amounts awarded are inconsistent with its determinations of total damages and percentages of fault, the trial court shall:

(1) inform the jury of such inconsistencies;

(2) order them to resume deliberations to correct the inconsistencies; and

(3) instruct them that they are at liberty to change any portion or portions of the verdicts to correct the inconsistencies.

34-4-33-10. Nonparty defense; assertion; burden of proof; pleadings; application. (a) In an action based on fault, a defendant may assert as a defense that the damages of the claimant were caused in full or in part by a nonparty. Such a defense is referred to in this section as a nonparty defense.

(b) The burden of proof of a nonparty defense is upon the defendant, who must affirmatively plead the defense. However, nothing in this chapter relieves the claimant of the burden of proving that fault on the part of the defendant or defendants caused, in whole or in part, the damages of the claimant.

(c) A nonparty defense that is known by the defendant when he files his first answer shall be pleaded as a part of the first answer. A defendant who gains actual knowledge of a nonparty defense after the filing of an answer may plead the defense with reasonable promptness. However, if the defendant was served with a complaint and summons more than one hundred fifty (150) days before the expiration of the limitation of action applicable to the claimant's claim against the nonparty, the defendant shall plead any nonparty defense not later than forty-five (45) days before the expiration of that limitation of action. The trial court may alter these time limitations or make other suitable time limitations in any manner that is consistent with:

(1) giving the defendant a reasonable opportunity to discover the existence of a nonparty defense; and

(2) giving the claimant a reasonable opportunity to add the nonparty as an additional defendant to the action before the expiration of the period of limitation applicable to the claim.

(d) This section applies to a claim filed with the insurance commissioner under IC 16-9.5 against a qualified health care provider, with the exception that the pleading of a nonparty defense, as required by subsections (b) and (c), must occur not later than ninety (90) days after the filing of the claim with the insurance commissioner. However, this time limitation may be enlarged or shortened by a court having jurisdiction over the claim in such matter as will give:

(1) the qualified health care provider reasonable opportunity to discover the existence of a nonparty defense; and

(2) the claimant reasonable opportunity to assert a claim against the nonparty before the expiration of the period of limitation applicable to the claim.

34-4-33-11. Actions against defendants who are qualified health care providers and who are not qualified health care providers; delay; joinder. When an action based on fault is brought by the claimant against one (1) or more defendants who are qualified health care providers under IC 16-9.5, and, also is brought by suit against one (1) or more defendants who are not qualified health care providers, upon application of the claimant, the trial court shall grant reasonable delays in the action brought against those defendants who are not qualified health care providers until the medical review panel procedure can be completed as to the qualified health care providers. When an action is permitted to be filed against the qualified health care providers, the trial court shall permit a joinder of the qualified health care providers as additional defendants in the action on file against the nonhealth care providers.

34-4-33-12. Liens or claims to diminish in same proportion as claimant's recovery is diminished. If a subrogation claim or other lien or claim, other than a lien under IC 22-3-2-13 or IC 22-3-7-36, that arose out of the payment of medical expenses or other benefits exists in respect to a claim for personal injuries or death and the claimant's recovery is diminished:

(1) by comparative fault; or

(2) by reason of the uncollectibility of the full value of the claim for personal injuries or death resulting from limited liability insurance or from any other cause;

the lien or claim shall be diminished in the same proportion as the claimant's recovery is diminished.

34-4-33-13. Application. This chapter does not apply in any manner to strict liability actions under IC 33-1-1.5 or to breach of warranty actions.

IOWA
Iowa Code Ann., § 619.17 (am. 70 G.A., H.F. 2487, § 13); §§ 668.1 to 668.10 (70 G.A., H.F. 2487, §§ 1 to 10)

619.17. Contributory fault—Burden. A plaintiff does not have the burden of pleading and proving the plaintiff's freedom from contributory fault. If a defendant relies upon contributory fault of a plaintiff to diminish the amount to be awarded as compensatory damages, the defendant has the burden of pleading and proving fault of the plaintiff, if any, and that it was a proximate cause of the injury or damage. As used in this section, "plaintiff" includes a defendant filing a counterclaim or cross-petition, and the term "defendant" includes a plaintiff against whom a counterclaim or cross-petition has been filed.

668.1. Fault defined. 1. As used in this chapter, "fault" means one or more acts or omissions that are in any measure negligent or reckless toward the person or property of the actor or others, or that subject a person to strict tort liability. The term also includes breach of warranty, unreasonable assumption of risk not constituting an enforceable express consent, misuse of a product for which the defendant otherwise would be liable, and unreasonable failure to avoid an injury or to mitigate damages.

2. The legal requirements of cause in fact and proximate cause apply both to fault as the basis for liability and to contributory fault.

668.2. Party defined. As used in this chapter, unless otherwise required, "party" means any of the following:
1. A claimant.
2. A person named as defendant.
3. A person who has been released pursuant to section 668.7.
4. A third-party defendant.

668.3. Comparative fault—Effect. 1. Contributory fault shall not bar recovery in an action by a claimant to recover damages for fault resulting in death or in injury to person or property unless the claimant bears a greater percentage of fault than the combined percentage of fault attributed to the defendants, third-party defendants and persons who have been released pursuant to section 668.7, but any damages allowed shall be diminished in proportion to the amount of fault attributable to the claimant.

2. In the trial of a claim involving the fault of more than one party to the claim, including third-party defendants and persons who have been released pursuant to section 668.7, the court, unless otherwise agreed by all parties, shall instruct the jury to answer special interrogatories or, if there is no jury, shall make findings, indicating all of the following:

a. The amount of damages each claimant will be entitled to recover if contributory fault is disregarded.

b. The percentage of the total fault allocated to each claimant, defendant, third-party defendant, and person who has been released from liability under section 668.7. For this purpose the court may determine that two or more persons are to be treated as a single party.

3. In determining the percentages of fault, the trier of fact shall consider

both the nature of the conduct of each party and the extent of the causal relation between the conduct and the damages claimed.

4. The court shall determine the amount of damages payable to each claimant by each other party, if any, in accordance with the findings of the court or jury.

5. If the claim is tried to a jury, the court shall give instructions and permit evidence and argument with respect to the effects of the answers to be returned to the interrogatories submitted under this section.

6. In an action brought under this chapter and tried to a jury, the court shall not discharge the jury until the court has determined that the verdict or verdicts are consistent with the total damages and percentages of fault, and if inconsistencies exist the court shall do all of the following:

    a. Inform the jury of the inconsistencies.

    b. Order the jury to resume deliberations to correct the inconsistencies.

    c. Instruct the jury that it is at liberty to change any portion or portions of the verdicts to correct the inconsistencies.

668.4. Joint and several liability. In actions brought under this chapter, the rule of joint and several liability shall not apply to defendants who are found to bear less than fifty percent of the total fault assigned to all parties.

668.5. Right of contribution. 1. A right of contribution exists between or among two or more persons who are liable upon the same indivisible claim for the same injury, death, or harm, whether or not judgment has been recovered against all or any of them. It may be enforced either in the original action or by a separate action brought for that purpose. The basis for contribution is each person's equitable share of the obligations, including the share of fault of a claimant, as determined in accordance with section 668.3.

2. Contribution is available to a person who enters into a settlement with the claimant only if the liability of the person against whom contribution is sought has been extinguished and only to the extent that the amount paid in settlement was reasonable.

668.6. Enforcement of contribution. 1. If the percentages of fault of each of the parties to a claim for contribution have been established previously by the court as provided in section 668.3, a party paying more than the party's percentage share of damages may recover judgment for contribution upon motion to the court or in a separate action.

2. If the percentages of fault of each of the parties to a claim for contribution have not been established by the court, contribution may be enforced in a separate action, whether or not a judgment has been rendered against either the person seeking contribution or the person from whom contribution is sought.

3. If a judgment has been rendered, an action for contribution must be commenced within one year after the judgment becomes final. If a judgment has not been rendered, a claim for contribution is enforceable only upon satisfaction of one of the following sets of conditions:

    a. The person bringing the action for contribution must have discharged the liability of the person from whom contribution is sought by payment made within the period of the statute of limitations applicable to the claimant's right of action and must have commenced the action for contribution within one year after the date of that payment.

    b. The person seeking contribution must have agreed while the action of the claimant was pending to discharge the liability of the person from whom contribution is sought and within one year after the date of the agreement must have discharged that liability and commenced the action for contribution.

668.7. Effect of release. A release, covenant not to sue, or similar agreement entered into by a claimant and a person liable discharges that person from all liability for contribution, but it does not discharge any other persons liable upon the same claim unless it so provides. However, the claim of the releasing person against other persons is reduced by the amount of the released person's equitable share of the obligation, as determined in section 668.3, subsection 4.

668.8. Tolling of statute. The filing of a petition under this chapter tolls the statute of limitations for the commencement of an action against all parties who may be assessed any percentage of fault under this chapter.

668.9. Insurance practice. It shall be an unfair trade practice, as defined in chapter 507B, if an insurer assigns a percentage of fault to a claimant, for the purpose of reducing a settlement, when there exists no reasonable evidence upon which the assigned percentage of fault could be based. The prohibitions and sanctions of chapter 507B shall apply to violations of this section.

668.10. Governmental exemptions. In any action brought pursuant to this chapter, the state or a municipality shall not be assigned a percentage of fault for any of the following:

1. The failure to place, erect, or install a stop sign, traffic control device, or other regulatory sign as defined in the uniform manual for traffic control devices adopted pursuant to section 321.252. However, once a regulatory device has been placed, created or installed, the state or municipality may be assigned a percentage of fault for its failure to maintain the device.

2. The failure to remove natural or unnatural accumulations of snow or ice, or to place sand, salt, or other abrasive material on a highway, road, or street if the state or municipality establishes that it has complied with its policy or level of service for snow and ice removal or placing sand, salt or other abrasive material on its highways, roads, or streets.

3. For contribution unless the party claiming contribution has given the state or municipality notice of the claim pursuant to sections 25A.13 and 613A.5.

Note: Section 15, 70 G.A., H.F. 2487, provides: "This Act, except for section 4 [668.4], applies to all cases filed on or after July 1, 1984. Section 4 of this Act applies to all cases tried on or after July 1, 1984."

KANSAS
Kan. Stat. Ann., §§ 60-258a, 60-258b (as am. L. 1976, ch. 251, § 4)

60-258a. Contributory negligence as bar to recovery in civil actions abolished, when; award of damages based on comparative negligence; imputation of negligence, when; special verdicts and findings; joinder of parties; proportioned liability. (a) The contributory negligence of any party in a civil action shall not bar such party or said party's legal representative from recovering damages for negligence resulting in death, personal injury or property damage, if such party's negligence was less than the causal negligence of the party or parties against whom claim for recovery is made, but the award of damages to any party in such action shall be diminished in proportion to the amount of negligence attributed to such party. If any such party is claiming damages for a decendent's wrongful death, the negligence of the decedent, if any, shall be imputed to such party.

(b) Where the comparative negligence of the parties in any such action is an issue, the jury shall return special verdicts, or in the absence of a jury, the court shall make special findings, determining the percentage of negligence attributable to each of the parties, and determining the total amount of damages sustained by each of the claimants, and the entry of judgment shall be made by the court. No general verdict shall be returned by the jury.

(c) On motion of any party against whom a claim is asserted for negligence resulting in death, personal injury or property damage, any other person whose causal negligence is claimed to have contributed to such death, personal injury or property damage shall be joined as an additional party to the action.

(d) Where the comparative negligence of the parties in any action is an issue and recovery is allowed against more than one party, each such party shall be liable for that portion of the total dollar amount awarded as damages to any claimant in the proportion that the amount of his or her causal negligence bears to the amount of the causal negligence attributed to all parties against whom such recovery is allowed.

(e) The provisions of this section shall be applicable to actions pursuant to this chapter and to actions commenced pursuant to the code of civil procedure for limited actions.

60-258b. Application of act. The provisions of this act shall not apply to any cause of action which has accrued prior to the effective date of this act.

LOUISIANA
La. Civ. Code Ann., arts. 1804, 1805 (Acts 1984, No. 331, § 1); 2323, 2324 (as am. Acts 1979, No. 431, § 1)

Civ. Code Art. 1804. Liability of solidary obligors between themselves. Among solidary obligors, each is liable for his virile portion. If the obligation arises from a contract or quasi-contract, virile portions are equal in the absence of agreement or judgment to the contrary. If the obligation arises from an offense or quasi-offense, a virile portion is proportionate to the fault of each obligor.

A solidary obligor who has rendered the whole performance, though subrogated to the right of the obligee, may claim from the other obligors no more than the virile portion of each.

If the circumstances giving rise to the solidary obligation concern only one of the obligors, that obligor is liable for the whole to the other obligors who are then considered only as his sureties.

Civ. Code Art. 1805. Enforcement of contribution. A party sued on an obligation that would be solidary if it exists may seek to enforce contribution against any solidary co-obligor by making him a third party defendant according to the rules of procedure, whether or not that third party has been initially sued, and whether the party seeking to enforce contribution admits or denies liability on the obligation alleged by plaintiff.

Civ. Code Art. 2323. Computation of damages. When contributory negligence is applicable to a claim for damages, its effect shall be as follows: If a person suffers injury, death or loss as the result partly of his own negligence and partly as a result of the fault of another person or persons, the claim for damages shall not thereby be defeated, but the amount of damages recoverable shall be reduced in proportion to the degree or percentage of negligence attributable to the person suffering the injury, death or loss.

Civ. Code Art. 2324. Liability for assisting or encouraging wrongful act. He who causes another person to do an unlawful act, or assists or encourages in the commission of it, is answerable, in solido, with that person, for the damage caused by such act.

Persons whose concurring fault has caused injury, death or loss to another are also answerable, in solido; provided, however, when the amount of recovery has been reduced in accordance with the preceding article, a judgment debtor shall not be liable for more than the degree of his fault to a judgment creditor to whom a greater degree of negligence has been attributed, reserving to all parties their respective rights of indemnity and contribution.

La. Code Civ. Proc., arts. 1812 (as am. Acts 1983, No. 534, § 8); 1917 (as am. Acts 1980, No. 112, § 1)

Code Civ. Proc. Art. 1812. Special verdicts. A. The court may require a jury to return only a special verdict in the form of a special written finding upon each issue of fact. In that event, the court may submit to the jury written questions susceptible of categorical or other brief answer, or may submit written forms of the several special findings which might properly be made under the pleadings and evidence, or may use any other appropriate method of submitting the issues and requiring the written findings thereon. The court shall give to the jury such explanation and instruction concerning the matter submitted as may be necessary to enable the jury to make its findings upon each issue. If the court omits any issue of fact raised by the pleadings or by the evidence, each party waives his right to a trial by jury of the issue omitted unless, before the jury retires, he demands its submission to the jury. As to an issue omitted without such demand the court may make a finding, or if it fails to do so, it shall be presumed to have made a finding in accord with the judgment on the special verdict.

B. The court shall inform the parties within a reasonable time prior to their argument to the jury of the special verdict form and instructions it intends to submit to the jury and the parties shall be given a reasonable opportunity to make objections.

C. In cases to recover damages for injury, death, or loss, the court may submit to the jury, unless waived by all parties, special written questions inquiring as to:

(1) Whether a party from whom damages are claimed, or the person for whom such party is legally responsible, was at fault, and, if so:

(a) Whether such fault was a legal cause of the damages, and, if so:

(b) The degree of such fault, expressed in percentage.

(2) If appropriate, whether another person, whether party or not, other than the person suffering injury, death, or loss, was at fault, and, if so:

(a) Whether such fault was a legal cause of the damages, and, if so:

(b) The degree of such fault, expressed in percentage.

(3) If appropriate, whether there was negligence attributable to any party claiming damages, and, if so:

(a) Whether such negligence was a legal cause of the damages, and, if so:

(b) The degree of such negligence, expressed in percentage.

(4) The total amount of damages sustained as a result of the injury, death, or loss, expressed in dollars.

D. The court shall then enter judgment in conformity with the jury's answers to these special questions and according to applicable law.

Code Civ. Proc. Art. 1917. Findings of the court and reasons for judgment. In all appealable contested cases, other than those tried by a jury, the court when requested to do so by a party shall give in writing its findings of fact and reasons for judgment, provided the request is made not later than ten days after the signing of the judgment.

In nonjury cases to recover damages for injury, death or loss, whether or not requested to do so by a party, the court shall make specific findings that shall include those matters to which reference is made in Paragraph C of Article 1812 of this Code. These findings need not include reasons for judgment.

MAINE
Me. Rev. Stat. Ann., tit. 14, § 156 (as am. L. 1971, ch. 8)

Tit. 14, § 156. Comparative negligence. Where any person suffers death or damage as a result partly of his own fault and partly of the fault of any other persons or persons, a claim in respect of that death or damage shall not be defeated by reason of the fault of the person suffering the damage, but the damages recoverable in respect thereof shall be reduced to such exent as the jury thinks just and equitable having regard to the claimant's share in the responsibility for the damage.

Where damages are recoverable by any person by virtue of this section, subject to such reduction as is mentioned, the court shall instruct the jury to find and record the total damages which would have been recoverable if the claimant had not been at fault, and further instruct the jury to reduce the total damages by dollars and cents, and not by percentage, to the extent deemed just and equitable, having regard to the claimant's share in the responsibility for the damages, and instruct the jury to return both amounts with the knowledge that the lesser figure is the final verdict in the case.

Fault means negligence, breach of statutory duty or other act or omission which gives rise to a liability in tort or would, apart from this section, give rise to the defense of contributory negligence.

If such claimant is found by the jury to be equally at fault, the claimant shall not recover.

In a case involving multi-party defendants, each defendant shall be jointly and severally liable to the plaintiff for the full amount of the plaintiff's damages. However, any defendant shall have the right through the use of special interrogatories to request of the jury the percentage of fault contributed by each defendant.

MASSACHUSETTS
Mass. Gen. Laws Ann., ch. 231, § 85 (as am. 1973 Acts, ch. 1123, § 1)

Ch. 231, § 85. Comparative negligence. Contributory negligence shall not bar recovery in any action by any person or legal representative to recover damages for negligence resulting in death or in injury to person or property, if such negligence was not greater than the total amount of negligence attributable to the person or persons against whom recovery is sought, but any damages allowed shall be diminished in proportion to the amount of negligence attributable to the person for whose injury, damage or death recovery is made. In determining by what amount the plaintiff's damages shall be diminished in such a case, the negligence of each plaintiff shall be compared to the total negligence of all persons against whom recovery is sought. The combined total of the plaintiff's negligence taken together with all of the negligence of all defendants shall equal one hundred per cent.

The violation of a criminal statute, ordinance or regulation by a plaintiff which contributed to said injury, death or damage, shall be considered as evidence of negligence of that plaintiff, but the violation of said statute, ordinance or regulation shall not as a matter of law and for that reason alone, serve to bar a plaintiff from recovery.

The defense of assumption of risk is hereby abolished in all actions hereunder.

The burden of alleging and proving negligence which serves to diminish a plaintiff's damages or bar recovery under this section shall be upon the person who seeks to establish such negligence, and the plaintiff shall be presumed to have been in the exercise of due care.

MINNESOTA
Minn. Stat. Ann., §§ 604.01, 604.02 (as am. Laws 1978, ch. 738, §§ 6, 7, 8)

604.01. Comparative fault; effect. Subdivision 1. Scope of application. Contributory fault shall not bar recovery in an action by any person or his legal representative to recover damages for fault resulting in death or in injury to person or property, if the contributory fault was not greater than the fault of the person against whom recovery is sought, but any damages allowed shall be diminished in proportion to the amount of fault attributable to the person recovering. The court may, and when requested by any party shall, direct the jury to find separate special verdicts determining the amount of damages and the percentage of fault attributable to each party; and the court shall then reduce the amount of damages in proportion to the amount of fault attributable to the person recovering.

Subd. 1a. Fault. "Fault" includes acts or omissions that are in any measure negligent or reckless toward the person or property of the actor or others, or that subject a person to strict tort liability. The term also includes breach of warranty, unreasonable assumption of risk not constituting an express consent, misuse of a product and unreasonable failure to avoid an injury or to mitigate damages. Legal requirements of causal relation apply both to fault as the basis for liability and to contributory fault.

Subd. 2. Personal injury or death; settlement or payment. Settlement with or any payment made to an injured person or to others on behalf of such injured person with the permission of such injured person or to anyone entitled to recover damages on account of injury or death of such person shall not constitute an admission of liability by the person making the payment or on whose behalf payment was made.

Subd. 3. Property damage; settlement or payment. Settlement with or any payment made to a person or on his behalf to others for damage to or destruction of property shall not constitute an admission of liability by the person making the payment or on whose behalf the payment was made.

Subd. 4. Settlement or payment; admissibility of evidence. Except in an action in which settlement and release has been pleaded as a defense, any settlement or payment referred to in subdivisions 2 and 3 shall be inadmissible in evidence on the trial of any legal action.

Subd. 5. Credit for settlements and payments; refund. All settlements and payments made under subdivisions 2 and 3 shall be credited against any final settlement or judgment; provided however that in the event that judgment is entered against the person seeking recovery or if a verdict is rendered for an amount less than the total of any such advance payments in favor of the recipient thereof, such person shall not be required to refund any portion of such advance payments voluntarily made. Upon motion to the court in the absence of a jury and upon proper proof thereof, prior to entry of judgment on a verdict, the court shall first apply the provisions of subdivision 1 and then shall reduce the amount of the damages so determined by the amount of the payments previously made to or on behalf of the person entitled to such damages.

604.02. Apportionment of damages. Subdivision 1. When two or more persons are jointly liable, contributions to awards shall be in proportion to the percentage of fault attributable to each, except that each is jointly and severally liable for the whole award.

Subd. 2. Upon motion made not later than one year after judgment is entered, the court shall determine whether all or part of a party's equitable share of the obligation is uncollectible from that party and shall reallocate any uncollectible amount among the other parties, including a claimant at fault, according to their respective percentages of fault. A party whose liability is reallocated is nonetheless subject to contribution and to any continuing liability to the claimant on the judgment.

Subd. 3. In the case of a claim arising from the manufacture, sale, use or consumption of a product, an amount uncollectible from any person in the chain of manufacture and distribution shall be reallocated among all other persons in the chain of manufacture and distribution but not among the claimant or others at fault who are not in the chain of manufacture or distribution of the product. Provided, however, that a person whose fault is less than that of a claimant is liable to the claimant only for that portion of the judgment which respresents the percentage of fault attributable to him.

MISSISSIPPI
Miss. Code Ann., § 11-7-15 (as am. Laws 1920, ch. 312)

11-7-15. Contributory negligence no bar to recovery of damages—jury may diminish damages. In all actions hereafter brought for personal injuries, or where such injuries have resulted in death, or for injury to property, the fact that the person injured, or the owner of the property, or person having control over the property may have been guilty of contributory negligence shall not bar a recovery, but damages shall be diminished by the jury in proportion to the amount of negligence attributable to the person injured, or the owner of the property, or the person having control over the property.

MONTANA
Mont. Code Ann., §§ 27-1-702 (L. 1975, ch. 60, § 1); 27-1-703 (as am. L. 1981, ch. 523, § 1)

27-1-702. Comparative negligence. Contributory negligence shall not bar recovery in an action by any person or his legal representative to recover damages for negligence resulting in death or injury to person or property if such negligence was not greater than the negligence of the person against whom recovery is sought, but any damages allowed shall be diminished in the proportion to the amount of negligence attributable to the person recovering.

27-1-703. Multiple defendants jointly and severally liable—right of contribution. (1) Whenever the negligence of any party in any action is an issue, each party against whom recovery may be allowed is jointly and severally liable for the amount that may be awarded to the claimant but has the right of contribution from any other person whose negligence may have contributed as a proximate cause to the injury complained of.

(2) On motion of any party against whom a claim is asserted for negligence resulting in death or injury to person or property, any other person whose negligence may have contributed as a proximate cause to the injury complained of may be joined as an additional party to the action. Whenever more than one person is found to have contributed as a proximate cause to the injury complained of, the trier of fact shall apportion the degree of fault among such persons. Contribution shall be proportional to the negligence of the parties against whom recovery is allowed. Nothing contained in this section shall make any party indispensable pursuant to Rule 19, M.R.Civ.P.

(3) If for any reason all or part of the contribution from a party liable for contribution cannot be obtained, each of the other parties against whom recovery is allowed is liable to contribute a proportional part of the unpaid portion of the noncontributing party's share and may obtain judgment in a pending or subsequent action for contribution from the noncontributing party.

NEBRASKA
Neb. Rev. Stat., § 25-1151 (as am. Laws 1978, LB 665, § 6)

25-1151. Actions for injuries to persons or property; contributory negligence; comparative negligence. In all actions brought to recover damages for injuries to a person or to his property caused by the negligence or act or omission giving rise to strict liability in tort of another, the fact that the plaintiff may have been guilty of contributory negligence shall not bar a recovery when the contributory negligence of the plaintiff was slight and the negligence or act

407

or omission giving rise to strict liability in tort of the defendant was gross in comparison, but the contributory negligence of the plaintiff shall be considered by the jury in the mitigation of damages in proportion to the amount of contributory negligence attributable to the plaintiff; and all questions of negligence or act or omission giving rise to strict liability in tort and contributory negligence shall be for the jury.

NEVADA
Nev. Rev. Stat., § 41.141 (as am. L. 1979, 1356)

41.141. Comparative negligence. 1. In any action to recover damages for death or injury to persons or for injury to property in which contributory negligence may be asserted as a defense, the contributory negligence of the plaintiff or his decedent does not bar a recovery if that negligence was not greater than the negligence or gross negligence of the person or persons against whom recovery is sought, but any damages allowed must be diminished in proportion to the amount of negligence attributable to the person seeking recovery or his decedent.

2. In those cases, the judge may and when requested by any party shall instruct the jury that:

(a) The plaintiff may not recover if his contributory negligence or that of his decedent has contributed more to the injury than the negligence of the defendant or the combined negligence of multiple defendants.

(b) If the jury determines the plaintiff is entitled to recover, it shall return:

(1) By general verdict the total amount of damages the plaintiff would be entitled to recover without regard to his contributory negligence.

(2) A special verdict indicating the percentage of negligence attributable to each party.

(3) By general verdict the net sum determined to be recoverable by the plaintiff.

3. Where recovery is allowed against more than one defendant in such an action, the defendants are jointly and severally liable to the plaintiff, except that a defendant whose negligence is less than that of the plaintiff or his decedent is not jointly liable and is severally liable to the plaintiff only for that portion of the judgment which represents the percentage of negligence attributable to him.

NEW HAMPSHIRE
N.H. Rev. Stat. Ann., § 507:7-a (as am. Laws 1970, 35:1)

507:7-a. Comparative negligence. Contributory negligence shall not bar recovery in an action by any plaintiff, or his legal representative, to recover damages for negligence resulting in death, personal injury, or property damage, if such negligence was not greater than the causal negligence of the defendant, but the damages awarded shall be diminished, by general verdict, in proportion to the amount of negligence attributed to the plaintiff; provided that where recovery is allowed against more than one defendant, each such defendant shall be liable for that proportion of the total dollar amount awarded as damages in the ratio of the amount of his causal negligence to the amount of causal negligence attributed to all defendants against whom recovery is allowed. The burden of proof as to the existence or amount of causal negligence alleged to be attributable to a party shall rest upon the party making such allegation.

NEW JERSEY

N.J. Stat. Ann., § 2A:15-5.1 (as am. L. 1982, c. 191, § 1); §§ 2A:15-5.2, 2A:15-5.3 (L. 1973, c. 146, §§ 2, 3)

2A:15-5.1. Comparative negligence to determine damages. Contributory negligence shall not bar recovery in an action by any person or his legal representative to recover damages for negligence resulting in death or injury to person or property, if such negligence was not greater than the negligence of the person against whom recovery is sought or was not greater than the combined negligence of the persons against whom recovery is sought. Any damages sustained shall be diminished by the percentage sustained of negligence attributable to the person recovering.

2A:15-5.2. Findings of fact; damages; percentage of fault; judgment. In all negligence actions in which the question of liability is in dispute, the trier of fact shall make the following as findings of fact:

a. The amount of damages which would be recoverable by the injured party regardless of any consideration of negligence, that is, the full value of the injured party's damages;

b. The extent, in the form of a percentage, of each party's negligence. The percentage of negligence of each party shall be based on 100% and the total of all percentages of negligence of all the parties to a suit shall be 100%.

c. The judge shall mold the judgment from the finding of fact made by the trier of fact.

2A:15-5.3. Recovery; contribution. The party so recovering, may recover the full amount of the molded verdict from any party against whom such recovering party is not barred from recovery. Any party who is so compelled to pay more than such party's percentage share may seek contribution from the other joint tortfeasors.

NEW YORK

N.Y. Civ. Prac. Law, §§ 1411 to 1413 (Laws 1975, c. 69, § 1)

1411. Damages when contributory negligence or assumption of risk established. In any action to recover damages for personal injury, injury to property, or wrongful death, the culpable conduct attributable to the claimant or to the decedent, including contributory negligence or assumption of risk, shall not bar recovery, but the amount of damages otherwise recoverable shall be diminished in the proportion which the culpable conduct attributable to the claimant or decedent bears to the culpable conduct which caused the damages.

1412. Pleading and proof. Culpable conduct claimed in diminution of damages, in accordance with section fourteen hundred eleven, shall be an affirmative defense to be pleaded and proved by the party asserting the defense.

1413. Applicability. This article shall apply to all causes of action accruing on or after September first, nineteen hundred seventy-five.

N.Y. Estates, Powers, Trusts Law, § 5-4.2 (as am. Laws 1975, c. 69, § 2); 11-3.2(b) (as am. Laws 1982, c. 100, § 2)

5-4.2. Trial and burden of proof. On the trial of an action accruing before September first, nineteen hundred seventy-five to recover damages for causing death, the contributory negligence of the decedent shall be a defense, to be pleaded and proved by the defendant.

11-3.2. (a) ***

(b) Action by personal representative for injury to person or property. No cause of action for injury to person or property is lost because of the death of the person in whose favor the cause of action existed. For any injury an action may be brought or continued by the personal representative of the decedent, but punitive damages shall not be awarded nor penalties adjudged in any such action brought to recover damages for personal injury where the death occurs on or before August thirty-first, nineteen hundred eighty-two. On the trial of any such action accruing before September first, nineteen hundred seventy-five, which is joined with an action for causing death, the contributory negligence of the decedent is a defense, to be pleaded and proved by the defendant. No cause of action for damages caused by an injury to a third person is lost because of the death of the third person.

NORTH DAKOTA
N.D. Cent. Code, § 9-10-07 (S.L. 1973, ch. 78, § 1)

9-10-07. Comparative negligence. Contributory negligence shall not bar recovery in an action by any person or his legal representative to recover damages for negligence resulting in death or in injury to person or property, if such negligence was not as great as the negligence of the person against whom recovery is sought, but any damages allowed shall be diminished in proportion to the amount of negligence attributable to the person recovering. The court may, and when requested by either party shall, direct the jury to find separate special verdicts determining the amount of damages and the percentage of negligence attributable to each party; and the court shall then reduce the amount of such damages in proportion to the amount of negligence attributable to the person recovering. When there are two or more persons who are jointly liable, contributions to awards shall be in proportion to the percentage of negligence attributable to each; provided, however, that each shall remain jointly and severally liable for the whole award. Upon the request of any party, this section shall be read by the court to the jury and the attorneys representing the parties may comment to the jury regarding this section.

OHIO
Ohio Rev. Code, § 2315.19 (1980 S 165, eff. 6-20-80)

2315.19. Contributory negligence not bar to recovery; damages to be diminished; calculation; procedures. (A)(1) In negligence actions, the contributory negligence of a person does not bar the person or his legal representative from recovering damages that have directly and proximately resulted from the negligence of one or more other persons, if the contributory negligence of the person bringing the action was no greater than the combined negligence of all other persons from whom recovery is sought. However, any damages recoverable by the person bringing the action shall be diminished by an amount that is proportionately equal to his percentage of negligence, which percentage is determined pursuant to division (B) of this section. This section does not apply to actions described in section 4113.03 of the Revised Code.

(2) If recovery for damages determined to be directly and proximately caused by the negligence of more than one person is allowed under division (A)(1) of this section, each person against whom recovery is allowed is liable to the person bringing the action for a portion of the total damages allowed under that division. The portion of damages for which each person is liable is calculated by multiplying the total damages allowed by a fraction in which the numerator is the person's percentage of negligence, which percentage is determined pursuant to division (B) of this section, and the denominator is the total of the percentages of negligence, which percentages are determined pursuant to division (B) of this section to be attributable to all persons from whom recovery is allowed. Any percentage of negligence attributable to the person bringing the action shall not be included in the total of percentages of negligence that is the denominator in the fraction.

410

(B)   In any negligence action in which contributory negligence is asserted as a defense, the court in a nonjury trial shall make findings of fact, and the jury in a jury trial shall return a general verdict accompanied by answers to interrogatories, that shall specify:

(1)   The total amount of damages that would have been recoverable by the complainant but for his negligence;

(2)   The percentage of negligence that directly and proximately caused the injury, in relation to one hundred per cent, that is attributable to each party to the action.

(C)   After the court makes its findings of fact or after the jury returns its general verdict accompanied by answers to interrogatories, the court shall diminish the total amount of damages recoverable by an amount that is proportionately equal to the percentage of negligence of the person bringing the action, which percentage is determined pursuant to division (B) of this section. If the percentage of the negligence of the person bringing the action is greater than the total of the percentages of the negligence of all other persons from whom recovery is sought, which percentages are determined pursuant to division (B) of this section, the court shall enter a judgement for the persons against whom recovery is sought.

OKLAHOMA
Okla. Stat. Ann., tit. 23, § 12 (L. 1973, c. 30, § 2); tit. 23, §§ 13, 14 (L. 1979, c. 38, §§ 1, 2)

Tit. 23, § 12.   Contributory negligence or assumption of risk question of fact.   The defense of contributory negligence or of assumption of risk shall, in all cases whatsoever, be a question of fact, and shall at all times be left to the jury, unless a jury is waived by the parties.

Tit. 23, § 13.   Contributory negligence not bar to recovery.   In all actions hereafter brought, whether arising before or after the effective date of this act, for negligence resulting in personal injuries or wrongful death or injury to property, contributory negligence shall not bar a recovery, unless any negligence of the person so injured, damaged or killed, is of greater degree than any negligence of the person, firm or corporation causing such damage, or unless any negligence of the person so injured, damaged or killed, is of greater degree than the combined negligence of any persons, firms or corporations causing such damage.

Tit. 23, § 14.   Recovery diminished.   Where such contributory negligence is shown on the part of the person injured, damaged or killed, the amount of the recovery shall be diminished in proportion to such person's contributory negligence.

OREGON
Ore. Rev. Stat., § 18.470 (L. 1971, c. 688, § 1); §§ 18.475 to 18.490 (L. 1975, c. 599, §§ 4, 2, 3, 5); § 18.510 (as am. L. 1981, c. 892, § 85c; 1981, c. 898, § 17)

18.470.   Contributory negligence not bar to recovery.   Contributory negligence shall not bar recovery in an action by any person or his legal representative to recover damages for death or injury to person or property if the fault attributable to the person seeking recovery was not greater than the combined fault of the person or persons against whom recovery is sought, but any damages allowed shall be diminished in the proportion to the percentage of fault attributable to the person recovering. This section is not intended to create or abolish any defense.

18.475.   Abolishment of last clear chance and assumption of risk.   (1) The doctrine of last clear chance is abolished.

411

(2) The doctrine of implied assumption of the risk is abolished.

18.480. Questions for trier of fact. (1) When requested by any party the trier of fact shall answer special questions indicating:

(a) The amount of damages to which a party seeking recovery would be entitled, assuming that party not to be at fault;

(b) The degree of each party's fault expressed as a percentage of the total fault attributable to all parties represented in the action.

(2) A jury shall be informed of the legal effect of its answer to the questions listed in subsection (1) of this section.

18.485. Joint tortfeasors. Each joint tortfeasor defendant is jointly and severally liable for the entire amount of the judgment awarded a plaintiff, except that a defendant whose percentage of fault is less than that allocated to the plaintiff is liable to the plaintiff only for that percentage of the recoverable damages.

18.490. Setoff. Setoff of damages shall not be granted in actions subject to ORS 18.470 to 18.490.

18.510. Disposition of advance payment. (1) If judgment is entered against a party on whose behalf an advance payment referred to in ORS 18.520 or 18.530 has been made and in favor of a party for whose benefit any such advance payment has been received, the amount of the judgment shall be reduced by the amount of any such payments in the manner provided in subsection (3) of this section. However, nothing in ORS 12.155, 18.520, 18.530 and this section authorizes the person making such payments to recover such advance payment if no damages are awarded or to recover any amount by which the advance payment exceeds the award of damages.

(2) If judgment is entered against a party who is insured under a policy of liability insurance against such judgment and in favor of a party who has received benefits that have been the basis for a reimbursement payment by such insurer under ORS 743.825, the amount of the judgment shall be reduced by reason of such benefits in the manner provided in subsection (3) of this section.

(3)

(a) The amount of any advance payment referred to in subsection (1) of this section may be submitted by the party making the payment, in the manner provided in ORCP 68 C.(4) for the submission of disbursements.

(b) The amount of any benefits referred to in subsection (2) of this section, diminished in proportion to the amount of negligence attributable to the party in favor of whom the judgment was entered and diminished to an amount no greater than the reimbursement payment made by the insurer under ORS 743.825, may be submitted by the insurer which has made the reimbursement payment, in the manner provided in ORCP 68 C.(4) for the submission of disbursements.

(c) Unless timely objections are filed as provided in ORCP 68 C.(4), the court clerk shall apply the amounts claimed pursuant to this subsection in partial satisfaction of the judgment. Such partial satisfaction shall be allowed without regard to whether the party claiming the reduction is otherwise entitled to costs and disbursements in the action.

PENNSYLVANIA
Pa. Stat. Ann., tit. 42, § 7102 (as am. L. 1982, P.L. 1409, No. 326, art. II, § 201)

Tit. 42, § 7102. (a) General rule.—In all actions brought to recover damages for negligence resulting in death or injury to person or property, the fact that the plaintiff may have been guilty of contributory negligence shall not bar a recovery by the plaintiff or his legal representative where such negligence was not greater than the causal negligence of the defendant or defendants against whom recovery is sought, but any damages sustained by the plaintiff shall be diminished in proportion to the amount of negligence attributed to the plaintiff.

(b) **Recovery against joint defendant; contribution.** —Where recovery is allowed against more than one defendant, each defendant shall be liable for that proportion of the total dollar amount awarded as damages in the ratio of the amount of his causal negligence to the amount of causal negligence attributed to all defendants against whom recovery is allowed. The plaintiff may recover the full amount of the allowed recovery from any defendant against whom the plaintiff is not barred from recovery. Any defendant who is so compelled to pay more than his percentage share may seek contribution.

(c) **Downhill skiing.**—(1) The General Assembly finds that the sport of downhill skiing is practiced by a large number of citizens of this Commonwealth and also attracts to this Commonwealth large numbers of nonresidents significantly contributing to the economy of this Commonwealth. It is recognized that as in some other sports, there are inherent risks in the sport of downhill skiing.

(2) The doctrine of voluntary assumption of risk as it applies to downhill skiing injuries and damages is not modified by subsections (a) and (b).

(d) **Definitions.**—As used in this section the following words and phrases shall have the meanings given to them in this subsection:

"Defendant or defendants against whom recovery is sought." Includes impleaded defendants.

"Plaintiff." Includes counterclaimants and cross-claimants.

PUERTO RICO
P.R. Laws Ann., tit. 31, § 5141 (Laws 1956, No. 28, p. 86)

Tit. 31, § 5141. Obligation when damage caused by fault or negligence. A person who by an act or omission causes damage to another through fault or negligence shall be obliged to repair the damage so done. Concurrent imprudence of the party aggrieved does not exempt from liability, but entails a reduction of the indemnity.

RHODE ISLAND
R.I. Gen. Laws, §§ 9-20-4, 9-20-4.1 (as am. P.L. 1972, ch. 18, § 1)

9-20-4. Comparative negligence. In all actions hereafter brought for personal injuries, or where such injuries have resulted in death, or for injury to property, the fact that the person injured, or the owner of the property, or person having control over the property may not have been in the exercise of due care shall not bar a recovery, but damages shall be diminished by the finder of fact in proportion to the amount of negligence attributable to the person injured, or the owner of the property or the person having control over the property.

9-20-4.1. No set-off. There shall be no set-off of damages between the respective parties.

SOUTH DAKOTA
S.D. Codified Laws, § 20-9-2 (as am. 1964, ch. 149)

20-9-2. Comparative negligence—Reduction of damages. In all actions brought to recover damages for injuries to a person or to his property caused by the negligence of another, the fact that the plaintiff may have been guilty of contributory negligence shall not bar a recovery when the contributory negligence of the plaintiff was slight in comparison with the negligence of the defendant, but in such case, the damages shall be reduced in proportion to the amount of plaintiff's contributory negligence.

TEXAS
Tex. Rev. Civ. Stat. Ann. (Vernon), art. 2212a (Acts 1973, p. 41, ch. 28, §§ 1, 2, eff. 9-1-73)

Art. 2212a, Sec. 1. Modified comparative negligence. Contributory negligence shall not bar recovery in an action by any person or party or the legal representative of any person or party to recover damages for negligence resulting in death or injury to persons or property if such negligence is not greater than the negligence of the person or party or persons or parties against whom recovery is sought, but any damages allowed shall be diminished in proportion to the amount of negligence attributed to the person or party recovering.

Sec. 2. Contribution. (a) In this section:

(1) "Claimant" means any party seeking relief, whether he is a plaintiff, counterclaimant, or cross-claimant.

(2) "Defendant" includes any party from whom a claimant seeks relief.

(b) In a case in which there is more than one defendant, and the claimant's negligence does not exceed the total negligence of all defendants, contribution to the damages awarded to the claimant shall be in proportion to the percentage of negligence attributable to each defendant.

(c) Each defendant is jointly and severally liable for the entire amount of the judgment awarded the claimant, except that a defendant whose negligence is less than that of the claimant is liable to the claimant only for that portion of the judgment which represents the percentage of negligence attributable to him.

(d) If an alleged joint tort-feasor pays an amount to a claimant in settlement, but is never joined as a party defendant, or having been joined, is dismissed or nonsuited after settlement with the claimant (for which reason the existence and amount of his negligence are not submitted to the jury), each defendant is entitled to deduct from the amount for which he is liable to the claimant a percentage of the amount of the settlement based on the relationship the defendant's own negligence bears to the total negligence of all defendants.

(e) If an alleged joint tort-feasor makes a settlement with a claimant but nevertheless is joined as a party defendant at the time of the submission of the case to the jury (so that the existence and amount of his negligence are submitted to the jury) and his percentage of negligence is found by the jury, the settlement is a complete release of the portion of the judgment attributable to the percentage of negligence found on the part of that joint tort-feasor.

(f) In the application of the rules contained in Subsections (a) through (e) of this section results in two claimants being liable to each other in damages, the claimant who is liable for the greater amount is entitled to a credit toward his liability in the amount of damages owed him by the other claimant.

(g) All claims for contribution between named defendants in the primary suit shall be determined in the primary suit, except that a named defendant may proceed against a person not a party to the primary suit who has not effected a settlement with the claimant.

(h) This section prevails over Article 2212, Revised Civil Statutes of Texas, 1925, and all other laws to the extent of any conflict.

UTAH
Utah Code Ann., §§ 78-27-37 to 78-27-43 (L. 1973, ch. 209, §§ 1 to 7)

78-27-37. Comparative negligence–Diminishment of damages–"Contributory negligence" includes "assumption of the risk."–Contributory negligence shall not bar recovery in an action by any person or his legal representative to recover damages for negligence or gross negligence resulting in death or in injury to person or property, if such negligence was not as great as the negligence or gross negligence of the person against whom recovery is sought, but any damages allowed shall be diminished in the proportion to the amount of negligence attributable to the person recovering. As used in this act, "contributory negligence" includes "assumption of the risk."

78-27-38. Separate special verdicts on damages and percentage of negligence—Reduction of damages.—The court may, and when requested by any party shall, direct the jury to find separate special verdicts determining (1) the total amount of damages suffered and (2) the percentage of negligence attributable to each party; and the court shall then reduce the amount of the damages in proportion to the amount of negligence attributable to the person seeking recovery.

78-27-39. Contribution among joint tort-feasors—Discharge of common liability by joint tort-feasor required.—(1) The right of contribution shall exist among joint tort-feasors, but a joint tort-feasor shall not be entitled to a money judgment for contribution until he has, by payment, discharged the common liability or more than his prorata share thereof.

78-27-40. Settlement by joint tort-feasor—Determination of relative degrees of fault of joint tort-feasors—"Joint tort-feasor" defined.—(1) A joint tort-feasor who enters into a settlement with the injured person shall not be entitled to recover contribution from another joint tort-feasor whose liability to the injured person is not extinguished by that settlement.

(2) When there is a disproportion of fault among joint tort-feasors to an extent that it would render inequitable an equal distribution by contribution among them of their common liability, the relative degrees of fault of the joint tort-feasors shall be considered in determining their prorata shares, solely for the purpose of determining their rights of contribution among themselves, each remaining severally liable to the injured person for the whole injury as at common law.

(3) As used in this section, "joint tort-feasor" means one of two or more persons, jointly or severally liable in tort for the same injury to person or property, whether or not judgment has been recovered against all or some of them.

78-27-41. Individual liability of joint tort-feasors, right of indemnity under law, and contractual right to contribution or indemnity not affected.—Nothing in this act shall affect:

(1) The common-law liability of the several joint tort-feasors to have judgment recovered, and payment made, from them individually by the injured person for the whole injury. However, the recovery of a judgment by the injured person against one joint tort-feasor does not discharge the other joint tort-feasors.

(2) Any right of indemnity which may exist under present law.

(3) Any right to contribution or indemnity arising from contract or agreement.

78-27-42. Release of joint tort-feasor—Reduction of injured person's claim.—A release by the injured person of one joint tort-feasor, whether before or after judgment, does not discharge the other tort-feasors, unless the release so provides, but reduces the claim against the other tort-feasors by the greater of: (1) The amount of the consideration paid for that release; or (2) the amount or proportion by which the release provides that the total claim shall be reduced.

78-27-43. Release of joint tort-feasor—Requirements for relief from liability to make contribution.—(1) A release by the injured person of one joint

415

tort-feasor does not relieve him from liability to make contribution to another joint tort-feasor unless that release:

(a) Is given before the right of the other tort-feasor to secure a money judgment for contribution has accrued; and

(b) Provides for a reduction, to the extent of the prorata share of the released tort-feasor, of the injured person's damages recoverable against all the other tort-feasors.

(2) This section shall apply only if the issue of proportionate fault is litigated between joint tort-feasors in the same action.

VERMONT
Vt. Stat. Ann., tit. 12, § 1036 (as am. 1979 Acts, No. 179)

Tit. 12, § 1036. Comparative negligence. Contributory negligence shall not bar recovery in an action by any plaintiff, or his legal representative, to recover damages for negligence resulting in death, personal injury or property damage, if the negligence was not greater than the causal total negligence of the defendant or defendants, but the damage shall be diminished by general verdict in proportion to the amount of negligence attributed to the plaintiff. Where recovery is allowed against more than one defendant, each defendant shall be liable for that proportion of the total dollar amount awarded as damages in the ratio of the amount of his causal negligence to the amount of causal negligence attributed to all defendants against whom recovery is allowed.

VIRGIN ISLANDS
V.I. Code Ann., tit. 5, § 1451 (added Feb. 15, 1973, No. 3382, 1973 Acts, p.10)

Tit. 5, § 1451. Comparative damages. (a) In any action based upon negligence to recover for injury to person or property, the contributory negligence of the plaintiff shall not bar a recovery, but the damages shall be diminished by the trier of fact in proportion to the amount of negligence attributable to the plaintiff. The burden of proving contributory negligence shall be on the defendant. If such claimant is found by the trier of fact to be more at fault than the defendant, or, in the case of multiple defendants, more at fault than the combined fault of the defendants, the claimant may not recover.

(b) This section does not apply to any action based upon a statute the violation of which imposes absolute liability, whether or not such statute comprehends negligent conduct.

(c) The trier of fact shall report by general verdict the total damages, in dollars and cents, not reduced by any contributory negligence of plaintiff, and if plaintiff is found to be contributorily negligent, shall also report the amount to which the damages are reduced by reason thereof, in dollars and cents, in which case the lesser monetary amount shall be the final verdict in the case.

(d) Where recovery is allowed against more than one defendant, the trier of fact shall apportion, in dollars and cents, the amount awarded against each defendant. Liability of defendants to plaintiff shall be joint and several but, for contribution between defendants, each defendant shall be liable for that proportion of the verdict as the trier of fact has apportioned against such defendant.

(e) This section shall apply to all causes of action accruing 60 days after the effective date of this chapter.

WASHINGTON
Wash. Rev. Code Ann., §§ 4.22.005 to 4.22.020 (as am. Laws 1981, ch. 27)

4.22.005. Effect of contributory fault. In an action based on fault seeking to recover damages for injury or death to person or harm to property, any contributory fault chargeable to the claimant diminishes proportionately the amount awarded as compensatory damages for an injury attributable to the claimant's contributory fault, but does not bar recovery. This rule applies whether or not under prior law the claimant's contributory fault constituted a defense or was disregarded under applicable legal doctrines, such as last clear chance.

4.22.010. [Repealed by Laws 1981, ch. 27, § 17.]
Note. This section, which provided that contributory negligence was not to bar recovery in a negligence action, was derived from Laws 1973, 1st Ex.Sess., ch. 138, § 1. See, now, § 4.22.005.

4.22.015. "Fault" defined. "Fault" includes acts or omissions, including misuse of a product, that are in any measure negligent or reckless toward the person or property of the actor or others, or that subject a person to strict tort liability or liability on a product liability claim. The term also includes breach of warranty, unreasonable assumption of risk, and unreasonable failure to avoid an injury or to mitigate damages. Legal requirements of causal relation apply both to fault as the basis for liability and to contributory fault.

A comparison of fault for any purpose under RCW 4.22.005 through 4.22.060 shall involve consideration of both the nature of the conduct of the parties to the action and the extent of the causal relation between such conduct and the damages.

4.22.020. Imputation of contributory fault—Spouse or minor child of spouse—Wrongful death actions. The contributory fault of one spouse shall not be imputed to the other spouse or the minor child of the spouse to diminish recovery in an action by the other spouse or the minor child of the spouse, or his or her legal representative, to recover damages caused by fault resulting in death or in injury to the person or property, whether separate or community, of the spouse. In an action brought for wrongful death, the contributory fault of the decedent shall be imputed to the claimant in that action.

WISCONSIN
Wis. Stat. Ann., § 895.045 (as am. L. 1971, ch. 47, eff. June 23, 1971)

895.045. Contributory negligence. Contributory negligence shall not bar recovery in an action by any person or his legal representative to recover damages for negligence resulting in death or in injury to person or property, if such negligence was not greater than the negligence of the person against whom recovery is sought, but any damages allowed shall be diminished in the proportion to the amount of negligence attributable to the person recovering.

WYOMING
Wyo. Stat. Ann., §§ 1-1-109 to 1-1-113 (as am. L. 1977, ch. 188, § 1)

§ 1-1-109. Comparative negligence. (a) Contributory negligence shall not bar a recovery in an action by any person or his legal representative to recover damages for negligence resulting in death or in injury to person or property, if the contributory negligence was not as great as the negligence of the person against whom recovery is sought. Any damages allowed shall be diminished in proportion to the amount of negligence attributed to the person recovering.

(b) The court may, and when requested by any party shall:
(i) If a jury trial, direct the jury to find separate special verdicts;
(ii) If a trial before the court without jury, make special findings of fact determining the amount of damages and the percentage of negligence attributable to each party. The court shall then reduce the amount of such damages in proportion to the amount of negligence attributed to the person recovering;

(iii)   Inform the jury of the consequences of its determination of the percentage of negligence.

§ 1-1-110.   **Contribution.**   (a) Except as otherwise provided in W.S. 1-1-110 through 1-1-113, where two (2) or more persons become jointly or severally liable in tort for the same injury to person or property or for the same wrongful death, there is a right of contribution among them even though judgment has not been recovered against all or any of them.

(b)   The right of contribution exists only in favor of a tortfeasor who has paid more than his pro rata share of the common liability, and his total recovery is limited to the amount paid by him in excess of his pro rata share. No tortfeasor is compelled to make contribution beyond his own pro rata share of the entire liability.

(c)   There is no right of contribution in favor of any tortfeasor who has intentionally, willfully or wantonly caused or contributed to the injury or wrongful death.

(d)   A tortfeasor who enters into a settlement with a claimant is not entitled to recover contribution from another tortfeasor whose liability for the injury or wrongful death is not extinguished by the settlement nor in respect to any amount paid in a settlement which is in excess of what was reasonable.

(e)   A liability insurer, who by payment has discharged in full or in part the liability of an insured tortfeasor and has discharged in full its obligation as insurer, is subrogated to the insured tortfeasor's right of contribution to the extent of the amount it has paid in excess of the insured tortfeasor's pro rata share of the common liability. This provision does not limit or impair any right of the subrogation arising from any other relationship.

(f)   W.S. 1-1-110 through 1-1-113 do not impair any right of indemnity under existing law. Where one (1) tortfeasor is entitled to indemnity from another, the right of the indemnity obligee is for indemnity and not contribution, and the indemnity obligor is not entitled to contribution from the obligee for any portion of his indemnity obligation.

(g)   W.S. 1-1-110 through 1-1-113 do not apply to breaches of trust or of other fiduciary obligation.

(h)   W.S. 1-1-110 through 1-1-113 do not affect the common law liability of the several joint tortfeasors to have judgments recovered and payment made from them individually by the injured person for the whole injury. The recovery of a judgment by the injured person against one (1) joint tortfeasor does not discharge the other joint tortfeasors, from liability to the injured party.

§ 1-1-111.   **Pro rata shares.**   (a) In determining the pro rata shares of tortfeasors in the entire liability:

(i)   The relative degrees of fault of the joint tortfeasors shall be considered in determining their pro rata shares solely for the purpose of determining their rights of contribution among themselves, each remaining severally liable to the injured person for the whole injury as at common law;

(ii)   If equity requires, the collective liability of some as a group shall constitute a single share;

(iii)   A final verdict in favor of an alleged joint tortfeasor as against the injured party shall be a conclusive determination that such successful party is not liable to make contribution to any other tortfeasor.

§ 1-1-112.   **Enforcement.**   (a)   Whether or not judgment has been entered in an action against two (2) or more tortfeasors for the same injury or wrongful death, contribution may be enforced by separate action.

(b)   Where a judgment has been entered in an action against two (2) or more tortfeasors for the same injury or wrongful death, contribution may be enforced in that action by judgment in favor of one (1) against other judgment defendant by motion upon notice to all parties to the action.

(c) If there is a judgment for the injury or wrongful death against the tortfeasor seeking contribution, any separate action by him to enforce contribution shall be commenced within one (1) year after the judgment has become final by lapse of time for appeal or the decision on appeal has become final.

(d) If there is no judgment for the injury or wrongful death against the tortfeasor seeking contribution, his right of contribution is barred unless he has either:

(i) Discharged by payment the common liability within the statute of limitations period applicable to claimant's right of action against him and has commenced his action for contribution within one (1) year after payment; or

(ii) Agreed while action is pending against him to discharge the common liability and has within one (1) year after the agreement paid the liability and commenced his action for contribution.

(e) The recovery of a judgment for an injury or wrongful death against one (1) tortfeasor does not of itself discharge the other tortfeasors from liability for the injury of wrongful death unless the judgment is satisfied. The satisfaction of the judgment does not impair any right of contribution.

(f) The judgment determining the liability of the several defendants to the claimant for an injury or wrongful death is binding as among defendants in determining their right to contribution.

§ 1-1-113. **Release.** (a) When a release or a covenant not to sue or not to enforce judgment is given in good faith to one (1) of two (2) or more persons liable in tort for the same injury or the same wrongful death:

(i) It does not discharge any of the other tortfeasors from liability for the injury or wrongful death unless its terms so provide; but it reduces the claim against the others to the extent of any amount stipulated by the release or the covenant, or in the amount of the consideration paid for it, whichever is the greater; and

(ii) It discharges the tortfeasor to whom it is given from all liability for contribution to any other tortfeasor.

APPENDIX C

COMPARATIVE NEGLIGENCE STATUTES OF LIMITED APPLICATION

Jurisdiction and Statute	Coverage	Contributory Negligence and Apportionment	Defenses Abrogated
Federal Employers' Liability Act [U.S. Code, Tit. 45, §§ 51 to 55 (as amd., Aug. 11, 1939, c. 685, § 1, 53 Stat. 1404)]	Personal injury or death in employment by interstate railroad caused by negligence of employer, including defect or insufficiency of equipment	No bar to recovery but damages diminished in proportion; defense not available when violation of safety statute contributed to injury	Assumption of risk abrogated where negligence or violation of safety statute contributed to injury
Jones Act [U.S. Code, Tit. 46, § 688 (as amd., Dec. 29, 1982, P.L. 97-389, Title V, § 503(a), 96 Stat. 1955)]	Personal injury or death of seaman; statutes of U.S. applicable to railway employees injured or killed in course of employment apply; applies to citizens or permanent resident aliens		
Alaska Stat., §§ 23.25.010 to 23.25.040	Personal injury, death or property damage in manufacturing, mining, construction, building or other business using machinery or appliances, due to negligence of employer, including defect or insufficiency of equipment	No bar to recovery where slight and employer's negligence gross in comparison; damages diminished by jury in proportion	

421

Jurisdiction and Statute	Coverage	Contributory Negligence and Apportionment	Defenses Abrogated
Ariz. Rev. Stat. Ann., §§ 23-801 to 23-808	Personal injury or death in mining, smelting, manufacturing, railroad, street railway, or industry defined as hazardous, not due to contributory negligence	No bar to recovery but damages diminished in proportion	Assumption of inherent risks of employment abrogated; common-law defenses abrogated except contributory negligence as sole cause
Ark. Stat. Ann., §§ 73-914 to 73-919	Personal injury, death or property damage in employment by railroad	No bar to recovery if of less degree than employer's negligence; no apportionment; defense not available when violation of safety statute contributed to injury	Assumption of risk abrogated
Ark. Stat. Ann., §§ 81-1201 to 81-1208	Personal injury or death in employment (except railroad) not covered by workmen's compensation	No bar to recovery but damages diminished by jury in proportion; defense not available when violation of safety statute contributed to injury	Assumption of risk abrogated where violation of safety statute contributed to injury
Cal. Labor Code, § 2801	Personal injury or death in course of employment	No bar to recovery where slight and employer's negligence gross in comparison; damages diminished in proportion; defense not available where violation of safety law contributed to injury	Express and implied assumption of risk abrogated as defense; fellow servant rule abolished

Colo. Rev. Stat., §§ 40-33-101 to 40-33-109	Personal injury or death in employment by railroad, due to negligence of employer	No bar to recovery but damages diminished in proportion; defense not available where violation of safety statute contributed to injury	Assumption of risk abrogated where injury caused by employer's negligence; presumption of negligence from fact of injury
D.C. Code Ann., §§ 44-401 to 44-404	Personal injury or death in employment by common carrier	No bar to recovery where slight and employer's negligence gross in comparison; damages diminished in proportion	
Fla. Stat. Ann., §§ 769.01 to 769.06	Personal injury or death in employment by railroad, street railway, electric utility, telephone, telegraph, express, blasting, automobiles for public use, power boats	No bar to recovery but damages diminished in proportion; fellow servant rule applies where plaintiff jointly negligent with fellow	Assumption of risk abrogated where injury caused by employer's negligence; presumption of negligence from fact of injury
Ga. Code Ann., §§ 34-7-41 to 34-7-44	Personal injury or death in employment by railroad	No bar to recovery unless employee could have avoided consequences by ordinary care; damages diminished in proportion; defense not available where violation of safety statute contributed to injury	Assumption of risk abrogated where violation of safety statute contributed to injury

Jurisdiction and Statute	Coverage	Contributory Negligence and Apportionment	Defenses Abrogated
Iowa Code Ann., §§ 327D.188, 327D.189	Personal injury or death in employment by railway corporation	No bar to recovery but damages diminished in proportion; defense not available where violation of safety statute contributed to injury	Assumption of risk abrogated
Kan. Stat. Ann., §§ 66-237 to 66-241	Personal injury or death in employment by railroad, due to negligence of employer, including defect or insufficiency of equipment	No bar to recovery but damages diminished in proportion; defense not available where violation of safety statute contributed to injury	Assumption of risk abrogated where violation of safety statute contributed to injury
Ky. Rev. Stat., §§ 277.310, 277.320	Personal injury or death in employment by railroad, due to negligence of employer, including defect or insufficiency of equipment	No bar to recovery but damages diminished in proportion; defense not available where violation of safety statute contributed to injury	Assumption of risk abrogated where violation of safety statute contributed to injury
Mich. Comp. Laws Ann., §§ 419.51 to 419.57	All damages sustained in employment by railroad, except employees working in shops or offices, due to negligence of employer, including defect or insufficiency of equipment	No bar to recovery where of less degree than employer's; no apportionment; defense not available where violation of safety statute contributed to injury	Assumption of risk abrogated where violation of safety statute contributed to injury

424

Minn. Stat. Ann., §§ 219.77, 219.79 to 219.83	Personal injury or death in employment by railroad	No bar to recovery but damages diminished in proportion; defense not available where violation of safety statute contributed to injury	Assumption of risk abrogated
Mont. Code Ann., § 69-14-1006	Personal injury or death in employment by railroad, due to negligence of employer, including defect or insufficiency of equipment	No bar to recovery but damages diminished in proportion; defense not available where violation of safety statute contributed to injury	Assumption of risk abrogated as to negligence of employer
Neb. Rev. Stat., §§ 25-1150, 74-703 to 74-705	Personal injury or death in employment by railway company, due to negligence of employer, including defect or insufficiency of equipment	No bar to recovery where slight and employer's negligence gross in comparison; damages diminished in proportion; no contributory negligence for furnishing substitutes for inadequate tools	Assumption of risk abrogated where employer negligent
N.C. Gen. Stat., § 62-242	Personal injury or death in employment by railroad, logging road or tram road, due to negligence of employer, including defect or insufficiency of equipment	No bar to recovery but damages diminished in proportion; defense not available where violation of safety statute contributed to injury	Assumption of risk abrogated where violation of safety statute contributed to injury

Jurisdiction and Statute	Coverage	Contributory Negligence and Apportionment	Defenses Abrogated
N.D. Cent. Code, §§ 49-16-02 to 49-16-05, 49-16-08	Personal injury or death in employment by railroad corporation, due to negligence, including defect or insufficiency of equipment	No bar to recovery but damages diminished in proportion; defense not available where violation of safety statute contributed to injury; no contributory negligence from continuation in employment with knowledge of unlawful use of equipment	Assumption of risk abrogated where violation of safety statute contributed to injury; no assumption of risk from continuation in employment with knowledge of unlawful use of equipment
Ohio Rev. Code Ann., § 4113.07	Personal injury or death in employment not covered by workmen's compensation	No bar to recovery where slight and employer's negligence gross in comparison; damages diminished in proportion; defense not available where violation of safety statute contributed to injury unless employee had duty but failed to report violation and employer had no knowledge	
Ohio Rev. Code Ann., §§ 4973.08, 4973.09	Personal injury or death in employment by railroad, due to negligence or defect in equipment; defect is prima facie evidence of negligence	No bar to recovery where slight and employer's negligence gross in comparison; damages diminished in proportion; no contributory negligence from continuation in employment with knowledge of defect in equipment	Assumption of risk not found from continuation in employment with knowledge of defect in equipment

426

Ore. Rev. Stat., §§ 654.305 to 654.335	Personal injury or death from employment in occupation defined as dangerous or hazardous, due to violation of safety statute	No bar to recovery but may be taken into account by jury in fixing damages	Fellow servant rule abrogated
S.C. Code Ann., §§ 58-17-3710 to 58-17-3800	Personal injury or death in employment by railroad, due to negligence of employer, including defect or insufficiency of equipment	No bar to recovery but damages diminished in proportion; defense not available where violation of safety statute contributed to injury	Assumption of risk abrogated where violation of safety statute contributed to injury
Tex. Rev. Civ. Stat. Ann. (Vernon), arts. 6439 to 6443	Personal injury or death in employment by railroad, due to negligence of employer, including defect or insufficiency of equipment	No bar to recovery but damages diminished in proportion; defense not available where violation of safety statute contributed to injury	Assumption of risk abrogated where violation of safety statute contributed to injury
Va. Code, §§ 8.01-57 to 8.01-62	Personal injury or death in hazardous employment by railroad, due to negligence, including defect or insufficiency of equipment	No bar to recovery but damages diminished in proportion; defense not available where violation of safety statute contributed to injury	Assumption of risk abrogated where violation of safety statute contributed to injury; knowledge of defect no bar to recovery
Va. Code, § 56-416	Personal injury, death or property damage to traveler on public highway due to railroad's failure to give required signal at crossing	No bar to recovery but may be considered in mitigation of damages	

427

Jurisdiction and Statute	Coverage	Contributory Negligence and Apportionment	Defenses Abrogated
Wyo. Stat., §§ 37-9-501 to 37-9-504	Personal injury or death in employment by railroad, due to negligence of employer, including defect or insufficiency of equipment	No bar to recovery but damages diminished in proportion; defense not available where violation of safety statute contributed to injury	Assumption of risk abrogated where risk created by employer's negligence

BIBLIOGRAPHY

Books and Pamphlets Cited in Text

Austin, J. *Lectures on Jurisprudence*. 2 vols. 5th ed. New York: Cockcroft, 1875.

Barron, W., and Holtzoff, A. *Federal Practice and Procedure*. Rules ed. St. Paul: West, 1961.

The Case Against Punitive Damages. Monograph Series. Milwaukee: Defense Research Institute, August, 1969.

Comparative Negligence. ATL Monograph Series. American Trial Lawyers Association, 1970.

Dollars, Delay and the Automobile Victim. Studies in Reparation for Highway Injuries and Related Court Problems. Supported by the Walter E. Meyer Research Institute of Law. Indianapolis: Bobbs-Merrill, 1968.

Ehrenzweig, A. *Conflict of Laws*. St. Paul: West, 1962.

Franklin, M. *Injuries and Remedies: Cases and Materials on Tort Law and Alternatives*. Mineola, N.Y.: Foundation Press, 1971.

Frumer, L., and Friedman, M. *Products Liability*. New York: Matthew Bender, 1984.

Gilmore, G., and Black, C. *The Law of Admiralty*. Mineola, N.Y.: Foundation Press, 1957.

Goodman, R. *Automobile Design Liability*. 2d ed. Rochester, N.Y.: Lawyers Co-operative, 1983.

Goodrich, H. *Handbook of the Conflict of Laws*. 4th ed., ed. E. Scoles. St. Paul: West, 1964.

Green, L. *Rationale of Proximate Cause*. Reprint of 1927 edition. South Hackensack, N.J.: Rothman Reprints, 1976.

Gregory, C. *Legislative Loss Distribution in Negligence Actions—A Study in Administrative Aspects of Comparative Negligence and Contribution in Tort Litigation*. Chicago: University of Chicago Press, 1936.

Harper, F., and James, F. *The Law of Torts*. Boston: Little, Brown, 1956.

Hart, H., and Honoré, M. *Causation in the Law*. New York: Oxford Univ. Press, 1959.

Hursh, R. *American Law of Products Liability*. Rochester, N.Y.: Lawyers Co-operative, 1961.

The Institutes of Justinian. English introduction, translation and notes by Thomas Collett Sandars. Reprint of 1922 ed. Westport, Conn.: Greenwood Press, 1970.

James, F., and Hazard, G. *Civil Procedure*. Boston: Little, Brown, 1977.

Keeton, R. *Legal Cause in the Law of Torts*. Columbus, Ohio: Ohio State Univ. Press, 1963.

Keeton, R., and O'Connell, J. *Basic Protection for the Traffic Victim; a Blueprint for Reforming Automobile Insurance*. Boston: Little, Brown, 1965.

Keeton, W.P., and Keeton, R. *Cases and Materials on the Law of Torts*. Mineola, N.Y.: Foundation Press, 1971.

Keeton, W.P.; Dobbs, D.; Keeton, R.; and Owen, D. *Prosser and Keeton on the Law of Torts*. 5th ed. St. Paul: West, 1984.

Harvard Legal Essays. Edited by Roscoe Pound. Reprint of 1934 ed. Freeport, N.Y.: Books for Libraries Press, 1967.

Larson, A. *Workmen's Compensation.* New York: Matthew Bender, 1984.

Leflar, R. *American Conflicts of Law.* Revised ed. Indianapolis: Bobbs-Merrill, 1968.

Marsden, R. *A Treatise on the Law of Collisions at Sea.* 11th ed. London: Stevens, 1961.

Moore, J. *Federal Practice.* 9 vols. New York: Matthew Bender, 1984.

Prosser, W. *Handbook of the Law of Torts.* 4th ed. St. Paul: West, 1971.

Prosser, W., and Wade, J. *Cases and Materials on Torts.* 5th ed. St. Paul: West, 1971.

Prosser, W.; Wade, J.; and Schwartz, V. *Cases and Materials on Torts.* 7th ed. Mineola, N.Y.: Foundation Press, 1982.

Responsible Reform: A Program to Improve the Liability Reparation System. Pamphlet No. 8. Milwaukee: Defense Research Institute, 1969.

Responsible Reform: An Update. Pamphlet No. 3. Milwaukee: Defense Research Institute, 1972.

Restatement of Torts. St. Paul: American Law Institute, 1934.

Restatement (Second) of Conflict of Laws. St. Paul: American Law Institute, 1971.

Restatement (Second) of Torts. St. Paul: American Law Institute, 1965.

Restatement (Second) of Torts. Tentative Draft. St. Paul: American Law Institute, 1979.

Restatement (Second) of Torts. Tentative Draft No. 10. St. Paul: American Law Institute, 1964.

Robinson, G. *Handbook of Admiralty Law in the United States.* St. Paul: West, 1939.

Schwartz, V. *Comparative Negligence.* Indianapolis: Allen Smith, 1974.

Schwartz, V. *Comparative Negligence: 1981 Supplement.* Indianapolis: Allen Smith, 1981.

The Seat Belt Defense in Practice. Monograph No. 6. Milwaukee: Defense Research Institute, 1970.

Speiser, S. *Recovery for Wrongful Death.* 2d ed. Rochester, N.Y.: Lawyers Co-operative, 1975.

Sutherland, J. *Statutes and Statutory Construction.* 3 vols., 3d ed., ed. F. Horack, Jr. Chicago: Callaghan, 1943.

Ulman, J. *A Judge Takes the Stand.* New York: Knopf, 1933.

Weintraub, R. *Commentary on the Conflicts of Laws.* 2d ed. Mineola, N.Y.: Foundation Press, 1980.

Words and Phrases. Permanent ed. 45 vols. St. Paul: West, 1940-45.

Wright, C. *The Law of Federal Courts.* 4th ed. St. Paul: West, 1983.

Articles in Addition
to Those Cited in Text

CHAPTERS 1 TO 3—
HISTORY, IMPACT, SYSTEMS

Abraham, *Adopting Comparative Negligence: Some Thoughts for the Late Reformer,* 41 Md. L. Rev. 300 (1982).

Beltz and Daly, *Comparative Negligence on Balance,* 58 Mich. B.J. 580 (1979).

Berg, *Comparative Negligence: A Substitute for the Rule of Contributory Negligence,* 9 S.D.B. J. 200 (1940).

BIBLIOGRAPHY

Boyle, *Comparative Negligence Law—A Descriptive Word Index*, 33 Wis. B. Bull. 13 (1960).

Bress, *Comparative Negligence: Let Us Hearken to the Call of Progress*, 43 A.B.A. J. 127 (1957).

Burns, *Comparative Negligence: A Law Professor Dissents*, 51 Ill. B.J. 708 (1963).

Comparative Fault Approach to the Due Diligence Requirement of Rule 10b-5, 49 Fordham L. Rev. 561 (1981).

Comparative Negligence, 81 Colum. L. Rev. 1668 (1981).

Comparative Negligence: Liability of Railroad Companies, 2 U. Fla. L. Rev. 124 (1949).

Comparative Negligence—The Developing Doctrine and the Death of Maki, 18 De Paul L. Rev. 203 (1968).

Comparative v. Contributory Negligence: The Effect of Plantiff's Fault, 6 N.M.L. Rev. 171 (1975).

Contributory Negligence and the Comparison of Fault, 91 Irish Law Times 175, 181 (1957).

Cooley, *Problems in Contributory Negligence*, 89 U. Pa. L. Rev. 335 (1941).

Cooper & Olson, *Constitutional Aspects of the Comparative Negligence Statutes*, 28 Okla. L. Rev. 49 (1975).

Cowan, *The Comparative Negligence Doctrine in Automobile Cases*, 20 Kan. Jud. Council Bull. 127 (1946).

Defense Research Institute, *Practice and Procedure—Comparative Negligence Primer* (monograph 1975).

Eldredge, *Contributory Negligence: An Outmoded Defense That Should Be Abolished*, 43 A.B.A. J. 52 (1957).

Ellerby & Gauhan, *Comparative Negligence by Judicial Fiat*, 42 Ins. Couns. J. 575 (1975).

Examining the Plaintiff's Conduct Under the Model Uniform Liability Act, 46 J. Air L. 419 (1981).

Fisher, *Comparative Negligence—Some Unanswered Questions*, 47 Fla. B.J. 566 (1973).

Fisher, Nugent & Lewis, *Comparative Negligence: An Exercise in Applied Justice*, 5 St. Mary's L.J. 655 (1973-74).

Gair, *Comparative Negligence*, 21 Queens B. Bull. 136 (1958).

Genard, *Notes on Comparative Negligence*, 51 L.A.B. J. 59 (1975).

Gerringer, *A Survey of Progress Toward the Comparative Negligence Rule*, 15 Law. Guild Rev. 1 (1955).

Hammond & Wade, *Comparative Negligence—Some Unanswered Questions*, 58 Mich. B.J. 232 (1979).

Heft, *Comparative Negligence: What It Is, How It Works, Why It's Fair*, 19 Fed'n Ins. Couns. Q. 79 (1969).

Heft & Heft, *Controversial Concepts Within Comparative Negligence*, 33 Fed'n Ins. Couns. Q. 49 (1982).

Judicial Activism in Tort Reform: The Guest Statute Exemplar and a Proposal for Comparative Negligence, 21 UCLA L. Rev. 1566 (1974).

Kightlinger, *The Doctrine of Comparative Negligence*, 16 Ohio B. 129 (1943).

Krause, *No-Fault's Alternative—The Case for Comparative Negligence and Compulsory Arbitration in New York*, 44 N.Y. St. B.J. 535 (1972).

Lambert, *Case for Comparative Negligence*, 2 Trial Law. Q. 16 (1965).

Liquor Law Liability—Comparative Negligence—Drunk Bar Patron Denied Recovery for His Injuries in a Suit Against the Bar, 17 Santa Clara L. Rev. 469 (1977).

Maury, *In Defense of Comparative Negligence*, 14 Cal. St. B.J. 297 (1939).

McConnell, *Comparative Negligence: Coping With the Changes*, 25 Trial Law. Guide 526 (1982).

Miller, *Extending the Fairness Principle of Li and American Motorcycle [Assn. v. Superior Court of Los Angeles County, 578 P. 2d 899 (Cal. 1978)]: Adoption of the Uniform Comparative Fault Act*, 14 Pac. L.J. 835 (1983).

Mooney, *Comparative Negligence—Reduction of Damages*, 17 Marq. L. Rev. 292 (1933).

O'Connell, *Proposal to Abolish Contributory and Comparative Fault with Compensatory Savings By Also Abolishing the Collateral Source Rule*, 1979 U. Ill. L.F. 591; Adaptations, 1980 Ins. L.J. 206.

Oliver, *Let Us All Be Frank About Comparative Negligence*, 28 L.A.B. Bull. 119, 140 (1953).

Palmer, *Let Us Be Frank About Comparative Negliegence*, 28 L.A.B. Bull. 37, 55 (1952).

Park, Jr., *Comparative Negligence Is Here Now?*, 39 Ky. Bench & B. 18 (1975).

Payne, *Reduction of Damages for Contributory Negligence*, 18 Mod. L. Rev. 344 (1955).

Pfankuch, *Comparative Negligence v. Contributory Negligence*, 1968 Ins. L.J. 725.

Phelan, Martin, & Scheid, *Comparative Negligence—Panacea or Pandora's Box?*, 1 J. Mar. J. Prac. & Proc. 270 (1968).

Pilot Error and Comparative Negligence: A Suggested Approach to Determining Relative Fault, 1980 Det. C.L. Rev. 1123.

Pound, *Comparative Negligence*, 6 Plaintiff's Advoc. 9 (1962).

Prosser, *Comparative Negligence*, 41 Calif. L. Rev. 1 (1953).

Redmond, *Fault and Apportionment Acts*, 31 Austl. L.J. 520 (1957).

Rizzo & Arnold, *Causal Apportionment in the Law of Torts: An Economic Theory*, 80 Colum. L. Rev. 1399 (1980).

Schroeder, *Courts and Comparative Negligence*, 1950 Ins. L.J. 791.

Schwartz, *Comparative Negligence*, 20 Prac. Law. 13 (1974).

Schwartz, *Comparative Negligence: Oiling the System*, 11 Trial 58 (1975).

Schwartz, *Contributory and Comparative Negligence: A Reappraisal*, 87 Yale L.J. 697 (1978).

Schwartz, *The Impact of Comparative Negligence*, 23 Def. L.J. 223 (1974).

Schwartz, *Pure Comparative Negligence in Action*, 34 A.T.L. L.J. 117 (1972).

Soule & Conkle, *Comparative Negligence versus the Constitutional Guarantee of Equal Protection: A Hypothetical Judicial Decision*, 1979 Duke L.J. 1083.

Tooze, *Contributory versus Comparative Negligence—A Judge Expresses His Views*, 12 N.A.C.C.A. L.J. 211 (1953).

Tort—Abolition of Defense of Contributory Negligence in Pedestrian-Motorist Cases, 53 Tul. L. Rev. 296 (1978).

Torts—Comparative Negligence—Adoption by Judicial Decree, 48 Tul. L. Rev. 746 (1974).

Torts—De Facto Abandonment of Contributory Negligence, 25 Ark. L. Rev. 559 (1972).

BIBLIOGRAPHY

Torts—Judicial Adoption of "Pure" Comparative Negligence, 7 U. Tol. L. Rev. 368 (1975).

Torts—Negligence—Contribution—Assumption of Risk and Gross Negligence Abolished Because Inconsistent with Comparative Negligence Act [McConville v. State Farm Mut. Auto. Ins. Co., 113 N.W.2d 14 (Wis. 1962); Bielski v. Schulze, 114 N.W.2d 105 (Wis. 1962)], 41 Tex. L. Rev. 459 (1963).

Twerski, *Selective Use of Comparative Fault*, 16 Trial 30 (1980).

Wade, *Uniform Comparative Fault Act*, 14 Forum 379 (1979).

Wade, *Uniform Comparative Fault Act—What Should It Provide?*, 10 U. Mich. J.L. Ref. 220 (1977).

Walker, *Question of Contributory Negligence*, 129 New L.J. 674 (1979).

Woods, *Quickening March of Comparative Fault*, 15 Trial 26 (1979).

Woods, *The Trend Toward Comparative Fault*, 20 Trial 16 (1984).

CHAPTERS 1 TO 3—
INDIVIDUAL JURISDICTIONS

Admiralty and Maritime:

Admiralty: Comparative Negligence in Collision Cases, 36 La. L. Rev. 288 (1975).

Admiralty—Division of Damages—Negligence—Failure of Ship to Use Radar as Determinative of Negligence [The Medford, 65 F. Supp. 622 (E.D. N.Y. 1946)], 33 Va. L. Rev. 86 (1947).

Admiralty—Strict Products Liability—Comparative Fault Principles Applicable to Strict Products Liability Actions in Admiralty, 49 Miss. L.J. 495 (1978).

Admiralty—Texas Wrongful Death and Survival Statutes—Unseaworthiness and Comparative Negligence [Vassallo v. Nederl-Amerik Stoomv Maats Holland, 344 S.W.2d 421 (Tex. 1961)], 16 Sw. L.J. 67 (1962).

Code Practice—Directed Verdicts Under the Comparative Negligence Statute [Campanelli v. Milwaukee Electric R. & Transport Co., 8 N.W.2d 390 (1943)], 27 Marq. L. Rev. 219 (1943).

Comparative Negligence Sails the High Seas: Have the Recovery Rights of Cargo Owners Been Jeopardized?, 7 Cal. W. Intl. L.J. 179 (1977).

Derby, *Divided Damages in Marine Cases*, 33 Va. L. Rev. 289 (1947).

The Doctrine of Comparative Fault Applies in an Admiralty Strict Products Liability Case: Lewis v. Timco, Inc., 716 F.2d 1425, 15 Tex. Tech L. Rev. 983 (1984).

Gorman, *Choice Between Proportionate Fault or Ryan Indemnity in Maritime Property Damage Cases*, 10 J. Mar. L. 325 (1979).

Owen & Moore, *Comparative Negligence in Maritime Personal Injury Cases*, 43 La. L. Rev. 941 (1983).

Stover & Plaetzer, *Comparative Negligence and the Harbor Workers' Act—History, Examination, Diagnosis and Treatment*, 63 Marq. L. Rev. 349 (1980).

United States v. Reliable Transfer Co. [95 S. Ct. 1708 (1975)], 10 Suffolk U.L. Rev. 116 (1975).

Federal:

FELA—Contributory Negligence [Rocco v. Lehigh Valley R.R., 53 S. Ct. 343 (1933)], 11 Tex. L. Rev. 552 (1933).

West, *Comparative Negligence in the Federal Courts*, 10 Ark. L. Rev. 75 (1955-56).

COMPARATIVE NEGLIGENCE

Alaska:

Williams, *Kaatz vs. State: The Rule of Comparative Negligence Afloat Upon Uncharted Alaskan Waters*, 6 U.C.L.A.-Alaska L. Rev. 175 (1977).

Arizona:

Comparative Negligence in Arizona, 1979 Ariz. St. L.J. 581.

Arkansas:

Comparative Negligence—A Survey of the Arkansas Experience, 22 Ark. L. Rev. 692 (1969).

Gilliam, *Comparative Negligence Under Earlier Arkansas Statute*, 10 Ark. L. Rev. 65 (1955-56).

Lindsey, *The Arkansas Experience with Comparative Negligence*, 10 Ark. L. Rev. 70 (1955-56).

California:

England, *Li v. Yellow Cab Co. [532 P.2d 1226 (Cal. 1975)]—A Belated and Inglorious Centennial of the California Civil Code*, 65 Calif. L. Rev. 5 (1977).

Levit, *California Supreme Court Abolishes Contributory Negligence as a Defense*, 1975 Ins. L.J. 221.

Nga Li v. Yellow Cab of Calif. [532 P.2d 1226 (Cal. 1975)], 30 Ark. L. Rev. 557 (1977).

Schwartz, *Comparative Negligence in California—Li v. Yellow Cab Company [532 P.2d 1226 (Cal. 1975)]: A Survey of California Practice Under Comparative Negligence*, 7 Pac. L.J. 747 (1976).

Schwartz, *Judicial Adoption of Comparative Negligence—The Supreme Court of California Takes a Historic Stand*, 51 Ind. L.J. 281 (1976).

Torts—Comparative Negligence—Contributory Negligence Judicially Abrogated by California Supreme Court, 6 Cum. L. Rev. 515 (1975).

Colorado:

Schwartz, *Comparative Negligence in Colorado*, 4 Colo. Law. 469 (1975).

Connecticut:

James, *Connecticut's Comparative Negligence Statute: An Analysis of Some Problems*, 1974 Ins. L.J. 375.

Saden, *Comparative Negligence Adopted in Connecticut*, 47 Conn. B.J. 416 (1973).

Florida:

Case for Comparative Contribution in Florida, 30 U. Miami L. Rev. 713 (1976).

Hoffman v. Jones [280 So. 2d 431 (Fla. 1973)], 4 Mem. St. U.L. Rev. 604 (1974).

Hoffman v. Jones [280 So. 2d 431 (Fla. 1973)], 28 U. Miami L. Rev. 473 (1974).

Walkowiak, *Innocent Injury and Loss Distribution: The Florida Pure Comparative Negligence System*, 5 Fla. St. U.L. Rev. 66 (1977).

Georgia:

Contributory Negligence, Comparative Negligence Doctrine [Southern R. Co. v. Bullock, 156 S.E. 456 (Ga. App. 1931)], 2 Ga. Law. 21 (1931).

Torts—Comparative Negligence [Georgia Stages, Inc. v. Pitman, 31 S.E.2d 887 (Ga. App. 1944)], 7 Ga. B.A.J. 355 (1945).

BIBLIOGRAPHY

Illinois:

Guy, *There is Nothing to Compare in Comparative Negligence*, 70 Ill. B.J. 484 (1982).

Kionka, *Comparative Negligence Comes to Illinois*, 70 Ill. B.J. 16 (1981).

Pure Comparative Negligence in Illinois, 58 Chi.-Kent L. Rev. 599 (1982).

Indiana:

Symposium on Indiana's Comparative Fault Act, 17 Ind. L. Rev. 687 (1984).

Yosha, *Indiana's Comparative Fault Act*, 27 Res Gestae 413, 476 (1984).

Kansas:

Comparative Negligence—A Look at the New Kansas Statute, 23 Kan. L. Rev. 113 (1974).

Torts: Causes Of Action Must Be Litigated at One Time Under the Comparative Negligence Principles of K.S.A. § 60-258a, 21 Washburn L.J. 725 (1982).

Vasos, *Comparative Negligence Update—A Discussion of Selected Issues*, 44 J. Kan. B.A. 13 (1975).

Woods, *New Kansas Comparative Negligence Act—An Idea Whose Time Has Come*, 14 Washburn L.J. 1 (1975).

Louisiana:

Robertson, *Ruminations on Comparative Fault, Duty-Risk Analysis, Affirmative Defenses, and Defensive Doctrines in Negligence and Strict Liability Litigation in Louisiana*, 44 La. L. Rev. 1341 (1984).

Symposium: Comparative Negligence in Louisiana, 40 La. L. Rev. 289 (1980).

Maine:

Comparative Negligence and Comparative Contribution in Maine: The Need for Guidelines, 24 Me. L. Rev. 243 (1972).

Maryland:

Digges & Klein, *Comparative Fault in Maryland: The Time Has Come*, 41 Md. L. Rev. 276 (1982).

Massachusetts:

Smith, *Comparative Negligence in Massachusetts*, 54 Mass. L.Q. 140 (1969).

Michigan:

Michigan Adopts Comparative Negligence: Will Comparative Contribution Follow?, 1980 Det. C.L. Rev. 1157 (1980).

Minnesota:

The Scope of Comparative Fault in Minnesota, 9 Wm. Mitchell L. Rev. 299 (1983).

Torts: Joint Ventures' Negligence Must Be Combined Under the Minnesota Comparative Negligence Statute, 58 Minn. L. Rev. 978 (1974).

Mississippi:

Mississippi Comparative Negligence Statute in Automobile Cases, 11 Miss. L.J. 221 (1938).

Negligence—Mississippi Comparative Negligence Statute—Wisconsin Statute Compared [Nelson v. Chicago, M., St. P. & Pac. Ry., 32 N.W.2d 340 (Wis. 1948)], 20 Miss. L.J. 99 (1948).

Missouri:

Anderson & Bruce, *Recent Developments in Missouri Tort Law: Gustafson v. Benda [661 S.W.2d 11 (Mo. 1983)]*, 52 U. Mo. K.C.L. Rev. 538 (1984).

Montana:

Comparative Negligence in Montana, 37 Mont. L. Rev. 152 (1976).

Nebraska:

Wiebusch, *Torts—Comparative Negligence in Nebraska—Effect of Statute*, 17 Neb. L. Bull. 68 (1938).

New Hampshire:

Nixon, *The Actual "Legislative Intent" Behind New Hampshire's Comparative Negligence Statute*, 12 N.H. B.J. 17 (1969).

New Mexico:

Torts—Negligence—Judicial Adoption of Comparative Negligence in New Mexico, 11 N.M.L. Rev. 487 (1981).

New York:

Homburger, *The 1975 New York Judicial Conference Package: Class Actions and Comparative Negligence*, 25 Buffalo L. Rev. 415 (1976).

Krause, *Comparative Negligence in New York*, 47 N.Y.S. B.J. 638 (1975).

North Dakota:

Erickson, *Comparative Negligence—North Dakota*, 51 N.D.L. Rev. 745 (1975).

Ohio:

Brant, *Practitioner's Guide to Comparative Negligence in Ohio*, 41 Ohio St. L.J. 585 (1980).

Hennemuth, *Ohio's Last Word on Comparative Negligence? Revised Code Section 2315.19*, 9 Ohio N.U.L. Rev. 31 (1982).

Judicial Adoption of Comparative Negligence in Ohio, 44 U. Cin. L. Rev. 811 (1975).

Wise, *Retroactive Application of Ohio's Comparative Negligence Statute—A Golden Opportunity*, 9 Ohio N.U.L. Rev. 63 (1982).

Oklahoma:

Gibbens, *Constitutionality of Oklahoma's Comparative Negligence Statute*, 28 Okla. L. Rev. 33 (1975).

Pennsylvania:

Pelaez & Gilardi, *Pennsylvania Comparative Negligence Act—An "Alien Intruder in the House of Common Law,"* 16 Duq. L. Rev. 739 (1978).

Pennsylvania Comparative Negligence Act: The Fifty-One Percent Solution, 50 Temp. L.Q. 352 (1977).

Symposium—Comparative Negligence in Pennsylvania, 24 Vill. L. Rev. 419 (1979).

Torts—Negligence—Pennsylvania Enacts Comparative Negligence Statute; Act of July 9, 1976, P.L. _____, No. 152, 81 Dick. L. Rev. 677 (1977).

Puerto Rico:

Wiesner, *Contributory and Comparative Negligence in Puerto Rico*, 11 Miami L.Q. 502 (1957).

South Carolina:

Call for the Adoption of Comparative Negligence in South Carolina, 31 S.C.L. Rev. 757 (1980).

Phillips, *Case for Judicial Adoption of Comparative Fault in South Carolina*, 32 S.C.L. Rev. 295 (1980).

Tennessee:

Wade, *Comparative Fault in Tennessee Tort Actions: Past, Present and Future*, 41 Tenn. L. Rev. 423, 461 (1974).

Texas:

Abraham & Riddle, *Comparative Negligence—A New Horizon*, 25 Baylor L. Rev. 411 (1973).

Comparative Negligence in Texas, 11 Hous. L. Rev. 101 (1974).

Dorsaneo & Robertson, *Comparative Negligence in Texas*, 10 Tex. Tech L. Rev. 933 (1979).

Texas Tort Law in Transition, 57 Tex. L. Rev. 381 (1979).

Utah:

Thode, *Comparative Negligence, Contribution Among Tortfeasors, and the Effect of a Release—A Triple Play by the Utah Legislature*, 1973 Utah L. Rev. 406.

Vermont:

Comparative Negligence in Vermont: A Solution or a Problem?, 40 Alb. L. Rev. 777 (1976).

West Virginia:

Symposium on Bradley v. Appalachian Power Co.—West Virginia Adopts Comparative Negligence, 82 W. Va. L. Rev. 473 (1980).

Wisconsin:

Heft & Heft, *Comparative Negligence: The Wisconsin Concept*, 1970 A.B.A. Sect. Ins. N. & C.L. 527.

Knoller, *Suggested Amendments to Wisconsin Comparative Negligence Law*, 19 Gavel 7 (1958).

Wisconsin Statute Law [Comparative Negligence], 7 Wis. L. Rev. 122 (1932).

Wyoming:

Comparative Negligence Practice in Wyoming, 18 Land & Water L. Rev. 713 (1983).

Canada:

Haines, *Canadian Comparative Negligence Law*, 23 Ins. Couns. J. 201 (1956).

CHAPTER 4—CAUSATION

Hoglund & Parsons, *Caveat Viator: The Duty to Wear Seat Belts Under Comparative Negligence Law*, 50 Wash. L. Rev. 1 (1974).

Legal Cause, Proximate Cause, and Comparative Negligence in the FELA, 18 Stan. L. Rev. 929 (1966).

Miller, *Seat Belt Defense Under Comparative Negligence*, 12 Idaho L. Rev. 59 (1975).

Sullivan, *Seat Belt Defense Should Be Resurrected Under Pure Comparative Negligence*, 61 Mich. B.J. 560 (1983).

CHAPTER 5—INTENTIONAL, RECKLESS AND GROSSLY NEGLIGENT CONDUCT

Comparative Fault and Intentional Torts, 12 Loy. L.A.L. Rev. 179 (1978).

Dear & Zipperstein, *Comparative Fault and Intentional Torts: Doctrinal Barriers and Policy Considerations*, 24 Santa Clara L. Rev. 1 (1984).

Role of Recklessness in American Systems of Comparative Fault, 43 Ohio St. L.J. 399 (1982).

Torts—Comparative Negligence—Action for Wanton and Willful Conduct is Beyond Purview of New Jersey Comparative Negligence Statute, 8 Rut.-Cam. L.J. 376 (1977).

Torts—Contribution Determined by Percentage of Causal Negligence; Gross Negligence No Longer Bars Contribution [Bielski v. Schulze, 16 Wis. 2d 1, 114 N.W.2d 105 (1962)], 14 Syracuse L. Rev. 140 (1962).

CHAPTER 7—LAST CLEAR CHANCE

Doctrine of Last Clear Chance—Should It Survive the Adoption of Comparative Negligence in Texas?, 6 Tex. Tech L. Rev. 131 (1974).

Effect of a Comparative Negligence Statute on the Humanitarian Doctrine, 9 Mo. L. Rev. 264 (1944).

Plaintiff's Last Clear Chance and Comparative Negligence in Georgia, 6 Ga. St. B.J. 47 (1969).

Torts: Comparative Negligence and the Doctrine of Last Clear Chance—Are They Compatible?, 28 Okla. L. Rev. 444 (1975).

CHAPTER 9—ASSUMPTION OF RISK

Anderson, *Defense of Assumption of Risk Under Comparative Negligence*, 5 St. Mary's L.J. 678 (1973-74).

Assumption of Risk in a Comparative Negligence System—Doctrinal, Practical, and Policy Issues, 39 Ohio St. L.J. 364 (1978).

Assumption of Risk in Alaska After the Adoption of Comparative Negligence, 6 U.C.L.A.-Alaska L. Rev. 244 (1977).

Colorado Comparative Negligence and Assumption of Risk, 46 U. Colo. L. Rev. 509 (1975).

Darling, *Patent Danger Rule: An Analysis and a Survey of Its Vitality*, 29 Mercer L. Rev. 583 (1978).

Negligence—Assumption of Risk—Comparative Negligence [Walker v. Kroger Grocery & Baking Co., 252 N.W. 721 (Wis. 1934)], 9 Wis. L. Rev. 319 (1934).

Parker v. Highland Park, Inc. [565 S.W.2d 512 (Tex. 1978)]—A Watershed in Landowner's Liability, 31 Baylor L. Rev. 121 (1979).

Role of Assumption of Risk in Systems of Comparative Negligence, 46 Ins. Couns. J. 360 (1979).

Tort Law—Assumption of Risk—Adoption of Comparative Negligence Requires that the Defense of Implied Assumption of Risk Be Eliminated as an Absolute Bar to Recovery, 6 Fla. St. U.L. Rev. 211 (1978).

Torts—Assumption of Risk and the Obvious Danger Rule. Primary or Secondary Assumption of Risk? [Sherman v. Platte County, 642 P.2d 787 (Wyo. 1982)], 18 Land & Water L. Rev. 373 (1983).

Torts—Assumption of Risk No Longer a Defense Separate from Contributory Negligence in Guest-Host Relationships Under the Wisconsin Comparative Negligence Statute [McConville v. State Farm Mut. Automobile Ins. Co., 113 N.W.2d 14 (Wis. 1962)], 8 Wayne L. Rev. 451 (1962).

BIBLIOGRAPHY

Torts—Assumption of the Risk—Comparative Negligence, 16 Duq. L. Rev. 417 (1979).

Torts: Comparative Negligence + Implied Assumption of Risk = Injustice, 27 Okla. L. Rev. 549 (1974).

CHAPTER 12—STRICT LIABILITY

Admiralty—Products Liability—The Contract-Tort Question, 50 Tul. L. Rev. 955 (1976).

Another Citadel Has Fallen—This Time the Plaintiff's. California Applies Comparative Negligence to Strict Products Liabilty, 6 Pepperdine L. Rev. 485 (1979).

The Application of Comparative Negligence to Strict Products Liability [Coney v. J.L.G. Industries, Inc., 454 N.E.2d 197 (Ill. 1983)], 59 Chi.-Kent L. Rev. 1043 (1983).

Application of Oregon Comparative Fault Law in Strict Products Liability Actions: Sanford v. Chevrolet Division of General Motors [642 P.2d 624 (Ore. 1982)], 19 Willamette L. Rev. 139 (1983).

Assumption of the Risk as the Only Affirmative Defense Available in Strict Product Liability Actions in Oregon, 17 Willamette L. Rev. 495 (1981).

Brewster, *Comparative Negligence in Strict Liability Cases*, 42 J. Air L. 107 (1976).

Butaud v. Suburban Marine & Sporting Goods [555 P.2d 42 (Alaska 1976)], 4 W. St. U.L. Rev. 283 (1977).

Comparative Contribution and Strict Tort Liability: A Proposed Reconciliation, 13 Creighton L. Rev. 889 (1980).

Comparative Fault and Strict Products Liability: Are They Compatible?, 5 Pepperdine L. Rev. 501 (1978).

Comparative Negligence Collides with Strict Liability: Will Tort Law Ever Be the Same?, 19 Washburn L.J. 76 (1979).

Comparative Principles and Product Liability in Montana, 41 Mont. L. Rev. 269 (1980).

Duncan v. Cessna Aircraft Company [665 S.W.2d 414 (Tex. 1984)]: "Sooner or Later" Is Now, 36 Baylor L. Rev. 429 (1984).

Feinberg, *Applicability of a Comparative Negligence Defense in a Strict Products Liability Suit Based on Section 402A of Restatement of Torts 2d (Can Oil and Water Mix?)*, 42 Ins. Couns. J. 39 (1975).

Hasten, *Comparative Liability Principles: Should They Now Apply to Strict Products Liability Actions in Ohio?*, 14 U. Tol. L. Rev. 1151 (1983).

Interaction of Comparative Negligence and Strict Products Liability—Where Are We?, 47 Ins. Couns. J. 53 (1980).

Levin & Burtz, *Torts on the Courts*, 14 Trial 28 (1978).

Levine, *Strict Products Liability and Comparative Negligence: The Collision of Fault and No-Fault*, 14 San Diego L. Rev. 337 (1977).

Merger of Comparative Fault Principles with Strict Liability in Utah, 1981 B.Y.U.L. Rev. 964 (1981).

Morton, *Strict Products Liability in Idaho: Avenues to Interpreting "Comparative Responsibility,"* 18 Idaho L. Rev. 521 (1982).

Nunnally & Ware, *Defenses in Personal Injury Product Liability Cases: Assumption of Risk and Misuse with a View Toward Comparative Fault*, 20 S. Tex. L.J. 221 (1979).

Pinto, *Comparative Responsibility—An Idea Whose Time Has Come*, 45 Ins. Couns. J. 115 (1978).

Products Liability—Comparative Negligence and Strict Products Liability, 1979 Ann. Surv. Am. L. 577.

Products Liability, Comparative Negligence, and the Allocation of Damages Among Multiple Defendants, 50 S. Cal. L. Rev. 73 (1976).

Richart, *Contributory Negligence—Or Assumption of Risk—What Is a Patient to Do?*, 55 N.D.L. Rev. 237 (1979).

Schwartz, *Products Liability and No-Fault Insurance: Can One Live Without the Other?*, 12 Forum 130 (1976).

Shelton, *Comparative Causation: A Legislative Proposal for the Equitable Allocation of Loss Between Strictly Liable and Negligent Parties*, 20 S. Tex. L.J. 123 (1979).

Timmerman v. Universal Corrugated Box Machinery Corp. [287 N.W.2d 316 (Mich. 1980)]—An Exception to the Doctrine of Comparative Negligence in Products Liability Litigation: Michigan Courts Speak Out on Public Act 495, 1981 Det. C.L. Rev. 223.

Torts—Doctrine of Strict Liability Meets a Comparative Negligence Statute [Dippel v. Sciano, 155 N.W.2d 55 (Wis. 1967)], 17 De Paul L. Rev. 614 (1968).

Twerski, *From Defect to Cause to Comparative Fault—Rethinking Some Product Liability Concepts*, 60 Marq. L. Rev. 297 (1977).

Various Risk Allocation Schemes Under the Model Uniform Product Liability Act: An Analysis of the Statute of Repose, Comparative Fault Principles, and the Conflicting Social Policies Arising from Workplace Product Injuries, 48 Geo. Wash. L. Rev. 588 (1980).

West v. Caterpillar Tractor Co. [504 F.2d 967 (5th Cir. Fla. 1974)], 29 U. Fla. L. Rev. 398 (1977).

Westerbeke & Meltzer, *Comparative Fault and Strict Products Liability in Kansas: Reflections on the Distinction Between Initial Liability and Ultimate Loss Allocation*, 28 Kan. L. Rev. 25 (1979).

Woods, *Product Liability: Is Comparative Fault Winning the Day?*, 36 Ark. L. Rev. 360 (1983).

Zahrte v. Sturm, Ruger & Co. [661 P.2d 17 (Mont. 1983)]: Montana Incorporates Comparative Principles into Strict Liability, 11 J. Contemp. L. 365 (1984).

CHAPTER 13—WRONGFUL DEATH

Wrongful Death Recoveries in California: Is the Decedent's Negligence a Defense After Li?, 11 Pac. L.J. 775 (1980).

CHAPTER 15—CHOICE OF LAW

Conflict of Laws—Conflict Between Mississippi Comparative Negligence Doctrine and Louisiana Contributory Negligence Doctrine, 43 Tul. L. Rev. 706 (1969).

Conflicts of Law—Federal Preemption— Aviation Law—Federal Common Law of Indemnity and Contribution on a Comparative Negligence Basis Will Govern in Mid-air Collisions, 28 Vand. L. Rev. 621 (1975).

Kennelly, *Transitory Tort Litigation—The Need for Uniform Rules Pertaining to In Personam Jurisdiction, Forum Non Conveniens, Choice of Laws, and Comparative Negligence*, 22 Trial Law. Guide 422 (1979).

McDougal, *Comprehensive Interest Analysis Versus Reformulated Governmental Interest Analysis: An Appraisal in the Context of Choice-of-Law Problems Concerning Contributory and Comparative Negligence*, 26 UCLA L. Rev. 439 (1979).

CHAPTER 16—MULTIPLE PARTIES

Adams, *Settlements After Li: But Is It "Fair"?*, 10 Pac. L.J. 729 (1979).

Article 2212A, Section 2(e), Abrogates the One Satisfaction Rule in Comparative Negli-

gence Actions: Cypress Creek Utility Service Co. v. Muller [640 S.W.2d 860 (Tex. 1982)], 14 Tex. Tech L. Rev. 679 (1983).

Assumption of Risk—Contribution—Imputed Negligence—Joint Tortfeasors—Comparative Negligence [Walker v. Kroger Grocery & Baking Co., 252 N.W. 721 (Wis. 1934)], 18 Marq. L. Rev. 192 (1934).

Baker, *Contributory Negligence, Contribution, and Comparative Negligence Questions*, 35 Wis. B. Bull. 31 (1962).

Boone, *Multiple-party Litigation and Comparative Negligence*, 45 Ins. Couns. J. 335 (1978).

Brown [Brown v. Keill, 580 P.2d 867 (Kan. 1978)] and West [Miles v. West, 580 P.2d 876 (Kan. 1978)]: At Last, An End to Ambiguity in the Kansas Law of Comparative Negligence, 27 Kan. L. Rev. 111 (1978).

Busick, *Contribution and Indemnity Between Tortfeasors in Nebraska*, 7 Creighton L. Rev. 182 (1974).

Change of the Wisconsin Comparative Negligence Statute in Multi-Defendant Suits, 62 Marq. L. Rev. 227 (1978).

Comparative Fault and Settlement in Joint Tortfeasor Cases: A Plea for Principle Over Policy, 16 San Diego L. Rev. 833 (1979).

Comparative Negligence as Applied to Contribution: The New Doctrine of "Comparative Contribution" [Bielski v. Schulze, 16 Wis. 2d 1, 114 N.W.2d 105 (1962)], 17 Sw. L.J. 155 (1963).

Comparative Negligence: The Multiple Defendant Dilemma, 36 Me. L. Rev. 345 (1984).

Comparative Negligence: The Role of the Absent Tortfeasor in Oklahoma, 34 Okla. L. Rev. 815 (1981).

Conley & Marsh, *Apportionment of Liability Among Concurrent Tortfeasors Based on Comparative Fault*, 29 Fed'n Ins. Couns. Q. 123 (1979).

Contribution and Indemnity Collide with Comparative Negligence—The New Doctrine of Equitable Indemnity, 18 Santa Clara L. Rev. 779 (1978).

Employer Liability to Third Parties Under the Workmen's Compensation and Comparative Negligence Statutes, 26 Kan. L. Rev. 485 (1978).

Fagelson, *Last Bastion of Fault? Contributory Negligence in Actions for Employers' Liability*, 42 Mod. L. Rev. 464 (1979).

Fleming, *Report to the Joint Committee of the California Legislature on Tort Liability on the Problems Associated with American Motorcycle Association v. Superior Court [of Los Angeles County, 578 P.2d 899 (1978)]*, 30 Hastings L.J. 1465 (1978).

George & Walkowiak, *Blame and Reparation in Pure Comparative Negligence: The Multi-party Action*, 8 Sw. U.L. Rev. 1 (1976).

Goldenberg, *Comparative Liability Among Joint Tortfeasors: The Aftermath of Li v. Yellow Cab Co. [532 P.2d 1226 (Cal. 1975)]*, 8 U. West L.A.L. Rev. 23 (1976).

Gordon & Crowley, *Indemnity Issues in Settlement of Multi-party Actions in Comparative Negligence Jurisdictions*, 48 Ins. Couns. J. 457 (1981).

Hummert, *Criticism of Judicially Adopted Comparative Partial Indemnity as a Means of Circumventing Pro Rata Contribution Statutes*, 47 J. Air L. 117 (1981).

Imputed Negligence Under the Arkansas Comparative Liability Statute, Exception: Stull, Admx. v. Ragsdale [620 S.W.2d 264 (Ark. 1981)], 35 Ark. L. Rev. 722 (1983).

McKay, *American Motorcycle Association vs. Superior Court [of Los Angeles County, 578 P.2d 899 (1978)]: From Comparative Negligence to Comparative Indemnity*, 5 Orange County B.J. 180 (1978).

441

McNichols, *Complexities of Oklahoma's Proportionate Several Liability Doctrine of Comparative Negligence: Is Products Liability Next?*, 35 Okla. L. Rev. 193 (1982).

McNichols, *Judicial Elimination of Joint and Several Liability Because of Comparative Negligence—A Puzzling Choice*, 32 Okla. L. Rev. 1 (1979).

Miller, *Filling the "Empty Chair": Some Thoughts About Sugue [v. F.L. Smithe Machine Co., 546 P.2d 527 (Hawaii 1976)]*, 15 Hawaii B.J. 69 (1980).

Multiple Party Litigation Under Comparative Negligence in Kansas—Damage Apportionment as a Replacement for Joint and Several Liability, 16 Washburn L.J. 672 (1977).

Nations & Cabello, *Contribution and Indemnity: The Intricate Web in Tort Litigation*, 24 S. Tex. L.J. 1 (1983).

Negligence—Comparative Negligence—Effect of Assumption of Risk as to One Tortfeasor on Recovery and Contribution [Walker v. Kroger Grocery & Baking Co., 252 N.W. 721 (Wis. 1934)], 48 Harv. L. Rev. 517 (1935).

Negligence—Defenses—Applying Comparative Negligence Among Joint Tortfeasors, 4 W. St. U.L. Rev. 292 (1977).

New Policies Bearing on the Negligent Employer's Immunity from Loss-Sharing, 29 Me. L. Rev. 243 (1978).

Raskoff, *Comparative Negligence in California: Multiple Party Litigation*, 7 Pac. L.J. 747 (1976).

Reppy, Jr., *Effect of the Adoption of Comparative Negligence on California Community Property Law: Has Imputed Negligence Been Revived?*, 28 Hastings L.J. 1359 (1977).

Third Party and Employer Liability After Nga Li v. Yellow Cab Company [532 P.2d 1226 (Cal. 1975)] for Injuries to Employees Covered by Workers' Compensation, 50 S. Cal. L. Rev. 1029 (1977).

Third-Party Tortfeasor's Right of Contribution Against Negligent Employer Covered Under Workmen's Compensation, 29 Mercer L. Rev. 635 (1978).

Torts: Comparative Negligence and Absent Parties, 18 Washburn L.J. 692 (1979).

Torts: Damage Apportionment Under the Kansas Comparative Negligence Statute—The Unjoined Tortfeasor, 17 Washburn L.J. 698 (1978).

Torts: Imputed Comparative Negligence, 28 Okla. L. Rev. 941 (1975).

Torts: Use of Comparative Fault in Apportioning Damages for Aggravated Injuries, 63 Minn. L. Rev. 1009 (1979).

Walkowiak, *Implied Indemnity: A Policy Analysis of the Total Loss Shifting Remedy in a Partial Loss Shifting Jurisdiction*, 30 U. Fla. L. Rev. 501 (1978).

Zavos, *Comparative Fault and the Insolvent Defendant: A Critique and Amplification of American Motorcycle Association v. Superior Court [of Los Angeles County, 578 P.2d 899 (1978)]*, 14 Loy. L.A.L. Rev. 775 (1981).

CHAPTERS 17 AND 18—FACT FINDING

Cadena, *Comparative Negligence and the Special Verdict*, 5 St. Mary's L.J. 688 (1973-74).

Civil Procedure: Informing Comparative Negligence Juries What Legal Consequences Their Special Verdicts Effect, 18 Washburn L.J. 606 (1979).

Comparative Negligence, Special Verdicts, 22 Gavel 16 (1955).

Effect of Colorado's Comparative Negligence Statute on the Doctrine of Res Ipsa Loquitur, 52 U. Colo. L. Rev. 565 (1981).

Informing the Jury of the Legal Effect of Its Answers to Special Verdict Questions Under Kansas Comparative Negligence Law—A Reply to the Masses; A Case for the Minority View, 16 Washburn L.J. 114 (1976).

BIBLIOGRAPHY

Informing the Jury of the Legal Effect of Special Verdict Answers in Comparative Negligence Actions, 1981 Duke L.J. 824 (1981).

Kansas Comparative Negligence Statute: Informing the Jury of the Legal Effect of Its Answers to Special Verdict Questions, 45 J. Kan. B.A. 91 (1976).

Keeton, *Legal Process in Comparative Negligence Cases*, 17 Harv. J. on Legis. 1 (1980).

Negligence—Comparative Negligence—Power of Court to Review Jury's Findings [Hammer v. Minneapolis, S. P. & S. S. M. R. Co., 255 N.W. 124 (Wis. 1934)], 12 N.Y.U. L.Q. 320 (1934).

Net Recovery Comparative Negligence: The Reasonable Alternative, 6 Willamette L.J. 551 (1970).

Smith, *Comparative Negligence Problems with the Special Verdict: Informing the Jury of the Legal Effects of Their Answers*, 10 Land & Water L. Rev. 199 (1975).

Special Verdict Procedure in Comparative Negligence Cases, 55 A.B.A. J. 129 (1969).

Torts: Issue of Comparative Fault Cannot Be Retried Independently of Issue of Liability, [Juvland v. Mattson, 289 Minn. 365, 184 N.W.2d 423 (1971)], 56 Minn. L. Rev. 973 (1972).

CHAPTER 19—COUNTERCLAIMS

Levy, *Pure Comparative Negligence: Set-Offs, Multiple Defendants and Loss Distribution*, 11 U.S.F.L. Rev. 405 (1977).

Torts—Remedies—Statutory Set-Off of Competing Claims Arising Under the Texas Comparative Negligence Act Is Mandatory, 9 Tex. Tech L. Rev. 367 (1978).

CHAPTER 20—STRATEGIC CONSIDERATIONS

Huff, *Defense Strategies with Comparative Negligence*, 44 Ins. Couns. J. 124 (1977).

Schwartz, *Trial Tactics Under a Comparative Negligence System*, 11 Forum 38 (1975).

TABLE OF CASES

References are to Sections

A

445

TABLE OF CASES

TABLE OF CASES

TABLE OF CASES

TABLE OF CASES

References are to Sections

TABLE OF CASES

TABLE OF CASES

TABLE OF CASES

References are to Sections

References are to Sections

TABLE OF CASES

References are to Sections

461

TABLE OF CASES

TABLE OF CASES

TABLE OF CASES

TABLE OF CASES

References are to Sections

TABLE OF CASES

S

TABLE OF CASES

References are to Sections

TABLE OF CASES

TABLE OF CASES

References are to Sections

T

U

TABLE OF CASES

TABLE OF CASES

References are to Sections

Y

Z

INDEX

477

INDEX

ARKANSAS

Assumption of risk, 2,3, 9.2, 9.4(A)
Comparative negligence statute discussed, 1.1, 1.4(B), 2.1, 3.1, 3.2, 3.5(B)
    "fault" statute, 2.2, 5.2
    text of statute, Appendix B
Joint tortfeasors, 16.4, 16.6
Last clear chance doctrine, 7.2
Special verdicts in comparative negligence cases, 2.3
Strict liability actions, 12.2
Wrongful death actions, 13.3

ASSUMPTION OF RISK

Comparative negligence as requiring adjustment of view of doctrine, 2.3
Defense in nuisance cases, 11.3, 11.4
Express assumption of risk
    definition, 9.1
    effect in comparative negligence jurisdictions, 9.2
    statutory provisions generally, 9.2
    Uniform Comparative Fault Act, 9.2
    validity of agreement to assume risk, 9.2
Implied assumption of risk
    arguments for and against retention as complete defense, 9.5
    basis of defense, 9.1
    complete defense in certain comparative negligence jurisdictions, 9.3
        Georgia precedents, 9.3
        Mississippi precedents, 9.3
        restricted application in certain states, 9.3
    defense as limitation upon defendant's duty, 9.1
    distinguished from contributory negligence, 9.1
    Federal Employers' Liability Act, 9.4(A)
    fireman's rule under comparative negligence, 9.4(C)
    historical background of defense, 9.1
    joint tortfeasors, application of assumption of risk to contribution between, 9.4(C)
    limited duty of defendant, 9.4(C)
    Longshoremen's and Harbor Worker's Compensation Act, 9.2, 9.4(A)
    merger of defense into contributory negligence, 9.1, 9.4(A), (B), 9.5
    primary assumption of risk, 9.1, 9.4(C)
    probable future treatment, 9.5
    reasonable conduct in assuming risk, availability as defense, 9.1 to 9.5
    spectator injuries, 9.3, 9.4(C)
    sports injuries, 9.4(C)
    statutory provisions generally, 9.4(A)
    treatment as negligence subject to comparison, 9.4(A) to (C)
        apportionment of damage award, 9.4(A) to (C)
        Federal Employers' Liability Act, unreasonable conduct by plaintiff required, 9.4(A)
    unreasonable conduct by plaintiff in assuming risk required, 9.4(A), (C)
        treatment as form of contributory negligence, 9.5

ATTORNEYS

Trial strategy under comparative negligence, 20.1 to 20.7–See TRIAL

B

BAILMENTS

Comparative negligence doctrine applied, 2.2

C

CALIFORNIA

Assumption of risk, 9.4(B), (C)
Comparative negligence doctrine adopted, discussed, 1.1, 1.5(E), 3.2
    limited retroactive effect, 8.2

D

E

F

INDEX

INDEX

INDEX

JUDICIAL CONTROL OF VERDICTS (Continued)

Pure comparative negligence systems
    assumptions indulged to uphold verdict, 18.5
    question of relative fault for jury, 18.1, 18.5
    remittitur and additur procedures, 18.5
    verdicts palpably against weight of evidence, 18.5
Slight-gross system
    new trial limited to damages only, 18.6
    plaintiff's contributory negligence more than slight as matter of law, 18.6
    question of relative fault for jury, 18.1, 18.6

JURIES

Apportionment of fault, 1.4(B)
    inexact nature of determination, 17.1
    informing jury as to effect, 17.5
Causation as issue for jury, 4.1
Comparative negligence as vesting too much power in jury, 3.1
Comparative negligence, submission to jury, 17.3
Contributory negligence as issue for jury determination, 1.5(A)
Federal Employers' Liability Act, reduction of award by jury, 1.4(A)
Instructions on contributory negligence modified, 1.2(A)
Interrogatories to jury, 17.4–See SPECIAL VERDICTS
    use in conjunction with general verdict, 17.4
Judicial control, 18.1 to 18.7–See JUDICIAL CONTROL OF VERDICTS
Maine, just and equitable reduction of award, 3.5
Negligence as jury question, 17.3
Proximate cause as issue for jury, 4.1, 4.3, 17.3
Reduction of award by percentage of fault, 3.5
Reduction of award under pure comparative negligence, 3.2
Slight-gross system, comparative negligence as issue for jury, 3.4(B)
    incorrect apportionment as basis for new trial, 3.4(B)
Special verdict practice in certain jurisdictions, 2.3, 17.4–See SPECIAL VERDICTS
    construed as substantive law, 15.4
    discretionary under federal rules, 15.4
    forms of special verdict, 17.4
Strict liability of defendant, determination of plaintiff's fault, 12.7

K

KANSAS

Comparative negligence statute discussed, 1.1, 1.4(B), 2.1, 3.1
    prospective application, 2.3, 8.3
    text of statute, Appendix B
Joint tortfeasors, 2.3, 16.2, 16.4 to 16.9
Special verdicts, statutory provisions for, 2.3
Strict liability actions, 12.2
Wrongful death actions, 13.6

KENTUCKY

Assumption of risk, 9.5
Comparative negligence doctrine discussed, 1.1, 1.5(E), 3.2
    retroactive effect, 8.2
Strict liability actions, 12.2

L

LAST CLEAR CHANCE DOCTRINE

Application of doctrine in comparative negligence jurisdictions, 7.2–See also Individual States
    arguments for and against application of doctrine, 7.2
    doctrine abolished in certain states, 7.2
    modified comparative negligence systems, application of doctrine in, 7.2
    plaintiff's last clear chance, application, 7.3

LAST CLEAR CHANCE DOCTRINE (Continued)

Application of doctrine (Continued)
 states in which doctrine retained, 7.2
 uncertainty in certain jurisdictions, 7.2
Applied as escape from equal division system, 3.3(C)
Conscious last clear chance, elements, 7.1
Effect upon contributory negligence defense, 1.2(A), 7.1
Historical background, 7.1
Plaintiff's last clear chance as contributory negligence, 7.1, 7.3
Proximate cause rationale, 7.1, 7.2
Purpose as limitation upon contributory negligence defense, 7.1
Rationale of doctrine, 7.1
Unconscious last clear chance, definition, application, 7.1

LEGAL MALPRACTICE

Comparative negligence inappropriate, 2.2

LONGSHOREMEN'S AND HARBOR WORKERS' COMPENSATION ACT

Assumption of risk precluded as defense, 9.4(A)

LOUISIANA

Comparative negligence statute discussed, 1.1, 1.3(A), 1.4(B), 3.2
 judicial adoption rejected, 1.5(B)
 prospective application, 2.3, 8.3
 text of statute, Appendix B
Strict liability actions, 12.2
Wrongful death actions, 13.3

M

MAINE

Assumption of risk, 9.4(B), (C)
Comparative negligence statute discussed, 1.1, 1.4(B), 2.1, 3.1, 3.5(B)
 effective date, 8.4
 "fault" statute, 2.2, 5.2
 text of statute, Appendix B
Intentional torts, statute ambiguous, 5.2
Joint tortfeasors, 2.3, 16.3, 16.6 to 16.8
Last clear chance doctrine not applicable, 7.2
Strict liability actions, 12.2
Verdicts in comparative negligence cases, statutory provisions, 2.3
Wrongful death actions, 13.6

MAJOR-MINOR RULE

Application in equal division system, 3.3(A)

MARYLAND

Contributory negligence doctrine preserved, 1.5(E)

MASSACHUSETTS

Assumption of risk, 2.3, 9.2, 9.4(A)
Comparative negligence statute discussed, 1.1, 1.4(B), 2.1, 3.1, 3.5(B)
 intentional torts not covered, 5.2
 prospective application, 2.3, 8.3
 text of statute, Appendix B
Joint tortfeasors, 16.6, 16.7
Skiing accidents, recovery limited, 2.2
Strict liability actions, 12.2
Violation of safety statute by plaintiff, 6.3
Wrongful death actions, 13.6

MENTAL INSTABILITY

Plaintiff's versus defendant's, under contributory negligence doctrine, 1.2(B)

MENTALLY INCOMPETENT PERSONS

Contributory negligence, absolute insanity or diminished mental capacity taken into account, 14.3
Held to standard of reasonable man, 14.3

MERCHANT MARINE ACT

Pure comparative negligence incorporated in provisions, 3.2, 3.3(B)

MICHIGAN

Assumption of risk, 9.4(B)
Comparative negligence doctrine discussed, 1.1, 1.5(E), 3.2
    early attempts to adopt, 1.4(B), 1.5(B)
    retroactive effect, 8.2
Employment discrimination claim, comparative negligence rule applied, 2.2
Joint tortfeasors, 16.5, 16.7
Last clear chance doctrine retained, 7.2
Wrongful death actions, 13.3

MINNESOTA

Assumption of risk, 2.3, 9.2, 9.4(A) to (C), 9.5
Comparative negligence statute discussed, 1.1, 1.4(B), 2.1, 3.1, 3.5(B)
    effective date, 2.3, 8.4, 8.5
    "fault" statute, 2.2
    judicial adoption rejected, 1.5(B)
    text of statute, Appendix B
Joint tortfeasors, 2.3, 16.4, 16.5, 16.7, 16.8
Special verdicts, statutory provisions for, 2.3
Wrongful death actions, 13.6

MISREPRESENTATION

Comparative negligence inapplicable to negligent misrepresentation, 2.2

MISSISSIPPI

Assumption of risk, 9.3, 9.4(B)
Comparative negligence statute discussed, 1.1, 1.4(B), 3.2
    text of statute, Appendix B
Joint tortfeasors, 16.4
Last clear chance doctrine, 7.2
Strict liability actions, 12.2
Wrongful death actions, 13.3

MISSOURI

Assumption of risk, 9.4(A)
Comparative negligence doctrine discussed, 1.1, 1.5(E), 3.2
    effective date, 8.2
    "fault" rule adopted, 12.2
    judicial adoption initially rejected, 1.5(B)
Last clear chance doctrine not applicable, 7.2
Strict liability actions, 12.2

MODIFIED COMPARATIVE NEGLIGENCE

Distinguished from pure comparative negligence, 3.1
Forms of, 2.1–See SYSTEMS OF COMPARATIVE NEGLIGENCE

MONTANA

Assumption of risk, 9.4(B)
Comparative negligence statute discussed, 1.1, 1.4(B), 2.1, 3.1, 3.5(B)
    effective date, 8.4
    text of statute, Appendix B
Joint tortfeasors, 16.5, 16.7, 16.8
Skiing accidents, recovery limited, 2.2
Strict liability actions, 12.2

N

NEBRASKA

Assumption of risk, 9.3
Comparative negligence statute discussed, 1.1, 1.4(B), 3.1, 3.4, 3.4(B)
    effective date, 8.4
    text of statute, Appendix B
Joint tortfeasors, 16.7, 16.8
Last clear chance doctrine retained, 7.2
Wrongful death actions, 13.1 to 13.3

NEGLIGENCE

Application of comparative negligence, 2.2
Assumption of risk as one form of contributory negligence, 9.4—See ASSUMPTION OF
  RISK
Children, standard of care required, 14.1
Contributory negligence—See CONTRIBUTORY NEGLIGENCE
Distinguished from intentional tort, 2.2, 5.3
Distinguished from "willful" or "reckless" conduct, 5.3, 10.3
"Fault" defined to include negligence, 5.2
Imputed negligence, 16.1—See IMPUTED NEGLIGENCE
Last clear chance rationale, 7.1, 7.2—See LAST CLEAR CHANCE DOCTRINE
"Reckless" and "wanton" conduct as something other than negligence, 10.3
Violation of criminal safety statute as negligence per se, 6.1
    defendant's violation, 6.2
    "outlaw" effect of violation, 6.3
    plaintiff's violation, 6.2
"Willful misconduct" as "negligent willful misconduct," 5.3

NEVADA

Comparative negligence statute discussed, 1.1, 1.4(B), 2.1, 3.1, 3.5(B)
    text of statute, Appendix B
Joint tortfeasors, 2.3, 16.6 to 16.8
Last clear chance doctrine not applicable, 7.2
Strict liability actions, 12.2
Wrongful death actions, 13.3

NEW HAMPSHIRE

Assumption of risk, 9.4(B), 9.5
Comparative negligence statute discussed, 1.1, 1.4(B), 2.1, 2.3, 3.1, 3.5(B)
    prospective application, 8.3
    text of statute, Appendix B
Joint tortfeasors, 2.3, 16.4, 16.6 to 16.8
Last clear chance doctrine retained, 7.2
Strict liability actions, 12.2
Verdicts in comparative negligence cases, statutory provisions, 2.3
Wrongful death actions, 13.6

NEW JERSEY

Assumption of risk, 9.4(B), 9.5
Comparative negligence statute discussed, 1.4(B), 2.1, 3.1
    prospective application, 2.3, 8.3
    text of statute, Appendix B
Joint tortfeasors, 2.3, 16.6 to 16.8
Special verdicts, statutory provisions for, 2.3
Strict liability actions, 12.2

NEW MEXICO

Comparative negligence doctrine discussed, 1.1, 1.5(E), 3.2
    earlier judicial adoption rejected, 1.5(B)
    retroactive effect, 8.2
Joint tortfeasors, 16.4, 16.5, 16.7
Strict liability actions, 12.2

O

INDEX

INDEX

SOLE PROXIMATE CAUSE

Application to pure comparative negligence, 3.2

SOUTH CAROLINA

Contributory negligence doctrine preserved, 1.5(E)

SOUTH DAKOTA

Assumption of risk, 9.3
Comparative negligence statute discussed, 1.1, 1.4(B), 2.1, 3.1, 3.4, 3.4(B)
    effective date, 8.4
    text of statute, Appendix B
Last clear chance doctrine retained, 7.2
Strict liability actions, 12.2
Wrongful death actions, 13.1 to 13.3

SPECIAL VERDICTS

Advantages of special verdict practice, 17.4
    control of jury, 17.4
        facilitating judicial review, 17.4
        simplification of instructions to jury, 17.4
Application in contributory negligence forum, 15.2–See CONFLICT OF LAWS
Authorized by judicial decision in Florida, 17.4
Control of jury by special verdict, 17.4
Criticism of practice, 17.4
Discretionary practice in certain jurisdictions, 2.3, 17.4
Federal Rules of Civil Procedure, procedure under, 17.4
Forms of special verdict interrogatories, 17.4
Informing jury of consequence of findings prohibited in certain jurisdictions, permitted in others, 17.5
Interrogatories to jury, when authorized, 17.4
    advantages in conjunction with general verdict, 17.4
    jurisdictions requiring reduction of damages for contributory negligence, 17.4
Mandatory in certain states, 2.1, 2.3, 17.4
Request by counsel required in certain states, 2.3, 17.4
Wisconsin practice, 2.3, 3.5, 17.4
    form of special verdict interrogatories, 17.4

STATE LEGISLATION

    See Individual States

STREET RAILWAY ACCIDENTS

Comparative negligence held to supersede statute relative to nonpassenger street railway accidents, 2.2

STRICT LIABILITY

Application of comparative "fault," 12.2, 12.4, 12.5
Application of comparative negligence, 2.2, 12.2 to 12.8
    assumption of risk by plaintiff, 12.6, 12.8
    judicial application, power of courts, 12.2
    patterns of plaintiff misconduct for application of comparative negligence, 12.3
        failure to discover or foresee dangers, 12.7, 12.8
        obvious hazards or risks, 12.6, 12.8
        statutory provisions generally, 12.2
        unintended foreseeable misuse by plaintiff, 12.5, 12.8
        unintended unforeseeable misuse by plaintiff as complete defense, 12.4, 12.8
        unreasonable assumption of risk by plaintiff, 12.6, 12.8
Contributory negligence as defense, 1.2(B)
Risk distribution considerations in applying comparative negligence, 12.7, 12.8
    modified systems, application as undermining policies, 12.8
Strict liability conduct as negligence per se, 12.2, 12.7
Uniform Product Liability Act, 12.2, 12.5, 12.7
Unintended unforeseeable misuse as complete defense, 12.4

INDEX

SUMMARY JUDGMENT

See TRIAL

SURVIVAL STATUTES

See WRONGFUL DEATH AND SURVIVAL STATUTES

SYSTEMS OF COMPARATIVE NEGLIGENCE

TRIAL (Continued)

Directed verdicts generally, 17.3
Interrogatories to jury, 17.4–See SPECIAL VERDICTS
Plaintiff's trial preparation and basic strategy, 20.2
    modified systems, 20.4
    pure comparative negligence systems, 20.3
Special verdict practice, 17.4–See SPECIAL VERDICTS
Summary judgment and directed verdict generally, 17.3
    fifty percent system jurisdictions, 17.3

U

UNIFORM COMMERCIAL CODE

Comparative negligence inapplicable in breach of contract of deposit and conversion case, 2.2

UNIFORM COMPARATIVE FAULT ACT

Act and comments, 21.4
Assumption of risk under, 2.3, 9.2
Effective date provision, 2.3
Joint tortfeasors, 2.3, 16.5

UNINSURED MOTORIST COVERAGE

Comparative negligence and uninsured motorist coverage, 2.4

UTAH

Assumption of risk, 2.3, 9.2, 9.4(A)
Comparative negligence statute discussed, 1.1, 1.4(B), 2.1, 3.1
    effective date, 8.4
    text of statute, Appendix B
Joint tortfeasors, 2.3, 16.6
Skiing accidents, recovery limited, 2.2
Special verdicts, statutory provisions for, 2.3
Strict liability actions, 12.2

V

VERDICT

    See JUDICIAL CONTROL OF VERDICTS; JURIES; SPECIAL VERDICTS

VERMONT

Assumption of risk, 9.4(B)
Comparative negligence statute discussed, 1.1, 1.4(B), 2.1, 3.1, 3.5(B)
    effective date, 2.3, 8.3
    text of statute, Appendix B
Joint tortfeasors, 2.3, 16.4, 16.6 to 16.8
Skiing accidents, recovery limited, 2.2
Strict liability actions, 12.2
Verdicts in comparative negligence cases, statutory provisions, 2.3

VIRGIN ISLANDS

Comparative negligence statute discussed, 1.1, 3.1, 3.5
    text of statute, Appendix B
Joint tortfeasors, 16.7
Strict liability actions, 12.2

VIRGINIA

Contributory negligence doctrine preserved, 1.5(E)

WASHINGTON

Assumption of risk, 2.3, 9.2, 9.4(A) to (C)
Comparative negligence statute discussed, 1.1, 1.4(B), 3.2
    effective date, 8.4, 8.5
    text of statute, Appendix B
Joint tortfeasors, 16.4, 16.8
Last clear chance doctrine not applicable, 7.2
Wrongful death actions, 13.3

WEST VIRGINIA

Comparative negligence doctrine discussed, 1.1, 1.5(E), 2.1, 3.1, 3.5(B)
    "fault" rule adopted, 12.2
    retroactive effect, 8.2
Joint tortfeasors, 16.4, 16.6, 16.8
Strict liability actions, 12.2

WILLFUL MISCONDUCT

Application of comparative negligence, 5.3
Construction of term, 5.3
Construed as "negligent willful misconduct," effect, 5.3
Contributory negligence, availability as defense, 5.1, 5.3
Distinguished from ordinary negligence, 5.3
Full recovery by plaintiff as deterrent, 5.3
Judicial interpretation of "willful," 5.3
Plaintiff's conduct willful, effect, 5.5
Punitive damages, 5.1, 5.4
Synonymous with "wanton" or "reckless" conduct, 5.3
"Willful" as synonymous with "knowing" or "intentional," 5.3

WISCONSIN

Assumption of risk, 9.4(B), (C), 9.5
Child safety seat laws, 4.6
Comparative negligence statute discussed, 1.1, 1.4(B), 2.1, 3.1, 3.5(A), (B)
    earlier attempt at judicial adoption, 1.5(A)
    effective date, 8.4
Joint tortfeasors, 16.4 to 16.9
Last clear chance doctrine not applicable, 7.2
Seat belt cases, 4.6
Special verdicts required in comparative negligence cases, 2.3
Wrongful death actions, 13.3, 13.6

WRONGFUL DEATH AND SURVIVAL STATUTES

Nature of statutes generally, 13.1
Survival statutes
    comparative negligence applicable in survival actions, 13.1
    continuation of decedent's action as purpose, 13.1
    negligence of beneficiaries immaterial, 13.1
Wrongful death statutes
    application of comparative negligence, 2.2, 13.1 to 13.6
        beneficiary's negligence, 13.4
        combined negligence of decedent and beneficiary, 13.5
        damages subject to statutory limit, apportionment, 13.6
        decedent's negligence, 13.3, 13.5

WYOMING

Assumption of risk, 9.4(B)
Comparative negligence statute discussed, 1.1, 1.4(B), 2.1, 3.1
    text of statute, Appendix B
Joint tortfeasors, 2.3, 16.6, 16.8